Baedeker
U.S.A.

Imprint

178 illustrations, 50 situation maps, 34 town plans, 11 ground-plans, 11 general maps, 9 drawings, 5 special maps, 4 geological profiles, 17 profiles of buildings, 4 special plans, 4 tables, 1 panoramic map, 1 large map of the United States

Original German text: Dr Peter H. Baumgarten, Annette Bickel, Dr Helmut Blume, Gisela Bockamp, Rainer Eisenschmid, Rolf Eisenschmid, Heidi Engelmann, Christine Gebhardt, Dr Wilfried Heinzler, Dr Cornelia Hermanns, Rupert Koppold, Dr Heinrich Lang, Heribert Langen, Helmut Linde, Dr Christina Melk-Haen, Dr Ruth Nestvold-Mack, Albert and Isolde Maier, Inge and Dr Georg Scherm, Lydia Störmer, Manfred Strobel, Martin Vogel, Werner Voran, Andrea Wurth, Dagmar Zimmermann

Editorial work: Baedeker-Redaktion (Helmut Linde, Rainer Eisenschmid)
English language edition: Alec Court

Cartography: Gert Oberländer, Munich; Christoph Gallus, Hohberg (Niederschopfheim); Mairs Geographischer Verlag GmbH & Co., Ostfildern (panoramic map, large map of USA)

General direction: Dr Peter H. Baumgarten, Baedeker Stuttgart

English translation: James Hogarth

Following the tradition established by Karl Baedeker in 1844, sights of particular interest and hotels and restaurants of particular quality are distinguished by either one or two stars. To make it easier to locate the various sights listed in the "A to Z" section of the Guide, their co-ordinates on the large city map are shown at the head of each entry.

The symbol (i) on a town plan indicates the local tourist office from which further information can be obtained. The post-horn symbol indicates a post office.

In a time of rapid change it is difficult to ensure that all the information given is entirely accurate and up to date, and the possibility of error can never be entirely eliminated. Although the publishers can accept no responsibility for inaccuracies and omissions, they are always grateful for corrections and suggestions for improvement.

1st English edition 1994

© Baedeker Stuttgart Original German edition

© 1994 Jarrold and Sons Limited English language edition worldwide

© 1994 The Automobile Association United Kingdom and Ireland

Distributed in the United Kingdom by the Publishing Division of the Automobile Association, Fanum House, Basingstoke, Hampshire RG21 2EA

All rights reserved. No part of this publication may be reproduced, stored in a retrieval system or transmitted in any form by any means – electronic, photocopying, recording or otherwise – unless the written permission of the publisher has been obtained.

Licensed user:
Mairs Geographischer Verlag GmbH & Co., Ostfildern-Kemnat bei Stuttgart

The name *Baedeker* is a registered trade mark
A CIP catalogue record of this book is available from the British Library

Printed in Italy by G. Canale & C.S.p.A – Borgaro T.se –Turin

Published in the United States by:
Macmillan Travel
A Prentice Hall Macmillan Company
15 Columbus Circle
New York, NY 10023

Macmillan is a registered trademark of Macmillan, Inc.

ISBN US and Canada 0–671–89689–X

UK 0–7495–0883–3

Contents

	Page
The Principal Places of Tourist Interest at a Glance	6 and 590
Preface	7
Facts and Figures	9

General · Topography and Geology· Climate · Flora and Fauna · Population; Towns and Other Settlements · The Indians of North America · Religion · Government and Society · Education · Economy Transport and Communications

History	63
Famous People	81
Art and Culture	94

Art · Architecture · Literature · Music · Film

Quotations	124
Suggested Routes	128
Sights from A to Z	139

Alabama · Alaska · Albuquerque · Arches National Park · Arizona · Arkansas · Atlanta · Badlands National Park · Baltimore · Big Bend National Park · Black Hills · Boston · Bryce Canyon National Park · California · Canyonlands National Park · Cape Canaveral/Kennedy Space Center · Cape Cod · Carlsbad Caverns National Park · Charleston · Charlottesville · Cheyenne · Chicago · Cincinnati · Cleveland · Cody · Colonial National Historical Park · Colorado · Colorado Springs · Connecticut · Crater Lake National Park · Dallas · Death Valley National Monument · Delaware · Denver · Detroit · Dinosaur National Monument · Everglades National Park · Florida · Georgia · Grand Canyon National Park · Grand Teton National Park · Great Smoky Mountains National Park · Gulf Islands National Seashore · Hawaii/Hawaiian Islands · Houston · Idaho · Illinois · Indiana · Indianapolis · Iowa · Jackson · Jacksonville · Joshua Tree National Monument · Kansas · Kansas City · Kentucky · Key West · Lake Tahoe/Squaw Valley · Las Vegas · Lassen Volcanic National Park · Lexington/Kentucky Horse Park · Los Angeles · Louisiana · Maine · Mammoth Cave National Park · Maryland · Massachusetts · Memphis · Mesa Verde National Park · Miami/Miami Beach · Michigan · Milwaukee · Minneapolis/St Paul · Minnesota · Mississippi · Missouri · Mojave Desert · Montana · Monterey · Monument Valley · Mount Rainier National Park · Napa Valley · Nashville · Navajo Country · Nebraska · Nevada · New Hampshire · New Jersey · New Mexico · New Orleans · New York · New York City · Niagara Falls · North Carolina · North Dakota · Ohio · Oklahoma · Oklahoma City · Olympic National Park · Omaha · Oregon · Orlando · Outer Banks · Palm Beach/West Palm Beach · Palm Springs · Pennsylvania · Pennsylvania Dutch Country · Petrified Forest National Park · Philadelphia · Phoenix · Pittsburgh · Portland · Puerto Rico · Redwood National Park · Rhode Island · Richmond · Rocky Mountain National Park · Sacramento · St Augustine · St Louis · St Petersburg · Salt Lake City · San Antonio · San Diego · San Francisco · San Jose · Santa Fe · Savannah · Seattle · Sequoia and Kings Canyon National Parks · Shenandoah National Park · South Carolina · South Dakota · Tampa · Tennessee · Texas · Tucson · US Virgin Islands · Utah · Vermont · Virginia · Washington · Washington DC · Waterton-Glacier International Peace Park · West Virginia · White Sands National Monument · Wisconsin · Wyoming · Yellowstone National Park · Yosemite National Park · Zion National Park

Practical Information	517

Air Travel · Alcohol · Amusement Parks · Angling · Bathing · Bed and Breakfast · Boat Trips · Business Hours · Bus Travel · Camping · Car Rental · Casinos · Chemists · Cruises · Currency · Customs Regulations · Diplomatic and Consular Offices · Diving · Dress · Electricity · Emergencies · Endangered Species Convention · Events · Food and Drink · Getting to the United States · Golf · Help for the Disabled · Holiday Apartments · Hotels/Motels/Resorts · Information · Language · Medical Care · Motoring in the United States · Museums · National Parks and Reserves · Newspapers and Periodicals · Photography · Postal Services · Public Holidays · Public Transport · Radio · Rail Travel · Restaurants · Riding · Rodeos · Safety and Security · Sailing · Shopping · Smoking · Sport · Taxis · Telephoning · Television · Tennis · Time · Tipping · Toilets · Travel Documents · Walking · Weights/Measures/Temperatures · When to Go · Winter Sports · Young People's Accommodation

Baedeker Specials

Religion and Agriculture	42/43
Land of the Skyscrapers	100/101
Living with San Andreas	177
Daredevils of Niagara	368
Index	585
Sources of Illustrations	590
Large Map	at end of book

The Principal Places of Tourist Interest at a Glance

**	Page
Amelia Island (FL)	264
Arches NP (UT)	146
Black Hills (SD, Y)	161
Boston (MA)	166
Bryce Canyon NP (UT)	175
Canyonlands NP (UT)	180
Cape Canaveral/ Kennedy Space Center (FL)	182
Carlsbad Caverns (NM)	185
Charleston (SC)	187
Chicago (IL)	194
Colonial Williamsburg (VA)	212
Death Valley (CA)	222
Denali NP (AK)	143
Everglades NP (FL)	234
Grand Canyon NP (AZ)	241
Hawaii (HI)	250
Kentucky Horse Park (KY)	278
Key West (FL)	270

**	Page
Lake Tahoe (CA, NV)	273
Los Angeles (CA)	280
Monticello (VA)	191
Monument Valley (AZ, UT)	322
Mount Vernon (VA)	497
Navajo Country (AZ, NM, UT)	327
New Orleans (LA)	339
New York City (NY)	349
Niagara Falls (NY)	367
Orlando (FL)	385
Philadelphia (PA)	400
Pueblos nr Santa Fe (NM)	456
Redwood NP (CA)	417
Rocky Mountain NP (CO)	420
San Francisco (CA)	441
Washington (DC)	484
White Sands (NM)	500
Yellowstone NP (WY, ID, MT)	506
Yosemite NP (CA)	510

*	Page
Acadia NP (ME)	292
Adirondacks (NY)	348
Atlanta (GA)	152
Atlantic City (NJ)	336
Badlands NP (SD)	155
Baltimore (MD)	157
Big Bend NP (TX)	161
Cape Cod (MA)	184
Channel Islands (CA)	178
Cody (WY)	209
Colorado Springs (CO)	215
Crater Lake NP (OR)	218
Cumberland Gap (KY)	269
Dallas (TX)	220
Denver (CO)	225
Detroit (MI)	229
Dinosaur National Monument (CO, UT)	233
El Paso (TX)	474
Florida Keys (FL)	237
Fort Laramie (WY)	505
Glacier Bay NP (AK)	144
Grand Teton NP (WY)	247
Great Smoky Mountains NP (NC, TN)	248
Hilton Head Island (SC)	467
Houston (TX)	252
Indianapolis (IN)	259
Isle Royale NP (MI)	309
Jackson (WY)	262
Kenai Peninsula (AK)	144
Lassen Volcanic NP (CA)	277

*	Page
Las Vegas (NV)	274
Louisville (KY)	269
Luray Caverns (VA)	482
Mammoth Cave NP (KY)	293
Memphis (TN)	296
Mesa Verde NP (CO)	298
Miami/Miami Beach (FL)	299
Milwaukee (WI)	309
Monterey (CA)	320
Mount Rainier NP (WA)	323
Mount Shasta (CA)	179
Napa Valley (CA)	325
North Cascades NP (WA)	483
Oklahoma City (OK)	378
Olympic NP (WA)	379
Organ Pipe National Monument (AZ)	149
Outer Banks (NC)	390
Ozark Mountains (AR)	151
Pennsylvania Dutch Country (PA)	396
Petrified Forest NP (AZ)	398
Phoenix (AZ)	406
Point Reyes (CA)	179
Puerto Rico (PR)	413
St Augustine (FL)	423
St Louis (MO)	424
St Petersburg (FL)	428
Salt Lake City (UT)	430
San Antonio (TX)	434
San Diego (CA)	437
Sanibel and Captiva (FL)	238
Santa Fe (NM)	452

(continued on page 590)

Preface

This guide to the United States is one of the new generation of Baedeker guides.

These guides, illustrated throughout in colour, are designed to meet the needs of the modern traveller. They are quick and easy to consult, with the principal places of interest described in alphabetical order, and the information is presented in a format that is both attractive and easy to follow.

This guide covers the whole of the United States, including the overseas states and territories. It is in three parts. The first part gives a general account of the country, its topography and geology, climate, flora and fauna, population, religion, government and society, educational system, economy, transport and communications, history, famous people, art and culture, with a special section on the Indian peoples of North America. A selection of literary quotations and a number of suggested itineraries lead in to the second part, in which places of tourist interest – states, towns and cities, National Parks, historic sites – are described. The third part contains a variety of practical information. Both the sights and the practical information are listed in alphabetical order.

The new Baedeker guides are noted for their concentration on essentials and their convenience of use. They contain numerous specially drawn plans and colour illustrations; and at the end of the book is a large map making it easy to locate the various places described in the "A to Z" section of the guide with the help of the co-ordinates given at the head of each entry.

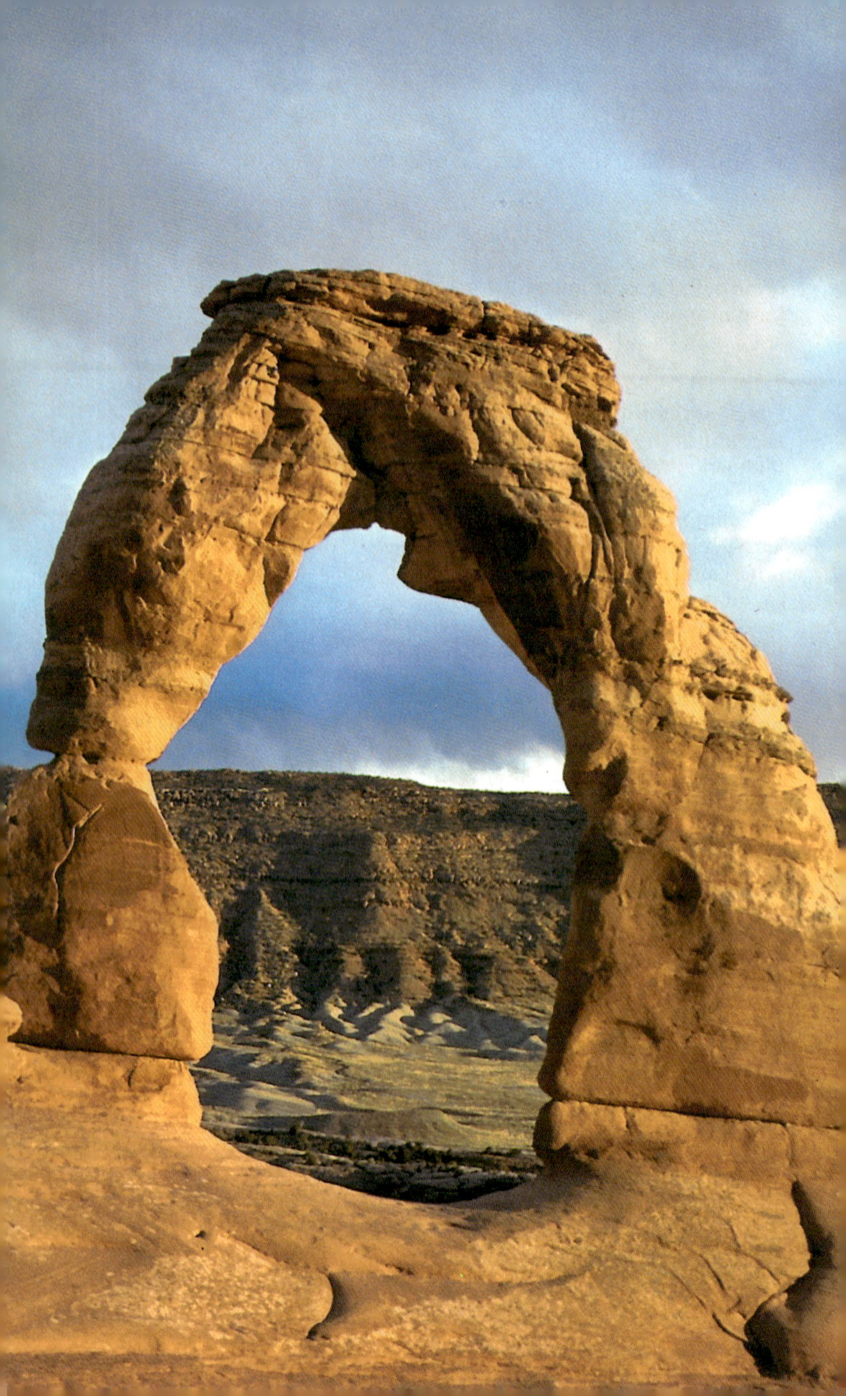

Facts and Figures

The United States offers an immense variety of attractions for holidaymakers. With awe-inspiring natural beauties such as the Grand Canyon and the Yosemite and Yellowstone National Parks, the immeasurable landscapes of the prairies, great historic cities like Philadelphia, Boston, New York, Washington, New Orleans and San Francisco, rapidly developing centres like Miami, Atlanta, Dallas, Houston, Phoenix and Denver, old colonial-style towns and mansions, the old Wild West, it has something for everyone – for those whose interests lie in the towns, for nature-lovers, for the adventurous, for both young and old. Within the limited compass of this guide it is possible to describe only a small selection of the places of interest to visitors in this immense country.

All the various natural regions of the United States, including the thinly populated areas of desert and steppe, are served by a magnificent network of roads, giving visitors easy access to a range of natural marvels hardly to be equalled anywhere on earth.

General

With an area of 3.6 million sq.miles/9.3 million sq.km, the United States of America is the world's fourth largest state (after Russia, Canada and the People's Republic of China). The main continental territory of the United States (48 of the 50 states, excluding Alaska and Hawaii) covers an area of some 3 million sq.miles/7.83 million sq.km, extending between the Atlantic and the Pacific and between Canada and the Gulf of Mexico. This continental heartland has broadly the form of a rectangle reaching for some 2800 miles/4500km from the Atlantic in the east to the Pacific in the west and extending over four time zones. From the Canadian frontier in the north (lat. 49° N) to the southern tip of Florida (lat. 24° N) it is some 1700 miles/2700km as the crow flies. The frontier with Canada (excluding Alaska) is almost 4000 miles/6400km long, that with Mexico some 2000 miles/3200km long. The total coastline of the continental United States ranges between 31,000 and 54,000 miles (50,000 and 87,000km) according to the method of measurement, taking account of all coasts washed by tidal waters, including bays and estuaries. With this large area, the continental United States extends into most of the natural regions of the North American continent, from the sub-Arctic expanses of Alaska to the fringes of the tropics in Florida; and in addition the United States reaches right into the tropics with the Hawaiian archipelago and the unincorporated territories of Guam and Samoa in the Pacific.

Situation and extent

The United States is the leading world power and industrial nation. The media constantly report new records in scientific research and technological development, in sport, in the economy and in many other fields. The

Super-power USA

◀ *Delicate arch in Utah State: The work of the wind and weather*

Topography and Geology

United States has eight of the ten largest industrial enterprises in the world, most of the world's wealthiest people, most jet aircraft and most automobiles, the largest consumption of energy, the greatest number of skyscrapers. The natural basis for all this is provided by the country's enormous mineral wealth (particularly coal, oil, natural gas and copper), its great expanses of productive agricultural land, forests and pasturage for immense numbers of livestock. The great scale of this territory and its climatic extremes have long been, and still are, a challenge to those who occupy it – a challenge calling for toughness and resource.

Population and density

At the last Census in 1990 the United States had a population of 248.7 million, at an average density of 71.5 to the sq. mile (27.6 to the sq. kilometre). This average conceals much higher figures in certain cities and conurbations: more than 20% of the total population live in the "Boswash" megalopolis (between Boston and Washington) alone.

Urbanisation

Although great stretches of this huge country are thinly populated and only superficially developed, nowhere else in the world does such a high proportion of the population live in towns and cities. Urbanisation has reached such a pitch that some of the larger cities have joined up along the highways linking them to form "strip cities". This development is particularly marked in the north-eastern USA (Boswash megalopolis, extending from Boston to Washington), the Middle West (Chipitts, from Chicago to Pittsburgh) and California (Sansan strip city, from San Diego to San Francisco).

A post-industrial service society

The dynamic development of the cities has made the United States the world's leading post-industrial service society, using the most modern communications technology.

Topography and Geology

Orographic and tectonic regions

Appalachians/ Cordilleras

Central Lowlands/ Coastal Plains

In the surface topography of the United States four main regions can be distinguished. The regional patterns result from the combination of differences of relief with differing climatic conditions. The four great natural regions, differing from one another but also differentiated within themselves, are the Appalachian mountain system; the Cordilleras, which can be divided into the Rocky Mountains, the intermontane region and the Pacific mountain system (extending into Alaska); the Central Lowlands, with basins and plateaux extending between these ranges of mountains; and the Coastal Plains on the Atlantic and the Gulf of Mexico. The fifth great natural region of North America, the Canadian Shield, extends only a short way into the United States, along Lake Superior and in the Adirondacks.

Climatic regions

The climatic pattern shows a transition from humidity in the east to aridity in the west, and from sub-Arctic conditions in Alaska to subtropical and tropical temperatures in the south. These broad trends in the two most important climatic factors – humidity (increasing from west to east) and temperature (increasing from north to south) – are subject to further differentiation in detail: thus in the arid regions the mountains represent islands of greater humidity.

Patterns of land use

The exploitation of the natural landscape by man was adapted to physical conditions in the different natural regions: a differentiation reflected particularly in patterns of agricultural development. In terms of settlement patterns and economic structure, however, it is possible to distinguish four broad regions. In spite of considerable differences within each region they show so many common features that their separate identities are unmistakable.

North-East: New England

The north-eastern United States, including New England and the middle Atlantic coast with its hinterland, was originally a farming region. It now

Topography and Geology

contains the largest conurbation in the country ("Megalopolis"), mainly consisting of the eastern parts of the manufacturing belt.

The Middle West, with Chicago as its principal centre, is the heartland of the United States. It is a region of highly productive agriculture, particularly in the maize (corn) and soya belt, and also of large-scale industrial production in the western part of the manufacturing belt.

Middle West

The South, extending from Virginia to Texas, was formerly the home of a plantation economy based on slave labour. Its economic development, in particular its industrial development, began relatively late. In some parts of the region, however, particularly on the western Gulf Coast and in the Piedmont area of the Appalachians, there has been an influx of important modern industries.

The South

The Sun Belt, mostly lying within the South, is a climatically favoured swathe of territory which takes in the hinterland of the Atlantic and Gulf coasts and also the arid region just north of the Mexican frontier. Since the 1970s this region has enjoyed a strong economic upswing as a result of the establishment of growth industries and has attracted many incomers from other parts of the country. The beneficial climate appeals particularly to older people, and there has been a sharp increase in the number of retirement homes, notably in Florida and Arizona.

Sun Belt

The West, the largest of the regions, takes in the arid territories of the Plains and the Cordilleras. Apart from the Pacific coast and a number of scattered concentrations of population it is relatively thinly settled. The dominant elements in its economy are mining and farming. In some areas modern industrial development is in progress.

The West

Relief and Geological Structure

The surface topography of the United States is determined by two mountain complexes running north–south, with an endless expanse of plains between them. The more easterly of the two ranges, the Appalachians, runs parallel to the Atlantic coast from New England in the north to Alabama in the south. Built up from sedimentary rocks of the Palaeozoic era, either subjected to folding at an early stage or horizontally bedded, then levelled down to a residual plateau and finally thrust up again during the formation of the Cordilleras, the Appalachians are a region of rounded hills of medium height, often reduced to a stepped outline, with occasional monadnocks rising above them, and of terraced plateaux.

Appalachians

From the highest hills – to the north Mount Washington (6288ft/1917m) in the White Mountains of New England, to the south the Great Smoky Mountains, with Clingmans Dome (6642ft/2025m), and above all Mount Mitchell (6684ft/2037m) in the Blue Ridge, rising steeply up from the Piedmont area below – there are wide-ranging views. The Appalachians are broken up by the picturesque transverse valleys of rivers flowing towards the Atlantic, particularly the Hudson, Delaware, Susquehanna and Potomac.

Mount Washington/ White Mountains/ Great Smoky Mountains/ Piedmont/ Blue Ridge

The longitudinal layout of the central and southern Appalachians reflects their geological structure. In passing through the mountain system from east to west four landscape zones can be distinguished: the rolling Piedmont Plateau, which falls down towards the Atlantic coastal plain in a steep gradient, with numerous rapids on the rivers; the long, high chain of the Blue Ridge; the Great Appalachian Valley (the Valley and Ridge Province), with numerous small ranges of folded rocks; and finally the Appalachian Plateau to the west, with a scarp face (the Allegheny Front and the Cumberland Front) which at some points is particularly marked.

Great Appalachian Valley/ Allegheny Front/ Cumberland Front

Topography and Geology

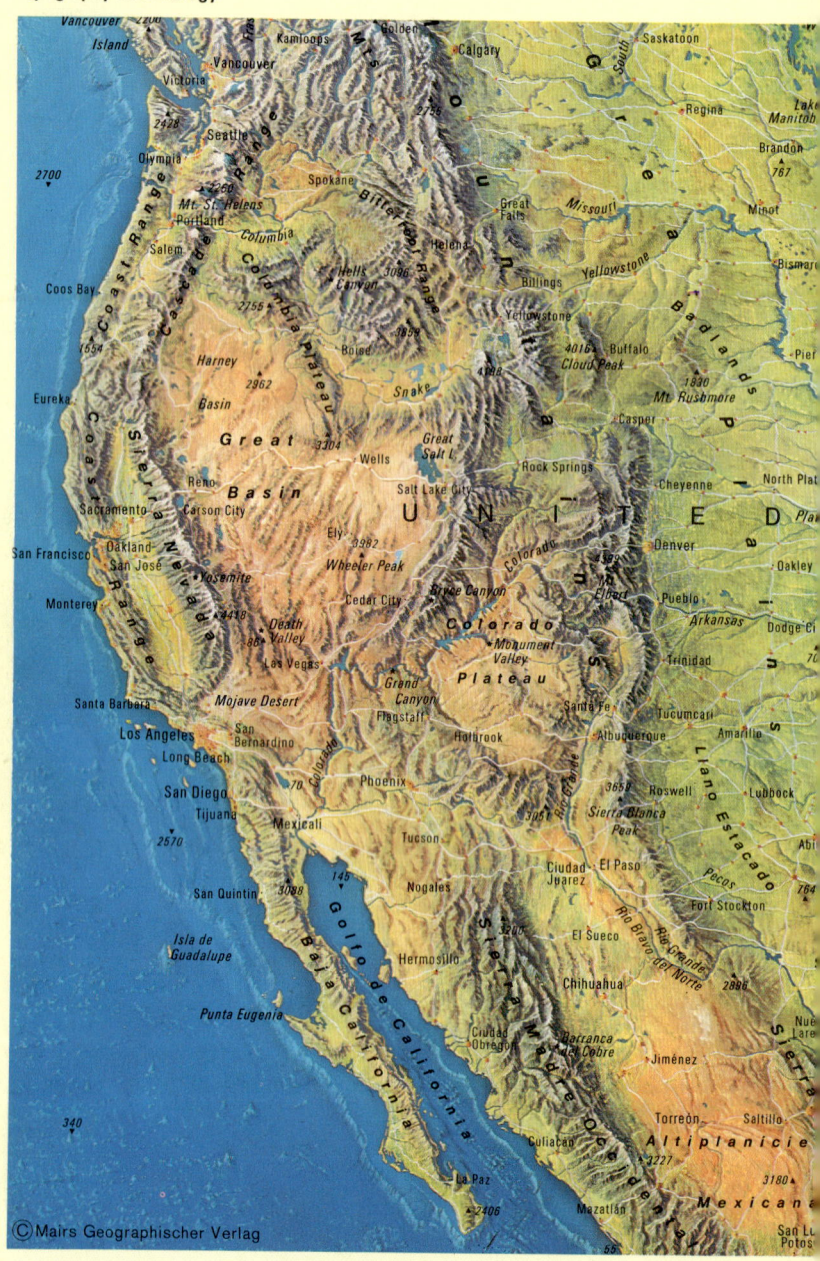

Topography and Geology

Topography and Geology

View into the Shenandoah Valley

Ozarks/ Ouachita Mountains	Beyond the alluvial Mississippi depression the Appalachians end in the Ozarks and the Ouachita Mountains, which rise to 2880ft/878m.
Cordilleras	The western range of mountains, the Cordilleras, occupy a much larger area. They consist of two mountain systems, the Rocky Mountains to the east and the Pacific Mountains to the west, between which lies an extensive region of intermontane plateaux and basins. The Cordilleras were the product of a stage-by-stage intrusion of oceanic crust and continental fragments during the thrust of the Pacific Plate under the North American Plate and the accompanying thickening of the earth's crust. The juxtaposition of upthrust and sunk rocks is the result of sharp fault movements in a geologically recent past. The continuing instability of the earth's crust at this boundary between convergent plates is reflected in active vulcanism and earthquakes, for example in the recent tremors in the San Francisco area and the volcanic eruptions in the north-western United States (Mount St Helens) and in Alaska.
Rocky Mountains	High alpine land-forms begin to appear in the Rocky Mountains at much higher altitudes than in the Alps – a consequence of the aridity of this region. Within the Pacific mountain system with its high rainfall, in Alaska, alpine forms with glaciers in the valleys reach right down to sea level, so that in this area the Pacific Ocean comes up against the mountains in a grandiose fjord landscape. The Cordilleras reach their greatest height in
Mount McKinley	Mount McKinley (20,320ft/6193m) in Alaska. In many places along their entire length they rise above 13,000ft/4000m – within the Pacific mountain
Cascade Mountains/ Sierra Nevada Front Range/ Sangre de Cristo Mountains	system in the Cascade Mountains and the Sierra Nevada, within the Rockies round the Yellowstone and Wyoming basins, and in the Front Range and Sangre de Cristo Mountains. Popular tourist sights, affording wide-ranging views, are Mount Evans (14,264ft/4348m), near Denver, and Pikes Peak (14,110ft/4301m) at Colorado Springs in the Front Range.

Topography and Geology

The arid intermontane regions in the rain shadow of the Pacific mountain system offer impressive steppe and desert landscapes. With scanty vegetation cover, the geological structure is revealed with great clarity, for example in the multi-coloured strata of the sedimentary rocks.

Intermontane regions

This can be seen at its most impressive in the world-famous Grand Canyon, which the Colorado River has cut through the horizontally bedded Palaeozoic strata of the Colorado Plateau.

Grand Canyon

Similar erosional forms can be seen in the basaltic lavas of the Columbia Plateau.

Columbia Plateau

The particularly arid southern section of the intermontane region, most of it without any drainage to the sea, is known as the Basin and Range Province, in which basins alternate with short, steep ranges of hills. The largest of these basins, much ramified, is the Great Basin, on the eastern edge of which is the Great Salt Lake and in its south-western part Death Valley, the lowest point in the United States (282ft/86m below sea level).

Basin and Range Province

The Central Lowlands, between the Appalachians and the Cordilleras, consist of horizontally bedded Mesozoic rocks. The steep edge of the High Plains facing the Missouri plateau, the Pine Ridge Escarpment, is – like the Coteau du Missouri and many other similar features – a scarp formed by the differing resistance to erosion of the horizontally bedded sedimentary rocks. Although much of the landscape of the Central Lowlands is monotonous, there are occasional features offering a little variety, particularly resulting from the glaciation of the Canadian Shield. Great areas of recent morainic landscape in the north, with rounded hills and numerous lakes, alternate with absolutely flat and featureless areas of alluvial deposits occupying former glacial lakes.

Central Lowlands
High Plains/
Pine Ridge
Escarpment

In the five Great Lakes (Superior, Huron, Michigan, Erie and Ontario), formed by the melting of the inland ice, the United States possesses a substantial share (60,600sq.miles/157,000sq.km) of one of the largest freshwater systems in the world, with a total area, including the Canadian section, of some 96,500sq.miles/250,000sq.km.

Great Lakes

The Great Lakes play a very important part in the North American system of inland waterways. They are linked with the open sea (the North Atlantic) by the St Lawrence Seaway, opened in 1959, and have various connections with the navigable Mississippi–Missouri river system.

To the south the Central Lowlands merge into the Gulf Coast Plain, which extends inland for some 550 miles/885km along the Mississippi and in Florida runs into the Atlantic Coast Plain. Both of these plains consist of geologically recent deposits (Tertiary and Quaternary). Along their coasts, fringing the Atlantic and the Gulf of Mexico, are numerous spits of land, which have frequently been cut off to form islands, as in the Sea Islands of Georgia. The coastal lagoons within the spits of land in the Gulf Coast Plain form the important Intracoastal Waterway.

Coastal Plains
Gulf Coast Plain
Atlantic Coast Plain

Intracoastal Waterway

Along the Atlantic coast, where the sea has encroached on the land, the wide funnel-shaped estuaries of the rivers, particularly the Delaware, Susquehanna and Potomac, give access for shipping to the inner reaches of Delaware Bay and Chesapeake Bay. The endless sandy beaches in both coastal plains offer ample scope for bathers; in the south bathing is possible throughout the year.

Minerals

The United States occupies a leading place in the world in the exploitation of its mineral resources, particularly oil and natural gas. In 1992 well over 500 million tons of gas and more than 420 million tons of oil were extracted. There are large oilfields in the western Gulf Coast plain (Texas), providing the basis for a massive petrochemical industry. There are also rich deposits

Oil, natural gas

15

Topography and Geology

of oil and gas in the Central Lowlands (Texas, Oklahoma, etc.), on the eastern edge of the Rockies (Colorado) and in the intermontane basins (e.g. the Wyoming basin). Oilfields of some size have also been found in the Central Valley of California, and in the early eighties considerable reserves of oil were discovered off the southern Californian coast. Since the completion of the Trans-Alaska Pipeline in 1977 oil has also been worked in the northern coastal plain of Alaska, on the Arctic Ocean. The Prudhoe field in this area is at present the largest working oilfield in North America.

Coal

The United States has the richest coal resources in the world, with 28% of total world reserves, and the coal can be extracted at a much more economic rate than in Europe, since the seams lie in relatively undisturbed rock and are close to the surface. In 1992 some 860 million tons of hard coal and 80 million tons of brown coal were extracted. Considerable reserves of hard coal have been discovered in the Appalachian plateaux and in the West (particularly in Colorado and Wyoming). The coal is worked by open-cast methods (30%) and by horizontal shafts (70%), which can be easily driven in from the slopes of the hills. The oldest-established coalfield is round Pittsburgh, which in the 19th century developed into the main centre of the US iron and steel industry. The large deposits of brown coal in the Central Lowlands (particularly North Dakota, Montana and Wyoming) are still being worked.

Iron ore

The largest reserves of iron ore are in the Canadian Shield, which is rich in minerals of all kinds and extends into the United States in the Great Lakes area. This area yields over 90% of total US production (in 1992 over 55 million tons). The high-grade haematite ores of the Mesabi Range (in the Superior Upland Range to the west of Lake Superior), with an iron content of 56%, established the world reputation of US iron ore. Following the gradual exhaustion of these stocks of high-grade ore since the end of the Second World War the lower-grade taconite ores, with an iron content of 20–35%, found in northern Minnesota have increasingly been worked. These ores can be brought up to a competitive level of quality by a concentration process. The ore is shipped from the port of Duluth to the centres of the steel industry on the Great Lakes and in the Appalachian region – earning the Great Lakes the name of the "inland ocean" of North American heavy industry. In spite of its rich deposits of ore, however, the Superior Upland region cannot meet the enormous demands of American industry, and considerable quantities of iron ore have to be imported.

Other minerals

Other important reserves of minerals are to be found mainly in the Cordilleras. There are large fully mechanised opencast copper-mines and associated non-ferrous metal smelting works in the states of Utah, Arizona and Montana. Uranium is worked mainly in the southern Rockies. Outside the Cordilleras the principal minerals worked are metals and industrial minerals. Gold is mined in Alaska and the Black Hills, and also in the Cordilleras (Rocky Mountains, Sierra Nevada). Large quantities of silver are worked in the Rockies. Lead comes mainly from the Ozark plateaux. Phosphate is worked in Florida and bauxite in Arkansas.

Rivers and Lakes

The United States shares with Canada the largest continuous area of fresh water in the world, the five Great Lakes, and much of the country is drained by the Mississippi and its tributaries. The Mississippi – "Old Man River" – is one of the longest and most abundantly flowing rivers in the world.

Rivers
Mississippi–Missouri river system

The largest catchment area among the river systems of the United States – with a length of over 3700 miles/6000km and an area of 1.25 million sq.miles/3.25 million sq.km – is that of the Mississippi and Missouri, which drains into the Gulf of Mexico. Its most important tributaries are the Arkan-

Topography and Geology

Lake landscapes in the Rockies

sas and the Ohio, with the Allegheny and the Tennessee. The Mississippi–Missouri river system plays an important part as an inland waterway: along with the Illinois Waterway it provides a link between the industrial regions of the Great Lakes and the Gulf of Mexico.

The Rio Grande, with a total length of 1885 miles/3034km and a catchment area of 220,000sq.miles/570,000sq.km, also flows into the Gulf of Mexico. The Colorado River, which flows through the arid region of the south-west, is 1450 miles/2334km long, with a catchment area of 165,000sq.miles/ 428,000sq.km. It flows into the Gulf of California, and in the course of its passage through the south-western United States has carved out a grandiose valley through the rock (see Sights from A to Z, Grand Canyon National Park).

Rio Grande
Colorado

The 1240 mile/2000km long Columbia River, with an abundant flow of water, rises in the Canadian Rockies and in its lower course flows through the north-western United States into the Pacific. It has a catchment area of 258,000sq.miles/668,000sq.km. Its most important tributary within the United States is the Snake River, whose source streams tumble down from the mountains of the Yellowstone and Grand Teton region.

Columbia River

Among the rivers draining into the Atlantic the St Lawrence, which flows out of Lake Ontario (length 800 miles/1287km; catchment area, including the Great Lakes, 398,000sq.miles/1,030,000sq.km), occupies a special position. As the St Lawrence Seaway, opened in 1959, it enables large ocean-going ships to reach the ports of the manufacturing belt on the Great Lakes.

St Lawrence

The river systems of the United States have been turned to good account. Dams have been constructed on most of the rivers, including some (on the Colorado, Columbia and Missouri) which are among the largest in the world. The prototype for all later developments was the Tennessee Valley project, begun in 1933. The dams provide protection against flooding, produce hydroelectric power and, in the arid regions, supply water for irrigation. Two important schemes in the Pacific West are the Central Valley

Dams

Topography and Geology

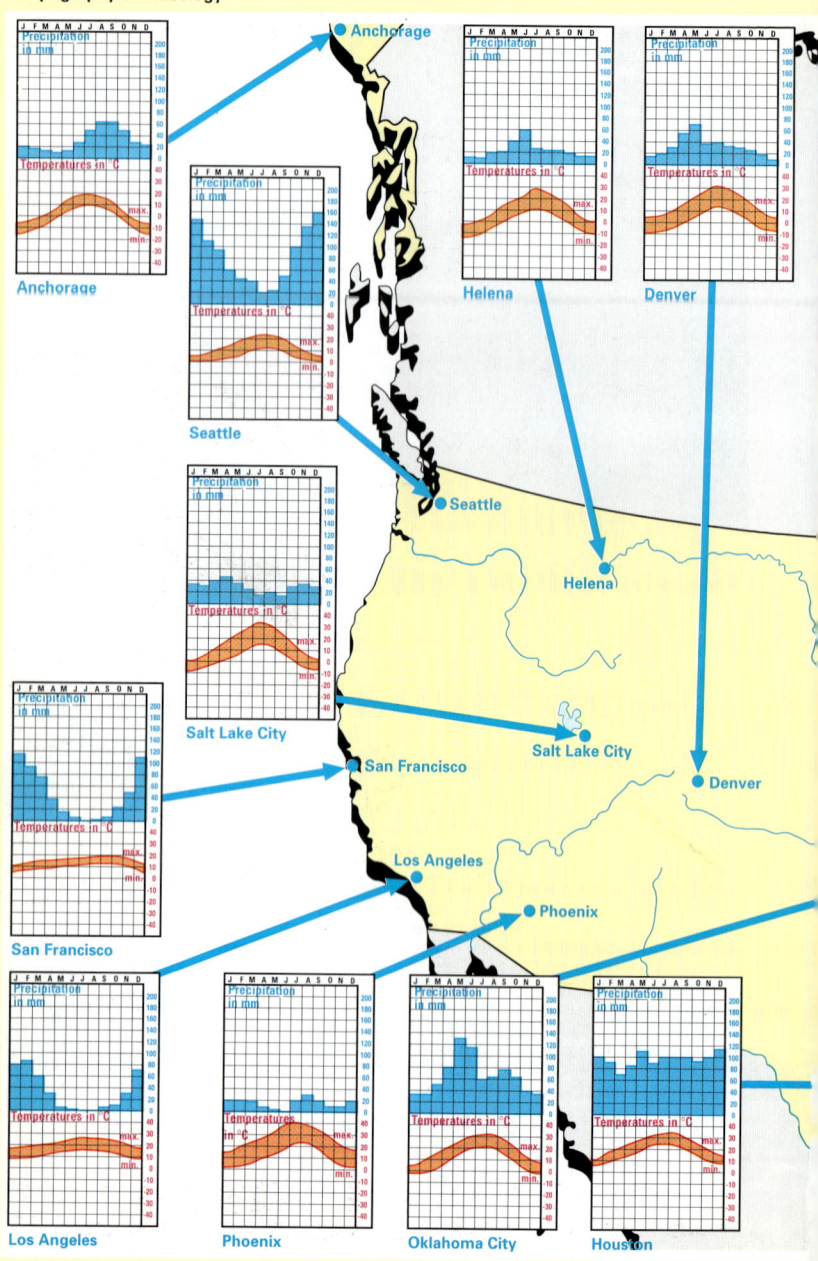

Anchorage

Seattle

Salt Lake City

San Francisco

Los Angeles

Phoenix

Oklahoma City

Houston

Helena

Denver

Topography and Geology

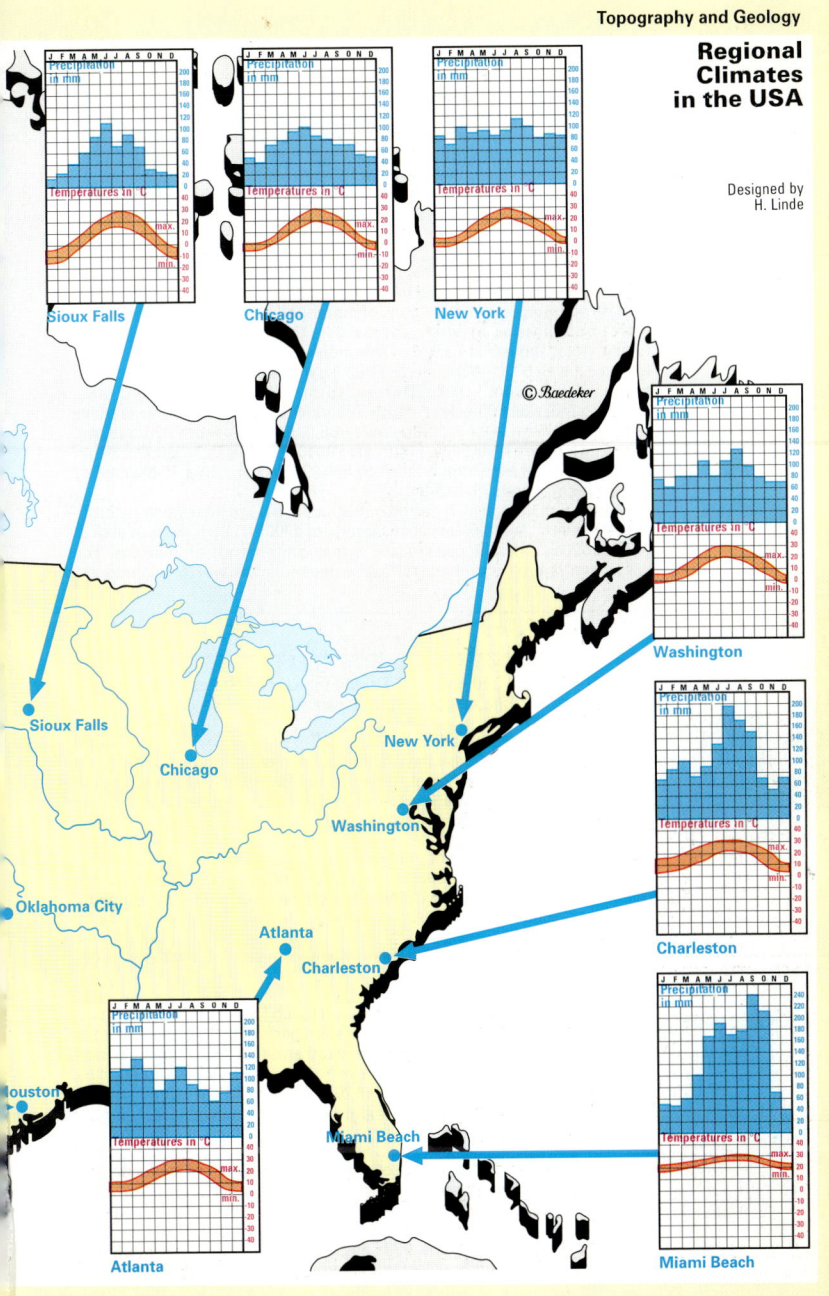

Regional Climates in the USA

Designed by H. Linde

© Baedeker

Sioux Falls

Chicago

New York

Washington

Charleston

Atlanta

Houston

Oklahoma City

Miami Beach

Climate

Project and the California State Water Project, which supply the densely populated arid region of southern California with water from the wetter north. To ensure that water will be available to meet the steadily increasing needs of the arid regions, schemes such as the Snake River–Colorado Project (to provide increased resources for the irrigation of the Columbia plateau) and the North American Water and Power Alliance (to supply the Central Valley of California) have been developed. The basic idea of such large-scale projects is to convey the surplus water resources of the northern Pacific states, with their abundance of rain, to the drought regions of the south.

Lakes
Great Lakes

As already noted, the five Great Lakes lying on the frontier with Canada are the largest continuous area of fresh water in the world. They influence the climate of the surrounding regions of the United States and are of predominant importance as an inland waterway for the transport of raw materials to the great industrial centres. The individual lakes are Lake Superior (surface level 600ft/183m; area 31,820sq.miles/82,414sq.km; maximum depth 1330ft/406m), Lake Huron (surface level 580ft/176m; area 23,000sq.miles/59,596sq.km; depth 785ft/239m), Lake Michigan (surface level 580ft/177m; area 22,400sq.miles/58,016sq.km; depth 925ft/282m), Lake Erie (surface level 570ft/174m; area 9940sq.miles/25,745sq.km; depth 210ft/64m) and Lake Ontario (surface level 245ft/75m; area 7540sq.miles/19,529sq.km; depth 797ft/243m).

Great Salt Lake

The Great Salt Lake, which has no outlet, lies in a huge intermontane basin in the western United States at an altitude of 4200ft/1280m, with an area of some 1500sq.miles/4000sq.km and a maximum depth of 35ft/10m. The water level is subject to sharp variations depending on weather conditions.

Climate (Map pp. 18–19)

Temperate zone

Apart from Alaska and southern Florida the United States lies within the temperate zone. The larger northern part is within the cool temperate climatic zone.

Travelling cyclones

In most of the United States the weather pattern is determined by cyclones (areas of low pressure) which travel throughout the year, bringing an alternation between cold and warm air masses and between overcast and clear skies and producing wide differences in rainfall.

Pacific coast

On the Pacific coast the mountains striking north–south form a barrier which gives the area an oceanic climate and high rainfall. In the coastal regions of the north-western United States the annual rainfall is frequently over 80in./2000mm.

Southern California

Southern California has a climate of Mediterranean type, with dry summers and winter rain.

West

The maritime influence, however, does not reach far inland. The intermontane region of the Cordilleras and the western parts of the Central Lowlands (the plains and prairies) are areas of marked aridity where the only period of precipitation of any quantity occurs in the hills. The leeward slopes of the hills have an annual rainfall of under 20in./500mm. In the south-western United States there are areas of extreme aridity in which there is only sporadic rainfall.

East

The eastern United States, on the other hand, have plenty of rain, since the masses of warm air moving north from the Gulf of Mexico are charged with moisture. The Gulf Coast and the Appalachians have annual precipitations of over 60in./1500mm. The boundary between the wetter east and the drier west runs roughly along the 98th degree of longitude. This important climatic frontier is clearly reflected in the different agricultural patterns in the transition from the humid to the arid regions. Since the level of precipitations varies widely from year to year the boundary of the arid zone moves this way or that way within a broad corridor.

The climate of the south-eastern United States is influenced by the masses of hot, moist air coming in from the Gulf of Mexico. Its characteristics are mild winters, hot summers and high rainfall.

South-East

The continental character of the climate, particularly in the central regions of the United States, means that visitors from Europe must be prepared for very high temperatures in summer and very low ones in winter. In the south-east the high humidity of the air frequently produces an unpleasant mugginess.

Continental climate

Since the mountain ranges run north–south there is a practically unhindered exchange of air masses between arctic and tropical latitudes. Cold air coming from Canada gives the north-eastern states extremely cool winters and springs, even though New York, for example, lies in the same latitude as central Italy. In summer, on the other hand, warm, moist air masses from the Gulf of Mexico can be carried to the north-eastern United States, bringing with them long periods of sultry weather.

Exchange of air masses

Particularly in the northern and north-eastern states inflows of cold air from Canada can produce extreme weather conditions in the form of unpleasant winter blizzards with heavy snowfalls.

Blizzards

The cold winds known as "northers" can reach far south and frequently cause considerable damage to subtropical crops on the Gulf Coast, particularly in Florida in winter.
The rapid change between warm and cold air leads to extreme variations in temperature, particularly in winter.

Northers

The collision between air masses at very different temperatures gives rise, particularly east of the Rockies, to tornadoes – violent storms with winds whirling round a small area of extremely low pressure which cause considerable damage in their passage.

Tornadoes

Hurricanes travelling in from the Caribbean in late summer and early autumn also cause great devastation, not so much from the high winds as from the tidal waves, heavy rain and flooding which they bring with them. Only the Gulf Coast plain and the Atlantic coastal plain lie in the path of these storms, against which there is now a well organised tracking and early warning system.

Hurricanes

Flora and Fauna

Flora

Apart from the arid western regions and the sub-Arctic tundra in Alaska the territory of the United States has a natural cover of forest. The boreal coniferous forest (spruce, fir, larch and pine) characteristic of great expanses of Canada extends far south into the United States only in the Cordilleras. Between the 60th and the 40th degrees of latitude there extends parallel to the coast the 90–180 mile/150–300km wide belt of coniferous forest of the Pacific coastal regions (Douglas fir, Sitka spruce, western red cedar, western hemlock), giving place towards the east to the pine forests and the sub-alpine coniferous forests of the mountain regions. These in turn are succeeded by the grassland of the Plains, the short-grass prairie, which around the 100th degree of longitude merges into the tall-grass prairie. Farther east the north-eastern mixed forest (hemlock, red

Northern regions

Flora and Fauna

pine, hickory, beech, yellow birch and maple species) extends by way of the oak–hickory deciduous forest of the Middle West and the Appalachian deciduous forest to the Atlantic coast.

Southern regions — Below the 40th degree of latitude, about the level of San Francisco, a narrow strip of sequoia forests gives place to the macchia and sclerophyllous (hard-leaved) forests of the Chaparral and beyond this the sagebrush region of the Great Basin. Farther east extend the plains and prairies, followed by the oak–pine mixed forests reaching to the Atlantic coast.

Other regions with characteristic vegetation patterns are the creosote bush area, a subtropical steppe with succulents, Covillea tridentata, cactuses, yuccas and agaves on the high plateaux of eastern Arizona and New Mexico, and the subtropical pine forests between New Orleans and Florida. In the swampy region of southern Florida (the Everglades) there are great expanses of palmetto scrub.

Fauna

Endemic species — The relatively late (in geological terms) separation of the American from the Eurasian continent has led to remarkable correspondences between the fauna of the two continents. Nevertheless a number of endemic species developed, among them the bison, pronghorn antelope, prairie dog, turkey and some amphibians and reptiles, the best known of which are the various species of rattlesnakes. At the end of the 19th century large nature reserves began to be established in order to preserve native species which had been decimated by human settlement.

North-East and East — In the hills of the north-eastern and eastern United States are found the Virginia or white-tailed deer, the raccoon, the opossum and the chipmunk; the black bear is now rare. The birds of the Atlantic coast are numerous and

The bison, once lord of the prairies

varied – various species of terns, the laughing gull, the American grey heron, the great white egret and the pelican.
The swamplands of the south-east are the habitat of the Mississippi alligator, once common but now found only in nature reserves. The few manatees living off the coast of Florida are now threatened with extinction.

The herds of bison (buffaloes) which once roamed the prairies are now represented only by a few survivors. They share this territory with prairie dogs, pronghorn antelopes and the American badger. Typical birds are the prairie chicken, the prairie falcon and the burrowing owl. The coyote now prefers to live in the cultivated land of the open grassland steppe.

Prairies

The mountains of the north-west and west and the northern forests are the home of the black and grizzly bears. Here too are found the bighorn sheep, the elk and the wapiti. There are small numbers of pumas (cougars) in the Rockies. The population of some species of lynx and of the wolf has shown an increase. The white-tailed eagle, the heraldic bird of the United States, lives along the edges of the waterways. Along the Pacific coasts of Oregon and California are found the Californian sealion, the grey whale and the sea elephant.

North-West and West

Alaska is the home of the Arctic fox, the wolverine and the otter. In the adjoining Bering Sea and the North Pacific there are bottle-nosed dolphins and various species of whale and seal.

Alaska

Protection of Nature and the Environment

Although claimed to be the "land of unlimited possibilities" and "God's own country", the United States – like every other country in the world – is threatened with the continuing destruction of the balance of nature by the activities of man. The process began when the traditional way of life of the native Indian inhabitants, living close to nature, was disturbed and displaced by the first settlers from the Old World, and reached a peak in the 19th century, when whole tribes were forced to leave their home territories, the buffaloes which roamed the prairies were almost completely wiped out and forests were ruthlessly cleared (involving the decimation of the giant redwoods of the Pacific West).

Destruction of the balance of nature

In farming country the crops are threatened by soil erosion and dust storms, and in order to increase yields recourse is had to dry farming (in which the land is regularly cultivated but not sown every year) and strip farming (in which strips of land of varying width are alternately sown with grain and left fallow). In some areas marginal land has been abandoned.

Erosion in the farmlands

The logging industry, which formerly supplied building timber and firewood, is now geared to paper and cellulose production. A common practice has been to clear whole areas of forest – leading, particularly in upland areas of high rainfall, to wholesale erosion of the soil. The practice of selective felling, accompanied by reafforestation, is only gradually becoming established.

Over-felling of timber

The problem of acid rain has not yet been solved, and much damage has been caused to the terrestrial eco-system (vegetation, soil structure, water quality), particularly in the north-eastern United States and round large cities. To this is added the pollution of rivers and lakes, mainly by agriculture but also by mining, industry, transport and urban development. In Florida and other parts of the country, for example, pesticides and fungicides have seeped into the ground-water, threatening the supply of drinking water. Round the Great Lakes much damage to the forests and dramatic changes in the stocks of freshwater fish have been reported, no doubt mainly due to the emission of harmful substances from the gigantic industrial concentrations in the Chicago–Indianapolis–Pittsburgh area.

Acid rain; water pollution

Flora and Fauna

Oil prospecting: test drill in Wyoming

Mineral working	Farther dangers to the environment are the large-scale development of opencast mining, the creation of huge spoil heaps and the uncontrolled prospecting for oil in ecologically sensitive areas. Some tracts of land already have the aspect of a lunar landscape. Memories are still vivid of the ecological catastrophe caused by the wreck of the super-tanker "Exxon Valdez" off the coast of Alaska.
Destruction of flora and fauna	The use of irrigation in agriculture and extensive building development in the sunshine states of Florida, Arizona and California have led not only to dramatic changes in the water table but also to the destruction of the balance of nature over a wide area. As a result of the expansion of agriculture, the demand for more houses and the growth of leisure activities more and more species of flora and fauna are threatened with extinction.
High-tech industry	The consequences for the environment of the uncontrolled expansion of high-tech industry have been the cause of increasing concern. In many areas harmful substances (solvents, radioactive materials, etc.) from leaking tanks and waste disposal sites have seeped into the ground and contaminated the ground-water. Many employees of the computer industry have suffered severe damage to their health from chemicals and harmful vapours. During the boom periods of the electronics industry there have been substantial emissions of harmful substances into the atmosphere.
Smog	The uncontrolled growth of building development, industry and transport has led to serious air pollution in many areas. The problem is particularly acute in Los Angeles, whose blanket of smog, caused mainly by its huge numbers of private automobiles, has become proverbial.
Efforts for the protection of nature	The native fauna of the United States was decimated, and in some cases completely destroyed, from an early stage in the country's development by the white man. In the latter part of the 19th century, however, a beginning

was made with the establishment of large national parks and nature reserves in order to limit human intrusion and provide refuges for the native flora and fauna. Pioneers in this development were the Scottish immigrant John Muir and the bird painter John James Audubon. In 1864 the Yosemite Valley and the surrounding forests of giant redwoods were given statutory protection by the Californian government, and in 1872 Yellowstone National Park was established.

In recent years the increasing pressure for development and the realisation of the grave dangers to the environment have led most of the states of the USA to amend their legislation on the protection of nature, and as a result many existing nature reserves have been extended and new ones have been established.

Many particularly sensitive natural regions have now been scheduled as protected zones, managed either by the federal government (National Park Service, etc.) or by individual states (usually by the Department of Resources). Among them are the Everglades of Florida, the redwood forests of the Pacific coast, stretches of the Atlantic, Gulf and Pacific coasts and beautiful mountain regions like the Grand Teton, Yosemite and Mount Rainier areas. Recently numbers of individual natural features, recreation areas, cycling and hiking trails and historic sites have also been given statutory protection.

National Parks/ National Forests/ National Seashores/ National Recreational Areas/ State Parks

The various protected areas have their own administrations, and there are strict regulations for visitors, with park rangers to secure their observance. There are also visitor centres which provide a wide range of information, literature and maps, together with audio-visual shows and special exhibitions.

In many parks – for most of which there are admission charges – there are refreshment facilities, campgrounds and picnic areas, and sometimes also hotels and motels. The most important of the National Parks are described in the "Sights from A to Z" section of this guide.

Population; Towns and Other Settlements

At the last Census (1990) the United States had a population of 248.7 million, with a density of 71.5 to the sq. mile (27.6 to the sq. kilometre). Density is very much higher in the highly urbanised Atlantic coastal region, where more than a fifth of the total population live in the Boswash (Boston–Washington) megalopolis. The highest density is found in Washington DC, with 10,132 inhabitants to the sq. mile (3912 to the sq. kilometre). The east coast states containing the great urban concentrations also show high densities: New Jersey 987 to the sq. mile (381 to the sq. kilometre), Rhode Island 826 (319), Massachusetts 728 (281), Connecticut 655 (253), Maryland 453 (175), New York State 363 (140). There are also large concentrations of population in the highly industrialised areas round the Great Lakes, on the Pacific coast (particularly in California) and on the west coast of the Gulf of Mexico. At the other end of the scale are the arid regions of the Plains and the intermontane areas of the Cordilleras, the boreal forests and the sub-Arctic tundra in Alaska. In the arid regions of the West the population density falls below 5 to the sq. mile; in Alaska it is only 0.9.

Population and population density

With a birth rate stabilised in the early nineties at 17 per 1000 and a death rate of 9 per 1000, the United States shows a healthy rate of natural increase. Along with the increase due to immigration this produced an average growth rate of 9% for the years 1980 to 1990. As a result of the mobility of the population there are very considerable differences between the states: thus between 1980 and 1990 there was a population increase of 50% in Nevada, 35% in Arizona, 33% in Florida, 26% in California and 20% in Texas, while over the same period the population fell by 8% in West Virginia and 4% in Iowa and Wyoming.

Population increase

Population; Towns and Other Settlements

Internal migration

Certain regions of the United States are particularly attractive to internal migrants. Thus there has for several decades been a steady movement of population to the Pacific coast, and there has been a continuing migration of coloured people from the South into the industrial regions of the Atlantic coast and the Middle West. The trend from the predominantly agricultural areas into the urbanised industrial regions is clear. The greatest increase of population is in the Sun Belt, the climatically favoured stretch of country in the South between the Atlantic and the Pacific.

Urbanisation

The population of the United States is highly urbanised. In 1990 75% of the population lived in towns of over 2500 inhabitants (compared with 64% in 1950); in the areas round the Atlantic megalopolises and in California the figure was over 90%. Urbanisation is proceeding at a great rate in these areas, though not so much in the city centres as on the urban fringes. There are in the United States 174 large cities with a total of some 60 million inhabitants, compared with 132 in 1960; 970 middle-sized towns (25,000–100,000 inhabitants) with just under 45 million inhabitants (633 in 1960); and 1770 small towns (10,000–25,000 inhabitants) with 28 million inhabitants (1134 in 1960). There are now nine cities with over a million inhabitants (New York, Los Angeles, Chicago, Houston, Philadelphia, San Diego, Detroit, Dallas, Phoenix) and 15 cities with over 500,000.

Population Groups

Immigrants from Europe

From the early 17th century onwards some 47 million Europeans left their old homes and found new ones in North America. Some were refugees from religious persecution or political oppression, but most of them came to seek a better life. The first mass movement was started by immigrants from England who landed in the territory of the Powhatan Indians in 1607 and founded the colony of Virginia. By then, however, Scots, Germans, Irishmen, Dutch, Swedes, Swiss and French were also crossing the Atlantic. After the formation of the United States a certain hostility to foreigners began to develop, but this declined during the Presidency of Thomas Jefferson (1801–09). In the hundred years between the Congress of Vienna (1815) and the outbreak of the First World War almost 30 million Europeans entered the United States in three great waves of immigration.

First wave of immigration

Between 1815 and 1860 there were some 5 million immigrants – more than the total population of the United States at that time. Most of them came from Ireland (2 million), England, Wales and Scotland (a quarter of a million each) and Germany (1.7 million). The most influential group was the Irish, who were almost exclusively Catholic; almost all of them settled in the large towns of the North, particularly New York, where they soon came to dominate the unskilled labour market and developed into a powerful political force. During the heyday of Irish "boss rule" between 1870 and 1920 every town with a high proportion of Irish in its population had an Irish political leader and an Irish mayor. Many old-established Americans, predominantly Protestant, saw the "papists" as a threat and organised themselves in such activities as the Nativist Movement. In 1844 there were riots in Philadelphia during which Roman Catholic churches were set on fire and Irishmen were killed.

Second wave of immigration

During the second wave of immigration, between 1860 and 1890, a further 10 million Europeans came to the United States, again predominantly British, Irish and German. Again, too, they settled mainly in the cities of the North: at this period half the population of New York, Chicago, Cincinnati, Milwaukee and Detroit had been born outside the United States.

Third wave of immigration

The third wave of immigration, between 1890 and 1914, brought another 15 million people to the United States, but this time they came from southern, south-eastern and eastern Europe. They were less rapidly assimilated than

Population; Towns and Other Settlements

In East Village, New York

their predecessors, and tended to live in separate districts of their own and to follow particular trades (Italians in the construction industries, Poles in heavy industry, etc.).

The increase in the number of immigrants gave rise to a new "nativist" movement and led finally to the Johnson Read Act of 1924, which restricted the number of immigrants to 150,000 a year and set quotas for different nationalities. In spite of this legislation, however, the United States was during the thirties the country which took in the largest numbers of refugees from Nazi persecution from all over Europe, particularly German Jews.

Restrictions on immigration

The 1990 Census showed that 29.9 million coloured people lived in the United States, representing 12.1% of the total population. In recent years the discriminatory term "negro" has fallen out of use, the terms "coloured" or "black" people being used instead. Increasingly, too, the black citizens of the United States like to refer to themselves as Afro-Americans. With the exception of the District of Columbia, where blacks make up 65.8% of the population, most of them live in the southern states of Mississippi (35.5% of the population), Louisiana (30.8%), South Carolina (29.8%) and Georgia (26.9%). The lowest proportions are in the states of Idaho (0.33%) and Montana (0.3%).

Afro-Americans

The first blacks arrived in Jamestown, in the British colony of Virginia, in 1619. They came not as slaves but as indentured labourers, who had bound themselves to pay the cost of their passage from Africa out of their wages, after which their earnings would be their own – an arrangement which also applied to many white workers. The bringing in of slaves began about 1660, and in the course of the 17th and 18th centuries the slave trade increased by leaps and bounds. By 1790 there were 610,000 slaves in Virginia, Georgia and North and South Carolina; in the other nine states there were only

Slavery

Population; Towns and Other Settlements

40,000. Their numbers had doubled by 1808, when the import of slaves was banned; and thereafter the need for additional labour was met by the children of slaves. The contrast between North and South was highlighted on the admission of Missouri to the Union in 1820, when under the Missouri Compromise slave-owning was prohibited north of latitude 36°30'. The Californian constitution of 1850 banned slave-owning, but it was permitted in other new territories. Federal officials were obliged by law to arrest runaway slaves and return them to their owners. In 1854 the Kansas–Nebraska Bill was passed, allowing slavery in these two states in spite of the fact that they lay north of the boundary line. This led to bloody riots and to the foundation of the Republican Party with its anti-slavery policy. The Republican victory in an election in 1860 sparked off the movement for secession.

"Free" blacks

In 1860 there were some 4 million black slaves in the southern states, owned by 384,000 whites. In addition there were in the United States 482,000 blacks who were not slaves, half of them in the slave-owning states. Neither in the South nor in the North, however, were these "free" blacks treated as equal with whites. In the South they were required by statutory restrictions to live as quasi-slaves, and in the North they were subject to discrimination, abuse and violence. During this period there was no public discussion of any change in their legal status: even the country's intellectual leaders, like Thomas Jefferson, who saw "natural and indelible lines of difference" between the white and black races, and Abraham Lincoln, in whose opinion blacks and whites could not be considered on the same level, had no thought of change.

Civil War

The Civil War (1861–65) began as a political conflict over the maintenance of the Union but ended as a war for the abolition of slavery. This war aim – if indeed it was one – was based primarily on pragmatic grounds. With the idea of weakening the economy of the South, attracting increased numbers of blacks into the army of the Union and stirring up unrest and risings among the blacks of the South, Lincoln issued in 1863 his proclamation of emancipation, which declared all black slaves in the southern states to be free. Some 190,000 slaves fled to the north, where they became competitors in the labour market. This led from 1863 onwards to the "draft riots", mainly involving Irish immigrants, in the course of which an orphanage for black children in New York was burned down.

Progressive developments

After the Civil War there were some progressive developments for the benefit of the black population. On September 18th 1865 the ban on slavery was incorporated in the Constitution under the 13th Amendment, and further constitutional amendments guaranteed the civil rights of blacks (1868) and granted them the vote (1870). Thus, theoretically, the liberation of blacks was achieved; but it was to be many years before further statutory measures were introduced to give them full equal rights. It was mainly from the fifties of the present century that they were granted rights which had been denied them since 1875 – the abolition of racial segregation in the armed forces between 1950 and 1955, the Civil Rights Acts of 1857 and 1964, the Voting Rights Act of 1965 and the Fair Housing Act of 1968. But all this still did not go far enough. As Martin Luther King declared, the black man was not fighting for some vague abstract rights but for a concrete and immediate improvement in his living conditions. What good did it do him if he could send his children to an integrated school if he had no money to buy school clothing, and what did he gain from permission to move into any part of his town if he could not afford it? Blacks not only wanted the right to make use of any institution open to the public: they had to be fitted into the economic system in such a way that they were able to exercise that right.

Civil rights movement

In spite of the bussing boycott of 1955 in Montgomery, Alabama, and the sending in of the National Guard in 1957 to end racial segregation in schools, not much had changed in the situation of the black population. They were more poorly housed, their wages were lower and they were frequently unemployed. The road to equality led by way of demonstrations in Birmingham, Alabama, in 1962, the march on Washington and the murder of Martin Luther King to the race riots of 1965–69, which brought the state to the brink of a new civil war. Martin Luther King had sought by his Peace Movement to achieve integration, while Malcolm X and Eldridge Cleaver, leaders of the Black Power movement, aimed at racial segregation, the separation of the black from the white population, each with the same rights, and were prepared to use violence to attain their ends.

The social situation of black Americans has undoubtedly improved, but openly racist discrimination has now given place to social discrimination. 31.9% of all blacks live below the poverty line, compared with 10.7% of whites, and the unemployment rate among black workers is twice as high as for whites. Visitors to the United States cannot but observe the high proportion of blacks among beggars and the homeless, and will notice how many blacks buying food in a supermarket pay for it with coupons. The slums of the cities are mainly occupied by blacks, for although the separation of black and white residential areas is banned it still happens in practice. Resistance to continuing discrimination still leads to violent outbreaks like the riots in Los Angeles in the summer of 1993. The United States is still a long way away from a solution of the problem.

Present situation

The second largest minority group in the United States, after the Afro-Americans, is the Hispano-Americans (22.3 million, or 9% of the total population), with their roots in the Latin American countries. 13.5 million of them are "Chicanos" (Americans of Mexican/Indian descent); the rest are mainly from Puerto Rico, a United States territory since 1848, and, over the last thirty years, from Cuba – refugees from the economic difficulties of Castro's Cuba, now numbering something like a million. The states with the largest numbers of Mexican Americans are New Mexico (39.4% of the population), California (25.8%) and Texas (25.5%). The Puerto Ricans make up a high proportion (12%) of the population of New York; the Cuban exiles have settled mainly in Miami.

Hispano-Americans

A major problem is presented by illegal immigration from Mexico, which the American authorities can barely control even with the aid of a fence along the frontier and increased patrols.

Americans of Asian origin (7.2 million, or 2.9% of total population) are the third largest ethnic minority in the United States. The largest group is the Chinese (1.6 million), with large Chinatowns in New York and San Francisco, followed by Filipinos (1.4 million) and Japanese (0.8 million).

Americans of Asian origin

Between 1850 and 1866 increased numbers of Chinese crossed the Pacific to the west coast of the United States, where they played a part in building up the state of California. Many of them worked on the construction of the transcontinental railroad, competing with European workers. In 1870 they numbered 63,000; a hundred years later there were 435,000 of them. In 1877 an Irishman founded the Working Man's Party, with the object of denying jobs to Chinese workers, and in 1880 there were anti-Chinese riots in Denver, Colorado. During the last thirty years of the 19th century the Chinese were permitted to live only in certain areas in the United States, and they were not allowed to become US citizens. The Chinese Exclusion Act of 1882 put a stop to further immigration and prevented those born abroad from obtaining naturalisation. The ban on immigration was extended for ten years in 1892, and in 1902 was continued indefinitely; it was confirmed in the Johnson Read Act of 1924, and was not finally done away with until 1943.

Chinese

Towns and Other Settlements

The 8000 or so towns of the United States show a considerable degree of uniformity, mainly because they were new foundations laid out on similar

Towns

Population; Towns and Other Settlements

Classical American townscape: the skyline of Denver

plans. Except in the towns of New England a regular grid is the norm. In the larger cities the centre (Downtown, the City, the Central Business District) is an area of high-rise blocks. The building of skyscrapers began in Chicago in 1885 and was pursued in central New York (Manhattan) – promoted by the invention of the electric elevator and the development of steel-framed construction. The high-rise buildings now common in cities of any size reflect the increasing importance of the services sector of the economy, now concentrated in the business districts.

The rapid growth of cities and the steady increase in the services sector have led not only to traffic problems but also to a radical change in the structure of cities. The more prosperous families have moved from districts near the centre to the outer fringes, and have been replaced by families lower in the social scale, particularly blacks. As a result the districts round the centre – severely overcrowded and mostly much dilapidated – have degenerated into slums. The result of the development of the cities has thus been to create social and ethnic ghettos.

Town planning

The town planners have tried to counter the negative developments resulting from continuing urbanisation. The separation of traffic into several levels and the provision of freeways into the central area have been achieved in many cities. The rehabilitation of areas round the centre, in a process of urban renewal, is well under way. The construction of tower apartment blocks is proceeding, with the object of restoring to the city centre its residential function. On the outskirts of the cities, where there is more space, carefully planned shopping centres (plazas) and industrial parks are being developed. In the great conurbations the planning of "strip cities" along the main highways is designed to obviate the spreading of development over large areas of the countryside.

Country settlements

Only a small proportion of the rural population of the United States live in towns, and villages of European type are almost non-existent. The settlements which have grown up at road intersections are centres providing essential facilities such as schools, churches, post offices, police stations, filling stations and garages, shops and cooperative institutions. Some 20% of the rural population live in settlements of this kind. Most of the farmers live in separate farmsteads. The regular layout of the fields and farms, like the grid plan in towns, reflects the original allocation of the territory of the states on the basis of "townships", square in plan and measuring six miles each way. The townships are divided into 36 "sections" with an area of 1 sq. mile (640 acres/260 hectares), and the sections into "quarter sections" with an area of 160 acres/65 hectares. The quarter section was originally intended to be worked by an individual farmer; but with the move of workers away from the land and the reduction in the number of separate farms the average size of farms has steadily increased and is now around 445 acres/180 hectares. The development of fully mechanised "farming factories" is illustrated by the fact that 3% of the total number of farms (with an average area of 2000 acres) work some 46% of the total agricultural land in the United States. In spite of this development the regular layout of the original division of the land is still reflected in the agricultural landscape. The roads, farm tracks and local government and state boundaries still run north–south and east–west, like the street grids of the cities. The featurelessness of the topography is thus paralleled by the monotony of the field pattern.

The Indians of North America

For many people the term "Indian" calls up a picture of redskins with eagle feathers in their hair roaming over the prairies on their mustangs. This is a romantic cliché which originated in the 18th century and has little to do with the indigenous inhabitants of North America. The very name "Indian" is misleading, derived from Columbus's erroneous belief that he had landed in India. The real "discoverers" of North America, the Indian peoples who occupied an immense area in more than a hundred different tribal groups and even more different languages and cultural forms, had no general sense of community or name for themselves. The tribal names like Sioux, Cheyenne and Comanche which came into use in the 18th and 19th centuries were either devised by whites or used by neighbouring tribes. As seen by the whites the Tsis-tsis-tas, Numenoi and Lakota, for example, were merely Cheyennes, Comanches and Sioux, referred to collectively as Indians; and, following traditional prejudices, denied their common humanity, for it was easier to make war on them, drive them from their territories, exterminate them and deceive them if they were not recognised as having human attributes. This treatment of the peoples of North America began with the European colonisation and left a bloody trail over the centuries. It is only in our own day that there has been some attempt to recognise the separate identity of these peoples.

When it was realised that the natives of North America were not Indians in the sense of inhabitants of India, speculation began about their origins. Since they were not mentioned in the Bible their membership of the human race was at first denied. It was only in 1512 that Pope Julius II declared publicly that the "Indians" of the New World were true descendants of Adam and Eve and must thus have come out of the Garden of Eden. One of the earliest theories to which this declaration gave rise was that they were descended from the "ten lost tribes of Israel".

Origins

In 1590, 150 years before the discovery of the Bering Strait, José de Acosta, a Jesuit, came astonishingly close to the answer to the problem of American Indian origins: "It is not probable that there was a second Noah's Ark which transported men to East India or that the first men were carried to this new world by an angel ... I come to the conclusion, therefore, that the first men came to this new world of America as the result of a shipwreck and foul stormy weather." But since a shipwreck could not explain the

José de Acosta

The Indians of North America

presence of animals in the New World he concluded that there must be, somewhere to the north, a piece of America "which was not completely separated and cut off, over which the animals travelled."

Edward Brerewood

In the 17th century the English antiquary Edward Brerewood observed that the Indians "showed little interest in the arts, science and culture of Europe, nor in those of China and civilised Asia" and because of their colour could not be descended from Africans. The only remaining possibility was the "Tartars", the term applied to the inhabitants of northern and central Asia. Brerewood believed that he had found in them cultural parallels with America. He concluded that there must be a land connection, which he thought would be "in that north-eastern part of Asia where the Tartars dwell". Although he was wrong in identifying Indian with Tartar culture, some of his conclusions were correct. 200 years later the German traveller Alexander von Humboldt drew attention to a "striking similarity between the Americans and the Mongol race". Modern scholarship has confirmed this view: it is now accepted that there is a close genetic relationship between the American Indians and the peoples of North-East Asia.

Settlement of the American Continent

Land bridge between Asia and America

The time of arrival of the first modern men in America was determined by the possibility of crossing the land bridge between Asia and America – somewhere in the region of the Bering Strait – and by the ability of men to exist for any length of time in Arctic cold. Thus the arrival of man in America cannot be set farther back than 40,000 years ago, for the land bridge has been crossable (that is, not covered by either water or ice) only twice during the last 40,000 years – some 32,000–26,000 years ago and, probably, 16,000–13,000 years ago. The most favourable route for further migration was through the valleys of the Yukon and Mackenzie Rivers and then south down the east side of the Rockies into the Dakotas. This line of separation between the eastward-flowing glaciers of the Pacific mountain system and those flowing down from the Laurentian Shield was no more than 25 miles/40km wide at some points, and before 20,000–13,000 years ago was completely impassable and ice-covered. After the retreat of the glaciers, for thousands of years, small groups of hunters followed the herds of mammoths, caribou and bison which ranged over these territories. Generation after generation men spread over the new land, while the land bridge from Asia was gradually reclaimed by the sea. Thus, cut off from their past, after their arduous journey over the Mackenzie watershed, the "Indians" from Asia settled the American continent.

Cultural phases

It is now believed that with high probability the advance of man into America took place in two phases – before 28,000–24,000 years ago and before 13,000–12,000 years ago. In the early days of settlement, the Palaeo-Indian period, men lived mainly by hunting large mammals and by about 9000 B.C., at the peak of this cultural phase, had spread over the whole of North America. The following Archaic period, which reached its greatest extension about 4000 B.C., was characterised by a semi-sedentary way of life in limited areas of settlement where men lived by hunting and gathering. This phase was gradually superseded by farming cultures, and there was a transition to the Formative phase, with settled communities living in villages and towns which were continuously occupied throughout the year and might have populations of several thousands. Around A.D. 100 this way of life was predominant down the whole of the east coast as far as Florida, round the Great Lakes and along the great rivers of the American prairies. The two other cultural phases, however, continued to co-exist.

North America on the eve of its "discovery"

The succession, co-existence and constant change of ways of life down to the end of the 18th century created a cultural variety in the American continent which found expression not only in more than a hundred different languages but also in a wide range of social and state structures. The

The Indians of North America

course of settlement in North America, however, cannot yet be conclusively established, since our information is based on archaeological evidence which is continually being supplemented by new material and may thus have to be reinterpreted. The evidence so far points to an early settlement of the east and west coasts, the river deltas along these coasts, the territory on the Pacific side of the Rockies and the Arctic regions. Traces of settlement have also been discovered round the Great Lakes, on the borders of the Canadian forest country and along the great rivers. Temporarily occupied hunting camps have been found at Folsom and Bascombe, fishing settlements on the east and west coasts, farming settlements in the Mississippi delta. In the south-west there are the remains of two large farming settlements: the ruins of Cliff Palace in the Mesa Verde National Park (see illustration, p. 555), which in its heyday was occupied by over 400 people in its 200 rooms, and Pueblo Bonito in the valley of the Charco River in New Mexico, built between A.D. 900 and 1100, which could accommodate some 1200 families in its 800 rooms. From western New York State to Nebraska, along the Gulf Coast from Florida to Texas and all over the interior of the United States there are thousands of conical mounds shaped into the form of birds, human figures and snakes. In the Ohio valley alone 10,000 artifacts have been found belonging to a people which had created a civilisation in the forests of the Middle West and built up a community of over 10,000 people living mainly by intensive farming and producing a wide range of luxury and utility articles. The valleys of the Mogollon range in New Mexico were settled from around 300 B.C. by a farming people, ancestors of the present-day Zuni Indians. The valleys of the Salt and Gila rivers were occupied by about 100 B.C.

Mandan feather headdress

by farming communities of the Hohokam, ancestors of the Papago and Pima. North of this were the Anasazi, among whose descendants are the Hopi Indians. Their villages are found from about A.D. 1200 in the Four Corners area where Arizona, New Mexico, Utah and Colorado meet. Comparable with historic sites in the Old World are the city states of the Mississippi Indians, who by A.D. 1200 had developed the most important culture so far found in North America. Their largest settlement at Cahohia, near present-day East St Louis in southern Illinois, had a population of over 20,000, whose cultural inheritors were the Natchez. Around the turn of the millennium there were primitive farming communities round the Great Lakes, forerunners of the Lakota-speaking tribes and the Algonquins. Within the Arctic Circle the Athabaskans and Inuits lived by hunting.

When the first Europeans arrived most of the North American subcontinent had long been occupied by flourishing cultures which had attained a high degree of economic wellbeing. Excluded from this development, however, were the prairies, since with the then available means of movement – on foot, with dogs as transport animals – their vast expanses formed a natural barrier to settlement.

The "Discovery" of America

Whether the Phoenicians actually had trading bases in what is now the United States and whether the lost tribes of Israel, Breton fishermen or Irish monks played a part in the discovery of America are matters of pure speculation. What is historically established is the landing in Newfoundland about A.D. 1000 of the Viking Leif Eriksson, followed about 1005 by the

The first Europeans

The Indians of North America

first attempt to establish a settlement in "Vineland" (probably Newfoundland) by a group of Vikings led by Thorfinn Karlsefni. They brought back the first accounts of the indigenous inhabitants of America, whom they called Skraelings – probably Eskimos. The relationship between the two groups, originally reserved but friendly, soon developed into conflict, and the Vikings were compelled to abandon their settlement at L'Anse aux Meadows in Canada. Thereafter the American continent disappeared from the consciousness of the Old World for almost 500 years: then on October 12th 1492 Columbus "discovered" America for the Spanish crown. From their base in Central America the Spaniards also prospected the new land to the north. Cabeza de Vaca's two-year journey through the southern part of North America was followed by military settlement by the Spaniards, whose objects, under the sign of the Cross, were to bring Christianity to the natives and to bring back gold and slaves to their royal masters.

Spain was followed by other powers. England established settlements on the east coast, moving from north to south, while the French occupied Louisiana and part of the Mississippi valley. Under this pressure the Indian societies were forced into movement and began to restructure themselves.

The Fate of the East Coast Indians

Iroquois League

Between 1559 and 1570 the Seneca, Onondaga, Cayuga, Mohawk and Oneida Indians founded the Iroquois League, a confederation of five nations bringing together both farming and hunting tribes which achieved such a high level of social and political progress that some of its democratic ideas influenced the American constitution. With the arrival of settlers in the territory of the Powhatan confederacy of the twenty Algonquin tribes (now Virginia) and the foundation of Jamestown in 1607 Britain established a foothold in North America; and in 1620 the Pilgrim Fathers landed in the territory of the double Algonquin tribe of the Wampanoags and Pokanokets at Cape Cod in the present-day state of Massachusetts. Their settlement was preserved from starvation during its first two years only by massive help from the Indians. Metacomet, son of the Wampanoag chief, known to the British as King Philip, saw the only future for his people in the expulsion of the whites and, allying himself with the Narragansett Indians of Rhode Island and other tribes, in 1675 launched "King Philip's War",

King Philip's War

which lasted two years and resulted in the destruction of twelve British settlements. The colonists struck ruthlessly back; Metacomet was killed

Pontiac

and his wife and son sold into slavery. In 1754 the Ottawa chief Pontiac rose against the British, and in 1763 formed an alliance of several tribes. This "Red Man's Revolution" was, from the Indian point of view, the greatest and most successful war of the 18th century.

The War of American Independence put an end to the Iroquois League, which in 1722, thanks to the influence of Hiawatha, had been enlarged to include the Tuscarora. The league was broken up as a result of shrewd negotiations and empty promises by both sides, and the individual tribes were set at odds with one another and reduced to insignificance. The Miami chief Little Turtle defeated the American general Arthur St Clair in the Ohio valley in 1791; but from 1830 onwards the flood of immigrants increased the pressure for the movement of settlement to the West. A policy of Indian resettlement was initiated under the Indian Removal Act,

Indian Removal Act

and during the 1830s and 1840s the "five civilised tribes" (Cherokee, Choctaw, Creek, Chickasaw, Seminole) were transported to distant Oklahoma (the "Trail of Tears"), though the Seminoles continued their resistance in a guerrilla war in the swamps of Florida until 1842.

The Indians of the Prairies and Plains

The European colonisation and settlement also led to dramatic changes in the heart of the continent. Until about the middle of the 17th century the

The Indians of North America

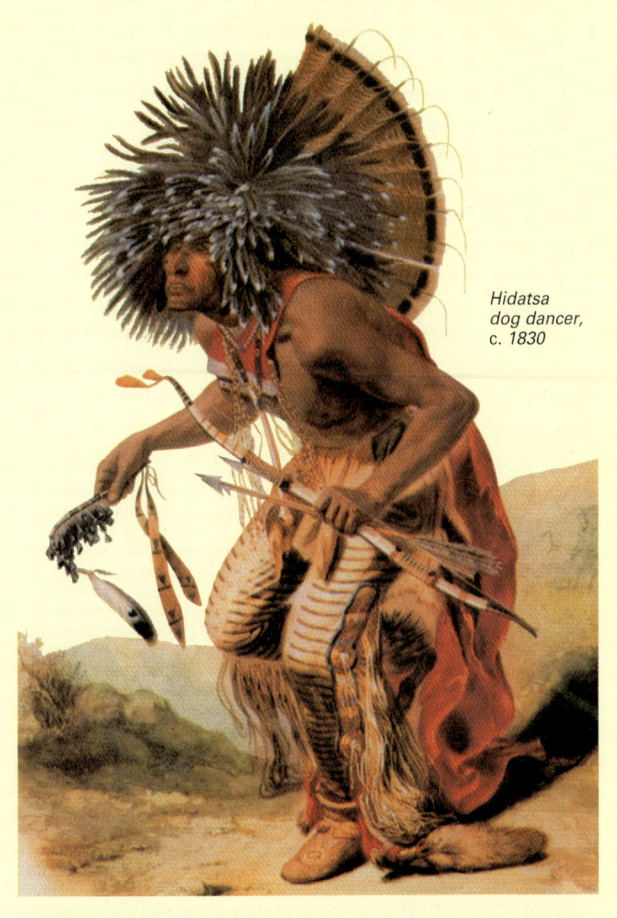

Hidatsa dog dancer, c. 1830

prairies and plains of the Middle West and South-West were occupied by Indian tribes practising simple arable farming only on the fringes and in areas with a water supply – on the southern edge of the grassland plain small groups of Apaches, known as Paducahs; in the north-west, in present-day Oregon, Cayuse; Comanche in Wyoming; Cheyenne, Arapaho and Absaroka round the Great Lakes. Blackfoots (Piegan) lived on the Canadian frontier and Sioux-speaking tribes hunted in the forest country of the North-West. For all these tribes the plains, with their immense empty expanses, were a closed territory, although these great areas of grassland supported millions of buffaloes, which were hunted only on a very modest scale. Two "technical innovations" changed this situation radically.

Around 1620, through the agency of the Hudson Bay Company, firearms began to come into the hands of the Indian tribes round the Great Lakes. Originally intended to increase the yield of the fur-hunters, they were used

Firearms and horses

35

The Indians of North America

by the Ojibway to attack smaller tribes in the area, which were compelled to move farther west to escape from their better armed neighbours.

In the Spanish-occupied South the Indians were, until the Pueblo Revolution which began in 1680, forbidden to own horses. After the expulsion of the Spaniards the numbers of horses living in freedom increased; they now became objects of trade, and were also distributed over the country by the widespread practice of horse-stealing. Herds of horses roamed over the prairies, and horses from Californian settlements found their way up the coast to Oregon. The Cayuse Indians were noted horse-breeders, rearing the famous Appaloosa breed; and these tribes carried the horse farther east. The first horsemen on the fringes of the plains were the Paducahs, who used their new power to raid the territory of their neighbours the Pawnees and other Cadda tribes. In the middle of the 18th century the horse reached the Uto-Aztec Comanches, who then left their homeland in Wyoming, advanced into the plains and drove out the Paducahs. The Cheyenne and Arapaho Indians moved westward, as did the Crow (Absarokee) and the related Mandan tribe. By about 1785 the way of life of the Sioux-speaking Lakota was centred on the horse. Somewhat later the Kiowa moved from Montana into the region between Texas and Oklahoma and from there, along with the Comanches, attacked Spanish and Pueblo Indian settlements. The Paducahs moved into the South-West and joined up with the related Apaches.

A buffalo-hunting culture

Apart from the Mandan and the Pawnees all the Indian tribes now gave up their traditional farming life and developed a hunting culture centred on the horse and the buffalo. For the prairie tribes buffaloes were the very basis of life: they provided food, clothing and dwellings and imposed on the Indians the rhythm of their existence. Wars – often bloody wars – were fought over hunting grounds, and for their own protection the nomadic tribes developed social structures involving warrior communities, special rites and complicated personal relationships. The struggle for survival always depended on the horse and the buffalo, and the slightest changes – for example if the herds of buffalo failed to appear after a hard winter – might lead to famine, while the loss of many men in battle might mean the ruin of a tribe. On the other hand the possession of horses and buffaloes brought great wealth and reputation to a tribe, a family group or an individual warrior, and wealth was used for lavish display.

It is an error to believe that this prairie culture was in harmony with nature. The Indians' herds of horses, some of them of great size, devastated great areas of pastureland, and there was often mass destruction of the buffalo herds. Even without the intervention of the whites this culture of warriors and hunters would probably have brought about its own destruction, particularly since almost all its essential elements – horses, firearms, metal – came from the world of the white man. The stylisation of fighting into a sport or a game, too, was a further indication that this type of civilisation had little chance of surviving. For many family groups and tribes the whole basis of life was destroyed by war; and the numbers were so small, and the ratio between numbers of men and women so unequal, that the prairie culture was unlikely to continue for any length of time.

In its variety and colour as well as in its freedom, however, this culture was unique in the world. Six different language families, with a total of 22 languages between them, were nevertheless able, in times of peace, to communicate with one another, discuss complicated matters and carry on trade with the help of a sign language developed for the purpose. In course of time the prairie tribes grew increasingly similar in their dress, their tools and implements and their dwellings, and many tribes developed similar forms of organisation. The chief of a tribe might be elected or might have inherited his title, but in either case, in almost all tribes, he could only advise and not command. Everywhere there were counselling and control organisations designed to guarantee peaceful coexistence and settle conflicts. The view of the majority of the tribe was always decisive. Only during

The Indians of North America

major hunting expeditions or when there was danger of war did the Indians submit to a severe and strictly policed discipline.

The Campaign against the Indians

As early as 1763 a British decree confirmed the Indians' right to their hereditary homeland, and settlers were prohibited from acquiring land beyond the Appalachians. The United States followed a similar line after achieving independence. At the beginning of the 19th century the noted lawyer and federal judge John Marshall expressly confirmed the status of the Indian tribes as nations and their natural right to the possession of the lands they occupied. Dealings with the Indians, he declared, must be conducted with the greatest possible honesty; land and property should never be taken from them without their agreement; and they should never be injured or restricted in their possessions and their rights and freedoms except in legally justified wars authorised by Congress. On this basis the United States concluded treaties with the Indians almost all of which were later broken.

Meaningless treaties

From 1837 and in subsequent decades, under the Indian Removal Act, almost the entire Indian population of the eastern United States was moved, sometimes with violence, to Indian territory in what is now Oklahoma. This territory was administered by the Ministry of War, and its area was repeatedly reduced. In 1889 part of it was opened to whites, and in 1907 it was incorporated in the state of Oklahoma.

Removal and resistance in the East and South-West

In the South-West the Indians had been able, from 1680 onwards, to hold up the Spanish advance, and from 1760 the Comanches and Apaches went over to the attack, in a war which was so murderous that after Spain was compelled to give up Mexico in 1824 most of the whites, after suffering huge losses, left New Mexico and New Spain. After the foundation of the state of Texas the extermination or expulsion of the Indians was seen there as the best solution, and a ruthless campaign was launched against them, until by 1855 all the Indian tribes had left the region; and in the following year Texas was declared "Indian-free". Only the Comanches were able to maintain their bare existence, withdrawing, with numerous rearguard actions, into the remote deserts of the Texas panhandle. In New Mexico and Arizona the resistance of the Apache guerrilla fighters was not finally broken until 1886.

The interest of the Europeans in the furs of the prairies and of the Plains Indians in the weapons and implements of the whites led to relatively peaceful trading activity between the two peoples during the fur-trading era of 1740 to 1840. From 1783, with the ending of the colonial period, the Indians had ever more frequent dealings with the American Fur Company of John Jacob Astor, who was ruthless in establishing his monopoly, undercutting the firms which supplied the independent traders until his competitors were bankrupted and the Indians were dependent on him alone. He also contrived to have competitors put out of business by accusing them of selling whiskey to the Indians, while if the Indians sold to rival firms the American Fur Company itself began to sell alcohol, leading inevitably to riots and to disciplinary measures by the government. The company thus succeeded in bringing a huge area under its control, in making the Indians dependent on it and in playing them off against each other.

Conquest of the plains

American Fur Company

Under treaties between the US government and various Indian tribes all the land west of the Mississippi–Missouri line had been confirmed as Indian territory in perpetuity. In order to ensure safe transit on the country's new roads, however, the Bureau of Indian Affairs which had been established in 1824 called a peace council of all the prairie tribes in 1841. Gifts to the value of 100,000 dollars were distributed, and the boundaries of the Indian hunting grounds were fixed by treaty: for the southern Dakota,

"So long as grass grows and water runs"; the 1841 treaty

The Indians of North America

Cheyenne and Arapaho tribes the area between the Arkansas and North Platte Rivers, the whole of Colorado east of the Rockies, part of present-day Kansas and the whole of southern Nebraska; for the northern Dakota, Cheyenne and Arapaho the whole of the Big Bend area on the northern Missouri; for the Crow, Assiniboin, Gros Ventre and Minnetaree Indians Montana and half of Wyoming. The Indians for their part pledged themselves to peaceful and friendly relations between the tribes, recognised the United States' right to build roads and establish posts on their territory and declared themselves ready in future to make good any damage caused by Indians to citizens of the United States or to their property. In return the United States promised to protect the Indians "so long as grass grows and water runs".

The beginning of conflict

The United States government kept a close watch on the observance of the treaty. When two Teton Dakota Indians stole a cow at Fort Laramie in 1854 a small army detachment moved into their encampment but was wiped out. The Dakotas now began to attack wagon trains on the roads, and in response the army marched into the valley of the Platte River and destroyed the village of the Brulé chief Little Thunder. For a time the roads were safe to travel – until 1862, when the government opened a new road through Indian territory, the Bozeman Trail to the goldfields of Montana. The Santee Indians led by Little Crow, who had for many years been cheated by traders and agents of the Bureau of Indian Affairs and had been thrust back ever farther into their reserve, rose in rebellion but were defeated in the battle of Cone Tree Lake on September 24th 1862. The survivors fled to the related Plains tribes, and their accounts of their experience led the northern Plains Indians – the Arapaho, Cheyenne and Dakota – to draw closer together. As a result of the gold and silver boom the Cheyenne were driven out of the territory which had been assigned to them under the 1851 treaty. Thereafter there were frequent conflicts, continuing until 1864.

Sand Creek massacre

Thanks to two shrewd chiefs, Black Kettle and White Antelope, the southern Cheyenne were able until that year to live undisturbed. Faced with the alternatives of living in peace with the United States and obtaining regular food or choosing war and winning their food by raids on the settlers, they put themselves under the protection of Fort Lyon, accepting the directions of the fort commandant that they should establish their camp on Sand Creek, hand in their arms and ammunition and live on prisoners' rations. In return they received confirmation in writing that they were "peaceful Indians under the protection of the United States" and an American flag which they flew prominently in their encampment. On November 29th 1864, when "no grass grew and no water ran", Col. John M. Chivington, a former Methodist pastor, appeared with the 1st and 3rd Colorado Cavalry and a battery of howitzers. The 500 inhabitants

Bow and quiver of the Crow

of the camp, among whom were practically no warriors, were attacked by 700 soldiers who had orders to take no prisoners and not to spare even children. 26 warriors and 274 women, children and old people were brutally murdered. The Sand Creek massacre became a rallying cry for the Indian wars.

Red Cloud

From 1866 onwards the Oglala chief Red Cloud successfully resisted the government's attempts to drive a road through Indian territory to the

38

The Indians of North America

Montana goldfields. After forcing the abandonment of three military outposts on the Bozeman Trail he and Gall, on behalf of Sitting Bull, signed a treaty in 1868 under which all of South Dakota to the west of the Missouri, the Powder River hunting grounds and the territory round the Bighorn Mountains were closed to whites. Soon afterwards, however, in 1872, a railway line for the North Pacific Railroad was surveyed through this territory.

In 1874 Col. Custer prospected the Black Hills, the sacred land of the Dakota, Paha Sapa, and when gold was discovered there a number of US settlements were established, contrary to treaty. On December 3rd 1875 the Department of the Interior ordered all tribes in the area to report to their agencies by January 31st 1876. The Indians were unwilling to expose their women, children and old people to the bitter cold of a particularly severe winter, but the government ultimatum was enforced by military units. The year of the Indian wars had begun.

The Indian wars

In March General Crook attacked an Oglala and Cheyenne village near the Powder River, but counter-attacks by Crazy Horse forced his 1400 men to retreat. In June, though warned against it, he crossed the Tongue River with fresh troops, and his 1400 men became involved in a one-day battle on the Rosebud River with equal numbers of Cheyenne, Arapaho and Oglala Indians led by Crazy Horse. On June 26th Colonel Custer, with 600 soldiers and 44 scouts, came on a huge camp of Dakota and Cheyenne and, without any reconnaissance to establish their numbers, attacked and was annihilated.

The campaign against the Indians had been a failure, but the Indians could not regard themselves as victors, for the deliberate slaughter of the buffalo herds had deprived them of their food stocks. Some Indian chiefs, among them Crazy Horse and Dull Knife, returned with their tribes into the reservations; Crazy Horse was killed in Camp Robinson, and the Cheyenne were sent to the reservation in Oklahoma. Some 800 of them fled from the catastrophic conditions there and sought to return to their old homeland but were hunted down and captured. Sitting Bull and Gall fled to Canada; then five years later, in 1881, Sitting Bull returned to the United States with the last 187 members of his tribe and gave himself up at Fort Buford. The General Allotment Act of 1887 divided the territory of the reservations among the Indians, making it their personal property. Then the Indian owners, driven by poverty, sold their land to white speculators at knockdown prices.

The last flare-up of Indian feeling was the Ghost Dance religion promoted by a young Paiute Indian, Wovoka, in the 1890s. He saw in a vision that a great flood would sweep away the whites, the buffaloes would return and the Indians would again be able to live as they had in past times. Until these events occurred the Indians were to dance and be ready to greet their ancestors and relatives on their return from the Beyond. 60,000 Indians of many different tribes joined the movement. The Dakota dressed in "bulletproof" Ghost Dance shirts, and their medicine-men foretold the expulsion of the whites. The Indians armed themselves, and there were battles with the whites. Sitting Bull was killed by Indian police officers in Standing Rock. A group of 146 men, women and children led by chief Bigfoot were massacred with the most modern weapons at Wounded Knee. The last military unit in Indian territory, a cavalry detachment, left Fort Yates on September 3rd 1903.

Ghost Dance

Wounded Knee

US Indian Policy in the 20th Century

After the abolition of collective Indian ownership of land under the General Allotment Act of 1908 further portions of the reservations were opened up

Legal advances and self-help

39

The Indians of North America

1 Hoopa, Yurok
2 Klamath, Modoc, Paiute
3 Paiute
4 Cheme-Huevi, Mohare
5 Cocopah
6 Pima
7 Walapai
8 Goshute
9 Paiute, Shoshone
10 Paiute, Tenino, Wasco
11 Umatilla, Cayuse, Walla Walla
12 Nez Perce
13 Cœur d'Alene
14 Colville, Spokane
15 Salish, Kootenai
16 Shoshone, Bannock
17 Gros Ventre, Assiniboin
18 Sioux, Assiniboin
19 Arikara, Mandan
20 Pueblo
21 **Oklahoma:** (Reservations and settlements) Cheyenne, Arapaho, Caddo, Delaware, Wichita, Kiowa, Comanche, Chickasaw, Choctaw, Pawnee, Shawnee, Seminole, Seneca, Cree, Cherokee, Ponca, Osaga, etc.
22 Sac, Fox
23 Alabama, Coushatta
24 Choctaw
25 Narragansett, Shinnecock

to whites by government decree. It was not until June 1924 that Congress passed a law making all Indians born in the United States US citizens with equal rights. Under the Indian Reorganisation Act of 1934 the tribes were granted the right to self-government and it was provided that all tribal territory not sold to whites was to be returned. This land, however, continued to be administered by the Bureau of Indian Affairs on behalf of the Indians. The Indian Claims Commission, a body independent of the Bureau, was set up in 1946 to establish Indian claims based on treaty undertakings which had not been fulfilled. So far over 1000 claims have been submitted; some have been accepted but many are still pending, including a million-dollar claim from the Sioux for the Black Hills, which were guaranteed to them by treaty. In the United Tribes Corporation, founded in 1967, tribes which were formerly opposed to one another are seeking to establish industry in the North Dakota reservations. In 1969 a family training centre was established in a joint operation by the United Tribes Corporation and the Bureau of Indian Affairs with the idea of preparing Indian families for entry into the world of the whites.

Indian resistance

Against progress of this kind must be set evidence of continuing discrimination against the Indian tribes and continuing exploitation of their natural resources. There have been harmful results from the abolition of the ban on alcohol in the reservations in 1951. Indians still, as in the 19th century, are exposed to further loss of land and destruction of their environment, for the reservations are rich in minerals. Thus the world's largest deposits of lead and zinc (85 million tons) are being worked in the territory of the Inupiah-Inuits, while the compensation promised by way of jobs and training facilities is slow in coming. Copper is worked on a large scale in the territory of the Courte Oreille Chippewa; and an attempt by the Chippewa to halt the extension of the workings by an action in the Wisconsin courts was frustrated by the high legal costs. 70% of world reserves of uranium lie within Indian territories, and the Lakota and Navajo tribes are opposed to mining operations.

All over the United States Indians, who traditionally see themselves as guardians of their land, are resisting removal from their territories, oppression and alienation from their culture – by spectacular actions like the occupation of Wounded Knee in 1973 by 200 armed members of the American Indian Movement, but also by a return to traditional values and ways of life.

Religion

Churches and religious communities in the United States have some 157 million members, in a wide variety of denominations and sects which reflects the pattern of settlement of the United States. Their influence on different parts of the country is related to their socio-economic structures, varying life styles, mentalities, marriage connections and international relationships.
In view of the largely European origins of the population the Christian churches are predominant, the largest groups being Protestants in various denominations, Catholics and Orthodox.

The largest of the Protestant denominations, which have a total of some 87 million members, are the Baptists, Methodists, Lutherans and Presbyterians. In addition there are some 3 million Mormons, 3 million members of the Churches of Christ, 2 million members of the United Church of Christ, 2½ million members of the Pentecostal churches and several hundred thousand Mennonites, Amish and Hutterites (see "Religion and Agriculture" on pp. 42–43). — Protestants

Just under 60 million Americans profess the Catholic faith, which is strongly represented in the North-East, Middle West and particularly in the West. There are around half a million Old Catholics. — Catholics

Roughly a quarter of the 4 million members of the Eastern churches are Greek Orthodox. There are also substantial numbers of Serbian, Syrian, Russian and Ukrainian Orthodox. — Orthodox

Some 6 million Americans profess the Jewish faith. There are three congregations, whose main strongholds are New York and Florida. — Jews

The varied population structure means that almost all the world's leading religions are represented in the United States. The largest non-Christian communities are Muslims (8 million), Buddhists (200,000), Baha'i (110,000), Taoists, Confucians, Shintoists, Sikhs and Hindus. — Other religions

Alongside the old-established religious denominations numerous sects have developed in the United States, particularly since the Second World War; many of them have split off from various evangelical communities. In addition there are a number of bizarre sects, many of them highly militant, which have come to considerable prominence in recent years. Notable for their missionary zeal and good organisation have been Jehovah's Witnesses and the Scientologists, who have achieved a considerable increase in membership in the last few years. The so-called "new religions" have now over 1.2 million members in the United States. — Sects

The number of Americans belonging to no religious denomination has been growing dramatically for many years; it is now well over 20 million. — Non-denominationals

The number of believers in natural and tribal religions – predominantly various Indian cults and religions – is estimated at about 40,000. — Natural and tribal religions

Baedeker Special
Religion and Agriculture

Soon after the beginning of Luther's Reformation the Baptist movement came into being. The term "Baptist" or "Anabaptist" reflected the belief that the only valid baptism was the baptism of an adult. The Anabaptist movement developed first in Switzerland, and by 1525 there was already a community of "Evangelical Baptists" in Zurich. The new teaching found many adherents, particularly among peasants and craftsmen, and spread from the Alpine region into Saxony and Moravia. From an early stage, however, the Baptists were exposed to ruthless persecution.

The **Mennonites**, a Baptist sect founded by a Frisian priest named Menno Simons (1497–1561), flourished mainly in North Germany and the Netherlands. There were also Mennonite groups in South Germany, from which the Amish (see below) later split off. The Mennonites, who had close affinities with Calvinism, rejected infant baptism, military service and state compulsion in matters of faith and sought to follow Christ in the spirit of the Sermon on the Mount. Their pacifism and opposition to the power of the state frequently brought them oppression and persecution, and as early as the 17th century some of them emigrated to the United States. Towards the end of the 18th century numbers of European Mennonites moved into the Ukraine. In the late 19th and early 20th centuries many Mennonites emigrated from Central Europe and the Ukraine to the United States.

In the late 17th century an Anabaptist from Switzerland named Jakob Ammann moved to Alsace, then liberal in matters of belief. He achieved his first great success as a preacher of his faith in 1692 at Markirch (Sainte-Marie-aux-Mines), where he called for a strict belief in Scripture and a chaste and virtuous community. Any who did not live in accordance with his prescriptions were to be expelled from the bed and board of members of the community. Ammann's followers, the Amish, could also be distinguished by their hair and dress (long beards for men, woven fabrics with no buttons). Ammann's rigorous demands drew criticism from other communities and led some to split off from the mainstream of Anabaptism. When Louis XIV decreed the expulsion of the Anabaptists from Alsace in 1712 they moved first into the Palatinate (particularly round Zweibrücken) and Hesse (particularly in the Kassel area). By this time a number of Mennonites had settled in America (Pennsylvania), and gradually this example was followed by some Amish families. The first Amish settlement was established at Northkill in Pennsylvania about 1738. From 1817 onwards several groups of Amish moved from Hesse to Ohio, and in subsequent years there was a regular emigration movement from Alsace, the Palatinate, Hesse and Bavaria to Ohio, Indiana, Illinois, Maryland, New York and Iowa.

There are now some 100,000 **Amish** living in 20 states of the Union. They adhere strictly to their traditions and reject the amenities of modern life – machinery, electricity, automobiles, insurance, etc. They pay their taxes but no social security contributions, since they care for their own members. They speak their old South German dialects and send their children to their own schools. The period of schooling lasts only eight years: in addition to reading, writing and arithmetic the children learn only what is necessary for their life on the farm, and further study is regarded as superfluous. A thorough knowledge of the Bible, however, is essential. The tradition established by Jakob Ammann of excluding from the community all who do not believe in its tenets is still maintained. All who live in sin – that is, those who infringe any of the Ten Commandments or bring discord into the community – are thus banned. The Amish, as the "enlightened", hold themselves apart from the "worldly" and live independently in their own world.

To the Amish work in the fields is the right way to fulfil the charge laid on them by the Bible, and particularly by the Sermon on the Mount. Through their old-world way of life the Amish avoid idleness. Children are of course involved in the work of the community, and the individual farms are of such a size that they can be worked by a family. The houses must be big enough to accommodate religious services once or twice a year for up to 200 members. The principal means of transport is a horse-drawn buggy, and horses are also used in the fields.

There are some 33,000 **Hutterites** in the United States, all sharing a small number of family names. They too are descended from the early Anabaptists and adhere to a fundamentalist view of Christianity. Their founder, Jakob Hutter, established a Baptist community based on common ownership of property in the manner of the early Christians at Nikolsburg (Mikulov) in Moravia in 1529. He was persecuted and burned at the stake in Innsbruck in 1536, and thereafter the Hutterites were driven out of their homeland to Hungary and then to Transylvania and Russia. In 1874 many Hutterites emigrated to the United States. Like the Amish, they maintain the traditions of their forebears and live an ascetic life working in the fields. They too have preserved their old South German dialect; they are convinced that, after the children of Israel, they are God's chosen people and daily await the Second Coming of Christ.

The **Mormons** maintain that their community was brought into being directly by God and was not merely an offshoot of an existing Christian church. They believe that their founder Joseph Smith (1805–44) was God's prophet, charged to restore the primitive church. From a collection of writings revealed to him by an angel he compiled a new Revelation, the "Book of Mormon", which he published in 1830. This is the sacred book of the Mormons. It contains accounts of the various peoples who have moved to America since the building of the tower of Babel and enjoyed Old Testament experiences of salvation with prophets, revelations and the appearance of Christ. In the Mormon view European Christians have fallen away from the true faith but the Mormons in America have restored the original Christian church with its offices and sacraments.

From Fayette in New York State the Mormon movement travelled west, and its first temple was built in Ohio in 1844. Others followed in Missouri and Illinois. In 1844 Joseph Smith was killed by a mob after the rumour that the Mormons practised polygamy proved to be true. A new leader and prophet was elected in the person of Brigham Young, who decided, in view of the severe persecution to which the Mormons were exposed, that they must move farther west. In 1847 some 15,000 Mormons, exhausted by their arduous journey, reached the valley of the Great Salt Lake, where they created a thriving agricultural community. Finally in 1896, after they had given up polygamy, their territory, centred on their capital of Salt Lake City, was admitted to the Union as the state of Utah.

The Mormon church has a priesthood on several levels, with differing powers and rituals, including sealing and the baptism of the dead. The unique practice of baptising the dead led to the Mormons' interest in genealogical research. The dead may also be sealed by proxy.

The Mormons have a positive conception of man and believe in progress. Joseph Smith's "words of wisdom" included much guidance for his followers on their manner of life and proper nourishment, including a ban on tobacco and alcohol and a directive on the very sparing consumption of meat.

Government and Society

Atheists — The number of atheists has increased sharply over the last two decades. A recent estimate puts it at 1.2 million.

Government and Society

National flag and coat of arms — The national flag of the United States, the Stars and Stripes, consists of seven red and six white horizontal bands, symbolising the original thirteen states of the Union, with fifty white stars on a blue ground in the top left-hand corner, representing the present fifty states. As first adopted in 1777, during the War of Independence, the flag originally showed a circle of thirteen stars. The coat of arms of the United States is a blue, white and red shield borne by the US heraldic bird, the white-headed sea eagle (the "bald eagle") – a former imperial symbol taken over by the American revolutionaries – holding in its beak a ribbon with the motto "E pluribus unum" ("Out of the many comes one").

National anthem — The text of the national anthem, the "Star-Spangled Banner", which was officially adopted only in 1931, was written by Francis Scott Key in 1814. It describes how, on the morning of September 14th 1814, the American flag was still flying over Fort Henry, near Baltimore, after a 25-hour bombardment by the British (see Quotations).

Political structure — The United States of America consist of the fifty states of the Union, the Federal District of Columbia round the national capital, Washington, and the four associated territories of Puerto Rico, US Virgin Islands, Guam and American Samoa.

Constitution and form of government

Checks and balances — The American constitution of 1787 was based on the then revolutionary premise that the best possible democratic government was ensured by a state ruled by law and not by a ruler's personal will ("government of laws and not of men"). The structure of American democracy is therefore based on the separation of powers and a system of checks and balances. In order to counter the danger of any form of absolute power each of the three branches of the state – the executive (the President and his ministers), the legislature (Congress) and the judiciary (with the Supreme Court as the highest instance) – has certain defined powers of control over the other two. The Supreme Court, for example, decides on the legality of laws put forward by Congress; the President has a power of veto on laws passed by Congress; and the Senate, as part of Congress, can refuse to confirm government appointments by the President. Congress and the President in particular are compelled by political realities to work together in mutual dependence on one another. In the tension-ridden relationship between the two members of this "antagonistic partnership" lies the core of the United States political system, which in this respect is very different from the parliamentary system.

Federal power and the states — When the "founding fathers", the creators of the Constitution, met in Philadelphia in May 1787 the first attempt, in the Articles of Confederation of 1777, to formulate a state organisation had already been shown to be inadequate. Out of fear of a powerful central authority – a fear inherited from the period of British colonial rule – the thirteen founding states had left the central government with practically no powers, not even the right to levy taxes. The new constitution of 1787 strengthened federal authority, but still held its rights to be derived from the original rights of the states. The primary competence of the states in certain fields is now much less extensive than in the early days of the Republic, but is still very considerable, mainly because their powers extend to all matters not expressly assigned to the federal government. Visitors travelling through the United

Government and Society

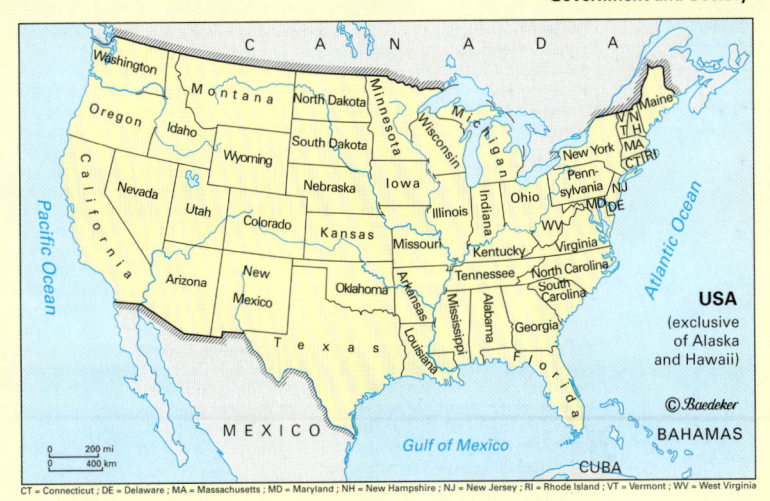

CT = Connecticut ; DE = Delaware ; MA = Massachusetts ; MD = Maryland ; NH = New Hampshire ; NJ = New Jersey ; RI = Rhode Island ; VT = Vermont ; WV = West Virginia

States will frequently come up against striking examples of the independence of the states in a variety of everyday concerns – the supply or sale of alcoholic liquor, the import of certain foodstuffs, the regulation of Summer Time, the interpretation of marriage law. Police, electoral law and education all fall within the competence of the states.

Since the 1787 Constitution contained no statement of basic human rights the first ten Amendments to the Constitution, adopted in 1791, constituted a Bill of Rights. Although the Bill of Rights is not formally part of the Constitution, for many representatives its passage was a necessary precondition for the ratification of the Constitution. The first two Amendments guarantee such basic rights as freedom of religion, speech, the press and assembly and the right to carry weapons. With the present high crime rate in the United States this last provision has been called in question; but any proposal for a more restrictive gun law is represented by the interest groups concerned – headed by the manufacturers and the National Rifle Association (NRA) – as an attack on a basic right and has therefore little chance of success. The 3rd and 4th Amendments are concerned with the security of private property, the 5th to 8th with the guarantee of the prosecution of offences in accordance with law. The 9th Amendment guarantees various rights of the citizen not mentioned in the Constitution, the 10th the rights of the states. Other important Amendments deal with the abolition of slavery (13th Amendment, 1865), the prohibition of any restriction on basic rights or electoral right on the grounds of race (14th, 1868; 15th, 1870) and the vote for women (19th, 1920). An attempt in the 1980s, mainly promoted by the feminist movement, to incorporate the principal of sexual equality in the Constitution (the Equal Rights Amendment) failed because the bill was not ratified by a sufficient number of states.

Bill of Rights

The President of the United States is elected by indirect popular vote every four years, on the Tuesday after the first Monday in November in a leap year. The President's term of office begins on January 20th in the year following the election and ends on the same day four years later. Under the 22nd Amendment (1951) a President can be re-elected only once (Franklin D. Roosevelt had served for four successive terms). If the President dies in office or resigns he is automatically succeeded by the Vice-President, who serves until the end of the current term.

The President and the government

Government and Society

Electoral procedure Primaries

The election of the President is a two-stage process. Most states hold primary elections in the spring of election year which decide which candidates in the two main parties will run against one another in the main election. Depending on voting results, the individual states send delegates to the National Congress of each of the parties, where the candidates will finally be selected. The primaries are as a rule open to all voters, though voters can take part only in the congress of one party. In some states the function of the primaries is taken over by party meetings ("caucuses") in which delegates are chosen by voters and party members. Candidates for other offices – e.g. state governors and Congressmen – are also selected in primaries. A candidate for the Presidency does not have to be put forward by one of the parties: independent candidates may submit themselves for election, but such candidates usually lack the financial resources and the organisation to make them serious contenders. In the main stage of the election voters formally choose the members of the Electoral College, which in practice amounts to the direct election of the President. The number of members a state sends to the Electoral College depends on its representation in Congress (reckoned as the number of its representatives in the House of Representatives plus two for its Senators). The candidate who wins a majority of votes in a state thereby wins the votes of all the state's members of the Electoral College – a provision which can produce a landslide victory even though the numbers of votes for the individual candidates are not so very far apart.

Electoral College

Position of the President

Although the President possesses great authority and influence, it is misleading to call the American system of government a presidential system, given the pattern of relationships between the President and Congress. The President alone appoints the ministers in his Cabinet; but the Senate are required to confirm his appointments and may refuse to do so. Moreover the President has no right to propose legislation and, apart from his annual "State of the Union" message, can speak in Congress only by invitation. On the other hand, since members of Congress are not bound by party directions, the President can exert considerable influence on them; and important decisions now tend to be preceded by long telephone calls from the President to undecided members. In addition to the members of the Cabinet (with the title of Secretary), at present sixteen in number, the President appoints considerable numbers of advisers and advisory bodies, among the most important and influential of which are the National Security Council and the staff of the White House.

Vice-President

Formally, the Vice-President has no decisive function in the government, and his position as President of the Senate is not one of great influence. His importance lies in his role as successor to the President if he should die or be removed from office.

Congress

The traditional counterpart of the President in the political process in the United States is Congress, which consists of two houses, the Senate and the House of Representatives. The Senate consists of two representatives of each state (irrespective of the state's population), who are elected for a six-year term. A third of the Senate retire every two years, so that the terms of office of individual senators overlap. The members of the House of Representatives are also elected in each state by majority voting for a two-year term, their number being determined in theory by the population of the various states as recorded in the Census; in practice, however, the number of representatives has remained at 435 since 1912.

Since there is no control by the parties over the actions of their members, even a President whose party is in a minority in Congress can still obtain a majority for a proposal he desires to put forward. Much more frequent, however, is the "gridlock" situation in which neither the President nor the opposing party is prepared to give way, thus holding up the work of government. Another consequence of the American system of checks and balances is that both houses of Congress must cooperate in the legislative process and that the President must sign all laws but has power to veto them – though his veto can be overridden by a two-thirds majority vote in

Government and Society

US Supreme Court, Washington, D.C.

both houses. Although the President is supreme commander of the armed forces only Congress can declare war. Congress is also responsible for the granting of budgetary funds and can initiate the procedure for the impeachment and removal from office of members of the executive, including the President, and the judiciary. The Senate has a key position mainly in foreign affairs, for the President can sign international treaties only with its approval by a two-thirds majority; he can, however, act independently in entering into agreements which are not classed as treaties.

Alongside the legislature (Congress) and the President as head of the executive the third element in the American government structure is the judiciary. United States law is based on English common law, a system of uncodified rules derived from judicial decisions in particular cases which are accepted as precedents. Judicial interpretation takes precedence over actual legislation – in complete contrast to the system of civil law, which attached greater importance to the examination and interpretation of legal texts by jurists. There is no such thing as a code of criminal or civil law in the United States.

The highest legal instance is the United States Supreme Court, which sits in Washington DC and has as one of its principal responsibilities the final decision on the constitutionality of legislation. The nine judges of the Supreme Court are appointed by the President for life, subject to confirmation of appointments by the Senate; and a President can thus influence the character of the court for many years after his period of office. Depending on its composition, the Supreme Court has frequently handed down judgments – on freedom of opinion, on race questions, on criminal law – which have had political implications and have given rise to controversy, for example on the abolition (1972) and reintroduction (1976) of the death penalty and on the right to abortion (1973).

As a result of the federal structure of the United States there are two judicial systems, the federal courts and the state courts, running side by side. In

Judiciary

Supreme Court

Two judicial systems

Education

contrast to the federal judges, who are appointed, the judges in the states are elected and thus frequently lose their political independence.

The states

The federal structure of the United States makes it difficult to generalise about the situation in the various states. The American states have wider powers than, for example, the *länder* in the German federal system: in a country of such vast extent the case for strong local decision-making authorities is still valid.

Governor

Each of the states is headed by a Governor. As at federal level, there is a legislature, the Congress, consisting of a Senate and a House of Representatives. Although the position of the Governor is politically important he is still bound by the decision of his Congress. This is seen, for example, in Congress's right to exercise a decisive voice in the appointment of officials. A veto by the Governor on a decision of Congress can be overridden by a simple majority vote. On the other hand a Governor's power to call out the National Guard to reinforce the state police in the event of riots or other disturbances has on occasion been a factor of great importance.

Parties

Since the Civil War and the election of Abraham Lincoln, a Republican, as President in 1860 the dominant parties in the United States have been the Republicans and the Democrats. There have been a number of other parties, but none of them has ever produced a President. There have been remarkable changes, however, in the two great parties. While it was the Republicans who originally stood for the freeing of the slaves, in opposition to the Democrats, and thereafter campaigned for civil rights for blacks, it is now the Democratic Party that tends to represent the interests of minorities. This is reflected in voting patterns: thus in the 1992 presidential election only 11% of black electors voted for the Republican candidate, George Bush.

Party programmes

For outside observers it is sometimes difficult to see much difference between the two great parties; but in view of the heterogeneous character of the electorate and the system of election by majority vote a high degree of flexibility and readiness to compromise is required of the parties. If a party moves too far from the centre its chances of gaining or retaining power are reduced. With a candidate like George McGovern (1972), for example, the Democrats were seen as too liberal, while the Republicans supporting George Bush in 1992 were too strongly influenced by religious fundamentalists and thus frightened off many voters. Although differences between the two parties are often difficult to detect, it can be observed that in the present political landscape the Republicans tend to appear conservative and to represent mainly economic interests. The Democrats have the reputation of being more in favour of reform, and appeal more to minorities, women and workers – though the trade unions avoid aligning themselves with any one political party. It is also difficult to assign the parties to any particular political trend because no party discipline is exercised in Congress and there are frequently inter-party alliances on particular problems or policies.

The organisation of the American parties is much looser than in Europe. There are no organised arrangements for party membership, no formal procedures for admission to the party and no regular subscriptions. To belong to a party a voter has only to declare himself a Republican or a Democrat by entering his name on the electoral register. This procedure is necessary for the primary elections, for only registered "members" of a party can take part in the primary within their party, and a voter automatically becomes a member of his party by taking part in the primary election.

Education

General

The educational system of the United States is neither centrally organised nor uniform throughout the country, for under the constitution education is a function of the states, which lay down the aims and principles of education and allot the necessary resources. Although within the Department of Health, Education and Welfare there is a US Office of Education, it can exert direct influence on the educational system only when federal funds are involved: its main field of operation is in educational research and advice. The running of the educational system is in the hands of elected school boards in over 15,000 school districts.

The public school system of the states ("public school" being used in a very different sense from the British public school), provided free of charge, comprises kindergartens, pre-school classes, primary schools, high schools, colleges and universities, together with various special types of school. Alongside the public schools are numerous private schools, run either by foundations or by churches. The Roman Catholic church is particularly active in this field, but Lutherans, Mormons, Jews, Quakers, Adventists and other religious communities also have their own schools. Renowned universities like Harvard, Yale and Stanford demonstrate the quality of private educational establishments, though because of their high costs they tend to be accessible only to students from better-off families. At all levels of the educational system the number of private establishments has been increasing, and more than half the country's colleges and universities are private. There are recurring complaints that the nation's educational level is steadily falling and that the 10% of the national income spent on education and training is too little in comparison with other fields. A 1982 study showed that some 13% of Americans over 21 could not read.

The American educational system consists of three main stages: elementary or primary education, with the elementary or primary schools; secondary education in high schools; and higher education in colleges, technical colleges and universities. School attendance is obligatory for twelve years – six years of elementary school and six of high school. Both stages may be included in comprehensive schools, when the elementary stage is increased to eight years and the high school stage reduced to four. Attendance at the pre-school classes which are attached to many schools is optional. A special type of elementary school is the "alternative" or "free" schools which experiment with unconventional teaching models.

Stages in the educational system

The high schools are divided into two stages, junior high schools (7th–9th years) and senior high schools (10th–12th years), which are usually separate establishments. In addition to a general stream and an academic (pre-college) stream there is also a vocational stream preparing pupils for future careers. The curricula of the three streams are interchangeable, and the core subjects (literary, scientific and social studies and sport) are common to all three streams. The pupils of vocational high schools also take practical courses in technical, commercial and domestic subjects, and these schools are usually well equipped with training workshops and laboratories and cooperate with industrial firms, banks and other commercial establishments. At the end of their final year pupils of high schools receive a high school diploma, which is granted without any special final examination and merely certifies that the pupil has regularly completed the obligatory twelve years' schooling. Unlike European school-leaving certificates, it does not necessarily qualify the pupil for admission to a university. Some 39% of high school pupils complete the full course, but there are very large numbers of dropouts who do not. It is one of the principal objectives of American educational policy to reduce their numbers.

High schools

The American school year is one of the shortest in the western world – 180 teaching days (differently regulated in different states). The school week has five days, each with six hours of teaching.

Half of all high school leavers continue to higher education, beginning with a higher education college. The conditions for admission to these colleges are laid down by the state authorities, or in the case of private colleges in the statutes of the college; in general they are related to the standard of achievement evidenced by the high school diploma. Gifted students can

Higher education colleges

Economy

leapfrog one or two college years if they pass additional examinations in particular subjects. The 3300 colleges in the United States had in 1987 some 15 million students. Although there is a free choice of subjects the teaching is on the same lines as in schools. The college course leads to a bachelor's degree (Bachelor of Arts or Bachelor of Science). The college year runs from September to June and is divided into two semesters, each lasting four and a half months, or into three "quarters" of three months each. The cost of a college education varies considerably; it is cheapest in a city or state college. Students can obtain some financial assistance towards the cost in the form of means-tested allowances, scholarships (the amount of which is dependent on academic attainment) and student loans from college or federal funds. More than two-fifths of all students at American colleges earn part of the cost themselves, and a fifth meet the cost without any external assistance.

Universities

Advanced higher education ("graduate studies") is provided by universities and professional schools of similar status (e.g. in technology or law). A master's degree (M.A., Master of Arts; M.S., Master of Science) can be obtained after a year's further study and the presentation of a thesis on some special subject. The doctorate is usually sought only by students aiming at a professional career as a scientist or scholar, college professor or physician. The teaching staff of a university consists of ordinary professors, extraordinary professors, assistant professors and lecturers. All the buildings of a university – including institutes and lecture halls, residences and refectories, recreation rooms and extensive sports facilities – are usually concentrated in in a single area, the university campus.

The Ivy League

The United States have numerous universities of world fame and high academic reputation, in particular the seven "Ivy League" universities in the north-eastern states – so named after the venerable ivy-clad walls of the oldest of them (Harvard, in Cambridge, Mass., founded in 1636). The other members of the Ivy League are Yale University, in New Haven, Connecticut; Princeton University, in Princeton, New Jersey; Columbia University in New York; the University of Pennsylvania in Philadelphia; Brown University, in Providence, Rhode Island; and Cornell University, in Ithaca, New York State. Newer universities of world reputation are the University of California in Berkeley, the Leland Stanford Junior University in Palo Alto, California, the University of Chicago, the State University of Michigan in Ann Arbor, the Massachusetts Institute of Technology in Cambridge and the California Institute of Technology in Pasadena. Berkeley University alone has produced eleven Nobel Prize winners since the Second World War.

Economy

A land of unlimited possibilities

Favoured by variety of topography, rich reserves of raw materials and a climatic range in which both temperate and subtropical crops can be grown, and with a domestic market which is the largest in the world, the United States has developed an economy which in numerous fields is one of the leading and most innovative economies in the world. The country's gross national product of 22,500 dollars (1991) per head of the population is one of the highest in the world, exceeded only by one or two small and Middle Eastern states.

The economy of the United States is a fully free market economy, characterised by the concentration of production and of services in large firms and organisations. The state plays a notably small part in the total economy, and so far has made only very minor contributions to social welfare spending.

It is difficult, therefore, to compare the economy of the United States with that of other states; and the extraordinary economic successes which in this setting can be achieved by individuals show that the United States is

Economy

still the "land of unlimited possibilities" which exerts such a powerful attraction.

In spite of the development of the economy along the main lines of communication and round certain administrative centres which is characteristic of the United States, and although decisions on the siting of industry and service organisations are sometimes difficult to explain on rational grounds, the economic structures of the United States are nevertheless closely related to physical conditions. This is seen particularly in the country's enormously productive agriculture, which supplies a quarter of the world's wheat crop, half of its maize crop and three-quarters of its soya bean crop.

The variety of topography, found even within the main natural regions, the varying climatic conditions and the vast extent of this great country produce both the opportunities and the problems of economic development. With a total area of 3.61 million sq.miles/9.36 million sq.km (3.02 million sq.miles/7.83 million sq.km in the mainland United States, excluding Alaska and Hawaii), the development of transport and communications was an important strategic factor and stimulus for the economy. The coastal regions, the plains, the grassland steppes, the deserts and the extensive humid and "amphibious" regions called for, and received, appropriate measures for their development. New technologies were developed and new industries grew up which played their part in making the United States in the 20th century the world's leading economic power.

Physical conditions

The roots of American economic history go back to the country's earliest days. The immigrants who came from the Old World, often from a narrow feudal social order, to the possibilities and opportunities of the New World were filled with a sense of mission and a drive to make good. They were deterred neither by the unaccustomed climate nor by the hardships which they had to endure. The first great economic centres developed first in the temperate North-East, then in the Middle West and California and finally, towards the end of the 19th century, in the prairies.

History of the economy

In the first place maritime trade began to develop, starting from the ports on the Atlantic coast. Peasants and craftsmen from Europe found an abundance of land and a steadily increasing market for products of all kinds. The combined skills of the new settlers, coming from different countries and backgrounds, made possible rapid technological progress.

In the east of the country metal processing and metalworking, mechanical and precision engineering made particularly rapid progress. Numerous inventions, like Samuel Colt's repeating revolver, John Deere's steel plough and Samuel Morse's telegraph which permitted communication over long distances, responded to the challenge of the land.

The first overland communications – the building of new roads and the establishment of postal services – were developed by private enterprise, as were shipyards, shipping services and canals. The most important contribution to the opening up of new territories was made by the private railroad companies, of which there were some 300 by about 1840. During the 19th century the railroads were the greatest stimulus to development, and at the end of the century something like two-thirds of all dealings in American stock exchanges were concerned with the shares of railroad companies. Railway construction and continuing technological advance were the basis on which great fortunes were amassed, including those of Cornelius Vanderbilt and Andrew Carnegie.

All this promoted the development of mining and steel production in the northern states, contributing to their economic superiority over the predominantly agricultural southern states and leading to one of the causes of the Civil War. The freeing of the slaves which was one of the consequences of the Civil War speeded up rationalisation and increased the use of machinery in agriculture.

An important spur to further economic development came from the use of electricity and the inventions of Thomas Alva Edison (including the light

Economy

bulb, the phonograph and the ciné camera) and Graham Bell (the telephone). The discovery of oil and the monopolistic development of the new form of energy by John D. Rockefeller and his Standard Oil Company (Esso), together with the rapid spread of the automobile – promoted by the cheap mass production methods introduced by Henry Ford – gave a great boost and a further technological lead to the American economy. The consumption of energy per head of the population grew enormously, and later was still further increased by the large-scale use of refrigerators and air conditioning. The United States are still, however, dependent to a high degree on the availability of fossil fuels. A further increase in mobility was brought by the development of aircraft. The first regular air services were started in 1926, and thanks to the huge domestic market American aircraft manufacturers still occupy a leading position in the world.

The north-eastern United States developed into the country's industrial heartland, with a particular concentration in the area bounded by New York, Detroit, Chicago and St Louis. After the Second World War there was a further expansion of the "manufacturing belt" to the west and south.

On the Gulf Coast new branches of industry (e.g. the manufacture of synthetic fibres) developed out of the traditional cotton and textile industries. The steel industry, which originally was mainly concentrated round Pittsburgh, established new centres on Lake Michigan and in the Detroit and Cleveland areas. The rich reserves of oil in Texas led to the establishment of gigantic petrochemical plants in the Gulf Coast plain. Major industrial areas also grew up on the Pacific coast, particularly round Los Angeles, San Francisco and Seattle. Then from the 1940s onwards "Silicon Valley" in California became the world centre of computer technology. And almost everywhere industrial development was followed by supply and service industries.

Social Differences

Prosperity

One result of relatively uncontrolled economic development in the United States has been a wide spread of prosperity. The average annual income in 1989 was $22,000. In recent years the middle income group ($30,000–50,000) has shrunk, while the numbers in the high income group and the seriously rich have increased.

Poverty

On the other hand the number of people classed as poor (with an annual income for a four-person household below $14,000) is increasing and now amounts to a sixth of the population. In the large cities in particular the abundance of consumer goods on display in the shops is in stark contrast to the need visible outside the business centres. Particularly hard hit are the blacks and the Hispanics.

Unemployment

As already noted, 72% of the working population of the United States are employed in the service industries (compared with 62% in the European Union). Although there are widespread complaints about unemployment in the United States the unemployment rate is in fact lower than in Europe; and only 6% of the unemployed have been without work for more than a year. Unemployment among young people is, however, a serious problem: more than a sixth of young whites, just under a quarter of young Hispano-Americans and a third of young blacks are unemployed.

Trade unions

The American trade unions, unlike their European counterparts, are by no means a mass movement. No more than a fifth of all workers belong to the AFL-CIO, formed in 1955 by the amalgamation of the American Federation of Labour (AFL) with the Congress of Industrial Organisations (CIO). The AFL-CIO, however, wields considerable influence when it is a matter of defending jobs against capital and management interests or pressing demands in the social welfare field (e.g. protection from sacking, sickness insurance for all workers).

Another cause of the increase in poverty in the United States, in addition to the downturn in the economy, is the inadequacy of social welfare legislation. Many Americans are not insured against either sickness or unemployment, and state expenditure on social welfare has been cut down in recent years to just under 8% of the gross domestic product.

There is some prospect of improvement in the Clinton administration's proposed reform of health insurance, launched in 1993. The additional expenditure involved is to be met in part by increased duties on tobacco products.

Social welfare expenditure

Economic and Social Policy

The essential foundation to the United States' rise into a leading economic power in the 20th century has been its massive resources of the fossil fuels (coal, oil and natural gas). For many years the United States accounted for almost a quarter of world national product. Over the last two decades, however, the economic situation of the United States in many fields has changed dramatically. Its self-sufficiency in many raw materials has declined; agricultural production has entered a phase of stagnation; and market share in the export of agricultural produce has fallen. During the 1970s there was a marked increase in the services sector of the economy, and since then some 90% of new jobs have been in that sector. At the same time there has been some neglect of capital and consumption goods industries. Only in the armaments and high-tech industries has there been lively investment activity.

The deficit on the US balance of trade has grown steadily, and even President Reagan's economic policy ("Reaganomics") was unable to halt the trend. The policy of "deficit spending" involved sharp tax reductions and enormously increased expenditure on armaments. The idea was that by increasing state indebtedness a boost would be given to the economy. During the eighties there was indeed an economic upswing; but this was soon seen to be a false dawn. Stock exchange quotations of American shares rose to unheard-of heights, only to fall through the floor in the October 1987 crash. The rate of exchange of the dollar also fell: worth 3.47 German marks in 1985, it was valued at only 1.58 marks two years later. And while the deficit on the balance of trade continued to increase, the budgetary deficit grew steadily larger, and the United States now became the greatest debtor nation in the world.

Negative balance of trade

In spite of these difficulties the average income was still rising, though mainly in the upper income groups. The number of people in the middle income ranges is now significantly smaller than in the seventies, and there has been an alarming rise in the numbers of those in the lowest income groups.

Towards the end of the eighties the unemployment rate fell to around 5%, but in spite of this some 32 million Americans were living below the official poverty line. Some 10% of the white population and over 30% of the coloured population now fall into this category. These social inequalities are accompanied by marked regional differences: in the New England states, for example, the income per head is twice as high as in the Middle West. Almost a third of the unemployed are not insured against unemployment, and almost 40 million US citizens have inadequate health insurance cover or none at all.

Sharp income disparities

The Clinton administration, in office since January 1993, plans to put a halt to these developments. During his 1992 election campaign Bill Clinton found his greatest support among ethnic and religious minorities and in areas which had suffered worst under the recession. The Clinton administration put forward an employment programme designed to halt the sharp rise in the number of jobless, to be financed by higher taxes (including an

Plans of the Clinton administration

Economy

increase in the peak rate of tax). In addition employers were given tax reliefs amounting in total to 15 billion dollars in the hope that this would give a boost to the economy. Confidence in the measures proposed by the Clinton administration has been reflected in a sharp rise in retail trade, and various economic institutions have predicted an upswing in the economy in the closing years of the century. Further stimulus to the economy is hoped for from the enlargement of the domestic market expected to result from the creation of the North American Free Trade Area (NAFTA), the common market formed by the United States, Canada and Mexico – though there has been controversy over the project in all three countries. In the United States there is concern about the possible export of jobs to Mexico, a low-wage country. It is unclear, too, how the huge state debt – interest payments on which accounts for 17% of total expenditure – is to be reduced. Numerous budgetary cuts, mainly in the defence field, have so far had little effect.

The efforts of the Clinton administration to reduce social disparities offer better prospects of success. Under the direction of Hillary Clinton, the President's wife, a reform of health services and social insurance is being developed. It is planned to introduce a compulsory system of social insurance and to lay down maximum charges for medical services so as to reduce the exorbitant cost of medical care.

Agriculture, Forestry and Fishing

Land use

Of the total area of the United States 30% is occupied by forests, 26% by pasture and 20% by arable land. The old division of the cultivated land into belts characterised by different monocultures is no longer so clearly recognisable as a result of increasing differentiation, but a number of classic production zones can still be distinguished:

Dairy belt

The North-East and the region round the Great Lakes belong to the dairy belt, in which dairy farming and the growing of fodder crops are predominant. Fruit and vegetables are now also grown in these areas, helping to feed the megalopolises on the east coast.

Corn belt

Immediately south of the dairy belt, mostly in the states of Ohio, Indiana, Illinois, Iowa and Missouri, is the corn belt, in which maize ("corn" in the United States) is the principal crop. The maize is used to feed cattle, pigs and poultry: it is estimated, for example, that ten pounds of maize produce one pound of pork. A quarter of all American cattle and half of all American pigs are reared in the corn belt. In the state of Iowa alone just under 3 billion eggs are produced every year.

Cotton belt

In the cotton belt, which extends across the southern states, the once dominant cotton crop has to a considerable extent given way to the growing of soya beans and peanuts. Tobacco is now also a crop of some importance.

Wheat belt

The wheat belt extends uninterruptedly northwards from Texas to the Canadian frontier.

Extensive pastoral farming

The arid areas farther west, mainly in the states of Colorado and Wyoming, are devoted to extensive cattle-rearing.

Irrigation agriculture/ Special crops

In the West and South-West great expanses of land have been irrigated since the beginning of the 20th century. The largest such areas are in the Great Plains and on the edge of the Rockies (particularly in the state of Colorado), along some rivers in Arizona, on the lower course of the Colorado River (Imperial Valley) and in the Central Valley of California. In these areas elaborate irrigation systems have made it possible to grow various special crops, including citrus and other fruits, rice, sugar-cane, vegetables, cotton and fodder plants.

Economy

Citrus fruit from Florida *Cotton plantation, South Carolina*

Productive crops are also grown on the Atlantic coast, under the influence of the warm Gulf Stream, and on the Gulf Coast. In addition to fruit and vegetables in the northern regions there are citrus fruits in Florida and sugar-cane plantations in Florida and along the Gulf Coast; and in some areas (e.g. in the Napa Valley) there are vineyards and a flourishing wine-making industry.

In the upland regions of the East, which were settled at an early stage, the traditional mixed farming is still practised, with intensive market-oriented livestock rearing (particularly poultry) in some areas.	Mixed farming
In 1935 the average size of American farms was 79 acres/32 hectares; by 1974 it had risen to 432 acres/175 hectares and in 1993 was estimated to be 470 acres/190 hectares. The number of farms fell from 6.8 million in 1935 to 3 million in 1970; it is now just over 2 million.	Farm sizes
Following restructuring and modernisation American agriculture has taken a leading place in the world in terms of productivity and yield. The value of agricultural and forestry exports in 1992, at $24 billion, is considerably more than the export value of computers and office machinery or of aircraft and aircraft parts, and is roughly on the same level as the export value of motor vehicles. The United States accounts for more than a third of world wheat exports, about two-thirds of world maize exports, some three-quarters of world soya bean exports, just under 30% of world cotton exports, a quarter of world production of citrus fruits, a fifth of world rice exports and a fifth of world meat production.	Production and export
The strong position of the American agricultural sector in export markets explains the tough stance of the United States in the recent GATT round, aimed at facilitating the access of US agricultural produce to the European market. It must be remembered that the United States produces half the	GATT negotiations

Economy

world crop of maize and 60% of the world crop of soya beans and that agriculture and forestry contribute some 7% of the total value of the country's exports. If the products of the foodstuffs and associated industries are included "agro-business" accounts for over 11% of the total value of US exports.

Forestry

With 1 million sq.miles/2.65 million sq.km of forests, the United States has one of the largest expanses of forest in the world. Two-thirds of this area are worked for timber; most of it is in private ownership, often in the hands of large woodworking and cellulose concerns.

The contribution made by agriculture and forestry to the gross domestic product is declining: some 3% in 1976, it had fallen to 2% in 1993. The work force employed in agriculture and forestry fell from 4% of the total working population in 1976 to 2.8% in 1993.

Fishing

The United States has rich fishing grounds, mainly off the Gulf and Pacific coasts but also in the Arctic Ocean and in inland waters. In 1976 the US government introduced a 200-mile exclusion zone round its coasts to protect its fishing grounds. The American fishing fleet, however, can supply only half the nation's needs; the rest must be imported. The US fishing industry employs some 350,000 people.

Mining

The United States has numerous large deposits of almost all useful minerals, and American output of coal, natural gas, oil, iron, copper, zinc, molybdenum, lead, gold, silver, uranium, bauxite, potassium, phosphates, sulphur and salt represents a high proportion of world production. The mining industry accounts for some 2% of gross domestic product.

Coal

With an output of around 900 million tons – roughly a quarter of total world output – the United States ranks after the People's Republic of China as the world's largest producer of coal. There are huge reserves of coal in the states of Wyoming and Colorado and elsewhere. Coal working was considerably extended in the 1980s. This "black gold" lies for the most part near the surface in rich continuous seams. This, combined with a high degree of mechanisation, makes for low mining costs, so that in spite of high transport charges American coal can be sold in Europe more cheaply than the native product.

Oil

With a daily output of over 8000 barrels of oil in 1989, the United States took second place only to the former Soviet Union (11,000 barrels) and outproduced Saudi Arabia (5000). In spite of the opening-up of new oilfields, however, American output is insufficient to meet domestic needs and 40% of national requirements must be imported. The largest oilfields in the United States are on the Gulf Coast, in Texas, Oklahoma and Louisiana, the eastern foreland of the Rockies (Colorado, Wyoming), the Wyoming Basin, southern California and above all in northern Alaska.

Natural gas

The United States is the world's largest producer of natural gas after Russia, with an output which is ample to meet domestic needs.

Energy

Consumption of energy

Of the total amount of energy consumed in the United States 65% is met by oil and natural gas, 23% by coal and 8% by nuclear power; the rest is provided by hydroelectric power, geo-thermal power and other alternative sources. The United States is the country with the highest rate of energy consumption per head in the world. A few years ago over a third of total world energy production was consumed in the USA, and appeals to save

Economy

Hoover Dam in Nevada

energy had no effect. More recently, however, there has been an increasing realisation of the need for economy; and if savings could be achieved in practice the United States could become self-sufficient in energy.

Around 25% of world energy production is generated in the United States. Some three-fifths of total output comes from coal-fired power stations, another fifth from nuclear power stations and smaller amounts from oil-fired and hydroelectric power stations and various alternative sources.

Electricity production

Industry

In spite of the problems of industrial development which arose in the late eighties and early nineties the United States is still one of the world's leading industrial nations, with six of the ten largest industrial concerns in the world. In 1992, however, industry accounted for no more than 20% of the gross domestic product.

The traditional heartland of American industry is the North-East, with the densest industrial concentration in the "manufacturing belt", occupying the triangular area between the cities of New York, Chicago and St Louis. Nowadays, however, this area, apart from some centres round Boston and the renowned New England universities, is a region of industrial stagnation, now known as the "rust belt". This is particularly evident in the partial decline of Detroit, the legendary centre of the American automobile industry. Many places show evidence of the "de-industrialisation" process and the increasing movement into the services sector. The number of workers employed in industry in this area has been falling steadily for years; and whereas before 1986 most of the 7.6 million private automobiles produced in the United States were made in the manufacturing belt, by 1990 the number had fallen below the 6 million mark.

The industrial heartland, the manufacturing belt

Economy

A new industrial region, the Sun Belt

Over the last two decades, with a speed and dynamism barely conceivable in Europe, new industrial regions have developed in the South and West, mainly in the "Sun Belt" which extends from Georgia (particularly round Atlanta) by way of Florida, Alabama, Texas, New Mexico and Colorado to California, on the Pacific coast. Numerous firms, mainly engaged in the aircraft and space industries, electronics, petrochemicals, chemicals and pharmaceuticals, have been established here, and half the 18.5 million workers employed in industry now work in the Sun Belt.

Major industrial products

The most important branch of industry, now showing a declining trend, is the automobile industry: a fifth of world automobile production is based in the United States. The highest growth rate, however, by a considerable margin, is in high-tech industry. The aircraft and space industry, based mainly in Florida, California and the Seattle area, which along with the electronics industry forms part of the military and industrial complex, produces three-quarters of world production of aircraft. In this area too well over 10 million personal computers and over 4000 mainframe computers were produced in 1990. The increase in refinery capacity has enabled the United States to achieve a leading place in the manufacture of petrochemical products and synthetic fibres. Other flourishing branches of industry – mainly in the Great Plains and the South – are tyre manufacture, textiles and clothing, paper and cellulose, and the foodstuffs and associated industries.

Service Industries

For many years the services sector of the American economy has been developing with particular dynamism. A survey in the year 1978 showed that two-thirds of the working population of the United States were employed in the services sector of the economy, which accounted for almost two-thirds of the gross domestic product. Now three-quarters of the working population are in the services sector, which accounts for just under 70% of GDP. Most of the jobs in this sector are in commerce, financial services, the tourist trade and not least in education and research.

The United States has a high potential in research and innovation. Industry and the universities, public and private research institutes work closely together with no barriers or hang-ups. Elites are deliberately fostered, and the large number of Nobel Prize winners in the United States suggests that the liberal American economic system has advantages over the less flexible Japanese or even European set-up. American scientific research, with its sights set on practical application, is now the real motive force behind the world economy. The American system has shown how it is possible to harness to development an extraordinarily high proportion of the gross domestic product and of the working population.

Foreign Trade

Exports

The United States still occupies a leading place among the commercial nations of the world. In 1991 it exported goods to the value of 400 billion dollars, mainly machinery, electrical and electronic products, motor vehicles, petrochemicals and other chemical products, maize, soya beans, wheat, fruit and vegetables, meat, coal and iron and steel. The main customers for American goods are Canada, the European Union (particularly Britain and Germany), Mexico, Japan, Taiwan and South Korea.

Imports

In 1991 the United States imported goods to the value of well over 500 billion dollars, principally motor vehicles, machinery, electrical and electronic equipment, oil and oil products, iron and steel, non-ferrous metals, chemicals, agricultural produce, fish and foodstuffs and related products.

Economy

Hectic activity in New York's Stock Exchange

The main suppliers were Japan, Canada, the European Union (particularly Germany, Britain, Italy and France), Taiwan, South Korea, Hong Kong, the People's Republic of China, Mexico and Brazil.

Negotiations between the United States and the neighbouring countries of Canada and Mexico on the formation of the strongest domestic market in the world, the North American Free Trade Agreement (NAFTA), were successfully concluded in the autumn of 1993 and approved by Congress. The agreement, which came into force in 1994, established a common market with a population of some 365 million and an annual economic product of some 6 billion dollars. The project, however, has aroused opposition, particularly in the United States, where there are apprehensions about the loss of several hundred thousand jobs to Mexico with its low wage costs.

NAFTA

Tourism

Over the last twenty years or so the United States has developed into a popular long distance holiday destination. The range of attractions for tourists is a wide one. Interesting cities like New York, Washington, Chicago, Los Angeles and San Francisco, breathtaking natural beauties like the Grand Canyon, Niagara Falls and the Yellowstone National Park and a variety of leisure and sporting facilities, including dream beaches on subtropical shores, some of the world's most beautiful golf courses and tennis courts and the "champagne snow" of the Rockies with their magnificent skiing pistes – these were among the attractions which brought over 45 million foreign tourists to the United States in 1992.

General

In 1978 just under 20 million foreign visitors came to the United States, 60% of them from Canada, 12% from Europe, 11% from Mexico and 4% from Japan. By 1992 the number of visitors had increased to 45.6 million – 47%

Development of tourism

Transport and Communications

from Canada, just under 20% from Europe, 17% from Mexico and just under 8% from Japan. This increase is no doubt partly due to the fall of the dollar and differing economic trends in the United States and the visitors' countries of origin.

The United States, served by all the leading airlines and with the largest chains of hotels and motels in the world, is well equipped to cope with this situation.

Income from tourism

The importance of tourism as an economic factor is indicated by a single figure: in 1991 alone foreign visitors spent 64.38 billion dollars. The main beneficiaries from tourism are the states of California, Florida, New York, Nevada (Las Vegas), Arizona and Texas. It is notable, however, that in the total picture of tourism in America tourism by the Americans themselves is still the major element.

Transport and Communications

General

The United States has an excellent transport and communications system to meet the needs of its economy and its great geographical extent. Its communications make use of the most modern technology: in this respect the United States is a world leader. Passenger transport is shared between the automobile and air services. In traffic in and around cities and regional traffic the automobile is predominant; for longer distances aircraft take over. Public transport for local travel, including buses and tram or rail systems, is well developed only in a few large cities (e.g. New York, San Francisco, Chicago and Miami). The railroads play only a subordinate part in passenger transport but are dominant in freight transport. Internal shipping services are of little importance.

Close encounter of the lonely kind

Transport and Communications

Road travel

The United States has well over 3.8 million miles/6.2 million kilometres of roads. Its highways (motorways) and national, regional and local roads are used by more than 136 million automobiles, 41 million lorries (trucks) and buses and some 5.5 million motorcycles. This is the most highly motorised nation in the world, with just under 600 automobiles per 1000 inhabitants.

Rail services

The private railroads which in the 19th century made such a major contribution to the opening up of the country and its economic development, still run a network of 154,000 miles/248,000km. They carry some 20 million passengers a year – only a small fraction of total passenger traffic. In 1971, following a decision of the US Congress, the Amtrak system was established by amalgamating 13 rail companies engaged in passenger transport; it carries intercity and tourist traffic. The development of the intercity system is to be given priority over the next few years.
The rail system still plays a major part in freight transport, carrying some 2 billion tons of goods annually. The Conrail system, the counterpart of Amtrak for freight traffic, was established in 1976.

Air services

After the Second World War air services in the United States developed at a tremendous pace, and now almost half the world's air traffic is handled in the USA. Between 1975 and 1990 alone the number of passengers carried rose from 206 million to over 450 million. The busiest airports are those of New York (John F. Kennedy, Newark and La Guardia), Chicago (O'Hare), Los Angeles, Atlanta, Miami and Denver. Chicago airport alone handled over 54 million passengers in 1992. The United States is the country with the most airports and the largest civil air fleet in the world. In addition to some 2200 commercial aircraft there are around 275,000 other aircraft (including light and sporting aircraft). In the early eighties, under the deregulation policy of the Reagan administration, the regulations on air traffic were liberalised and the airlines were relieved of much state control, including the fixing of fares. The consequences were cutthroat competition on fares and falling profits. After a fierce battle for predominance between the airlines during which there were some spectacular failures (including the collapse of Pan Am) the economic situation of air travel in the United States – now dominated by six large airlines – is stable.

Inland shipping

Inland shipping in the United States serves predominantly to carry freight traffic. The most important inland waterways are the Mississippi–Missouri river system, including the Tennessee and Ohio Rivers, the Great Lakes, the St Lawrence Seaway and the Intracoastal Waterway. There are some tourist steamboats and passenger ships on the Mississippi, Missouri, Ohio and Tennessee Rivers and on the Great Lakes.

Seagoing shipping

The United States has a seagoing fleet of some 6500 vessels, with a total capacity of over 20 million tons. The principal seaports are New York, New Orleans, Baltimore, Newport, Houston, San Francisco and Los Angeles. Some 300 million tons of freight are loaded annually and some 400 million tons discharged. The most important import is oil; the principal exports are agricultural produce (wheat, maize, etc.), coal and petrochemical products.

Pipelines

Pipelines are increasingly being used for the transport of gaseous and fluid raw materials and basic industrial materials. They have been installed not only in the oil states of Texas and Oklahoma but also in distant Alaska. There are now special networks for natural gas, oil and refinery products; and some 7 billion barrels of oil and over 4.5 billion barrels of refinery products annually are now pumped through long-distance pipelines. There are plans (including in particular the Kern River Project) to supply California with natural gas from Wyoming and Canada.

Telecommunications

With the exception of the postal service telecommunications are in the hands of fiercely competitive private companies. Rapid communication is provided by six communications satellites and 26 cable systems, and there

Transport and Communications

are some 130 million telephone subscribers. Telephone corporations have efficient communications networks which carry radio and television programmes and electronic mail as well as telephone calls. Other facilities in course of development are the remote monitoring of raw material prospection, environmental monitoring by satellite and satellite control of traffic movements by land and sea.

History

The ethnic origins of the earliest inhabitants of the North American subcontinent are still the subject of controversy, but the generally accepted view is that the indigenous inhabitants of North America, wrongly identified by Columbus as Indians, came from northern Asia in two waves some 28,000–24,000 and 13,000–12,000 years ago, travelling over the land bridge which then still existed in the area of the Bering Strait. For their further spread and subsequent history see the chapter on the Indians of North America (pp. 31 ff.).

Original inhabitants

Discovery

The Viking Leif Eriksson, coming from Greenland, lands on the coast of Newfoundland and calls the country Vineland. A first attempt at settlement led by Thorfinn Karlsefni is a failure.

c. 1000–1005

Christopher Columbus, looking for the western seaway to India, lands on October 12th 1492 on the small island of San Salvador (Guanahani, Watling Island) in the Bahamas. Between 1492 and 1504, on this and three subsequent voyages, he reconnoitres the West Indies, the north coast of South America and the Central American coast. Although he never set foot on the territory of the United States, his fame outshines that of the other discoverers.

Discoveries in modern times

John Cabot (Giovanni Caboto), a Venetian in the service of the English crown, sails along the coasts of Newfoundland and Delaware.

1497–98

After the much-travelled Florentine Amerigo Vespucci claims in his writings that the New World is a continent the German cartographer Martin Waldseemüller names the continent America in Vespucci's honour.

1507

The Spanish navigator Juan Ponce de León discovers Florida.

1513

Colonisation

Spain becomes the first European nation to establish a colonial empire in the New World. The ruthless conquistadors, seeking rapid success and wealth for themselves and their country, destroy the flourishing empires of the Aztecs and the Incas in Central and South America. The southern regions of North America also attract their interest.

Spain

Hernando de Soto, starting from Florida, explores the coast of the Gulf of Mexico as far as the Mississippi and presses on into Arkansas and Oklahoma.

1539–43

Francisco Vásquez de Coronado leads an expedition into the territory of Arizona and New Mexico. Hernando de Alarcón reaches the Colorado River. García López de Cardenas discovers the Grand Canyon.

1540

Pedro Menendez founds the first enduring Spanish colony in North America at what is now St Augustine in Florida.

1565

While Spanish and Portuguese colonising activity is mainly in Central and South America, the French establish their colonial empire of Nouvelle France in North America, extending from Canada to the Mississippi.

France

Giovanni da Verrazano, a Florentine in the French service, reconnoitres the east coast of North America. He is probably the first European to sail into the estuary of the Hudson River, now the port of New York.

1524

Jacques Cartier discovers the river St Lawrence.

1534

Samuel de Champlain (1570–1635) founds the first French colony in the New World at Québec.

1608

History

1673	The Jesuit Jacques Marquette and Louis Joliet advance south to the Mississippi and claim the whole river for France.
1682	René Robert Cavelier, Sieur de la Salle, reaches the Mississippi delta and takes possession of the whole river basin in the name of Louis XIV, calling it Louisiana.
1718	Jean-Baptiste Le Moyne, Sieur de Bienville (1680–1768), founds Nouvelle Orléans (New Orleans).
Conflicts with Britain	France thus theoretically controls the whole of known North America. Towards the end of the 17th century it becomes involved in war with Britain (King William's War). During the War of the Spanish Succession (1704–13) France and Britain are also at war in North America (Queen Anne's War). Under the treaty of Utrecht in 1713 Britain receives the territory round Hudson Bay, Nova Scotia and Newfoundland. After King George's War (1744–48) and the French and Indian War (1754–63), during the Seven Years' War, France loses Canada and the territory east of the Mississippi.
1803	In the Louisiana Purchase the United States buys the French colony of Louisiana.

Holland	Dutch interest in the New World is concentrated on the area round New York and New Jersey.
1609	Henry Hudson, an Englishman in the service of the Dutch East India Company who is looking for the North-West Passage, sails up the Hudson River and claims the territory for Holland.
1614	The area round Long Island Sound is named Nieuw Holland.
1626	Peter Minuit buys the island of Manhattan from the Indians – it is said with trinkets worth 24 dollars – and founds Nieuw Amsterdam.
1664	British forces occupy Nieuw Amsterdam, of which Peter Stuyvesant is governor, and rename it New York.

Britain	Britain is the last of the great powers to establish a colonial empire in North America. Around 1700 there are some 2500 British settlers; by 1750 two-thirds of the inhabitants have been born in the colonies.
1584	Sir Walter Raleigh founds the first English settlements on Roanoke Island in North Carolina. They are later abandoned.
1607	British colonisation of North America begins in earnest with the arrival of 105 settlers led by Captain John Smith. Their settlement of Jamestown is the nucleus of the colony of Virginia.
1619	The first black Africans, voluntarily engaged as indentured labourers, arrive in Jamestown.
1620/21	In November 102 Puritans, the Pilgrim Fathers, land from the "Mayflower" at Cape Cod in Massachusetts, after signing the Mayflower Compact, an agreement promising obedience to the laws and ordinances introduced by the leaders of the enterprise. This government by the people is seen as foreshadowing one of the basic principles of American democracy. The Pilgrims' first harvest in 1621 is still commemorated on Thanksgiving Day.
1623	Foundation of the colony of New Hampshire.
1629	Robert Heath receives from King Charles I the originally Spanish colony of Carolina (later, in 1730, divided into North and South Carolina).
1634	Foundation of the Catholic colony of Maryland.
1635	Foundation of the colony of Connecticut.
1636	Foundation of the colony of Rhode Island. Harvard College founded in Boston.
1650	Slave-owning is officially permitted.
1664	British forces occupy Nieuw Amsterdam, Nieuw Holland and Delaware.
1676	The Wampanoag and Narragansett Indians, living on the east coast, rebel against the British (King Philip's War).
1681/83	The Quaker William Penn founds the colony of Pennsylvania. Its capital, Philadelphia, is founded in 1683.
1704	The first newspaper in the colonies, the "Boston News Letter", appears.
1732	James Oglethorpe founds Georgia, the thirteenth and last British colony in North America.

History

The American Revolution

The colonists, increasingly self-confident, their trade restricted by the Navigation Act of 1660, without any political weight in London and governed from there, with ever new regulations and taxes, strive to achieve independence.

The Currency Act prohibits the colonies from issuing their own currency. The Sugar Act reintroduces a tax on sugar. The Stamp Act (repealed in 1766) requires all documents and printed works to be stamped. The Quartering Act obliges the colonies to meet the cost of reinforcing the British garrisons. The Townshend Acts impose import duties on tea, paint, glass, paper and other items. The colonists' resentment is expressed in passive resistance and soon also in a demand for representation in Parliament ("No taxation without representation"), made at a congress of representatives from nine colonies at New York in November 1767.

1764–67

Thomas Jefferson's draft of the Declaration of Independence

History

1770 During a riot in Boston on March 5th three civilians are killed by British troops. This "Boston Massacre" further alienates the colonists from the mother country.

1773/74 The Boston Tea Party. In protest against the banning of trade with other countries a party of Boston citizens disguised as Indians throw several cargoes of tea into Boston harbour. The British government introduces a series of restrictive Acts (the "Intolerable Acts") and closes Boston harbour.
Representatives of all the colonies except Georgia meet in Philadelphia in the first Continental Congress and resolve to break off all commercial relations with Britain and with other British colonies throughout the world.

1775 The first clashes between British "redcoats" and American "minutemen" (patriots ready for action at a moment's notice) occur at Concord and Lexington, near Boston. This marks the beginning of the War of American Independence. On June 15th the second Continental Congress appoints George Washington commander in chief of American forces. On June 17th the patriots are defeated in the battle of Bunker Hill.

1776 On July 4th 1776 the Congress in Philadelphia proclaims the independence of the colonies from Britain in the Declaration of Independence. This day, the foundation date of the United States of America, is now a national holiday (Independence Day).
The military situation is characterised by varying fortunes. Washington drives the British out of Boston, but is defeated on Long Island in August. In December, after crossing the frozen Delaware River, he defeats British forces at Trenton. British troops, with mercenaries from Hesse and Brunswick, occupy New York.

1777 The British occupy Philadelphia, but are defeated at Saratoga on October 17th. On December 17th France recognises the independence of the thirteen colonies.

1778–80 On February 6th 1780 France concludes an assistance pact with the United States and sends a fleet to support the American patriots. In June the British leave Philadelphia. In 1779 Washington is condemned by shortage of men to inactivity in his camp at West Point. On May 12th 1780 British forces take Charleston in what is now South Carolina.

1781 The British army, commanded by General Cornwallis, withdraws to Yorktown, Virginia. A French fleet under the command of Admiral de Grasse then closes the Hampton Roads, and the combined American and French forces, commanded by Washington and General Rochambeau, defeat the British army and force Cornwallis to surrender (October 19th). This victory decides the war in favour of the Americans.

1782 On November 30th Britain and its former colonies sign a preliminary peace treaty in Paris.

1783 On September 3rd the independence of the thirteen American states is recognised in the treaty of Versailles. Canada, the American North-West and Nova Scotia remain in British hands, but the western frontier of the United States moves west to the Mississippi, incorporating the territories ceded by France in 1763. Some 100,000 pro-British Loyalists flee to Canada or join the British army to escape the hatred and revenge of the patriots.

Foundation, Consolidation and Extension of the Union

1787 In the Northwest Ordinance of July 13th the Continental Congress establishes the territory west of New York and north of the Ohio River as a state.

History

Territorial Development of the USA

- The 13 founding states
- Ceded by Britain 1783
- Bought from France 1803 (Louisiana Purchase)
- Annexed 1819 and 1813
- Bought from Spain 1819
- Ceded by Britain 1842
- Admitted to the Union 1845
- Incorporated in the Union 1818–46 (North-West Territories)
- Ceded by Mexico 1848
- Bought from Mexico 1853 (Gadsden Purchase)

On September 17th the Constitutional Convention approves the Constitution of the Union.

The first Congress of the United States meets in Federal Hall in New York and elects Washington unanimously as first President of the Union. On March 4th the Constitution comes into force, and on April 30th the Supreme Court is established.	1789
The Bill of Rights, promulgated on December 15th, guarantees basic rights such as freedom of religion, assembly and the press and the inviolability of persons and property.	1791
The United States Mint is established in Philadelphia on April 2nd.	1792
The invention of the cotton gin by Eli Whitney leads to the extension of cotton monoculture. A direct consequence is a rapid increase in the slave trade.	1793
Washington ends his second term of office with the Farewell Address of September 19th, in which he warns against long-term alliances with other powers and against high state debts.	1796
The population of the United States, with around a third of its present-day territory, is about 4 million. There are only five towns of more than 10,000 inhabitants. Washington DC becomes the official residence of the President and the seat of Congress.	1800
In the Louisiana Purchase the United States acquires the largely unexplored French territory of Louisiana and thus doubles its area.	1803
On May 14th 1804 Meriwether Lewis and William Clark set out from St Louis on a 2½-year-long expedition in the course of which they explore the territory now occupied by the states of the North-West and reach the Pacific coast.	1804–06

History

1807	Maiden trip of Robert Fulton's steamboat.
1808	Congress bans the import of slaves.
1812–14	Napoleon's Continental System, British counter-measures which seriously injure American trade and British support of a rebellion by the Shawnees lead to war with Britain. The American attempt to take Canada fails; British troops occupy Washington and burn down the Capitol and the White House. The status quo is restored by the treaty of Ghent on December 24th 1814. In the battle of New Orleans in January 1815 – fought before news of the peace treaty is received – there are heavy losses, particularly on the British side.
1819	The United States buys Florida from Spain.
1820	The Missouri Compromise permits slave-owning in the new state of Missouri but prohibits it in all territories west of the Mississippi and north of latitude 36°30' N.
1823	President James Monroe sets out the Monroe Doctrine: the United States renounces any idea of exerting American influence in Europe and rejects any intervention by European powers in the western hemisphere ("America for the Americans").
1825	The Erie Canal is opened on October 26th.
1829	Andrew Jackson becomes President – the first representative of the farmers of the West to reach the highest office.
1830s	During the 1830s there is a threat of secession from the Union by the farming and slave-owning Southern states because of the introduction of taxes favouring the industrial Northern states and the Northern demand for the abolition of slavery. The dispute is settled for the time being by new tax laws.
1830	Joseph Smith founds the Mormon sect in Fayette, New York State.
1832	War against the Sac and Fox Indians in Illinois and Wisconsin. The Democrats hold their first party convention in Baltimore.
1833	William Lloyd Garrison founds the radical Antislavery Society.
1835	The Seminole Indians of Florida launch a war against the whites which lasts eight years. Texas declares its independence from Mexico.
1836	Mexican troops occupy San Antonio in Texas and wipe out the defenders of the Alamo mission there. Six weeks later Texan forces, with the battle-cry "Remember the Alamo!", defeat the Mexicans at San Jacinto.
1838	The Cherokee Indians are deported from their hereditary territory in the Smoky Mountains to Oklahoma (the "Trail of Tears").
1840	75,000 slaves escape to Canada on the secret "underground railway".
1841/42	On May 1st 1841 the first wagon trek sets out from Independence, Missouri, for California. A year later the Oregon Trail is opened. In 1841 the United States government guarantees various Indian tribes possession of the territory west of the Mississippi "so long as grass grows and water runs".
1844	On May 24th Samuel Morse sends the first message by telegraph from Washington to Baltimore.

History

Texas is admitted to the Union.	1845

After the signature of a frontier agreement with Britain the North-Western Territories are incorporated in the Union.
In the war with Mexico which is sparked off by the incorporation of Texas in the Union American troops occupy Veracruz and Mexico City. The war ends in 1847 with an agreement by Mexico, in return for compensation, to renounce any claim to Texas, New Mexico, Colorado, Arizona, Utah, Nevada and northern California.
In July 1847 the Mormons, led by Brigham Young, travel to Utah. — 1846/47

Gold is found on the American River in California, and by 1849 80,000 gold-seekers have made their way to California. In July the world's first conference on women's rights is held in Seneca Falls, New York State. — 1848

The Southern states prevent the banning of slavery in the territories acquired from Mexico except California. — 1850

Harriet Beecher Stowe publishes her novel "Uncle Tom's Cabin", the success of which exacerbates the conflict between North and South. — 1852

The Kansas–Nebraska Bill permits the inhabitants of these states to own slaves – in effect abrogating the Missouri Compromise. There are conflicts in Kansas and Nebraska between the supporters and opponents of slavery; the opponents are members of the Republican Party. — 1854

The first transcontinental mail service reaches the Pacific coast. — 1858

John Brown attacks the military post at Harpers Ferry in Virginia in order to get arms for the fight against slavery. — 1859

Abraham Lincoln, a Republican, is elected President.
The population of the United States passes the 30 million mark. — 1860

Civil War

The election of Lincoln as President brings the conflict between the South and the North to crisis point. At the end of 1860 South Carolina withdraws from the Union, to be followed in 1861 by Mississippi, Florida, Alabama, Georgia, Louisiana, Texas, Virginia, Arkansas, North Carolina and Tennessee. Representatives of these states, meeting in Montgomery, Alabama, form the Confederate States of America, with Richmond, Virginia, as capital and Jefferson Davis as President. On April 12th 1861 the Confederates open hostilities with the bombardment of Fort Sumter in the harbour of Charleston, South Carolina; thereupon Lincoln calls up 75,000 volunteers. From April 19th the ports of the Southern states are blockaded. In the first battle of the war, at Bull Run (Manassas, Virginia), the Union forces are defeated.
The first transcontinental telegraph line comes into operation. — 1860/61

Union troops win successes in the West and occupy New Orleans. In the East there are no decisive results. A naval battle in the Hampton Roads (Williamsburg, Virginia) is the first encounter in history between two armour-clad warships, the "Monitor" on the Union side and the Confederacy's "Virginia". A seven-day battle at Mechanicsville, Virginia, ends in the retreat of the Union forces. The Confederates win another victory at Bull Run and advance on Washington, but after the battle of Antietam (Sharpsburg, Maryland) are compelled to retreat. At Fredericksburg, Virginia, the Union army is again defeated. — 1862

On January 1st, in the Emancipation Declaration, Lincoln declares all slaves in the rebel Southern states to be free. The Civil War now becomes a — 1863

History

war for the liberation of the slaves, though this is a subsidiary war aim in comparison with the maintenance of the Union. On the same day the Homestead Act comes into force, enabling any citizen of full age to acquire land, subject to an obligation to build a homestead and cultivate the land. On July 1st, at Gettysburg, Union troops commanded by General Meade defeat the Confederate army, which, under the command of General Lee, has advanced into Pennsylvania and Maryland. Thereafter the Southern army is in more or less continuous retreat. On July 4th, in the Gettysburg Address, Lincoln sets out his ideas on the future form of the Union. Union forces under the command of General Grant take Vicksburg, the principal Confederate base on the Mississippi.

1864 Grant throws Lee's Confederate army back to Richmond and Petersburg, Virginia. A Union army led by General Sherman takes Atlanta and then drives through Georgia to Savannah, leaving a trail of devastation.
On November 29th, at Sand Creek, a cavalry unit shoots down some 300 peaceable Cheyenne Indians (the Sand Creek Massacre).

1865 The Confederates abandon Columbia and Charleston in South Carolina and Petersburg and Richmond in Virginia. On April 9th, at Appomattox, Virginia, the main Confederate army, commanded by Lee, surrenders unconditionally to Grant. At the end of the war, which has cost 385,000 dead and 282,000 wounded, the Union is restored to its unity, the slaves are, formally, freed and the South is devastated. Tensions remain, however, between the South, whose pride has been wounded, and the "progressive" North, and indeed are exacerbated by the social and economic differences between North and South as well as by the race question.
On April 14th Lincoln is shot in Ford's Theatre in Washington by John Wilkes Booth, a fanatical Southerner.
With the adoption of the 13th Amendment to the Constitution on December 18th slavery is abolished throughout the United States and some 3 million blacks are formally granted their freedom.

Reconstruction and the Rise to World Power

The two decades after the Civil War are an unsettled period in which events are dictated by war profiteers and speculators. In the second half of the 19th century the population of the United States grows at a tremendous rate (from 23 million in 1850 to 76 million in 1900), and technological development proceeds at a breathtaking pace. Commercial trusts are formed, and the magnates of the oil and steel industries lay the foundations of their fortunes. At the same time social contrasts become more acute, leading, particularly in the industrialised cities of the North, in strikes and sometimes in violent riots. Trade unions are now formed.
By the end of the 19th century the United States has established itself as a world power which does not hesitate to intervene in other countries' affairs, particularly in Latin America (the policy of the "big stick").

1866 Foundation of the Ku Klux Klan in the Southern states. It commits its first atrocities.

1867 The United States acquires Alaska from Russia for 7.2 million dollars.

1866–68 The Sioux, headed by their chief Red Cloud, successfully resist an attempt to drive the Bozeman Trail through their territory.

1869 The Central Pacific and Union Pacific Railroads meet in Promontory, Utah, completing the transcontinental line.

1870 The 15th Amendment to the Constitution gives blacks the vote.

1872 The Yellowstone National Park is established – the first National Park in the United States.

History

May 10th 1869: completion of the first transcontinental railway

The centenary of the foundation of the United States is marked by the World's Fair in Philadelphia. On June 15th Sioux and Cheyenne Indians wipe out the 7th US Cavalry, commanded by George Custer, on the Little Bighorn River in Montana. — 1876

During the Presidency of Rutherford B. Hayes Carl Schurz, Secretary of the Interior, builds up a professional civil service. — 1877

President James A. Garfield, who had taken up office in January, dies on September 19th from the consequences of an attack on his life in Washington on July 2nd. — 1881

In May eleven people are killed in eight days of fighting between anarchists, workers and the police in Chicago (the Haymarket Riot). On December 8th the American Federation of Labour is founded.
In September the Apache rebel leader Geronimo surrenders to the police. — 1886

The General Allotment Act divides collectively owned Indian land into individual holdings. The Indians, to whom this form of land ownership is unknown, become the victims of speculators. — 1887

Oklahoma, hitherto guaranteed Indian territory, is opened up for settlement by whites. — 1889

The Sherman Anti-Trust Law is the first of a series of laws against the formation of cartels which restrict competition.
The Ghost Dance movement makes rapid headway among the Indians. The government seeks to control its spread by repressive measures. On December 29th US troops kill Chief Bigfoot and 200 of his followers at Wounded Knee – the last battle between Indians and whites.
The Federal Bureau of Census officially records the end of the "frontier" period in the history of the United States, the three hundred years of continuing acquisition of land. — 1890

History

1898

The declared aim of the United States in the war with Mexico during the Presidency of William McKinley is to free Cuba from Spanish rule. After annihilating defeats of the Spanish fleet in naval battles at Cavite (Manila Bay, Philippines) and Santiago de Cuba Spain cedes to the United States in the treaty of Paris the Philippines (in return for a payment of 20 million dollars), Puerto Rico and Guam. Cuba's independence is guaranteed. Congress annexes the Hawaiian Islands.

1900

The United States sends an auxiliary corps to China to assist in the crushing of the Boxer rebellion.

1901

President McKinley dies on September 14th after being shot by an anarchist on September 6th. He is succeeded by Theodore ("Teddy") Roosevelt, who restricts the power of the trusts and makes a name as a "trust buster".

1903

The independent state of Panama is established, under US protection, to safeguard work on the Panama Canal.
Henry Ford founds his first automobile factory. The brothers Orville and Wilbur Wright make the first powered flight in history on the coast of North Carolina (December 17th).

1906

San Francisco is destroyed by an earthquake and a great fire on April 18th and 19th.

1913

The Federal Reserve Act establishes twelve federal reserve banks to mobilise banking reserves and issue currency notes.

1914–18

On August 15th 1914 the first ship passes through the Panama Canal. The United States continues its policy of intervention in its own back yard, landing troops in Haiti in July 1915, intervening in the Mexican civil war and installing a military government in the Dominican Republic in 1917.
On the outbreak of the First World War in Europe President Woodrow Wilson declares the neutrality of the United States. The sinking of two British passenger ships, the "Lusitania" and the "Arabic", by German submarines in May 1915 sparks off a wave of violent protests against Germany, which apologises. After an unsuccessful attempt at mediation in 1916 the United States begins to rearm and increases its relief supplies to the Allies. When Germany declares unrestricted submarine warfare in February 1917 the United States breaks off diplomatic relations, and on April 6th declares war on Germany. Universal military service is introduced on May 18th. By the summer of 1918 the American expeditionary corps is in action on the western front, and by the end of the war it amounts to over a million men and has had 116,000 men killed and 204,000 wounded. The "Fourteen Points" put forward by President Wilson at the beginning of 1918 as the basis for a lasting peace prepare the way for an armistice on November 11th 1918. The Senate refuses to ratify the treaty of Versailles or to join the League of Nations.

Prosperity and Neo-Isolationism

By the end of the First World War the United States has become the world's leading economic power. After a brief period of readjustment the American economy enjoys an unprecedented boom. Technological progress combined with new methods of rationalisation and an apparently irrepressible optimism brings in an era of extraordinary prosperity – counterbalanced, however, by the inadequate purchasing power of the mass of the people, the bootlegging which flourishes during the period of Prohibition and an alarming increase in gangster activity. Uncontrolled speculation increasingly endangers the liberal economic system, and the Stock Exchange crash of 1929 not only leads to the collapse of the American capital market but triggers off one of the world's worst economic crises. By the end of the thirties the crisis appears to be over, and even after the outbreak of the Second World War the American people favour pacifism and neutrality. After Hitler comes to power in Germany the United States takes in great numbers of refugees from the Nazis.

1920 During the period of Prohibition, which continues until 1933, the production, sale, transport, import and export of alcoholic drinks are banned. The first radio programmes are transmitted. The 19th Amendment to the Constitution gives American women the vote.
The trial for murder of two anarchists, Sacco and Vanzetti, and their execution in 1921 create a worldwide sensation.

1921 On August 25th the United States concludes a separate peace with Germany, Austria and Hungary which takes over only some of the provisions of the treaty of Versailles.
After many years of inactivity the Ku Klux Klan resumes its acts of violence against blacks in the southern states.

1922 A miners' strike in Herrin, Illinois, leaves 36 dead.

1924 All Indians are granted full civil rights. The Johnson Read Act drastically restricts the number of immigrants and puts a total ban on Chinese and Japanese immigrants.

1927 Charles Lindbergh makes the first non-stop flight across the Atlantic. The first talking film, the "Jazz Singer", is shown.

1929 A great Stock Exchange crash on October 29th ("Black Friday") ends the period of prosperity.

1930/31 There are 8 million unemployed in the United States. President Hoover tries to counter the depression by great construction projects (the Hoover Dam), the granting of credits, tax increases and a moratorium on international payments.

1932 The number of unemployed reaches 15 million.

1933 President Franklin D. Roosevelt announces his New Deal, a programme for recovery which involves a series of far-reaching measures (declaration of a state of national emergency, agricultural subsidies, the huge Tennessee Valley construction project, etc.).

1934 The devaluation of the dollar by 41% leads to a considerable increase in exports.
The United States gives up its special rights in Cuba and its protection of Haiti.

1935 A new social programme gives workers extensive rights and lays the basis of a pension scheme.

1936–38 The law on the permanent neutrality of the United States comes into force on April 1st, but by the following year the government shows signs of departing from its isolationist policy. Roosevelt threatens states which endanger world peace with "political quarantine".

The United States in the Second World War

1939 The first splitting of the atom is achieved at New York's Columbia University. When the Second World War breaks out in Europe the United States again declares its neutrality and bans the export of war materials. Soon, however, Britain is excepted from the embargo and receives military equipment from the United States.

History

1940 — In spite of its neutrality the United States embarks on comprehensive rearmament, particularly of the navy. Roosevelt is re-elected President for an unprecedented third term and a National Defence Council is established.

1941 — In a speech to Congress Roosevelt sets out the "four freedoms" which he sees as the foundations of a future world order: freedom of speech, freedom of religious belief, freedom from want and freedom from fear. The Lend-Lease Act enables Britain, and later the Soviet Union, to acquire American war materials. In July American troops land in Greenland and Iceland. On August 14th Roosevelt and the British prime minister, Winston Churchill, agree on the Atlantic Charter, which is to become the basis for the creation of the United Nations. The Japanese air attack on the American base of Pearl Harbor on the Hawaiian island of Oahu on December 7th 1941 sparks off the war in the Pacific. On December 11th Germany and Italy declare war on the United States. On December 12th universal military service is introduced. 120,000 Japanese living in the United States, two-thirds of them US citizens, are interned.

1942 — The Japanese conquer the Philippines, but suffer heavy losses in sea and air battles in the Coral Sea and Midway Islands. At the beginning of November American and British troops land in French North Africa.
On December 2nd Enrico Fermi achieves the first nuclear chain reaction at the University of Chicago.

1943 — At the Casablanca Conference in January Roosevelt and Churchill resolve to carry on the war until the unconditional surrender of the enemy. After bitter fighting (begun in August 1942) US troops capture the Japanese air base of Guadalcanal in the south-western Pacific. In September Allied troops land in Sicily. The air war against Germany, based mainly in Britain, is stepped up and continues on an increased scale until 1945. At the Teheran Conference Roosevelt and Churchill meet with Stalin for the first time and discuss common military action and cooperation after the end of the war.

1944 — On June 6th ("D Day") Allied forces land in Normandy: the opening of the second front called for by Stalin. Paris is freed in August, and in October Aachen is taken by the Americans – the first German city to fall to the Allies. In the same month US troops land in the Philippines.
Roosevelt is re-elected President for a fourth term.

1945 — At the Yalta Conference in February Roosevelt, Churchill and Stalin agree on guidelines for the further conduct of the war and the occupation of Germany. On April 12th Roosevelt dies and is succeeded by the Vice-President, Harry S. Truman. On April 25th American and Soviet troops meet at Torgau on the Elbe. On May 7th the German Wehrmacht surrenders unconditionally.
The tactic of "island-hopping" has brought American forces in the Pacific steadily closer to Japan. Iwo Jima falls in February, Okinawa in April. On July 16th the first atom bomb is detonated at the Alamogordo test site in New Mexico. On August 6th and 9th two atom bombs are dropped on Hiroshima (killing between 80,000 and 200,000) and Nagasaki (killing between 39,000 and 74,000). Japan surrenders on September 2nd.
Of the 16 million US soldiers involved in the war 292,000 have been killed and 671,000 wounded.
On June 26th representatives of 51 states meet in San Francisco and found the United Nations. During the last two years of the war there have been ever clearer signs of the power-political trends which lead after the war to the split between the western capitalist and the eastern socialist camps.

From the Cold War to Détente

1947 — Under the "Truman doctrine" the United States gives military and economic aid to Greece and Turkey in order to prevent a Communist takeover.

History

The controversial Taft-Hartley Labor Act curtails the authority of trade unions.

The Soviet blockade of West Berlin is broken by the American and British airlift. The Marshall Plan for the rebuilding of western Europe, initiated by Secretary of State George Marshall in 1947, begins to operate. — 1948

Truman, re-elected President, outlines a 21-point domestic programme which comes to be known as the Fair Deal. The United States is the leading power in the North Atlantic Treaty Organisation (NATO) which is established on April 4th. — 1949

In January President Truman gives approval to the development of the hydrogen bomb.
Senator Joseph McCarthy launches his first attack on "Communists" in the country's political and cultural life. The following years are marked by anti-Communist hysteria and an atmosphere of denunciation and mistrust.
After North Korea's invasion of South Korea US troops commanded by General MacArthur intervene on behalf of the United Nations. In October they reach the frontier with China and clash with Chinese troops. — 1950

Truman recalls MacArthur, who wants to carry the war into Chinese territory. Negotiations on a cease-fire begin.
Australia, New Zealand and the United States conclude the ANZUS pact in San Francisco. — 1951

The United States, Britain and France sign a peace treaty with the German Federal Republic.
On November 1st the first hydrogen bomb is detonated on Eniwetok atoll in the Marshall Islands. — 1952

On July 27th an armistice in the Korean War is signed at Panmunjong. Of the 5.7 million US soldiers engaged more than 54,000 were killed and 103,000 wounded. — 1953

Senator McCarthy's pursuit of Communists reaches a final peak in a series of televised hearings; at the end of the year, however, his activities are condemned by the Senate. The Supreme Court declares racial segregation in public schools unconstitutional.
ANZUS is replaced by the wider SEATO (South-East Asia Treaty Organisation). — 1954

The two largest American trade unions, AFL and CIO, join to form AFL-CIO, with a total of 15 million members. In Montgomery, Alabama, a black woman refuses for the first time to give up her seat to a white; the buses are boycotted by blacks; and a federal court declares segregation in buses unconstitutional.
The first military advisers are sent to South Vietnam. — 1955

In September troops of the National Guard are called out by the Governor of Arkansas to prevent nine black children from entering the previously white Central High School in Little Rock. President Eisenhower sends federal troops to enforce the Supreme Court's declaration that racial segregation in public schools is unconstitutional.
The successful launch on October 4th of the Soviet satellite "Sputnik 1" is a shock to Americans' belief in their technological superiority. — 1957

On January 31st the United States' first earth satellite, "Explorer", is put into orbit.
US troops land in Lebanon to forestall an attempted coup d'état. — 1958

Alaska and Hawaii are admitted to the Union as the 49th and 50th states. On April 25th the St Lawrence Seaway is opened, giving the ports on the Great Lakes a direct link with the Atlantic. — 1959

History

	Nikita Khrushchov becomes the first Soviet head of state to visit the United States.
1960	On May 1st an American U 2 reconnaissance aircraft is shot down over the Soviet Union. As a result a planned summit conference in Paris is called off. Black and white students demonstrate against racial discrimination with sit-ins all over the country. The Democrat John F. Kennedy, a Roman Catholic, is elected President by a narrow majority over the Republican Richard Nixon. Kennedy's "New Frontier" programme shakes up the nation and makes him the idol of a new and more hopeful era.
1961	The "Sugar War" between the United States and Fidel Castro's Cuba leads in January to the breaking off of diplomatic relations. The invasion of Cuba, with US support, by Cuban exiles landing in the Bay of Pigs is a fiasco. On April 12th the Soviet cosmonaut Yury Gagarin becomes the first man to fly into space. He is followed on May 5th by the United States' first man in space, Alan B. Shepard.
1962	President Kennedy strengthens the US presence in South Vietnam. In October the Cuban missiles crisis brings the world to the verge of a third world war, when the Soviet Union stations troops and medium-range rockets on the island. The United States calls for them to be dismantled and mounts an air and sea blockade of Cuba. After days of worldwide tension the Soviet Union gives way on condition that the United States withdraws its rockets from Turkey. Kennedy's successful handling of the crisis is his greatest foreign policy achievement.
1963	On August 5th the United States, Soviet Union and Britain sign a nuclear test-ban treaty. At the end of August some 200,000 people, mainly coloured, demonstrate in Washington against racial discrimination. They are led by Martin Luther

March on Washington, August 28th 1963

King, who makes his famous speech, "I have a dream". On November 22nd President Kennedy is shot in Dallas, Texas.
At the end of the year there are 15,000 US troops in South Vietnam.

1964
A new civil rights law is directed against racial discrimination in employment, housing and political actiivity.
On August 2nd two American warships are attacked by North Vietnamese torpedo-boats in the Gulf of Tonkin. Congress thereupon gives President Lyndon Johnson unlimited authority for action in South-East Asia. The Vietnam War now officially begins.

1965
President Johnson orders the bombing of North Vietnam north of the 20th parallel. By the end of the year the number of US troops in South Vietnam has risen to 184,000.
Martin Luther King leads thousands of civil rights supporters in a protest march from Selma to Montgomery, Alabama. In race riots in Los Angeles in August 35 people are killed.

1966
The strength of US forces in Vietnam, Laos and Thailand has risen to 480,000.

1967
President Johnson and the Soviet prime minister, Kosygin, meet in Glassborough, New Jersey, in June and agree that an atomic war must be avoided at all costs.
During the summer the National Guard is called in to quell violent race riots in Newark and Detroit which leave 66 dead and thousands of injured. Thurgood Marshall becomes the first black judge in the Supreme Court.
Protests against the war in Vietnam increase. On October 21st and 22nd 35,000 people demonstrate in Washington.

1968
The Tet offensive by the Vietcong and the North Vietnamese causes heavy American and South Vietnamese losses. The bombing of North Vietnam is called off, and peace negotiations begin in Paris.
On April 4th Martin Luther King is shot in Memphis, leading to race riots in many states. On June 5th Senator Robert Kennedy is shot in Los Angeles. The Republican Richard Nixon is elected President.

1969
The Supreme Court recognises the right of objection to military service on moral as well as on religious grounds.
In April there are 534,000 US servicemen in Vietnam. Their withdrawal begins in July. On November 15th 250,000 people demonstrate in Washington against the Vietnam war. On the following day there is news of the My Lai massacre, in which US troops are said to have killed several hundred South Vietnamese civilians.
Climaxing the series of manned space flights which have been carried out since 1961 (Mercury, Gemini, Apollo), Apollo 11 lands on the moon on July 20th, with the two astronauts Neil Armstrong and Edwin Aldrin.
SALT negotiations, aimed at the limitation of American and Soviet strategic arms, begin in Helsinki. Relationships between the two super-powers enter a period of détente.

Crisis and New Hope

From the beginning of his term of office President Nixon is faced with a variety of problems – racial discrimination, poverty, economic stagnation and the fall of the dollar, unemployment, environmental pollution, increasing protests against the war in Vietnam – which raise doubts throughout the world about the "land of unlimited possibilities". The state of shock in America at the end of the Vietnam War – the realisation that the world's mightiest military machine had been defeated by poorly equipped jungle

History

fighters, the split in the nation between opponents and supporters of the war, the gradual revelation of the real reasons for US involvement – shatters the collective consciousness of the United States for years if not decades to come. The Watergate scandal and the deplorable behaviour of President Nixon increase doubts about the "American dream".

1970 The nuclear weapons non-proliferation treaty comes into force on March 5th.
On Earth Day (April 22nd) millions of Americans demonstrate in a call for effective protection of the environment.
President Nixon authorises American forces to enter Cambodian territory. During protests against this action at Kent State University in Ohio four students are shot by the National Guard.

1971 The voting age is reduced to 18.
On June 13th the "New York Times" begins to publish the "Pentagon Papers", which reveal the deliberate intervention of the United States in Vietnam at an early stage and sparks off a violent controversy. The number of American servicemen in Vietnam is reduced to 140,000.

1972 At the end of February President Nixon pays a "friendly" visit to the Chinese People's Republic, and in May travels to Moscow. The United States and the Soviet Union sign the SALT 1 agreement in Moscow.
Nixon orders the mining of North Vietnam ports. The last US troops leave Vietnam on August 11th.
An Amendment to the Constitution declares discrimination against women unconstitutional, and the Supreme Court declares the death sentence unconstitutional. In June there is a break-in at the Democratic Party's headquarters in the Watergate building in Washington. Nixon wins the Presidential election with a large majority.

1973 An armistice in the Vietnam War is signed in Paris on January 24th. US losses in the war are 56,000 dead and over 303,000 wounded. Universal military service is abolished on June 30th.
Militant Indians occupy the hamlet of Wounded Knee and hold it for ten weeks in protest against the continuing discrimination.
In the course of the year the direct involvement of President Nixon's closest advisers in the Watergate break-in and the President's attempts to hush the matter up become increasingly clear. After the resignation of Vice-President Spiro Agnew, accused of tax evasion, Gerald Ford becomes Vice-President.
In October the oil-producing Arab states put an oil embargo on the United States because of its support for Israel in the Yom Kippur War.
The Supreme Court declares abortion during the first six months of pregnancy to be legal.

1974 During the further course of the Watergate affair impeachment proceedings are started against Nixon. He resigns on August 8th. He is granted a pardon by the new President, Gerald Ford, in spite of strong public protests.

1975 After the capture of Saigon by North Vietnamese forces Vietnam capitulates on April 30th. The last American citizens are evacuated from the roof of the US embassy by helicopter. The United States take in 140,000 refugees from South Vietnam. In September SEATO is dissolved.

1976 The 200th anniversary of the Declaration of Independence is celebrated in July. The Supreme Court, reversing its previous decision, declares the death sentence to be constitutional. In the Presidential election on November 2nd Jimmy Carter, a Democrat from Georgia, wins a narrow victory over his Republican opponent, President Gerald Ford.

History

President Carter grants a pardon to some 10,000 objectors to service in Vietnam.	1977
A peace treaty between Egypt and Israel is signed in Washington on March 26th. On June 18th the United States and the Soviet Union sign the SALT 2 treaty in Vienna. On November 4th Iranian revolutionaries storm the US embassy in Teheran and take 63 diplomats hostage; their object is to secure the return to Iran of the Shah, who has taken refuge in the United States. There is a nuclear accident, classed in the highest category, in the Three Miles Island reactor at Harrisburg, Pennsylvania.	1979
Following the Soviet intervention in Afghanistan (1979) the United States imposes a grain embargo on the USSR. In subsequent years the policy of détente suffers setbacks. The United States boycotts the Olympic Games in Moscow. An attempt to free the Teheran hostages by military means ends in fiasco. Mount St Helens, a volcano in Washington state, erupts on May 18th with a force equal to 500 bombs of Hiroshima type. Ronald Reagan, a Republican, wins the Presidential election.	1980
On January 20th, the day on which President Reagan takes up office, the Teheran hostages are released. Reagan's economic programme ("Reaganomics") is based on reductions in taxes and government expenditure and an increase in the defence budget; his aim is to restore American self-confidence and overcome the trauma of Vietnam. The space shuttle "Columbia", the first reusable spacecraft, is launched on April 12th. Sandra Day O'Connor is appointed assessor to the Supreme Court, the first woman to join the court.	1981
The Peace Movement is formed and, with the slogan "Freeze nuclear arms!", calls for an end to nuclear weapons. On June 12th half a million people demonstrate in New York. Over 12 million Americans are unemployed.	1982
In a television address President Reagan puts forward his idea of an anti-rocket defence system based in space, the "Strategic Defence Initiative". 241 American soldiers, part of an international peace-keeping force in Lebanon, are killed in a bomb attack in Beirut on October 23rd. On October 25th US troops land on the Caribbean island of Grenada, an independent Commonwealth state, to overthrow the left-wing Military Council.	1983
The Olympic Games in Los Angeles are boycotted by the countries of the Eastern Bloc. Ronald Reagan has a triumphal victory in the Presidential election. The Democratic candidate for the Vice-Presidency is Geraldine Ferraro, the first woman to be nominated for the post.	1984
President Reagan and the Soviet leader, Mikhail Gorbachov, meet in Geneva. A fresh boost is given to the policy of détente.	1985
The space shuttle "Challenger" blows up soon after its launch on January 28th, killing all seven of its crew. After terrorist attacks in Europe the United States accuses Libya of being responsible, and US aircraft bomb Tripoli and Benghazi. At the end of the year details of the "Irangate" affair, in which the proceeds of arms sales to Iran went to the Contra rebels in Nicaragua, begin to leak out. On June 12th official sources draw attention for the first time to the threat from AIDS.	1986

History

1987	On October 19th the fall in share prices on the New York Stock Exchange brings heavier losses than on "Black Friday" in 1929. Presidents Reagan and Gorbachov sign an agreement in Washington on the destruction of land-based medium-range missiles.
1988	A Republican, George Bush, is elected President.

A New World Order?

After the dissolution of the Soviet Union the United States, in President Ford's view, is the only real world power, whose task is to defend and protect the free world. It must be ready, therefore, to intervene militarily in international crisis areas – in the Third World and where it is necessary to defend American Interests.

1989	The wreck of the supertanker "Exxon Valdez" on the coast of Alaska in March leads to catastrophic oil pollution. On October 17th the strongest earthquake since 1906 hits San Francisco, causing over 59 deaths. The Supreme Court restricts the right to abortion. In December 25,000 US troops occupy Panama and arrest the President, General Noriega, who is suspected of drug dealing.
1990	After the occupation of Kuwait by Iraq US troops are sent to Saudi Arabia.
1991	Under US command, American, British, French, Saudi and other troops attack Iraq and liberate Kuwait. After the collapse of the Eastern Bloc the United States begins to reduce its military presence in Europe and Asia and to cut down its atomic weaponry.
1992	Serious race riots in Los Angeles following the acquittal of four white policeman who maltreated a black motorist: 58 people are killed and damage estimated at a billion dollars is caused. President Bush announces the creation of the North American Free Trade Area (NAFTA), which comes into force at the beginning of 1994 and removes restrictions on trade between Mexico, the United States and Canada. A Democrat, Bill Clinton, wins the Presidential election, ending twelve years of Republican Presidency which have seen severe cuts in expenditure on social welfare and raising the hopes of millions of socially disadvantaged Americans. In December US troops land in Somalia as part of a UN peacekeeping force aimed at ending the civil war in the country.
1993	The Clinton administration launches a health service reform. Devastating floods in the Mississippi/Missouri valley. In November a referendum in Puerto Rico produces a majority against incorporation in the USA as the 51st state. Congress approves the establishment of NAFTA. In December President Clintom signs a law making it more difficult to buy guns. In September representatives of Israel and the Palestine Liberation Organisation, meeting in Washington, agree on the peace process.
1994	In January a severe earthquake shakes the northern districts of Los Angeles, causing many deaths and much destruction.

Famous People

This section contains brief biographies of notable people who have lived, worked or died in the United States. It is necessarily only a small selection.

The jazz trumpeter and singer Louis Armstrong, born in New Orleans, made a name for himself at the age of 18 with his new-style solos and husky voice, performing in small jazz spots in the South. In the early twenties he played in the bands of "King" Oliver and Fletcher Henderson, and later was equally successful as soloist in various smaller groups. With his extraordinary virtuosity and infectious musicality "Satchmo" became a central figure in the world of jazz and had a decisive influence on its development.

Louis Armstrong (1900–71)

Leonard Bernstein, born in Lawrence, Mass., studied composition under Walter Riston and conducting under Fritz Reiner and Serge Koussevitzky. His brilliant career as a conductor took off when he stood in at the last minute for Bruno Walter in 1943. From 1958 to 1969 he was permanent conductor of the New York Philharmonic – the first occupant of the post to have been born and trained in the United States. He composed symphonies, ballet music, musicals and chamber music. Among his best known works are the Jeremiah Symphony (1942), the ballet "Fancy Free" (1944) and above all the very popular musical "West Side Story" (1957) with its catchy tunes. He also wrote a number of works on the theory and appreciation of music.

Leonard Bernstein (1918–90)

William H. Bonney, known as Billy the Kid, was born in New York. He is said to have committed his first murder at the age of 12 (the victim had insulted his mother), and by 1877 was credited with eleven other murders. When the Cattle War broke out in Lincoln County, New Mexico in 1878 he became leader of a band which murdered a sheriff and his deputy and was ruthlessly hunted down by Pat Garrett, a former friend of Billy's. Billy was captured and condemned to death but managed to escape from prison. Three months later, however, Garrett cornered him in Fort Sumner, New Mexico, and shot him. Billy the Kid is said to have killed a total of 21 people. Why he committed the murders even Pat Garrett, who wrote the first biography of him, was unable to explain.

Billy the Kid (1859–81)

The great opponent of slavery, born in Torrington, Connecticut, believed that he had a divine mission to fight slavery, by violent means if necessary. In 1858 he founded an organisation of both coloured people and whites which set about establishing a refuge for runaway slaves in the mountains of Maryland and Virginia and forming an armed force. He led his men in an attack on a military post at Harpers Ferry in West Virginia with the object of seizing arms for a nation-wide rising of the slaves. After a bloody battle, however, Brown's men were overpowered by a force of US Marines commanded by Robert E. Lee. Brown was condemned to death and hanged in Charles Town, West Virginia. Although his plan to bring about a general rising of the slaves had failed, the battle of Harpers Ferry underlined the conflict between North and South which finally led to the Civil War. John Brown is commemorated by the song "John Brown's Body".

John Brown (1800–59)

Al (Alfonso) Capone, the most famous of American gangsters, was born in Naples and grew up in a New York slum. In 1920 he moved to Chicago, where he became a much feared underworld boss, establishing his position by bootlegging during the period of Prohibition. Although he was suspected of being involved in numerous murders and attacks he was never brought to court, due to fear of reprisals. Finally in 1931 he was sentenced to eleven years in prison for tax evasion, but in 1939 was released on health grounds and retired to Miami.

Al Capone (1899–1947)

Famous People

Louis Armstrong *John Brown* *William F. Cody*

William F. Cody "Buffalo Bill" (1846–1917)

The most celebrated Wild West hero of them all was born in Scott County, Iowa. After working in his youth as a Pony Express rider he became a gold-hunter in Colorado, fought against the Indians and served in the Civil War in the forces of Tennessee and Missouri. During the construction of the Kansas–Pacific Railroad he contributed to the food supply of the construction workers by – according to his own account – killing over 4000 buffaloes in 17 months. This exploit and his fights with the Sioux and Cheyenne Indians were recounted by Ned Buntline in "Buffalo Bill", published in popular form, which brought the hero of the stories world fame and established the mythology of the Wild West. In 1883 Cody organised his Wild West show, with performers who included the markswoman Annie Oakley and chief Sitting Bull, and travelled with it throughout the United States and Europe. In 1890 he retired to a ranch near the township of Cody, Wyoming, which he had founded. Despite his fame as a hero of the Wild West, he must also bear a share of the blame for the extinction of the buffalo and thus for the destruction of the basis of Indian life.

Jefferson Davis (1808–89)

Jefferson Davis, born in Abbeville, Kentucky, served in the American–Mexican War in 1845–47 and then became a Senator and from 1853 to 1857 Secretary of War. Originally a supporter of an expansionist federal policy, after the election of Abraham Lincoln as President he fought for the secession of the Southern states from the Union. In 1861 he was elected President of the Confederated States of America, and along with General Lee was the driving force on the Southern side during the Civil War. After the surrender of the South in April 1865 he was imprisoned but was pardoned in 1868. He died in Beauvoir, Mississippi.

Miles Davis (1926–91)

When the jazz trumpeter Miles Davis (born in Alton, Illinois) was asked by a politician's wife at a party in Washington what he had achieved in life he replied that he had five or six times changed something in music and asked in return what she had achieved apart from being white. He had some justification for his claim; for Miles Davis, the "man with the horn", had since 1945, when he first performed in Charlie Parker's quintet, influenced or initiated all the various schools of jazz. His greatest hit was the combination of jazz, rock and African rhythms in the album "Bitches' Brew" (1970), which was a powerful stimulus to almost all the leading jazzmen of the day, including Herbie Hancock, Wayne Shorter and Tony Williams.

Walt Disney (1901–66)

Walt Disney, a native of Chicago, laid the foundations of his fame with the creation and animation, along with his brother Roy, of Mickey Mouse in 1925. The appearance of Mickey Mouse in "Steamboat Willie" (1928) established the popularity of the animated cartoon film. It was followed by

Famous People

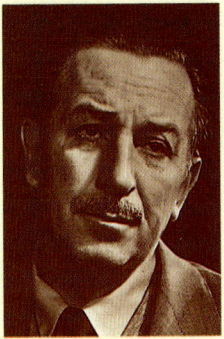

Walt Disney *Amelia Earhart* *Wyatt Earp*

the first feature-length cartoon film, "Snow White and the Seven Dwarfs" (1937) and then by "Fantasia" (1940) and "Bambi" (1942) – all classics of the cartoon film. Then came adventure films ("20,000 Leagues under the Sea", 1955), documentary nature films ("The Living Desert", 1953; "The Vanishing Prairie", 1954) and television films ("Mickey Mouse Club", "Davy Crockett", "Walt Disney's Wonderful World of Color"). Disney's modest original studio in a garage developed over the years into a great film production company and finally into an international entertainment corporation, running Disneyland in Anaheim, near Los Angeles (established 1955), Disney World at Orlando, Miami (1971) and Euro Disney Resort, near Paris (1992).

Donald Duck can claim to be the most famous duck in the world. He first appeared in the film "The Wise Little Hen" in 1934, and since then has not only improved his appearance but has launched a whole series of (usually unsuccessful) attempts to achieve fame and fortune – as an auxiliary fireman, a sales representative, Emperor of America, a scientist (investigating, for example, the hens in the Andes which lay square eggs) and Sheriff of Bullet Valley. Although bad-tempered by nature, he is kind and affectionate to his nephews Louie, Huey and Dewey; but his relationship with his immensely rich Uncle Scrooge is marred by profound differences of view, largely based on difference in social standing. Nevertheless he is immensely popular: his portrait appears on stamps (for example in San Marino) and he is internationally known – as Paperino in Italy, Donald Furioso in Spain, Pato Donald in Brazil, Kalle Anka in Sweden and Anders And in Denmark. It has not been possible to establish his new Russian name.

Donald Duck
(b. 1934)

Amelia Earhart, born in Atchison, Kansas, became the first woman to fly solo across the Atlantic. After studying at Columbia University, New York, she took up flying as a hobby and in 1928 was the first woman passenger on a transatlantic flight. Thereafter she flew only on her own: in 1932 across the Atlantic from Newfoundland to Ireland, in 1935 on the first solo flight from Hawaii to the American mainland. In 1937 she set out with her navigator Frederick J. Norman on a flight round the world, but after completing two-thirds of the distance her plane disappeared near Howland Island in the Pacific.

Amelia Earhart
(1897–1937?)

Wyatt Earp, born in Monmouth, Illinois, became one of the great figures of the Wild West and the hero of numerous films – though it is still not clear whether he should be remembered as an upholder of the law or as a gun-happy criminal. Somewhere on the way from Kansas, where he is known to have been an upholder of law and order in a number of towns, to Arizona he and his two brothers seem to have crossed the boundary

Wyatt Earp
(1848–1929)

Famous People

Thomas A. Edison  *Benjamin Franklin*  *Thomas Jefferson*

between the status of marshal and that of outlaw. At any rate the event which made him a legend, the shoot-out with the Clanton gang at the O.K. Corral in Tombstone, Arizona, was regarded by many contemporaries as cold-blooded murder. But Earp survived this and later shoot-outs and died peacefully in Los Angeles. His legendary ally Doc Holliday died of consumption and heavy drinking.

Thomas Alva Edison (1847–1931)

Thomas Alva Edison, a native of Milan, Ohio, ranks as one of the world's most productive inventors – in spite of the fact that he had only three months regular schooling. He was active throughout his life as an experimenter and inventor, patenting over a period of 50 years something like 1100 inventions, including the carbon filament lamp, the phonograph (using wax records) and the Ediphone, a dictating machine, motion-picture cameras and projectors and a concrete-pouring process.

Henry Ford (1863–1947)

The automobile manufacturer Henry Ford, born in Dearborn, Michigan, started life as a mechanic and engineer; then in 1892 he built his first automobile and in 1903 founded the Ford Motor Company in Detroit. He was the first to introduce assembly-line manufacture, an idea which revolutionised industrial production. Within 25 years the Ford works grew into an industrial giant, whose legendary Model T, 15 million of which were produced, dominated the roads of the United States in the 1920s. The firm continued to be family-owned until the thirties. The Ford Foundation, established in 1936, is now one of the wealthiest American foundations, active particularly in the educational field in the United States and in promoting technical aid programmes in developing countries.

Benjamin Franklin (1706–90)

Benjamin Franklin – statesman, scientist and publicist, a man learned in many fields – was born in Boston, Massachusetts, the 17th child of a soapmaker and candlemaker who had emigrated to the United States from Oxfordshire. As a printer and publisher, he soon began to take an interest in politics. In 1732 he founded the influential "Pennsylvania Gazette", and between 1753 and 1758 published "Poor Richard", a witty annual almanac. He was also concerned for his fellow-men in practical life, and was involved in the foundation of Pennsylvania's first university, the first hospital in the North American colonies and a learned society which became the American Philosophical Society. He earned a place in the history of science with his invention of the lightning conductor (1752) and of binoculars, and was also responsible for numerous discoveries and publications in the most varied fields – education and science, international relations and the public service, engineering, medicine and health services, printing, publishing and graphic art, finance and insurance, religion and freemasonry, agriculture and botany, music. In spite of all this activity he refused to take out

Famous People

patents for any of his inventions, for he believed that all inventions should be for the public benefit. He supported the strivings of the colonies for independence from an early stage, and as their ambassador in France from 1776 to 1785 exerted so powerful an influence that the French support for the Americans must be attributed to him. He was one of the signatories of the Declaration of Independence, the alliance with France against Britain, the peace treaty with Britain and the Constitution of 1787. In 1788 he was elected president of the first society for the abolition of slavery. He died in Pennsylvania.

Clark Gable, born in Cadiz, Ohio, established his reputation as one of the great screen heart-throbs in his role as Rhett Butler in "Gone with the Wind" – a part which he was at first disposed to turn down. At that time (1939) he was already an established Hollywood figure, having won an Oscar for his part in the comedy "It Happened One Night". After serving as a pilot in the Second World War he returned to Hollywood, but he was not in great demand and was unable to repeat his previous successes. He put up a brilliant performance in John Huston's "Misfits" (1960), alongside Marilyn Monroe and Montgomery Clift, but it was too late for a comeback. Soon after the shooting of the film he died of a heart attack.

Clark Gable
(1901–60)

The New Yorker George Gershwin, creator of so many marvellous tunes, grew up without any contact with music; later he had piano lessons, and finally studied music. At first he was drawn to jazz, and wrote popular songs and musicals; then, beginning with "Rhapsody in Blue" (1924), he turned away from light music and developed his own conception of classical music, in which he mingled elements of the everyday music of the twenties, jazz and serious music: Piano Concerto in F Major (1925); the tone poem "An American in Paris" (1928); "Of Thee I Sing" (1931), a satire on the American political system; and the still popular opera "Porgy and Bess" (1935). He died of a brain tumour in Hollywood at the height of his fame.

George Gershwin
(1898–1937)

Ernest Miller Hemingway, born in Oak Park, Illinois, ranks as the principal representative of the "lost generation" after the First World War, with which his first novel "The Sun Also Rises" ("Fiesta"), published in 1926, was concerned; it was also a celebration of Spanish machismo. "A Farewell to Arms", a novel of love and war, appeared in 1929. "For Whom the Bell Tolls" (1940) dealt with the Spanish Civil War from the point of view of an American – like himself – fighting on the Republican side. His short novel "The Old Man and the Sea" (1952) was another international success, and in 1954 he was awarded the Nobel Prize for literature. Hemingway's novels are written in a spare, laconic and virile style. Writing in the novels of strong-willed men facing a variety of challenges, he tried to act the same part in his own life, with bullfighting, big game hunting and deep-sea angling as his favourite recreations. Unable to face his greatest challenge – dealing with his own personality and with alcohol – he finally shot himself.

Ernest Hemingway
(1899–1961)

One of the most eccentric figures in the history of the United States was the billionaire, aviator and film producer Howard Hughes, a native of Houston, Texas. In 1924 he inherited his father's tool factory, the large profits from which he invested in film productions, airlines and aircraft production. In his factory were built the first retractable undercarriage and the "Spruce Goose", a huge wooden seaplane – the largest aircraft then in existence – which he himself piloted. In 1938 he made a record 91-hour flight round the world. After a series of legal proceedings against him for various commercial offences he became increasingly reclusive, and from 1958 onwards never appeared in public. He became a legend the subject of speculation by the press, which regularly carried reports of his death or his appearance somewhere in the world. In fact he continued to run his financial empire

Howard Hughes
(1905–76)

Famous People

from various hiding-places. He died in 1976 on a flight from Mexico to Texas.

Jesse James (1847–82)

Legend and reality were so mingled in the life of Jesse Woodson James, the son of a Baptist preacher in western Missouri, that many people, seeing him as a kind of Robin Hood of the Wild West, refused to believe in his death. On February 13th 1866 Jesse, his brother Frank and their gang raided a bank in Liberty, Montana – the first bank robbery in the United States in time of peace but by no means the last. The brothers meanwhile continued to live peacefully on their mother's farm, until information pointing to them began to emerge in 1869. Thereafter they were blamed for a wide range of other holdups and robberies, to such an extent that Jesse disclaimed responsibility in the press. The legend, however, was born. The gang then specialised in train robbery, pursuing their activities in Texas, Arkansas, Montana and Colorado. Jesse James was never caught, for he was always able to return to an ordinary quiet existence. He settled with his wife and two children in St Joseph, Montana, living under a false name, but was tracked down by Robert Ford, a member of the gang, and shot for the sake of the reward. He it was who died as a hero, while Ford was the villain.

Thomas Jefferson (1743–1826)

Thomas Jefferson, third President of the United States (1801–09), was a man of universal learning. Born in Shadwell, Virginia, he attended William and Mary College and began his career as a lawyer and politician in Virginia. A brilliant polemical writer, he came to prominence in 1774 with a broadside directed against Britain, "A Summary View of the Rights of British America", and in 1776 was one of the drafters of the Declaration of Independence. He succeeded Benjamin Franklin as US ambassador in France (1784–89), and thereafter became Secretary of State under Washington. Jefferson's party of Democratic Republicans (forerunners of the Democrats) was opposed by the Federalists led by Alexander Hamilton, and in 1793 the disagreements became so acute that Jefferson resigned. Under John Adams, however, he became Vice-President, and in 1801 became President – the first to be inaugurated in Washington DC. As President he sought to achieve simplicity in administration and the restriction of federal powers to foreign affairs but to maintain close control on Congress. His greatest foreign policy success was the acquisition of the French territory of Louisiana (the Louisiana Purchase). At the end of his term of office he retired to his well-managed estate and country house, Monticello, which he had designed himself and developed for forty years. In 1819 he founded the University of Virginia in Charlottesville.

John F. Kennedy (1917–83)

John Fitzgerald Kennedy, scion of a wealthy Massachusetts family and great-grandson of an Irishman who emigrated to the United States about 1850, was the first Roman Catholic President of the United States. After studying at the best universities in the country (Princeton, Harvard and Stanford) he commanded a torpedo-boat in the Pacific during the Second World War. In 1946 he entered the House of Representatives as a Democrat, and in 1952 was elected to the Senate. Eight years later, after narrowly defeating Richard Nixon, he became the 35th President of the United States. His inaugural address – "Ask not what your country can do for you: ask what you can do for your country" – appealed to Americans and raised high hopes for his Presidency. John F. Kennedy, who had constantly to take strong drugs for a severe kidney disease and back problems, was murdered on November 22nd 1963 in Dallas, Texas. Since then there has been much speculation about the motives for the shooting.

With hindsight it is astonishing to see how the Kennedy myth grew up. His foreign policy was marked by more misjudgments than successes. During his period of office 16,000 American servicemen were sent to Vietnam, the Bay of Pigs invasion was a fiasco and even the success of his tough stance in the Cuba missiles crisis was bought at the price (which was kept secret) of the withdrawal of American missiles from Turkey and an undertaking not to intervene in Cuba. In domestic policy the moving spirits in such matters

Famous People

John F. Kennedy  *Martin Luther King, Jr.*  *Abraham Lincoln*

as reform and civil rights were his brother Robert and Vice-President Johnson rather than the President himself.
The President's younger brother Robert, his closest adviser and Attorney General in his government, was murdered on June 8th 1968 while running for the Presidency.

Coloured Americans still revere the memory of the theologian and Baptist preacher Martin Luther King Jr, a native of Atlanta, Georgia, who was murdered in April 1968. He was one of the first to oppose racism in his country: in 1955/56 he organised a boycott of the public transport system in Montgomery, Alabama, in protest against racial segregation in public buses. Through this and similar actions and above all through his speeches and preaching, expressing a charisma which captivated his listeners, he made racial discrimination a matter of public concern – leaving no doubt, however, about his insistence on non-violence in the struggle for civil rights. The high point of his work was the peaceful march on Washington in 1963, when he made his famous "I have a dream" speech. In 1964 he became the youngest recipient of the Nobel Peace Prize. He was shot by a Southern racist in Memphis, Tennessee.

Martin Luther King Jr (1929–68)

General Robert E. Lee was the hero of the South during the American Civil War – in spite of the fact that he had been appointed commander in chief of the Confederate army rather against his will. Yet there is no doubt that he felt more strongly bound to his home state of Virginia than to the Union in which he had begun his military career. He inflicted heavy losses on the Northern army, particularly at Fredericksburg, but suffered a decisive defeat at Gettysburg. Thereafter the Confederates could fight only delaying actions, and Lee was finally compelled to surrender to Ulysses S. Grant on April 9th 1865. After the war he supported the cause of reconciliation, and his name is now honoured both in the South and the North.

Robert E. Lee (1807–70)

Abraham Lincoln, son of a poor family of farmers and craftsmen, was born in a small township in Kentucky and spent much of his early life, which was marked by hard work and study of the Bible, in Illinois. He trained as a lawyer in Springfield, Illinois, and was active in politics as a Democrat. Then, believing that slavery was irreconcilable with the principles of freedom and equality, he went over to the Republicans and was elected to the Senate in 1858. In 1860 he was elected President, and soon after he took up office the Civil War broke out. From the beginning he insisted that the Union must be preserved, and called up a citizens' militia, strengthened the army and suspended Habeas Corpus in the Southern states. After the Northern victory at Antietam, Maryland, in 1862 he made the liberation of all slaves in those states which on January 1st 1863 were still "in rebellion"

Abraham Lincoln (1809–65)

Famous People

one of the objectives of the war. The Civil War thus became also a war for the liberation of the slaves. Only five days after General Lee's surrender Lincoln was shot in Ford's Theatre in Washington by an actor named John Wilkes Booth.

Lincoln owes his place in American history to the abolition of slavery (under the 13th Amendment to the Constitution, December 18th 1865) and his determination to preserve the Union. His vision of "government of the people, by the people, for the people" was given its clearest expression in his Gettysburg Address on November 19th 1863.

Charles Lindbergh (1902–74)	On May 20th and 21st 1927 Charles Lindbergh, a native of Detroit, made the first non-stop solo flight across the Atlantic from west to east. His plane, the "Spirit of St Louis", took 33½ hours to fly from Long Island, New Jersey, to Le Bourget near Paris. In 1932 his son was kidnapped and murdered. Lindbergh opposed the United States' entry into the Second World War in 1941, and was rehabilitated only in 1954. He died on the island of Maui (Hawaii).
Joe Louis (1914–81)	The "Brown Bomber" of Lafayette, Alabama, was one of the most successful boxers of all time: in 71 professional fights between 1934 and 1951 he suffered only three defeats, and between 1937 and 1949, when he retired, he successfully defended his title 25 times.
Malcolm X (1925–65)	Malcolm Little of Omaha, Nebraska, left school early and thereafter went to the bad, spending the years 1946–52 in prison. There he was converted to the Nation of Islam (Black Muslim) faith and began to call himself Malcolm X (as an ex-smoker, ex-drinker, ex-Christian and ex-slave). As spokesman for the radical militant blacks he preached black nationalism in a way that went too far for the Black Muslim leader Elijah Muhammad, who ordered him in 1963 to call a halt to his preaching. Thereupon Malcolm X left the Black Muslims (1964) and founded the Muslim Mosque. Soon afterwards he established the Organisation for Afro-American Unity, the object of which was to combine the fight of black Americans and that of the oppressed peoples of the Third World. Malcolm X was murdered in Harlem by three blacks.
Mark Twain (1835–1910)	Samuel Langhorne Clemens, born in Florida, Missouri, made an international name for himself, under the pseudonym Mark Twain, with his two principal novels, "Tom Sawyer" (1876) and "Huckleberry Finn" (1884), which rank as the finest works of American prose of the later 19th century. He started his working life as apprentice to a local printer, but then became an apprentice steamboat pilot on the Mississippi (hence his pseudonym, from the call of the man sounding the depth of the river) and an unsuccessful gold prospector. Finally he became a newspaper reporter and began his career as a writer with a series of humorous and sometimes grotesque sketches. It is easy to forget, however, that Mark Twain also saw himself as a critic of social conditions.
Glenn Miller (1904–44)	The band leader Glenn Miller, a native of Clarinda, Iowa, wrote a series of catchy tunes which are still popular, notably "Tuxedo Junction", "Moonlight Serenade" and above all "In the Mood". A trombonist, he spent years as an ordinary member of various bands until in 1937 he realised his dream of founding his own band, which soon became by far the most popular group of the big band era. During the Second World War he conducted the US Air Force Band in Europe. He disappeared without trace on a flight from England to Paris.
Marilyn Monroe (1926–62)	Marilyn Monroe (real name Norma Jean Baker) was born in Los Angeles, an illegitimate child, and grew up in various foster homes. In films such as "Gentlemen Prefer Blondes" and "How to Marry a Millionaire" she acquired a reputation as an attractive but dumb blonde, and soon became known as the "sex goddess of the fifties". She herself disliked this image

Famous People

Marilyn Monroe  *Edgar Allan Poe*  *Franklin D. Roosevelt*

and tried to establish herself as a serious actress with a great gift for comedy; and indeed achieved this in the very successful films "The Seven Year Itch" and "Some Like It Hot". She never managed, however, to get her anxieties and depression under control, either through her three marriages (to such varied husbands as the baseball player Joe Di Maggio and the dramatist Arthur Miller) or by recourse to the bottle. Her constant absences from the set led to her dismissal from the film "Something Has Got to Give". Soon afterwards she died of an overdose of sleeping pills.

Edgar Allan Poe, born in Boston, Massachusetts, achieved his first great literary success with his "Tales of Ratiocination", published between 1841 and 1845. These tales, including "The Murders in the Rue Morgue", made him the creator of the modern detective story – in Arthur Conan Doyle's words, "the master of us all". His fame was enhanced by the publication of a collection of poems ("The Raven and Other Poems", 1845) on fantastic and frightening themes – themes found also in his tales ("The Fall of the House of Usher"). As the leading member of the American Romantic movement Poe had great influence on European literature. Throughout his life, however, he was always short of money, lonely and given to the use of alcohol and later, in consequence of a serious nervous illness, of opium. His death might have come from one of his stories: he was found unconscious in a bar in Baltimore and the cause of his death remained a mystery.

Edgar Allan Poe (1809–49)

Elvis Aron Presley, born in Tupelo, Mississippi, was mainly employed as a truck driver before the meteoric rise to a mega-star of the rock and roll era, the "King", which began between 1956 and 1958. The songs which he moaned into the microphone – usually expressing an innocent teenage eroticism – and the gyrations which accompanied them (earning him the name of Elvis the Pelvis) drove his young audiences into a kind of mass hysteria. Unusually for a white singer, he drew from the style of black performers, giving it his own interpretation. His first hit "Love Me Tender", the later "In the Ghetto" and many other songs are still popular. In the course of his career Elvis Presley sold over half a million records, and his satellite television show "Aloha from Hawaii" on January 14th 1973 drew a worldwide audience of a billion viewers. By then – without any future artistically or, after a failed marriage, in his private life – he was addicted to alcohol and drug misuse. He died wretchedly in his mansion of Graceland in Memphis, Tennessee.

Elvis Presley (1935–77)

One of the bitterest and most effective opponents of the expansion of the whites in North America was Red Cloud, a chief of the Oglala Sioux, whose Indian name was Che-ton-waka-wa-mani ("The hawk who hunts on foot"). In 1866 and 1867 he opposed the government's plan to drive the Bozeman Trail through what is now Wyoming to the goldfields of Montana and to

Red Cloud (1822–1909)

Famous People

establish three forts. The route ran through the richest Sioux hunting grounds east of the Bighorn River. Under Red Cloud's leadership a combined Sioux and Cheyenne force launched one of the most celebrated raids of the Indian Wars, the attack on Colonel Fetterman's force at Fort Phil Kearny in December 1866. The Indians' activities inflicted such heavy losses on the whites that in 1868 the government signed a treaty with Red Cloud and gave up the idea of the Bozeman Trail. Red Cloud observed the treaty for the rest of his life; but in the 1880s his tribe was moved to the Pine River reserve in South Dakota, where he died.

Rockefeller dynasty

Perhaps no other family was more archetypical of the "land of unlimited possibilities", in which it is possible to rise from dish-washer to millionaire, than the Rockefellers. The founder of the family was John D. Rockefeller (1839–1937), who made his fortune in the oil and steel industries. He founded the Standard Oil Company in 1870, and by 1882 controlled practically the whole American oil industry. Retiring from business in 1896, he devoted himself to the Rockefeller Foundation he had established, which is mainly active in the medical field. His only son, John D. Rockefeller Jr (1874–1960), made over to the United Nations the site on New York's East River now occupied by its headquarters (1947), founded the Museum of Primitive Art in New York (1957) and financed the reconstruction of Williamsburg, one-time capital of the colony of Virginia. Two of his sons, Republicans, became Governors – Nelson Aldrich Rockefeller (1908–79) in New York State and Winthrop Rockefeller (1912–73) in Arkansas; and Nelson Aldrich was Vice-President of the United States from 1974 to 1977. Winthrop's grandson John D. Rockefeller IV was Democratic Governor of West Virginia from 1977 to 1985.

Franklin Delano Roosevelt (1882–1945)

The greatest President of the United States in the 20th century, Franklin Delano Roosevelt, was born in Hyde Park, New York State. After studying law at Harvard and the Columbia Law School he worked as a lawyer for some time and then entered politics. Although stricken with polio in 1921 he remained politically active, and in 1932 became the 32nd President of the United States. During his four successive terms of office he helped by the reforming policies of his "New Deal" to overcome the country's economic crisis and took the United States well prepared into the Second World War, in which he fought the Axis powers with great determination. He also played a major part in the formulation of the Atlantic Charter, which led to the foundation of the United Nations. His sudden death came as a shock to the nation. His wife Eleanor (1884–1962) saw her role as First Lady as more than a background figure and played an active part in politics.

Babe Ruth (1895–1948)

George Herman Ruth, the great hero of American baseball, was born in Baltimore, Maryland. Playing for the New York Yankees, he revolutionised the game, putting the emphasis on power rather than speed. With his tremendous strength, he drove the ball across the field and frequently out of the ground altogether, enabling him to make his home runs at leisure. In the 1927 season he established a record of 60 home runs in 154 games which was not beaten until 1960.

Carl Schurz (1829–1906)

The statesman and reformer Carl Schurz was born near Cologne. As a student at Bonn University he was involved in the 1848 Revolution and was obliged to leave Germany. In 1852, with his wife, he emigrated to the United States, where he soon felt himself an American and became a firm supporter of the Republicans. In 1861 he was sent to Spain as the American ambassador, but on the outbreak of the Civil War returned to the United States to become a general in the Union forces. As editor of the "Detroit Post" and the German-language "St Louis Westliche Post" he advocated a policy of reconstruction and opposed the expansionist trends in United States foreign policy. As Secretary of the Interior under President Hayes (1877–81) he promoted reforms and a humaner treatment of Indians. After retiring from politics he wrote for "Harper's Weekly", still showing himself

Famous People

an eloquent advocate of political morality and the principles of freedom. His wife Margarethe Meyer-Schurz established the first kindergarten in the United States.

Sitting Bull (in the Sioux language Tatanka Yotanka), of the Hunkpapa Sioux tribe, is perhaps the most legendary of the Indian chiefs. Born on the Grand River in South Dakota, by his refusal to move with his tribe into the reservation assigned to them he brought about the greatest defeat suffered by the US army in the Indian Wars, the annihilation of a detachment of the 7th US Cavalry led by George Custer in the battle of the Little Bighorn on June 25th 1876. He himself took no direct part in the battle, for as medicineman he had the task of seeking "good medicine" (that is, the support of the spirits for the warriors). The military victory was mainly due to the tactical skill of Crazy Horse. In spite of this success Sitting Bull was compelled to flee to Canada, but in 1881, after an amnesty, he was able to return to the Standing Rock reservation. Then, for reasons that are obscure, he allowed himself to be persuaded to take part for a year in Buffalo Bill's Wild West show. When in 1890 the Ghost Dance movement led to the threat of unrest among the Indians the United States government, still fearing his popularity among the Indians, ordered his arrest by the Indian police. In the affray which followed Sitting Bull and his son Crow Foot were shot. His grave is in Mobridge, South Dakota.

Sitting Bull
(1834?–1890)

Joseph Smith, a farm worker of Windsor County, Vermont, claimed that God had appeared to him in 1823 and charged him to form a religious community which should exceed all others in perfection; in the same revelation he had been instructed where to find a number of gold plates inscribed with the "Book of Mormon", recording the history of an elect people which had emigrated from Israel to America. Joseph Smith maintained that he had received the gold plates from an angel called Moroni in 1827 – though no one has ever set eyes on the plates themselves. At any rate Smith became priest and prophet of the new faith and in 1830 founded in Fayette, New York State, the Church of Jesus Christ of Latter Day Saints – the Mormons. After a number of unsuccessful attempts he founded a settlement at Nauvoo, Illinois, in 1841. The new sect attracted much criticism and hostility, particularly on account of its practice of polygamy, to which Smith reacted intransigently and violently. After the destruction of the premises of a local newspaper which had attacked him Joseph Smith and his brother Hyrum were arrested and lynched in prison by an angry mob. His successor Brigham Young (1801–77) led the Mormons from Illinois by way of Missouri to Utah.

Joseph Smith
(1805–44)

John Sutter, "King of New Helvetia", was a character who could have come to the fore only in the pioneering days of the United States. Originally called Johann August Sutter, he was of Swiss origin but was born in Germany. Fleeing from bankruptcy, he emigrated to North America in 1834, and within a short time had acquired a vast area of land (50,000 acres/20,000 hectares) in California, then almost uninhabited. He named the territory New Helvetia and styled himself its king. In 1848 the first Californian gold was found near its capital, Sacramento, which Sutter had founded, and during the subsequent gold rush Sutter's model farming settlement of New Helvetia was totally devastated. After California joined the Union he was unable to establish a legal claim to his territory and spent the rest of his life in poverty, a ruined man.

John Sutter
(1803–80)

Booker Taliaferro Washington, born in a slave hut in Virginia, was one of the first blacks in the United States to call publicly for equal rights for all races and to work actively to achieve that aim. He became a teacher at the Hampton Institute for blacks and Indians in Virginia, and in 1881 was selected to head the Tuskegee Institute in Alabama, established to give the blacks of the South better educational opportunities. He believed that

Booker T.
Washington
(1856–1915)

Famous People

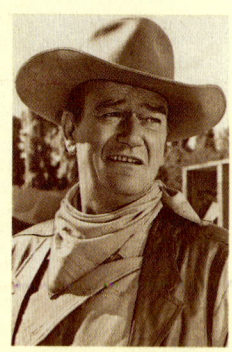

Sitting Bull *George Washington* *John Wayne*

practical vocational training was more important than higher intellectual education and that equal rights for blacks could be achieved only through improving their training and their standard of living. In 1900 he founded the Negro Business League.

George Washington (1732–99)

The leading figure in American history, commander in chief during the War of Independence and first President of the United States, was born on the estate of Pope's Creek in Virginia, the son of English immigrants. After working for some time as a land surveyor he served in the British forces against the French in the Ohio valley (1753) and in securing the western frontier of Virginia (1755). In 1774–75 he was a delegate at the first Continental Congress in Philadelphia, and on the outbreak of the War of Independence was appointed commander in chief of the "continental" forces. In spite of inferior numbers and inadequate equipment he won the victory at Yorktown, Virginia, in 1781 which decided the war in favour of the Americans. Nominated by the Constitutional Convention in 1787, he was appointed first President of the United States in 1789. During his two terms of office he established a national currency and a national bank, a postal service, a customs system and patent and copyright protection, reorganised the army and the fleet, founding the West Point Military Academy in New York State, and ordered the construction of fortifications on the east coast and the western frontier. In 1796 he withdrew to his Mount Vernon estate, setting out his political testament in his farewell address.

John Wayne (1907–79)

The film actor John Wayne was born Marion Michael Morrison, the son of a chemist in Winterset, Iowa, but was given the name under which he became famous by the film director Raoul Walsh. His first breakthrough came with "Stagecoach" (1939). Thereafter, in a succession of films like "Red River", "El Dorado", "Rio Grande" and "The Sons of Katie Elder", under such directors as Howard Hawks, John Ford and Henry Hathaway Wayne, known as the "Duke", became the archetypal man of the West. He was less successful in excursions into other fields (as Genghis Khan, as Police Officer Brannigan, or as an officer in the super-patriotic Vietnam film "The Green Berets", which was panned by the critics), for without cowboy gear it became clear that John Wayne's best role was the hard-hitting tough guy – himself.

Frank Lloyd Wright (1867–1959)

Frank Lloyd Wright, recognised as the leading American architect of the 20th century, studied at the University of Wisconsin and in 1888 entered the progressive Chicago architectural firm of Adler and Sullivan. In 1893 he branched out on his own, and around 1900 began to build a series of private country houses in "prairie style", with long horizontal forms adapted to the natural setting. Examples in and around Chicago are Willis House (1902)

Famous People

and Robie House (1909). Later he also used concrete (Falling Water, Bear Run, Pennsylvania, 1938). Other examples of his work are the John Wax Building (1939) in Racine, Wisconsin, the Price Tower (1955) in Bartlesville, Oklahoma, and the Guggenheim Museum (1959) in New York, one of his most spectacular creations. He left numerous plans and sketches of other buildings, so far unbuilt, including a high-rise residential block of over 500 storeys.

The Wright brothers of Dayton, Ohio, had a factory manufacturing printing machinery and bicycles, but after learning about Otto Lilienthal's gliding experiments began to experiment with gliders, carrying out their first flights at Kitty Hawk, on the Outer Banks of North Carolina, in 1901 and 1902. Their real ambition, however, was to construct and fly the first powered aircraft. On December 17th 1903 they achieved the first powered flight in history, in which their plane covered a distance of 118 feet (36 metres) in 12 seconds – not a great distance, but nevertheless a revolutionary technological achievement. The brothers were finally granted a patent for their flying machine in 1906. In 1908 Wilbur Wright carried out a series of exhibition flights in Europe; in 1909 Orville Wright passed the first official flying test; and in the same year the brothers won a US Army contract for the world's first military plane.

Wilbur Wright (1867–1912)
Orville Wright (1871–1948)

Art and Culture

Art

Apart from the art and the crafts of the indigenous Indian peoples American art is as young as the nation itself. The Puritan founding fathers, who tended in any event to be disapproving of art, had their hands full in the early days of settlement with the practical requirements of everyday life. The first artistic products were therefore purely utilitarian objects. Nevertheless American painting has a considerably longer history than is generally believed in Europe, where it is generally identified with art since the Second World War, when American artists began to set the tone in the international art scene with Abstract Expressionism, Pop Art and Minimal Art: that there was any American art before then is not commonly realised. American art achieved a first flowering in the 19th century, when the structures of the state were being consolidated and the towns were growing rapidly. During this period landscape painting – influenced by the great expanses of unspoiled natural landscape in North America – developed as a genre in its own right. American sculpture, on the other hand, remained traditional, becoming of greater interest only in the 20th century. The earliest American paintings, in the late 18th century, took the form of portraits, mainly representing the sitters as they liked to see themselves.

Painting

Painters

Most painters of the 18th and early 19th centuries either came from Britain or at any rate were strongly influenced by British art. In art as in other fields the mother country only gradually lost its influence. The artistic centre of the United States in this period was Boston. The leading painters were John Singleton Copley (1738–1815), John Trumbull (1756–1843), Charles Wilson Peale (1741–1827), Benjamin West (1738–1820) and Gilbert Charles Stuart (1755–1828), who painted several portraits of Washington (including the one that appears on the one-dollar bill). J. S. Copley ranks as the "father of American painting", and some of his pictures, like the portrait of the American hero Paul Revere, are familiar to every schoolchild in the United States. On the outbreak of the War of Independence, in 1775, Copley and his family moved to London, where he lived for the rest of his life. Benjamin West, well known as a historical painter, moved to Britain in 1763 and in 1792 succeeded Sir Joshua Reynolds as President of the Royal Academy. It is symptomatic of early American painting that its best known representatives were more successful in Europe than in their home country.

Landscape painting

Landscape painting became of increasing importance in the 19th century. After the War of Independence Americans were concerned in art as in other matters to cut loose from Europe and in particular from Britain. The new genre of landscape painting satisfied the American need for artistic independence. (In Europe too landscape painting developed as a separate genre in the 19th century). The unspoiled American wilderness was depicted as a kind of Garden of Eden in which the ideal society could be brought into being. Favoured compositions were mountain and lake landscapes, panoramas of the American wilderness, forest scenes and coastal scenery. Representations of everyday life and pictures of Indians also began to appear. The artists who practised this last type of genre painting, rather in the manner of naïve art, were mostly self-taught. Among them were Edward Hicks (1780–1849), George Caleb Bingham (1811–79) and Charles Wimar (1818–62).

Art

Albert Bierstadt: "The Last of the Buffalo"

Landscape painting was practised particularly by the Hudson River school, with its artistic centre in New York (which lies on the Hudson). It established itself around 1825 and reached its peak in the middle of the century. The "father of American landscape painting" was Thomas Cole (1801–48), an Englishman who emigrated to the United States at the age of 18. He studied at the Pennsylvania Academy of Fine Arts while working in his father's business but was otherwise self-taught, like many American artists. In 1825 he moved to New York, where his paintings of scenery on the Hudson River – which were to give the school its name – soon attracted attention. Cole was friendly with two other important representatives of the Hudson River school, Asher B. Durand (1796–1886) and Frederic Edwin Church (1826–1900). Durand's painting "Kindred Spirits" (1849), one of his best known pictures, is a memorial to Thomas Cole: it shows Cole and the writer William Cullen Bryant contemplating a grandiose landscape. "Mount Katahdin" (the highest peak in the state of Maine; 1853) and "Niagara Falls" (1857) are two of F. E. Church's best known works; the latter won him a medal at the Paris International Exposition of 1867.

Hudson River school

Fritz H. Lane (1804–65), the best known American seascape painter, was, like Church, trained exclusively in America: he regarded study visits to Europe as unnecessary. Although artists of this period were fascinated by the American West, most of their landscapes were painted in their own part of the country, the east coast. Albert Bierstadt (1830–1902) was the first artist to concentrate, in the sixties and seventies, on the landscapes of the West. Of German origin, he came to the United States with his parents at the age of two, and apart from two years at the Düsseldorf Academy was self-taught. In 1859 he took part in an expedition to the Rocky Mountains which produced a rich harvest of landscape paintings. The success of his landscapes brought him a commission for two historical paintings in the Capitol in Washington, "Discovery of the Hudson" and "Landing of the Vizcaino Expedition in Monterey, 1601".

Other painters

Towards the end of the 19th century American landscape painting once again came under European – mainly French – influence, from the Barbizon school and from the Impressionists. One member of the group was George

Influence of Barbizon school and Impressionists

Art

Innes (1825–94), who had been trained in Europe. William Merritt Chase (1849–1916) and above all Mary Cassatt (1844–1926), a close friend of Degas, had a particular affinity with the Impressionists. The development of abstract painting is foreshadowed in the landscapes of James McNeill Whistler (1834–1903), one of the most innovative and most controversial painters of his time. Although an American, he was trained in Paris and spent much of his life in London. Another London resident was the American painter John Singer Sargent (1856–1925), who received numerous commissions in the United States, including murals in Harvard's Wildener Library and the Boston Museum of Fine Arts and Public Library.

Ashcan school	In the early years of the 19th century the Ashcan school – so called because its members frequently depicted the poverty and misery of life in the slums in a spirit of social criticism – grew up round Robert Henri (1865–1929).
Hard Realism	The Ashcan school reached its culmination in the Hard Realism of the 1930s. In addition to Max Beckmann, an immigrant from Germany, the members of this school included Ben Shan (1898–1969), Philip Evergood (1901–73) and Jack Levine (b. 1915). A realism of a very distinctive type is seen in the pictures of Edward Hopper (1882–1967), who frequently took as his subject the loneliness of man in modern society.
Refugees from Nazi persecution	The exodus of European artists after the Nazis came to power in Germany brought new impulses to American painting. Among the many artists who sought refuge in the United States were Piet Mondrian, Joseph and Anni Albers, Marcel Duchamp and Georg Grosz.
Abstract Expressionism	After 1945 Abstract Expressionism came to the fore, with Jackson Pollock as its leading representative. The picture was now not only the expression of an artistic idea but was also affected by the accidental combination of painting technique, colour and technical aids. Other members of this

Pop Art: Richard Lindner's "Ice" and Andy Warhol's "Ethel Scull"

school were Robert Rauschenberg, Willem de Kooning, Arshile Gorky and Franz Kline.

Abstract Expressionism was succeeded by Minimal Art, which sought to reduce the various art forms to a minimum.   *Minimal Art*

Perhaps the most controversial art trend of the post-war period was Pop Art, whose best known exponent was Andy Warhol. Other practitioners of Pop Art included Roy Lichtenstein with his outsize pictures in the style of the comic strip, Jasper Johns, Richard Lindner, Claes Oldenburg and George Segal. Oldenburg and Segal became best known for their sculpture.   *Pop Art*

During the seventies there developed, in reaction against total artistic freedom, the school of Hyperrealism, which aimed at a photographically exact reproduction of reality. Among its best known representatives were Richard Estes and Howard Kanovitz.   *Hyperrealism*

Sculpture

American sculpture of the 18th and 19th centuries tended to be traditional in style and had little new to offer. The only notable sculptor of the period was Horatio Greenouth (1805–52), a pupil of the Danish neo-classical sculptor Bertel Thorvaldsen (1768–1844).   *18th and 19th centuries*

Right into the 20th century American sculptors showed a marked predilection for realistic monumental sculpture. The best known example is the Statue of Liberty (1871–84), by the Alsatian sculptor Frédéric-Auguste Bartholdi. Others are the Jefferson Memorial (by Daniel Chester French, 1943) and the Lincoln Memorial (by Rudolph Evans, 1915–22). The climax of this trend is to be seen at Mount Rushmore, South Dakota, where from 1927 onwards Gutzom Borglum and his son Lincoln hewed from the living rock figures of Presidents George Washington, Thomas Jefferson, Abraham Lincoln and Theodore Roosevelt.   *Monumental sculpture*

Under the influence of émigrés from Europe American sculpture enjoyed a considerable upswing in the course of the 20th century and produced a number of new native sculptors. Among the most important émigrés were the Russians Naum Gabo (1890–1977) and Alexander Archipenko (1887–1964).   *Emigré art*

The moving spirit of modern American sculpture was Alexander Calder (1898–1976), who achieved world fame with his mobiles. David Smith (1906–65) became known for his metal sculpture. Among more recent sculptors are Edward Kienholz and George Segal. Asian influence can be seen in the work of the Los Angeles sculptor Isamu Noguchi (b. 1904). A very particular position is occupied by Christo, famous for his spectacular "packaging" operations, in which buildings and whole areas are wrapped in various fabrics. The Californian artist Bruce Naumann, with his "Negative Art", stands between different disciplines, using also films and photographs in his installations.   *Modern sculpture*

Photography

With the invention of photography a new art form soon developed. By the 1920s photography had been recognised in the United States as an artistic genre in its own right; among its most notable exponents were Alfred Stieglitz, lifetime companion of the famous painter Georgia O'Keeffe, and Edward Streichen, who together ran in New York one of the first galleries devoted to photography. Man Ray, Duane Michals, Paul Strand and Walter

Architecture

Evans were among other artistic personalities who worked in the new medium. The history of photography is now taught in the universities as part of the history of art – a situation which is still exceptional in Europe – and there are photographic collections in many American museums.

Architecture

While American painting and sculpture have been for the most part influenced by Europe, architecture has become the distinctively American form of artistic expression. During the second half of the 19th century in particular many cities in the United States were in process of rapid growth and accordingly attracted gifted young architects. A new type of building, the skyscraper, now came into being. Among the most lucrative commissions for young architects were the huge new office and commercial blocks now required, for the exteriors of which a whole new language of forms was developed.

New and old: Transamerica Pyramid and Columbus Tower, San Francisco

Architecture

Residential buildings, on the other hand, remained for many years traditional in style, following neo-classical or neo-Gothic models. Typical examples are the shingle-clad façades of the frequently bizarre wooden buildings on the north-east coast (the "shingle style") and the neo-classical imitations in the tradition of Thomas Jefferson's buildings in Virginia, in particular the University of Virginia in Charlottesville and Jefferson's own mansion of Monticello. Houses of this type still set the pattern of many American residential areas.

Residential buildings

A distinctive modern architecture began to emerge only about 1900 with the houses built by Frank Lloyd Wright (see Famous People) in Chicago. He remained, however, an isolated figure: most people preferred houses in eclectic styles. Nevertheless Frank Lloyd Wright is one of the few architects of his period whose influence has continued into our own time. His houses establish a unity between nature and architecture: a striking example of this is the house Falling Water at Bear Run, Pennsylvania, built in 1936. He was not afraid to leave natural materials like stone and timber visible and to use them as a stylistic feature – an idea which is now taken as a matter of course but at the beginning of the 20th century was revolutionary. He was one of the most creative architects in history. One of his late works of the mid 20th century, the Guggenheim Museum in New York, is more like a work of sculpture than a building; and the interior likewise bears witness to its architect's very personal interpretation of architecture.

Frank Lloyd Wright

An important development in the history of architecture was the appearance of the skyscrapers which have become such characteristic features of American cities. Their construction was made possible by a number of technological innovations, new building methods like the use of steel and concrete, and Elisha Otis's invention of the passenger lift (elevator). The steel-framed type of structure made possible the construction of higher buildings than did traditional methods and materials. The earliest high-rise

Skyscrapers

Guggenheim Museum in New York: Frank Lloyd Wright's only museum

Baedeker Special
USA: Home of the Skyscrapers

The construction of high-rise buildings – skyscrapers – developed from the late 19th century onwards in the United States, particularly in the two cities of New York and Chicago, which from the outset vied with one another for possession of the highest building in the world.

The first multi-storey office blocks equipped with elevators were built in New York about 1870. Chicago, after a great fire in 1871, adopted the steel-framed structure for office and commercial buildings devised by the local school of architects (Burnham, Root, etc.).

From the turn of the century onwards every conceivable type of high-rise structure was built in New York – tall blocks soaring vertically up, tapering to a

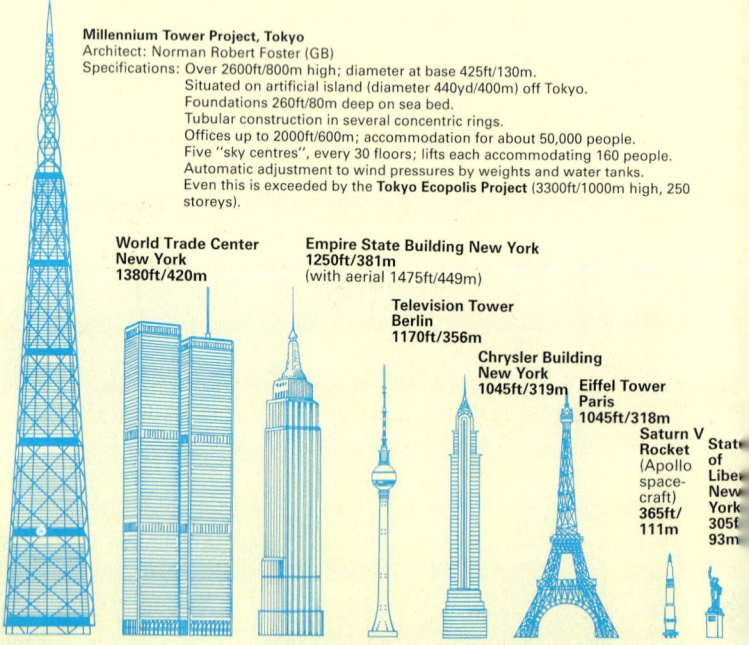

Millennium Tower Project, Tokyo
Architect: Norman Robert Foster (GB)
Specifications: Over 2600ft/800m high; diameter at base 425ft/130m.
Situated on artificial island (diameter 440yd/400m) off Tokyo.
Foundations 260ft/80m deep on sea bed.
Tubular construction in several concentric rings.
Offices up to 2000ft/600m; accommodation for about 50,000 people.
Five "sky centres", every 30 floors; lifts each accommodating 160 people.
Automatic adjustment to wind pressures by weights and water tanks.
Even this is exceeded by the **Tokyo Ecopolis Project** (3300ft/1000m high, 250 storeys).

World Trade Center New York 1380ft/420m

Empire State Building New York 1250ft/381m (with aerial 1475ft/449m)

Television Tower Berlin 1170ft/356m

Chrysler Building New York 1045ft/319m

Eiffel Tower Paris 1045ft/318m

Saturn V Rocket (Apollo spacecraft) 365ft/111m

Statue of Liberty New York 305ft/93m

point or set back in stages, with traditional or stylised decoration on the façades.

The essential elements determining the form of skyscrapers are the structural system and the provision for services. Consideration must always be given to the ratio between usable floor-space and costs of construction. Much of the area is occupied by structural and service requirements. An important element in the economics of a high-rise building is the "sway factor": that is, the ratio between horizontal distortion at the top and total height. In very tall buildings the determining factor is not the vertical load but the horizontal forces exerted by building is the "sway factor": that is, the ratio between horizontal distortion at the top and total height. In very tall buildings the determining factor is not the vertical load but the horizontal forces exerted by wind. Thus framed buildings over 10 storeys and conventional steel-framed structures over 20 storeys are uneconomic. For greater heights only a tubular structure is practicable, as in the John Hancock Center in Chicago (see diagram below).

High-rise building was slow to reach out beyond the frontiers of the United States: only after the end of the Second World War did it set out on its – not universally acclaimed – triumphal progress round the globe. Nowadays, however, it seems that no great city can do without skyscrapers. The tallest building in Europe is the 840ft/256m high Trade Fair Tower in Frankfurt am

Skyscrapers

Comparisons of Height

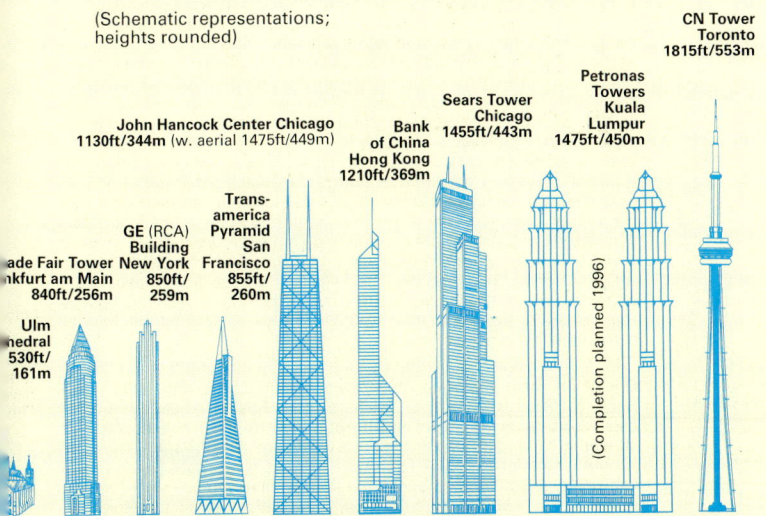

(Schematic representations; heights rounded)

CN Tower Toronto 1815ft/553m

Petronas Towers Kuala Lumpur 1475ft/450m

Sears Tower Chicago 1455ft/443m

Bank of China Hong Kong 1210ft/369m

John Hancock Center Chicago 1130ft/344m (w. aerial 1475ft/449m)

Transamerica Pyramid San Francisco 855ft/260m

GE (RCA) Building New York 850ft/259m

ade Fair Tower kfurt am Main 840ft/256m

Ulm edral 530ft/161m

(Completion planned 1996)

Main; but the capital for its construction came from New York, and the architect was a German American, Helmut Jahn, based in Chicago.

The famous Empire State Building on New York's Fifth Avenue, built in 1932, was for forty years the tallest skyscraper in the world. It lost its place in 1973 to the twin towers of the World Trade Center in southern Manhattan, which in turn were overtopped in 1974 by the Sears Tower in Chicago.

Shown above, for purposes of comparison, are the tallest skyscrapers in the United States together with high-rise buildings and other tall structures elsewhere in the world.

Architecture

buildings were erected in New York in the 1870s. Rising to heights of between 245ft/75m and 295ft/90m, they were still, by present-day standards, relatively low. Among the first such skyscrapers were the Tribune Building and Western Union Building in New York City, neither of which has survived.

High-rise building was given a great boost by the invention of the passenger lift. Hitherto it had not been thought possible to ask people to walk up more than 4 or 5 floors, which necessarily imposed restrictions on the height of office buildings. The first elevator was installed in an office block in New York's Broadway in 1857.

The first half of the 20th century saw the erection of such famous skyscrapers as the Empire State Building and the Chrysler Building. Later there was a move away from the type of tower block tapering towards the top in favour of square or slab-shaped buildings. The Sears Tower in Chicago (1453ft/443m high; 110 floors) and the twin towers of the World Trade Center in New York (1368ft/417m; 110 floors) are at present the highest office blocks in the world.

Architectural centres

As with painting and sculpture, the main architectural centres were originally Boston and New York. Towards the end of the 19th century, however, Chicago took over as the capital of American architecture, with such architects as Daniel H. Burnham (1846–1912), John Wellburn Root (1850–91), William LeBaron Jenney (1832–1907), Louis H. Sullivan (1856–1924) and his pupil Frank Lloyd Wright (1867–1959) all working there. After a great fire in 1871 and the construction of the railroad Chicago became an important traffic junction and a commercial centre of major importance, and the population of the city doubled within ten years. The rapidly growing city attracted many young and talented architects, including the young Louis H. Sullivan, who had received his architectural training in Boston. His famous statement that "form follows function" was later much quoted and is said to have influenced the Bauhaus school. In contrast to later Bauhaus buildings, however, Sullivan's buildings have rich floral ornament and can be seen as a Chicago version of Art Nouveau. Five or six years before Art Nouveau ornament appeared in Europe Sullivan used similar forms of ornament. One of his best known buildings, designed in association with his partner Dankmar Adler, is the Wainwright Building in St Louis (1890–91). In spite of its ornament the building is much more modern in effect than Sullivan's Auditorium Building in Chicago, built a few years earlier, which still shows neo-Romanesque stylistic influences and is reminiscent of the Marshall Field Wholesale Store in Chicago (not preserved), built by Henry Richardson (see below) in 1887. This early steel-framed building was still fronted by an ashlar façade.

Henry H. Richardson

One of the most important American architects of the 19th century was Henry H. Richardson (1838–86), also trained in Boston, where some of his best known buildings (including Trinity Church) are still to be seen. After his studies in Harvard he went to the Ecole des Beaux-Arts in Paris and worked for some time for Théodore Labrouste, brother of the more famous Henri Labrouste. Labrouste was one of the first architects to use steel-framing. Richardson's buildings were technically innovative but still employed traditional forms, mainly Romanesque.

Architecture of the 1930s

American architecture received important new impulses in the 1930s which led to the formation of new schools and gave the United States a leading place in modern architecture. Great architects like Mies van der Rohe, Walter Gropius, Richard Joseph Neutra and the Finns Eliel and Eero Saarinen emigrated to the USA and gave the International Style almost a monopoly position in American architecture over the next two decades. From 1938 Mies van der Rohe taught at the Illinois Institute of Technology in Chicago and built a number of high-rise buildings in Chicago and New York.

Architecture

The influence of Mies van der Rohe can be detected particularly in the work of Philip Johnson, Gordon Sunshaft and Eero Saarinen. Johnson was associated with Mies van der Rohe in the design of the Seagram Building (1956–58) in New York, and he made his name with his "Glass House" in New Canaan, Connecticut, with walls of huge steel-framed glass panels on a clinker-brick base. Johnson's design is very clearly in the tradition of Mies van der Rohe's buildings. The almost exactly contemporary Farnsworth House in Plano, Illinois, shows how the two architects each inspired the other.

Postwar architecture; the International Style

Walter Gropius, former head of the Bauhaus, taught at Harvard University and influenced such architects as Paul Rudolph, Hugh Stubbins and his pupil I. M. Pei. Gropius lived until his death in a house designed by himself in the Boston suburb of Lincoln. The Graduate Center in Harvard was built to his design.

Walter Gropius

Harvard University gave numerous commissions to leading architects of the day, including, in addition to Richardson and Gropius, Le Corbusier, who designed the Graduate Center of the Visual Arts. More recently the Fogg Art Museum was built by the noted British architect James Stirling.

Architecture in Harvard

One of the largest architectural firms of the postwar period was Skidmore, Owings and Merrill, who established their reputation in the design of complex office and commercial buildings and through the development of a particular type of steel construction for high-rise buildings (Lever Building, New York, 1952; Sears Tower, Chicago, 1972–74).

Skidmore, Owings and Merrill

In the mid fifties, with the exhaustion of the reduced language of forms of the International Style, there was a quest for new possibilities of expression – for example in the work of Minoru Yamasaki, who along with Emery Roth and Sons built the World Trade Center (1966–73) in New York, and I. M. Pei, who designed the remarkable East Wing of the National Gallery in Washington DC, a building which has something of the effect of sculpture with its simple forms and smooth, luxurious-seeming, surface treatment. In sharp contrast are the buildings of Paul Rudolph, an exponent of the New Brutalism, who experimented with concrete as a building material. Characteristic of this school were the rough surface treatment of the concrete buildings and their often fortress-like aspect.

New trends

A place apart in American postwar architecture was occupied by Louis I. Kahn, an architect who had few immediate followers but paved the way for the move from the International Style to the new architectural styles of the seventies and eighties.

One of the pioneers of Post-Modernism was Robert Venturi, who in the sixties had rejected the principles of modern architecture and argued for the separation of function and decoration. Post-Modern architecture, like the Historicism of the late 19th century, returned to traditional forms (columns, porticoes, etc.) and admitted the use of colour and decoration. A characteristic feature, however, was the playful and sometimes almost ironic application of traditional forms, which thus were given a fresh interpretation.

Post-Modernism

In sharp contrast to Post-Modernism, in the late sixties and early seventies, were the "New York Five", a group of young architects led by Richard Meier who were influenced by the rationalism and functionalism of the 1920s and in particular by Le Corbusier. For their elegant buildings, invariably faced in white (hence their nickname of the "Whites", in opposition to the "Greys"), they favoured the use of glass, steel and concrete.

Richard Meier and the "New York Five"

In the 1980s the German-born architect Helmut Jahn, who from 1981 headed the Murphy and Jahn partnership, revolutionised the construction of high-rise buildings, combining the technological advances in steel-framing with a playful use of Post-Modern forms.

Helmut Jahn

Literature

The beginnings

The literature of North America goes back to the beginnings of English settlement. The first works written in New England were predominantly theological, like the first book published in the Puritan colonies, the "Bay Psalm Book" (1640). The poets of the early colonial period, including Anne Bradstreet (1612–72) and Edward Taylor (1644–1729), also favoured religious themes.

When the ideas of the Enlightenment reached the American colonies in the 18th century the subject matter of books became increasingly political. Alexander Hamilton (1757–1804), Thomas Paine (1737–1809) and Thomas Jefferson (1743–1826; see Famous People), one of the authors of the Declaration of Independence, wrote polemical works supporting the American striving for Independence. Benjamin Franklin (1706–90; see Famous People), whose autobiography, with its stress on rationalism and individualism, was one of the most important works of the revolutionary period, promoted the development of an independent American literature by establishing and supporting magazines and newspapers. The first American theatres were built in Philadelphia, New York and Charleston before the Revolution, though their repertoire consisted mainly of works by British authors.

Benjamin Franklin

19th Century

Prose

It was only after the Revolution that a few American authors were able to make a living by writing – in each case only for a short time. The first professional writer in the United States was Charles Brockden Brown (1771–1810), whose Gothic novel "Wieland" was published in 1799. The first American works to achieve success in Europe were the fairytale-like stories of the early Romantic writer Washington Irving (1783–1859) and the adventure novels of James Fenimore Cooper (1789–1851).

James Fenimore Cooper

Transcendentalism
Ralph Waldo Emerson

The first major literary movement in the new country was Transcendentalism, an influential representative of which was the essayist and philosopher Ralph Waldo Emerson (1803–82). Although Emerson regarded himself as a thoroughly religious man he rejected organised religion, believing instead in a "super-reality", the presence of God in man and nature. With his conviction that the individual must rely on intuitive knowledge and reject any adaptation to the ideas of society he reflected on an intellectual level the individualistic trend of American ideology. He created a philosophy in which the individual and not religious doctrine, tradition or society is the measure of all things.

Another Transcendentalist was Henry David Thoreau (1817–62), whose idea of civil disobedience – the doctrine of peaceful resistance – influenced such leading 20th century figures as Gandhi and Martin Luther King Jr. Margaret Fuller (1810–50), a pioneer of the feminist movement, was editor of the Transcendentalist journal the "Dial" and an inspirer of other writers of the period. Nathaniel Hawthorne (1804–64) is believed to have taken her as the model for Zenobia in "The Blithedale Romance" (1852).

The break with English literature
Nathaniel Hawthorne

With this generation of writers the United States achieved its first literary flowering and began to distance itself from English literature. Nathaniel Hawthorne, one of the leading literary figures of his day, stressed in the foreword to "The House of the Seven Gables" the writer's entitlement to go beyond the purely realistic treatment of reality. He argued for a literature which should represent individual truths in symbolic and allegorical fashion. Edgar Allan Poe (1809–49; see Famous People) was another writer who detached himself from the English tradition in tales and poems which draw their horror from extreme conditions of the human psyche. Both in practice and in theory he made a major contribution to the development of the short story. Baudelaire admired his comic fantasy and translated some of his works.

Edgar Allan Poe

The first page of the manuscript of "Uncle Tom's Cabin"

The greatest literary achievement of this period was the novel by Herman Melville (1819–91), "Moby Dick" (1851), a masterpiece in which the mythic theme of Captain Ahab's obsession with the capture of the White Whale is set against a realistic contemporary background of whaling. In his own time Melville was better known for his South Seas novels, and "Moby Dick" was rediscovered only at the beginning of the 20th century.

Herman Melville

The publication of the famous novel by Harriet Beecher Stowe (1811–96), "Uncle Tom's Cabin", in 1852 was not a purely literary event; it also gave a decisive stimulus to the move for the abolition of slavery. With its moving depiction of the life of slaves it made a major contribution to public awareness of the miseries of slavery and thus to the course of the conflict between Northern and Southern states. The novel occupies a unique situation in American literary history and must rank as one of the most influential works of the 19th century.

Harriet Beecher Stowe

After the Civil War the angle of vision of American literature became narrower and sharper. The subject matter was now regional, not transcendental; the treatment was predominantly realist, not allegorical. Every part of the country had its chroniclers, who mostly depicted the life, the people and the dialect of a particular region. Sarah Orne Jewett (1849–1909) and Mary E. Wilkins Freeman (1852–1930) concentrated on depicting the life of small New England towns in short stories. Kate Chopin (1851–1904) described the life of people of French origin, Cajuns and Creoles, in Louisiana. Her novel "The Awakening" (1899), the story of a married woman who slowly discovers her sexuality, caused a scandal from which she never recovered. Bret Harte (1836–1902) depicted the rough life of California for curious readers in the East. Mark Twain (1835–1910; see Famous People) wrote stories about the West and life on the Mississippi; his most famous work, the "Adventures of Huckleberry Finn" (1884), is a classic of American literature.

Regionalism

Kate Chopin

Mark Twain

With the beginnings of industrialisation after the Civil War the first forerunners of the great novels of social criticism of the turn of the century began to appear, like "Life in the Iron Mills" by Rebecca Harding Davis (1831–1910) and "The Silent Partner" by Elizabeth Stuart Phelps (1844–1911). These

Social criticism

Literature

Realism

two writers belonged to a realist tradition which had more in common with the works of their European contemporaries than with Hawthorne and Melville.

During the last quarter of the 19th century realism increasingly came to the fore. Among the leading figures of this period were William Dean Howells (1837–1920), Edith Wharton (1862–1937) and above all Henry James (1843–1916). James, however, felt himself more at home in the intellectual atmosphere of Europe than in his own country, and a year before his death became a British citizen. Although he made his name as a realist, his works became increasingly experimental in the course of his career. His narrative and technical innovations paved the way for the development of the modern psychological novel; and some of the great English and Irish writers of recent times, like Virginia Woolf and James Joyce, owe a great deal to Henry James.

Poetry

In the second half of the 19th century American lyric poetry also turned in new directions. In his "Leaves of Grass" Walt Whitman (1819–92) revealed a completely new form and subject matter reflecting the immeasurable landscapes of America and the individualism of Americans. Emily Dickinson (1830–86), on the other hand, led the life of a hermit and wrote poems which with their brief, precise observations were at the opposite extreme from Whitman's excesses. Nevertheless the new forms developed by Dickinson and Whitman were of far-reaching importance to the poetry of the 20th century.

Drama

While American poetry, novels and short stories had towards the end of the 19th century established their place in the literature of the world, American drama remained of little significance until the early years of the 20th century. Around the turn of the century, however, William Vaughn Moody (1869–1910) wrote plays which had a decisive influence on later developments. Before the success of his play "The Great Divide" the dramatic repertoire in North America consisted mainly of English imports and adaptations of successful prose works. The works of dramatists like David Belasco (1859–1931), who in 1905 founded the Belasco Theater in New York, and Susan Glaspell (1882–1948), who was particularly concerned with the studio theatre, made possible the development of an independent theatrical culture in subsequent decades.

20th Century

Naturalists

The economic upswing of the late 19th century and the peopling of the whole continent, now largely completed, gave American literature round the turn of the century a new character. The problems of industrialisation, the flood of new immigrants and the consequent formation of slums provided material for novels of social criticism by the "Naturalists" Theodore Dreiser (1871–1945), Stephen Crane (1871–1900), Frank Norris (1870–1902) and Jack London (1876–1916). Influenced by Zola and a philosophy of determinism, the Naturalists mostly depicted the dark side of the American dream. The critical attitude displayed in the satirical novels of Sinclair Lewis (1885–1951), the first American to win the Nobel Prize for literature, and the denunciatory works of Upton Sinclair (1878–1968) is derived from the Naturalists. A more temperate realism is seen in the works of Willa Cather (1873–1947), Ellen Glasgow (1874–1945) and John O'Hara (1905–70).

Sinclair Lewis

The "Lost Generation"

The results of industrialisation and the events of the First World War shattered American optimism. A new cynicism found expression in the works of writers of the "Lost Generation", as Gertrude Stein (1874–1946) called them. Among them were F. Scott Fitzgerald (1896–1940), with his depictions of the wild but empty social life of the 1920s, and Ernest Hemingway (1898–1961; see Famous People), whose rootless heroes sought to

Ernest Hemingway

Literature

preserve their dignity even in defeat. Henry Miller (1891–1980) wrote novels of such meticulous detail in the depiction of sexual encounters that for many years they were banned in the United States and Britain.

This generation of writers, to which the poets Ezra Pound (1885–1972) and T. S. Eliot (1888–1965) also belonged, was born in the last decades of the 19th century and grew up in isolationist prewar America, only to be confronted with the reality of the First World War. The disillusion expressed in the works of these writers is encapsulated in Eliot's "Waste Land". Harriet Monroe's journal "Poetry", in which Eliot's first works were published, proclaimed a revolution in the art of poetry. As an element of the Modern movement in literature, the poetry of the Imagists – an important member of whom, in addition to Pound and Eliot, was H. D. (Hilda Doolittle, 1886–1961) – was deliberately experimental. These poets explored new directions, particularly in the form of their poetry. Carl Sandburg (1878–1967) and Robert Frost (1874–1963), although belonging to the same generation, were less concerned with form than with their subject matter – the language, life and dreams of America and its people. More accessible than Pound and Eliot, Sandburg and Frost are still widely popular.

Imagists

The novelist William Faulkner (1897–1962), a pioneer of modern narrative technique, also belongs to the Modern movement. In his novels he depicts, with sympathetic insight and philosophical depth, the history and life of the Southern states and assesses the consequences of slavery.

William Faulkner

While the Modern movement was essentially apolitical – T. S. Eliot was a conservative, Pound a convinced fascist – John Dos Passos's (1896–1970) trilogy of novels "U.S.A." was driven by socialist commitment. During the 1930s – the "Red Decade" – political commitment was widespread in the literary scene. American drama in particular, which with Eugene O'Neill (1888–1953) at last attained international significance, was imbued with social consciousness. O'Neill's plays marked the beginning of a flowering of the drama in the United States; after him came Thornton Wilder (1897–1975) and Tennessee Williams (1911–83). In the 1950s some writers, particularly dramatists, who achieved success during the "Red Decade" were hauled before the notorious McCarthy commission, which was officially charged with rooting out Communism in the United States: among them were Lillian Hellman (1905–84) and Arthur Miller (b. 1915), whose play "The Crucible" dramatised the witch hunts of the 17th century in America and had obvious parallels to McCarthy's pursuit of dissidents.

The Red Decade

Eugene O'Neill

A conservative reaction against left-wing trends in the intellectual scene was expressed during the thirties by a group of writers from the Southern states who published mainly in a journal called "The Fugitive" and accordingly were known as the Fugitives. Writers belonging to the school of "New Criticism", particularly John Crowe Ransom (1888–1974) and Robert Penn Warren (1905–89), exerted influence on academic circles. Eliot's theory of the autonomy of the poetical imagination, which reflected a profound disillusion with politics and social reality, was the basis of the New Criticism, which for many years determined the intellectual climate in America.

New Criticism

Partly as a result of the regional pride which the New Critics were concerned to promote, and also because of Faulkner's reputation, the Southern states became in the 1940s an important centre of literary production. Led by Katherine Anne Porter (1890–1980), a group of women writers came to the fore who depicted predominantly grotesque and abnormal aspects of life; among them were Eudora Welty (b. 1909), Carson McCullers (1917–67) and Flannery O'Connor (1925–64). Other representatives of this "Southern Gothic" school were Walker Percy (1916–90) and Truman Capote (1924–84).

Southern Gothic

The quest for meaning in modern American life became the most important theme for the writers of the fifties and sixties. In 1958 Vladimir Nabokov (1899–1977), who had emigrated from Russia in 1919 and lived in the

Postwar period

Literature

United States since 1940, published his novel "Lolita", a satirical consideration of American society which brought him worldwide success and scandal. Other works of social criticism were the early novels of Norman Mailer (b. 1923) and Ken Kesey (b. 1935), two writers who returned in their writings to the individualist trends of American ideology. The writers of the "Beat Generation" – Jack Kerouac (1922–69) in prose and Alan Ginsberg (b. 1926) in poetry – also saw the only possibility of individual fulfilment outside the compulsions of society. Many publications of this period were lightly fictionalised autobiography. The important thing was the "authenticity" of the work, and the writers were concerned to achieve an exact reproduction of their experiences. The process of adolescence became a genre on its own, and weltschmerz an everyday matter. The prototype in this field was J. D. Salinger's (b. 1919) "Catcher in the Rye". While Saul Bellow (b. 1915), Bernard Malamud (1914–86) and Philip Roth (b. 1933) gave expression to the problems of (usually Jewish) intellectuals, John Updike (b. 1932) and John Cheever (b. 1912) depicted the monotony of everyday life from the viewpoint of the white middle classes. Joyce Carol Oates (b. 1938) repeatedly depicted the violence of life at all levels of United States society.

Black writers

Like some of the Jewish writers mentioned above, many black writers also produced autobiographical novels. The novel "Invisible Man" by Ralph Ellison (b. 1914) describes how attempts by black Americans to live in the white culture finally end in the "invisibility" of the protagonist. Richard Wright (1908–60), James Baldwin (1924–87) and Maya Angelou (b. 1928), in both fictional and non-fictional confessions, all made the quest for their own identity the central theme of their writing.

Women's writing

In the seventies Erica Jong (b. 1943) and Marilyn French (b. 1929) did for women what Bellow and Updike had done for their own particular social class: with light self-irony they gave expression to weltschmerz from a very particular, feminine, point of view. Tillie Olsen (b. 1913) and Grace Paley (b. 1922), on the other hand, wrote humorous stories about domestic life.

Poetry

This trend was followed also by the poets of the period, particularly in the poems of the so-called "confessional" poets – Robert Lowell (1917–77), John Berryman (1914–72), Anne Sexton (1928–74) and Sylvia Plath (1932–63). Denise Levertov (b. 1923) and Adrienne Rich (b. 1929) took up feminist themes in their poetry, while Gwendolyn Brooks (b. 1917) and Imamu Amiri Baraka (b. LeRoi Jones, 1934) supported the cause of the blacks. Gary Snyder (b. 1930) mingled her confessions with ecological themes and Far Eastern mysticism.

New Journalism

Truman Capote and Norman Mailer carried the quest for authenticity to its extreme, combining journalism and fiction in an experimental fashion. Tom Wolfe (b. 1931), one of the leading representatives of the so-called "New Journalism", sought to achieve a new type of social novel through the mingling of fiction and reportage in his hugely successful novel "The Bonfire of the Vanities".

Irrealism

In parallel to the "non-fictional novels" there developed another trend, marked by unashamed delight in story-telling, in which the authors explore unrealistic and even unreal premisses. Thomas Pynchon (b. 1937), John Barth (b. 1930), John Hawkes (b. 1925), Kurt Vonnegut Jr (b. 1922), Joseph Heller (b. 1923) and Don DeLillo (b. 1936) depict a world in which paranoia is normal, logic is turned on its head and black humour is the only possible reaction to the lunacy of everyday life.

Black women writers

A new generation of black women writers were not content with autobiographical accounts of the miseries of life. The works of Toni Morrison (b. 1931) and Alice Walker (b. 1944) do not disregard historic and social injustices but still find some hope of a better future. With best-sellers like

Walker's "The Color Purple" and Morrison's "Beloved" the Afro-American experience and literature move into the mainstream of American culture. This is nothing new: as in the earlier case of the writers from the Southern states, the Nobel Prizes awarded to Saul Bellow and Isaak Bashevis Singer (1904–78) and the popularity of feminist authors show how a formerly marginal consciousness can come to occupy a place in the centre of cultural development. A further confirmation of this is the award of the Nobel Prize for literature to Toni Morrison in 1993.

Current trends

It is inevitably difficult to categorise contemporary literature. Among the trends of the moment are Post-Modernism, Minimalism, Magical Realism and Metahistory; but if there is one overall trend it is perhaps the turning away from traditional realist forms. Of the movements just mentioned only Minimalism is thoroughly realist. John Barth takes the impossibility of reproducing reality as a ground for concerning himself mainly with other literary phenomena, and thus deliberately draws attention to the fictional character of the novel. John Gardner (1933–82), in his "Grendel", retells the Old English epic "Beowulf" from the point of view of the monster Grendel. The crazy fictional games of Tom Robbins (b. 1936) appear repeatedly in the best-seller lists. In E. L. Doctorow's (b. 1931) "Ragtime" the traditional cultural history of the turn of the century is rewritten from top to bottom. "The Woman Warrior", by Maxine Hong Kingston (b. 1940), blurs the boundary between fiction and autobiography. Lisa Alther (b. 1944) parodies the autobiographical novel in "Kinflicks". During the eighties some authors who hitherto had traditionally been realists joined this trend. John Updike's "The Witches of Eastwick" was a farce about witches in New England in the sixties, and Joyce Carol Oates took over ideas from Magical Realism and played with the literary conventions of the family saga in her novel "Bellefleur".

Recent American plays, on the other hand, have been traditional in form, though not in content: for example Harvey Fierstein's (b. 1954) depiction of the dangerous life of a transvestite in the "Torch Song Trilogy" and Marsha Norman's shattering account of a mother–daughter relationship in "Night Mother". In Tony Kushner's play on AIDS, "Angels in America", however, the provocative plot is combined with a new form. Sam Shepard (b. 1943) is one of the most productive and most important contemporary playwrights in America.

Drama

Music

Dancing in the Street: America's Pop Music

The history of popular music was for decades identical with the history of 20th century American music. Light music produced outside the United States was usually a mere imitation of American originals. This dominance was challenged only in the mid sixties by the Beatles, but even they originally copied Chuck Berry, Buddy Holly and Little Richard.

Mingling of styles

Surprisingly, the genuinely American music, the music of the indigenous inhabitants, played no part in the development of the different styles. The origins of the music of the United States lie mainly in Europe, Africa and the Caribbean – brought by immigrants and slaves. A musical identity had first to emerge from the crucible of cultures alien to one another. Most of the immigrants brought with them their own folk music, which had frequently to be shielded from alien influences. Only when the Irish, the British, the Poles and the Germans felt themselves to be Americans and the former slaves were also permitted to become Americans could an independent American musical tradition develop.

The distinction made in Europe between serious music and light music could not establish itself in the United States, at any rate so far as the

Black music

Music

styles which had developed in America were concerned. It was not until rock'n'roll came along that the strict separation between "normal" music and "race music" could be relaxed. Until then records by black performers were produced only for a market of black people – though the labels established for the purpose were still subsidiaries of white record companies. "Jungle music", with its frequent sexual allusions, was regarded as inferior and suspect. This cultural racism compelled the blacks to seek their own musical identity. They themselves were much less narrow-minded: they had an ear for European harmonies, they adopted many of the European instruments which had previously been unknown to them and combined them with their own favourite instrument, the drum. There thus came into being a form of music which for the first time combined rhythm and melody on an equal basis.

"It don't mean a thing, it ain't got that swing": Jazz

Origins and antecedents

Jazz was not "invented" solely by black musicians, though the performers who formed its various styles were mainly coloured. The frequently cited characteristic "blue notes" were the result of an attempt to reconcile the five-note scale of the African savanna with the European eight-note scale.

Spirituals and blues

In addition racial segregation gave rise to hybrid forms like spirituals and the blues – in effect the earliest independent styles produced in North America. Spirituals, already popular in the early 19th century, expressed the deep religious feeling of the blacks. A hundred years later the blues grew out of the spirituals and the work songs or "field-hollers" sung by blacks at work in the fields.

Ragtime

A forerunner of jazz was ragtime, which became popular about the turn of the 19th century; its characteristic feature was syncopation, and any type of music, from operetta to marches, was grist to its mill. Its outstanding exponent was Scott Joplin, who as early as 1899 had sold more than 400,000 scores of his "Maple Leaf Rag".

New Orleans

Jazz, which is said to have originated in New Orleans, was played about the same time in other parts of the United States – in Memphis (Tennessee) and in Indiana, Texas and Oklahoma. New Orleans, however, is of importance in the history of traditional jazz because it got its name there. Apparently in the mixed French-English language of the Creoles the Biblical Jezebel (a female of very questionable repute) became the "Jazz Belle"; and the bars and brothels of the New Orleans district of Storyville, in which prostitution was legalised in 1898 in order to keep the rest of the city "clean", were the only places where black musicians could find paid employment. Originally only pianists were employed, like Jelly Roll Morton, later famous as a band leader; but the marching bands (still employed to accompany funeral corteges) soon gave rise to small jazz combos which also sought to exploit this lucrative market. The most popular bands were those of Kid Ory and King Oliver, who employed musicians like Louis Armstrong (see Famous People) and Sidney Bechet. The characteristic division of the band into the rhythm group and the wind players who provide the melody was soon accomplished.

Dixieland

The first group to make a record, in 1917, was a white ensemble, the Original Dixieland Jazz Band; and Dixieland is still the name applied to the white interpretation of New Orleans jazz. The compositions of the Dixieland Band, however, were invariably longer than the three minutes' capacity of the wax matrix and had to be reduced in length by being played at a breakneck tempo. This technical problem is the main reason why Dixieland music is still played at such a cracking pace.

The move north

During the First World War large numbers of impoverished land workers moved into the industrial cities of the North and the east coast, and many jazz musicians followed the same route. The new jazz centres were Kansas

Music

City (with Count Basie), New York (with Fletcher Henderson and Duke Ellington) and above all Chicago. Here most of the New Orleans musicians met, including Louis Armstrong, who as early as 1928 had preferred his small group, the Hot Five, to the big bands which were steadily growing bigger. In the Prohibition era a small group also had practical advantages: it could be more easily accommodated in a small and crowded speakeasy, it made less noise and so attracted less attention, and in the event of a police raid the instruments could be quickly spirited away.

During the 1930s jazz was dominated by big band swing, with Benny Goodman, Woody Herman and Tommy Dorsey among the best known white band leaders. Also very popular was the almost improvisation-free dance music of Paul Whiteman and Glenn Miller (see Famous People), which can only with difficulty be regarded as jazz at all. The more exciting jazz was mostly played by black bands under such leaders as Duke Ellington or Count Basie, who were readier to experiment, allowed more scope for improvisation and solo performances and engaged fine singers like Billie Holiday, who sang with Count Basie before embarking on her solo career.

The big bands

During the 1940s many performers, finding their creativity restricted by membership of a big band, founded their own small combos. Charlie Parker (saxophone), Dizzy Gillespie (trumpet) and Thelonious Monk (piano) were the best known exponents of bebop, which with its complex rhythms, breakneck tempo and apparently unconnected shreds of melody was totally unsuited for dancing and for many people was difficult to take. Accordingly jazz came increasingly to be regarded as an elite form of music for intellectuals. The cool jazz of the 1950s – a gentler style with relaxed rhythms and a mood of melancholy created by such musicians as Lester Young, Gerry Mulligan and Miles Davis (see Famous People) – did little to change this view. This was followed by the free jazz of such as Ornette Coleman, Cecil Taylor, John Coltrane and Albert Ayler, which broke completely away from all accepted styles and was met with a general lack of appreciation. Jazz now lost its leading role in popular music.

Bebop, cool and free jazz

Jazz lives on, however, in the big bang rock of Blood, Sweat and Tears and the jazz rock of Chick Corea, Herbie Hancock and Pat Metheny, who learnt from the great master Miles Davis. In recent years, too, musicians like the Wynton brothers, Branford and Delfeayo Marsalis have achieved success with a return to the original forms of jazz.

Jazz today

"How blue can you get?": Blues

In contrast to jazz, which was a city music, the blues were the form of musical expression of the blacks who had remained in the rural South – not only in the Mississippi delta but all over the region; they are better referred to, therefore, as country blues rather than Delta blues. The structure of the blues is simple and relatively inflexible: a system of "call and response" in a pattern that is always the same. The first line of the song, usually a cry or a question, is repeated in the second line and then receives an answer in the third. This structure is similar to that of the spirituals and work songs, in which the audience responded to the soloist or the workers to the foreman.

In the mid twenties the first records were produced of blues singers like Blind Lemon Jefferson, Tampa Red and Son House, who accompanied themselves on the acoustic guitar. The finest interpreter of this style, ten years later, was Robert Johnson, who legend said had sold his soul to the devil in order to become the leading singer and guitarist of the blues. Unlike his contemporaries, Johnson sang not so much of the injustices of life as of the irrepressible craving for luxury, sex and alcohol and the fear that this would mean literally going to the devil ("Hellhound on my Trail"); and in

Acoustic blues

Music

fact Johnson himself died of poisoning at the age of 25 in mysterious circumstances. Among the many other singers with big and expressive voices and sparse guitar accompaniment were Big Bill Broonzy, Skip James, Leadbelly and Mississippi John Hurt, who travelled around the South singing of unrequited love, hard times and the misfortune of being born with the wrong colour of skin.

Barrelhouse

At the same time there developed out of the boogie-woogie of Meade Lux Lewis and Pinetop Smith a version of the blues which was soon to be heard in every bar and dive. Pianists like Roosevelt Sykes, Memphis Slim and Champion Jack Dupree introduced a fast tempo and demonstrated in the Barrelhouse style that blues did not always need to sound melancholy.

City blues

During the Second World War many blacks again moved north, looking for jobs in the armaments and automobile industries. Chicago now became the centre of modern city blues. Among the musicians who settled there were Muddy Waters, Howlin' Wolf and Elmore James, who recorded classics such as "Hoochie Coochie Man", "Little Red Rooster" and "Dust my Broom". In order to make themselves heard in the din of the great city they

Electric blues
Rhythm and blues

reinforced their music electrically. With bass, percussion, guitar, piano and mouth organ they produced a hard sound: rhythm and blues. B. B. King and T-Bone Walker became famous as virtuosos of the solo guitar. John Lee Hooker demonstrated with items like "Boom Boom" that a stamping boot could be an impressive rhythm instrument.

Orchestral blues and soul

From the mid fifties it became almost impossible to assign particular performers to this or that school. Most of them followed musicians like Ray Charles and Bo Diddley, who performed blues, rhythm and blues and black rock'n'roll. With the blacks' increasing self-confidence they lost taste for the blues, now seen as antiquated and uncultivated, and too reminiscent of their country origins. In the sixties the more sophisticated orchestral style of Ray Charles and Sam Cooke was enriched with Gospel elements and developed into soul by Otis Redding and James Brown.

The blues today

Had it not been for the success of young whites like Alexis Korner and John Mayall in Britain and Johnny Winter, Paul Butterfield and Canned Heat in the United States in winning a new audience, the blues might have fallen into oblivion. Of the grand old men of the blues only B. B. King (b. 1924) and John Lee Hooker (b. 1917) still regularly perform, and hardly a year passes without news of the death of another veteran. Musicians like Robert Cray and Eric Clapton, however, still ensure that the blues do not completely disappear from the hit parade.

"Take me Home Country Roads": Country Music

Hillbillies

In 1904 "Harper's Magazine" drew attention to a breed of men living hidden in the hills of Kentucky, Tennessee and Carolina whose music was not only distinctive but, like the men themselves, distinctively American. There, in the recesses of the Appalachians, settlers of Anglo-Saxon origin, mocked as "hillbillies", played their old folksongs, though usually forced by poverty to make do with home-made fiddles, banjos and mandolines. The themes of this "mountain music", like the performers, were ultra-conservative, inspired by the Bible and anti-pleasure. In 1927 Ralph Peer discovered the Carter family and recorded their songs, celebrating their life on the land and the fear of God, often with something of the musical style of Christian chorales. The records sold astonishingly well, and the Carters' style was carried on by singers like Ernest Tubb and Roy Acuff.

Bluegrass

Instrumentalists like Bill Monroe, Lester Flatt and Earl Scruggs soon began to play this music at double the normal tempo, creating in items like "Orange Blossom Special" and "Foggy Mountain Breakdown" the Bluegrass style, which became the very epitome of traditional country music. It owed its wide popularity to the radio: although the Grand Ole Opry programme transmitted by station WSM in Nashville, Tennessee, was not the earliest radio show devoted to country music it was undoubtedly the most important. First presented in 1925, it gave the white music of the Southern states a wider audience; it launched many leading performers on their careers (though the young Elvis Presley's appearance on the show was a flop); and it made Nashville "Music City USA", the capital of country music.

Only two days after the Carter family the itinerant white singer Jimmy Rodgers, who had travelled all over the South as a railway worker and had thus seen more of life than the sedentary Carters, made his first record. His "Blue Yodel" sold half a million copies right off the reel. His example was followed by the "Storytellers", from Hank Williams, Johnny Cash and Merle Haggard to the "Outlaws", Willie Nelson and Waylon Jennings. — Storytellers

The leading song-writer in this field was Hank Williams, who contrived in the early fifties to free country music from its rustic backwoods image and make it the music of middle-class America. The whimpering sound of the pedal steel guitar was soon heard across the United States, from California to Alaska. In 1973 there were more than 800 radio stations which played nothing but country music and were able to make stars: Dolly Parton has been for decades the female Number 1, Charley Pride has achieved fame as the only black in this field, and Chet Atkins is not only an exceptional guitarist but one of the most successful producers of country music. — Middle-class music

In the mid seventies young bands like the Flying Burrito Brothers and the Nitty Gritty Dirt Band combined rock'n'roll with country music, and the style, though criticised as reactionary, found a sympathetic audience in the Woodstock generation. Townes van Zandt and Dong Sahm remain outsiders, though outsiders of great talent, while the ancestral line of superstars is continued in the nineties by Dwight Yoakam and Garth Brooks, the latter of whom sold more discs in 1992 than megastar Michael Jackson. — New faces

"The Blues had a Baby and they named it Rock'n'Roll"

... So at least assert renowned blues musicians like Willie Dixon, though Johnny Cash maintains that country music must have had a share in its paternity. The principal characteristic (and the recipe for success) of rock'n'roll, however, was not so much the mingling of black and white styles as the age and comportment of its interpreters. In the eyes of their distraught elders, who wanted a quiet life after the depression and the war to enjoy their unaccustomed prosperity, it was pure rebellion. Bill Haley with his "Rock Around the Clock" was nerve-racking but was not seen as a sex symbol for teenagers or a figure for them to identify with; but swinging-hips Elvis Presley with his bedroom eyes was a potential threat to domestic peace. — Rebellion

Musically Elvis Presley was no innovator, but he was the right man at the right time, who showed millions of adolescents that there was another attitude to life than that of their parents, and that it found expression in music rather different from that of Bing Crosby, Frank Sinatra and Perry Como. Presley got his first chance from Sam Phillips, owner of Sun Records in Memphis, Tennessee, who was convinced that a good-looking young white man who could play black rhythm and blues was bound to be a success – and a look at contemporary photographs of his competitors shows why Elvis became king of rock'n'roll. After his first successes Sam Phillips sold him to RCA Records for 50,000 dollars, thinking that he had made the best deal of his life; then when "Heartbreak Hotel" and "Hound Dog" reached the top of the charts he began to wonder. The whole entertainment industry wondered likewise, and then tried desperately to jump — Elvis Presley

Music

Elvis 1956 – Front page of "Der Spiegel"

on to the bandwagon. Although the bosses of the record companies found his braying and screaming repulsive, they quickly realised the massive economic potential of teenagers' pocket-money. Eddie Cochran, Gene Vincent, Buddy Holly and the Everley brothers were among the "panic buys" now made by the big record companies.

Black rock'n'roll

The hardest sound still came from the ghetto, and since the white public's appetite was insatiable Little Richard, Bo Diddley and Chuck Berry, by far the best song-writer of rock'n'roll, now got their chance. In 1956 Fats Domino became a black rock star with his comfortable "Blueberry Hill", and hardly anyone knew that he had been performing hard numbers like "The Fat Man" since 1929 – when Elvis Presley was 14 years old. Characteristic of black rock'n'roll were vocal groups of several voices, with a repertoire which ranged from the rough Gospel music of the Coasters ("Poison Ivy") by way of the refined harmonies of the Drifters ("Under the Boardwalk") to the schmaltzy doo-wop style of the Platters ("Only You").

The end of rock'n'roll

The wild time of rock'n'roll, however, was soon over. In the early sixties the aggressive sound of "Tutti Frutti", "Summertime Blues", "Roll Over,

Music

Beethoven" and "Great Balls of Fire" was toned down. Although musical "fabric-softeners" like Fabian, Paul Anka and Frankie Avalon still took after Elvis Presley, it was after "Love Me Tender" rather than "Jailhouse Rock". It was a black lookout for fans of hard rhythms: Buddy Holly and Eddie Cochran were dead, Gene Vincent was crippled, Elvis was in the army and Chuck Berry in prison, Little Richard had become a convert to Gospel and Jerry Lee Lewis to country music. Bert Kaempfert and Billy Vaughn now dominated the hit parade: the young people of America seemed to have been domesticated.

The Beat Goes On

Friday October 5th 1962 was the day that changed the world, or at any rate the world of pop music. On that day the Beatles published their first official single, "Love Me, Do", and thereafter Beatlemania overran the American entertainments industry so rapidly and violently that to this day it has still not completely recovered. Between February and June 1964 the Beatles had four successive hits at the top of the charts. In September they were displaced by another British band, the Animals ("House of the Rising Sun"), and in October by Manfred Mann; but the main thrust of the British invasion was still to come, with the Rolling Stones, the Kinks and The Who – to name only the best known. US dominance was broken, and the imitation of American models was replaced, with increasing self-confidence, by the independent style of British beat groups, though the most important of these still had their roots in the blues and rock'n'roll.

The British invasion

Apart from the "surf sound" of the Beach Boys, which had enjoyed success since 1962, the United States had little to oppose to the British bands. New groups were founded almost daily, hoping to become the American Beatles; and the Lovin' Spoonful, the Turtles, the Monkees, the Young Rascals, Sam the Sham, the Pharaohs and many others had hits selling a million records.

In the middle of the "crisis" the first independent record company run wholly by blacks was established. The leading exponents of what came to be known as Motown sound (after the automobile town of Detroit) included Stevie Wonder, Marvin Gaye, the Supremes and the Temptations. Tamla Motown soul was a successful attempt to appeal to a mass white public with black music. It was catchier and more lightweight than the soul music of Otis Redding, Aretha Franklin and Wilson Pickett produced in Memphis and Harlem.

Motown sound

Bands like Mamas and Papas, Buffalo Springfield and above all the Byrds married beat music with the American folksong tradition to produce folk rock. Its leading representative, apart from Arlo Guthrie and Pete Seeger with their protest songs and trade union songs, was Bob Dylan, who had just discovered the electric guitar and published his first long-playing record just six months before the Beatles. Accompanying himself on mouth-organ and guitar, he denounced war profiteers, racial discrimination and social abuses, and became the voice of "the other America", the spokesman of all those who had not found the fulfilment of their dreams in the American way of life. When he appeared for the first time with a fully electric band in 1965 he put off some of his hearers but won a wider audience through a combination of intelligent texts, elements of social criticism and rough rock music. He prepared the way for the increasingly rebellious attitudes of American schoolchildren and students from 1966 onwards.

Folk rock

Bob Dylan

From the "Summer of Love" in 1967 to the Woodstock Festival of 1969 the rebellious youth of America was very much in the news, with love-ins, experiments with LSD, hippies, Flower Power and anti-Vietnam demonstrations. Terms like the Underground, psychedelic, acid rock and progressive music were coined to describe the music which was to lead to an

From the Summer of Love to Woodstock

Music

enlargement of consciousness and to revolution. The contribution of British groups like Cream, Pink Floyd and the Jimi Hendrix Experience (though Hendrix himself was an American) was no less important than that of the San Francisco scene, with the Grateful Dead and Jefferson Airplane, Janis Joplin, plagued by alcohol, drugs and loneliness, New York's uncompromising and illusionless Velvet Underground, Detroit's radical socialist MC5, the Doors group led by the egomaniac Jim Morrison, who left no taboo unbroken, from incest to exhibitionism, and Frank Zappa's Mothers of Invention, who made such inimitable fun of Mr and Mrs America. As had happened with rock'n'roll, the industry resolved to follow the principle "If you can't beat them, join them"; and by the early seventies most of the important bands were under contract and thus stripped of their wildness.

The "boring seventies"

The seventies were not quite so boring as was often claimed. Iggy Pop and the Stooges, the New York Dolls and the Dictators dedicated themselves to hard city rock'n'roll, swimming stubbornly against the stream. Neil Young took his fans aback with his astonishing variety of styles and his fireworks with the guitar, which could have been equalled only by Jimi Hendrix, who had died in 1970. Bob Dylan, The Band, Randy Newman, Lou Reed, Little Feat, the Eagles and many others still continued to produce fine music, and in 1973 the superstar of our own day, Bruce Springsteen, made his first record, which was hailed by the critics as "the future of rock'n'roll".

Bombast rock

The entertainment industry, however – now consisting of billion-dollar international corporations – managed to establish its idea of "adult-oriented rock", which was more a marketing strategy than a musical style. It changed the image of rock music, so that the average young American, newly married and with a good job, could still identify with it. The result of these efforts was the bombast rock, dominated by keyboard instruments, of Boston, Kansas and Styx. In Britain this was the heyday of Supertramp, Yes, Genesis and Queen. Country and rock'n'roll elements had almost completely disappeared from this music.

"Hey, Ho! Let's Go!!": But Where To?

Punk

The term "punk" which cropped up in American slang in the sixties meant the kind of young hooligan who would trip his grandmother up rather than help her across the street. Punk as a musical style achieved world notoriety in 1977 when British groups like the Sex Pistols, The Clash and the Stranglers, in deliberately shocking rig-out and with provocative texts and ear-shattering volume, bellowed their contempt for the Establishment and the rock music which was inherent in the system. Their slogan "No future" was an expression of frustration with a society which could not offer its young people enough jobs, even as labourers. A similarly noticed political line appeared in the United States only in 1980 with the Dead Kennedys, and their protest expressed their disgust with superfluity. But Punk as a form of musical expression was nothing new in America. Johnny Thunder's Heartbreakers had branched off from the New York Dolls; Patti Smith had published their debut in 1975; and the first album of the Ramones was on the market in 1976, before the Sex Pistols had produced even a single.

Mixture of styles

The industry was not much taken with these violent sounds, but it had learned from experience. It soon had everything that could be called punk under contract, and coined the term New Wave for a more polished and rather less coarse version of the new music. Numbers of groups with a readiness to experiment and with very varying styles now got their chance. Talking Heads, Blondie, the B 52s, even Tom Petty and Mink de Ville took advantage of the fresh wind and put the fear of death in the dinosaurs of rock. They also found inspiration in rock'n'roll and the music of the sixties; and the electric guitar came back into favour. The number of new bands that were now founded was huge, and many of them established their own labels. The Independent scene which resulted is now a well of talent for the

record firms, constantly producing new bands which are brought under contract.
Instead of being caught unawares and overrun by new waves the industry, equipped with large advertising budgets, now creates them itself. Market research is used to identify target groups, to which the latest new trend can be "sold" by the massive use of videos on cable television. Thus the fusion of punk and heavy metal produced a style from which a steadily increasing number of groups have hived off – Hardcore, Grunge, Speed Metal, Grindcore, Thrash and Death Metal – which are often easier to distinguish from one another by the type of fans than by musical criteria.

The rap of the angry young men from the ghetto like Tone-Loc, Run D M C and Ice Cube, which combines hard funk with radical texts in rapid speech-song, was quickly depoliticised and declared the sound of the nineties, and now forms part of the standard repertoire of every producer of advertising spots. The same fate is likely to befall the hip hop of the Beastie Boys or the Red Hot Chilli Peppers, which crosses rap with hard guitar riffs and in equally unambiguous language aims well below the belt. With the immense technical resources of modern recording studios and with sampling techniques it is easy to produce "crossovers" (minglings of different styles from old recordings) – though the frequency with which these new artificial creations appear considerably shortens their own life.

Rap and hip hop

Since the end of the beat era there has been no single dominating style in popular music. Pop and Rock have become part of everyday life throughout the world. Nowadays even the mainstream accommodates such very different artistes as Prince, Dire Straits, Madonna, Michael Jackson, Bruce Springsteen and Tina Turner. The old guard, in so far as it has not been carried off by sex and drugs or by rock'n'roll, is still (or is back) in business. Paul Simon, Paul McCartney and Eric Clapton have no need to worry about paying the rent, the Beach Boys are still busily touring, the Kinks produced an extraordinary record in 1993, and the Rolling Stones have not yet found a stadium big enough to ensure that it will not be sold out over night.

Taming of the Shrew

A spectacular video seems nowadays to be a more effective way of selling records and discs than a song of above-average quality. Now that rock music is no longer the privilege of youth, the battle between the generations is no longer fought in the musical field and the entertainment industry is almost unshockable, we can only wait for the next great revolution. At present, however, no Elvis, no Beatles, no Sex Pistols are in sight.

Musicals and Serious Music

In comparison with the great prominence of "popular" music, "serious" music occupies a relatively modest position. James W. Johnson and Randall Thompson, for example, took over themes and techniques from jazz and country music and formed them into appealing symphonic music, which George Gershwin (see Famous People) stylised into music of serious artistic quality in "Rhapsody in Blue" and above all in "Porgy and Bess". Leonard Bernstein (see Famous People) and Paul Creston were more strongly influenced by European music. John Philip Sousa, inventor of the sousaphone and composer of "The Stars and Stripes Forever", wrote popular march music.

New York's Broadway is the home of the musical, the American counterpart to the European operetta. Its most important representatives, composers of many immortal tunes, are Frederick Loewe ("My Fair Lady"), Irving Berlin ("Annie Get Your Gun") and Leonard Bernstein ("West Side Story"), and in more recent times Galt McDermot ("Hair") and Marvin Hamlisch ("A Chorus Line"). Since then London has replaced New York as the musicals capital of the world, particularly with Andrew Lloyd Webber's productions ("Jesus Christ Superstar", "Cats").

Musicals

Film

Serious music

Serious music was produced in the second half of the 19th century by such American composers as John Knowles Paine and Arthur William Foote – though this "New England school" looked to European models. The breakaway began with Charles Edward Ives, who, along with colleagues like Walter Piston, took up themes from American folklore. Emigrants from Europe brought new impulses to American music, in particular Arnold Schönberg, who brought the twelve-tone system with him and influenced Ross Lee Finney, Milton Babbitt and other American composers. Breaking away from all traditions, Edgar Varese composed pure background music, while Henry Dixon Cowell was the creator of "tone clusters". John Cage ranks as the father of the avant-garde composers and Nestor of the experimentalists. In recent years Philip Glass has attained an international reputation as an exponent of "minimal music".

Film

Beginnings

Hollywood

When Mr and Mrs Horace Wilcox bought land in southern California in the 1880s and called it Hollywood they could not foresee that this area would develop into the largest and mightiest centre of production of moving pictures in the world and that the name Hollywood would become a synonym for the American film industry. A strictly Puritan couple, they would probably not have approved of what later happened to Hollywood, either as to the content of the films produced or the life led by the stars in their luxury villas.

But when Hollywood first received its name all this was in the future. The cinematograph had to be invented by Thomas Alva Edison in 1891 and further developed by the French Lumière brothers before the first public film show could be held in New York in 1895. A popular feature in fairgrounds for many years was the nickelodeon, a machine operated by inserting a 5-cent coin which allowed one person to look at a one-minute-long film strip which might depict, for example, à man sneezing. Thereafter the film developed with giant strides into a mass medium. The small shops in which films were originally shown gave place to proper cinemas and later to huge and showy film palaces. For many years the middle classes remained sceptical about the cinema, but from the outset they were immensely popular with the masses, including new immigrants who had little English but could follow the pictures.

At first the film makers were content to film actual events – sometimes frightening their audiences with the sight of a train heading straight for them – but they soon began to experiment with the language of film. There is still room for argument about which film can claim to be the first; but current histories of the cinema assign that honour to an eleven-minute western, Edwin S. Porter's "Great Train Robbery", shot in 1903. Thus American film history begins with that characteristically American genre, the western.

"The Great Train Robbery"

Pioneering days

In the pioneering days of the American cinema, before the First World War, businessmen began to take an interest in the new medium. Edison, whose patent rights were not absolutely watertight, spent some time fighting with his competitors before deciding to form a trust with the biggest of them, which then proceeded to pursue all the others in the courts, and sometimes also by sending in hired thugs to interrupt the shooting of the rivals' films and destroy the cameras. (In order to escape such attacks some of the independent producers moved their operations for the first time to California). The trust was never able, however, to cut out completely the independent producers, among whom were William Fox and Carl Laemmle. Moreover in comparison with the cheeky newcomers the trust was too inflexible, for example in holding to the usual ten-minute one-

Film

acters after innovative producers had been experimenting for some time with longer films.

This led D. W. Griffith, the greatest producer-director of his time, to leave Edison's firm in 1913, and two years later he shot a film in which the cinema finally found its own language: "The Birth of a Nation". Griffith, who in his revolutionary innovations (e.g. parallel editing, in which he cuts in and out of different settings) was inspired by Dickens's technique in the novel, made the cinema respectable: henceforth good middle-class citizens could be seen at the movies.

D. W. Griffith "The Birth of a Nation"

In the years after the First World War Hollywood became the main centre of the film industry. There was enough room for the studios, the weather made open-air shooting almost risk-free and the variety of scenery provided the settings. During the twenties, when the American economy was booming, huge sums of money flowed into the cinema. By then, too – although the producers were at first reluctant to reveal the names of their actors and only did so after massive pressure from the public – a star system had developed. It was this system, which enabled actors to live a life of luxury, that led finally to Hollywood's reputation as "Sin City". After a series of scandals about orgies, murders and other killings the Puritan element in American society imposed a form of self-censorship on the film industry. The Hays Code prescribed exactly what the stars – at least in their films – could do and not do. One film-maker described the effect of the code in these words: "Hollywood buys a good story about a bad girl and turns it into a bad story about a good girl". Nevertheless resourceful directors found plenty of ways of making good films in spite of the code.

Hollywood as Babylon

By the mid twenties the big producing and distributing companies had been established: Paramount, First National and Metro-Goldwyn-Mayer, followed by Fox, Universal and United Artists, formed by stars like Charlie Chaplin, Mary Pickford and Douglas Fairbanks along with D. W. Griffith to avoid being too dependent on the big companies. The young Irving Thalberg (later portrayed by Scott Fitzgerald in "The Last Tycoon") became production manager at MGM and in that capacity was able to oversee the shooting of the company's films. Production managers were soon appointed in other studios, leading to constant friction with directors concerned for their artistic freedom. During the twenties a great variety of genres developed in Hollywood to satisfy almost every public taste: Rudolph Valentino, Gloria Swanson and Lilian Gish provided the love interest in melodramas, Douglas Fairbanks fought his way through adventure films, Tom Mix and company rode in the West, and in a series of slapstick comedies ("The Gold Rush", 1925) Charlie Chaplin's tramp became celebrated throughout the world. Since Hollywood offered the world's best production facilities, European directors like Friedrich Wilhelm Murnau, Ernst Lubitsch and Viktor Sjöström made their way there, producing such masterpieces as Erich von Stroheim's "Greed" (1923), King Vidor's "The Crowd" (1928) and Murnau's "Sunrise" (1927).

The Greats

The Talkies

There had been earlier experiments with sound film, but the breakthrough came only on October 6th 1927, when Al Jolson spoke a few sentences and sang a few songs in "The Jazz Singer". Many stars, unable to cope with the requirements of the new medium, became unemployed; actors with theatrical experience were now in demand, and many were recruited from Broadway. The technical teething troubles of the sound film were soon overcome, and new film genres developed such as the revue and the musical, in which Busby Berkeley in particular made a name for himself with his mass choreographies. The thirties saw the beginning of the fabulous career of Fred Astaire and Ginger Rogers, who danced their way through a series of successful musicals.

Film

Screwball comedy

Ernst Lubitsch, who had begun his career in Germany, seized on the new possibilities of the sound film with enthusiasm and developed a type of elegant drawing-room comedy with polished dialogue which was unmistakably his own (the "Lubitsch touch"). This was also the great age of the screwball comedy, in which masterful women angle for shy and eccentric men, with quick-fire verbal sparring between the two. In Howard Hawks's "Bringing Up Baby" (1938), a classic of the genre, an energetic Katharine Hepburn snaps up an awkward Cary Grant. Finally Walt Disney (see Famous People) established a highly specialised studio and in 1937 produced "Snow White", the first feature-length animated cartoon film.

Animated cartoon

The dream factory

These light entertainment films reflect only indirectly the years of the American depression during which they were produced. They offered entertainment and an escape from an existence which for most cinemagoers was very different from that depicted on the screen. During the early years of the depression at least Hollywood, the dream factory, was one of the few industries which increased their turnover.

Film

In parallel with these films – which reached the extreme of remoteness from reality and of kitsch in the films constructed round the child star Shirley Temple – Hollywood also turned out films which dealt directly and robustly with reality, including the darker sides of life: the first gangster films and the first "films noirs" were now produced. Films like "Scarface" (1932), "Little Caesar" (1932) and "The Public Enemy" (1931), in which a violent James Cagney crushes a grapefruit on the face of his female opposite number, depict the rise and fall of the gangster and, as the critic Robert Warshow observed, give the audience the double satisfaction of joining in the gangster's sadism by proxy and seeing how this sadism is directed against the gangster himself.

Gangster films

On the eve of the Second World War the rigidly organised studios had achieved a high degree of efficiency. The year 1939 marked a high point in the history of Hollywood. The 15,000 American movie houses had a weekly audience of 85 million (four times the present figure), and more than 400 films were produced during the year, including some of the most famous in the history of the cinema. John Ford shot the classic western "Ringo", which gave John Wayne his first big break; William Wyler earned rave notices with his filming of "Wuthering Heights", starring Laurence Olivier and Merle Oberon; Greta Garbo laughed for the first time in Lubitsch's "Ninochka"; Judy Garland sang "Somewhere Over the Rainbow" in the fairytale musical "The Wizard of Oz"; and Vivien Leigh and Clark Gable pursued their love and hate affair through "Gone with the Wind", perhaps the greatest melodrama of them all and claimed by the posters as "the most magnificent picture ever".

Hollywood's high point

During the Second World War and immediately after it gangster and detective films and thrillers grew ever bleaker. Many German directors who had emigrated from Hitler's Third Reich were now working in America. Fritz Lang ("Fury", 1936), Robert Siodmak ("The Spiral Staircase", 1945), Billy Wilder ("Double Indemnity", 1944) and others produced pessimistic films with an atmosphere of shadiness and often with a shady hero. John Huston's "Maltese Falcon" (1941) and Howard Hawks's "The Big Sleep" (1946), both starring Humphrey Bogart in the principal role, paint the picture of a morally corrupt America. The other side of the picture was presented by Frank Capra ("Mr Smith Goes to Washington", 1939), whose heroes – usually James Stewart or Gary Cooper – at first almost fall victim to political machinations and intrigues but then pull themselves together and courageously save democracy.

Light and shadow

Hollywood in Crisis

In 1941 the multi-talented Orson Welles, aged only 25, produced his first film, "Citizen Kane", which opinion polls among critics repeatedly rate as the finest film of all time. In the postwar years, however, Hollywood, like Welles's career, slid into crisis. An anti-trust law aimed at separating production from distribution compelled the large film corporations to divest themselves of their chains of movie houses. At the same time Senator McCarthy launched a campaign against "unAmerican activities" which in the early and middle fifties led to a witch-hunt directed against all who were or might be "left-wing". Stars, directors and script-writers were summoned to appear before investigating committees; black lists were drawn up which amounted to a ban on the employment of those who appeared on them; and an atmosphere of mutual suspicion and denunciation built up. Charlie Chaplin was driven out of the country (taking his revenge in 1957 with his malicious comedy "A King in New York") and the famous "Hollywood Ten" were imprisoned for their convictions, while others betrayed their best friends.

"Citizen Kane"

As if this was not trouble enough, the film industry was now faced with competition from television – competition which, in spite of technical

Competition from television

Film

innovations like the wide screen (e.g. Cinemascope) and the 3 D film they were never to shake off. Between 1946 and 1952 the number of cinemagoers was almost halved, and although the downward trend later slowed it could not be halted. The industry was compelled to reach an accommodation with its competitor: it sold transmission rights on older feature films, hired out studios which could no longer be fully used and finally bought into television. Soon, however, television was able to make some return to the cinema: directors like Sidney Lumet ("Twelve Angry Men", 1957), Martin Ritt ("Hombre", 1967), Arthur Penn ("Bonnie and Clyde", 1967) and later Robert Altman ("Nashville", 1975) and Sam Peckinpah ("The Wild Bunch", 1969), who had all learned their trade in television studios, brought a fresh wind to Hollywood.

New talents

The decline of the old studio and star system offered – and still offers – opportunities to independent directors, new talents and outsiders. In 1969 Dennis Hopper produced "Easy Rider", a tale of two motorcyclists trekking across the country to a meaningless death which created the genre of the road movie. Others who now achieved success included the directors Peter Bogdanovich ("What's Up, Doc?", 1972), Francis Ford Coppola ("The Godfather", 1972) and Martin Scorsese ("Taxi Driver", 1976) and the stars Jack Nicholson, Robert de Niro and Al Pacino. The greatest successes of the seventies, however, were achieved by George Lucas and Steven Spielberg with their fantasy and science fiction spectaculars "Star Wars" (1977) and "Close Encounters of the Third Kind" (1977), later followed by "Star Wars" 2 and 3 and "E.T." (1982), which is claimed to be the most successful film of all time.

Hollywood today

Hollywood no longer lives by maintaining a healthy level of production, or even by producing good average films, but almost exclusively by turning out increasingly expensive blockbusters, from the success of which the whole future of the company sometimes depends. When Michael Cimino's epic of immigration "Heaven's Gate" reached the movie houses in the eighties, at a time when Ronald Reagan was spreading an atmosphere of optimism, audiences were not interested in such a critical view of America; and the flop of "Heaven's Gate" meant ruin for United Artists.

The merry-go-round of Hollywood personalities is now revolving at a frantic rate, in an industry now supported by much foreign, particularly Japanese, capital. Directors are appointed who have rarely any special commitment to the subject of the film but are more familiar with bookkeeping and financial management. They try to meet the public taste but have no clear idea of what they want to do. In consequence directors are often sacked as suddenly as they are appointed. (Robert Altman's film "The Player", issued in 1992, on which many stars worked without pay, is a sarcastic account of the present climate in the dream industry). Hollywood now seldom produces films for adults but aims mainly at the youth market. Films by Woody Allen and other independent film-makers reach only a restricted audience and are often more popular in Europe than in their country of origin. Films which devote time to their subject, like the Indian epic "Dancing with Wolves" (1992), are increasingly becoming the exception. The common feature which distinguishes almost all new Hollywood productions from the films of twenty or more years ago is the great pace at which they run. Not only action films like the Schwarzenegger vehicles "Total Recall" (1991) and "Terminator II" (1992) but thrillers and comedies move at full speed compared with their counterparts of yesteryear.

Hollywood has thus become a little more childish and, in its attempt to track down the latest trends, rather short-winded. Nevertheless it still controls the world market. One reason for this is that film production in every other country is in crisis; another, perhaps, is that – as in the case of the two "Batman" films (1992) and the dinosaur film "Jurassic Park" (1993) – the film itself is almost fading into the background in comparison with the huge marketing campaign for film-related products like stickers, T-shirts, caps and models. The fact remains, however, that Hollywood still sets the standards – perhaps now not so much the artistic standards, but certainly the entertainment standards. It still celebrates the annual presentation of Oscars with the usual razzmatazz as if nothing had happened, while the world looks on in fascination, and perhaps also with a touch of envy.

Quotations

[Sheet music: "The Star-Spangled Banner," Maestoso, with lyrics: "Oh, say, can you see, by the dawn's early light, what so proudly we hailed at the twilight's last gleaming? Whose stripes and bright stars, thro' the perilous fight, o'er the ramparts we watch'd, were so gallantly streaming? And the rocket's red glare, bombs bursting in air, gave proof thro' the night that our flag was still there. Oh, say, does the star-spangled banner still wave o'er the land of the free and the home of the brave?"]

National anthem	Text of the national anthem by Francis Scott Key (1780–1843), written after the British siege of Fort Henry, Baltimore, on September 14th 1814; tune by John Stafford Smith (1750–1836), after the English song "To Anacreon in Heaven".
James Fenimore Cooper (1789–1851) American writer	And, truly, the scene was of a nature deeply to impress the imagination of the beholder. Towards the west, in which direction the faces of the party were turned, and in which alone could much be seen, the eye ranged over an ocean of leaves, glorious and rich in the varied but lively verdure of a generous vegetation, and shaded by the luxuriant tints that belong to the forty second degree of latitude. The elm, with its graceful and weeping top, the rich varieties of the maple, most of the noble oaks of the American forest, with the broad leafed linden, known in the parlance of the country as the bass-wood, mingled their uppermost branches, forming one broad and seemingly interminable carpet of foliage, that stretched away towards the setting sun, until it bounded the horizon, by blending with the clouds, as the waves and sky meet at the base of the vault of Heaven. Here and there, by some accident of the tempests, or by a caprice of nature, a trifling opening among these giant members of the forest, permitted an inferior tree to struggle upward toward the light, and to lift its modest head nearly to a level with the surrounding surface of verdure. Of this class were the birch, a tree of some account in regions less favored, the quivering aspen, various generous nut-woods, and divers others, that resembled the ignoble and vulgar, thrown by circumstances into the presence of the stately and great. Here and there, too, the tall, straight trunk of the pine pierced the vast field, rising high above it, like some grand monument reared by art on the plain of leaves.

Quotations

It was the vastness of the view, the nearly unbroken surface of verdure, that contained the principle of grandeur. The beauty was to be traced in the delicate tints, relieved by gradations of light and shadow, while the solemn repose induced a feeling allied to awe.

From "The Pathfinder" (1840)

Every part of this soil is sacred in the estimation of my people. Every hillside, every valley, every plain and grove, has been hallowed by some happy or sad event in days long vanished. Even the rocks, which seem to be dumb and dead as they swelter in the sun along the silent shore, thrill with memories of stirring events connected with the lives of my people . . . Our departed braves, fond mothers, glad, happy-hearted maidens, and even our little children who lived here and rejoiced here for a brief season, will love these sombre solitudes and at eventide they greet shadowy returning spirits. And when the last Red Man shall have perished, and the memory of my tribe shall have become a myth among the White Men, these shores will swarm with the invisible dead of my tribe . . . At night when the streets of your cities and villages are silent and you think them deserted, they will throng with the returning hosts that once filled them and still love this beautiful land.

Chief Seattle

Speech during the negotiations in 1850 on the division of the Oregon Territory.

Four score and seven years ago our fathers brought forth on this continent a new nation, conceived in Liberty, and dedicated to the proposition that all men are created equal.
Now we are engaged in a great civil war, testing whether that nation, or any nation so conceived and so dedicated, can long endure. We are met on a great battlefield of that war. We have come to declare a portion of that field, as a final resting place for those who here gave their lives that that nation might live. It is altogether fitting and proper that we should do this.
But, in a larger sense, we can not dedicate – we can not consecrate – we can not hallow – this ground. The brave men, living and dead, who struggled here, have consecrated it, far above our poor power to add or detract. The world will little note, nor long remember what we say here, but it can never forget what they did here. It is for us the living, rather, to be dedicated here to the unfinished work which they who fought here have thus far so nobly advanced. It is rather for us to be here dedicated to the great task remaining before us – that from these honoured dead we take increased devotion to that cause for which they gave the last full measure of devotion – that we here highly resolve that these dead shall not have died in vain – that this nation, under God, shall have a new birth of freedom – and that government of the people, by the people, for the people, shall not perish from the earth.

Abraham Lincoln (1809–65) President of the United States

Address delivered at the dedication of the cemetery at Gettysburg, November 19th 1863

The great advantage, it seems to me, that America possesses over the Old World is its material and moral plasticity. Even among the giant structures of this city, one feels that there is nothing rigid, nothing oppressive, nothing inaccessible to the influence of changing conditions. If the buildings are Cyclopean, so is the race that reared them. The material world seems as clay on the potter's wheel, visibly taking on the impress of the human spirit; and the human spirit, as embodied in this superbly vital people, seems to be visibly thrilling to all the forces of civilisation.

William Archer

From "America Today" (1900)

In a great many ways travelling in the United States is, to one who understands it, more comfortable than in Europe. The average Englishman will probably find the chief physical discomforts in the dirt of the city streets,

Baedeker's "United States"

125

Quotations

the roughness of the country roads, the winter overheating of hotels and railway cars (70–75° Fahr. being by no means unusual), and (in many places) the habit of spitting on the floor; but the Americans themselves are now keenly alive to these weak points and are doing their best to remove them ... Throughout almost the whole country travelling is now as safe as in the most civilised parts of Europe, and the carrying of arms, which indeed is forbidden in many states, is as unnecessary here as there. – No limit is placed on the number of passengers admitted to public conveyances, and straps are provided in the cars of tramways and elevated railways to enable those who cannot obtain seats to maintain their equilibrium. – Indoor clothing for American use should be rather thinner in texture than is usual in England, but winter wraps for outdoor use require to be much thicker. The thick woollen gowns that English ladies wear in winter would be uncomfortably warm in the ordinary winter temperatures of American hotels and railway carriages; and a thin soft silk will, perhaps, be found the most comfortable travelling dress on account of its non-absorption of dust. Overshoes ("arctics" and "rubbers") are quite necessary in winter and are worn almost as much by men as by women.

From "The United States, with an Excursion to Mexico. Handbook for Travellers" (1893)

Stephen Vincent Benét
(1898–1943)
American poet

I have fallen in love with American names,
The sharp names that never get fat,
The snakeskin titles of mining claims,
The plumed war-bonnet of Medicine Hat,
Tucson and Deadwood and Lost Mule Flat.

Seine and Piave are silver spoons,
But the spoonbowl-metal is thin and worn.
There are English counties like hunting-tunes,
Played on the keys of a postboy's horn,
But I will remember where I was born.

I will remember Carquinez Straits,
Little French Lick and Lundy's Lane,
The Yankee ships and the Yankee dates
And the bullet-towns of Calamity Jane.
I will remember Skunktown Plain.

I will fall in love with a Salem tree
And a rawhide quirt from Santa Cruz,
I will get me a bottle of Boston sea
And a blue-gum nigger to sing me blues.
I am tired of loving a foreign muse.

Rue des Martyrs and Bleeding-Heart-Yard,
Senlis, Pisa, and Blindman's Oast.
It is a magic ghost you guard
But I am sick for a newer ghost,
Hamburg, Spartanburg, Painted Post ...

I shall not rest quiet in Montparnasse.
I shall not lie easy at Winchelsea.
You may bury my body in Sussex grass,
You may bury my tongue at Champmedy.
I shall not be there. I shall rise and pass.
Bury my heart at Wounded Knee.

"American Names" (1931)

A. G. Macdonell
English writer

The truth of the matter is, and I record it with misgiving, reluctance, and a sense of imminent calamity, that the American does not like strangers to say that America is a new country. He himself will say it, over and over again, but it is as much as your life is worth to say it yourself. It is risky even to agree with him when he says it. In fact it is safer either to say nothing at all in answer to him, or to confine yourself to a muttered reference to Karlsefne or Leif Ericson.

It is a peculiar business, the American attitude to Antiquity. Of all the citizens of the world there is no one so alive as the American to the values of modernity, so fertile in experiment, so feverish in the search for something new. There is nothing, from Architecture to Contract Bridge, from the Immortality of the Soul to the Ventilation of Railroad-Cars, from Golf to God, that he does not pounce upon and examine critically to see if it cannot be improved. And then, having pulled it to pieces, mastered its fundamental theory, and reassembled it in a novel and efficient design, he laments bitterly because it is not old.

From "A Visit to America" (1935)

This land is your land, this land is my land.
From California to the New York Island,
From the redwood forest to the Gulfstream Waters
This land was made for you and me.

As I went walking that ribbon of highway
I saw above me that endless skyway,
I saw below me that golden valley.
This land was made for you and me.

I've roamed and rambled and I followed my footsteps
To the sparkling sands of her diamond deserts,
And all around me a voice was sounding.
This land was made for you and me.

When the sun comes shining and I was strolling
And the wheatfields waving and the dust clouds rolling
A voice was chanting and the fog was lifting.
This land was made for you and me.

Woody Guthrie
(1912–67)
American
folk singer

I am not unmindful that some of you have come here out of excessive trials and tribulation. Some of you have come fresh from narrow jail cells. Some of you have come from areas where your quest for freedom left you battered by the storms of persecution and staggered by the winds of police brutality. You have been the veterans of creative suffering. Continue to work with the faith that unearned suffering is redemptive.

Go back to Mississippi; go back to Alabama; go back to South Carolina; go back to Georgia; go back to Louisiana; go back to the slums and ghettos of the northern cities, knowing that somehow this situation can, and will be changed. Let us not wallow in the valley of despair.

So I say to you, my friends, that even though we must face the difficulties of today and tomorrow, I still have a dream. It is a dream deeply rooted in the American dream that one day this nation will rise up and live out the true meaning of its creed – we hold these truths to be self-evident, that all men are created equal.

I have a dream that one day on the red hills of Georgia, sons of former slaves and sons of former slave-owners will be able to sit down together at the table of brotherhood.

I have a dream that one day even the state of Mississippi, a state sweltering with the heat of injustice, sweltering with the heat of oppression, will be transformed into an oasis of freedom and justice.

I have a dream my four little children will one day live in a nation where they will not be judged by the colour of their skin but by the content of their character. I have a dream!

Martin Luther
King Jr
(1929–68)
Civil rights
activist

From a speech in Washington on August 28th 1963

Suggested Routes

Dream Roads of the USA

The best way of seeing the United States is by car or motorcycle. All the major scenic beauties are accessible by road. Municipal tourist offices and the visitor centres of National Parks and State Parks (see Practical Information, National Parks) are well supplied with good maps and descriptions of the area. With the help of the map of the United States at the end of this guide it is easy to work out individual routes and round trips. In the main part of the guide (Sights from A to Z) a number of particularly attractive routes are briefly described: for example the Blue Ridge Parkway in Virginia (see entry) and North Carolina, the Needles Skyway in the Black Hills (see entry) and the Skyway to the Sun in the Waterton-Glacier International Peace Park (see entry). In the following pages a number of the most interesting routes and round trips for visitors with several weeks at their disposal are briefly sketched.

Route 66

History

Route 66, 2448 miles/3941km long, was opened in 1926, the first transcontinental highway with an all-weather surface. It linked Chicago, the pulsating economic metropolis on Lake Michigan, with Los Angeles, the then still relatively young boom town on the Pacific. It followed much activity by the Good Roadas Movement, bringing together representatives of all road

Get your kicks on Route 66

(by Bobby Troup)

If you ever plan to motor west
Travel my way, take the highway that's the best,
Get your kicks on Route 66

It winds from Chicago to L.A.
More that 2,000 miles all the way
Get your kicks on Route 66

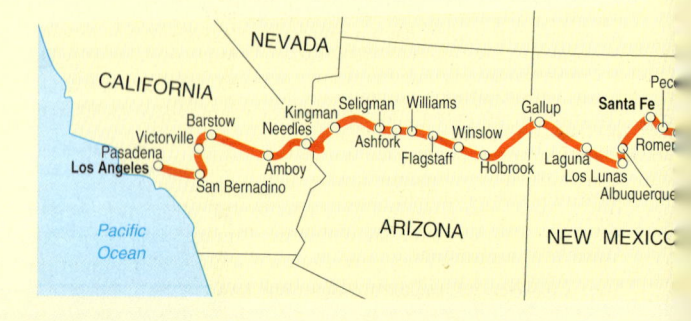

Dream Roads of the USA

users, particularly motorists and farmers, which developed in the early twenties. The authorities then began, following the old slogan "Go west!", to link up with one another old pioneering trails, farm tracks and existing country roads and to supplement the network by building new roads.

In the thirties Route 66 became a legend when, after a number of rainless years in the Middle West, tens of thousands of farmers left the dust bowl of the prairies (particularly in Oklahoma) and made their way to the "golden land" of California. In his famous novel "The Grapes of Wrath" John Steinbeck pictured the life of these victims of drought and their journey along Route 66.

During the Second World War military transports and the training camps in the Mojave Desert increased the importance of Route 66, and after the war Nat King Cole's interpretation of Bobby Troup's song "Get your kicks on Route 66" made the road world-famous.

In the early fifties the federal government launched a roads programme designed to give the United States a modern highway network, and by 1984 the old US 66 had been replaced, section by section, by new roads. The modern interstate highways I 55, I 44 and I 40 took over its functions, and the old road was left to itself. Its gas stations, snack bars, restaurants, motels and hotels remained, but were now in the backwoods. The legend, however, still lives on.

Course of Route 66

Between Chicago and St Louis only sections of the old Route 66, running parallel to I 55, survive as rather bumpy country roads. South of Bloomington U 66 serves as a local link road or "business loop". Interesting relics of better days are Funk's Grove, the old maple syrup factory south of Shirley, the Dixie Truckers' Home in McLean, Mort's Roadhouse in Glenarm, now a bikers' rendezvous, and the Ariston Café in Lichfield.

Illinois

Now you go through St. Louis, Joplin, Missouri
And Oklahoma City looks mighty pretty
Now you'll see Amarillo, Gallup, New Mexico
Flagstaff, Arizona, don't forget Winona,
Klingman, Barstow, San Bernardino

Won't you get hip to this timely trip
When you make that California trip
Get your kicks on Route 66

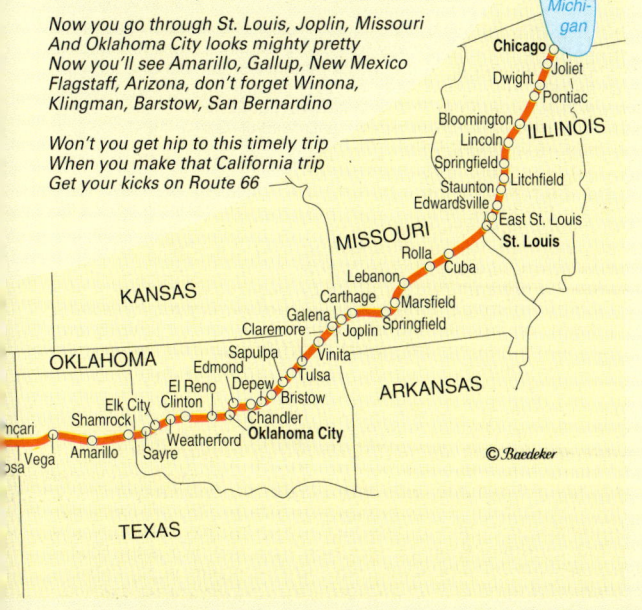

Dream Roads of the USA

Missouri

In the state of Missouri, particularly in the south-west, round Springfield and between Lebanon and Joplin, Route 66, here running parallel to I 44, is well preserved. Many little townships founded in the heyday of Route 66 are visibly in decline. From Stanton a side trip can be made to the Meramec Caverns, where the bank robber Jesse James and his gang are said to have concealed themselves.

Kansas

Between Joplin, Missouri, and Quapaw, Oklahoma, Route 66 cuts across the southernmost tip of Kansas. The road runs on a zigzag course with many right-angled bends, following old district and farm boundaries. In Baxter Springs is Murphy's Restaurant, in which Jesse James stayed when there was still a bank here.

Oklahoma

In the state of Oklahoma Route 66 has memories of the more recent past, when in the thirties thousands of impoverished farmers ("Okies") travelled along it on their way to the West. The road is still well preserved and carries considerable traffic – a paradoxical result of modern road development. The people of Oklahoma were in the forefront of the movement for the construction of the new highways, calling as early as the 1950s for the building of new freeways, to be financed by tolls; and because the new I 44 is still a toll road many drivers branch off into the old US 66, which here is still in excellent condition. Features of interest on the route are the Lincoln Hotel in Chandler, the Cowboy Hall of Fame in Oklahoma City and Pop Hicks Hotel in Clinton.

Texas

Early travellers over the dreary plateau of the High Plains in Texas were dismayed rather than impressed. On the Llano Estacado stakes were driven into the ground to mark the route. On the western outskirts of Amarillo ten old Cadillacs, half buried in the ground on Cadillac Farm, which belongs to the art collector Stanley Marsh III, now perform the same function – marking, as it were, the frontier of the motorised society.

New Mexico

Between Santa Rosa and Albuquerque, where I 40 now cuts across the barren plateau, US 66 formerly followed a winding course to Santa Fe. West of Albuquerque, in the neighbourhood of Laguna and between Grants and the continental watershed at Thoreau there are very fine scenic stretches of the old Route 66, now state road NM 122. In the centre of Gallup there are many old buildings reminiscent of earlier days; and the town's 1st Street is part of the old US 66.

Arizona

In western Arizona, between Ashfork and the boundary with California, a 160 mile/258km long stretch of Route 66 is preserved. Particularly fine is the section between Seligman and Kingman. The road here is dead straight, as if drawn by a ruler. The road between Kingman and the Californian border, on the other hand, is a real challenge for the driver, even in a cross-country vehicle. Travellers who are not put off by rough roads and the Sitgreave Pass, the steepest parts of which could be negotiated by the automobiles of the thirties only in reverse, can see a Western show in the gold-mining town of Oatman and visit the hotel in which Clark Gable spent his wedding night with Carole Lombard.

California

There is another fine stretch of Route 66 between Essex and Ludlow, California. The road runs through the Mojave Desert for some 60 miles/100km, passing a salt lake and the crater of an extinct volcano at Ambay. It runs through the godforsaken township of Bagdad, where scenes from the film "Out of Rosenheim" were shot, and the little settlement of Siberia, where the temperatures are very far from Siberian. There is also a well preserved section of the road between Barstow and Victorville to the south. At San Bernardino Route 66 turns west again and follows the Foothill Boulevard (CA 66) to Pasadena. From there it continues on the Colorado Boulevard to Glendale and from there on the Los Felíz Boulevard to Holly-

Dream Roads of the USA

wood. The last few miles are on the Santa Monica Boulevard through Beverly Hills and Santa Monica, and so down to the Pacific.

Coast to Coast

Distance: about 5000 miles/8000km. Time required: at least 4 weeks.
Boston – Cape Cod – New York – Philadelphia – Baltimore – Washington – Gettysburg – Pennsylvania Dutch Country – Niagara Falls – Toronto (Canada) – Detroit – Chicago – Sioux City – Badlands National Park (side trip to Wounded Knee) – Rapid City – Mount Rushmore National Monument – Black Hills (side trip to Hot Springs and Devil's Tower) – Buffalo, Wyoming – Bighorn Mountains – Ten Sleep – Cody – Yellowstone National Park – Grand Teton National Park – Jackson – Idaho Falls – Salt Lake City – Bryce Canyon National Park – Grand Canyon National Park – Lake Mead National Recreation Area – Las Vegas – Los Angeles (side trip to San Diego) – Hollywood – Beverly Hills – Santa Monica – Malibu – Santa Barbara – San Luis Obispo – Monterey – San Francisco.

USA Highlights
Boston to
San Francisco

Distance: about 4350 miles/7000km. Time required: at least 4 weeks.
Boston – Cape Cod – New York (side trip to Niagara Falls) – Philadelphia – Baltimore – Washington – Pittsburgh – Cleveland – Detroit – Chicago – Milwaukee – Minneapolis/St Paul – Sioux Falls – Badlands National Park (side trip to Pine Ridge Indian Reservation, with Wounded Knee) – Rapid City – Mount Rushmore National Monument – Black Hills (side trip to Devil's Tower) – Buffalo, Wyoming – Bighorn Mountains – Cody – Yellowstone National Park – Grand Teton National Park – Idaho Falls – Butte – Waterton-Glacier National Park (Skyway to the Sun) – Spokane – Seattle.

Northern Route
Boston to Seattle

Distance: about 3400 miles/5500km. Time required: at least 4 weeks.
Washington – Allegheny Mountains (Spruce Knob) – Charleston, West Virginia – Lexington, Kentucky (side trip to Cincinnati) – Louisville – St Louis – Kansas City – Denver – Rocky Mountain National Park – Cheyenne – Laramie – Medicine Bow Mountains – Rock Springs – Flaming Gorge National Recreation Area – Dinosaur National Monument – Uintah Mountains – Salt Lake City – Great Basin – Reno – Carson City – Lake Tahoe – Sacramento – Oakland – San Francisco.

Middle Route
Washington to
San Francisco

Distance: about 3400 miles/5500km. Time required: at least 3 weeks.
Miami – Miami Beach (side trip to Florida Keys, with Key West) – Everglades National Park – Naples – Fort Myers (side trip to Sanibel/Captiva) – Sarasota – Bradenton – Sunshine Skyway – St Petersburg (side trip to Tampa and Orlando, with Walt Disney World) – Pinellas Suncoast – Tallahassee – Panama City – Gulf Islands National Seashore – Pensacola – Mobile – Biloxi – New Orleans – Baton Rouge – Lafayette – Houston (side trip to Galveston and Texas Gulf Coast) – San Antonio – El Paso (side trip to El Paso National Monument) – Tucson – Phoenix (side trip to Montezuma Castle) – Blythe (side trip to Colorado River and Lake Havasu) – Joshua Tree National Monument – Palm Springs – San Bernardino – Los Angeles.

Southern Route
Miami to
Los Angeles

East Coast / West Coast

Distance. about 2100 miles/3400km. Time required: at least 14 days.
Boston – Cape Cod – New York (side trip to valley of Hudson River and Niagara Falls) – Philadelphia (side trip to Atlantic City) – Baltimore – Washington – Norfolk – Outer Banks, Cape Hatteras – Wilmington – Myrtle Beach – Charleston – Savannah (side trip to Hilton Head Island) – Amelia Island – Jacksonville – St Augustine – Daytona Beach – Cape Canaveral (Kennedy

Atlantic Coast
Boston to
Key West

Dream Roads of the USA

Space Center; side trip to Orlando and Walt Disney World) – Palm Beach – Fort Lauderdale – Miami/Miami Beach – Florida City (side trip to Everglades National Park) – Key West.

Pacific Coast
Seattle to
San Diego

Distance: about 1600 miles/2600km. Time required: at least 14 days.
Seattle to – (side trip to Olympic National Park and Mount Rainier National Park) – Portland (possible side trip to Mount St Helens) – Salem – Eugene – Oregon Dunes National Recreation Area – Crescent City – Redwood National Park – Eureka – Point Reyes National Seashore – San Francisco – Monterey – Big Sur – San Luis Obispo – Santa Barbara – Malibu – Santa Monica – Los Angeles (with Hollywood, Beverly Hills and Anaheim/Disneyland) – Huntington Beach – San Clemente – San Diego (side trip to Tijuana in Mexico).

Special Interest Tours

New England

Round trip: about 2300 miles/3700km. Time required: at least 14 days.
New York – Philadelphia – Baltimore – Washington – Williamsburg – Richmond – Charlottesville – Shenandoah National Park – Gettysburg – Pennsylvania Dutch Country – Niagara Falls – Rochester – Syracuse – Albany – Boston – Cape Cod – New York.

**The Historic
East and
Old South**
Boston to
New Orleans

Distance: about 2000 miles/3200km. Time required: at least 14 days.
Boston – Cape Cod – Philadelphia (side trip to Amish Country) – Baltimore – Washington (side trip to Gettysburg) – Williamsburg – Durham – Cherokee Indian Reservation – Great Smoky Mountains – Knoxville – Nashville – Memphis – Natchez – Vicksburg – New Orleans.

The South-East
Atlanta to
Miami

Distance: about 2000 miles/3200km. Time required: at least 14 days.
Atlanta – Birmingham – Tuscaloosa – Jackson – Vicksburg – Natchez – Baton Rouge – Lafayette – New Orleans – Biloxi – Mobile – Tallahassee – Wakulla Springs – St Augustine – Orlando – Tampa – Naples – Everglades National Park – Miami (side trip to Key West).

**Florida Sunshine
Circle**

Round trip: about 1100 miles/1800km. Time required: at least 7 days.
Miami – Miami Beach – Fort Lauderdale – Palm Beach – Space Coast (with Cape Canaveral, Kennedy Space Center and Cape Canaveral National Seashore; side trip to Daytona Beach and St Augustine) – Orlando (side trip to Walt Disney World) – Ocala National Forest – Crystal River – Weeki Wachee Spring – Pinellas Suncoast – Tampa – Sarasota – Venice – Fort Myers (side trip to Sanibel/Captiva) – Naples – Port Everglades – Everglades National Park – Florida City (side trip to Florida Keys, with Key West) – Miami.

Land of Dixie
Savannah to
Dallas

Distance: about 2200 miles/3500km. Time required: at least 14 days.
Savannah – Charleston – Atlanta – Chattanooga – Nashville – Memphis – Natchez – New Orleans – Baton Rouge – Houston (side trip to Galveston and Texas Gulf Coast National Recreation Area) – San Antonio – Austin – Dallas.

Rose of Texas
Texas-Oklahoma-
New Mexico

Round trip: about 2500 miles/4000km. Time required: 14 days.
Dallas – Oklahoma City – Amarillo – Las Vegas – Santa Fe – Albuquerque – White Sands National Monument – El Paso – Guadalupe Mountains National Park – Carlsbad Caverns – Pecos – Balmorhea – Big Bend National Park – Fort Stockton – Fort Lancaster National Historic Site – San Antonio – Corpus Christi (side trip to Padre Island National Seashore) – Houston – Dallas.

Rocky Mountains

Round trip: about 2400 miles/3900km. Time required: at least 14 days.
Denver – Idaho Springs – Mount Evans – Rocky Mountain National Park – North Platte River – Medicine Bow Peak – Laramie – Laramie Mountains –

Dream Roads of the USA

Casper – Wind River Indian Reservation – Thermopolis – Cody – Yellowstone National Park – Grand Teton National Park – Idaho Falls – Wasatch Range – Salt Lake City – Provo – Price – Green River – Capitol Reef National Park – Glen Canyon National Recreation Area – Canyonlands National Park – Arches National Park – Grand Junction – Black Canyon of the Gunnison – Aspen – Mount Elbert – Florissant Beds National Monument – Colorado Springs (side trip to Pikes Peak) – Denver.

Round trip: about 2300 miles/3700km. Time required: at least 3 weeks. **Canyons and** Denver – Colorado Springs – Black Canyon of the Gunnison – Silverton – **Indian Country** Mesa Verde National Park – Durango – Santa Fe (side trip to Taos) – Albuquerque – Window Rock – Canyon de Chelly – Kayenta – Monument Valley – Navajo Indian Reservation – Grand Canyon National Park – Sedona (Montezuma Castle) – Phoenix/Scottsdale (side trip to Tucson, Tombstone and Yuma) – Las Vegas – Zion National Park – Bryce Canyon National Park – Capitol Reef National Park – Moab – Grand Junction – Vail – Denver.

Round trip: about 2300 miles/3700km. Time required: at least 2½ weeks. **Pacific Coast and** Los Angeles – Anaheim (Disneyland) – San Diego – Palm Springs – Phoenix **Canyon Country** (side trip to Tucson and Tombstone) – Montezuma Castle – Flagstaff – Grand Canyon National Park – Monument Valley – Navajo Indian Reservation – Lake Powell – Page – Bryce Canyon National Park – Zion National Park – Las Vegas – Death Valley – Mono Lake – Yosemite National Park – Lake Tahoe – San Francisco – Monterey – San Luis Obispo – Santa Barbara – Los Angeles.

Round trip: about 3800 miles/6100km. Time required: at least 4 weeks. **Western** San Francisco – Sacramento (side trip to Lake Tahoe) – Lassen Volcanic **Highlights** National Park – Mount Shasta – Lava Beds National Monument – Crater Lake National Park – Bend – Portland – Mount Rainier National Park – Seattle (side trip to Olympic National Park) – North Cascades National Park – Spokane – Kalispell – Waterton-Glacier National Park (Skyway to the Sun) – Great Falls – Butte – Bozeman – Yellowstone National Park – Grand Teton National Park – Jackson – Salt Lake City – Bryce Canyon National Park – Zion National Park – Grand Canyon National Park – Lake Mead National Recreation Area – Las Vegas – Death Valley – Mono Lake – Yosemite National Park – San Francisco.

Other Scenic Routes

Arkansas Highway 7 runs through the magnificent scenery of the Ouachita **Arkansas** Mountains west of Little Rock and the cave country on the Buffalo River, **Highway 7** near the boundary with Missouri. It begins in Diamond City, on Bull Shoals Lake, in the north, and ends in the little artists' town of El Dorado in the south.

From Portland there is an attractive trip to the wild and romantic valleys **Columbia River** which the Columbia River has carved through the Cascade Range and the **and Gorge,** Coast Range. Particularly impressive is the gorge with its tumbling white **Oregon** water between Mount St Helens in the north and Mount Hood (11,240ft/3426m) to the south.

From the little town of Twin Falls on I 84 a very rewarding excursion can be **Craters of the** made – first north-eastward to the Craters of the Moon, an extraordinary **Moon/Salmon** lunar landscape created by volcanic activity and erosion; then through the **River/** Lost River Range into the valley of the Salmon River. In the Sawtooth **Sawtooth,** region are two gold-mining ghost towns, Bonanza and Custer. Farther **Idaho** south are the two well-known winter sports resorts of Ketchum and Sun Valley and the Shoshone ice cave.

Through the United States by Rail

Finger Lakes,
New York State

There is very attractive country round the Finger Lakes, in a landscape created in the last ice age. It is particularly fine south of Seneca Falls (Seneca Lake, Cayuga Lake and Watkins Glen State Parks, Montour Falls, Ithaca, Buttermilk Falls).

Lake Michigan
Circle

From Chicago the route runs north along the western shores of the lake to Milwaukee and on to Sturgeon Bay. From there the narrow peninsula to the north, with its beautiful State Parks, can be explored. The route then continues up the west side of Lake Michigan to Escanaba and Lake Superior; then east to the great locks at Sault Ste Marie, on the Canadian frontier. A few miles to the south the road crosses the narrow channel between Lake Michigan and Lake Huron. The north-eastern shore of Lake Michigan, with its little offshore islands, is particularly beautiful. The Sleeping Bear Dunes are now a nature reserve, Traverse City is widely famed for its cherries. Farther south are the little towns of Holland and Saugatuck, from which a short excursion can be made to Grand Rapids. At the southern tip of the lake, near Michigan City, is the Indiana Dunes National Lakeshore.

Oregon Trail
Nebraska/Wyoming

A very interesting and beautiful part of the Oregon Trail is the prairie region traversed by the North Platte River, in the border area between the states of Wyoming and Nebraska. The imposing rock formations of Chimney Rock (near Bridgeport) and Scotts Bluff were prominent landmarks for settlers moving west in the 19th century. Along the trail there are many places scheduled as historic monuments. The area round Crescent Lake is one of the largest resting places for migrant birds in North America.

Ozark Mountains
Arkansas/Missouri

In the border region between the states of Arkansas and Missouri is a particularly beautiful part of the Ozark Mountains centred on Table Rock Lake and Beaver Lake. In this area, with numerous springs and caves, there are a number of State Parks and two National Forests. A good base for excursions is the town of Eureka Springs.

Vermont
Highway 100

Vermont's Highway 100 runs through the beautiful upland scenery of Green Mountain National Forest, which lies between the valley of the Connecticut River and the border with New York State.

Through the United States by Rail

The section on rail travel in the Practical Information part of this guide shows the main railroad lines in the United States and lists the most important express trains. It also lists a selection of the best known old-time railroads.

By Steamboat on Old Man River

River cruises

A very special holiday experience is a trip on one of the old-style paddle steamers which run cruises on the Mississippi and the Ohio River and its tributaries the Tennessee and Cumberland Rivers. The steamers operate on three stretches of the Mississippi: from Minneapolis/St Paul to St Louis, from St Louis to Memphis, Tennessee, and from Memphis to New Orleans. On the Ohio River cruises start from Pittsburgh, Cincinnati and Louisville, Kentucky. Other ports of call are Nashville on the Cumberland River and Chattanooga on the Tennessee River. See Practical Information, Cruises.

Mississippi
The Old South

From New Orleans the boat sails upstream through the Old South, the region once dominated by the plantation economy, passing handsome old mansions and estates (e.g. Nottoway Plantation of 1857, once owned by

By Steamboat on Old Man River

the sugar baron John Hampden Randolph), and comes to Baton Rouge, capital of the state of Louisiana, and St Francisville, with the extravagantly beautiful Rosedown Plantation (1835), once the home of Martha and Daniel Turnbull. The next port of call is Natchez, with its magnificent antebellum (pre-Civil-War) buildings. Farther upstream is Vicksburg, the "Gibraltar of the Old South", which was the scene of bloody fighting in the Civil War. Then by way of the port of Helena to Memphis, the legendary cotton-growing centre, which has associations with W. C. Handy, father of the blues, and Elvis Presley.

The section of the river between Memphis and St Louis is known as the "crossroads of America". In this area the Mississippi is joined by its most important tributaries, the Missouri and the Ohio, major north–south and east–west roads and railroads intersect and the most important economic and cultural regions of the United States meet.

Crossroads of America

From Memphis the boat continues upstream, negotiating the great New Madrid Bend, and comes to New Madrid, Missouri, which was shaken in 1811 by the most violent earthquake so far recorded in the United States. It was also the scene of fighting in the Civil War. Farther north the Mississippi is joined by the Ohio River, which drains large territories in the Middle West and the Appalachians. For several miles arms of the two rivers, differing in the colour of their water, run parallel to one another. The boat passes the little towns of Cairo and Cape Girardeau, with the very interesting River Heritage Museum. Then come Chester, Illinois, with its buildings recalling the French colonial period, and Ste Genevieve, the oldest French base in this area, founded in the mid 18th century, where the townscape is still dominated by French-style buildings. This section of the river ends at St Louis, Missouri, "Gateway of the West", with the world-famed Gateway Arch. A few miles above the city the Missouri, bringing an abundant flow of water from the prairies and the Rockies, flows into the Mississippi.

The region between St Louis in the south and Minneapolis/St Paul in the north is known as "America's Heartland". This section of the Mississippi, formerly difficult to navigate on account of its rapids and its wide meanders, has been tamed by the construction of more than two dozen lock systems and now offers a comfortable journey through "God's own country" with its carefully tended farmland, large orchards, great expanses of arable land and ancient riverine woodland.

America's Heartland

In the summer of 1993 this area was devastated by one of the most catastrophic floods in living memory. The flooding was attributed to global climatic changes on the one hand and to the measures taken to regulate the flow of the river on the other. The Mississippi–Missouri river system has now been canalised, straightened and enclosed by protective works over long stretches, and farming and settlement have ventured far into the former flood plain. The great masses of water resulting from heavy falls of rain in the prairies and the Rockies now surge unhindered down the straight reaches of the river and, instead of dispersing in a maze of meanders, dead arms and subsidiary arms, pile up against locks and bridges, seeking new ways through: hence the flooding.

From St Louis the journey continues past the junction with the Missouri to the small town of Hannibal, Missouri, where Samuel Clemens, who later, as Mark Twain, was to introduce the Mississippi into world literature, spent his early years. Farther upstream is the picturesque little town of Burlington. The boat sails past a number of old ports from which the early settlers shipped minerals, timber and agricultural produce and comes to Dubuque, Iowa, a little town founded in 1788 where lead was formerly mined. Beyond this is Prairie du Chien, Wisconsin, an old fur-trading town where the Sioux, Winnebago and Fox Indians exchanged their furs for firearms, brandy and a variety of trinkets. Another interesting place is Winona, Wisconsin, set-

By Steamboat on Old Man River

tled in the 1860s by large numbers of immigrants from Germany, Poland and Ireland, which developed into the fourth largest grain market in the United States, with more than a dozen large mills. 35 miles farther upstream is Wabasha, Minnesota, a picturesque little town from which large quantities of timber were formerly shipped. The cruise on the Mississippi ends at Minneapolis/St Paul, a very busy double city with an active cultural life.

Ohio River

The second finest river cruise in the United States runs down the Ohio River from Pittsburgh through country of great scenic beauty and historic interest. At the Pittsburgh Golden Triangle the Allegheny River and the Monongahela River join to form the Ohio. Here the first steamboat was launched in 1811. From Pittsburgh the boat sails south-west down the river to Wellsburg, West Virginia, a port over 200 years old which formerly shipped mainly grain and whiskey; it has preserved a number of handsome 19th century buildings. At Parkersburg, also in West Virginia, is Blennerhasset Island, with a magnificent old mansion. At Marietta, the oldest European settlement in the state of Ohio, is the Steamboat and Ohio River Museum, housed in an old steamboat, the "W. P. Snyder Jr". Then comes Portsmouth, Ohio, chief town of the Bonneyfiddle Country, which is famed as the home of the legendary cowboy Roy Rogers. The gateway to the Bluegrass Country is Maysville, Kentucky, where the old Natchez Trace crosses the Ohio River.

In the heyday of the steamboats Cincinnati, Ohio, was a boom town, in which over 1000 buildings were erected in the year 1846 alone. Now a very modern industrial city, in the past it was derisively called Porkopolis because it had for many years one of the largest stock markets (mainly pigs) in the United States; to Longfellow, on the other hand, it was "queen among the cities of the West". The next place is Madison, Indiana, which has preserved numbers of trim 19th century buildings. Then comes Louisville, Kentucky, which claims to be the "horse-racing capital of the world". Here every year in spring is held the famous Kentucky Derby, preceded by a 14 mile race on the river between two aged paddle steamers, the "Delta Queen" and the "Belle of Louisville". Farther downstream is the little town of Henderson, Kentucky, founded in 1779, with a carefully tended park. A few miles beyond this is the Cave in Rock, a cavern scooped out by the river from which is the late 18th century bandits and robbers lay in wait for passing ships. The notorious Samuel Mason invited the crews of ships into his House of Entertainment, where they were robbed of all their possessions. Just below the junction with the Tennessee River is Paducah, founded by white settlers in 1821 and named after an Indian chief, where during the Civil War 42,000 Union troops embarked on 173 steamboats and twelve gunboats and sailed for Shiloh on the Tennessee River (see below).

Tennessee River/ Cumberland River

From Paducah, on the Ohio River, boats sail up the Tennessee River into Kentucky Lake (formed by a dam on the Tennessee) and Lake Barkley (on the Cumberland River). The first place of interest is Dover, Tennessee, where Union forces won their first considerable victory in the Civil War. The boat then continues up the Cumberland River to Nashville, Tennessee, world-famed as the home of country and western music. From Nashville it returns to Kentucky Lake and sails up the Tennessee River to Shiloh, scene of a battle on April 6th 1862 between General Grant's Northern forces and a Southern army led by Johnston and Beauregard. The next place up river is Florence, Alabama, a little town founded in 1818 where slavery lingered on for many years; in more recent times it has been famed as the birthplace of W. C. Handy, "father of the blues". Farther upstream, to the east, is Decatur, Alabama, built round two old settlements (Rhodes Ferry or Decatur and Albany) which rank among the finest ensembles of Victorian buildings in the United States. Near the point where the states of Alabama, Georgia and

By Steamboat on Old Man River

Tennessee meet the boat sails through Guntersville Lake and comes to the railway town of Chattanooga, Tennessee. In the time of the Cherokee Indians this was already a place of some consequence, which was reconnoitred by the Spanish conquistador Hernando de Soto in 1540.

The "Delta Queen" now (since 1994) sails up the Arkansas River from its junction with the Mississippi to Little Rock.

Arkansas River

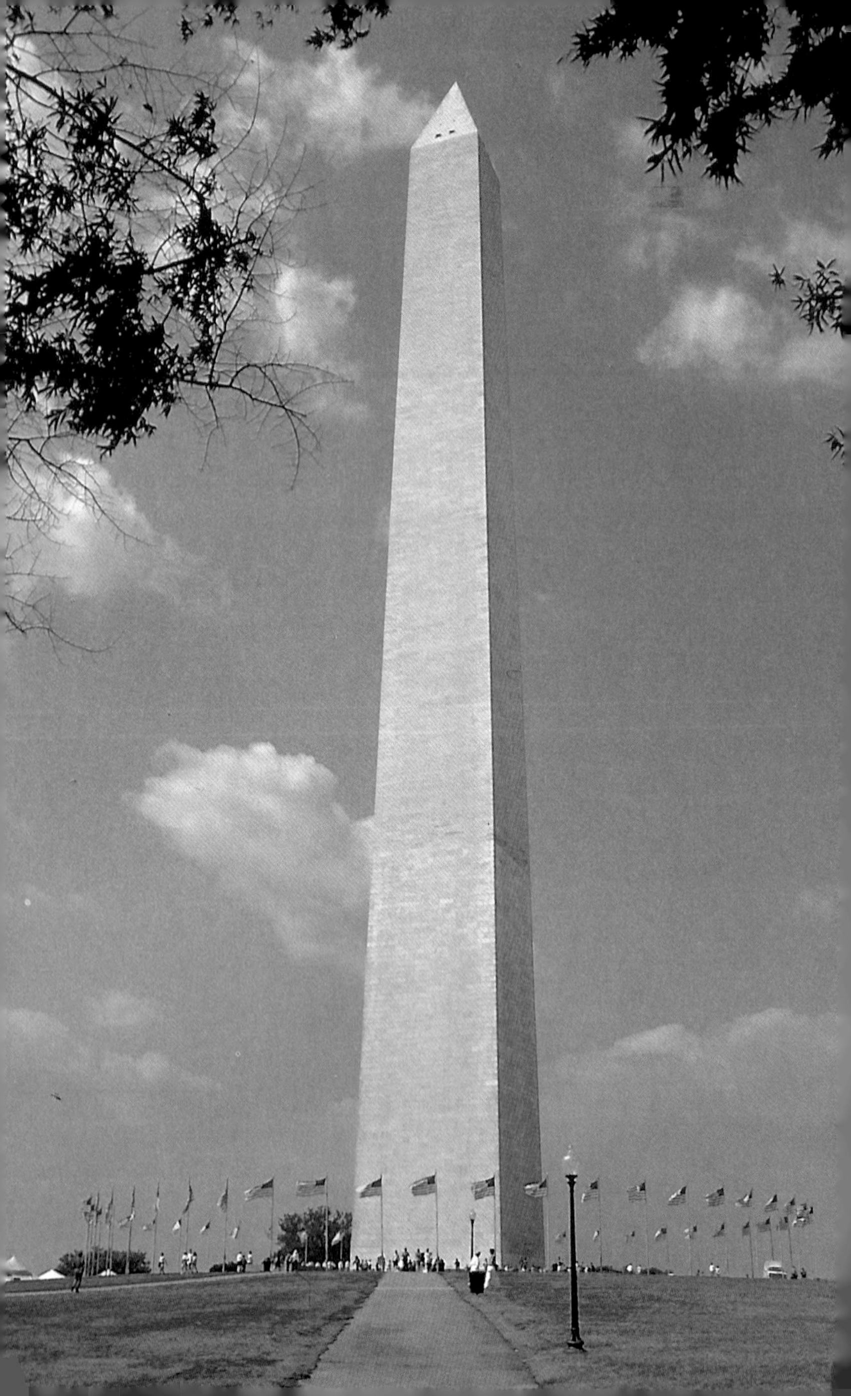

Sights from A to Z

Within the compass of this guide it is possible to give only a selection of the innumerable places of interest and scenic beauty in the vast expanses of the United States.

N.B.

Alabama (State; AL)

P–T 37–41

Area:
 51,610sq.miles/133,667sq.km
Population: 4.09 million
Capital: Montgomery
Popular names: Heart of Dixie, Camellia State

The state of Alabama (from the Choctaw word *alibamu*, "clearing of the bush") lies in the south-eastern United States, extending into three great natural regions. In the north and east the landscape is patterned by the southern outliers of the Appalachians and part of the Cumberland and Piedmont Plateaux. The north-west of the state is occupied by the North-West Plateau in the central lowlands. The greater part of the state, to the south, takes in part of the Gulf Coast plain, descending in terraces from the Piedmont Plateau, with the fertile Black Belt. On both sides of the Alabama River estuary and Mobile Bay Alabama reaches down to the Gulf of Mexico. The climate is warm and humid, with high summer temperatures and mild winters. The coast is exposed to the danger of hurricanes. Much of the state is covered by forest (particularly oak, hickory and pine).

Situation and topography

The area was explored by the Spanish at the beginning of the 16th century. In 1702 French immigrants, disregarding British claims, settled the area round the Mobile River, but in 1763 France was compelled to cede the territory to Britain. Twenty years later the southern part of the area fell to Spain. In 1817 Alabama was incorporated as a US territory and only two years later, in 1819, became the 22nd state of the Union. For many years cotton-growing was a major element in the economy. Racial segregation in education was abolished only in 1963.

History

Alabama lies in the Cotton Belt, but in recent decades cotton-growing has considerably declined, and maize, soya beans and peanuts are now important crops. Most of the abandoned cotton fields have now been given over to extensive cattle-rearing. The forested southern part of the state supplies firewood and woodpulp for papermaking. The iron and coal mined in the southern Appalachians led to the development of Birmingham's iron and steel industry. Other important contributions to the state's economy are made by the chemical, textile and foodstuffs industries. Hydroelectric power stations have been established on the Tennessee and Alabama Rivers and some of their tributaries. There is lively inland shipping traffic on the dense network of rivers and waterways. Mobile has one of the largest and most important ports on the Gulf Coast. The beautiful bathing beaches on the Gulf of Mexico are attracting increasing numbers of holidaymakers.

Economy

◀ *The Washington Memorial, Washington, DC*

Alaska

Places of Interest in Alabama

Birmingham	The industrial city of Birmingham (pop. 266,000; iron and steel) has three museums: the Museum of Art (including Renaissance art), the Red Mountain Museum and the Southern Museum of Flight. On Red Mountain is a statue of the god Vulcan (by G. Moretti, 1904). There is a fine antebellum (pre-Civil-War) mansion, Arlington (1842; period furniture). South-east of Birmingham is an interesting karstic region with over a thousand sinkholes. In this area too is the Oak Mountain State Park. South-west of the city is Tannehill Historic State Park, with a 19th century village.
Dauphin Island	Dauphin Island, now a bird sanctuary, lies at the south-west entrance to Mobile Bay. The island, which has white sandy beaches, was occupied by French settlers in the early 18th century. Its main sight is Fort Gaines, which played a part in the Civil War.
Huntsville	The main attraction in Huntsville (pop. 160,000), which has preserved some attractive old quarters, is the US Space and Rocket Center, where visitors can try out flight simulators and see the newest spacecraft.
Mobile	Mobile (pop. 197,000), one of the more important ports and industrial towns on the Gulf of Mexico, lies in a bay in south-western Alabama which reaches over 25 miles/40km inland. The town was founded by French immigrants at the beginning of the 18th century. Mardi Gras (Carnival) is still a lively annual event. A number of well preserved antebellum houses (e.g. Oakleigh Mansion, De Tonti Square) and beautiful gardens planted with azaleas give the town its special atmosphere. An interesting modern building is the new Civic Center. Other features of interest are the Museum of the South, the Museum of the City of Mobile, the Cathedral (1835) and an old French fort (rebuilt), Fort Condé. In Battleship Memorial Park are the destroyer "Alabama" and the submarine "Drum", which fought in the Second World War and the Korean War. 20 miles/32km south of Mobile are the beautiful Bellingrath Gardens, with thousands of azaleas.
Montgomery	Montgomery (pop. 187,000), capital of Alabama, lies in the centre of the state on the east bank of the Alabama River. Old Alabama Town with its 19th century houses preserves something of the atmosphere of old Montgomery, once an important cotton market. Other features of interest are the Capitol and the White House, the oldest in the Confederate states. On the eastern outskirts of the town are the Museum of Fine Arts and the renowned Alabama Shakespeare Festival Theater. 43 miles/70km east of Montgomery is Tuskegee University, which originated as a college for the education of blacks founded by the former negro slave Booker T. Washington (see Famous People) in 1881.
Tuscaloosa	Tuscaloosa (pop. 78,000), former capital of Alabama and seat of the University of Alabama (founded 1831), lies on the Black Warrior River in the west of the state. It preserves a number of historic old houses. 16 miles/26km south of the town is the Mound State Monument, a prehistoric Indian cult centre or settlement site.
Vance	In the little town of Vance, near Tuscaloosa, Mercedes-Benz are in process of building an automobile assembly plant.

Alaska (State; AK)   **Inset in map of USA**

Area: 591 million sq.miles/1531 million sq.km
Population: 552,000
Capital: Juneau
Popular name: Last Frontier

Alaska

Alaska, the largest and most northerly of the states of the Union, lies in the extreme north-west of the North American sub-continent, separated from the Asiatic land mass by the Bering Strait and Bering Sea. Its western and southern coasts are washed by the north-eastern Pacific and its north coast lies on the ice-cold Arctic Ocean. Just under 20% of its population are Inuits (Eskimos), Aleuts and Indians. The name Alaska means "great land" in the language of the Aleuts. Alaska is separated from the main United States by western Canada. The southern tip of the state, the Panhandle, reaches down to latitude 54°40' north, with numerous fjords and islands. The most northerly point in the United States is Cape Barrow on the Arctic Ocean. Some two-thirds of the area of Alaska is under permafrost, with the soil frozen to depths of up to 1300ft/400m.

Situation and topography

Alaska is made up of three main regions: a narrow southern coastal strip, with the Panhandle to the south-east and the Aleutians to the south-west; the interior plains and tablelands; and the Arctic North.

Regions of Alaska

The topography of south-eastern Alaska is dominated by the Coast Mountains, a range which suffered folding at a geologically recent period and is slashed by numerous tectonic faults. Rising to 8200ft/2500m, it cuts off the Panhandle from Canada. Between Glacier Bay in the east and the Kenai Peninsula in the south numerous glaciers calve into the sea.

Coast Mountains

The Gulf of Alaska in enclosed by the Chugach Mountains (Mount Marcus Baker, 13,176ft/4016m) and the Kenai Mountains, which extend into the Kodiak Peninsula. Other ranges of mountains striking farther inland reach considerable heights: the St Elias Mountains (Mount Logan, 19,555ft/5960m), the Wrangell Mountains (Mount Blackburn, 16,523ft/5036m) and the mighty arc of the Alaska Range, with Mount McKinley (20,320ft/6193m), the highest peak in the whole United States. These mountains and the coastal region with its deep bays and fjords all show very typical examples of the effects of glaciation (U-shaped valleys, morainic ridges, glacial drift, *roches moutonnées*, etc.).

Chugach Mountains/ Kenai Mountains/ St Elias Mountains/ Wrangell Mountains/ Alaska Range

The whole of the south-west coast of Alaska forms part of the "Ring of Fire", the very active circum-Pacific volcanic and earthquake zone. This has been demonstrated by recent volcanic activity on Mount Redoubt and in the Katmai National Park.

Ring of Fire

The interior tablelands of Alaska, with their extensive plateaux and relatively low hills, are traversed by the 2000 mile/3200km long Yukon River, which rises in the Yukon Territory in Canada and flows into the Bering Sea in a wide delta.

Interior tablelands/ Yukon River

The interior tablelands are bounded on the north by the 600 mile/1000km long Brooks Range, which rises from 4900ft/1500m in the west to 9239ft/2816m in Mount Michelson in the east.

Brooks Range

The coastal mountains have very high precipitations. The Yukon Basin, in the lee of the mountains, has a very cold and dry continental climate: an extreme temperature of −65°F/−54°C has been recorded at Fort Yukon. The coasts on the Arctic Ocean are ice-bound almost all year round. The Bering Strait is ice-free from June to October. Some two-fifths of Alaska is forest-covered, with hemlock, Sitka spruce, birch and willow most strongly represented. The Arctic tree-line is approximately on the 68th parallel. Beyond

Climate and vegetation

141

Alaska

this and at higher altitudes the vegetation cover is that of the treeless tundra, characterised by dwarf pine, various shrubs, lichens and mosses.

History
In 1741 Vitus Bering, a Dane in the Russian service, discovered the south coast of Alaska, then thinly peopled by Eskimos, Aleuts and Indians. Subsequently Spanish, British, Russian and American fur-traders made their way into the territory, then administered by Russia. From 1799 the Russian-American Company had a monopoly of the fur trade in Alaska. In 1867 Russia sold the territory to the United States for 7.2 million dollars, and 17 years later, in 1884, it was given its own civil administration and a constitution modelled on that of Oregon. The discovery of gold on the Yukon River in 1897 led to an increase in population; and later the discovery of other raw materials, notably the deposits of oil found on the north coast in 1968, increased the economic importance of Alaska. In 1912 it became an independent territory. During the Second World War it was of strategic importance (construction of the Alaska Highway; US military bases). In 1959 it became the 49th state of the Union.

Economy
The economic wealth of Alaska lies in its enormous reserves of raw materials (timber, coal, copper, platinum, silver, oil). The extraction of oil and natural gas (since 1968) on the Arctic Ocean plays a major part in the economy of the state. Fishing and fish-processing are also important sources of income. The timber industry is active mainly in the south-east of the territory. Agriculture, confined to small areas round Anchorage and Fairbanks, is in decline.

Features of Interest in Alaska

Alaska Highway
The 1510 mile/2430km long Alaska Highway runs from Dawson Creek in British Columbia (Canada) through the Yukon Territory to Fairbanks, in the centre of Alaska. It was built for military purposes in 1942, during the

Denali National Park

Alaska

Second World War, in the record time of only eight months, and since the end of the war has been the most important means of access by land to the Yukon Territory and southern Alaska. For most of the way it is asphalted (with a gravel surface only in Canada), but at certain times of year is in only moderately good condition. There are motels, shops and gas stations at intervals of 30–50 miles (50–80km).

From Dawson Creek the road runs north-west over the plain of the Peace River, passing Stone Mountain and Muncho Lake Provincial Park. Beyond Fort Nelson (about 310 miles/500km) it approaches the Rockies. The first place of any size in the Yukon Territory is Watson Lake, the "Gateway to the Yukon", with an information centre on the construction of the Highway and a famous collection of signposts. The route continues by way of Teslin, on the 800 mile/1300km long lake of that name, to Whitehorse (930 miles/1500km), capital of the Yukon Territory. Beyond Whitehorse the road heads for the St Elias Mountains. At the little township of Haines Junction is the entrance to Kluane National Park, a unique nature reserve with Canada's highest peak, Mount Logan (19,525ft/5951m). At Soldiers Summit (1060 miles/1707km) the Alaska Highway was officially opened on November 20th 1942. On the right of the road, some 37 miles/60km beyond Haines Junction, is the 46 mile/74km long Kluane Lake (campgrounds, good fishing). After 1240 miles/2000km the Highway comes to the Canadian–US frontier and moves from the Pacific into the Alaska time zone. On the final 310 miles/500km to Fairbanks it runs through the fertile Tana Valley. At Tok Junction (about 1320 miles/2120km) the Glen Highway branches off, running by way of Glacier Park, with the Matanuska Glacier, to Fairbanks (see below).

The port of Anchorage (pop. 250,000) lies at the head of Cook Inlet, surrounded by the Chugach Mountains. It is Alaska's largest town and its commercial and economic centre and its most important traffic hub (intercontinental air services; the world's largest seaplane base). Among features of interest are the Anchorage Museum of History and Art and Earthquake Park, which commemorates the devastating 1964 earthquake. Anchorage appeals to visitors as a good base for excursions by air or boat and for the scenic attractions of its immediate surroundings. Within easy reach of the town are Mount Alyeska Ski Resort, which offers skiing throughout the year, the magnificent Portage Glacier (50 miles/80km south-east) and the Kenai Peninsula (see below). Chugach National Forest and Chugach State Park offer unspoiled natural landscapes.

Anchorage

Point Barrow is the most northerly point in Alaska and in the United States, where even in summer the temperature seldom rises as high as 50°F/10°C. Here the Midnight Sun can be seen on 82 days in the year. The 3000 inhabitants of the Eskimo settlement of Barrow live by fishing and ivory-carving.

Barrow

In the northern part of the Alaska Range is the Denali National Park (open mid May to mid September), the second largest National Park in the United States, with an area of 9375sq.miles/24,280sq.km – a region of depressions and wide river valleys, areas of tundra and high alpine ranges of mountains from which glaciers flow down. In the south-west of the park is majestic Mount McKinley (20,320ft/6194m), the highest mountain in the United States. This is the home of grizzly bears, wolves, reindeer, elk and other animals.

**Denali National Park

Fairbanks, Alaska's second largest town and the terminus of the Alaska Highway, developed around 1900 from a gold-diggers' camp. The University of Alaska Museum has a collection illustrating the history of the territory. In the Alaskaland leisure park are reconstructions of a gold-diggers' village and Eskimo and Indian settlements. In the Large Animal Research Station wild animals can be seen living in natural conditions.

Fairbanks

Alaska

There are paddle-steamer trips on the Chena and Tanana Rivers. The Midnight Sun is visible from September to April. Fairbanks is a good base for excursions (by air) to northern and eastern Alaska, for example to Fort Yukon, the largest Indian settlement in Alaska.

*Glacier Bay National Park

An impressive natural spectacle is to be seen at Glacier Bay, 60 miles/100km north-west of Juneau, an inlet between two promontories where sixteen glaciers reach down to the sea. There are cruises to the bay (day trips and longer trips) in the course of which whales are sometimes seen.

Juneau

Juneau, capital of Alaska, was originally a gold-diggers' settlement (founded in the 1880s) on Gold Creek. It lies in the most southerly part of the state on the Panhandle, a narrow tongue of land slashed by fjord-like inlets which is separated from the sea by a string of small islands. There is no road to Juneau, and it can be reached only by sea or air. Features of interest are the Alaska State Museum, the House of Judge Wickersham and the Russian Orthodox church (1894). Juneau is a good base from which to explore the scenic beauties of the Panhandle, either by sea or by air. Particularly worthwhile are the Admiralty Island National Monument, the Tongass National Forest and Glacier Bay National Park (see above).

*Kenai Peninsula

The Kenai Peninsula, south of Anchorage, is a popular excursion and holiday destination. The larger settlements on the peninsula – Homer, Seward and Kenai, the chief town, are easily accessible on Highway 1 or 9; and Seward, a fishing port, is also the terminus of the Alaska Railroad. Seward is an excellent base for excursions into Kenai Fjords National Park. With its glaciers and fjords, the scenery of this National Park, centred on the Harding Icefield, is reminiscent of the west coast of Norway; there is a motorable road to the Exit Glacier. Here bird-watchers will be able to observe many species of birds. Highway 1 ends in the fishing village of Homer, a popular resort for visitors with its comparatively mild climate and beautiful situation on Kachemak Bay (Pratt Museum, with exhibits illustrating the culture of the Eskimos, Aleuts and early Russian settlers; camping, fishing, boat trips).

Kodiak

Most of this island off the south-west coast of Alaska (boats from Homer and Seward on Kenai Peninsula) is now the Kodiak National Wildlife Refuge, established to protect the Kodiak bear and other rare animals. The waters round Kodiak are among the richest fishing grounds in Alaska. The town of Kodiak at the north-eastern tip of the peninsula, now an important fishing port, was occupied for over 6000 years by the indigenous Aleuts, until Russian fur-traders settled here in 1784 and made the town first capital of the Russian territory. Features of interest are the old Russian Orthodox church and a small museum on the history of the island.

Kotzebue

Just north of the Arctic Circle, at the north end of a narrow peninsula reaching out into Kotzebue Sound, is the old Eskimo village of Kotzebue (reached only by air from Nome or Anchorage), which is named after Otto von Kotzebue (1786–1946), a German living in the Baltic area. The pack ice in the bay does not usually break up until the first half of June. In the hinterland (reached only by air) are the Kobuk Valley National Park and the Cape Krusenstern National Monument (no accommodation available).

Nome

The port of Nome, situated some 500 miles/800km west of Fairbanks on the Seward Peninsula (Bering Sea), can be reached only by air. Founded by gold-diggers about 1900, during the gold rush, it is the economic and commercial centre of north-western Alaska; gold-panning is now only a show for tourists. Nome is the end-point of the 1049 mile/1688km Iditarod dog-sled race from Anchorage, lasting anything from two to four weeks, which is run annually in March. The Eskimo villages in the surrounding area can be visited either by air or by hired car.

The fishing port of Sitka on the west side of Baranoff Island in the Alexander Archipelago, founded by Alexander Baranoff in 1804, was once the chief town of Russian America. Features of interest are icons and vestments from the Orthodox church of St Michael (built 1844, burned down 1966) and the Sheldon Jackson Museum (artifacts, masks, craft products and clothing of Eskimos and Indians). In the Sitka National Historical Park are a display of material illustrating the culture of the original Indian tribes and the Russian settlers and the scene of the last battle (1804) between Russians and Tlingit Indians, commemorated by Indian totem poles.

Sitka

The old gold-diggers' town of Skagway lies in the Klondike Gold Rush National Historical Park. It can be reached either by road or by way of the Inside Passage, the shipping route which links the towns and settlements on the Panhandle with one another.

Skagway

The Wrangell-St Elias National Park is the largest and most magnificent of the National Parks of Alaska, with nine of the 16 highest peaks in the United States. This grandiose mountain region on the frontier with Canada contains numerous glaciers, lakes and mountain streams and is home to a rich variety of wild life. It is superb country for climbers, walkers and water sports enthusiasts.

*Wrangell-St Elias National Park

Albuquerque

O 19

State: New Mexico
Altitude: 5005ft/1525m
Population: 385,000

The city of Albuquerque lies on the Rio Grande, surrounded by the Sandia Hills. The climate is dry, with hot summers and cold winters. A quarter of the total population of New Mexico live in the city, on which Indians, Spaniards and Anglo-Americans have all left their mark. Albuquerque has long been an important commercial town and traffic hub. It is an important centre of research and development, with many institutes and laboratories (including nuclear research), as well as the University of New Mexico.

Situation and characteristics

The Spanish colonial settlement of Albuquerque, situated on the trade route between Santa Fe and Mexico City, was founded in 1706 and soon developed into a considerable town. The Stars and Stripes was hoisted over the town in 1846 by General Stephen Kearny when he established a military post here. A boost was given to the town when the railway reached it in 1880. A new town was established which soon outstripped and incorporated the old Spanish colonial settlement.

History

Sights in Albuquerque

The Old Town of Albuquerque is the picturesque core of the old Spanish colonial settlement. Dominating the Spanish-style Plaza is the church of San Felipe de Neri, built in 1706. Round the square, on which various craftsmen (not only Indians) offer their products for sale, are a range of shops, galleries, cafés, etc. Between April and October there are guided tours of the Old Town.

*Old Town/Rio Grande Boulevard

The New Mexico Museum of Natural History (1801 Mountain Road) offers a fascinating survey of the natural history of the American South-West from prehistoric times to the present day. Particularly impressive are a life-size model of a dinosaur, an artificial volcano, a reproduction of an Ice Age cave habitation and a "time machine". There is also a cinema in which spectacular nature films are shown.

*New Mexico Museum of Natural History

The Indian Pueblo Cultural Center (2401 12th Street NW) gives an informative picture of the history and culture of the Pueblo Indians. Visitors

*Indian Pueblo Cultural Center

Arches National Park

can watch as beautiful craft objects are produced by traditional techniques and can sample Indian cooking. At weekends there are performances of traditional Indian dances.

National Atomic Museum
The National Atomic Museum (Kirtland Air Force Base, Wyoming Boulevard, Building 20358; pass must be obtained from military police) illustrates the development of atomic weapons. There is also an exhibition on the development of alternative sources of energy.

University of New Mexico
The University of New Mexico (Central Avenue) is built in the style of an Indian pueblo. It contains three fine museums – the Geology Museum, the Meteorite Museum and the Maxwell Museum of Anthropology.

Surroundings of Albuquerque

*Indian Petroglyph Park
7 miles/11km north-west of the city is the Indian Petroglyph State Park, with symbols and drawings scratched in the rock by prehistoric Indians, the significance of which has not been established.

Arches National Park   L 16

State: Utah
Area: 120sq.miles/310sq.km
Established: 1929

Season
The Park is open throughout the year. The best time to visit it is from April to September.

Natural architecture in the Arches National Park

Arizona

Within the Park there is only a small campground near the Devil's Garden. There are motels in Moab.	Accommodation
Arches National Park lies at altitudes between 3900ft/1200m and 5600ft/1700m in the desert-like south-eastern part of Utah, through which flows the Colorado River. It is world-famed for its extraordinary rock formations – several hundred sandstone arches, some of them of gigantic size, mushroom-shaped rocks, high sandstone rock faces, pinnacles, battlements, buttresses and ridges – created mainly by the action of wind and weather. The reddish Entrada sandstone laid down some 150 million years ago was subjected to tectonic movements of the earth's crust and thereafter was exposed to severe chemical and physical erosion.	Situation and **topography
With luck visitors to the Park may encounter desert hares, deer, coyotes. red foxes and porcupines.	Animals
The 21 mile/38km long Scenic Drive takes visitors round the most impressive features in the National Park (nature reserve). From Moab Canyon it runs to the LaSal Mountains View Point, from which mountains rising to almost 13,000ft/4000m can be seen in the distance. Then follow the Courthouse Towers, a series of unusual rock formations (including the Three Gossips and the Tower of Babel). The road continues along the Great Wall and past the Petrified Dunes. At the Balanced Rock, which is almost 130ft/40m high, a road goes off on the right to the Windows Section with its rock arches (Cove Arch, Double Arch, etc.) and rock windows (North Window, South Window, etc.). Then down into Salt Valley, with a road branching off on the right to the Wolfe Ranch (once owned by a Civil War veteran) and the Delicate Arch View Point. From Salt Valley the road continues past Salt Valley Overlook, the Fiery Furnace Viewpoint and the Skyline Arch to end at the Devil's Garden car park.	Scenic Drive
In view of the very fragile desert vegetation there are only a few hiking routes in the National Park. Among them are the Devil's Garden Trail (2 miles/3.2km), on which there are eight rock arches, including the Landscape Arch, one of the largest of its kind, and the Delicate Arch Trail (1½ miles/2.5km), which starts from the Wolfe Ranch. The rock labyrinth known as the Fiery Furnace, in which it is easy to lose your way, should be entered only on a guided walk conducted by a park ranger. There is an attractive walk from the car park at Klondike Bluffs to the Tower Arch area on the north-western edge of the National Park.	Walking
To the west of the National Park is the Dead Horse State Park, with magnificent views of the northern part of the Canyonlands National Park and the junction of the Colorado River and Green River. From there it is worth taking a short trip into the Island in the Sky area of the park. At Moab is Castle Valley, with picturesque castle-like rock formations. Moab is also the starting-point of organised rafting trips on the Colorado River.	Surroundings

Arizona (State; AZ)   N–S 12–16

Area: 114,000sq.miles/
  295,260sq.km
Population: 3.75 million
Capital: Phoenix
Popular name: Grand Canyon
State

Arizona (from the Indian *arizo-nac*, "land of the little rivers") lies in the south-western United States, bounded on the south by

Situation and topography

Arizona

Mexico. It consists of two different geological and morphological regions within the intermontane zone of the Cordilleras. Northern Arizona forms part of the Colorado Plateau, with the Grand Canyon, hewn from the rock to depths of up to 6600ft/2000m. The plateau, traversed by innumerable faults and flexures, falls away to the south and west in a series of steep scarps. In this area are the highest mountains in the state, rising to 12,668ft/3861m in the San Francisco Peaks. In the south of Arizona is the Basin and Range Province, its north-eastern part reaching into the highlands of Mexico, its south-western part ending in the Gila Desert. As a result of the hot and very dry climate steppeland and desert predominate, accounting for some two-thirds of the state's area. Giant cactuses and yuccas are characteristic of its drought-loving vegetation. At higher altitudes, with a more humid climate, the hills are partly forest-covered.

History

Some areas in Arizona are among the longest-settled parts of North America. Archaeological evidence points to continuous human occupation for some 11,000 years. In the 16th century A.D. Spaniards began to move into Arizona from Mexico. Under the peace of Guadalupe Hidalgo at the end of the Mexican War (1846–48) Arizona passed to the United States (the Gadsden Purchase), and in 1912 it was admitted to the Union as the 48th state. Arizona is now the state with the highest proportion of Indians (mostly Apache, Navajo and Hopi) in its population.

Economy

A major element in Arizona's economy is cattle-rearing, but in the valleys of the Gila and Salt Rivers arable farming is made possible by irrigation. Huge artificial lakes formed by damming the rivers provide water throughout the year for lucrative crops of cotton, citrus fruits, winter vegetables and forage cereals. The mining of the state's large deposits of copper ore (roughly half total US output) and its processing make an important contribution to the economy. Other important minerals are molybdenum, gold, silver, zinc, lead and oil. Important industries in the secondary sector are metalworking and electronics (aircraft, rockets, etc.), foodstuffs and textiles. Tourism has also developed rapidly and become an important element in the state's economy, thanks to Arizona's magnificent scenery (e.g. the Grand Canyon), its pleasant climate and the numerous remains of old Indian cultures.

Places of Interest in Arizona

Flagstaff

The university town of Flagstaff (alt. 7028ft/2142m; pop. 46,000), within the Coconino National Forest, is a good base from which to visit the Grand Canyon and the Navajo Country (see entries). Features of interest in and around the town are the Pioneer Museum of the Arizona Historical Society, the Coconino Center for the Arts (art exhibition) and the Museum of Northern Arizona (3 miles/5km north-west of the town; crafts of the Navajo and Hopi Indians). On Mars Hill, to the west of the town, is the Lovell Observatory, from which the planet Pluto was discovered in 1930.

Walnut Canyon

16 miles/26km east of Flagstaff is the deep Walnut Canyon, with some 300 rock dwellings of the old Indian Sinagua culture (12th/13th c.; the name Sinagua in Spanish means "waterless"). Some 30 miles/48km farther east is the best preserved meteorite crater on earth, which has been used for the training of astronauts.

*Montezuma Castle

An hour's drive south of Flagstaff is Montezuma Castle, a dwelling of the Sinagua culture built into a recess in a sandstone cliff which rises to a height of 100ft/30m above Beaver Creek. The first whites who came here thought that this was an Aztec settlement. The dwelling has 20 rooms on five levels and could be entered only on ladders.

Globe

The old mining town of Globe (copper, silver) is a good place from which to visit the cave dwellings occupied by Salado Indians in the 13th and 14th centuries (Besh-Ba-Gowah, Tonto). 30 miles/48km north-west of the town

Arizona

Montezuma Castle, Arizona

is Theodore Roosevelt Lake, formed by a massive dam, which is much frequented by water sports enthusiasts.
An hour's drive north-east is the imposing Salt River Canyon.

Salt River Canyon

In the far west of Arizona, on the border with California, is Lake Havasu, a popular resort with water sports enthusiasts. Lake Havasu City (alt. 600ft/183m; pop. 25,000) was founded only in 1964. Its main attraction is the 1831 London Bridge which was bought in 1968 and re-erected here.

Lake Havasu City

In south-western Arizona, on the frontier with Mexico, is Organ Pipe National Monument, in which are three distinct desertic vegetation zones with some 30 different species of cactus, in particular the characteristic organ pipe cactus, up to 23ft/7m high, which blooms from May to July but because of the great heat during the day opens up its flowers only after sunset. The area can be explored on various roads and hiking trails.

*Organ Pipe National Monument

Prescott (alt. 5368ft/1636m; pop. 27,000), north-west of Phoenix (see entry) in the beautiful Prescott National Forest, has developed in recent years into a popular tourist centre. Its features of interest are Sharlot Hall (1864; historical museum), home of the first Governor of Arizona, the Smoki Museum (Indian crafts) and the Phippen Museum (art).
38 miles/61km south-west is the settlement of Arcosanti, designed by the Soleri firm of architects with careful concern for ecological considerations.

Prescott

Arcosanti

The Saguaro National Monument, part of the Sonora Desert, extends east and west of Tucson (see entry). The characteristic feature of this desert area, the lowest in North America, is the abundant and varied flora and fauna which flourish in spite of the great heat: the typical saguaro or candelabra cactuses, which are the tallest species in North America, birds like the Gila woodpecker and cactus wren which live on the cactuses, rattlesnakes, desert tortoises and the Gila monster (a large lizard).

*Saguaro National Monument

Arkansas

Arizona-Sonora Desert Museum
In the south-west of the park is the very interesting Arizona-Sonora Desert Museum, with more than 200 species of animals and 300 species of plants.

*Tombstone
In the south-eastern corner of Arizona is Tombstone (pop. 1200), the famous Wild West township of the silver boom. Many buildings of that period, including the printing office of the town's daily newspaper "Epitaph", the Bird Cage Theatre, the Crystal Palace Saloon, the Rose Tree Inn and the Court House, have been lovingly restored. The OK Corral, scene of the famous shoot-out in 1881 between the Earp and Clanton gangs, is also preserved.

Yuma
The town of Yuma (pop. 45,000) lies in the extreme south-west of Arizona, in a region of great heat which has been made fertile by irrigation. It preserves a number of buildings, including an adobe-built prison and the US Army Quartermaster Depot, which recall the troubled history of earlier days.

Other sights in Arizona
Canyon de Chelly (see Navajo Country), Grand Canyon, Petrified Forest National Park, Phoenix (see entries), Scottsdale (see Phoenix), Tucson (see entry).

Arkansas (State; AR) N–Q 31–36

Area:
    53,187sq.miles/137,754sq.km
Population: 2.38 million
Capital: Little Rock
Popular names: Land of
    Opportunity, Natural State

Situation and topography
The state of Arkansas, in the southern USA, is divided into two by the Arkansas River, which flows from north-west to south-east to join the Mississippi. In the north of the state the Boston Mountains, part of the Ozark Plateau, rise to heights of up to 2900ft/884m; in the south are the Ouachita Mountains (2950ft/899m). To the south the flood plain of the Mississippi merges almost imperceptibly into the Gulf Coast plain. Roughly half the state is forest-covered. The climate is marked by mild winters, warm summers and precipitations which are distributed evenly over the year.

History
The first European to pass through the region, then occupied by the indigenous Indian inhabitants, was the Spanish explorer Hernando de Soto, who was looking for the legendary Well of Eternal Youth (1541). In the 17th century the territory was occupied by France and in 1731 became part of Louisiana. In 1763 it passed to Spain but was recovered by France in 1799. Under the Louisiana Purchase it was acquired by the United States for 15 million dollars. On June 15th 1836 it became the 25th state of the Union.

Economy
Arkansas lies in the climatically favoured Sun Belt. Its agriculture is mainly devoted to the growing of soya beans, rice and fruit and to cattle rearing and poultry farming. Its industry is mainly concerned with the processing of local produce (e.g. attar of roses for use in the manufacture of perfume) and timber.
Arkansas also has substantial mineral resources, including oil, natural gas, coal, manganese and diamonds. It also produces some 95% of the total American output of bauxite. Tourism is still relatively little developed.

Arkansas

Places of Interest in Arkansas

In south-eastern Arkansas is the Arkansas Post National Memorial, commemorating the first permanent French settlement, established in 1686.	Arkansas Post
In northern Arkansas, round the Buffalo River, is a popular and very beautiful recreation area which in summer attracts large numbers of canoeists.	*Buffalo River
In south-western Arkansas, a few minutes' drive from Murfreesboro, is the Crater of Diamonds State Park, the only source of natural diamonds in the United States which is open to the public.	Crater of Diamonds
Within the area of Eureka Springs, a tourist resort in the extreme north-west of Arkansas, there are more than sixty springs. With its attractive old Victorian buildings, an artists' colony, two small museums, a varied programme of entertainments (including a Passion Play) and the old-time Eureka Springs and North Arkansas Railway, it draws visitors throughout the year. To the east of the town is the interesting Onyx Cave; to the west is the Blue Spring, one of the most abundant springs in the Ozark Mountains.	Eureka Springs
In the north-western corner of Arkansas is the town of Fayetteville (pop. 38,000), seat of the University of Arkansas. Features of interest are the Fine Arts Center (with a collection of Indian crafts) and the Walton Art Center (modern art). South of the town is the picturesque Devil's Den State Park.	Fayetteville
The town of Fort Smith, situated on a bend in the Arkansas River on the border with Oklahoma, grew out of a fort established in 1817 to protect the westward trek of settlers. During the Californian gold rush it became the haunt of gun-happy bandits. The Belle Grove Historic District has been beautifully restored.	Fort Smith
Hot Springs, 55 miles/88km south-west of Little Rock, is one of the most popular spa resorts in the United States. The heyday of this little town of rather European aspect was in the twenties and thirties, but it still attracts large numbers of visitors to "take the cure", practise various sports or walk in Hot Springs National Park, part of the Ouachita Mountains. The old Fordyce Bathhouse still gives some impression of spa life in earlier times.	***Hot Springs** *Hot Springs National Park
Little Rock, political and economic centre of Arkansas, lies in the heart of the state, separated from its sister city of North Little Rock by the Arkansas River. The town, founded in 1812, took its name from the French "petite roche"; it became capital of the state in 1821. The Quapaw Historic District (named after a local Indian tribe) preserves some handsome remains of old Little Rock, including the classical-style Old State House and the Arkansas Museum of Science and History in MacArthur Park, housed in the only surviving building of Little Rock's Arsenal (1836), in which General Douglas MacArthur (1880–1964) was born. Fans of "Gone with the Wind" will want to visit the Old Mill (a watermill of 1828) in North Little Rock, where the early scenes of the film were shot.	**Little Rock**
Large areas of the beautiful Ozark Mountains are now protected as a National Forest. Their lakes, waterfalls, wild gorges and hills offering magnificent views, like Magazine Mountain, draw large numbers of visitors in summer. Also of interest is the Ozark Folk Center (folk art) at the little town of Mountain View.	*Ozark Mountains
Stuttgart, founded around 1880 by a German from Swabia in southern Germany and named after the Swabian capital, is now a rice-growing and poultry-farming centre. It has an interesting Agricultural Museum illustrating the development of farming in the prairies.	Stuttgart

Atlanta

State: Georgia
Altitude: 1050ft/320m
Population: 394,000 (Greater Metropolitan Area 2.8 million)

Situation and characteristics

Atlanta, capital of the state of Georgia, is in almost all respects the principal centre of the American South. It lies in the foreland of the southern foothills of the Piedmont Plateau, on the watershed between the Gulf of Mexico and the Atlantic. The city was originally planned as a railway junction, and rapidly developed into an important commercial town. In recent years it has become a major economic and cultural centre in the American South-East and an important hub of air traffic. Internationally famed businesses (e.g. Coca-Cola) have their headquarters here. Atlanta is also the seat of renowned institutes of higher education and the venue of numerous conferences and congresses.

History

A military outpost was established in 1814 in the Indian village of Standing Peachtrees on the east bank of the Chattahoochee River, and in 1837 this became the terminus of the Western and Atlantic Railroad. The settlement which grew up was at first known simply as Terminus; then in 1843 it was renamed Marthasville in honour of the daughter of the then governor. Only two years later, in 1845, it was given its present name of Atlanta. During the Civil War it was an important Confederate stronghold, supply base and hospital centre. In 1864 the Union General William Sherman, noted for his ruthless conduct of the war, captured the town and reduced it to rubble. These events were described by Margaret Mitchell in her best-selling novel "Gone with the Wind", which won her the Pulitzer Prize. In 1868 Atlanta became capital of the young state of Georgia. In 1886 the soft drink with the largest world sale was created in Atlanta. Large areas of the city were

Skyline of Atlanta

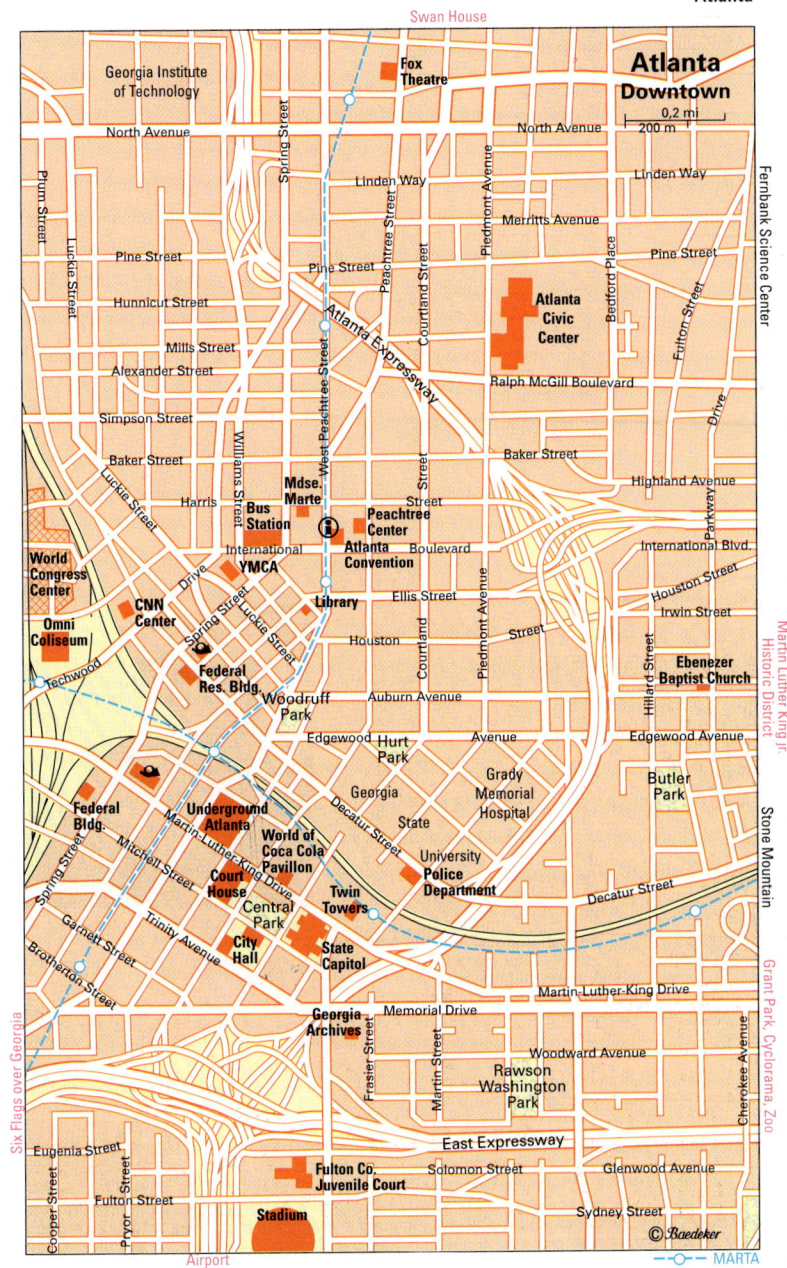

Atlanta

Atlanta Downtown

Atlanta

destroyed by a great fire in 1917. In 1929 Martin Luther King (see Famous People) was born in Atlanta.
After the Second World War Atlanta, as the metropolis of the dynamically developing Sun Belt, enjoyed an unprecedented boom. The Summer Olympics are due to be held in the city in 1996.

Sights in Atlanta

Underground Atlanta

At the point where two covered shopping malls now meet (Alabama Street, between Peachtree Street and Central Avenue) there once stood the terminus of the Western and Atlantic Railroad, the nucleus of the present city. During the Civil War there was an assembly point for wounded here. Since 1865 this area has lain below the present street level. For many years it was hidden and forgotten; then in the 1980s, when its possibilities were realised, it was restored in period (1880–1900) style and reopened in 1989. The underground passages, enlivened by musicians, entertainers and street traders, are now occupied by restaurants, bars and over a hundred shops and boutiques.

*The World of Coca-Cola

Mon.–Sat. 10am–9.30pm, Sun. noon–6pm

In 1886 a chemist named Dr John Pemberton devised a syrup designed to relieve headaches. A friend of his mixed the glutinous liquid with water and carbonic acid, and the result of the mixture soon became the world's most popular soft drink. The World of Coca-Cola (55 Martin Luther King Jr Drive) entertainingly illustrates the history and triumphal progress of the world-famed drink.

*Martin Luther King Jr National Historic Site

Two blocks on Auburn Avenue are now protected as a National Historic Site. They include the birthplace of the civil rights campaigner Martin Luther King Jr at 501 Auburn Avenue, which dates from 1895, and the Ebenezer Baptist Church (407–413 Auburn Avenue), in which he and his father were ministers. Immediately adjoining, in the Freedom Hall Complex, is his grave. The Martin Luther King Jr Center for Nonviolent Social Change (with an exhibition) is also in this area. Conducted tours are run by the Visitor Center at 522 Auburn Avenue.

Birthplace of Martin Luther King Jr

Georgia State Capitol

On Capitol Square and Washington Street is the State Capitol of Georgia, completed in 1889, with a gilded dome 236ft/72m high.

CNN Center

On Marietta Street and Techwood Drive is the CNN Center, the headquarters of Cable Network News (conducted tours daily between 9am and 5pm), where visitors can see something of the work (including the television studios) of the most famous and most up-to-the-minute news broadcasting system in the world.

Peachtree Center

The Peachtree Center, a futuristic complex of tower blocks designed by John Portman (between Baker Street, Ellis Street, Williams Street and Courtland Street), with the world's tallest hotel, rises to varying heights between 302ft/92m and 722ft/220m. With numerous offices and a wide variety of shopping, dining and entertainment facilities, it forms a second city centre.

Badlands National Park

In a 32 acre/13 hectare park at 3101 Andrews Drive NW / West Paces Ferry Road are two handsome but very different buildings: Swan House, an elegant Renaissance-style mansion built in 1928 which now houses the Atlanta Historical Society and the Tullie Smith House, a plain Georgian farmhouse built in 1840. The McElreath Hall contains extensive collections on the Civil War and the history of Atlanta.

Atlanta History Center

In Grant Park (Georgia and Cherokee Avenues) is the Atlanta Cyclorama, with a large circular painting (by German artists, 1885–86) depicting the battle for Atlanta in 1864.

Atlanta Cyclorama

The Fernbank Science Center (156 Heaton Park Drive) contains an observatory, one of the largest planetariums in the United States and extensive natural history collections, with an aquarium and a large botanic garden.

Fernbank Science Center

The Robert W. Woodruff Arts Center (1280 Peachtree Street NE), a striking modern building, was built to commemorate 122 members of the Atlanta Arts Association who died in an air crash in Paris in 1962. It is the home of the Atlanta Symphony Orchestra, several theatre companies and an art school. Within the complex is the High Museum of Art, with works by internationally known artists.

***Robert W. Woodruff Arts Center**

High Museum of Art

The Jimmy Carter Library houses documents from the Presidency of Jimmy Carter, a former Governor of Georgia. The Museum (at 1 Copenhill) is devoted to the President's life and his concern with human rights.

Jimmy Carter Library and Museum

On the northern outskirts of the city is the select residential district of Buckhead. In addition to the sumptuous houses it has fashionable boutiques, unusual galleries and high-class restaurants.

*Buckhead

Surroundings of Atlanta

Atlanta's international airport (Hartsfield Airport), 10 miles/16km south of the city centre, is one of the largest and busiest airports in the United States (over 42 million passengers in 1992). It is at present being expanded to enable it to handle more than 100 aircraft an hour. Its most striking architectural feature is the Atrium, opened in 1994.

*Atlanta International Airport

16 miles/26km east of the city centre, at 6867 Memorial Drive, is Stone Mountain Park (area 5sq.miles/13sq.km), commemorating the soldiers of the Southern states who fell in the Civil War. In the centre of the park is Stone Mountain, an 863ft/263m high mass of exposed granite with a circumference of 5 miles/8km. On the east flank of the hill is an equestrian relief, hewn from the rock between 1923 and 1970, depicting the three Confederate leaders, President Jefferson Davis and his two generals, Stonewall Jackson and Robert E. Lee. The top of the hill can be reached by cable car, and round it runs an old steam railway. Nearby is an artificial lake on which there are paddle-steamer cruises. Other features are a museum devoted to the early days of industrialisation in the Southern states, a Civil War Museum and an antebellum plantation (restored).

*Stone Mountain Park

This amusement park (7561 Six Flags Road, near I 20 West), named after the flags of the six countries which have ruled in Georgia since the age of discovery, has a varied range of over a hundred attractions, from a hair-raising roller coaster to the Batman Stunt Show.

Six Flags Over Georgia

Badlands National Park

F 23/24

State: South Dakota
Area: 422sq.miles/1093sq.km
Established: 1939

Badlands National Park

View over the Badlands National Park

Season	The Badlands National Park is open throughout the year; its facilities operate from May to September. In summer it can be very hot and there may be violent storms. The best times of year to visit the park are spring and autumn.
Accommodation	There is only limited accommodation for visitors in the National Park. The Cedar Pass Lodge is open only from May to the middle of October. There is only one campground open all year, with 110 places. Outside the park there are motels at Wall and Kadoka. The nearest town of any size is Rapid City (see South Dakota).
Situation and topography	Badlands National Park lies in the south-west of the state of South Dakota. It was originally scheduled as a National Monument in 1939 and became a National Park in 1978. In 1978 its area was almost doubled and the Pine Ridge Indian Reservation was incorporated in it. In 1992 it attained world fame as one of the settings of the Kevin Kostner film "Dancing with Wolves". The "bad lands" – a name originally given to the area by the Prairie Indians because of the rough nature of the terrain – are a prairie plateau up to 200ft/60m high which has been furrowed by erosion, with deeply indented dry valleys and bizarre rock formations (pinnacles, towers, ridges, small tabular hills, etc.) in multi-coloured strata (numerous fossils) consisting mainly of solidified clay, sand, slate and volcanic ash. The National Park includes the most rugged and fissured part of the bad lands.
By road through the National Park	A road runs through the park from the north-western entrance (Pinnacles Entrance), lined with parking places and viewpoints which offer changing vistas of the rugged rock formations to the south and of the Buffalo Gap National Grassland, one of the last remaining intact prairie landscapes in North America.

Throughout the park, particularly in the Cedar Pass area, there are way-marked hiking trails. Maps can be obtained from the park administration (see Practical Information, National Parks) or from visitor centres. There are guided walks on nature trails.

Walking in the park

On either side of the unsurfaced Sage Creek Rim Road (10 miles/16km) in the north-west of the park grazes a herd of bison which has now increased to over 300 head. In this area too is a colony of prairie dogs (Robert Prairie Dog Town). Other animals to be seen in the park include mole and white-tailed deer, pronghorn antelopes and bighorn sheep.

Wild life

In the early days of white settlement the Indians living round the Badlands and Pine Ridge put up fierce resistance to the takeover of their land, and there were frequent bloody encounters with US troops. On December 29th 1890 several hundred Indians were massacred by the US Cavalry at Wounded Knee Creek – an inglorious operation which broke the resistance of the Indians. The massacre of Wounded Knee, however, is still not forgotten: in 1973 members of the American Indian Movement occupied the area around Wounded Knee, and in 1993 there was a further protest there against the US government's Indian policy.

Pine Ridge Indian Reservation/ Wounded Knee

Baltimore   K 49

State: Maryland
Altitude: 0–446ft/0–136m
Population: 736,000 (Greater Metropolitan Area 2.4 million)

Baltimore, the largest city in Maryland (see entry) and an important seaport, lies north of Washington on the wide estuary of the Patapsco River, which forms a much ramified natural harbour, 14 miles/23km from Chesapeake Bay and 170 miles/275km from the Atlantic. Its industries include shipbuilding, aircraft construction, automobile manufacture, engineering, the production of electronic apparatus and oil processing. With several famous universities, in particular the Johns Hopkins University, museums and a renowned symphony orchestra, Baltimore is a major east coast cultural centre. It was the birthplace of Edgar Allan Poe (see Famous People).

Situation and characteristics

The settlement of Baltimore was established in 1729 and named after the Barons Baltimore, founders of the colony of Maryland. Commerce and shipping brought it prosperity, and in 1796 it was granted its municipal charter. Its place in American history was won in 1814, when British forces bombarded Fort Henry for 25 hours without bringing about its surrender. The sight of the American flag still flying over the fort on the morning after the bombardment inspired Francis Scott Key's poem "The Star Spangled Banner", which became the text of the national anthem. Over the last twenty years the old town centre and the inner harbour area have been thoroughly renovated.

History

Downtown Baltimore

In the northern part of the central area is park-like Mount Vernon Place, with the Washington Monument. On the south-east side of the square is the Peabody Institute, founded by George Peabody to promote scientific and artistic education (library).

Mount Vernon Place

Near Mount Vernon Place, in Centre Street, is the Walters Art Gallery, with a collection, originally assembled by the Walters family, which has grown to become one of the finest in the United States. The high points of the collection include Islamic art, European old masters, particularly from Italy (Pietro Lorenzetti, Carlo da Camerino, Giovanni Bellini, Raphael, Guido

*Walters Art Gallery

Tue.–Sun. 11am–5pm

Baltimore

Maryland Historical Society	Reni) and Spain (El Greco), Fabergé Easter eggs from Russia and 19th century European painting. The Maryland Historical Society (201 West Monument Street) has a fine library and historical collections, including Francis Scott Key's original manuscript of "The Star-Spangled Banner" and War of Independence uniforms.
Basilica of the Assumption	South of the Walters Art Gallery, in Cathedral Street, is the Basilica of the Assumption, the oldest Roman Catholic cathedral in the United States, built in the time of Archbishop John Carroll. In the crypt are the tombs of Archbishop Carroll (1735–1815) and Cardinal James Gibbons (1834–1921).
*Charles Center	To the south of the cathedral, on Charles Street and Lombard Street, is the busy Charles Center, a complex of office buildings and apartment blocks

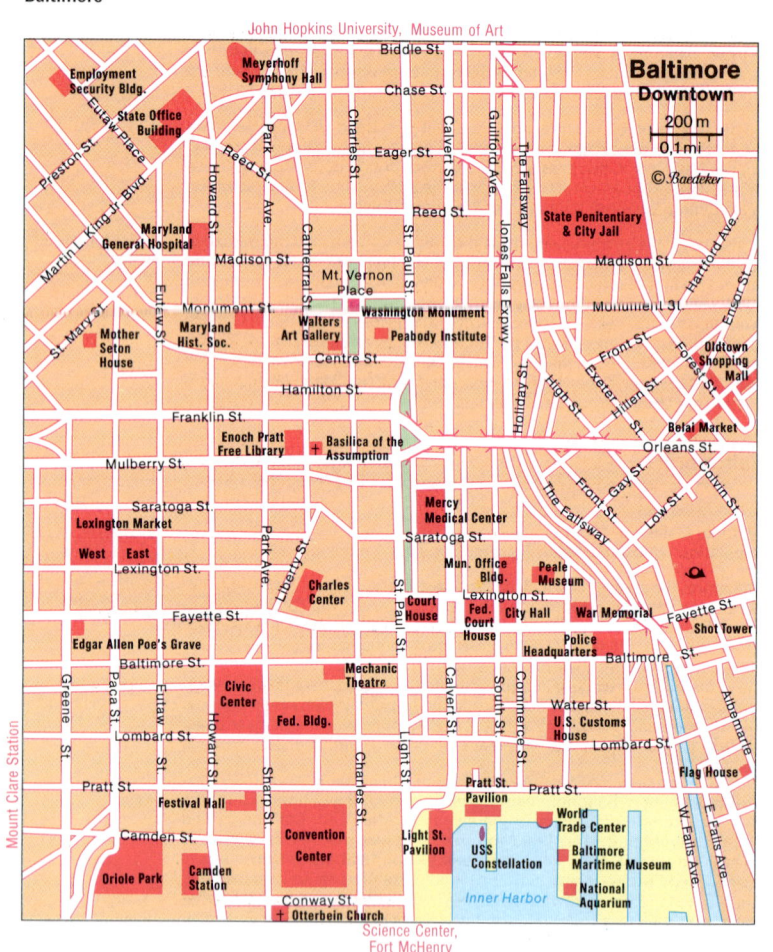

158

Baltimore

built from 1959 onwards. The building at One Charles Center was designed by Mies van der Rohe (1962). Farther south, on Baltimore Street and Charles Street, is the Morris Mechanic Theatre, which puts on Broadway productions. Adjoining this is the Hopkins Plaza (concerts and theatrical shows). Also on Charles Street is the granite and steel façade of the Sun Life Building, with the 26-storey Charles Center South immediately south of it. In the streets to the south and east are other striking high-rise buildings, including the USF & G Building, the city's tallest (525ft/160m). South-west of the Charles Center is the Baltimore Arena, used mainly for sporting events.

Farther west is the Babe Ruth Birthplace and Baltimore Orioles Museum (216 Emory Street). The house in which the famous baseball player (see Famous People) was born is now a baseball museum.

Babe Ruth Birthplace

Pratt Street runs west to the Mount Clare Railroad Station of the Baltimore and Ohio Railroad, from which the first passenger train in the United States ran west to Ellicott's Mills in 1830.

Mount Clare Railroad Station

Wed.–Sun. 10am–4pm

The Baltimore and Ohio Railroad Museum takes in the Mount Clare Station (1851), the Print Shop (1884) and a roundhouse which now houses an excellent collection of historic locomotives. The centrepiece is the turntable, which connects with 22 lines containing locomotives and coaches. With only a few exceptions all the exhibits are originals and in working order. In front of the building is a large open area with more locomotives. There is also a miniature railway system.

The grave of the writer Edgar Allan Poe (see Famous People) is in the churchyard of the Westminster Presbyterian Church. His house, at 203 North Amity Street, is now a museum.

Poe's Grave and House

East of the Charles Center stands the Battle Monument (1815). Farther east is the 19th century City Hall (100 Holliday Street). Nearby is the War Memorial to the dead of the First World War.

City Hall

South-east of the War Memorial, on East Lafayette and Front Streets, is the Shot Tower (1828), which until 1892 produced most of the American forces' requirements of ammunition. Close by will be found the Lloyd Street Synagogue (1845), the oldest in Maryland.

Shot Tower

*Inner Harbor

In 1968 the redevelopment of the area round the Inner Harbor began. Old factories and other buildings were cleared away to make room for modern apartment blocks and shops. A year later USS "Constellation" moored at Pier 1, and in 1973 US submarine "Torsk" took up her moorings at Pier 4. In 1976 the Maryland Science Center was opened, in 1977 the Baltimore World Trade Center, in 1980 Harborplace.

Renovation plan

Harborplace, an attractive modern complex with two glass-enclosed pavilions in historical style, is both a shopping centre and a market-place, with a plethora of shops, restaurants and open spaces. Street artists display their skills in the Amphitheater on the Promenade.

*Harborplace

The Inner Harbor area is dominated by the Baltimore World Trade Center (401 Pratt Street), a pentagonal tower designed by I. M. Pei. From the viewing platform on the 27th floor there are fine views of the harbour and the city. There are multi-media shows on the history of Baltimore.

Baltimore World Trade Center

At Pier 1 lies the frigate "Constellation", the first vessel in the US Navy, built in 1797; it is now a museum ship. It fought in the British–American War and the Civil War, and still served in the Second World War as the flagship of the Atlantic Fleet. On board are cannon, weapons and nautical equipment, and there is a small museum on the history of the vessel.

USS "Constellation"

Baltimore

Baltimore Harbor

*Aquarium

Maryland
Science Center

Museum
of Industry

Fell's Point

Convention
Center/
Otterbein Church/
Camden Station

Fort McHenry

Summer daily
8am–8pm

Other museum ships are moored at Pier 3, in front of the Aquarium – the lightship "Chesapeake" and the submarine "Torsk", the last United States vessel to sink a Japanese submarine during the Second World War. On Pier 5 is the Knoll Lighthouse (1856), transferred here in 1988 from the mouth of the Patapsco River; it contains an exhibition on the history of the harbour. On Pier 3 is the ultra-modern National Aquarium, built in 1981. Features of particular interest are the five-storey Tropical Basin, the Open Ocean Exhibit (sharks) and the "Wings under Water" basin, with various species of ray. On Pier 4 is a separate Marine Mammals Pavilion.

The south-west corner of the Inner Harbor is occupied by the modern Maryland Science Center, with a planetarium. On its three floors are scientific displays, particularly on space travel and physics, and experiments are laid on in which visitors can take part.

Farther south-west, on Key Highway, is the Baltimore Museum of Industry, which is devoted to the industrial history of the city. Among the exhibits are reconstructions of an old workshop, a printing office and a canning factory. At the quay is moored the tug "Baltimore".

The old harbour quarter of Fell's Point was once the shipbuilding district of Baltimore, with places of entertainment for the seamen. Behind the brick façades of this beautifully restored quarter are now mainly restaurants.

To the west of the Inner Harbor is the Convention Center, with a fine piece of sculpture by Henry Moore in the lobby. Close by, to the south-west, is Old Otterbein Church, built in 1786 by German immigrants. To the west is Camden Station, which was renovated some years ago.

3 miles/5km south-east of the city centre via Key Highway and Fort Avenue is Fort McHenry, built between 1798 and 1803 to command the harbour entrance. In 1814 it withstood a 24-hour bombardment by a British warship and thus saved Baltimore from occupation. In the fort's Visitor Center are displays and a film on the history of the fort, referring to the origins of the national anthem.

Black Hills

The Great Blacks in Wax Museum (1601 North Avenue) is devoted to Afro-American history. It contains wax figures of black personalities and tableaux on important historical themes such as slavery, the Civil War and the civil rights movement.

Wax Museum

In the north of the city (Museum Drive and Charles and 31st Streets) is the Baltimore Museum of Art, the largest art museum in Maryland. The high point of the museum is the Cone Collection, mainly of French art, with an excellent representation of works by Matisse – the result of the artist's friendship with Etta Cone.

*Baltimore Museum of Art
Wed.–Fri. 10am–4pm,
Sat. and Sun. 11am–6pm

Big Bend National Park U 22

State: Texas. Established: 1935
Area: 1250sq.miles/3240sq.km

The park is open throughout the year. The best months for a visit are March and April. In summer it is often extremely hot.

Season

Visitors should fill up with gas before driving to Big Bend: there are only two filling stations in the park, both closing at 5pm. There are only 74 hotel rooms in the park; advance reservation is therefore advisable. See Practical Information, National Parks.

Big Bend National Park is in south-western Texas, on the frontier with Mexico, round the great bend in the Rio Grande from which it takes its name. Lying at altitudes of between 1870ft/570m and 7875ft/2400m, it is made up of three different zones: the valley of the Rio Grande, the desolate landscape of the Chihuan Desert and the Chisos Mountains. Thanks to its great extent and to its range of altitudes it is home to over 400 species of birds, including the golden eagle and the roadrunner, and over 1100 species of plants – a paradise for nature-lovers.

Situation and *topography

Altogether the park has some 240 miles/380km of hiking trails. Among the shorter routes are the Lost Mine Trail, a 5 mile/8km long nature trail affording beautiful views, the Window Trail and 17 miles/27km of other waymarked trails in the Chisos Mountains. There are a number of longer trails into the desert, allowing hikes of several days. On these trails it is essential to take enough drinking water – at least 7 pints/4 litres per person per day.

Hiking trails

Apart from the flora and fauna the great attractions of Big Bend National Park are the three canyons on the Rio Grande, the Mariscal, Boquillas and Santa Elena Canyons, with rock faces rising almost 1650ft/500m above the river, and the Chisos Mountains, with Emory Peak (7835ft/2388m), once a refuge of the Comanche Indians, a region of wild gorges, precipitous rock faces and gentle valleys.

***Canyons**

Boat trips through the breathtaking canyons on the Rio Grande can be booked in the Park headquarters at Panther Junction (the intersection of US 385 and SR 118).

Boat trips

This region is rich in fossils, some of which can be seen in an exhibition 7 miles/11km north of the Park headquarters at Panther Junction.

Fossils

On the western edge of the park is the ghost town of Terlingua, now only a tourist attraction, where mercury was mined between 1900 and 1946.

Terlingua

Black Hills E/F 22

States: South Dakota and Wyoming

Black Hills

Situation and *topography

The Black Hills, now mostly a National Forest, are a fairly isolated range of hills in the northern Great Plains and on the border between the states of South Dakota and Wyoming, some 125 miles/200km east of the Rockies as the crow flies.

The range was thrust up during the Tertiary era. Its nucleus consists of Pre-Cambrian schists and granites, with some basaltic masses. In some places the more resistant rocks have been left exposed as bizarrely shaped rock pinnacles. The highest point is Harney Peak (7242ft/2207m). The crystalline rock is rich in minerals, particularly gold and silver. The Palaeozoic and Mesozoic surface layers (Cambrian, Carboniferous, Triassic, Cretaceous) have been eroded away in the centre of the range but round the edges have formed a limestone plateau with marked differences of level in the strata of the different rocks.

The Black Hills are also of interest for their flora, lying as they do on the boundary between the western (Pacific) and eastern (Atlantic) plant worlds. By far the commonest conifer is the western yellow pine (*Pinus ponderosa*).

Indian country

To the western Dakota Indians (Teton-Sioux or Lakota) the Black Hills are a sacred region, the place of origin of their people. In the past they were also very conscious of the material value of this region with its rich stores of gold, uranium and other ores. In 1868, in the treaty of Laramie, the American government guaranteed the Indians possession of the Black Hills. When gold was found in the area in 1874, however, they were anxious to get it back. Negotiations with the chiefs Red Cloud (see Famous People) and Spotted Tail broke down; but in 1876 the Americans compelled the Lakota Indians to hand the land back without compensation. The Indians are still fighting in the US courts for appropriate reparation for the rich lands they have lost.

Places of Interest in the Black Hills

**Mount Rushmore

Visitor Center:
Mid May to mid Sept. daily
8am–10pm;
rest of year
8am–5pm

Mount Rushmore, the "shrine of American democracy", attracts millions of visitors every year. The American sculptor Gutzom Borglum (1867–1941), a great admirer of Abraham Lincoln, began the task of hewing heads of Presidents George Washington, Thomas Jefferson, Abraham Lincoln and Theodore Roosevelt, each over 60ft/18m high, out of the granite rock of Mount Rushmore (5725ft/1745m). Work continued until 1941, involving the blasting away of no less than 400,000 tons of rock. After Gutzom Borglum's death in March 1941 his son Lincoln carried on the work. Shortage of money and the uncertainties of the Second World War led to the suspension of the project in October 1941; but fifty years later, in a ceremony on July 3rd 1991, President George Bush was able formally to declare the huge work of sculpture completed. An avenue flanked by the flags of all the states of the Union now leads to the Visitor Center.

From mid May to mid September the monument is illuminated. The lights are switched on every evening at 9pm in a ceremony accompanied by the playing of the national anthem, which many spectators join in singing.

Keystone

A few miles below Mount Rushmore is the little town of Keystone, which in recent years has developed into a busy tourist centre, with souvenir shops, eating places and a variety of attractions appealing to every taste.

Rushmore Cave

5 miles/8km east of Keystone is the Rushmore Cave, one of the largest show caves in the Black Hills.

Hot Springs

The little town of Hot Springs, in the south of the Black Hills, has long been a popular tourist resort thanks to the mineral springs, whose qualities were already known to the Sioux and Cheyenne Indians. The springs now supply Evans Plunge, the world's largest natural warm-water indoor pool.

Black Hills

Mount Rushmore: a shrine of American democracy

Mammoth cemetery at Mammoth Site

Black Hills

**Mammoth Site

Mid May–Aug.
daily 8am–8pm,
Apr.–mid May
and Sept.–Oct.
9am–5pm

Hot Springs hit the international headlines in 1974, when during building operations on the outskirts of the town the remains of mammoths were found. The site, now roofed over, is a Mecca for both professional and amateur palaeontologists. Some 26,000 years ago it lay on the edge of a steep-sided sinkhole some 80ft/25m deep filled with water from a hot spring, whose luxuriant vegetation, even during the Ice Age, attracted the mammoths which lived in this region. Many of these heavy creatures, standing up to 13ft/4m high, tumbled over the edge of the hole or sank into the soft soil. Painstaking work on the site has brought to light the remains of some four dozen Columbus mammoths. Surprisingly, none of the bones were broken. In addition to the mammoths remains of other inhabitants of the tundra and steppe landscape of the Ice Age, including squirrels, marmots, wolves and large bears, together with quantities of birds' feathers, were also found. In the Visitor Center enclosing the site are informative displays on the Quaternary era and the development of life in North America over the past 2 million years.

*Wind Cave

June–Aug. daily
8.30am–6pm;
rest of year
very restricted
opening times

10 miles/16km north of Hot Springs is the Wind Cave, part of one of the largest karstic cave systems so far found on earth. It was discovered in 1881 when a hunter noticed a strong current of air emerging from a narrow cleft in the rock. Differing air pressures inside and outside the cave produce air currents which can reach a speed of up to 50 miles/80km an hour. Inside the cave there are interesting but not particularly spectacular rock formations and mineral efflorescences. A local peculiarity is the occurrence of very delicate honeycomb-like structures of brown calcareous spar. Part of the cave system can be visited, and the park rangers run conducted tours of varying length adjusted to the interests of particular groups of visitors.

*Wind Cave
National Park

On the beautiful park-like "roof" of the cave system, now a National Park, several hundred bison graze. Some of these indigenous inhabitants of America – whom it is advisable not to approach too closely – featured in the background of the film "Dancing with Wolves". See Practical Information, National Parks.

Custer State Park

North of Wind Cave National Park is Custer State Park, which is no less beautiful and is richly stocked with game. A drive on the Wildlife Loop Road, particularly in the early morning or late afternoon, is a rewarding experience.

*Needles Highway

The Needles Highway is a magnificent scenic mountain road through the imposing landscapes of the central Black Hills, with their bizarre rock pinnacles and the fairytale Sylvan Lake.

Custer

The little town of Custer is a popular tourist resort. Its particular attraction is Flintstone's Bedrock City, a theme park dedicated to dinosaurs and the Stone Age. The town also has the interesting National Museum of Woodcarving.

Crazy Horse
Memorial

A few miles north of Custer is the Crazy Horse Memorial – a kind of Indian counterpart to Mount Rushmore National Monument. The initiative for this other gigantic piece of rock sculpture came from a Lakota chief named Standing Bear, who sought thereby to remind the world that the Indians too had produced great heroes like Crazy Horse, the real victor in the battle on the Little Bighorn River. Work on the monument was begun in 1947 by Korczak Ziolkowski (1908–82), a sculptor of Polish origin, and continued after his death by members of his family.

*Jewel Cave

13 miles/21km west of Custer is the Jewel Cave National Monument, a karstic cave in which crystals of calcareous spar sparkle like jewels. With a maze of passages over 75 miles/120km long, this is one of the largest cave systems in the United States.

The legendary Devil's Tower ▶

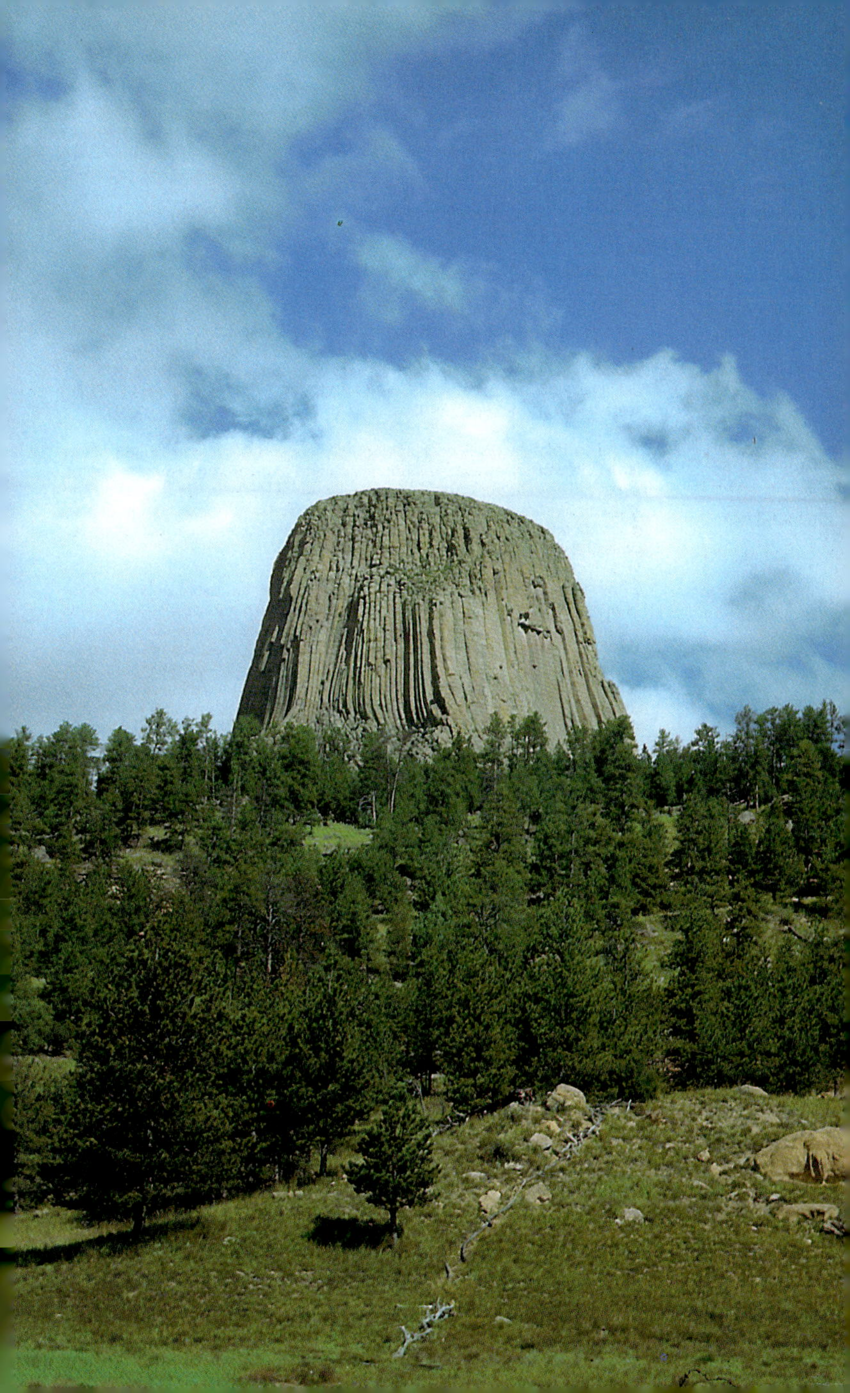

Boston

Sturgis	In the north-eastern Black Hills is Sturgis, where thousands of Harley Davidson enthusiasts – not all of them belonging to the "Easy Rider" generation – gather every summer. East of the town is the Fort Meade Cavalry Museum, recalling the days when this really was the Wild West.
*Lead	The little town of Lead is a centre of the Black Hills gold-mining industry. Homestake Surface Tours (weekdays only) show visitors round one of the largest operating goldmines in the western hemisphere. Also of interest is the Black Hills Mining Museum, which gives an excellent survey of the history of gold-mining, going back more than 100 years.
Deadwood	A few minutes' drive north-east of Lead is Deadwood, with the Adams Memorial Museum (recalling the time of the Black Hills gold rush) and the old Broken Boot goldmine. During the main holiday season there are highly realistic performances of the Wild West play "The Trial of Jack McCall" every evening (except Sundays).
Spearfish	In the north of the Black Hills is Spearfish, where the Black Hills Passion Play is performed during the summer. From here a rewarding excursion can be made to the wild Spearfish Canyon, with two waterfalls, the Bridal Veil and the Rough Lock Falls, and two striking hills, Spearfish Peak and Little Crow Peak. A few miles north of Spearfish is the geographical centre of the United States.
**Devil's Tower	27 miles/43km north-west of Sundance is the Devil's Tower, an extraordinary natural monument and a landmark visible from many miles away. This huge isolated crag (alt. 5118ft/1560m) was declared a National Monument, the first in the United States, in 1906. In the early Tertiary era, some 60 million years ago, hot liquid magma thrust its way up into rock strata near the surface, where it cooled and hardened into a highly resistant and tightly packed cluster of columns. In course of time the surrounding sediments were eroded away, leaving this monadnock, 865ft/264m high and 1000ft/305m in diameter at the base, standing by itself. It is now a Mecca for rock climbers. The crag, known to the local Indians as Mateo Tipi, was the subject of an old legend. A giant bear, it was said, was pursuing two children when suddenly the land on which the children were standing was thrust up into the air, out of the bear's reach; and the grooves in the crag were made by the bear's claws as it scrabbled at the rock to get at them. Under the south-east side of the Devil's Tower, which is particularly impressive in the morning or evening sun, lives a large colony of prairie dogs.
Rapid City	See South Dakota

Boston G 65

State: Massachusetts
Altitude: 0–300ft/0–91m
Population: 574,000 (Greater Metropolitan Area 2.87 million)

Situation and characteristics	Boston, capital of the state of Massachusetts and the largest city in New England, lies at the mouth of the Charles River in Massachusetts Bay, some 185 miles/300km north-east of New York City. The city centre occupies a peninsula between the Charles River and the arm of the sea known as Boston Harbor and is linked with the university town of Cambridge by several bridges. During the War of Independence Boston, capital of the British colony, played a prominent role. It is now the leading economic, commercial and cultural metropolis of New England, with a variety of industry (including fish processing), renowned universities and research

Boston

centres, many publishing houses and numerous cultural institutions and events.

Boston was originally built on three hills, still commemorated in the names of the Beacon Hill, Copp's Hill and Fort Hill districts. The English settlers who came here in the mid 17th century named their new home after the birthplace of one of their leaders, Boston in Lincolnshire. Governor John Winthrop made Boston capital of the new colony. The little town, governed by strict Puritan principles, grew rapidly. The inhabitants soon developed an overseas trade, and the town's first shipyard was built in 1673. By the middle of the 18th century Boston was the largest and most important town in North America, overshadowing New York and Philadelphia with its 25,000 inhabitants. The first American newspaper was printed here in 1704. The main centre of opposition to the mother country as early as the reign of Charles II (1660–85), Boston became the starting-point of the War of Independence. It was the scene of the Boston Massacre on March 5th 1770 and of the Boston Tea Party on December 16th 1773, when a mob threw tea imported from Britain into the sea. During the War of Independence Boston was occupied by British troops, until on March 4th 1776 Washington's forces crossed the Charles River, took the Dorchester Heights and drove the British out. After the United States achieved independence Boston grew steadily, with only brief interruptions, and by 1900 its population had passed the half-million mark. In 1872 a great fire caused much destruction in the central area, which has since then been more than doubled in size by the reclamation of land from the sea.

Boston was the birthplace of a number of notable Americans, including Benjamin Franklin (see Famous People), Samuel Morse, inventor of morse telegraphy, and John F. Kennedy (see Famous People).

History

**Freedom Trail

The 3 mile/5km Freedom Trail, which takes in the city's principal historic monuments and sites, starts from Boston Common. Some of the sights form part of Boston National Historical Park.

The Freedom Trail is marked by a line of red bricks in the sidewalk and by footprints at street crossings.

The starting-point of the Freedom Trail is the Visitor Center on Boston Common, the large park which lies between downtown Boston and the Black Bay area. This is the oldest public park in the United States, municipal property since 1634, and throughout its history the home of free speech and free assembly. In the park are monuments commemorating the War of Independence and the Civil War. At the south end is the Central Burying Ground of 1756.

***Boston Common**

Adjoining Boston Common, on the west side of Charles Street, is the Public Garden (opened 1859), with a large artificial lake (boating; skating in winter). It contains numbers of Victorian-style monuments and statues, including an equestrian statue of George Washington (1869) near Arlington Street.

Public Garden

The trail cuts across Boston Common to Beacon Street, with the State House (1798) of Massachusetts, on Beacon Hill. The middle section, with a high gilded dome, was designed by Charles Bulfinch, who built the Capitol in Washington DC. On the terrace in front of the buildings are statues of two New England statesmen, Daniel Webster (1782–1852) and Horace Mann (1796–1859). On the first floor are the Doric Hall, which is used for civic occasions, the Hall of Flags (with flags and historical paintings) and the Great Hall (1990). On the second floor are the Governor's offices, the Senate Chamber, the Senate Reception Room and the Chamber of the House of Representatives. In the north wing is the State Library.

***State House**

Guided tours
Mon.–Fri.
10am–4pm

Boston

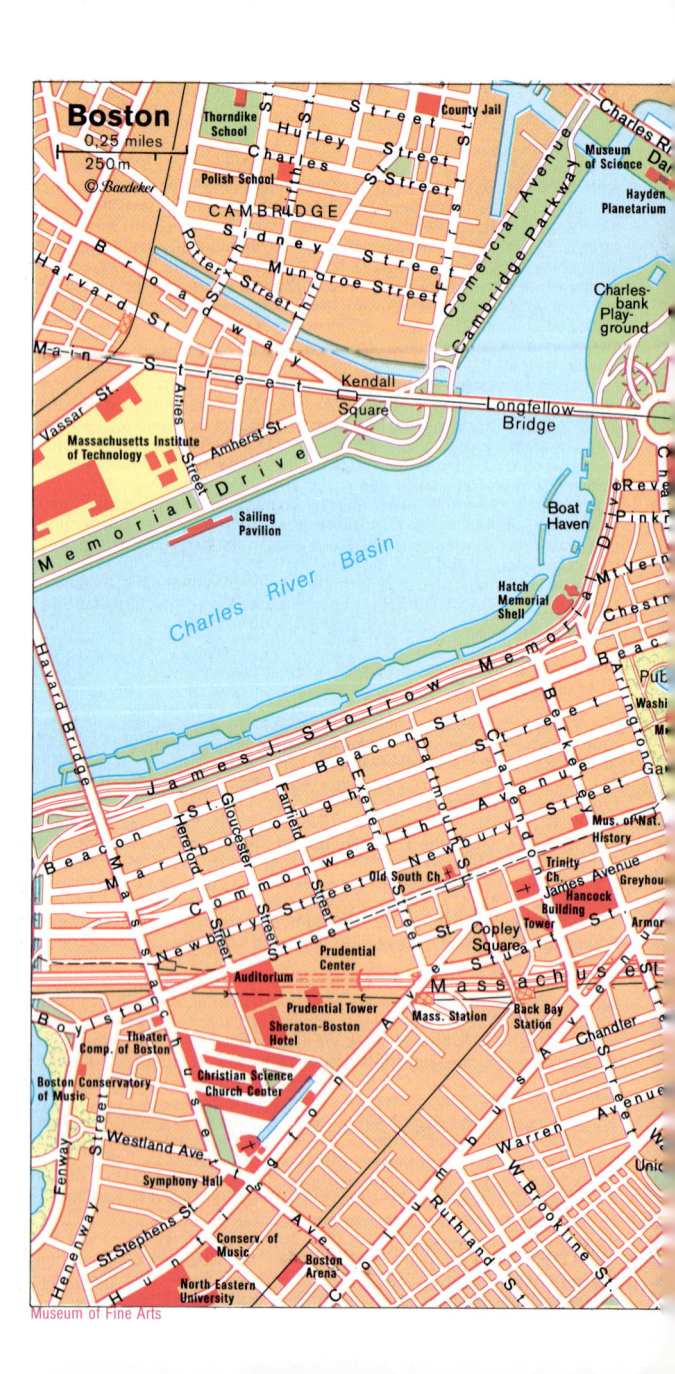

City Centre

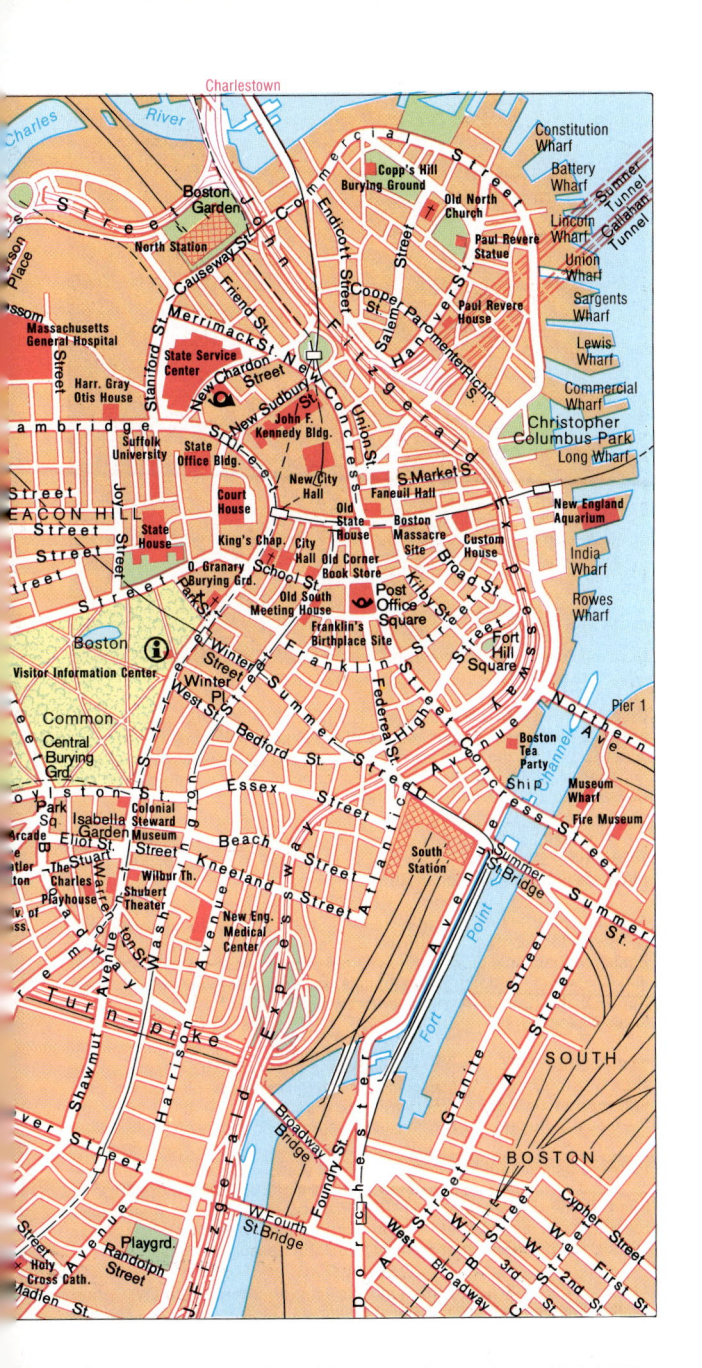

Boston

City Centre

Boston

Old State House

Archives Museum

Guided visits Mon.–Fri. 10am–4pm

On the ground floor of State House is the Archives Museum, whose most precious possession is the "History of the Plimouth Plantation", a manuscript account by the governor of Plymouth Colony. Other items of particular interest are a number of treaties signed with the Indians and the Constitution of 1780, which is still in force.

Park Street Church

From State House Park Street runs south-east to Park Street Church, built in 1810 on the site of an old granary. Here in 1829 William Lloyd Garrison made his first speech against slavery.

Old Granary Burying Ground

Adjoining Park Street Church, in Tremont Street, is the Old Granary Burying Ground, which contains the graves of several governors of Massachusetts, Benjamin Franklin's parents, the victims of the Boston Massacre of 1770 and a number of notable Bostonians, including Samuel Adams, John Hancock and Robert Treat Paine, three signatories of the Declaration of Independence.

King's Chapel and Burying Ground

At the corner of Tremont Street and School Street is King's Chapel, on the site of Boston's first Anglican church of 1686. This modest place of worship, Episcopalian until 1787, now belongs to the Unitarians. In the churchyard, the oldest in Boston, is the grave of Governor John Winthrop (1588–1649).

Old City Hall

Farther along School Street, set back from the street, is Old City Hall, now occupied by offices and a restaurant. In front of it are statues of Benjamin Franklin and Josiah Quincy (1772–1864), second mayor of Boston and founder of Quincy Market. Also in School Street is Boston's first public school, at which Benjamin Franklin and John Hancock were pupils.

Old Corner Book Store

At the corner of School Street and Washington Street is the Old Corner Book Store, one of Boston's oldest buildings. Originally built in 1712 as a

Boston

dwelling house and business house, in the mid 18th century it was occupied by a publishing house. In the 19th century it was a meeting-place of writers and poets.

A little way south, at the corner of Washington Street and Milk Street, is the Old South Meeting House, built in 1729 as the Old South Church and Meeting Hall. A number of lively meetings were held here during the War of Independence, and it was from here that the people of Boston set out to throw a British ship's cargo of tea into the harbour (the Boston Tea Party). The Old South Meeting House is now occupied by a Historical Museum.

Old South
Meeting House

Opposite the Old South Meeting House, at 7 Milk Street, is the site of the house in which Benjamin Franklin was born and spent his early years.

Franklin Birthplace
Site

From here Devonshire Street runs north to Old State House. Built in 1713 and subsequently several times restored, this was the seat of the British colonial government. From the balcony on the east end John Adams read out the Declaration of Independence in 1776. John Hancock resided in the house from 1780 as first Governor of Massachusetts. Thoroughly restored in the early nineties, it now houses a museum of Boston history.

A stone cross outside the east end of the building marks the site of the Boston Massacre of March 5th 1770, in which five people were shot down by British troops.

*Old State House

Daily 9.30am–5pm

The next section of the Freedom Trail runs along Congress Street, with the Government Center (see below) on the left-hand side. On Dock Square is Faneuil Hall, known as the "cradle of liberty". Originally built in 1740–42 by a Huguenot merchant, Peter Faneuil, as a market hall, it was presented to the city on condition that it should always be open to the public. The ground floor is still occupied by market stalls; on the upper floor is a council chamber which in the 18th and 19th centuries was the meeting-place of revolutionaries and later of abolitionists.

East of Faneuil Hall is Faneuil Hall Marketplace, a successful example of urban renewal. Its three long halls (Quincy Market, North Market and South Market), dating from the early 19th century, are now occupied by a lively assortment of shops, restaurants and exhibitions.

*Faneuil Hall

*Faneuil Hall
Marketplace

The Freedom Trail continues by way of Marshal Street (Ebenezer Hancock House, 1767) and under a freeway to North End, the oldest and one of the most interesting parts of the town, now mainly occupied by Italians (good restaurants).

North End

At 19 North Square is the shingle-clad Paul Revere House (now a museum), one of Boston's oldest buildings, dating from about 1680, which now seems incredibly tiny. From 1770 to 1800 it was the home of Paul Revere, famed for his ride to Lexington on April 18th 1775 to warn the patriots of an impending British attack.

*Paul Revere
House

The route continues along Prince Street to Hanover Street. At St Stephen's Church (1804) it turns north-west towards Paul Revere Mall, with an equestrian statue of Paul Revere. Adjoining, at 123 Salem Street, is the Old North Church or Christ Church, Boston's oldest church (1723). In 1775 lanterns were hung from the church tower to warn the citizens of the British advance.

Old North Church

The red line of the Freedom Trail now heads north-west over Charlestown Bridge into the district of Charlestown and beyond the bridge turns north-east. Alternatively there is a ferry from Long Wharf to Charlestown Navy Yard. The first point on the Freedom Trail is Bunker Hill Pavilion, with a multi-media show on the battle of Bunker Hill.

Charlestown Navy Yard, part of Boston National Historical Park, occupies the site of an old naval dockyard. The only vessels to be seen here now are museum ships like USS "Constitution", a warship launched in 1797 (visits daily 9.30am–3.50pm). There is a Visitor Center with displays on the Navy

Charlestown

Bunker Hill
Pavilion

Navy Yard

*USS
"Constitution"

Boston

Bunker Hill Monument

Yard. To the north-east is the USS Constitution Museum (ship models, etc.). Farther north-west the Freedom Trail ends in Monument Square, with the Bunker Hill Monument, a 220ft/67m high granite obelisk commemorating the battle of Bunker Hill on June 17th 1775; a spiral staircase leads up to the top. The battle, which was actually fought on Breed's Hill and not on Bunker Hill, ended in a British victory over the American militia.

*Government Center and Beacon Hill

Along Congress Street and Merrimack Street extends the Government Center, with the offices of the city and state authorities as well as some federal departments.

New City Hall

In the south-east part of the area is New City Hall, on the south side of which is Government Square. To the north is the John F. Kennedy Federal Building.

Court House

Between New City Hall and State House on Pemberton Square is the Suffolk County Court House in Somerset Street, a granite building in German Renaissance style. A little way south-west of this, in Beacon Street (No. 10), is the Boston Athenaeum, which has a fine library and collections of art and antiquities.

Houses in Beacon Hill

Between Beacon Street and Cambridge Street, to the west of State House, is the picturesque Beacon Hill district, with many red brick houses belonging to old Boston families.

Black Heritage Trail

In the 19th century Beacon Hill had many black residents. The Black Heritage Trail (guided walks) takes in many places which have featured in the history of the black population of Boston, including the African Meeting House (8 Smith Court), the first church of the Afro-American population (established 1806), the Museum of Afro-American History (46 Joy Street), the Smith Court Residences (typical 18th and 19th century houses), the George Middleton House (Pinkney Street), the oldest surviving house (1797) of a black resident in Beacon Hill, and, at the corner of Beacon Street and Park Street, a monument to Robert Gould Shaw and the Massachusetts 54th Regiment, the first regiment recruited from blacks to serve in the Civil War.

The Lewis and Harriet Hayden House at 66 Phillips Street was once a "safe house" on the legendary "underground railroad" which enabled large numbers of blacks to flee to Canada.

Science Park
Museum of Science

Tue.–Sat. 9am–5pm, Fri. to 9pm

1 mile/1.6km north of Beacon Hill, on an artificial island in the river linked with Boston by the Charles River Dam, is the Science Park, with the Museum of Science and the Hayden Planetarium. The Museum has a permanent collection and special exhibitions covering many branches of science and technology, including oceanography, astronomy, medicine and space travel.

On the south side of the same building is the Hayden Planetarium, which puts on presentations on the planets and a 3-D laser show.

Back Bay and Brookline

Situation

South-west of Boston Common, between the Charles River and Huntington Avenue, is the Back Bay area, laid out on a regular grid, with numerous office and commercial tower blocks and cultural institutions. South of Boylston Street are many modern skyscrapers. On Berkeley Street (No. 200) is the 495ft/151m high John Hancock Building, with a pyramidal top, headquarters of the insurance corporation of that name.

*Hancock Tower

The 790ft/241m high Hancock Tower not only overtops its immediate neighbours but is in fact the highest building in the whole city. Its forty floors are concealed behind a reflective glass façade. The finest panoramic view of Boston is to be had from the observatory on the top floor.

Boston

Skyline of Boston Habor

To the west of the Hancock Tower is Copley Square, the main square of the Back Bay area, surrounded by both old and ultra-modern buildings, department stores, hotels and shops. On the east side of the square is Trinity Church, a neo-Romanesque red sandstone building with fine stained glass, some of it by Edward Burne-Jones and William Morris. On the west side is Boston Public Library (1895), in Italian Renaissance style. Farther west is the ultra-modern Prudential Center, with the Prudential Tower.

Between Huntington Avenue and Fens Park is the Museum of Fine Arts, with comprehensive collections from every major period. Of particular interest are the departments of European painting (with works by leading masters from El Greco to Monet and Max Beckmann) and Asian art and the representative collection of American art, which ranges from the 18th century Boston painter John Singleton Copley to such modern masters as Edward Hopper and Jackson Pollock. There is also an interesting exhibition of American decorative arts.

Near the south-west end of the Fens (280 The Fenway) is the Isabella Stewart Gardner Museum, with a small but distinguished collection of furniture, tapestries, sculpture, decorative art and European art. The charm of this museum lies in its character as a former private collection reflecting the personal preferences of the owners.

To the south of Commonwealth Avenue is the suburb of Brookline (pop. 55,000). In Beals Street (No. 83; open daily 10am–4.30pm) is the house in which John F. Kennedy was born, with mementoes of the 35th President of the United States.

Copley Square
*Trinity Church
*Public Library
Prudential Center

*Museum of Fine Arts

Tue.–Sun. 10am–5pm, Wed. to 10pm

*Isabella Stewart Gardner Museum

J. F. Kennedy Birthplace

Inner Harbor

To the east of Faneuil Hall Marketplace is the waterfront on the Inner Harbor. The Harbor Walk (indicated by blue markings) takes visitors round the main sights of Boston's former harbour.

Harbor Walk

173

Boston

New England Aquarium

On Central Wharf is the very interesting New England Aquarium. Its main attraction is the four-storeys-high Giant Ocean Tank, containing some 180,000 gallons/680,000 litres of water, with tropical fish, sharks, giant turtles and other marine creatures (which are fed by divers several times a day). The Aquarium runs boat trips to observe whales off the coast.

Boston Tea Party Ship and Museum

To the south of Central Wharf, at the point where Congress Street crosses Fort Point Channel, is moored the Boston Tea Party Ship, a replica of the brig "Beaver II". The scene is re-enacted for visitors several times daily. In the Museum are audio-visual shows and a model of old Boston.

Computer Museum Children's Museum

On the far side of Fort Point Channel (300 Congress Street/Sleeper Street), housed in an old warehouse, are two museums. The Children's Museum is laid out in the form of a 1930s house, with hands-on exhibits which encourage children to play and make discoveries. The Computer Museum has informative displays on the development of information and data-processing technology and allows visitors to play computer games and try their hand at programming and computer graphics. Other fascinating features are a walk-through computer and an exhibition on artificial intelligence.

Surroundings of Boston

J. F. Kennedy Library and Museum

5 miles/8km south of the city, in the Columbia Point Campus of the University of Massachusetts on Dorchester Bay, is the John F. Kennedy Library and Museum, designed by I. M. Pei and opened in 1979. The Museum contains mementoes of President Kennedy (films, photographs, slides, letters, etc.).

Cambridge

From Boston Massachusetts Avenue leads over the Charles River on Harvard Bridge into Cambridge, an independent town with a population of 95,000. The quickest way to reach it from downtown Boston is on the Red Line of the subway. Cambridge, named after its English counterpart, has an international reputation as a centre of teaching and research, with Harvard University and the Massachusetts Institute of Technology.

Massachusetts Institute of Technology

Immediately beyond Harvard Bridge, on both sides of Massachusetts Avenue, is the extensive campus of the Massachusetts Institute of Technology (MIT), one of the most important in the United States. Originally founded in 1861, it moved to its present site in 1916.
On the east side of Massachusetts Avenue is the Main Building, with the F. R. Hart Nautical Museum (55 Massachusetts Avenue). On the south-east side of the building is the Charles Hayden Memorial Library (77 Massachusetts Avenue), with the Hayden Gallery (art exhibitions). The MIT Chapel and the Kresge Auditorium were designed by the Finnish-born architect Eero Saarinen.

Harvard University

From the MIT Massachusetts Avenue runs north to Harvard University, the oldest university in the United States (founded 1636), at which many prominent Americans have been students, including Presidents John Adams, John Quincy Adams, Rutherford B. Hayes, Theodore Roosevelt, Franklin D. Roosevelt, and John F. Kennedy.

Art museums

To the east of the University campus are the Carpenter Center for the Visual Arts, designed by Le Corbusier, with displays on visual communication, and the Fogg Art Museum (32 Quincy Street), with old prints, drawings, paintings, etc. Farther north, beyond Broadway, is the Arthur M. Sackler Museum (opened 1985), with collections of Oriental and Islamic art. At 29 Kirkland Street is the Busch-Reisinger Museum, with an excellent collection of pictures of the German Modernist school and one of the largest Bauhaus collections outside Germany.

Bryce Canyon National Park

Also well worth visiting are the University Museums of Cultural and Natural History at 24 Oxford Street. In the south wing is the Peabody Museum (ethnology of the Indians of North, Central and South America), in the west wing Museums of Geology and Mineralogy and in the north wing the Museum of Comparative Zoology and the Botanical Museum.

University Museums

Bryce Canyon National Park   M 13/14

State: Utah
Area: 56sq.miles/145sq.km
Established: 1928

The park is open throughout the year; the best time to visit it is from April to October. On account of its altitude (8000–9000ft/2400–2700m) the nights can be cool even in summer.

Season

The bizarre rock formations of Bryce Canyon National Park in south-western Utah were created at a relatively late period in geological history. The park lies on the eastern edge of the Paunsaugunt Plateau, which was formed by marine deposits around 60 million years ago. The forces of erosion began to operate on the scarped rim of the limestone tableland, creating huge semicircular amphitheatres, a fairytale landscape of intricately patterned rock formations in brilliant shades of colour ranging from salmon-pink to red. Bryce Canyon is one of the most magnificent scenic spectacles in the North American West, whose magical and quickly changing play of colour is seen at its finest at sunrise.

Situation and
**topography

There is evidence of occupation in this area by Anasazi Indians from A.D. 700, and later by Paiute Indians. The latter gave the canyon the very appropriate name of the "red rocks which stand like men in the shell-shaped gorge". The first white settlers reached this area with the Mormons about 1870. The canyon is named after Ebenezer Bryce, who tried for some years to rear cattle here.

Squirrels and jays (Steller's jay) are frequent visitors to picnic and campgrounds. Other animals which may be spotted are mule deer, foxes, coyotes, skunks, marmots and prairie dogs.

Fauna

SR 63 runs south through the park, passing the Visitor Center, the two campgrounds and the lodges, to Rainbow Point (35 miles/56km), with viewpoints offering wide and ever-changing prospects. From the viewpoints there are hiking trails of varying length and strenuousness leading down into the canyon.

Scenic road

The Navajo Trail (2¼ miles/3.5km) and the Queen's Garden Trail (1½ miles/2.4km) are the best choice for visitors who want a quick look into the canyon; the highlights of this route are Thor's Hammer, Two Bridges and a view of the Silent City. The Rim Trail (5½ miles/8.9km) is a level route, also with magnificent views, running from Fairyland Point by way of Sunrise Point, Sunset Point and Inspiration Point to Bryce Point. The Peekaboo Loop Trail (5½ miles/8.9km) leads to the Cathedral, the Wall of Windows, the Alligator and the Fairy Castle. The Fairyland Loop Trail (8 miles/12.9km), which can be combined with a short side trip to the Tower Bridge, runs past the Chinese Wall and innumerable unnamed formations which may stimulate visitors' imagination to devise names of their own and affords views of Fairyland Canyon and the Boat Mesa. Those who want only to see the Tower Bridge can take the Tower Bridge Trail (3 miles/4.8km), which also runs past the Chinese Wall. The Bristlecone Loop (1 mile/1.6km), a short level walk, is a good introduction to the park's vegetation, particularly its conifers. The Under the Rim Trail (22 miles/35.4km) runs below the rim of the canyon from Bryce Point to Rainbow Point.

Hiking trails

California

The park rangers in the Visitor Center run guided walks amd rides (see Practical Information, National Parks).

Cedar Breaks National Monument

A rewarding day trip (which can also be done by coach) is to the Cedar Breaks National Monument, 65 miles/105km west. This, like Bryce Canyon, is an amphitheatre which has been eroded out of a sedimentary tableland (the Markagund Plateau), with brilliantly coloured though less elaborately patterned rock formations than those of Bryce Canyon.

California (State; CA) H–R 1–11

Area: 158,704sq.miles/
411,043sq.km
Population: 30.38 million
Capital: Sacramento
Popular name: Golden State

Situation and topography

California, the third largest state of the Union (after Alaska and Texas), is the most southerly of the four Pacific mainland states. It has a very varied landscape pattern. The coastal strip along the Pacific, much of it of great beauty, is sheltered by the Coast Range, which reaches its highest point in Thompson Peak (9003ft/2744m). East of this is the Central Valley, running along a geological fault zone which from time to time gives evidence of its existence in the form of violent earthquakes. The northern part of this wide and very fertile valley is watered by the Sacramento River, the southern part by the San Joaquín River, both flowing into San Francisco Bay. Farther east again is the Sierra Nevada with its snow-capped peaks, rising to 14,495ft/4418m in Mount Whitney, the highest point in the continental United States.

To the south-east California occupies part of the Great Basin, an enclosed basin with no outlet, with the hot and arid Death Valley, in which is the lowest point in the western hemisphere, 282ft/86m below sea level. In the extreme south California extends into the Mojave and Colorado Deserts. In the forests of the Coast Range grow the world's tallest trees, the sequoia and the redwood. The Central Valley, originally covered by scrub and grassland, now yields rich crops of wine grapes, fruit and vegetables.

The climate of California ranges between Mediterranean and subtropical, with dry, warm summers and heavy rain in winter. Only to the east of the Sierra Nevada, in the lee of the mountains, and in the far south is it dry throughout the year. Occasionally warm desert winds (the Santa Ana winds) reach even into the coastal regions and the Los Angeles area.

History

Long before the arrival of pioneers and settlers from Europe California had a relatively dense Indian population, including the Na-Dene, Hoka, Penuti and Aztek-Tano tribes. In 1542 the Portuguese navigator Cabrilho sailed along the Pacific coast of California, the first European to reach this area. From 1769 onwards the Spaniards established themselves on the Californian coast, setting up no fewer than 21 mission stations. In 1821 California became a province of Mexico, now independent of Spain. In 1846, when war broke out between Mexico and the United States, California sought to achieve independence; but two years later, under the treaty of Guadalupe Hidalgo, it was assigned to the United States. On September 9th 1850 it became the 31st state of the Union. Between 1846 and 1848 some 250,000 new settlers streamed into California, almost all of them bitten by gold fever. Thereafter California soon developed into the economic leader of the West.

Baedeker Special
Living with San Andreas

On January 17th 1994, at 4.31am, the inhabitants of Los Angeles had a rude awakening, when an earthquake of medium strength (6.6 on the Richter scale) hit the city, causing billions of dollars worth of damage and killing over 40 people, many of the deaths being caused by the collapse of buildings and bridges. Five years before, in 1989, San Francisco Bay had been struck by one of the most violent earthquakes ever recorded in California, with the loss of 59 lives.

The cause of these movements in the earth's crust lay in the process of "continental drift" first postulated by the German scientist Alfred Wegener. California, with its many zones of tectonic weakness and lines of disturbance, is the American state most exposed to the threat of earthquakes. The best known of these stress lines, and the most spectacularly evident in the landscape, is the San Andreas Fault, which runs north-west from the north end of the Gulf of California through Imperial Valley and the Mojave Desert to the San Bernardino range. From there it turns west, and then at Santa Barbara resumes its north-westerly course. It then runs along the side of the Coastal Range, skirting the west side of the Central Valley, to Point Arena, which projects into the Pacific 110 miles/180km north-west of San Francisco, and from there continues under the sea. Along the San Andreas Fault the Pacific Plate, drifting north-west, and the North American Plate, advancing south-east, come up against one another. Over the past 140 million years the two continental plates have pushed over one another for a distance of some 350 miles/560km, creating severe tensions in the earth's crust which have repeatedly produced strong earth tremors.

The city of San Francisco, which extends along the San Andreas Fault, has frequently suffered severe earthquakes – in 1857, 1865 and 1868, but particularly in 1906, 1940, 1986 and most recently in 1989. There are likely to be further earthquakes – perhaps in the not too distant future – but in spite of all warnings the construction of dams and canals and the development of towns has continued on land which is basically unstable.

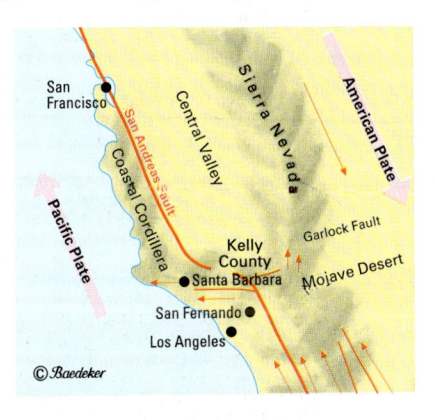

California

Economy

California has considerable mineral resources (non-ferrous metals, oil, natural gas), but the economy of the "Golden State" is centred on "agro-business", largely dependent on irrigated agriculture. In addition to grain, fruit and vegetables the principal crops are cotton, citrus fruits, wine grapes and walnuts. Some 80% of all American wine is produced in California. Industrial development took off in the 1940s, stimulated by arms production and aircraft construction, which promoted the development of a flourishing electronics and computer industry. "Silicon Valley", south-east of San Francisco, was later to enjoy an unprecedented boom. Other important branches of industry are automobile construction and foodstuffs.

Film industry

Hollywood, a suburb of Los Angeles, is the centre of the American film industry, which dominates the international market. Since the end of the Second World War California has attracted increasing numbers of visitors, drawn not only by Hollywood but also by the state's many interesting cities, world-famed amusement parks (including Disneyland and Universal Studios) and great range of leisure and recreational facilities.

Places of Interest in California

*Channel Islands
(Santa Barbara Islands)

Lying in the Pacific north-west of Los Angeles are a series of islands which attract many divers and nature-lovers – Santa Cruz, Santa Rosa and San Miguel, together with the small Anacapa group and the little islet of Santa Barbara, which together form the Channel Islands National Park (see Practical Information, National Parks). Here visitors can see various species of seals (including sealions) and in winter whales.

*Colorado Valley

The eastern boundary of the state of California is formed by the lower course of the Colorado River, which is dammed by the Parker and Imperial Dams. Water pounded by the Imperial Dam is fed into the All-American Canal, which runs through the desert along the southern boundary of California, powering a series of three hydroelectric stations and supplying water for the irrigation of Imperial Valley (see below), the "winter garden of the United States". Below Blythe the river is a popular rafting area.

Fresno

The city of Fresno (pop. 300,000), on the eastern edge of the very fertile San Joaquín Valley, is the economic centre of a very productive fruit-growing region (particularly wine grapes and raisins), with many large wineries. Immigrants from all over Europe came here at the end of the 19th century and built up a town with an active cultural life, now the seat of California State University. It is a good base for excursions to Sequoia and Kings Canyon National Parks and Yosemite National Park (see entries).

*Golden Chain Highway
(Route 49)

The Golden Chain Highway runs along the west side of the Sierra Nevada from Oakhurst, north of Fresno, to the Yuba Pass north of Sacramento (see entry), giving access to the Gold Country, with the gold-diggers' towns of Columbia, Sutter Creek, Placerville, Coloma (where James Marshall's discovery of gold started the gold rush; Marshall Gold Discovery State Historic Park), Auburn, Grass Valley (home of Lola Montez, the dancer who became mistress of King Ludwig I of Bavaria) and Nevada City (see below; some miles north is the Malakoff Diggins Historic State Park).

Imperial Valley

Imperial Valley in southern California ranks along with Death Valley (see entry) as the hottest region in North America, with summer temperatures of up to 126°F/52°C. Thanks to irrigation with water brought from the Colorado River by the All-American Canal the valley has developed highly productive agriculture and stock-rearing and all-year-round fruit- and vegetable-growing and horticulture, earning it the name of the "winter garden of the United States". On the eastern edge of Imperial Valley are the fascinating Imperial Sand Dunes, whose fragile eco-system is now increasingly threatened by thoughtless sand buggy and jeep drivers.

Imperial
Sand Dunes

California

In a beautiful coastal setting in northern California is Mendocino (pop. 1000), a picturesque little town founded in the mid 18th century. | *Mendocino

In northern central California Mount Shasta (14,162ft/4316m), the south-western buttress of the Cascade Mountains, rears its twin peaks. From this extinct volcano with its deep crater five glaciers flow down. The Everett Memorial Highway affords magnificent views. Some miles east of the town of Mount Shasta is a large ski circus. | ***Mount Shasta**

From Mount Shasta a road runs south, following the upper course of the Sacramento River, to Lake Shasta, a much ramified artificial lake which is now a popular recreation area (many houseboats). The lake was formed by the construction of the 600ft/183m high Shasta Dam. On the McCloud arm of the lake, to the north, are the Lake Shasta Caverns, with magnificent stalactites and stalagmites. | Lake Shasta

A good base from which to visit Lake Shasta and Mount Shasta is Redding (pop. 48,000), a station on the California and Oregon Railroad established in the late 19th century. | Redding

An hour's drive north of San Francisco (see entry) is the Muir Woods National Monument, a 500 acre/200 hectare forest area with giant redwoods (*Sequoia sempervirens*) over 230ft/70m high and 20ft/6m in diameter, some of which are over 2000 years old. The forest is named after John Muir, the 19th century Scottish immigrant who promoted the conservation of the natural landscape and the establishment of National Parks. | *Muir Woods National Monument

Nevada City (pop. 3000), now a tourist resort, was one of the main centres of the gold rush. There are many well preserved buildings and other relics of gold-digging days. | Nevada City

Point Reyes National Seashore is a very beautiful promontory reaching into the Pacific north-west of San Francisco which attracts holidaymakers all year round with its magnificent beaches, luxuriant vegetation and over 125 miles/200km of hiking trails. | *Point Reyes National Seashore

In the centre of the Southern Californian desert is the Salton Sea, lying 235ft/72m below sea level, which was filled with water conveyed from the Colorado River in 1905. Round it there is now a flourishing oasis, with forests of date-palms and plantations of wine grapes and citrus fruits. On its north-eastern shore is the popular Salton Sea State Recreation Area (water sports, fishing). | Salton Sea

1½ hours' drive from Los Angeles is the town of San Bernardino (pop. 130,000), which originally grew up round a Franciscan mission established in 1810. Later the Mormons also passed this way. The town is now a centre of citrus fruit growing. From San Bernardino a scenic highway, the Rim of the World Drive (CA 18) runs east into a magnificent mountain region, with Lake Arrowhead, Big Bear Lake and Baldwin Lake. | San Bernardino

The commercial and university town of San Luis Obispo (pop. 40,000), lying a few miles inland to the north-west of Los Angeles, was founded by Junípero Serra in 1772 as the Franciscan mission of San Luis Obispo de Tolosa. The church and museum of the mission are well worth a visit. A popular hotel is the Madonna Inn with its 110 rooms in lush and kitschy style. | San Luis Obispo

Santa Barbara (pop. 80,000), a bathing resort with a distinctly Spanish atmosphere in a beautiful setting, is also a university town and a centre of the electronics industry. The Franciscan mission founded by Junípero Serra in 1786 is surrounded by olive-groves. On the university campus is an interesting art museum. On the seafront is Stearns Wharf, with a variety of shops and restaurants. Every Sunday there is an arts and crafts show in | Santa Barbara

Canyonlands National Park

Dolphin fountain in Santa Barbara

Palm Park, displaying work by Californian artists. On Moreton Bay is a huge fig-tree with a crown 150ft/46m across. Round Santa Barbara are 30 miles/50km of sandy beaches with facilities for surfing, swimming, diving and sailing.

Other places of interest

Lassen Volcanic Park, Los Angeles, Mojave Desert, Monterey, Napa Valley, Redwood National Park, Sacramento, San Diego, San Francisco, San Jose, Yosemite National Park (see entries).

Canyonlands National Park L 16

State: Utah
Area: 527sq.miles/1366sq.km
Established: 1964

Season

The National Park is open throughout the year. It is best, however, to avoid the hot summer and visit it in spring or autumn.

Situation and topography

The Canyonlands National Park lies in the dry, hot and relatively remote south-east of Utah. The Colorado River and its tributary the Green River have in the course of some 300 million years carved out of the sandstone of the Colorado Plateau a basin some 45 miles/70km across and 2000ft/600m deep with fantastic rock formations, narrow gorges and rugged cliffs.
Rock drawings discovered by archaeologists (e.g. in the Great Gallery in Horseshoe Canyon, All American Man in the southern part of the National Park) show that this region was occupied by man some 3000 years before the Christian era.

Island in the Sky

The National Park consists of three parts. The plateau to the north, dissected by numerous streams, is known as the Island in the Sky. It is

Canyonlands National Park

View of the Canyonlands National Park

bounded by the White Rim (up to 4800ft/1460m), which falls down almost 1000ft/300m to the valleys of the Green River (Stillwater Canyon) and the Colorado River.

To the south of the junction of the Green and Colorado Rivers is the Needles District, with a profusion of rock pinnacles, buttresses and battlements.

*Needles District

To the west of the Green and Colorado Rivers is the Maze, a landscape of rock faces banded red and yellow, gorges, fissures and spurs of rock.

The Maze

There is a very attractive walk on the White Rim Trail, with fine views into the deep valleys of the Green and Colorado Rivers. From Grandview Point (6650ft/1860m) there are spectacular panoramic views. Another trail runs from the Needles District to the Confluence Overlook at the junction of the Green and Colorado Rivers.

Hiking trails

A rafting trip through the spectacular Cataract Canyon on the Colorado River or the Stillwater Canyon on the Green River will provide a memorable experience.

*Rafting trips

Round Canyonlands National Park

South-west of Canyonlands National Park, round the 185 mile/300km long Lake Powell (formed by a dam on the Colorado River), is the Glen Canyon National Recreation Area. Here, in the middle of the desert, has been created an all-year-round leisure centre which attracts large numbers of anglers and sailing and water sports enthusiasts. The massive dam is a tourist sight in itself.

*Glen Canyon

60 miles/100km west of Canyonlands National Park is the Capitol Reef, a reef-like wall of banded sandstone rising above the Fremont River. It is the

*Capitol Reef

Cape Canaveral / Kennedy Space Center

most impressive section of the Waterpocket Fold, which strikes north–south for some 100 miles/160km. This geological flexure (an S-shaped fold of the strata) is the largest of its kind in the United States, with a variety of bizarre rock formations and chimneys carved out by erosion. Round the Capitol Reef and Fremont River there are remains (rock paintings, etc.) of the Indian Fremont culture. In the 19th century Mormons laid out a fertile garden landscape round the township of Fruita. The Capitol Reef National Park, with an area of 375sq.miles/972sq.km, was established in 1971.

*Westwater Canyon

80 miles/130km north-east of Canyonlands National Park is a popular rafting area in the Westwater Canyon on the Colorado River.

*Natural Bridges National Monument

Just under 100 miles/160km south-east of Canyonlands National Park is the Natural Bridges National Monument. Other features of interest in this area are remains of the prehistoric Anasazi culture and the largest solar field in the world, with an area of 11½sq.miles/30sq.km.

Cape Canaveral / Kennedy Space Center   V 45

State: Florida

Situation and characteristics

On the east coast of Florida is Cape Canaveral, a promontory studded with lagoons, mangrove swamps and marshland which is now world-famed as the site of the US Air Force's largest rocket testing and launching area (23sq.miles/60sq.km). From 1963 to 1973 Cape Canaveral was known as Cape Kennedy in honour of the murdered President. On its west side is Merritt Island, on which is the Kennedy Space Center (area 130sq.miles/340sq.km), with Spaceport USA, from which manned space flights are launched.

**John. F. Kennedy Space Center/ Spaceport USA

The NASA (National Aeronautics and Space Administration) installations on the Atlantic coast of Florida are one of the most popular tourist sights in the United States. From this rocket-testing site, established in 1949, the first men were launched into orbit and sent to the moon, and from here, at irregular intervals, the US space shuttle is launched. In the heyday of American space travel anything up to 25,000 people were employed here.

Spacecraft launches

If they are lucky visitors can watch the launch of a space shuttle. The Space Center itself and the southern part of Cape Canaveral National Seashore are closed to the public on launch days, but on such days great crowds of spectators gather on the west bank of the Indian River between Titusville and the Bennett Causeway or in Jetty Park on Highway A1A on Cape Canaveral, while others watch from boats. For information about forthcoming launches telephone 1 800 432 2135 (Florida only; toll-free) or 1 900 321 LIFT OFF (rest of USA; small charge).

... 3 ... 2 ... 1 ... 0 – Lift off!

History

The rocket testing area was established in 1949, and in July 1950 a German V 2 was tested here. The first rockets developed by Wernher von Braun and his colleagues for space travel were launched from Cape Canaveral Air Force Station, where experiments with ballistic missiles had been carried

Cape Canaveral / Kennedy Space Center

out since 1953; but it was only with the establishment of NASA in 1958 that the development of civil space travel in the United States really got under way. On January 31st 1958 the first US satellite, Explorer 1 (weighing only 30 pounds/13.5kg), was sent into orbit round the earth, and on May 5th 1961 Alan Shepard, in Mercury 1, became the first American to be sent into space. This first manned space flight was followed by other Mercury and Gemini flights. With the start of the Apollo moon programme the rocket-launching area, now known as the Kennedy Space Center, was extended on to neighbouring Merritt Island. Cape Canaveral continued to be used, however, for the launch of unmanned rockets carrying satellites. The high point of the Apollo programme was the Apollo 11 mission, which on July 20th 1969 landed the first men on the moon. In 1976 the Kennedy Space Center was enlarged to become Spaceport USA, from which the reusable space shuttles were launched.

Spaceport USA

Spaceport USA, Visitor Center TWRS, Kennedy Space Center, FL 32899. Opening times: daily 9am–6pm; guided tours from 9.45am.

Visitor Center

Cape Cod

*Rocket Garden
In the Rocket Garden are displayed various types of spacecraft, including the rockets that launched some of the early space shots, a lunar module, a space shuttle and the prototype of a future space glider. Occasionally there also appears a "spaceman" in a space suit.

Galaxy Center, **IMAX Theatre
The development of American space flight is illustrated in an extensive exhibition and cinema complex.

**Bus tours
Red Tour
The Red Tour is the only way to see the rest of the space complex on Merritt Island. It first runs through the Industrial Area, with the Kennedy Space Center headquarters. In the former space control centre visitors can experience the first landing on the moon with the aid of a film show and exhibits such as a lunar module and a moon buggy. In the 525ft/160m high Vehicle Assembly Building, one of the largest structures in the world, the shuttles are assembled and fitted with their payload. Near this is the Orbiter Processing Facility, another huge building in front of which is a Saturn V rocket. Rockets of this type were used from 1967 to 1972 in the Apollo missions, and also in the moon flights of 1969–72 and the Skylab mission. Also to be seen are the gigantic "crawlers" which transport the assembled spacecraft to the launching ramps. If there is no launch in immediate prospect the tour will also take in the two launching ramps in Complex 39 (Pads A and B) from which the space shuttles are launched.

Blue Tour
The Blue Tour, which is more concerned with the earlier history of American space travel, takes visitors round the Cape Canaveral Air Force Station, with the Atlantic Missile Range where the US space programme began. Here can be seen the ramps from which the Mercury and Gemini rockets were launched in the sixties and seventies. Visitors also learn about the various scientific, commercial and military programmes, in the course of which numerous unmanned satellites have been launched into space.

Cape Cod (The Cape) H 57

State: Massachusetts

Situation and topography
South-east of Boston (see entry) the Cape Cod peninsula reaches out into the Atlantic like a gigantic crab's claw. Its western end is an outlier of a range of hills belonging to the Appalachian system; the central part consists of an Ice Age terminal moraine and associated glacial drift; and the eastern section, curling round to the north, is made up of narrow spits of land and dunes. The gently undulating landscape of sandy and gravel soil, once covered with forests of oak and pine, has long been an area of small farms specialising in the growing of cranberries. With its beautiful sandy beaches Cape Cod is now also a popular holiday area for the people of nearby Boston and New York.

Sandwich
Sandwich (pop. 16,000), an attractive little New England town at the west end of Cape Cod, was a considerable centre of the glass industry in the 19th century, as is illustrated in the local Glass Museum.

Brewster
In Brewster, on Cape Cod Bay, are the Cape Cod Aquarium and the Drummer Boy Museum (story of the American Revolution). Outside the town is the interesting Cape Cod Museum of Natural History, devoted to the natural history of the peninsula.

Hyannis
The ferry port of Hyannis, on the south coast of the peninsula, is the busy hub of Cape Cod life. On Lewis Bay, in which many yachts sway at anchor, is a monument commemorating the murdered President Kennedy. (The Kennedy family have a holiday retreat in the Hyannis Port district.)

Carlsbad Caverns National Park

Almost the whole of the east coast of Cape Cod is under protection as Cape Cod National Seashore. Its marvellous beaches, beautiful coniferous woodland (particularly Atlantic white cedar) and many attractive hiking trails draw thousands of visitors, particularly during the summer months. Information about the area can be obtained at the Salt Pond and Provincetown Visitor Centers.
**Cape Cod National Seashore

The picturesque little tourist resort and artists' haunt of Provincetown (pop. 4000), at the northern tip of Cape Cod, was the landing-place in 1620 of the first Pilgrim Fathers. On High Pole Hill (253ft/77m; wide views) is the Pilgrim Monument. Provincetown Heritage Museum is devoted to the history of the town. There are boat trips out to sea to look for whales.
*Provincetown

Popular bathing beaches on Cape Cod are Scusset Beach, at the north entrance to Cape Cod Canal; Old Silver Beach on the south-west coast (Buzzard's Bay); Craigville Beach and West Dennis Beach on the south coast; and Nauset Beach, Coast Guard Beach and Head of the Meadow Beach on the east coast. On Cape Cod Bay is the favourite Sandy Neck Beach.
Bathing beaches

Surroundings of Cape Cod

A popular holiday resort is the island of Martha's Vineyard (pop. 12,000), off the south-west coast of Cape Cod. 20 miles/32km long by 10 miles/16km across, it is surrounded by beautiful beaches. There are a number of handsome Victorian houses in Vineyard Haven, Oak Bluffs and Edgartown Harbor.
Martha's Vineyard

Also popular with holidaymakers is Nantucket Island (pop. 6000), 12 miles/20km long by 6 miles/10km across, off the south-west coast of Cape Cod. It too has beautiful beaches. The Whaling Museum recalls the great days of the Nantucket whalers in the 18th and 19th centuries.
Nantucket Island

On December 21st 1620 the Pilgrim Fathers landed from the "Mayflower" in what is now Plymouth Bay, west of the northern tip of Cape Cod. At Plymouth's State Pier is moored "Mayflower II", an accurate replica of the original "Mayflower". From Town Wharf boats take visitors out to look for whales.
***Plymouth**

3 miles/5km south-east of the town of Plymouth is the Plimoth Plantation, an open-air museum with a reconstruction of the first colony. It presents "living history", with actors in period costume re-living the everyday life of the 17th century. Relics of the Pilgrim Fathers are also displayed in the Pilgrim Hall Museum.
*Plimoth Plantation

Carlsbad Caverns National Park   R 21

State: New Mexico
Area: 73sq.miles/190sq.km
Established: 1930

The National Park is open throughout the year. It is particularly beautiful in spring, when the desert blossoms; in the hot summer the caves are pleasantly cool; and in autumn temperatures are perfectly tolerable even outside the caves.
Season

The Carlsbad Caverns lie in south-western New Mexico, on the northern edge of the arid Chihuahua region, a desert area covered with thorny scrub.
Situation

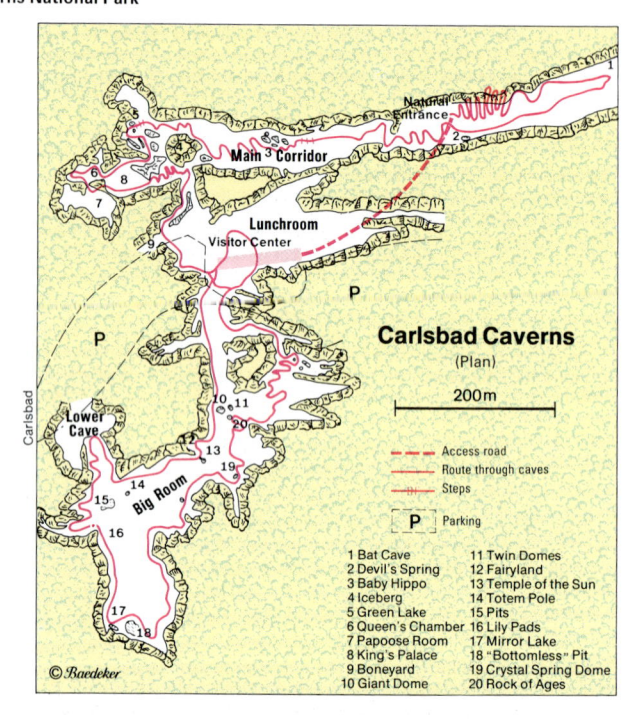

Carlsbad Caverns National Park

Carlsbad Caverns (Plan)

200m

- - - Access road
— Route through caves
—II— Steps
P Parking

1 Bat Cave
2 Devil's Spring
3 Baby Hippo
4 Iceberg
5 Green Lake
6 Queen's Chamber
7 Papoose Room
8 King's Palace
9 Boneyard
10 Giant Dome
11 Twin Domes
12 Fairyland
13 Temple of the Sun
14 Totem Pole
15 Pits
16 Lily Pads
17 Mirror Lake
18 "Bottomless" Pit
19 Crystal Spring Dome
20 Rock of Ages

**Stalactitic caves

The Carlsbad Caverns are one of the largest and most impressive cave systems in the world, notable for the variety and beauty of their stalactites and stalagmites and as the home of great swarms of bats. The caves were already known to the local Indians in the 10th and 11th centuries, as a rock carving at the entrance shows. The first systematic exploration of a small part of the cave system was carried out by James L. White in 1901. Until the 1920s the abundant supplies of bat guano in the outer reaches of the caves provided a valued source of fertiliser. So far some 22 miles/35km of passages have been explored. A 3 mile/5km tour takes visitors through the main cave and a series of spectacular chambers containing stalactites and stalagmites.

Origin of the caves

The cave system has been created over many millions of years, and the process is still continuing. Some 200–250 million years ago calcareous sediments were deposited by a warm sea, and thereafter upthrusts and subsidences of the earth's crust in this part of the world, advances and retreats of the sea and varying climatic conditions brought about chemical disintegration processes which were particularly active during the rise in the level of the land which took place some 40–20 million years ago. Groundwater and rainwater seeped into the limestone through fissures and crevices, creating cavities which grew steadily larger. In course of time the water filtering through the rock, with its high lime content, created the marvellous stalactites and stalagmites and the waterfall-like limestone terraces to be seen today.

*Tours of the caves

There are different types of tours, starting from the Visitor Center. For visitors who are pressed for time there is the Red Tour, which takes them down by elevator to see the finest cave chambers, 750ft/230m below the surface. Much more interesting is the Blue Tour (1½ hours on foot; stout footwear essential), which leads down through the main passage to the fascinating Big Room. It first runs down into the first chamber, the Bat Cave, and then past the Devil's Spring (with stalactites and stalagmites still in course of formation) and the Natural Bridge to reach the main show caves, with the Veiled Statue, the Green Lake Room, the Queen's Chamber, the King's Palace and Iceberg Rock. The tour continues past the elevator to the striking stalactitic formations in the Hall of Giants, the Twin Domes and the Temple of the Sun; then on to the Lower Cave and the Big Room. Particularly fascinating is the Top of the Cross, a huge chamber 255ft/78m high. The route continues by way of Mirror Lake and the Bottomless Pit, a sinkhole over 130ft/40m deep, to the Crystal Spring Dome, with stalagmites still in process of formation, and the Painted Grotto, where water containing iron has coloured the rocks in tones of red.

56 miles/90km south-west of Carlsbad is the Guadalupe Mountains National Park, an area of 135sq.miles/350sq.km in the state of Texas which is still ill-provided with roads. Within the park are mountains of Permian age, with the Guadalupe Peak (8750ft/2667m), the highest point in Texas, and the prominent mass of rock known as El Capitán (8078ft/2462m). There is evidence of human occupation in this area 12,000 years ago,

*Guadalupe Mountains National Park

Charleston

R 46

State: South Carolina
Altitude: 10ft/3m
Population: 80,400 (Metropolitan Area 506,900)

If you want to see a well preserved "Southern belle" and breathe the atmosphere of the old white South, you must go to Charleston. Built on a peninsula where the Cooper River and the Ashley River flow into the Atlantic, it retains, to a greater extent than any other town in the Southern states, the luxurious, almost aristocratic, ambience of the great days of plantation society – dependent as it was on the sweat and the misery of the blacks. A walk or a drive in a horse-drawn carriage through the Historic District, with its Georgian mansions fronted by verandas and classical columns and its slender church towers, makes it easy to see why the heroine of "Gone with the Wind" preferred to live in Charleston.

Situation and characteristics

**Townscape

Tourism is now a major element in the economy of Charleston, but the armed forces also make a considerable contribution. Transport planes of the US Air Force drone almost constantly over the town, and ships of the US Navy set out from the port on exercises.

Economy

The first British settlers landed on the marshy banks of the Kiawah (now the Ashley) River in April 1670, naming their settlement Charles Towne in honour of Charles II. A few years later, however, they moved to the more conveniently situated peninsula and began to develop a new town. Reinforced by new settlers, including French Huguenots, Charles Towne grew to become an important port which owed its prosperity to the trade in skins, rice and indigo. The planters living in the interior sought entertainment and relaxation in the town, and it acquired the first theatre, the first museum and the first college in North America. In 1773 Charleston was described as the wealthiest town in the American South. During the War of Independence the town was occupied in 1780 by British forces, who held it until December 1781. Eighty years later the bombardment of Fort Sumter, at the entrance to Charleston harbour, marked the beginning of the Civil War. The town suffered much damage during the war, but was rebuilt in the old style. It was similarly rebuilt in 1989 after being devastated by Hurricane Hugo.

History

Charleston

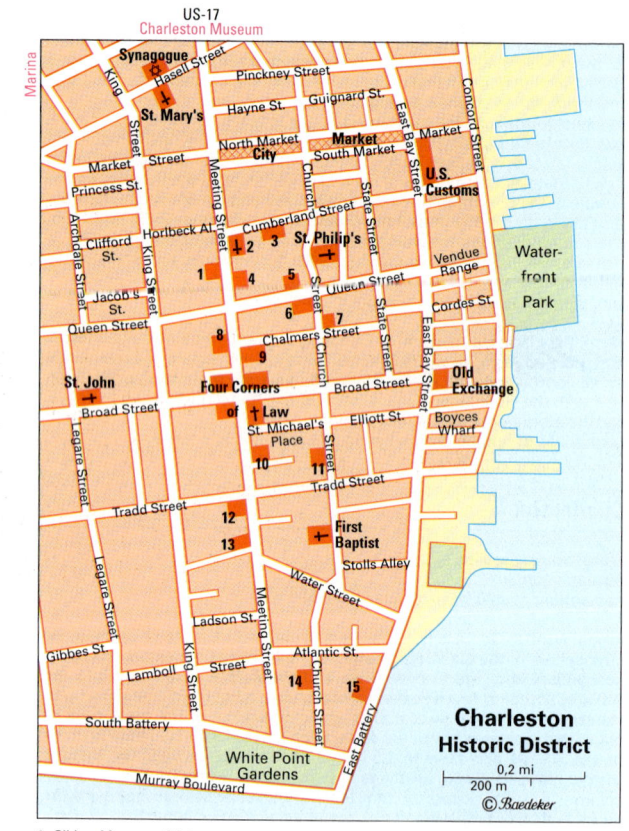

1. Gibbes Museum of Art
2. Circular Congregational Church
3. Old Powder Magazine
4. 134 Meeting Street
5. Thomas Elfe Workshop
6. Dock Street Theatre
7. French Huguenot Church
8. Hibernian Hall
9. Fireproof Building
10. S.C. Society Hall
11. Heyward-Washington House
12. First (Scots) Presbyterian Church
13. Nathaniel Russell House
14. Calhoun Mansion
15. Edmonston-Alston House

**Historic District

Sightseeing walk

City Market

The best starting-point for a walk through old Charleston is the intersection of Meeting and Market Streets, in the heart of the town. Here is the main building of the City Market (1841), now housing the Confederate Museum. Beyond this are the market halls, bustling with life and colour. Farther down Meeting Street is Cumberland Street, with the Powder Magazine (1713). Beyond it, in Church Street, can be seen the tower of St Philip's Church (1835–38; Protestant), occupying the site of the first church founded in 1670. Back on Meeting Street is the circular Congregational Church (1891; originally founded 1681), the meeting-house which gave its name to the street. At 135 Meeting Street is the Gibbes Museum of Art, with a very fine collection of paintings and graphic art, including old views of

Charleston

Sumptuous mansions on East Bay Street, Charleston

Charleston. At No. 134 is the house in which the secession of South Carolina was signed on December 20th 1860. Beyond this is the intersection with Broad Street, known as the Four Corners of Law. On the north-east corner is Old City Hall (1801), originally built as a bank; it now houses a collection of pictures, including John Trumbull's fine portrait of Washington. At the north-west corner is the County Court House (1752), originally State House. At the south-west corner is the Federal Court, built in 1886 on the site of the old Town Guardhouse; and at the south-east corner is St Michael's Church (1752–61; Protestant), which has the town's finest church tower. At the east end of Broad Street is the Old Exchange (1771), the last building to be erected by the British in Charleston; originally a stock exchange and custom house, it was used during the War of Independence as a prison.

Farther down Meeting Street are the quieter residential districts of Charleston. Among the handsome mansions open to the public are the Heyward-Washington House (87 Church Street), built in 1752, with a particularly fine 18th century bookcase; the Adam-style Nathaniel Russell House (51 Meeting Street), built in 1808, with a marvellously light staircase; and the sumptuous Edmonston-Alston House (21 East Battery), built in 1828 for a wealthy shipowner and remodelled in Greek Revival style in 1838. We are now in the elegant Battery district, with other splendid mansions lining the seafront promenade. The return to the City Market can be either along King Street, lined by antique dealers' shops, or on East Battery, with the beautiful Waterfront Park, from which there is a good view of the gigantic steel structure of the Grace Memorial Bridge, a double bridge spanning the Cooper River.

Four Corners of Law

Old Exchange

*Old houses

Waterfront Park

Other Sights in Charleston

The Charleston Museum (360 Meeting Street, opposite the Visitor Center) is the oldest municipal museum in North America, founded in 1773. It is

*Charleston Museum

Charleston

Mon.–Sat. 9am–5pm, Sun. 1–5pm

devoted to the history and natural history of the coastal region. In front of the building is a replica of the Confederate submarine "Hunley", which carried out the first underwater attack in history. Nearby are two luxuriously furnished old mansions which are managed by the Museum: the Aiken-Rhett House (1817) at 48 Elizabeth Street and the Joseph Manigault House (1802) at 350 Meeting Street.

*Fort Sumter

From the Charleston Marina on Lockwood Drive there are boat trips (for departure times ring 722 1691) to Fort Sumter, which guards the harbour entrance. From the boat there are fine views of the town and the handsome mansions on the Battery.

The bombardment of Fort Sumter, held by Union forces, from Fort Johnson on April 12th 1861 marked the beginning of the Civil War. After 34 hours of artillery bombardment the garrison surrendered, and thereafter Fort Sumter was held by the Confederates until February 1865. After withstanding incessant attacks from 1863 onwards the Confederate forces at last withdrew, leaving the fort a heap of rubble. The history of the fort is documented on the site.

Patriot's Point

On the east bank of the Cooper River, clearly visible from the town, lies the aircraft carrier USS "Yorktown", which recovered the crew of Apollo 8 in 1968. It is now part of the Maritime Museum on Patriot's Point, whose other major attraction is the nuclear-powered freighter USS "Savannah".

Surroundings of Charleston

Charles Towne Landing

From Charleston US 17 and SR 171 lead to the site of the landing by the first settlers in 1670 (reconstructed timber fortifications).

**Boone Hall Plantation

8 miles/5km north-east of Charleston on US 17 a signpost points to Boone Hall Plantation, one of the finest plantations in the Southern states, origi-

Slave hut at Boone Hall

Magnolia Gardens

nally established by Major Boone in 1681. During the 18th and 19th centuries cotton was grown on the plantation, which then switched to pecan nuts. The mansion (restored), with its gardens and its magnificent half-mile long avenue of oaks, has been a favourite setting for film and television producers. A reminder of the slaves who made this splendour possible is provided by nine 18th century brick huts, among the few surviving examples of original slave huts in the United States.

Equally beautiful is Drayton Hall (9 miles/15km north-west of Charleston), one of the oldest plantations in the South to survive the Civil War unscathed. The fine Georgian mansion built in 1738 by the Draytons, who came here in 1679 and owned the estate for seven generations, can thus be seen in its original condition.

**Drayton Hall

1 mile/1.6km beyond Drayton Hall on the same road is the Magnolia Plantation. The most impressive feature here is not so much the house as the gardens, lavishly laid out around 1680 – the oldest man-made gardens in North America. The bridges over the quiet ponds and arms of the river have a fairytale look. Also within the estate are the Swamp Gardens, which give some impression of the swamp country inhabited by alligators which the first settlers found here.

**Magnolia Plantation and Gardens

The last of the series of plantations on SR 61 is Middleton Place, once the home of Henry Middleton, first President of the Continental Congress. In 1941 he laid out the oldest surviving landscaped garden in North America, which falls away in grassy terraces to the Ashley River.

*Middleton Place

Charlottesville

L 47

State: Virginia
Altitude: 480ft/146m
Population: 40,300

Amid the gentle hills of central Virginia is the town of Charlottesville, founded in 1762, the development of which was much influenced by Thomas Jefferson (see Famous People), third- President of the United States, who was born near here.
Charlottesville is the centre of a region in which tobacco was once the main crop; it is now farming and horse-breeding country. It is the seat of the important University of Virginia, which has some 18,000 students.

Situation and characteristics

Sights in Charlottesville

The University of Virginia was founded by Jefferson in 1819, and its redbrick buildings, centred on the Rotunda, together with the gardens and the road system of the extensive campus (at the west end of Main Street) were designed by him. Among students here was Edgar Allan Poe (see Famous People), whose room (No. 13 in the West Building) can be visited.

University of Virginia

Surroundings of Charlottesville

One of the finest country houses in the United States (featured on the reverse side of the 5-cent coin) is Jefferson's villa of Monticello. He himself designed the Palladian-style mansion, beautifully situated on a hill, and continued altering and improving it over a period of forty years, from 1768 to 1809. The guided tour through the house takes visitors into Jefferson's study, the parlour and other living rooms, all filled with works of art and

**Monticello

Mar.–Oct.
daily 8am–5pm;
Nov.–Feb.
daily 9am–4.30pm

Cheyenne

Thomas Jefferson's country house, Monticello

personal mementoes. The whole house shows the versatile genius of its owner, who eased the tasks of domestic life by a variety of inventions.

Gardens
To the rear of the house are the gardens, also designed by Jefferson: flower gardens and, on a lower terrace, vegetable gardens and a vineyard. Between them runs Mulberry Row, on which were the workshops of the estate craftsmen – all slaves. Jefferson, who called slavery an "abominable crime", himself owned almost 200 slaves.

Cemetery
Below the gardens is the family cemetery, still in use, in which an obelisk marks Thomas Jefferson's grave.

Ash Lawn Highland
A short distance from Monticello is Ash Lawn Highland, the country house of James Monroe (1758–1831), fifth President of the United States. It too was designed by Thomas Jefferson. There are guided tours of the house.

Cheyenne   H 21

State: Wyoming
Altitude: 6060ft/1847m
Population: 55,000

Situation and characteristics
The capital of the state of Wyoming, named after the Cheyenne Indians, lies in the rolling upland country of the Great Plains in the eastern foreland of the Rockies. The town was founded in 1867 in what was then the Wild West as a station on the Union Pacific Railroad, and two years later became the chief town in the territory of Wyoming. In the town was the largest outpost of the US Cavalry, whose task was to protect the settlers and railroad workers from Indian attack. It is now an important traffic hub, at the intersection of busy trunk roads (Highways I 80 and I 25) and rail lines (mainly goods traffic on the Union Pacific and Burlington Northern). By far

Downtown Cheyenne

the largest employer is the military, which has an intercontinental ballistic missile base here, of great strategic importance. In the surrounding area there are oil wells and iron ore workings.

Sights in Cheyenne

The town's principal sight is the prominently situated State Capitol on Capitol Avenue, round which are various state government buildings. The foundation stone of the Capitol was laid in 1867 but it was completed only thirty years later. The dome was regilded in 1986. Notable features of the central Rotunda are the marble floor and the cherrywood staircase.

State Capitol

Wyoming State Museum (south-east of the Capitol, on 24th and Central Streets) has interesting collections of material on the Prairie Indians and the development of cattle ranching in Wyoming.

Wyoming State Museum

On 17th Street, famed as Cattle Barons' Row, are a number of handsome Victorian-style mansions which belonged to 19th century cattle barons.

Cattle Barons' Row

At the south end of Capitol Avenue is the Union Pacific Railroad Depot, a notable example of industrial architecture built in 1886.

Union Pacific Railroad Depot

North-east of the Depot is a Big Boy locomotive, one of the largest steam engines ever built.

Big Boy

In the north of the town, in Frontier Park (adjoining the rodeo arena), is the interesting Frontier Days Old West Museum, with much information about rodeos and a number of the old coaches and wagons in which the first settlers came to the Wild West. Open: July–Sept. Mon.–Sat. 8am–7pm. Sun. 10am–6pm; rest of year Mon.–Fri. 9am–5pm, Sat. and Sun. 11.30am–4.30pm.

*Frontier Days Old West Museum

Chicago

**Frontier Days In the Frontier Days festival, held annually in the last week in July, the Wild West comes to life again. Hundreds of thousands of spectators come to watch spectacular rodeos, cowboy shows, chuckwagon races, parades and a mock battle between Sioux Indians and the US Cavalry.

Surroundings of Cheyenne

F. E. Warren Air Force Base On the western outskirts of the town (west of Frontier Park) is the extensive area occupied by the F. E. Warren Air Force Base. The site was originally occupied by a 19th century fort. During the Second World War it was a prisoner of war camp. Since 1958 it has been an intercontinental ballistic missile base. There is an informative Air Base Museum.

Chicago   H 38

State: Illinois
Altitude: 580ft/177m
Population: 3 million (Metropolitan Area 8 million)

Situation Chicago, the "city of superlatives", widely known also as the "windy city", extends, including its suburbs, for more than 60 miles/100km along the south-western shores of Lake Michigan, from which the canalised Chicago River flows south as part of the Illinois Waterway, heading towards the Mississippi. Farther to the south the Calumet River flows into the lake.

Climate The climate of the city is characterised by extremes, with winds – sometimes very violent winds – blowing throughout the year. In spite of its situation on Lake Michigan the city can become intolerably hot in summer. In winter influxes of cold air, accompanied by heavy snowfalls and very low temperatures, lead almost regularly to catastrophic conditions in the city.

**Skyline Chicago has a strikingly impressive skyline, with numerous recently built skyscrapers, some of them unconventional in form (among them two of the world's tallest buildings), on the Lakefront, part of which is land reclaimed from the lake.

Economic importance The metropolis of the American Middle West has the world's busiest airport and largest inland port and is one of the most important road and rail hubs in the United States. It is the world's leading commodity futures market, the most important financial centre in the United States after New York and a long-established major industrial centre. Originally the foodstuffs industries (meat-processing, milling), with such firms as Kraft and Libby, played a major part; later came mechanical engineering (including agricultural machinery) and motor vehicle construction (Pullman, International Harvesters, etc.) and the steel industry (particularly in the suburb of Gary); and in recent years high-tech industries have flourished. A brilliant future is predicted for Chicago as an industrial centre following the coming into force in 1994 of NAFTA (North American Free Trade Association, consisting of the United States, Canada and Mexico), the strongest economic region in the world.

A cultural metropolis Chicago is, after New York, the most important cultural metropolis in the United States. It is a focal point of modern American architecture, represented by such great names as Louis Sullivan, Frank Lloyd Wright, Mies van der Rohe and Helmut Jahn. Works of open-air sculpture by Picasso, Miró, Dubuffet and Chagall enrich the townscape of Chicago. The city has no fewer than nine universities and numerous internationally renowned research institutes. Other important cultural institutions are the Chicago

Chicago

The skyline of Chicago with the Hancock Tower

Symphony Orchestra, the Art Institute of Chicago, the Lyric Opera of Chicago, the Steppenwolf Theater, the Goodman Theater, the Field Museum of Natural History, the Museum of Science and Industry and the world-famed Oriental Institute of the University of Chicago. In Chicago – often claimed to be the true "home of the blues" – a distinctive style of jazz was developed during the "wild twenties". And that Chicago has also much to offer in the sporting field is demonstrated weekly by the Chicago Bulls (basketball), the Chicago Bears (American football) and the Chicago White Sox (baseball).

Chicago's rapidly growing population – from 20,000 in 1848 to 1.6 million at the turn of the century and 3.2 million in the 1940s – has recently shown a falling trend, resulting from a move to the suburbs, and now stands at around 3 million. The heterogeneous make-up of the population is demonstrated by the growth of districts of particular ethnic or national origin, like Bronzeville, inhabited by the coloured population, Chinatown, a Polish quarter which is the third largest concentration of Poles in the world and other districts with predominantly Lithuanian, Swedish, German, Italian, Greek and Jewish populations.

Population

The first whites to come to this area, in 1673, were French prospectors and fur-traders, who met with an unfriendly reception from the local Indians. The first real settlement on the site of Chicago grew up round Fort Dearborn, which was established in 1803, and was incorporated as a town in 1837. Boosts were given to its growth by the development of the rail network and steam-powered shipping on the Great Lakes. After the Civil War Chicago became the country's leading centre of major industry, attracting a great influx of immigrants from all over the world. Temporary economic difficulties and the enormous pressure of population led to social and ethnic conflicts, reflected in such incidents as the Hay Market riot of 1886 and the Pullman strike in 1894. Gangster activity, too, developed on

History

Chicago

an unprecedented scale. In October 1871 large areas of the city were destroyed in a catastrophic fire; but recovery was swift, and only 22 years later, in 1893, Chicago hosted the World's Columbian Exposition. After the great fire, too, the Chicago school of architects, including such masters as L. H. Sullivan, D. H. Burnham and D. Adler, established their reputation. During the Prohibition era (1919–33) Chicago was tyrannised by gangs, often with the co-operation of bribed police and government officials. One of the leading gangsters of this period was Al Capone (see Famous People). In the twenties, too, the city became the great centre of jazz, which although born in New Orleans (see entry) enjoyed a fresh flowering in Chicago. In 1933–34 another very successful world's fair was held in the city. During the economic difficulties of the thirties a neo-liberal school of economists came to the fore in Chicago. In the forties the "second Chicago school" of architects, led by Mies van der Rohe, established their reputation. In 1942 the first controlled atomic chain reaction was achieved in Chicago. In 1959 the opening of the St Lawrence Seaway gave the city access to the oceans of the world; and in the last thirty years Chicago has developed into one of the busiest metropolises in the western hemisphere.

Near North Side/Gold Coast

The Near North Side and Gold Coast district is a very handsome part of the city, fronted by the gleaming façades of modern skyscrapers, behind which are two- and three-storey 19th century houses, now much sought after. In this area there are excellent jazz spots, one or two night clubs, good restaurants, interesting boutiques, antique dealers and well-stocked bookshops.

Practically in the middle of the city the Oak Street Beach offers scope for relaxation.

*Astor Street district

Between East Division Street and East North Boulevard is the Astor Street district – six blocks with notable modern buildings by famous architects (Frank Lloyd Wright, David Adler, Bertrand Goldberg, etc.).

International Museum of Surgical Sciences

The International Museum of Surgical Sciences (1524 North Lake Shore Drive) has one of the world's largest collections of material on the history of medicine, extending from the simple implements of primitive peoples to the most modern technical apparatus.

New East Side/Cityfront Center

In the last few years the area round the mouth of the Chicago River has been refurbished and smartened up at great expense, and further new building is planned.

*North Pier

The focal point of the refurbishment programme is the recently completed new North Pier, now a multi-functional centre with ship and yacht landing-places, museums (including the Maritime Museum and the Children's Museum), luxury shops, good restaurants, sidewalk cafés and a variety of indoor entertainment facilities.

*Centennial Fountain and Arch

A little way south is the Centennial Fountain, which every ten minutes shoots an arch of water up to 100ft/30m high across the Chicago River, and when the sun is shining produces a marvellous rainbow-like play of colour.

Navy Pier

North-east of the mouth of the Chicago River is the Navy Pier, constructed in 1916, from which there is a breathtaking view of Chicago's skyline. This is the scene of all-year-round festivities, including the Chicago Festival in August.

Chicago Downtown

400 m
0,3 mi

Milwaukee, Sault Ste. Marie
Hyde Park, Univ. of Chicago, Lincoln Park, Old Town

Lake Michigan

W. Goethe St.
W. Division St.
W. Elm St.
W. Hill St.
Seward Park
W. Oak St.
Newberry Library
E. Oak St.
E. Walton St.
W. Chestnut St.
John Hancock Center
E. Chestnut St.
Loyola University of Chicago
Water Tower
Armory
W. Chicago Ave.
Moody Bible Institute
E. Chicago Ave.
Northwestern University
W. Huron St.
Peace Museum
E. Huron St.
Terra Museum
Water Filtration Plant
W. Ontario St.
Museum of Contemporary Art
E. Ontario St.
Olive Park
W. Grand Ave.
E. Grand Ave.
Time Life Building
Lake Point Tower
Tribune Tower
NBC Tower
Navy Pier
W. Hubbard St.
Wrigley Building
North Pier Maritime Museum
E. North Water St.
Merchandise Mart
W. Carroll Ave.
Equitable Building
Centennial Fountain
Marina City
E. Wacker Dr.
Chicago
W. Wacker Dr.
Illinois Center
State of Illinois Center
W. Randolph St.
Prudential Building
Amoco Building
City Hall & Co. Bldg.
Daley Center
E. Randolph St.
Northwestern Atrium Center
W. Washington St.
Brunswick Plaza
Public Library
Civic Opera House
Chicago Exchange
First National
Carson Pirie Scott
W. Monroe St.
E. Monroe St.
U.S. Gypsum
Union Station
Sears Tower
Orchestra Hall
Art Institute
Federal Center
W. Jackson Blvd.
E. Jackson Dr.
Midwest Stock Exchange
Grant Park
Lake Chicago
Eisenhower Expwy.
W. Congress Pkwy.
Buckingham Fountain
Printers Row Printing Museum
Columbia College
E. Balbo Dr.
W. Polk St.
E. 8th St.
Museum of Broadcast & Communications
Dearborn Station
E. 9th St.
Lake Michigan
W. Taylor St.
Logan Monument
Chicago Fire Dept. Academy
E. 11th St.
W. Roosevelt Rd.
E. Roosevelt Rd.
Field Museum of Natural History
Shedd Aquarium
Adler Planetarium
E. 13th St.
Solidarity Dr.
E. 14th St.
Soldier Field
Burnham Park Harbor
W. 15th St.
Chicago Merrill C. Meigs Field
W. 16th St.
E. 16th St.
Waldron Dr.

© Baedeker

///// The Loop   CHINATOWN, Police Museum   — Elevated   McCormick Place, Glessner House, Museum of Science & Industry

197

Chicago

333 North Michigan Avenue Building

South-west of the NBC Building, beyond the Chicago River, is the 35-storey 333 North Michigan Avenue Building (1928), on the site of Fort Dearborn (see History). Regarded at the time of its erection as an ultra-modern building, it is now protected as a historic monument.

*Amoco Building

Farther south is the 80-storey Amoco Building (1973), its white marble façade soaring up to a height of 1135ft/346m.

North Michigan Avenue/Oak Street

Magnificent Mile

The section of Michigan Avenue north of the Chicago River, with its numerous galleries, boutiques and luxury shops, is known as the "Magnificent Mile".

*Water Tower/ Pumping Station/ "Here's Chicago"

The only buildings in this area to survive the devastating 1871 fire were the 205ft/62m high Water Tower (800 North Michigan Avenue) and the associated Pumping Station. Here now are housed the tourist information office and "Here's Chicago", a multi-media show about the city.

Water Tower Place

To the north-west, housed in the 74-storey Water Tower Place Building, is a shopping mall centred on a seven-storey atrium (over 120 shops, restaurants, seven movie houses).

*John Hancock Center

The John Hancock Center, an 1125ft/343m high tower, tapering towards the top, which has something of the appearance of a pit winding station, was completed in 1970 to the design of the renowned SOM firm of architects (architect B. Graham, constructor F. Kahn). Its cross-braced steel structure has a facing of oxidised aluminium with a slightly reflective surface. From the observatory on the 94th floor (1030ft/314m above ground level; open 9am–midnight) there are magnificent panoramic views. On the roof are two 345ft/105m high telecommunications aerials.

*Oak Street

Farther north is Oak Street, an exclusive shopping street between Michigan Avenue and State Street.

*Terra Museum of American Art

Farther south, at 666 North Michigan Avenue, is the Terra Museum of American Art, with one of the largest collections of American art, covering two centuries (many famous works by John Singer Sargent, W. M. Chase, Mary Cassat, Samuel F. B. Morse, Winslow Homer and E. Hopper). Open: Tue. noon–5pm, Wed.–Sat. 10am–5pm, Sun. noon–5pm.

*Museum of Contemporary Art

South-east of the Water Tower, at 237 Ontario Street, is the Museum of Contemporary Art (open: Tue.–Sat. 10am–5pm, Sun. noon–5pm), one of the outstanding collections of contemporary art. It displays the work of both established and lesser artists of the Modernist and Avantgarde schools, and offers very informative guided tours.

Wrigley Building

Another architectural landmark is the Wrigley Building at 400 North Michigan Avenue, a 32-storey tower in French Renaissance style built for the chewing-gum firm in 1924.

River North

The River North district caters for those interested in art, galleries and fashion. Here too there are a number of imposing buildings.

*Marina City

An architectural highlight of the area is Marina City (by Bertrand Goldberg, 1963–64), a 590ft/179m high twin-towered 61-storey office and apartment complex on the Chicago River.

Merchandise Mart

Some 550yd/500m farther west is the gigantic Merchandise Mart, which belongs to the Kennedy family. This furniture and building materials "supermarket", originally built in 1928 and since then repeatedly enlarged,

Chicago

now has no fewer than 1800 showrooms. It was extended in 1991 by the addition of a large shopping mall.

¾ mile/1km north-west of Marina City, running east–west, is Superior Street, the pulsating centre of Chicago's gallery quarter. — *Superior Street

A little way south-west, at 430 West Erie Street, is the only Peace Museum in the United States. — Peace Museum

The Loop

Chicago's financial and business district is known as the Loop: in the strict sense only the area enclosed by the "El" (elevated railway), but in practice taking in a dozen or so blocks on both sides of the Chicago River. The El follows Wabash Street, Lake Street, Wells Street and Van Buren Street, on which are many buildings designed by great architects. On the squares and in the public buildings of the Loop there are over 60 works by well-known artists, including Picasso, Chagall and Alexander Calder.

The classical-style City Hall and County Building, in the northern part of the Loop, was completed in 1910. — City Hall and County Building

In the north-western part of the Loop, at 100 West Randolph Street, is the very handsome modern complex of the State of Illinois Center, regarded by many as the German-born architect Helmut Jahn's masterpiece. Its interior is strikingly impressive, with a huge atrium mall housing many excellent shops, cafés and restaurants. Here too is the State of Illinois Art Gallery (open: Mon.–Fri. 9am–6pm), a branch of the State Museum in Springfield which puts on periodic exhibitions of works by well-known Middle West artists. — **State of Illinois Center and Art Gallery

Adjoining, to the east, is the Richard J. Daley Center (1965), a 31-storey tower containing government offices and lawcourts. In the plaza in front of the building is a 50ft/15m high piece of abstract sculpture by Picasso (1967). An eternal flame commemorates the dead of many wars. — Richard J. Daley Center

Still farther east is State Street Mall, a shoppers' paradise, with the 450 departments of Marshall Field's great store. — *State Street Mall

The next block to the south, between Madison Street and Monroe Street, is occupied by the 60-storey First National Bank Building (1969, by Murphy, Perkins and Will). In its attractively laid out plaza are a mosaic of the "Four Seasons" by Marc Chagall (1974) and a fountain by Samuel Hamel. — *First National Bank Building

Farther south-east, at 30 West Monroe Street, is the Inland Steel Building, supported by massive steel columns on the Dearborn Street front. — **Dearborn Street** / Inland Steel Building

At the corner of Monroe Street and Dearborn Street is the eye-catching Xerox Building, its aluminium and glass façade reflecting the neighbouring buildings. — Xerox Building

A few minutes' walk farther south, at 230 South Dearborn Street, is the Federal Center, with the low Central Post Office, the 45-storey Federal Office Building and the 30-storey Court House (by Mies van der Rohe, 1964). In the plaza is a 50ft/16m high stabile by Alexander Calder, "Flamingo". — *Federal Center

Farther south (330 South Dearborn Street and 53 West Jackson Boulevard) is the Monadnock Building of 1893, still the tallest masonry-built office block. It now houses the ArchiCenter, with an exhibition gallery and a wide selection of good architectural books, which also offers guided walking tours of the Loop and neighbouring districts. — Monadnock Building, ArchiCenter

Chicago

Fisher Building
Farther south, at 343 South Dearborn Street, is the Fisher Building (designed by Daniel H. Burnham), with a particularly handsome façade.

Old Colony Building
Farther south again, at 407 South Dearborn Street, is the Old Colony Building (by Holabird and Roche, 1894).

Manhattan Building
Nearby, at 431 South Dearborn Street, is the Manhattan Building, the first steel-framed high-rise building (designed by William LeBaron Jenney, c. 1890).

State Street

*Carson Pirie Scott Building
To the east of the First National Bank, at 1 South State Street, is the Carson Pirie Scott Building, a richly ornamented turn-of-the-century department store designed by Louis Sullivan.

LaSalle Street

LaSalle Street, which runs north–south to the west of the Federal Center, is known as Chicago's "financial heart".

Midwest Stock Exchange
At 440 South LaSalle Street is the Midwest Stock Exchange, the second largest in the United States (Visitors' Gallery, guided tours).

Chicago Board of Options Exchange
Immediately north is the Chicago Board of Options Exchange, one of the largest commodity futures exchanges in the United States (Visitors' Gallery).

*Chicago Board of Trade
A few minutes' walk north, at South LaSalle Street/141 West Jackson Boulevard, is the 44-storey Chicago Board of Trade, the largest grain exchange in the world. On the 5th floor is a Visitors' Gallery (open: Mon.–Fri. 9.30am–1pm). The building is topped by an aluminium statue of Ceres, goddess of fertility.

Wacker Drive

On Wacker Drive, which runs along the west side of the Loop, roughly parallel to the Chicago River, are some outstanding architectural achievements.

**Sears Tower
Dominating the skyline of Chicago is the 110-storey Sears Tower (233 South Wacker Drive), which rises to a height of 1450ft/443m in successively smaller stages. It was built in 1974 for the then powerful Sears, Roebuck company and became the highest office block in the world. In the lobby is a mobile by Alexander Calder, "Universe". From the observatory on the 103rd floor there are spectacular views, particularly in the evening.

Main Post Office
South-west of the Sears Tower, beyond the Chicago River, is the Main Post Office (433 West Van Buren Street), the largest post office in the world (conducted tours by appointment, tel. 312-765 3007).

Chicago Mercantile Exchange and International Monetary Market
North of the Sears Tower, at 30 South Wacker Drive, is the Chicago Mercantile Exchange and International Monetary Market (the "Merc"), one of the largest commodity and financial markets in the world (Visitors' Gallery on 4th floor; guided tours).

US Gypsum Building
At 101 South Wacker Drive is the US Gypsum Building, a striking structure faced with slate and white marble which has something of the appearance of a gigantic crystal of gypsum.

*Civic Center for the Performing Arts
Farther north, at 20 North Wacker Drive, is the imposing Civic Center for the Performing Arts (1929), with the Civic Theatre and Civic Opera, home of the world-famed Chicago Lyric Opera.

*333 West Wacker Drive Building
At the bend into West Wacker Drive is the slightly curved 333 West Wacker Drive Building, its gleaming steel and glass façade reflecting the Chicago River and neighbouring buildings. It is particularly eye-catching at sunset.

North Michigan Avenue

North Michigan Avenue runs along the east side of the Loop. Here too there are a number of notable buildings.

Carbide and Carbon Building
The dark-coloured Carbide and Carbon Building (1929) at 230 North Michigan Avenue was designed by the Burnham brothers.

Stone Container Building
Farther north, at 360 North Michigan Avenue, is the imposing classical-style Stone Container Building (1923), with a dome borne on columns.

Sears Tower: one of the tallest skyscrapers ▶

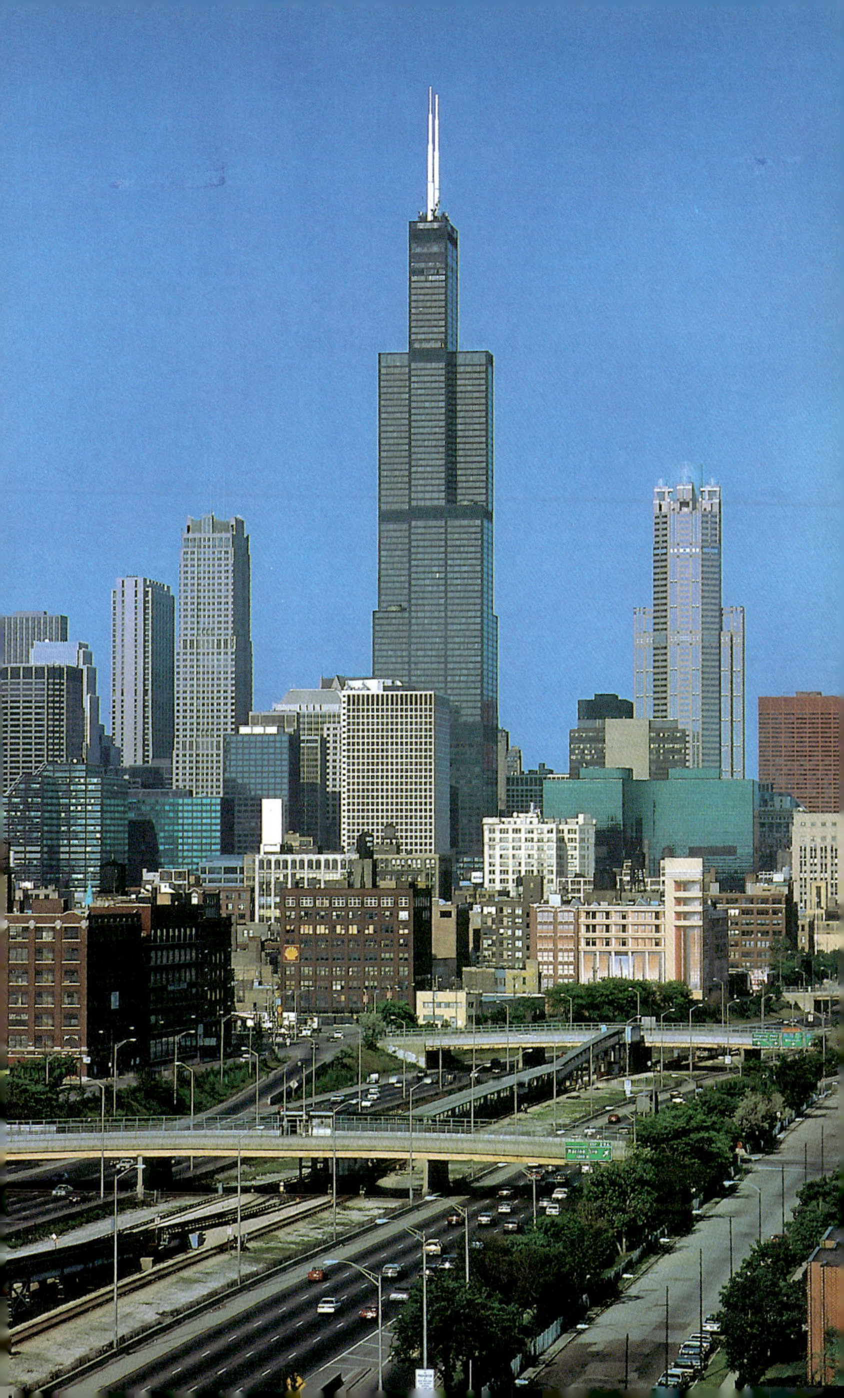

Chicago

Jewelers' Building — Nearby, at 35 East Wacker Drive, is the striking Jewelers' Building. Erected in 1926, this cream-coloured building in neo-Rococo style with an attractive terracotta façade originally housed a large number of jewellers' businesses.

Grant Park / South Michigan Avenue

The Grant Park and South Michigan Avenue area attracts millions of visitors annually with its world-famed cultural institutions and its architecture by Louis Sullivan and Daniel Burnham.

**Art Institute of Chicago

Mon., Wed., Thur., Fri. 10.30am–4.30pm, Tue. 10.30am–8pm, Sat. 10am–5pm, Sun. and pub. hols. noon–5pm

The Art Institute of Chicago (Michigan Avenue and Adams Street), one of the largest art collections in the world, is housed in a building in Italian Renaissance style erected by Shepley, Rutan and Coolidge for the World's Columbian Exposition of 1893. The collections cover every field of art from antiquity to the present day – paintings, graphic art, sculpture, photography, applied and decorative art and ethnographic material from Asia, Africa and America. The French Impressionists and Post-Impressionists are particularly well represented, with works by Monet, Renoir, Cézanne, Gauguin, Seurat, Degas and Van Gogh. On the lower floor are the Thorne Miniature Rooms, a kind of gigantic dolls' house with 68 different rooms (representing every type of dwelling from a peasant's hut to a palace) reproduced on the scale of 1:12. Also within the complex are an art school, a Children's Museum, the Film Center and the renowned Goodman Theater.

Chicago Symphony Orchestra Hall

A little way south of the Art Institute, at 220 South Michigan Avenue, is the home of the world-famed Chicago Symphony Orchestra, built in 1900 to the design of Daniel Burnham.

*Grant Park

Grant Park extends eastward to Lake Michigan and south to the Field Museum of Natural History, 2 miles/3km away. Its central feature is the pink marble Buckingham Fountain (1927), a magnet for visitors. The fountain plays from May to September, and is illuminated in the evening.

Fine Arts Building / *Auditorium Theater

To the west of the Buckingham Fountain are the Fine Arts Building (410 South Michigan Avenue), formerly the city's cultural centre, and the striking Auditorium Theater (by Dankmar Adler and Louis Sullivan), which is famed for its excellent acoustics.

Auditorium Building

At 430 South Michigan Avenue is the Auditorium Building (by Adler and Sullivan, 1887–89), which now houses the private Roosevelt University (founded 1945; 6000 students), the O'Malley Theater and the Ganz Recital Hall. To the south are a number of large hotels, including the Conrad Hilton Hotel ("mother house" of the renowned Hilton chain).

Lake Shore Drive

Lake Shore Drive runs along the shores of Lake Michigan, with some beautiful stretches of beach.

**Field Museum of Natural History

Daily 9am–5pm

At the south end of Grant Park is the Field Museum of Natural History (Roosevelt Road and Lake Shore Drive), named after the department store proprietor and art patron Marshall Field. The collection, founded in 1893, covers geology, botany, zoology and anthropology, with permanent displays on travels in the Pacific, ancient Egypt and the cultures of North, Central and South America. Not to be missed are the fine collection of minerals and the spectacular dinosaur presentation.

*John G. Shedd Aquarium

North-west of the Field Museum, at 1200 South Lake Shore Drive, is the John G. Shedd Aquarium, the largest of its kind in the world, with well over 6000 different marine creatures. On an artificial coral reef divers feed sharks, turtles and other denizens of the Caribbean (daily at 1 and 2pm). In

Chicago

View over the McCormick Trade Fair Center

the new Oceanarium live inhabitants of the north-western Pacific, including whales, dolphins and sea-otters.

Farther south, on an area of land reclaimed from Lake Michigan, is the Adler Planetarium (1300 South Lakeshore Drive), from which there is a particularly fine view of the skyline of Chicago. The Planetarium puts on regular presentations (with special sessions for children), accompanied by exhibitions on astronomy and space travel.

*Adler Planetarium

South of the Field Museum is Soldier Field, a huge sports stadium built between 1922 and 1940, with seating for up to 200,000 spectators.

Soldier Field

South-west of Soldier Field is the Prairie Avenue Historic District, centred on this exclusive 19th century residential street (recently restored), once the home of such wealthy citizens of Chicago as the department store magnates Marshall Field and Joseph Sears. Of particular interest are the neo-Romanesque Glessner House (1886) at 1800 South Prairie Avenue, now the headquarters of the Chicago Architecture Foundation, and Clarke House, in Greek Revival style, one of the oldest houses in Chicago.

*Prairie Avenue Historic District

The McCormick Place-on-the-Lake, the largest trade fair ground in the United States, extends southward towards Lake Michigan.

McCormick Place-on-the-Lake

West Loop / Near Southwest Side

The Chicago Fire Academy at 558 West Dekoven Street stands on the precise spot where in October 1871 Mrs O'Leary's cow upset a lamp and started the fire which devastated Chicago.

Chicago Fire Academy

North-west of the Fire Academy, at 800 South Halsted Street, is Jane Addams' Hull House, a social work settlement modelled on London's

*Jane Addams' Hull House

Chicago

	Toynbee Hall which was founded in 1889 by the social reformer Jane Addams (1860–1935), later awarded the Nobel Peace Prize. It lies on the eastern edge of the campus of the University of Illinois (20,000 students).
*Mexican Fine Arts Museum	The Mexican Fine Arts Museum at 1852 West 19th Street, the largest establishment of the kind in the northern United States, displays the work of both well-known and lesser known Mexican artists and also folk art.
Chicago Stadium	The Chicago Stadium at 1800 West Madison Street is the home of the Chicago Bulls baseball team, one of whose stars is Michael "Air" Jordan.

Burnham Park / Chinatown

Burnham Park	The area round Burnham Park, formerly neglected, has recently been refurbished at great expense. Its excellent shops, restaurants, bars, cafés, entertainment facilities and various features of interest attract numbers of visitors as well as locals.
*Dearborn Station	At 47 West Polk Street is Dearborn Station, the city's oldest railroad station, built in the 1880s. Now lovingly restored and protected as a national monument, it is a popular and photogenic meeting-place, with a variety of attractive shops and restaurants.
Printers Row/ Printing Museum	A little to the north-east is Printers Row, once occupied by printing offices and warehouses but now a luxury shopping area, with only the Printing Museum (731 South Plymouth Court) as a reminder of earlier days.
Police Museum	The Police Museum at 17025 South State Street has relics of the Haymarket Riot of 1886 and of the gangsters of the 1920s and 1930s (Al Capone, John Dillinger, etc.).
Chinatown	South of the Burnham Park area, round Cermark Road and Wentworth Avenue, is Chicago's lively Chinatown, with its own town hall and temple and the interesting Ling Long Museum.
Illinois Institute of Technology	1 mile/1.5km south of Chinatown is the renowned Illinois Institute of Technology, built between 1942 and 1958 to the design of Mies van der Rohe.
*DuSable Museum	Still farther south, at 740 East 56th Street, is the DuSable Museum of African-American History, with a rich collection of pictures and documents on the history of blacks in America.

Hyde Park / University of Chicago

University of Chicago	To the south of the city is the large campus of the University of Chicago, one of the leading US universities, which was founded in 1890 by John D. Rockefeller and now has some 10,000 students. On the campus is Robie House, built by Frank Lloyd Wright in 1909 as a private residence, which is now occupied by the Institute of International Studies. There are also buildings designed by Mies van der Rohe and Eero Saarinen. The first controlled nuclear chain reaction was achieved by University scientists in 1942.
**Oriental Institute Tue.–Sat. 10am–4pm, Sun. noon–4pm	The University has a number of interesting museums, the most famous of which is the Museum of the Oriental Institute (1155 East 58th Street), which has valuable collections illustrating the development of the civilisations of the Near and Middle East. Among the most notable exhibits are Egyptian mummies, a statue of Tutankhamun, gold from Iran and a massive animal relief from an Assyrian palace.
**Museum of Science and Industry Daily 9.30am–5.30pm	At the north end of nearby Jackson Park (South Lakeshore Drive and 57th Street) is the Museum of Science and Industry, founded in 1933, which is devoted to the application of natural laws in technological and industrial development. Among many notable exhibits are the Apollo 8 space module, a German submarine captured during the Second World War, a walk-

through model of the human heart and a representation of the human brain. Other items of interest include Coleen Moore's House, a dolls' house in the form of a fairytale castle, and a large model railway layout.
The Henry Crown Space Center illustrates the latest developments in space travel, and the Omnimax Theater puts on impressive film shows.

Henry Crown Space Center

North of the University of Chicago, at 1100 East Hyde Park Boulevard, is the Morton B. Weiss Museum, a museum of Jewry, housed in a Byzantine-style synagogue, which possesses rare documents on the Jewish-Persian and Jewish-Kurdish heritage.

*Morton B. Weiss Museum

Lakefront / Old Town / Lincoln Park

A few miles north of the city centre is the Lakefront, with beautifully laid out parkland, beaches, marinas and a variety of sporting and leisure facilities (golf, tennis, jogging, cycle tracks, cross-country skiing, etc.).

*Lakefront

The renowned Chicago Academy of Science (2001 North Clark Street) was founded in 1857 to promote the study of science. Its excellently presented and informative displays illustrate many aspects of the biosphere, concentrating particularly on the development of animal species in the different periods of the earth's history. There is a special "hands-on" section for children.

*Chicago Academy of Science

In Lincoln Park are one of the largest municipal zoos in the United States and the Lincoln Park Conservatory (designed by J. L. Silsbee), with a large collection of exotic plants.

Lincoln Park

North-west of Lincoln Park, at 2433 North Lincoln Street, is the Biograph Theater, in front of which the notorious gangster John Dillinger was shot down on July 22nd 1934.

Biograph Theater

Farther north-west is Wrigley Field, one of the oldest baseball pitches in North America, home of the Chicago Cubs.

Wrigley Field

Between Lincoln Avenue and the Chicago River, at 909 West Armitage Avenue, is the Scholl Museum of Folk Culture, with a large collection of musical instruments and music.

Scholl Museum of Folk Culture

Chicago's oldest cultural institution is the Historical Society's museum on the history of the city (Clark Street and North Avenue), where visitors can see, among much else, Chicago's first locomotive and a film reconstruction of the great fire of 1871. The "Please touch" section enables both children and grown-ups to "get the feel" of the city's history.

*Historical Society Museum

The Old Town of Chicago, an area of just over 1sq.mile/3sq.km between North Wells Street and Eugene Street, has recently been cleaned up and refurbished on the model of New York's Greenwich Village. Many of the houses built here after the 1871 fire are now occupied by boutiques, souvenir shops, restaurants and bars. In the past there was a considerable German element in the population, as is reflected in the streets named after German writers. Those interested in curious facts may like to visit Ripley's "Believe it or not" Museum in Wells Street.

Old Town

Surroundings of Chicago

A visit to Oak Park, a suburb on the west side of Chicago, is a must for anyone interested in modern architecture. A major part in the development of this district was taken by Frank Lloyd Wright and the Prairie School of architects, including George C. Maher (1864–1926), Robert C. Spencer Jr (1864–1953) and Thomas Eddy Tallmadge (1876–1940). Particularly notable examples of their work are the Frank Lloyd Wright Home and Studio, the Unity Temple (1908; an early example of the use of concrete), the Fricke

*Oak Park

Chicago

House and Heurtly House (both 1902), the Martin House (1903) and the Cheney House (1904).

Brookfield Zoo
11 miles/18km west of Chicago is the popular Brookfield Zoo, in which more than 2000 species of animals can be seen in enclosures as close as possible to their natural conditions. There are a children's zoo, a safari train and dolphin shows.

Evanston
North of Chicago is the suburb of Evanston, with the Northwestern University. The Mary and Leigh Block Gallery has a notable art collection covering the period from the 15th to the 20th century. The sculpture garden has works by Henry Moore, Barbara Hepworth, Jacques Lipschitz, Joan Miró and other modern sculptors.

Botanic Garden
Farther north, in Glencoe, is the 300-acre (120 hectare) Botanic Garden, covering 20 different botanical fields. There are daily guided visits and tram tours.

Six Flags Great America
West of Waukegan is the gigantic theme park Six Flags Great America, with a large roller coaster and numerous other attractions.

New Salem Historic Site
New Salem, to the south of Chicago, was the home of Abraham Lincoln from 1831 to 1837. The 23 log cabins in the little settlement have been reconstructed and furnished exactly as they were in Lincoln's time. During the main summer holiday season "living history" programmes are run here.

Cincinnati K 41

State: Ohio
Altitude: 540ft/165m
Population: 364,000 (Metropolitan Area 1.75 million)

Situation and characteristics
The city of Cincinnati lies in a wide basin on the north bank of the Ohio River, surrounded by hills. In the past its beautiful situation earned it the styles of the "Pearl of the West" and the "Queen City". It is now a busy industrial city, with the headquarters of several large firms, and the seat of a well-reputed university. It has a wide range of cultural and recreational facilities.

History
The first white settlers established themselves here in 1788, to be followed a few years later by the US Army. The town was given its name by a group of revolutionary admirers of the Roman general Cincinnatus. Its excellent situation on the navigable Ohio River promoted its further development, and for many years it was the dominant centre of the Middle West. The coming of the railway reduced the importance of the river and of the town, but it soon recovered from this setback.

Tyler Davidson Fountain

By 1869 it could boast the first professional baseball team in the world, the Cincinnati Reds. Until the First World War the city's life showed the influence of its many German immigrants, and it still holds annually a large Oktoberfest on the Munich model.

Cincinnati

Sights in Cincinnati

The focal point of the city centre with its modern tower blocks is Fountain Square, in which is the Tylor Davidson Fountain (cast in Munich in 1871).
Downtown/ *Fountain Square

From the roof of the 575ft/175m high Carew Tower (5th and Vine Streets) there are superb views of the city and the valley of the Ohio River. From here there is access to the Skywalk, a network of arcades and flyovers spanning sixteen city blocks which offers abundant opportunities for shopping and window-shopping.
Carew Tower/ Skywalk

The Cincinnati Zoo and Botanical Gardens (3400 Vine Street) are famed for their white Bengal tigers and gorillas. Here too there is one of the largest insectariums in the world.
*Cincinnati Zoo and Botanical Gardens

The Cincinnati Union Terminal at 1301 Western Avenue, an Art Deco railroad station built in 1933, has been occupied since 1990 by the Museum Center (natural history and history of the city; cinema shows).
*Museum Center, Cincinnati Union Terminal

In Eden Park is the Cincinnati Art Museum, with works of art (sculpture, ceramics, pictures, etc.) from the great civilisations of five millennia.
Cincinnati Art Museum

To the south of Eden Park is the picturesque Mount Adams quarter with its popular bars and cafés.
Mount Adams

The Taft Museum, housed in an elegant villa of 1820 at 316 Pike Street, has an excellent collection of Chinese porcelain and European painting.
*Taft Museum

The venerable old house in which William Howard Taft (1857–1930), 27th President of the United States, was born is now a museum.
William Howard Taft National Historic Site

Surroundings of Cincinnati

In Covington (Kentucky) on the side of the Ohio River is the district of Main Strasse, showing the influence of German immigrants. A carillon in the bell-tower plays the "Ratcatcher of Hamelin" tune.
Covington (Kentucky)

Popular race meetings are held on the River Downs racecourse at 6301 Kellogg Avenue and the Turfway course in Florence (Kentucky).
Horse-racing

23 miles/38km north-east of Cincinnati on I 71 (exit 25A) is Kings Island, with a large amusement park.
Kings Island

54 miles/87km north of Cincinnati is the industrial town of Dayton, headquarters of NCR (National Cash Registers) and other major firms. Founded in 1776 and named after a General Dayton, the town was the home of the air pioneers the Wright brothers. On Old Wright Field (enter by Gate 28B) is the US Air Force Museum, the oldest and largest museum of military aviation, with over 200 aircraft and missiles. Near here is a monument to the Wright brothers. In Carillon Historic Park (2001 South Patterson Boulevard) are reproductions of the Wright brothers' bicycle factory, one of their aircraft and the covered wagons and log cabins of the early settlers. In the Old Courthouse (3rd and Main Streets) are numerous relics and documents on the Wright brothers. Other interesting collections are the Dayton Art Institute (Forest and Riverview Avenues) and the Dayton Museum of Natural History (2600 De Weese Parkway).
Dayton

Cleveland

State: Ohio
Altitude: 575–865ft (175–264m)
Population: 506,000 (Metropolitan Area 2.7 million)

Situation and characteristics

Cleveland, the second largest city in the state of Ohio, lies at the outflow of the Cuyahoga River into Lake Erie. Immediately south begins the long Appalachian Plateau; to the west are the Central Lowlands. The city has a strong economic base, with steel and metal processing and the manufacture of machine tools and automobile parts. Its traditional position as a centre of the oil industry is carried on by BP, which after its takeover of the Standard Oil Company of Ohio established its US headquarters in Cleveland. In the cultural field, the Cleveland Orchestra has a high reputation.

History

The newly acquired territory of New Connecticut, an area of 770 sq.miles/2000sq.km, was mapped by Moses Cleveland in 1796 for the Connecticut Land Company, but the settlement which he founded (on the site of the present city centre) was soon abandoned. Three years later Lorenzo Carter established a permanent community, in whose harbour the first cargoes were discharged in 1813. With the completion of the system of canals between the Ohio River and Lake Erie and the coming of the railroad the town developed into one of the most important ports in the eastern United States and an industrial centre in which some of the biggest American entrepreneurs made their fortunes – demonstrating their wealth in luxury residences on Euclid Avenue, known as Millionaires' Row. Among those who lived here around the turn of the century were John D. Rockefeller, founder of the Standard Oil Company, and Samuel Mather, who made his fortune in steel production and transport – though almost nothing is left to show for it. After the Second World War Cleveland suffered an economic decline, which even the efforts of Carl B. Stokes, the first black to be elected mayor of a major American city, were unable to stem. In the eighties, however, a restructuring of the economy produced positive results, and in recent years the city has been largely modernised.

Sights in Cleveland

Public Square

The central feature of Cleveland is Public Square, which in 1870 became the first public square in the United States to be lit by electricity. Round it are the Tower City Center, a shopping centre converted from an old railroad station, with the 52-storey Terminal Tower (viewing platform on 42nd floor), and the 46-storey BP America Building. North-east of Public Square is the Mall, the largest square in the city centre, which is decorated with fountains and sculpture and dominated by the Society Center, Cleveland's tallest building (890ft/271m).

North Coast Harbor

North Coast Harbor, at the north end of East 9th Street, was thoroughly cleaned up and refurbished in 1988 as a promenade and a setting for festivals. Here too is the Rock'n'Roll Hall of Fame (by I. M. Pei, 1994). Moored at the quay is the "William G. Mather", an ore and coal carrier built in 1925. Some distance away, at Burke Lakefront Airport, is USS "Cod", a Second World War submarine.

Flats

The Flats, the low-lying area of old industrial buildings round the outflow of the Cuyahoga River into Lake Erie which was the original nucleus of Cleveland, is now a favourite haunt of nightbirds, attracted by its numerous restaurants, cafés and bars. On the west bank of the river is the Powerhouse of 1892, which until 1954 supplied the city's streetcars with electricity; it is now occupied by shops and restaurants.

Round University Circle, 5 miles/8km east of the city centre on Wade Park, are a number of interesting museums. In Severance Hall the Cleveland Orchestra performs in a series of concerts from September to June. The Cleveland Museum of Art at 11150 East Boulevard is particularly strong on medieval art from Europe and Asia and American art. Among notable American artists represented are John Singleton Copley ("Portrait of Anna Dummer Powell", 1764), Frederic Edwin Church ("Twilight in the Wilderness", 1860) and Thomas Eakins ("The Biglin Brothers Turning the Stake", 1873). Highlights of the Asian collection are the figures of Krishna Govardhana (6th c.) and the Buddhist monk Kakushin (1300). Medieval European art is represented by nine items from Brunswick Cathedral, modern art by the French Impressionists and Picasso.

University Circle

*Cleveland Museum of Art

Tue.–Sat. 10am–5.45pm Sun. 1–5.30pm Mon. to 9.45pm

The Cleveland Museum of Natural History on Wade Oval presents a survey of prehistory and the history of mankind, with departments of astronomy, geology and ecology.

Cleveland Museum of Natural History

The Western Reserve Historical Society (10825 East Boulevard) runs the Frederick C. Crawford Auto Aviation Museum, with 200 antique automobiles and old planes dating from 1895 onwards.

Western Reserve Historical Society

Surroundings of Cleveland

5 miles/8km south of the city centre, to the east of Brookside Metropolitan Park, is the Cleveland Metroparks Zoo, one of the oldest in the United States. A particular feature is an artificial rain forest.

*Cleveland Metroparks Zoo

South-west of the city, on the northern edge of the Cleveland Hopkins International Airport, is the NASA Lewis Research Center (21000 Brookpark Road), which is responsible for the propulsion systems of the space shuttles. Visitors can see an exhibition on space research and examples of spacecraft and satellites.

NASA Lewis Research Center

South of Cleveland is the popular Cuyahoga Valley National Recreation Area, a 22 mile/35km long stretch of country along the Cuyahoga River which has been restored to its original state. Through the northern part of the park runs the old Ohio and Erie Canal. To the south is Hale Farm, an open-air museum with restored early 19th century houses in which old crafts are demonstrated.

Cuyahoga Valley National Recreation Area

Cody

E 16

State: Wyoming
Altitude: 5095ft/1553m
Population: 8000

The little town of Cody, founded by "Buffalo Bill" (Colonel William F. Cody; see Famous People), lies on the western edge of the Bighorn Basin in Wyoming, an area rich in raw materials, where the land begins to rise to the Absaroka Range in the Rockies. It is a good base from which to visit Yellowstone National Park (see entry). The well preserved old town centre, once the domain of cowboys and prospectors, is now crowded, particularly in summer, with tourists anxious to experience something of the atmosphere of the old Wild West.

Situation and characteristics

Sights in Cody

Cody's main sight is the Buffalo Bill Historical Center at 720 Sheridan Avenue (variable opening times), a four-part museum complex which gives a lively impression of the history of the Wild West. The Buffalo Bill

**Buffalo Bill Historical Center

Cody

Farewell to the Wild West in Old Trail Town

Museum displays saddles, guns, photographs and other personal possessions of Buffalo Bill. The Cody Fire Arms Museum has the largest collection of hand guns in the world – over 4000 items illustrating the development of firearms from the old muzzle-loaders by way of the famous Winchester repeating rifle to the latest types of revolvers and hand guns. The Whitney Gallery of Western Art possesses what must be one of the finest collections of pictures on Wild West themes, including works by Albert Bierstadt, George Catlin, Charles M. Russell, Frederic Remington and many other artists. The Plains Indian Museum contains tepees, implements, weapons, clothing and cult objects of the Prairie Indians (Arapaho, Blackfoot, Cheyenne, Crow, Shoshone and Sioux). In front of the museum is a statue by Gertrude Vanderbilt Whitney of Buffalo Bill on his horse Smoky.

Irma Hotel

One of the oldest buildings in the town centre is the Irma Hotel (12th and Sheridan Streets), built by Buffalo Bill in 1902 for his daughter. Its attractive Victorian furniture and mementoes of the Wild West draw large numbers of visitors.

*Old Trail Town

On the west side of the town (West Yellowtone Highway) is the Old Trail Town, with 24 old buildings dating from the eighties and nineties of the 19th century which give some impression of Wild West life in the time of the great bandits Butch Cassidy and the Sundance Kid.

*Cody Nite Rodeo

Close by is the arena for the wild rodeos, held every evening at 8.30pm from the first Saturday in June to the last Saturday in August, in which the best cowboys of the Wild West compete.

Cody Mural

In the Church of Jesus Christ of the Latter Day Saints (Bighorn Avenue, on the east side of the town) is a large mural showing scenes from the early days of the Mormon settlement in the Bighorn basin.

Colonial National Historical Park

Surroundings of Cody

Rafting trips on the Shoshone River, starting from Cody, are a popular attraction from May to September. **Shoshone River**

West of Cody is Shoshone National Forest, which offers scope for a variety of outdoor activities, including mountain hiking. Shoshone National Forest

Also to the west of Cody, only a few miles from the entrance to Yellowstone National Park (see entry), is the Sleeping Giant, a hill much frequented by winter sports enthusiasts. Sleeping Giant

North-east of Cody is the Bighorn Canyon National Recreation Area, centred on the deep gorge on the Bighorn River, which offers a wide variety of recreational activities, including riding, golf and surfing. *Bighorn Canyon National Recreation Area

Colonial National Historical Park M 49

State: Virginia
Length: 23 miles/37km

The Colonial Historical Parkway runs along the coast of Virginia, linking three places which played important roles in the history of the United States. Starting from Yorktown, it follows the York River, turns inland to Williamsburg and ends in Jamestown, on the James River. Situation

The victory of Washington's American and French force over Cornwallis's British troops at Yorktown on October 9th–17th 1781 ended the American revolutionary wars. In the Yorktown Battlefield Visitor Center an exhibition of relics of the battle (including Washington's tent) and a film show prepare visitors for a tour of the battlefield, passing British earthworks, French gun positions and Washington's headquarters. Yorktown

Taking a rest in Williamsburg

211

Colorado

**Colonial Williamsburg

Visitor Center:
daily 8am–8pm

One of the most interesting sites in Virginia is Colonial Williamsburg, which was rebuilt from 1926 onwards with financial help from John D. Rockefeller. The town, founded in 1633, was capital of the colony and for a time capital of the state of Virginia. Its great charm lies not only in the 88 restored and over 50 reconstructed 18th century buildings but also because it is a living museum, whose "inhabitants", wearing period costume, go about their daily business as cobblers, smiths, barbers, printers, shopkeepers, innkeepers and so on, re-creating round the main street (Gloucester Street) the pattern of life in colonial Virginia. The handsomest and most historic buildings are the Capitol (1705) and the Governor's Palace (1720). Visitors can also watch a trial in the Court House (1770) or attend an open-air theatrical performance. Outside the historic centre is the College of William and Mary (founded 1693), with the oldest academic building in the United States, the Wren Building (1695–99).

If you merely want to stroll about the streets of Colonial Williamsburg (best access on the east side, on North Henry Street) without going into any of the buildings, there is no charge. For admission to the buildings it is necessary to buy a (fairly expensive) ticket at the Visitor Center.

Jamestown

At the west end of the Colonial Parkway is Jamestown, the oldest British settlement on North American soil. It was established on Jamestown Island on May 13th 1607 by 104 settlers from all over Europe led by Captain John Smith. Not much is left of the original settlement apart from the foundations of the church tower (1639), the churchyard (probably the oldest British churchyard in North America) and the outlines of a few other buildings. In the Jamestown Settlement are a re-creation of a Powhatan Indian village and replicas of the three ships which brought the settlers from England. A memorial stone commemorates Pocahontas (*c.* 1595–1617), the daughter of an Indian chief who married John Rolfe and contributed to the reconciliation between Indians and Europeans. There is also a very interesting reconstruction of a 17th century glassblower's workshop, in which glasses are made on old models.

Colorado (State; CO)   J–M 16–23

Area: 104,332sq.miles/
    270,219sq.km
Population: 3,295,000
Capital: Denver
Popular name: Centennial State

Situation and topography

The state of Colorado (from Spanish *colorado*, "coloured") lies in the western United States. The smaller eastern part of the state belongs to the Great Plains, lying at altitudes between 3300ft/1000m and 5900ft/1800m. The soils of this region, originally short-grass steppeland, yield abundant crops with the help of irrigation. The larger western part of Colorado lies in the Rocky Mountains, which are made up mainly of two parallel ranges striking north–south and separate two widely different climatic zones. The Front Range, rising in places to over 13,000ft/4000m, forms the imposing eastern boundary of the Rockies. The Savage Range in western Colorado is the watershed between the Pacific and the Atlantic (Gulf of Mexico), rising to 14,433ft/4399m in Mount Ebert, the highest peak in Colorado. In the mountains coniferous forests predominate, giving place above the 11,500ft/3500m mark to a vegetation of alpine type dominated by mountain pines.

History

From the 11th to the 13th century the farming culture of the Anasazi Indians, now well documented, flourished in south-western Colorado.

Colorado

Their heirs are believed to have been the Ute Indians and the bison-hunting Cheyenne and Arapaho tribes. In the 17th century Spanish conquistadors explored at least the southern part of the territory and gave it its name (the "coloured" country, after the rocks in light and dark reddish tones which outcrop here). Soon afterwards French prospectors pushed into eastern Colorado from Louisiana. Thereafter the French and Spanish fought for predominance until 1763, when the territory passed to the Spanish crown. In the first half of the 19th century the United States gained control of the area; then in 1861 it was incorporated as a US territory, and fifteen years later became the 38th state of the Union. In 1913 a Norwegian introduced skiing to the Rockies and thus sparked off the development of the tourist trade.

Agriculture is well developed in the Great Plains. In the south and east irrigated arable farming predominates; the north-west is given up to cattle-ranching. In the eastern foreland of the Rockies (particularly in north-western Colorado) considerable quantities of oil and natural gas are extracted, and there are rich mineral resources in the mountainous west of the state – coal, silver, gold, zinc, vanadium, uranium and, in the Sawatch Range, molybdenum. Steel manufacture and metalworking, as well as arms production, are old-established industries; also of importance are the foodstuffs industries. Younger, but highly successful, is the electronics industry, with its dynamic centre round Colorado Springs. Tourism also makes a major contribution to the economy: the Rockies are increasingly popular with summer vacationists, and they also have a number of world-famed winter sports centres, notably Aspen, Vail, Keystone and Steamboat Springs.

Economy

Places of Interest in Colorado

The internationally renowned resort of Aspen lies in the valley of the Roaring Fork River, some 160 miles/256km south-west of Denver (see entry). Originally an important mining town, Aspen is now an exclusive winter sports resort and a rather less expensive summer holiday resort. In the surrounding area are a number of ghost towns, still occupied by miners only a few decades ago, and the beautiful Maroon Lake, set against the backdrop of three mountains over 13,000ft/4000m (Maroon Peak, North Maroon Peak and Pyramid Peak).

Aspen

From Aspen SR 82 runs up into the grandiose mountain world of Independence Pass (12,095ft/3686m and Mount Elbert (14,433ft/4399m), the highest peak in the state of Colorado.

*Independence Pass

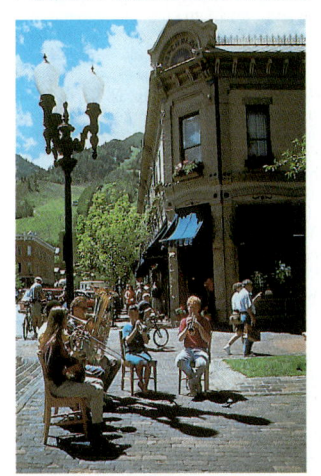

Concert on the square, Aspen

Among the finest skiing areas round Aspen are Aspen Mountain, the Aspen Highlands, Snowmass and Buttermilk Mountain.

*Skiing areas

At Dolores, in the south-western corner of Colorado, is the Anasazi Heritage Center, with a collection of material on the Anasazi farming culture of the 11th–13th centuries.

Dolores/*Anasazi Heritage Center

213

Colorado

Durango

Also in south-western Colorado is the old mining town of Durango (pop. 13,000), which flourished during the gold and silver boom of the 19th century. It is a good base for excursions into the San Juan Mountains. From here the "Million Dollar Highway" (US 550) runs north through magnificent scenery. Another attraction is the Durango and Silverton Narrow Gauge Railroad, on which old-time trains run up the narrow valley of the Animas River into the San Juan National Forest.

Fort Collins

An hour's drive north of Denver, in the oil-rich eastern foreland of the Front Range, is Fort Collins (pop. 68,000), a town founded in 1864 which is now the seat of Colorado State University. Features of interest are the lovingly restored old town centre with its attractive shops and restaurants, the Western Museum and the large Anheuser-Busch brewery on the north-eastern outskirts of the town.

Grand Junction

The town of Grand Junction (pop. 28,000) lies in the far west of Colorado at the junction of the Gunnison River with the Colorado. Its attractions are the Museum of Western Colorado (natural and cultural history of the region), Dinosaur Valley (fossils) and the Cross Orchards Historical Site (history of agricultural development in the region).

*Colorado National Monument

A few miles west of Grand Junction is Colorado National Monument, a nature reserve with bizarre rock formations and canyons.

*Black Canyon of the Gunnison

130 miles/210km south-east of Grand Junction is the spectacular Black Canyon of the Gunnison, a narrow gorge, over 2600ft/800m deep in places, cut through dark-coloured rocks of the Palaeozoic era.

*Great Sand Dunes National Monument

In southern Colorado are the impressive Great Sand Dunes (now protected as a national monument). Over a period of 15,000 years the wind has carried great masses of sand from the semi-arid San Luis Valley to the foot of the Sangre de Cristo Mountains. Some of the dunes are over 650ft/200m high.

*Leadville

High up in the Rockies is Leadville (alt. 10,190ft/3105m; pop. 2500), once an important silver-mining centre. Gold and silver are still worked in the area. The National Mining Hall of Fame and Museum has a large collection of material on the history of mining. Leadville is now also an important winter sports centre which, thanks to its high altitude, has a very long season. Features of interest are the restored Healy House, a reminder of the great days of the gold and silver boom, and the Matchless Mine Cabin, home of "Baby Doe", the wife of Horace Tabor, a storekeeper who became a wealthy mine-owner but died a ruined man. Their story became the subject of a musical, "The Ballad of Baby Doe". From Leadville you can take a rail trip through the mining country to Climax on the Leadville, Colorado and Southern Railroad.

*Steamboat Springs

In the mountains of northern Colorado is the beautiful Yampa Valley, the chief town in which is Steamboat Springs (pop. 7000), with more than 150 hot mineral springs. In 1913 Carl Howelsen, a Norwegian, made this a centre of Nordic (langlauf) skiing, and it is now one of the leading winter sports resorts in the United States. Notable sights in the area are the Thunderhead (aerial cableway), the Fish Creek Falls and Routt National Forest.

Telluride

In the mountains of south-western Colorado is Telluride (alt. 8745ft/2665m; pop. 1400), where gold and silver were found in the 19th century. The town then acquired a luxury hotel, the Sheridan, and even an opera house. In 1889 the notorious bank robber Butch Cassidy made a haul of 30,000 dollars here. Telluride is now a popular winter sports centre. Outside the town are the beautiful Bridal Veil and Bear Creek Falls.

Colorado Springs

Vail, like Aspen, is a world-famed winter sports resort. It lies in the Rockies 100 miles/160km west of Denver on I 90. The town's lightning development began after the Second World War, and it is now an important centre on the international skiing circuit. Features of interest are the Ski Museum, with the Ski Hall of Fame, and the charming Betty Ford Alpine Garden, named in honour of President Ford's wife.

In White River National Forest is the world's largest skiing area on a single mountain, with more than two dozen cableways and lifts. The season is from the end of November to the middle of April.

Colorado Springs, Denver, Dinosaur National Monument, Mesa Verde National Park, Rocky Mountain National Park (see entries).

Vail

*Colorado Ski Museum and Hall of Fame

**Skiing area

Other places of interest

Colorado Springs

L 21

State: Colorado
Altitude: 5980ft/1823m
Population: 281,000 (Metropolitan Area 390,000)

The city of Colorado Springs, a popular resort both in summer and in winter, lies on the eastern slope of the Front Range, here dominated by Pikes Peak (14,110ft/4301m). In recent years it has developed into an important centre of the electronics industry, not least because of the presence in the surrounding area of several highly sensitive military establishments (including an underground command centre and the North American Aerospace Command).

Situation and characteristics

Colorado Springs was founded in 1871, following the construction of the railroad, near the existing town of El Dorado City (later Colorado City and for a time capital of the state of Colorado). In the 1890s the gold rush on Cripple Creek drew large numbers of people to Colorado Springs. By 1917 it had grown so much that it was amalgamated with the neighbouring little town of Colorado City. The establishment of various military installations after the Second World War gave a further boost to the town.

History

Sights in Colorado Springs

The lovingly restored old town of Colorado City still retains something of the atmosphere of the Wild West.

*Colorado City

In the Fine Arts Center (30 West Dale Street) notable exhibits include Indian sand paintings and works of art of the Spanish colonial period (e.g. the carved figures known as "santos"). There are other interesting exhibitions in the El Pomar Carriage House Museum on Lake Circle (including two Presidential carriages); the Pioneers Museum at 215 South Tejon Street; the McAllister House (furnishings of 1873) at 423 North Cascade Avenue; the Pro Rodeo Hall of Fame (history of the rodeo) on the northern outskirts of the city, near I 25; and the Peterson Air and Space Museum on the eastern outskirts.

Museums (a selection)

Surroundings of Colorado Springs

6 miles/10km north-west of the city is the Garden of the Gods, a nature reserve with bizarrely shaped red sandstone formations (the Kissing Camels, the Balanced Rock, etc.) and ancient cypresses. It is at its most impressive in the early morning light or at twilight.

*Garden of the Gods

7 miles/12km north-west of Colorado Springs is Manitou Springs (pop. 5000; mineral springs), a spa which has seen better days. The name comes

Manitou Springs

Colorado Springs

The "Garden of the Gods"

from Indian word manitou, a great god or spirit. Features of interest are the Manitou Cliff Dwellings Museum (reconstructions of Indian cliff dwellings, etc.) and the Cave of the Winds, a stalactitic cave to the north-west of the town. From the south-western outskirts of the town Pikes Peak Cog Railway runs up to the summit of Pikes Peak.

**Pikes Peak

Pikes Peak (14,110ft/4301m), 3 miles/5km north-west of Manitou Springs, can also be climbed on a difficult toll road (car rally annually at beginning of July). From the summit there are breathtaking views, extending on clear days as far as Denver (see entry) and into New Mexico, which attract large numbers of visitors throughout the year. Katherine Lee Bates was inspired by Pikes Peak to write the words of the song "America the Beautiful". The whole of the mountain is now protected as Pike National Forest.

North Cheyenne Canyon/Seven Falls/Gold Camp Road

South-west of Colorado Springs are the wild North Cheyenne Canyon and the Seven Falls. There are magnificent views from the Gold Camp Road, originally built by gold-diggers, which runs up into Pike National Forest.

Cripple Creek

44 miles/71km west of Colorado Springs, at a height of 10,000ft/3000m, is the old gold-diggers' town of Cripple Creek (which can be reached by all-terrain vehicles from the Gold Camp Road). In the 1890s there was a swarming population of over 10,000 gold prospectors; nowadays Cripple Creek – in which gaming is now legal – has no more than 600 inhabitants. Visitors can take an interesting excursion through the area on a steam train of the Cripple Creek and Victor Narrow Gauge Railroad.

*Florissant Fossil Beds

37 miles/60km west of Colorado Springs on US 24 (Ute Pass) are the very interesting Florissant Fossil Beds (stumps of fossil trees, etc.).

Connecticut

12 miles/20km north of Colorado Springs, at the foot of the Front Range, is the US Air Force Academy, where over 4000 Air Force cadets are trained. The "Moon Meal Parade" is held daily at noon, and there is also a large parade on Saturdays at 11am. The dominant architectural feature of the establishment is the Chapel, with pointed gables resembling rockets, which serves Protestants, Catholics and Jews alike.
Near the Academy is the North American Aerospace Command (NORAD).

Air Force Academy

Connecticut (State; CT)   H 14/15

Area:
  5018sq.miles/12,997sq.km
Population: 3.3 million
Capital: Hartford
Popular names: Constitution
  State, Nutmeg State

The relatively small state of Connecticut (from the Indian *quinnehtukqut*, "on the long tidal river") in the north-eastern United States lies between Long Island Sound on the Atlantic and the foothills of the northern Appalachians. The hilly western part of the state, rising to a height of 2380ft/725m in Mount Frissell, is separated from the gently rolling country, up to 1000ft/300m high, of the eastern part by the wide valley (up to 20 miles/30km across) of the Connecticut River. The temperate climate, with warm summers and abundant snow in winter, makes possible a wide variety of outdoor activities throughout the year, with bathing in the Atlantic in summer and skiing in the Mohawk Mountains in winter. The forests of deciduous trees (mainly oak, chestnut, hickory and poplar) make the state's "Indian summer" in autumn a memorable experience.

Situation and topography

The land on the Connecticut River was settled by Indians long before the coming of the Europeans. In 1614 a Dutchman, Adrian Block, explored the course of the river, and twenty years later English Puritans founded Windsor, the first permanent white settlement. The local Pequot Indians put up a stubborn resistance, which was not overcome until 1637. In 1662 the British colony was granted a considerable degree of self-government, with its own constitution. In 1776 the independent state of Connecticut was proclaimed, and on January 9th 1788 it became the fifth state of the Union.

History

Soon after the Declaration of Independence the state's economy began to develop rapidly. One of the factors in this development was Connecticut's abundant supply of water power, which made possible a remarkably early process of industrialisation. The timber industry, shipbuilding, arms production and engineering are still major pillars of the economy; but the proximity of markets in neighbouring cities has also provided a powerful stimulus to the development of agriculture (particularly dairy farming, poultry and fruit and vegetable growing). Tobacco-growing, which formerly flourished in the valley of the Connecticut River, has declined considerably in recent years, partly as a result of successful anti-smoking campaigns.

Economy

Places of Interest in Connecticut

Bridgeport (pop. 142,000) has a museum devoted to the celebrated showman and circus proprietor Phineas T. Barnum and a Discovery Museum.

Bridgeport

Crater Lake National Park

Bristol	Features of interest in Bristol (pop. 61,000) are the American Clock and Watch Museum and the New England Carousel Museum (over 200 old-time roundabouts).
Hartford	Hartford (pop. 140,000), capital of the state of Connecticut, is also the "insurance capital of the United States" and has a large plant manufacturing aircraft engines. In the town are houses once occupied by Mark Twain, who wrote "Tom Sawyer" here, and Harriet Beecher Stowe, author of "Uncle Tom's Cabin". Other features of interest are the Wadsworth Atheneum, one of finest American collections (works of the Hudson River school), and the State Library, with the large Colt Collection of hand guns.
Mystic	The old boatbuilding and whaling town of Mystic is now a popular tourist resort, with its old harbour and the Marinelife Aquarium as its principal attractions.
New Canaan	New Canaan is a very typical New England colonial town, with the renowned Silvermine Guild Arts Center.
New Haven Yale University	The port of New Haven (pop. 131,000), at the mouth of the Quinnipiac River, was founded by English Puritans in 1638, and has been famed since 1716 as the seat of Yale University. On the university campus are the Peabody Museum (natural history; Dinosaur Hall), the Art Gallery (with important finds from Mesopotamia), the Reinecke Rare Book and Manuscript Library (whose principal treasure is a Gutenberg Bible), the Sterling Memorial Library (4 million volumes; archives of the University) and the Center for British Art (particularly art of the 16th–19th centuries). Popular with children (and with adults) are the Children's Museum and the Shoreline Trolley Museum (old streetcars).
New London	The old whaling port of New London (pop. 29,000), now the seat of the US Coast Guard Academy, has preserved a number of handsome old 17th, 18th and 19th century buildings. Other features of interest are Monte Cristo Cottage (home of the playwright Eugene O'Neill), the Lyman Art Museum (dolls' houses, etc.) and the Arboretum, on the campus of Connecticut College. Ocean Beach Park is a popular recreation area. From New London there are ferries to Block Island, Fisher Island and Long Island, which attract many visitors.

Crater Lake National Park   G 3

State: Oregon
Area: 251sq.miles/649sq.km
Established: 1902

Season	The National Park and Visitor Center are open throughout the year; the Rim Drive, however, is negotiable only between July and mid October, and the facilities in Rim Village operate only from June to September. Even in summer it is advisable to take warm clothing.
Situation and topography	Crater Lake National Park lies in the Cascade Mountains in south-western Oregon. The striking feature of Crater Lake is the intense blue colour of its water. This unusually deep lake (1935ft/590m) is almost exactly circular, with a diameter ranging between 4½ miles/7.2km and 6½ miles/9km and a circumference of 26 miles/42km, and is surrounded by lava cliffs rising to heights of between 500ft/152m and 2000ft/610m. Crater Lake is the water-filled caldera of Mount Mazama, an extinct volcano which was once 12,000ft/3660m high. Continuing eruptions hollowed out the summit of the mountain, which collapsed some 6850 years ago, leaving the present circular cavity. Later eruptions within the crater gave rise to a volcanic cone which now emerges from the lake as Wizard Island. When volcanic activity

Crater Lake National Park

Wizard Island in Crater Lake

ceased some 4000 years ago the crater began to fill up with melt-water and rainwater. It has no other sources of water.
There is an informative display on the geology and formation of the lake on the Sinnott Memorial viewing terrace on the southern rim of the crater.

Rim Drive runs round the lake in a clockwise direction a short distance from the edge of the crater, beginning at Rim Village; its total length is 33 miles/55km. The first spectacular viewpoint is the Watchman, to the west of Wizard Island; a path (1400yd/1300m) leads up to the top, from which there are magnificent views extending, in good weather, as far as Mount Shasta (14,162ft/4316m) in northern California. To the north of the Watchman is Hillman Peak (8189ft/2496m), the highest point on the rim of the crater. Then to the east of North Junction, on the north side of a lake, is Llao Rock (8045ft/2452m), a former glacier valley filled up with obsidian. Farther on the Cleetwood Trail (1 mile/1.6km) runs down from the Rim Drive to Cleetwood Cove, from which there are hourly cruises on the lake, with a landing on Wizard Island. Thereafter the road turns south, opening up a view of Mount Scott, to the east of the crater rim – the highest point (8928ft/2721m) in the National Park. The Mount Scott Trail (2½ miles/4km) leads up to the top of the hill, while a side road runs up to the Cloudcamp viewpoint, the highest point on the Rim Drive (8061ft/2457m). From Kerr Notch there are good views of the curious Pinnacles, carved from the pumice rock by erosion, and the Phantom Ship, a bizarrely shaped rocky island near the steep shore of the lake (also seen from the Sun Notch viewpoint). The Rim Drive then continues over the Tututni Pass (6600ft/2012m) and the Vidae Ridge to the park offices, where it meets the road coming from the west and south entrances to the National Park. From here it is another 3 miles/4.8km to Rim Village.

In addition to those already mentioned there are a number of other hiking trails in the National Park, including the Garfield Peak Trail (1¾ miles/

Rim Drive

Watchman

Wizard Island

Phantom Ship

Hiking trails

Dallas

2.7km), which runs up to the top of Garfield Peak; the Discovery Point Trail (2¼ miles/3.6km), running along the crater rim from Crater Lake Lodge; the Godfrey Glen Trail (2¼ miles/3.6km) to the Duwee Falls on Munson Creek; and the Annie Creek Canyon Trail (1¼ miles/2km) along Annie Creek with its basalt columns. The Pacific Crest Trail (here called the Oregon Skyline Trail) also cuts through the western part of the National Park. This long-distance trail follows the crest ridges of the Cascade Mountains and the Sierra Nevada for a total distance of 2350 miles/3780km from the Canadian to the Mexican frontier. Further information about hiking and other activities in the National Park can be obtained from the Park administration (see Practical Information, National Parks).

Dallas   R 29

State: Texas
Altitude: 465ft/142m
Population: 1 million (Metropolitan Area 3.8 million)

Situation and characteristics

Dallas, now the largest city in Texas after Houston (see entry), owes its origin to John Neely Bryan, who in 1841 built himself a hut on the banks of the Trinity River in north-eastern Texas. Until after the Civil War Dallas was overshadowed by its sister city Fort Worth, but after the coming of the railroad in 1873 Dallas grew rapidly. While until the Second World War the city's economy depended on the grain and cotton grown in the surrounding area and later on oil, it has now become, with its numerous insurance corporations and banks, the business and financial centre not only of Texas but of the whole of the South-West. It was natural, therefore, that the famous soap opera of power, money and intrigue should have Dallas as its setting. The city's main industrial products are electronic apparatus, oil drilling equipment, chemicals and, since the Second World War, aircraft, rockets and micro-electronics. Important contributions to the economy are also made by textiles and publishing.

Sights in Dallas

Dallas County Historical Plaza

On Dallas County Historical Plaza (Main and Record Streets) is the log cabin (restored) in which John Neely Bryan is said to have lived.

JFK Memorial

Immediately adjoining, on Kennedy Plaza, is the John F. Kennedy Memorial, a monumental open granite cube commemorating the murder of President Kennedy here on November 22nd 1963.

*The Sixth Floor

The presumed murderer of President Kennedy, Lee Harvey Oswald, is believed to have fired the fatal shots from the sixth floor of the Texas School Book Depository at the intersection of Houston and Elm Streets. Here now is the Kennedy museum known as the Sixth Floor, devoted to John F. Kennedy's life, work and death (open: Sun.–Fri. 10am–5pm, Sat. 10am–6pm).

*Reunion Tower

Dallas's great landmark is the Reunion Tower in Reunion Park (viewing platform). In the same complex is the restored Union Station (400 South Houston Street), now housing the tourist information office.

Historic districts
West End District

Many of Dallas's older districts and buildings have been restored in recent years, for example the West End Historic District between Elm, Record and Lamar Streets, a rebuilt warehouse district now occupied by clubs, movie houses and restaurants. Here too (Main and Houston Streets) is the Old Courthouse of 1892. In the Old City Park (1717 Gano Street) are a number of restored buildings dating from between 1840 and 1910 – some of them originally situated here, some brought here from other sites – which form an interesting open-air museum.

Old City Park

Dallas

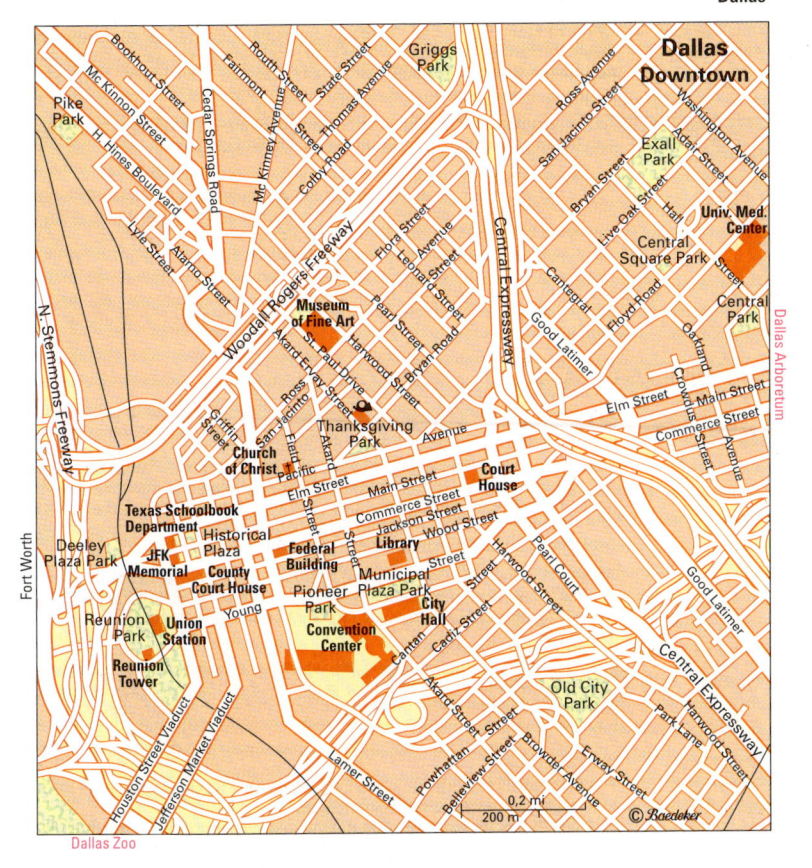

Dallas Downtown

Among important examples of modern architecture in Dallas are City Hall (by I. M. Pei), a huge pyramid lying on edge; the Dallas Theater Center on Turtle Creek Boulevard, the only theatre designed by Frank Lloyd Wright, set in beautiful gardens; and the Crescent Court Center (by Philip Johnson) to the north of the city centre, a complex occupied by restaurants, clubs, antique shops and art galleries. Thanksgiving Square, between Pacific Avenue, Bryan Street and Ervay Street, was also designed by Philip Johnson.	Modern architecture
Fair Park (on 2nd Avenue, to the south of US 67/I 30), Dallas's Civic Center and scene of the annual State Fair, is dominated by the Big Tex Towers. Originally laid out for the Texas Centennial Exposition of 1936, the park contains a number of museums: the Age of Steam Museum, the Museum of Natural History, Science Place I and II, and the Museum of African-American Life and Culture. Also in the park are the Art Deco Hall of State (commemorating great Texans), the Sports Stadium of the Southern Methodist University, the Cotton Bowl, the Music Hall (opera and ballet; Dallas Summer Festival) and the Dallas Aquarium.	Fair Park

Death Valley National Monument

Dallas Museum of Fine Art	North of Main Street and Thanksgiving Square, at 1717 North Harwood Street, is the Dallas Museum of Fine Art, notable particularly for its collection of pre-Columbian sculpture (open: Tue.–Sat. 10am–5pm, Sun. and pub. hols. noon–5pm).
Dallas Arboretum and Botanical Garden	To the north-east of the city, at 8617 Garland Road, is the Dallas Arboretum and Botanical Garden, on the shores of White Rock Lake.
Northern districts	To the north of the city, on Hillcrest Avenue, between Dallas North Tollway and US 75, is the extensive campus of the Southern Methodist University, with the Meadows Museum (Spanish painting of the 15th–20th centuries) and the Meadows Sculpture Garden (modern sculpture). Farther north, near Hillcrest Memorial Park, is the Biblical Arts Center, with a collection of religious works of art – pictures, icons, liturgical utensils, a reproduction of the Holy Sepulchre and an outside painting of the Resurrection, with *son et lumière* effects.

Surroundings of Dallas

Six Flags Over Texas	In Arlington, between Dallas and Fort Worth, is the Six Flags Over Texas entertainment park, with a variety of typically American rides, shows and attractions, including a cable railway, an old-time steam railway, boat trips and a number of hair-raising roller coasters, including one with three loops (taken both forwards and backwards) and a track which rises to the height of a 14-storey building. (The "six flags" are the flags of the six countries which ruled in Texas from the time of Columbus onwards.)
Southfork Ranch	Southfork Ranch, home of the Ewing family in the television soap opera "Dallas", has been reopened as a tourist attraction. It lies in Plano, 6 miles/9km east of US 75 by way of Parker and Hogge Roads. Open: daily 9am–6pm.
Fort Worth "Cowtown"	The city of Fort Worth (pop. 450,000), which has now almost joined up with Dallas, grew out of a military post established in 1849 and rapidly developed into a leading cattle-ranching centre, where cattle were collected for transport to the slaughterhouses of the North – earning it the nickname of "Cowtown". Fort Worth itself prefers to be known as "the city where the Wild West begins".
*Stockyards Historic Area	The Stockyards Historic Area (123 East Exchange Street) takes visitors back to the great days of the cattle round-ups.
Museums	Fort Worth has three interesting museums: the Amon Carter Museum of Western Art (Camp Bowie Boulevard), in a building designed by Philip Johnson; the Kimbell Art Museum (3333 Camp Bowie Boulevard; art of the Aztecs and Mayas); and the Cattle Raisers Museum (1301 West 17th Street), which is informative on cattle-ranching and the famous Texan longhorns.
Log Cabin Village	Log Cabin Village, a restored settlement of log cabins in Forest Park, to the south-west of the city, gives some impression of life in Texas in the time of the cattle barons.

Death Valley National Monument M–P 8/9

	State: California Altitude: up to 282ft/86m below sea level
When to go	The best time to visit Death Valley is from October to May, when temperatures range between 68°F/20°C and 91°F/33°C. From June to September it can be intolerably hot, with average maximum temperatures above 104°F/40°C; a July temperature of 134.1°F/56.7°C has been recorded. The average annual rainfall is about 0.2in./50mm.
Warning	A drive through Death Valley in summer can be hazardous, and on no account should drivers disregard any restriction or ban on driving. It should

Death Valley National Monument

Badwater, the lowest point in the United States

be borne in mind, too, that accommodation in the area is limited: advance reservation is essential in the Furnace Creek Inn, the Furnace Creek Ranch, Stove Pipe Wells Village and the few campgrounds.

Furnace Creek Visitor Center, Hwy 190; open daily 8am–5pm, in winter to 8pm.

Information

Death Valley, a nature reserve, has an area of 3000sq.miles/7800sq.km, centred on a depression 140 miles/230km long and between 4 miles/6km and 16 miles/26km across which is bounded on the west by the Panamint Range and on the east by the Amargosa Range. Something like a fifth of the area lies at or below sea level.
At Badwater is the lowest point on the North American continent (282ft/86m below sea level).

Situation

Death Valley was given its name in 1849, when a party of gold prospectors, seeking a short cut to the Californian goldfields, lost their way here and some of them died in the inhospitable terrain. Other prospectors and adventurers were attracted to the area by the hope of finding gold. Apart from some unproductive ore deposits they found only borax, a salt used in the manufacture of soap, detergents and cosmetics and in the industrial production of glass and enamel. In 1881 the Harmony Borax Works were opened at Furnace Creek, and thereafter there was a regular borax boom. This "white gold" was transported by mule train to the railroad station of Mojave, 164 miles/264km away.

History

In spite of the extreme natural conditions Death Valley has, thanks to a number of hidden springs, a relatively varied flora (mainly succulents) and fauna (lizards, rattlesnakes and even coyotes). This varied desert landscape appeals to many visitors with its rugged rocks, salt lakes and sand-dunes. There are impressive sand-dunes at Stove Pie Wells. The Devil's Golf-

**Topography, flora and fauna

Delaware

course is a white salt flat with thousands of salt pinnacles. The bizarrely eroded badlands of Zabriskie Point are at their most magical at sunrise and sunset. From Dante's View there is a magnificent prospect of the salt lakes and barren hills. The Devil's Cornfield is so called after its great expanses of arrowhead (*Sagittaria sagittifolia*). Badwater, the lowest point in America (282ft/86m below sea level), lies on the edge of a salt lake which never completely dries out even in summer, occupied by waterweeds and myriads of tiny flies. A striking geological feature is the Ubehebe Crater, 875yd/800m in diameter and 500ft/150m deep. In Grapevine Canyon (on the northern edge of Death Valley) is Scotty's Castle, a house in Spanish colonial style built by Albert W. Johnson and Walter E. Scott ("Death Valley Scotty").

Harmony Borax Works — The ruins of the Harmony Borax Works (partly restored) recall the prosperous borax-mining days.

Delaware (State; DE) K/I 51

Area: 2045sq.miles/5296sq.km
Population: 680,000
Capital: Dover
Popular names: First State, Diamond State

Situation and topography — Delaware (named after Baron De La Warr, governor of Virginia), the first of the thirteen founding states of the Union and its second smallest, lies in the eastern United States on a well watered peninsula reaching out into the Atlantic between Delaware Bay and Chesapeake Bay. In the north it extends on to the Piedmont Plateau. It has a temperate maritime climate.

History — The first European to explore this section of the North American coast, then inhabited by Indians, seems to have been John Cabot (1498), who was followed in the early 17th century by Dutch navigators. The first permanent settlement, however, was established by Swedes in 1638. In 1655 Ny Sverige (New Sweden) passed to Holland and nine years later to Britain. In 1682 Delaware was incorporated in the colony of Pennsylvania, but in 1775 recovered its independence and in 1787 was the first state to sign the new Constitution of the Union.

Economy — Delaware is highly industrialised, and benefits from its proximity to Philadelphia (see entry). In addition to its dominant chemical and petrochemical industries (Wilmington area) it has a number of major metalworking firms (including automobile construction and steelworks), textiles and foodstuffs industries. Agriculture also makes an important contribution to the state's economy, and the holiday and tourist trade is of importance in the coastal areas.

Places of Interest in Delaware

Delaware Bay — Delaware Bay, over 50 miles/80km long and up to 30 miles/50km across, is the estuary of the 280 mile/450km long Delaware River, which flows down from the Catskill Mountains on the Allegheny Plateau, a region richly stocked with raw materials. The bay carries heavy shipping traffic.

Dover — The state capital, Dover (pop. 25,000), was founded by William Penn in 1717, and has preserved something of its colonial-period charm. Features of interest include the Old State House (1787), the Delaware State Museum

Denver

(history of the state), the Delaware Agricultural Museum and the John Dickinson Mansion (1740), 5 miles/8km south-east of the town.

31 miles/50km south-west of Philadelphia (see entry) is the port and industrial city of Wilmington, founded by Swedish immigrants in 1638. It is an important centre of the chemical industry (DuPont).

Wilmington

Denver   K 21

State: Colorado
Altitude: 5280ft/1609m
Population: 470,000 (Metropolitan Area 1.8 million)

The "mile high city", as Denver, capital of the state of Colorado, is known, lies at the junction of Cherry Creek with the South Platte River, at the foot of the Front Range (Rocky Mountains). It is the dynamically developing economic and cultural centre of a wide hinterland extending widely over the Great Plains and into the Rockies. It has an agreeable continental climate, with plenty of sunshine and low rainfall.

Situation and characteristics

Denver is the see of a Roman Catholic archbishop and the seat of the University of Denver and the renowned University of Colorado Medical Center. It is also an important industrial centre, with over 180 large firms (power production, electrical apparatus, petro-chemicals, foodstuffs, publishing), a major destination for business travel and a good base for vacation trips into the Rockies.

In 1858 gold was discovered on Cherry Creek, and the three gold-diggers' settlements of Aurora, Highland and Denver which grew up there amalgamated in 1860–61 to form the town of Denver. In 1868, when it had a population of over 4000, it became capital of the territory of Colorado. After the coming of the railroad in 1870 Denver was a boom town, and in 1876 became capital of the 38th state of the Union. In the late eighties it became involved in the silver and gold rush, when increasing numbers of people passed through Denver on their way to the Rockies or settled in the town. By the turn of the century it had a population of 134,000. Thereafter it developed into an important traffic hub and industrial centre. It has also been popular for many years as a good base from which to explore the beauties of the Front Range. The importance of the business and tourist trade was recognised by the opening of a large new airport in 1994.

History

Sights in Denver

In the heart of Denver is the green and in summer agreeably shady Civic Center Park, laid out in classical style, with numerous monuments. Round the park are the principal administrative buildings of the state of Colorado, and along its north side runs Colfax Avenue, the city's principal traffic artery.

Civic Center Park

On a low hill on the east side of the park is the classical-style State Capitol, crowned by a gilded dome 250ft/76m high. From the viewing platform on the drum of the dome there are magnificent views of the city's imposing skyline and the Front Range. The 13th step on the west side of the Capitol is exactly one mile above sea level (the "mile high city").

*Colorado State Capitol

To the west of the park is the City and County Building, another imposing classical-style complex.

City and County Building

Immediately beyond the City and County Building is the US Mint, one of the United States' three mints (the others being in Philadelphia and San Francisco). Part of the country's gold reserves is also stored here. There is a small museum on the history of coining (open: Mon.–Fri. 10am–3pm).

*US Mint

To the south-west is the massive, fortress-like Denver Art Museum, with a collection which includes the art of the Indians as well as outstanding

*Denver Art Museum

Denver

Tue.–Sat. 10am–5pm, Sun. noon–5pm

works from Europe and the Far East. Of particular interest are the "santos", figures of saints carved by Indian craftsmen following models brought in by Spanish missionaries in the 17th century. Among notable European works is Degas' "Rehearsal" (1879).

*State Historical Museum

To the south-east of Civic Center Park is the State Historical Museum (prehistoric Indian cultures, including the Anasazi; relics of pioneering days; gold-mining. Opening times as for the Art Museum.

Molly Brown House

A few minutes' walk south-east of the State Capitol, at 1340 Pennsylvania Street, is the Molly Brown House (guided visits daily), which belonged to a

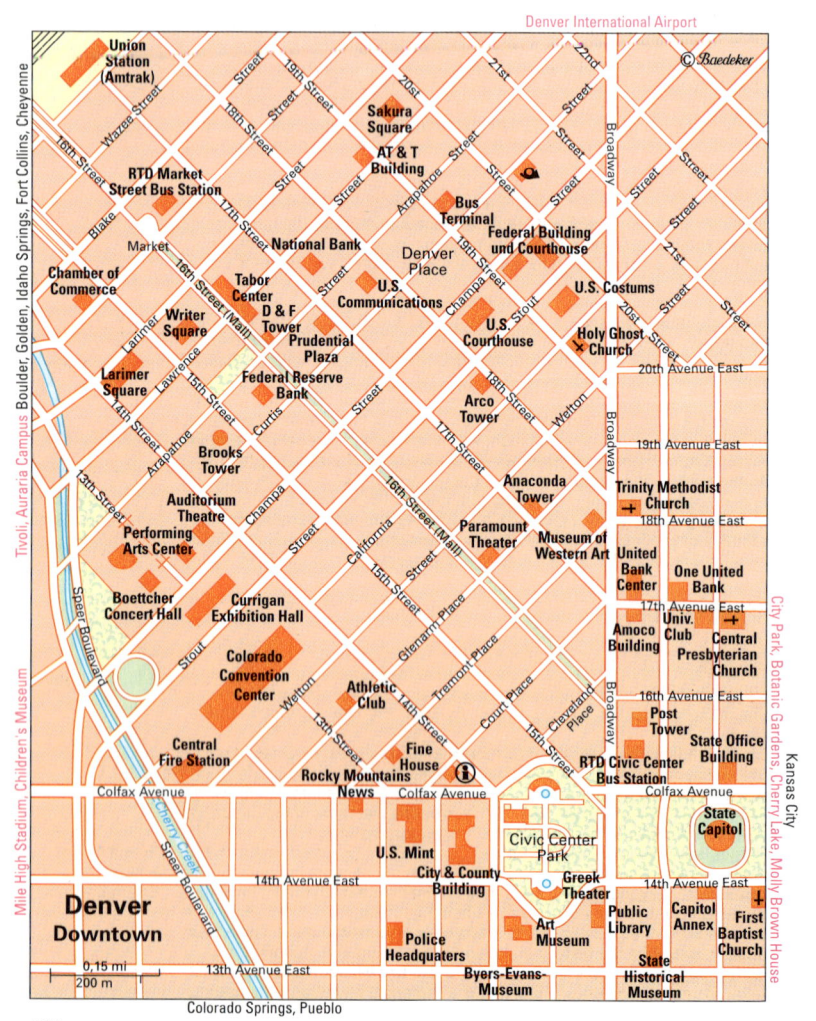

Denver

survivor of the "Titanic" disaster (celebrated in the musical "Unsinkable Molly Brown") who was famed for her lavish parties.

In an effort to bring a little more life into downtown Denver amid the skyscrapers 16th Street, which runs through the city centre, has been made a European-style pedestrian precinct, with shady trees, flowerbeds and park benches, in which the only traffic is a free shuttle bus. The street is lined with department stores, boutiques, souvenir shops, restaurants and the stalls of street traders (mostly "Indios" from Latin America).	**16th Street Mall**
Particularly round the south end of the street there are numerous modern and Post-Modern skyscrapers. Among the tallest are the 56-storey Republic Plaza, the 690ft/210m high United Bank Center, the Denver Post Tower, the Amoco Building, the Anaconda Tower and the Denver Club Building.	*Skyscrapers
On north-western 16th Street (corner of Arapahoe Street) is the D. and F. Tower, which was modelled on the Campanile in St Mark's Square in Venice. Adjoining is the modern Tabor Center, with some sixty shops and a number of friendly restaurants.	D. and F. Tower/ Tabor Center
On the opposite side of 16th Street is attractive Writer Square, part of a recent programme of refurbishment and redevelopment in the traditional architectural style of the South-West.	Writer Square
Another successful example of urban refurbishment is nearby Larimer Square, where Buffalo Bill (see Famous People) lived at one time, with well restored buildings of the Civil War period, art galleries, gift shops, cheerful restaurants and gas lamps.	*Larimer Square
On the south side of Larimer Square is the Denver Center for the Performing Arts, a gigantic cultural centre with the Boettcher Concert Hall, the Auditorium Theatre and the DOPA Theatre. To the south-east are the Currigan Convention Hall and the Colorado Convention Center.	Denver Center for the Performing Arts
To the west of the Performing Arts Center is the extensive Auraria Campus, with the modern buildings of the University of Colorado, the Learning Resources Center, the Metropolitan State College, etc.	Auraria Campus
Nearby, beyond Cherry Creek, is the Tivoli shopping and entertainment centre, housed in a former brewery.	Tivoli
At 1727 Tremont Place is the Museum of Western Art (open: Tue.–Sat. 10am–4.30pm), with a collection which includes important pictures by Albert Bierstadt, Frederick Remington and Georgia O'Keeffe, three artists who found their inspiration in the American West.	*Museum of Western Art
Immediately south is the Brown Plaza Hotel (1892), with a fine Art Deco interior.	Brown Plaza Hotel
To the east of the city centre is City Park, with a variety of facilities for entertainment and relaxation.	**City Park**
The Denver Zoo is beautifully laid out, with enclosures adapted to different species (polar bears' den, monkeys' island, "stroke the animals" zoo).	*Denver Zoo
In the south-east of City Park is the Natural History Museum (open: daily 9am–5pm). Among the most notable exhibits are imposing dinosaur skeletons, remains of Ice Age animals, the collection of minerals presented by the Coors brewing family, one of the largest nuggets of gold found in Colorado and artifacts of prehistoric Indian peoples. Attached to the Museum are the C. H. Gates Planetarium and an IMAX cinema with a giant screen.	*Natural History Museum
1 mile/1.5km farther south are the Botanic Gardens, laid out in the 1950s, with large glasshouses.	Botanic Gardens

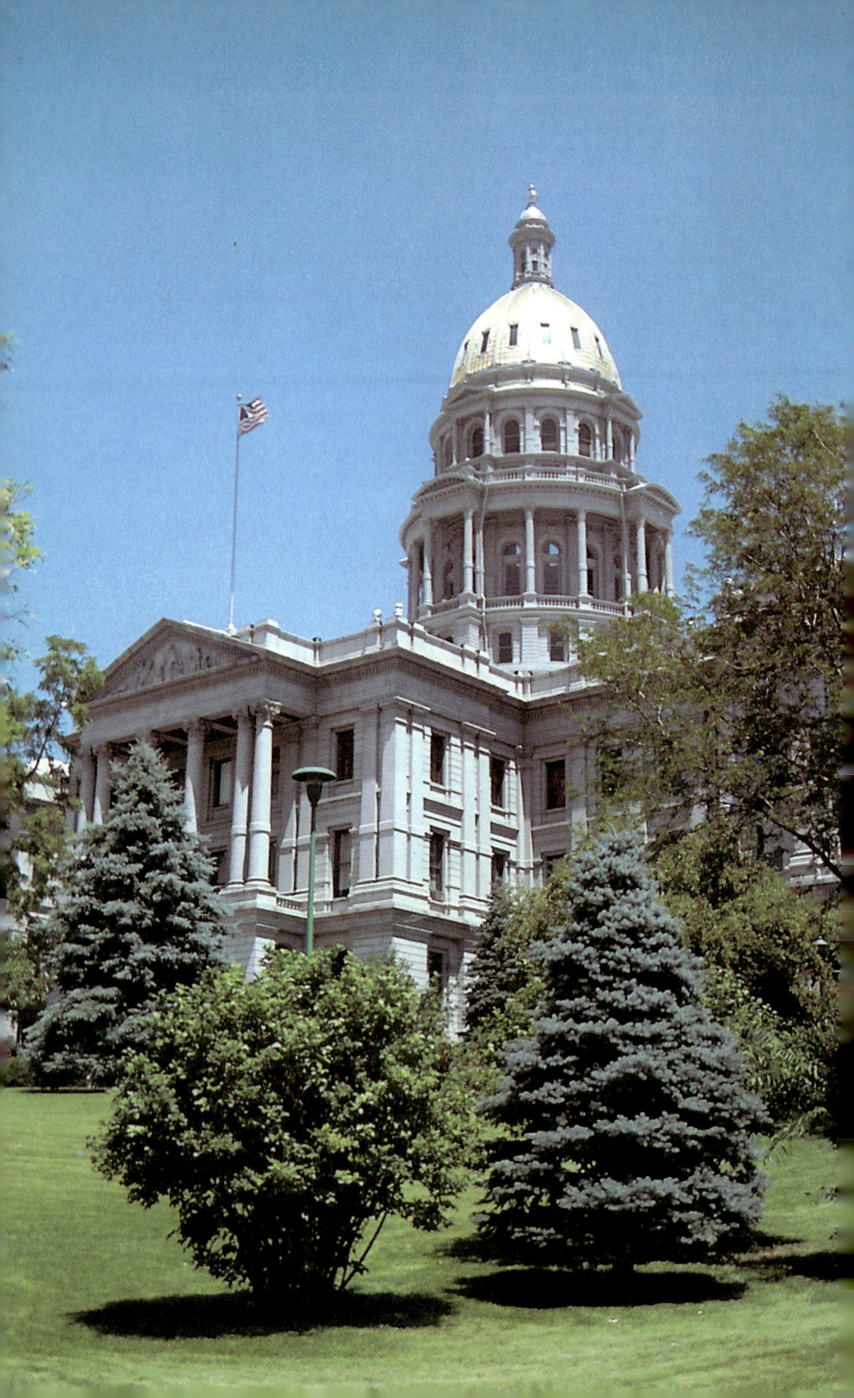

Surroundings of Denver

On the south-eastern outskirts of the city is Cherry Creek Lake, formed by a dam on the river. Round the lake is a large recreation area. — Cherry Creek Lake

A few miles west of the city, on the eastern slopes of the Front Range, are the Denver Mountain Parks, a popular recreation area. — **Denver Mountain Parks**

Between the brilliant red rocks of the Front Range foothills is a natural amphitheatre which can accommodate an audience of several thousand. During the summer concerts in a wide variety of musical styles are given here. — *Red Rocks Park Amphitheater

From Lookout Mountain Park there are superb views of the city of Denver and the eastern foreland of the Rockies. High up in the hills is Buffalo Bill's grave, with a small museum devoted to his memory. In a nearby enclosure a herd of buffaloes (bison) graze. — *Lookout Mountain Park

In a narrow valley 37 miles/60km east of Denver is the old gold-diggers' town of Idaho Springs (alt. 7550ft/2300m). At many places in the surrounding area various ores (including gold) are still mined. Some mines (among them the Phoenix Gold Mine) can be visited. — **Idaho Springs**

From Idaho Springs the highest mountain road in the United States runs steeply up past the beautifully situated Echo Lake to the alpine pastures on Mount Evans (14,266ft/4348m), from the summit of which there are breathtaking panoramic views. — *Echo Lake / **Mount Evans

14 miles/23km west of Denver is the town of Golden (pop. 16,000), founded in 1859 after the discovery of gold in Clear Creek Canyon, which from 1862 to 1867 was capital of Colorado. Features of interest are the 12th Street Historic District; the Colorado Railroad Museum; the geological and mineralogical collections and earthquake observatory of the Colorado School of Mines (founded 1874); and the large Coors Brewery, established by a German immigrant of that name (open: Mon.–Sat. 10am–4pm). — **Golden**

In a deep V-shaped valley north-west of Golden, still frequented by numerous hopeful gold-prospectors, is the old Western settlement of Black Hawk, nostalgically refurbished, with various gaming houses and saloons to tempt the tourist. — *Black Hawk

North-west of Denver is Boulder, a good centre from which to explore the Arapahoe National Forest and the Rocky Mountain National Park (see entry). — **Boulder**

23 miles/37km north-east of downtown Denver is the huge new Denver International Airport, opened in 1994, which has six runways and three terminal buildings with a total of 100 gates and is expected to handle 32 million passengers in its first year of operation. The terminal building has an imposing tent roof. — *Denver International Airport

Detroit G 42

State: Michigan
Altitude: 597ft/182m
Population: 1,028,000 (Metropolitan Area 4.66 million)

Detroit, by far the largest city in the state of Michigan, lies on the north-west bank of the Detroit River and on Lake St Clair, between Lakes Huron and Erie. The "metropolis of the automobile", Detroit ranks with New York and Chicago as one of the largest industrial cities in the United States. It is the country's busiest inland port after Chicago and Duluth – accessible, since the construction of the St Lawrence Seaway, to ocean-going vessels of up to 25,000 tons. — Situation and characteristics

◀ *State Capitol, Denver*

Detroit

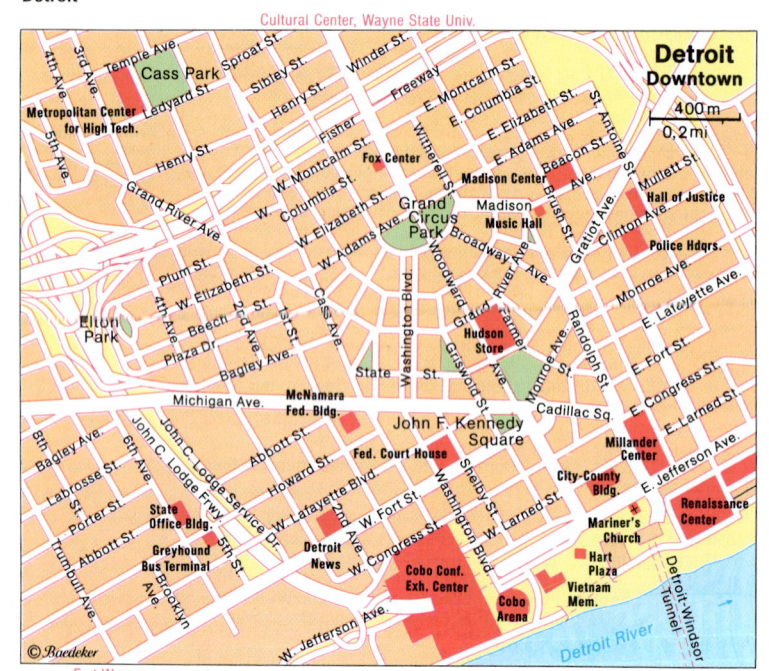

History

The city's name is derived from the French *détroit* (strait), referring to the narrow waterway between Lakes Huron and Erie. In 1701 Antoine de la Mothe Cadillac established a fort on the site of the present-day city. In 1760 this passed into British hands, and in 1796, after the American victory in the battle of Fallen Timber, was incorporated in the United States. After being incorporated as a town in 1802 and suffering great devastation in a fire in 1805, Detroit was from 1807 to 1847 capital of the state of Michigan. Its economic rise began in earnest with the opening of the Erie Canal in 1825 and the development of steamship traffic and was accompanied by a rapid increase in population. The automobile industry, founded by Henry Ford around the turn of the century, soon took the city's population above the million mark (and by 1930 to 1.5 million); and in spite of its considerable chemical, electrical and electronics industries, its shipyards and its oil refineries, there can be few cities more heavily dependent on automobile production than Detroit. As a result of the severe crisis in the automobile industry in recent years and the resultant plant closures and loss of employment Detroit has recently found itself in serious economic and political difficulties.

Sights in Detroit

*Renaissance Center and Civic Center

Along the Detroit River are the huge skyscraper complexes which since the 1970s have formed the new city centre. Dominating them all is the Renaissance Center (RenCen for short), with the 73-storey Detroit Plaza Hotel and five other 39-storey towers containing hotels, shops, theatres, restaurants and public institutions.

To the west of the Renaissance Center is the Mariners' Church (1849), the

Detroit

oldest in the city, which was moved 260yd/240m east to make room for the Civic Center with its extensive congress and conference facilities and exhibition halls. Among them are the Convention Arena, with seating for 11,000, and the Cobo Hall, one of the largest exhibition halls in the United States, with numerous conference rooms of all sizes. Immediately west of the Cobo Hall is the Joe Louis Arena, with seating for 21,000, which houses major sporting events; in front of it is a bronze statue of the Detroit-born boxer whose name it bears. Between the Renaissance Center and the Civic Center is Hart Plaza, a riverfront playground designed by the Japanese sculptor Isamu Noguchi which is a popular meeting-place in spring and summer (concerts and other performances, including part of the Montreux-Detroit Jazz Festival in May).

There are many interesting high-rise blocks to the north of the Civic and Renaissance Centers, on Griswold Street and Woodward Avenue, Detroit's main north–south axis. Between these two streets is the 32-storey Michigan Consolidation Gas Building, designed by Minoru Yamasaki. Beyond this, on the right-hand side of Griswold Street, is the 40-storey Guardian Building (485ft/148m), and on the left the 26-storey Buhl Building (350ft/107m). Then come, on the right, the National Bank of Detroit Building, opposite which is the imposing 47-storey City National Bank Building (558ft/170m). Farther along Griswold Street, on the right, is John F. Kennedy Square, south-east of which, on Cadillac Square, is the 40-storey Cadillac Tower.

Griswold Street
Woodward
Avenue

Beyond John F. Kennedy Square, between Griswold Street and Woodward Avenue, are the 23-storey First Federal Savings Building (427ft/130m) and the 38-storey David Stott Building. Farther along Woodward Avenue, on the right, is one of the world's largest department stores, the J. L. Hudson Store, on the front of which the largest Stars and Stripes in the country (236ft/72m long) is hung on Flag Day. Farther north, on the semicircular Grand Circus Park (with the Edison Fountain), is the 34-storey David Broderick Tower. On the wide Washington Boulevard, which runs south from the park, is the 35-storey Book Building (472ft/144m). Diagonally opposite it is St Aloysius' Church (R.C.).

Farther south-west, at 6325 West Jefferson Avenue, is the well preserved Fort Wayne (1843–48), with casemates, tunnels, powder magazines and numerous exhibits and displays illustrating the fort's history.

Fort Wayne
Military Museum

3 miles/5km north-west of the city centre along Woodward Avenue is the modern Cultural Center, where a number of fine museums lie close to one another.

Cultural Center

The Detroit Institute of Arts (5200 Woodward Avenue) displays a representative cross-section of man's artistic creation from the earliest cultures to the present day. Its strong points are the art of China; the art and culture of the Near East and classical antiquity; works of art, arms and armour of medieval Europe; and American art and culture (including 18th century domestic interiors in Whiteby Hall, a mansion of 1754). The collection includes many masterpieces of European painting, including works by Rembrandt, Van Gogh, Matisse and Picasso, as well as a mural by the Mexican painter Diego Rivera, "Detroit Industry" (1932), a work of social criticism.

*Institute of Arts

Wed.–Sun.
9.30am–5.30pm

Opposite the Institute of Arts is the Public Library, with a large collection on the history of the automobile. Immediately adjoining is Detroit Historical Museum (5401 Woodward Avenue), with reconstructions of old Detroit streets, model railways, dioramas and periodic special exhibitions on the history of the city.

Public Library/
Historical Museum

A little way east, at 301 Frederick Douglas Street, is the Museum of African-American History, which illustrates the role of blacks in the history of the United States and their position in the city of Detroit. An interesting feature is the "underground railway" which enabled slaves to flee from Michigan into Canada.

Museum of
African-American
History

Detroit

Detroit Science Center

South-east of the Institute of Art, at 5020 John R Street, is Detroit Science Center, with displays on science and technology (facilities for carrying out experiments, space travel simulator, etc.).

Wayne State University

One block west of the Cultural Center, beyond Cass Avenue, is the campus of Wayne State University (founded 1868), with more than forty buildings, mainly erected since the Second World War. Some of them are of outstanding architectural quality, such as the College of Education Building, the Kresge Science Library, the Shapero Hall of Pharmacy, the McGregor Memorial Community Conference Center, the DeRoy Auditorium and the Prentis Building (much of it designed by Minoru Yamasaki).

New Center Area

1¼ miles/2km north of Wayne State University, at the intersection of Second Boulevard and Grand Boulevard, is the New Center Area, with the General Motors Building, which is made up of several parallel wings.

Motown Museum

At 2648 West Grand Boulevard is the Motown Museum, the small shingle-clad building which was occupied from 1957 to 1972 by the studio where records of the "Motown sound" were produced. Visitors can see the actual recording studio. On the upper floor the walls are decorated with record sleeves, photographs and other mementoes.

*Belle Isle

Grand Boulevard and the General MacArthur Bridge over an arm of the Detroit River lead on to Belle Isle, an island in the river (3 miles/5km long and up to 1 mile/1.5km wide) laid out with beautiful parkland, hiking trails, sports facilities and other attractions, including an Aquarium (freshwater fishes), a Safari Zoo, a Botanical Museum and the Dossin Great Lakes Museum (numerous ship models and other exhibits illustrating the history of shipping on the Great Lakes).

Surroundings of Detroit

*Henry Ford Museum

Daily 9am–5pm
Greenfield Village closed Jan.–Mar.

11 miles/18km west of the city centre is the suburb of Dearborn, in which the automobile manufacturer Henry Ford (see Famous People) was born (20900 Oakwood Boulevard). Here in 1929 he established two exhibition complexes as memorials to himself: the Henry Ford Museum (area 12 acres/5 hectares) and an open-air museum, Greenfield Village (reached from Kennedy Square by way of Michigan Avenue, going west; bus 200 or 250). The Henry Ford Museum offers a general survey of the development of American life and technological advances from pioneering days to the present time. On the long entrance front of the building are representations of three historic buildings in Philadelphia (see entry): Independence Hall, Congress Hall and Old City Hall.

Inside, along the front, are the Decorative Arts Galleries, a series of rooms decorated in appropriate period style showing the development of American decorative and applied art and the furnishing styles of different social groups. The exhibits include furniture, textiles, porcelain, pottery, glass and silverware, including masterpieces by the Boston silversmith Paul Revere. At the entrance to the main hall is a reconstruction of an early 19th century street, with 22 different shops and workshops, including a drugstore, shops selling hats, furs, fiddles and toys, a hairdresser's shop, a smithy and a gunsmith's workshop.

The Main Exhibition Hall, in seven sections, is devoted to the history of technology in the United States, from agricultural machinery by way of craftsmen's equipment to industrial machinery; also illustrated are the development of transport, electrical engineering and communications. Among the most notable exhibits are George Stephenson's first steam locomotive (1829); some 200 automobiles, including the first Ford and early Daimler and Benz models; historic aircraft, including the Fokker in which Admiral Byrd made the first flight over the North Pole in 1926 and the Junkers W 33 in which Hermann Köhl, Freiherr von Hünefeld and James Fitzmaurice made the first east–west crossing of the Atlantic in 1928.

Towers of the Renaissance Centre, Detroit

A little way north of the Henry Ford Museum is the entrance to Greenfield Village, an open-air museum with some 100 historic buildings of the 18th and 19th centuries from all over the United States. Among them, in addition to different types of houses, are a school, a railroad station and other public buildings, the house in which Henry Ford was born, Edison's laboratory and the Wright brothers' bicycle factory. The numerous shops in the Village Craft Center sell the products of the various workshops in the village.

Greenfield Village

Dinosaur National Monument   J 16/17

States: Colorado, Utah
Area: 330sq.miles/855sq.km

The area is open throughout the year. The best time for a visit is between May and October.

Season

Dinosaur National Monument, famed for its fossils, lies in north-western Colorado, with a tip reaching into Utah. It occupies part of the Yampa plateau, which is cut by the spectacular canyons on the Yampa River and Green River. This extraordinary natural landscape has been created by movements in the earth's crust and the erosive forces of water and wind.

Situation and *topography

The area round the Yampa and Green Rivers became world-famous when the fossilised remains of saurians (dinosaurs), crocodiles and tortoises were found there. In the Jurassic period giant creatures, including Allosaurus, Apatosaurus, Brontosaurus and Stegosaurus, roamed over this part of America. 7 miles/11km north of Jensen (Utah) is the very informative

**Fossils

Everglades National Park

Dinosaur Quarry Visitor Center, and outside it visitors can watch specially trained workers as they carefully prise fossils (and occasionally dinosaur bones) out of the rock.

*Canyon Country Scenic Drive

From the Park offices in Dinosaur (Colorado) a 31 mile/50km long road runs round the finest sites in Canyon Country. From Harpers Corner there is a spectacular view into the 2950ft/900m deep gorge at the junction of the Yampa and Green Rivers. Other impressive spots are Steamboat Rock, Whirlpool Canyon and Echo Park.

**Rafting

There are facilities for adventurous rafting trips on the Yampa River (from Deerlodge Park) and the Green River (from Gates of Lodore). Finest of all is a trip through the Split Mountain Gorge.

Everglades National Park

Y 44/45

State Florida
Area: 2186sq.miles/5661sq.km
Established: 1947. UNESCO World Heritage Site since 1982

Season

The National Park is open throughout the year. The best time for a visit is in winter, preferably towards the end of the dry season (March/April). In summer (May–November), when the climate is predominantly hot and humid, an insect-repellent is a must.

**Situation and topography

The National Park occupies the whole of the southern tip of Florida.

Known to the Indians as Pa-hay-okee ("River of Grass"), this great expanse of subtropical swamplands, famed for its alligators (plus a small number of crocodiles) and its innumerable species of birds, is the surviving southern part of an area of swamp and marshland which originally covered fully a third of the Florida peninsula. To the north and east the Everglades have largely been drained and converted into fertile farming country. Down to the northern boundary of the National Park the land is now under cultivation (producing mainly winter vegetables for the northern states). Before being drained the Everglades were often under water for anything up to nine months in the year. The great attractions of this exotic landscape are the extraordinarily rich subtropical and sometimes tropical flora and fauna, without parallel anywhere else in the world, and the largely unspoiled and inaccessible wilderness. This is not country for the motorised tourist in a hurry: it requires plenty of time, and is best seen by boat (boat hire available in Flamingo City and in Everglades City, at the west end of the park), or alternatively on a guided walk. Visitors during the summer months are often disappointed to see only a few alligators or birds. This is because during the rainy season much of the National Park is under water and the animals and birds have no difficulty in finding food: it is only during the dry winter season that they gather at the few water points. At this time of year, too, millions of migrant birds arrive in the National Park. Nowadays the sensitive eco-system of this unique wilderness region is under threat from agricultural development and the uncontrolled building developments on the east and west coasts. The Everglades are a major source of water for these developments.

Dangerous animals

When walking away from the surfaced roads or when camping or picnicking visitors should watch out for possible encounters with dangerous animals. Among the snakes which live in the Everglades are the venomous coral snake, the black water mocassin snake, which may be anything up to 10ft/3m long, the diamondback snake and a dwarf rattlesnake. Caution is also required in approaching too close to alligators; and even raccoons, which like to forage or to beg for remains of food, are best kept at a distance. It is strictly forbidden to feed animals in the National Park.

One of the few crocodiles in the Everglades

There are also a number of poisonous species of plants in the Everglades, including poison ivy (*Rhus radicans*) and poisonwood (*Metopium toxiferum*), which is related to the sumach. Contact with these plants, particularly with the sap, can have unpleasant consequences.

Poisonous plants

Florida (State; FL)

T–Z 38–45

Area:
 58,560sq.miles/151,670sq.km
Population: 13 million
Capital: Tallahassee
Popular name: Sunshine State

The state of Florida (from the Spanish Pascua Florida = Palm Sunday, the day on which it was discovered in 1513) occupies the peninsula of that name in the south-eastern United States, which separates the Atlantic Ocean from the Gulf of Mexico, together with the "Panhandle", a narrow strip of land on the north-eastern Gulf Coast. The Sunshine State is one of the great centres of both American and international tourism. Its wide beaches of white sand, its unspoiled expanses of swampland still inhabited by alligators and panthers, its crystal-clear springs and coral reefs with their colourful underwater life, its huge theme parks (Walt Disney World, Busch Gardens, Universal Studios, etc.) and not least Spaceport USA on Cape Canaveral make a visit to Florida a very special holiday experience.

The Florida peninsula is a region of sedimentary rocks with great expanses

Situation and topography

Florida

of sand, limestone tableland much dissected by karstic action and wide areas of swamp. The landscape is patterned by numerous lakes (often formed in dolines or poljes), coastal lagoons and spits of land, mangrove swamps in the south and south-east, wide estuaries and offshore coral reefs. Seen from the air, it is clear that not so long ago the northern part of the peninsula was mainly covered with pine forests, the south with marshy grassland, cypress swamps and "hammocks" (patches of primeval forest).

History

Between about 10,000 and 8000 B.C. hunters and food-gatherers began to move into the Florida peninsula. There is evidence of a first cultural flowering in the 6th and 5th centuries B.C. Around A.D. 1500 European navigators sailed along the coasts, and on Palm Sunday (Pascua Florida) in 1513 Ponce de León landed in the estuary of the St John's River. Soon afterwards Spaniards and Frenchmen were fighting for predominance in the newly discovered territory. In 1565 the first European settlement in the United States was established at St Augustine. In the 18th and 19th centuries Florida was a bone of contention between Spain and Britain; then in 1819 it passed to the United States. After the Seminole War (1835–42) most of the Indians were deported to Oklahoma. During the American Civil War (1861–65) Florida sided with the Confederates. Towards the end of the 19th century the railroad magnates Flagler and Plant began to open up the south-eastern United States for tourism. Florida suffered setbacks to its development as a result of the war with Spain in 1898 and devastating hurricanes in 1926 and 1928. During the Second World War training camps, military camps and rest homes were established in the state, and aircraft construction and shipbuilding flourished. In 1958 the first American space satellite was launched from Cape Canaveral, followed three years later by the first manned space flights, culminating in Neil Armstrong and Edwin Aldrin's landing on the moon in 1969. In 1980 there were violent race riots in the city of Miami. Then more than 140,000 Cuban refugees poured into southern Florida. The "Challenger" catastrophe of 1986 was a severe setback to the American space programme. In 1992 race riots in Los Angeles sparked off similar disturbances in Tampa and Miami, and in the same year Hurricane Andrew brought devastation to southern Florida.

Economy

The most important branch of Florida's economy is the holiday and tourist trade, centred mainly on the Atlantic and Gulf coasts and round Orlando with its giant theme parks. In 1992 Florida had some 40 million visitors. It is also becoming an increasingly important financial centre, with over 170 international financial institutions based in Miami alone. In the industrial sector the most important elements are the processing of agricultural produce (particularly fruit juices and concentrates, sweets, essential oils, preservatives) and aircraft and space technology. The main agricultural crops are citrus fruits, sugar-cane and vegetables. Stock farming, fishing and forestry also make important contributions to the economy. Other sources of income are phosphates (one-third of world output), titanium and zircon from dune sands, lime and cement production and offshore oil and natural gas.

Places of Interest in Florida

*Apalachicola

The little town of Apalachicola (pop. 3000) in the Panhandle of Florida has a charming old Historic District. It is now the centre of Florida's oyster fisheries (Apalachicola Bay). Within easy reach of the town are the offshore St George Island with its beautiful beaches; St Vincent Island, a nature reserve (turtles, various species of birds); and the St Joseph Peninsula, an unspoiled region with magnificent beaches. Two areas popular with nature-lovers are the Apalachicola National Estuarine Reserve (the estuary of the Apalachicola River) and, farther inland, the Apalachicola National Forest. On the southern edge of the Apalachicola Forest is Fort Gadsden (1814).

Florida

View of Fort Lauderdale

Daytona Beach, famed for the 20 mile/32km stretch of firm sand on which Malcolm Campbell five times broke the world land speed record, now also has an international racing circuit, the Daytona International Speedway. A recent tradition has been the "spring break" during the university vacation (beginning of March to Easter), when hundreds of thousands of young people converge on Daytona, the scene is dominated by brilliantly chrome-plated motorcycles, convertibles, beach buggies, jeeps and pickups and there are almost daily concerts of deafening rock music.

Daytona Beach

To the south of Miami (see entry) are the Florida Keys (from the Spanish *cayo,* "islet, reef"), a chain of coral islands of varying size which extends for more than 110 miles/180km between the Atlantic and the Gulf of Mexico. Until a devastating hurricane in 1935 they were linked by a rail line extending to Key West, from which there were boats to Havana (Cuba). The boldly engineered Overseas Highway (US 1) now runs over 42 bridges and numerous artificial causeways to the south-eastern tip of the United States. The little islands of Sands Key, Elliot Key, Cotton Key and Old Rhodes Key, lying off Biscayne Bay, are now part of the Biscayne National Underwater Park, established in 1980. Off Key Largo (pop. 11,000) are the John Pennekamp Coral Reef State Park and the Key Largo National Marine Sanctuary, the only living coral reef in the continental United States. The rich underwater life and a number of wrecks attract large numbers of snorkellers and scuba divers. Islamorada claims to be the "sport fishing capital of the world". On Grassy Key is the Dolphin Research Center, where the TV series "Flipper" was filmed. Marathon (pop. 10,000) is the second largest town on the Keys. The new Seven Miles Bridge (1982) leads to the Bahia Honda State Recreational Area, with a beautiful bathing beach. On Big Pine Key is the National Key Deer Refuge, home to the last few hundred of the shy, miniature (only 2ft/60cm high) roe-deer of the Keys.

*Florida Keys

Florida

*Fort Lauderdale
: The military and trading post of Fort Lauderdale, established in 1837, has now developed into the "Venice of the United States". Its 160 miles/260km of palm-fringed artificial waterways, tens of thousands of moorings for pleasure craft, elegant holiday apartments and beautiful 6 mile/10km long beach draw visitors from all over the world throughout the year. Particular attractions are Ocean World (trained dolphins and seals), the International Swimming Hall of Fame (with mementoes of Johnny Weissmuller, famous as a swimmer and as Tarzan, the record-breaking swimmer Mark Spitz and many others), the beautiful Flamingo Groves (planted with various species of citrus fruits) and Butterfly World on Coconut Creek. From the offshore Port Everglades, the second largest cruising port in the United States, there are daily departures of musical and gambling cruises to the Bahamas and the Caribbean.

*Fort Myers
: Fort Myers, a town in process of dynamic development, lies on the Gulf of Mexico at the mouth of the Caloosahatchee River. Abundant traces of human settlement going back 7000 years have been found in the surrounding area. The town became widely known in the 1880s, when Thomas Alva Edison (see Famous People) began to establish his home and his laboratory here during the winter. His example was followed in 1916 by his friend Henry Ford (see Famous People), who also built himself a winter home opposite Edison's. There are guided tours round the two "Winter Homes" (Mon.–Sat. 9am–4pm, Sun. 12.30–4pm). From Fort Myers the select Palm Alley (planted with royal palms from Cuba) runs down to the Gulf Coast, with the beautiful bathing resorts of Fort Myers Beach, Estero Island and the islands of Sanibel and Captiva (see below).

Fort Walton Beach
: The family resort of Fort Walton Beach lies on the north-western Gulf Coast. The Temple Mound Museum illustrates the history of Indian settlement and culture over 10,000 years. Off Fort Walton Beach is the narrow coral island of Santa Rosa, part of the Gulf Islands National Seashore (see entry). Inland from Fort Walton Beach is the Eglin Air Force Base, the largest in the United States; there is an Air Force Museum, open: daily 9.30am–4.30pm.

Naples
: The town of Naples (pop. 20,000) on the Gulf coast of south-western Florida was founded in 1877 at a time of much speculation in land. It is now a popular holiday resort with elegant shopping streets and a famous wooden pier. Round Naples are a number of beautiful bathing beaches (Vanderbilt Beach, Wiggins Pass, Marco Island, etc.).

Ocala
: Ocala (pop. 43,000), a country town in "Cracker Country" (northern central Florida), is a horse-breeding centre. Within easy reach of the town are Silver Springs, setting of the James Bond film "Never Say Never Again"; Orange Lake, an anglers' paradise; and Ocala National Forest.

Pensacola
: The port of Pensacola (pop. 60,000), situated on the best and largest natural harbour in Florida, is the economic centre of the western edge of the Panhandle, the "Miracle Strip". Its history goes back more than 400 years, and the carefully restored Historic Village contains buildings of the Spanish, French and British colonial periods.
Features of interest in the surrounding area are the US Naval Aviation Museum; Fort Pickens (1834), at the west end of Santa Rosa Island; and Pensacola Beach with its expanses of brilliantly white sand.

*Sanibel and Captiva
: To the west of Fort Myers (see above) are the islands of Sanibel and Captiva, famed for their magically beautiful beaches, strewn with a great variety of seashells. On the shores facing the mainland are areas of marshland and mangroves, home to a wide variety of animal life. On the north-east coast of Sanibel is the "Ding" Darling National Wildlife Refuge.

*Sarasota
: In a bay on the south-western Gulf coast of Florida is Sarasota (pop. 52,000), founded in 1842, now a rather exclusive retreat for the well-to-do known as a centre of the arts. It owes this reputation mainly to the million-

Georgia

aire circus owner John Ringling and his wife, who established here not only a circus museum but an important art museum and a theatre. The Ringling Museum of Art possesses major works by Cranach, Rubens, Van Dyck and many other European artists. The Theatre, a faithful reproduction of the Baroque theatre in the Italian town of Asolo, is the home of a successful drama company. The Ringlings' winter residence (1926) is in the form of a Venetian Renaissance palazzo. Other sights in Sarasota are Belim's Cars and Music of Yesterday Museum (veteran and vintage cars, old musical boxes, mechanical musical instruments, gambling machines), the Sarasota Jungle Gardens (with flamingoes, etc.), the Mary Selby Botanical Gardens (orchids, etc.) and the Mote Science Aquarium (marine flora and fauna). There are beautiful bathing beaches on the narrow little offshore islets of St Amands, Lido, Longboat and Siesta Keys.

To the east of Sarasota is the Myakka River State Park, a still largely intact eco-system in which the original flora and fauna of the Sunshine State can be studied.

In the hilly country of central Florida is Sebring, a town well known to motor-racing enthusiasts for the races held at the end of March and in October on the old military airfield. To the west of Sebring lies the Highland Hammock State Park.

Sebring

Tallahassee (founded 1824), capital of the state of Florida, is a quiet town of some 127,000 inhabitants at the east end of the Panhandle. Its main features of interest are the Old Capitol (1839), the New Capitol (1978) and the richly stocked Museum of Florida History. Outside the town are the Lake Jackson Indian Mounds (an Indian cult site), the Lafayette Vineyards, the Natural Bridge Battlefield (on which the defenders of Tallahassee defeated the Union forces), the Spanish fort of San Marcos de Apalache (1679) and Wakulla Springs, with one of the biggest karstic springs in Florida, part of an extensive cave system of which little has so far been explored.

Tallahassee

Round Winter Haven are a number of beautiful little lakes which draw many holidaymakers. The main attraction, however, is Cypress Gardens, opened in 1936, where glamorously costumed "Southern belles" pose for photographers and a famous water-skiing show is presented.

Winter Haven
*Cypress Gardens

Amelia Island (see Jacksonville); Cape Canaveral, Everglades National Park, Jacksonville, Key West, Miami, Orlando, Palm Beach, St Augustine, St Petersburg, Tampa (see entries); Walt Disney World (see Orlando).

Other places of interest

Georgia (State; GA)

P–T 40–44

Area:
  58,910sq.miles/152,576sq.km
Population: 6.63 million
Capital: Atlanta
Popular names: Empire State of the South, Peach State

The state of Georgia (named after King George II) lies in the south-eastern United States, bounded on the south by Florida. Most of the state lies in the Atlantic coastal plain. Offshore are numerous islands, on which there are beautiful bathing beaches. Inland there are extensive areas of marshland. To the north-east the land rises gradually to the Appalachians and the Cumberland Plateau. The highest point in the state is the hill of Brasstown Bold (4784ft/1458m). The warm temperate and humid climate fosters a lush growth of vegetation. Some two-thirds of the state is covered by forest, with oak, hickory, fir and pine predominating in

Situation and topography

Georgia

the hills. In the coastal plain and the marshland areas there are cypresses, various species of palms and arbor vitae.

History

The territory of Georgia, discovered by Europeans in 1540, had long been settled by Indians. During the 16th, 17th and 18th centuries Britain, Spain and France fought for predominance in the south-east of the North American continent. In 1733 the British established a settlement, and in 1754 the territory became a Crown colony. In 1776 the colony ratified the Declaration of Independence, and twelve years later signed the Constitution of the United States as the fourth of the founding states. Cotton-growing on plantations worked by slave labour soon became the basis of the state's economy. During the Civil War Georgia set out to play a leading role, but was devastated by Sherman's march through the state. It was re-admitted to the Union only in 1870. The abolition of slavery and competition from other parts of the world brought Georgia's plantation economy into crisis. In more recent times the banning of racial segregation and the granting of full civil rights to blacks led to serious social conflicts. During this period Martin Luther King (see Famous People) became a symbol of the awakening Afro-American consciousness.

Economy

Agriculture is still one of the main pillars of Georgia's economy. In addition to cotton, dominant for 150 years, the main crops are soya beans, maize and peanuts. Stock farming (cattle, pigs) and above all poultry farming have gained greatly in importance. The great forests of pines provide raw material for papermaking and the manufacture of turpentine. Considerable quantities of granite, marble and kaolin are also worked in Georgia. Alongside the highly developed cotton and textile industries chemical and foodstuffs industries have also been established in recent decades. Georgia lies in the Sun Belt, a region remarkable for its dynamic economic development. This is particularly true of the Atlanta region, with over 500 businesses operating on an international scale.

Places of Interest in Georgia

Athens

Athens (pop. 48,000), seat of the University of Georgia, is noted for its Greek Revival architecture. There are a number of particularly fine classical-style buildings on Prince Avenue. The Georgia Museum of Art has a notable collection of pictures.

Augusta

On the eastern borders of Georgia, on the Savannah River, is Augusta, founded by James Oglethorpe in 1735, long the centre of a large cotton- and tobacco-growing area.

Chickamauga and Chattanooga National Military Park

In north-western Georgia are the Civil War battlefields of Chickamauga and Chattanooga, where 34,000 Union and Confederate troops fell.

Columbus

In the far west of Georgia, on the Chattahoochee River, is the town of Columbus (pop. 170,000), with its well restored and refurbished Historic District. During the Civil War it was an important supply base. Features of interest are the Springer Opera House; the Confederate Naval Museum, with the armoured warships "Muscogee" and "Jackson"; the Columbus Museum; and the National Infantry Museum in Fort Benning, outside the town.

Dahlonega

Gold was discovered in 1828 near the township of Dahlonega, and this led to a gold rush here and in the surrounding area (with the ghost town of Auraria, Clarksville, Cleveland and Helen).

*Macon

Macon (pop. 120,000), formerly an important inland port on the Ocmulgee River, is now the cultural and economic centre of a large surrounding area.

It has a number of well preserved old buildings, including City Hall, the Grand Opera House, Hay House, in Italian Renaissance style, and the birthplace of the poet Sydney Clayton Lanier.
To the east of the town is the Ocmulgee National Monument. Originally (10,000 years ago) an Indian settlement of the prehistoric Mound Builder culture, the site was still occupied in the 19th century.

Between Atlanta (see entry) and Macon is Milledgeville, former capital of Georgia, which still preserves something of the atmosphere of antebellum times.

Milledgeville

The Okefenokee Swamp, known to the Indians as the "Land of the Quaking Earth", is an area of swampland in southern Georgia, over 770sq.miles/ 2000sq.km in extent – a maze of watercourses, cypress swamps and swamp grassland. Interesting features are the "floating islands", which quake under foot but nevertheless support whole forests and in the past provided protection for Indian settlements. The swamp is home to many endangered species and has no fewer that 10,000 alligators. From the little town of Waycross there are boat trips into the swamp.

*Okefenokee Swamp

North of Columbus (see above), on Pine Mountain, is a popular leisure centre established by the industrialist Cason Callaway, with artificial lakes, gardens of magnolias and azaleas, a butterfly house, a golf course, cycle tracks and a variety of sports facilities.

*Callaway Gardens

Atlanta, Savannah (see entries)

Other places of interest

Grand Canyon National Park

N 12–14

State: Arizona
Area: 1905sq.miles/4934sq.km
Established: 1919

The National Park is open throughout the year. The best times for a visit are from April to June and from September to mid November. In summer it can be intolerably hot. During the main holiday season, too, the National Park's facilities tend to be overstrained. In winter the North Rim is under heavy snow, and most of the roads and tracks are closed from November to mid May.

Season

The Grand Canyon National Park lies in north-western Arizona, bounded on the west by Lake Mead National Recreation Area, where the Colorado River is dammed by the Hoover Dam, and on the north-east (following the course of the Colorado River) by Canyonlands National Park and the Glen Canyon. The South Rim can be reached from Williams or Flagstaff on SR 64 and US 180, the North Rim from Jacob Lake on SR 67. Although the North and South Rims are only 10 miles/16km apart as the crow flies, the distance by road is 215 miles/346km. During the main summer holiday season there are bus services between the two.

Preliminary information
Situation and access

Since the Grand Canyon is at times overrun by tourists it is advisable to book accommodation or a camping site and to apply for a "backcountry permit" (required for hiking in the National Park) in plenty of time – during the main holiday season months in advance.

Reservations

The Visitor Center on the South Rim, which is much more heavily visited than the North Rim, is on South Rim Drive, 1¼ miles/2km east of Grand Canyon Village (open: Sept.–May daily 8am–5pm, June–Aug. 7.30am–8.30pm). On the North Rim information can be obtained in Grand Canyon Lodge or the Ranger Station.

Visitor Centers

There are daily lectures and guided walks by well informed park rangers.

Park ranger services

Grand Canyon National Park

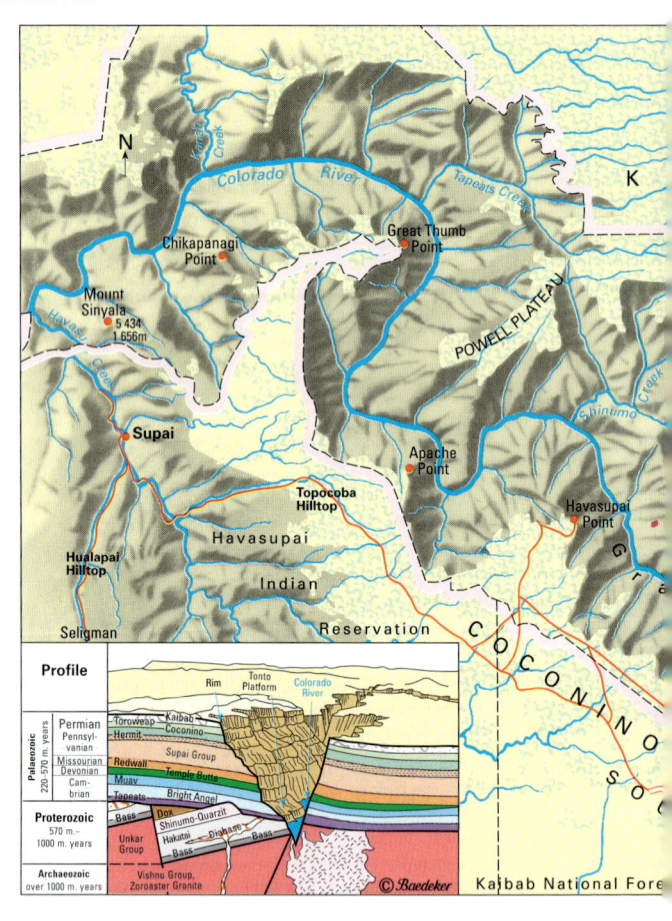

Sightseeing flights	There are sightseeing flights by helicopter and light aircraft from the Grand Canyon Airport at Tusayan (5 miles/8km south of Grand Canyon Village) and from airfields at Flagstaff, Page, Phoenix and Williams.
Bus trips	On the South Rim there are bus trips (with commentary) along the Rim Drive, starting from Grand Canyon Village. On the North Rim there are buses between Grand Canyon Lodge and the Cape Royal viewpoint.
Mule treks	On both the North and South Rims there are half-day and whole-day trips into the Canyon on muleback; also two-day trips, spending the night in the Phantom Ranch.
Rafting	For the adventurous there are rafting trips in rubber dinghies (from 2 to 18 days) down the Colorado River. There are operators in Flagstaff, Page and Peach Springs (Arizona) and in Kanab, Orem and Salt Lake City (Utah).
Hiking	For hikers there are three dozen maintained trails with a total length of over 400 miles/640km.

Grand Canyon National Park

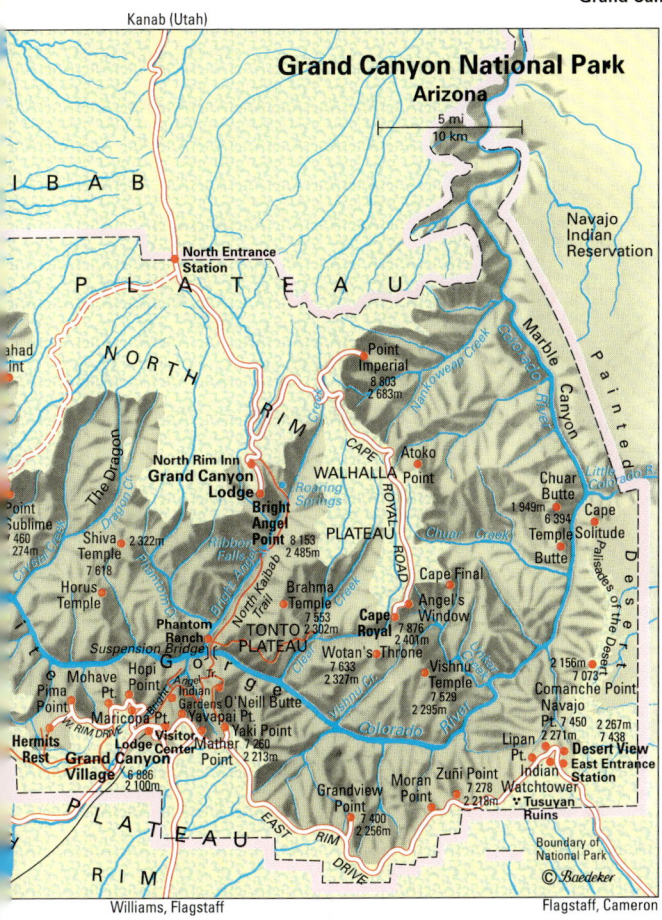

A descent into the Grand Canyon is an exceptionally strenuous undertaking, requiring both fitness and stamina. Essential items of equipment are stout footwear, protection against the sun and plenty of drinking water. Before setting out you must inform a park ranger of your intention. Bear in mind, too, that the Grand Canyon National Park is rattlesnake country, and keep a watchful eye for these venomous reptiles.

Warning

Grand Canyon

The Grand Canyon created by the Colorado River was described by the Scottish-born pioneer of conservation John Muir as the grandest place on God's earth. The breathtaking width and depth of this canyon, its beauty, its forms and colours, leave even the most travelled visitor lost in admiration. Here the river winds its way for a distance of 277 miles/446km through the Kaibab plateau, into which it has cut a deep yawning gorge ranging in width between 4 miles/6km and 18 miles/29km. On the south side the rock

*Topography

Grand Canyon National Park

Panorama of the Grand Canyon

face falls down 5000ft/1500m to the river below (alt. 2400ft/730m), on the north side no less than 6000ft/1800m.

Origins

The history of the formation of the Grand Canyon has not been certainly established, but the general view is that the reduction in the height of the Colorado river-bed has been brought about mainly over the past 9 million years. The lowest level of erosional activity now runs through a narrow gorge cut out of Palaeozoic rocks up to 1700 million years old. The canyon becomes wider towards the top, where younger, horizontally bedded sedimentary rocks of varying degrees of resistance have been eroded away. These layers of sandstone and limestone, in brilliant reddish, bluish-grey and yellowish tones, depending on light conditions, were laid down during the Cambrian, Devonian, Carboniferous and Permian periods, and the steep rock faces descending in steps to the bottom of the canyon display a complete stratigraphical sequence. Going down into the canyon, you pass 1700 million years of the earth's history.

History

Much evidence has been found of Indian settlement in the Grand Canyon dating back more than 4000 years. The most impressive remains are the 1000 year old rock dwellings of the Anasazi Indians. When a member of Francisco Vásquez de Coronado's expedition questing for gold became the first European to discover the Grand Canyon in 1540 these had probably long been abandoned. In 1869 Major John Wesley Powell, later director of the US Geological Survey, travelled by boat through the inhospitable gorges of the Colorado and Green Rivers, starting from Wyoming. In the 1880s the tourist potential of the Grand Canyon began to be realised; the first hotel was built on Grand View Point in 1892, and ten years later visitors were able to visit the Grand Canyon by rail. Thereafter the numbers of visitors grew steadily, particularly after the establishment of the Grand Canyon National Park in 1919. In 1965 the number of visitors was over 1.6 million, and by 1992 the figure had risen to 4 million.

Grand Canyon National Park

Sights on the South Rim of the Grand Canyon

From Grand Canyon Village the Rim Drive runs east and west along the edge of the canyon, affording magnificent views into the canyon.

The East Rim Drive (25 miles/40km) runs east from the Visitor Center, passing Yavapai Point and the Yavapai Museum, to Desert View and on to the east exit of the National Park, towards Cameron. Halts can be made at a number of viewpoints – Yaki Point, Grandview Point, Moran Point, Lipan Point and finally Navajo Point, with the Indian Watchtower.

The West Rim Drive (8 miles/13km) also offers spectacular views into the canyon, with viewpoints at Trailview Overlook, Maricopa Point, Hopi Point, Mohave Point, the Abyss, Pima Point and Hermits Rest. The West Rim Drive is barred to private automobiles from May to September; instead there is a free shuttle bus.

1 mile/1.6km east of the Visitor Center is the Yavapai Museum, which has interesting displays illustrating the origins and geology of the Grand Canyon. From here too there are breathtaking views.

3 miles/5km west of Desert View on the East Rim Drive is the Tusayan Ruin, one of over 2000 remains of Indian settlements in the Grand Canyon region. In the late 12th century the Tusayan pueblo was home to some three dozen Anasazi Indians, but – like most of the pueblos in this region – it was abandoned in the 13th century. The Tusayan Museum surveys the history of the Anasazi culture.

From the Watchtower at Desert View, built in 1932 on the model of Indian watchtowers, there are tremendous views of the Painted Desert to the east and into the Grand Canyon.

The South Rim Nature Trail (3 miles/5km) is an easy walk from the Yavapai Museum along the rim of the canyon to Maricopa Point. Part of this scenic route is signposted as a nature trail.

The Bright Angel Trail (8 miles/13km) starts from Bright Angel Lodge (6861ft/2091m) and runs down by way of the Indian Gardens (3806ft/1160m; campground) either to Plateau Point (3780ft/1152m), or right down to the Colorado River (2395ft/730m).

The South Kaibab Trail (6 miles/10km) runs steeply down from Yaki Point to the Colorado River, 4865ft/1483m below.

The Bright Angel and South Kaibab Trails are linked by the Tonto Trail (4 miles/6km) and the River Trail (2 miles/3km).

The Colorado River is spanned by two bridges leading to the Bright Angel Campground and the Phantom Ranch, which provide board and lodging (reservation essential).

**Scenic drives

East Rim Drive

West Rim Drive

*Yavapai Museum

Tusayan Ruin and Museum

Watchtower

*Hiking trails

Bright Angel Trail

South Kaibab Trail

Tonto Trail/ River Trail

Bridges

Sights on the North Rim of the Grand Canyon

Since the North Rim of the Grand Canyon is between 1000 and 1250ft (300 and 380m) higher than the South Rim, it offers a whole range of new and spectacular prospects. The most popular viewpoints are Bright Angel Point, Point Imperial and Cape Royal.

Bright Angel Point, at the end of SR 67 near Grand Canyon Lodge, lies high above the gorge of Bright Angel Creek and opens up a grandiose prospect of the Grand Canyon landscape.

A few miles north of Bright Angel Point a 22 mile/35km road branches off. This then forks, one road running north-east to Point Imperial, the other south-east over the Walhalla Plateau to Cape Royal. Point Imperial, the highest point in the National Park (8803ft/2683m), affords views into the Marble Canyon to the east and of the Painted Desert on the south side of

*Viewpoints

Bright Angel Point

Point Imperial/ Cape Royal

Grand Canyon National Park

the Grand Canyon. From Cape Royal there are views of the Painted Desert and of the striking rock towers known as Wotan's Throne and the Vishnu Temple.

Hiking trails
Transept Canyon Trail

From Grand Canyon Lodge the Transept Canyon Trail (2 miles/3km) runs to the North Rim Inn. There is also a short trail to Bright Angel Point.

North Kaibab Trail

The North Kaibab Trail (14 miles/23km) starts at a parking area (8242ft/2512m) at the head of Roaring Springs Canyon, 2½ miles/4km before Grand Canyon Lodge, and runs through Bright Angel Canyon, passing the Cottonwood Campground (4003ft/1220m), the Phantom Ranch (see above) and Bright Angel Campground, to the Colorado River (2395ft/730m).

Surroundings of the Grand Canyon

*Havasupai Indian Reservation

In the canyon of Havasu Creek, a tributary of the Colorado River, some 450 Havasupai Indians (the "people of the blue-green water") live a secluded life, subsisting on their modest farming activities but now mainly dependent on the tourist trade. In this paradisiac valley the Havasu has created a number of waterfalls and carved out basins in the travertine rock which form attractive bathing pools. The Indian village of Supai can be reached only by helicopter from Grand Canyon Airport or on foot or horseback on an arduous 8 mile/13km long trail from Hualapai Hilltop (70 miles/112km north-east of Peach Springs). Accommodation, camping sites and horses must be booked in advance. Information from Havasupai Tourist Enterprise. Supai, AZ 86435, tel. (602) 448 2121.

*Grand Canyon Caverns

The romantic Grand Canyon Caverns lie 12 miles/19km east of Peach Springs on the legendary Route 66. An elevator takes visitors down into the

Havasu Falls in the Grand Canyon

Grand Teton National Park

caves with their beautiful mineral formations and a constant temperature of 55°F/13°C.

The road from Flagstaff to Grand Canyon Village runs past Sunset Crater, Arizona's youngest volcano, which erupted for the first time about 1064. — *Sunset Crater

The Wupakti National Monument has remains of settlements of the Sinagua and Anasazi Indians. — Wupakti National Monument

The Glen Canyon and Lake Mead National Recreation Areas offer facilities for a variety of water sports and other leisure activities. — Glen Canyon/Lake Mead

Grand Teton National Park   F 15

State: Wyoming
Area: 485sq.miles/1257sq.km
Established: 1929

The Grand Teton National Park is open throughout the year. The best time for a visit is between June and September. In winter all the facilities except the Moose Visitor Center are closed, but there is ample scope for winter sports (downhill and langlauf skiing, skating; trips in dog-, horse- or motor sleighs; ice fishing). — Season

Grand Teton National Park, established in 1929 and enlarged in 1950 by the inclusion of Jackson Hole, lies in north-western Wyoming a few miles south of Yellowstone National Park (see entry), with which it is linked by the John D. Rockefeller Jr Memorial Parkway. It consists of Jackson Hole, a mountain valley 50 miles/80km long and up to 14 miles/23km wide lying at a height of almost 6500ft/2000m, and the jagged Teton Range, whose — Situation and *topography

Grand Teton: view from Signal Hill

Great Smoky Mountains National Park

highest peaks rise to around 13,000ft/4000m (Grand Teton, 13,770ft/4197m; Middle Teton, 12,804ft/3903m; South Teton, 12,514ft/3814m; Mount Owen, 12,927ft/3940m). The range was named Grand Teton by French fur-trappers (*grands tétons* = "big breasts"). The landscape of the National Park is of extraordinary beauty. Jackson Hole is surrounded by lakes, some of them of considerable size, and traversed by the beautiful Snake River. Popular leisure activities here are hiking, fishing and canoeing, and for experienced climbers there are a variety of challenging routes.

Wild life

This well watered mountain valley is the home of elk, wapiti and mule deer; on the lakes and rivers there are beavers, trumpeter swans, white pelicans, wild ducks, wild geese and ospreys; and a herd of bison is usually to be seen grazing to the east of the Oxbow Bend on the Snake River (near the Buffalo Entrance at Moran). Black bears are now rare. On the south side of the National Park is the National Elk Refuge, where the largest herd of wapiti in the United States regularly winters.

Scenic roads

Two scenic roads offer magnificent views of the mountains: the Rockefeller Parkway, which runs north–south, following the east side of Jackson Lake and the Snake River, and the Teton Park Road, which runs south-east from Jackson Lake and along Cottonwood Creek.

Hiking trails

The National Park has more than 200 miles/320km of hiking trails and footpaths running through the forests, to the various lakes and into the mountains. Among the easiest are the path from the east side of Jenny Lake to Inspiration Point (2½ miles/4km) and the Colter Bay Nature Trail (2 miles/3.2km). A whole-day hike is from Jackson Lake Lodge to Emma Matilda Lake and Two Ocean Lake. A longer trail, taking several days but offering magnificent views, starts from the upper cableway station at Teton Village (outside the park to the south) and runs north along the west side of the Grand Teton range, returning to the valley by way of Death Canyon, Cascade Canyon or Paintbrush Canyon. Information about other activities (horse trekking, climbing) can be obtained from the Park administration (see Practical Information, National Parks).

Indian Arts Museum

In the Visitor Center in Colter Bay on the east side of Jackson Lake is the Indian Arts Museum (Indian arts and crafts, implements, clothing).

Great Smoky Mountains National Park   O 42

States: North Carolina, Tennessee
Area: 814sq.miles/2107sq.km
Established: 1934

Season

The Great Smoky Mountains National Park, the most visited National Park in the United States, is open throughout the year – though in winter some roads may be impassable.

Situation and *topography

The Great Smoky Mountains, a central range of the Appalachians running roughly east–west, are one of the finest forest regions in the United States. The name of the National Park, through which runs the border between the states of North Carolina and Tennessee, comes from the clouds and mist which frequently rise out of the lonely mountain valleys like smoke signals and swathe the mountains rising above the valleys to heights of over 6500ft/2000m.

Flora and fauna

With its abundant rainfall, mainly in the summer months, and fertile soils, the National Park has a wide variety of flora and fauna (including bears). At lower levels dense deciduous forests predominate; higher up there are conifers. Well over 1400 species of flowering plants can be found here, including mountain magnolias, wild azaleas, mountain laurels and

Gulf Islands National Seashore

orchids; from the beginning of June to the middle of July there are splendid shows of rhododendrons.

**Rhododendron blossom

The full beauty of the National Park can best be appreciated by exploring it on foot. There are a total of some 900 miles/1440km of hiking trails: information from Visitor Centers and the Park administration (see Practical Information, National Parks).

Hiking trails

The National Park can be approached from the east on the Blue Ridge Skyway (see Virginia), which ends at the Oconaluftee Visitor Center. Here, in the extreme west of North Carolina, is the largest Indian reservation east of the Mississippi, the Qualla Reservation, occupied by the descendants of the Cherokees who refused in 1838 to follow the "Trail of Tears" to Oklahoma. In the little town of Cherokee there is an informative museum, and the Oconaluftee Indian Village above the town seeks to re-create the old life of the tribe.

Cherokee Indian Reservation

To the west, reached by way of Gatlinburg, a little town now given over to the tourist trade, and the Sugarlands Visitor Center, is Newfound Gap (5050ft/1539m), on the crest line of the mountains, which offers a magnificent view of the mountain forests. Still finer is the prospect from the viewpoint (closed in winter) on Clingmans Dome (6642ft/2024m), the highest hill in Tennessee, which can be climbed from Newfound Gap either by road or on a 6 mile/9.6km long section of the Appalachian Trail (see Practical Information, National Parks).

Newfound Gap

Clingmans Dome

Round Cades Cove, in the western part of the National Park, runs an 11 mile/18km long road, passing the fields, houses, wooden churches and mills of the pioneers who settled here in the 19th century.

Cades Cove

Gulf Islands National Seashore

T 38/39

States: Florida, Alabama, Mississippi

The Gulf Islands National Seashore takes in large areas of the long series of islands and peninsulas which extend for more than 150 miles/240km along the coast from West Ship Island, off the Mississippi delta, to the east end of Santa Rosa Island, off the Panhandle of Florida, together with certain areas on the mainland. Florida's share of the National Seashore includes parts of Perdido Key, to the west of Pensacola (see Florida), the Naval Live Oaks Reservation to the east of Gulf Breeze, the fortifications on Pensacola Naval Station and much of Santa Rosa Island (Fort Pickens, Santa Rosa Day Use Area, Okaloosa).

Situation and **topography

The National Seashore is administered by the National Park Service, which runs a Visitor Center. There are excellent recreational faciliities on the beautiful beaches of fine sand, and fishing in the gentle surf (no permit required) is also popular. There are a number of nature trails introducing visitors to the flora and fauna of the barrier islands. For the historically minded there are the remains of fortifications dating from the first half of the 19th century.

The flat sandy islands which protect the mainland from storms are subject to constant change and displacement (mainly towards the west) through the action of winds and currents. Strong winds and hurricanes sometimes partly flood the islands and break sections of them off. In 1979 Hurricane Frederick moved a whole range of dunes on Santa Rosa Island. Along the coast of the Gulf of Mexico extends a belt of dunes covered with marram grass, and behind this, sheltered from the salt spray, grow low trees and palmetto scrub. On the older dunes are low-growing live oaks, magnolias and pines. Beyond these again are areas of salt and freshwater marshland frequented by herons and ospreys, various species of waterfowl, alligators, turtles and snakes.

Dunes

Hawaii / Hawaiian Islands (State; HI)

Area: 6385sq.miles/16,540sq.km
Population: 1.1 million
Capital: Honolulu
Popular name: Aloha State

Situation and topography

The Hawaiian Islands lie in the northern Pacific some 2400 miles/3860km south-west of San Francisco (see entry). The archipelago consists of eight larger islands – from east to west Hawaii, Maui, Kahoolawe, Lanai, Molokai, Oahu, Kauai and Niihau – and over a hundred small islands and coral atolls, the North-western Hawaiian Islands. The eight large islands lie in the tropics and have lush tropical vegetation, while most of the north-western islands are north of the Tropic of Cancer. The mild climate, beautiful scenery and good bathing and surfing beaches attract large numbers of visitors from the United States, Europe and Japan. In spite of heavy Americanisation the islands have preserved much of their native culture and unspoiled natural beauty.

Origins

The Hawaiian archipelago consists of the tips of volcanoes of the type known as Hawaiian (i.e. open craters with expulsion of lava but no explosive activity). Only two volcanoes on the island of Hawaii, Mauna Loa and Kilauea, are still active. The formation of Hawaii, in a seismically unstable zone of the Pacific, began in the Middle Tertiary era and continued over a period of 70 million years. This activity is explained by the theory of "hot spots": at certain points on the earth's mantle magma accumulates and is then released through faults and crevices in the crust in the form of volcanic eruptions and cools to form new land. Since the Hawaiian Islands lie on the Pacific Plate, which is drifting from south-east to north-west, the islands are also moving north-west at the rate of 3 to 4 inches (8–10cm) a year. As a result of this movement the "hot spot" under Hawaii has given rise not merely to one volcano but to a whole chain of volcanoes, with the oldest on the Kure atoll to the north-west and the youngest on Hawaii to the south-east.

History

The Hawaiian Islands were settled by Polynesians between A.D. 300 and 600. In 1778 Captain James Cook landed on the islands, but thereafter they remained an independent kingdom, though during the 19th century they became increasingly dependent on the United States both economically and politically. A coup d'état against Queen Liliuokalani in 1893 put an end to the monarchy, and in 1894 a republic was proclaimed. Soon after the outbreak of the war with Mexico in 1898 the United States annexed

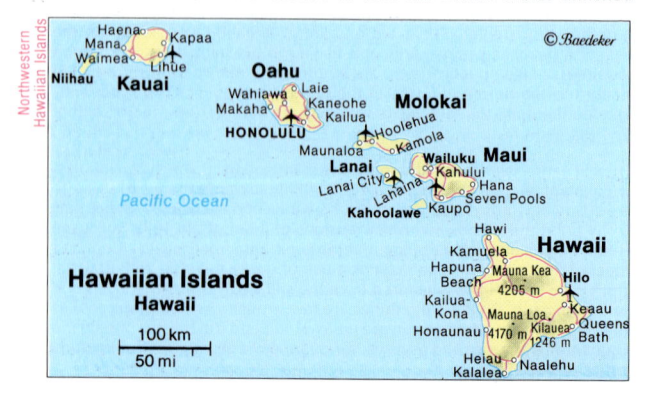

Hawaii / Hawaiian Islands

the islands, which in 1900 were incorporated as a United States territory. In 1959 Hawaii became the 50th state of the Union. The Japanese attack on the American naval base of Pearl Harbor in the Hawaiian archipelago on December 7th 1941 brought the United States into the Second World War.

The most important element in the economy of Hawaii by a long way is tourism, followed by agriculture (sugar, canned pineapples) and fishing. The US Navy continues to be a major employer.

Economy

Places of Interest on the Hawaiian Islands

This section is deliberately abridged, since there is a special AA/Baedeker guide "Hawaii".

On Hawaii, the largest and most south-easterly island in the archipelago, are the two active volcanoes of Mauna Loa (13,672ft/4167m) and Mauna Kea (13,797ft/4205m). Kilauea, a subsidiary of Mauna Loa, is the world's most active volcano. Both of these volcanoes are included within the Hawaiian Volcanoes National Park, which offers unique opportunities to see an active volcano, for example from the Crater Rim Road round the caldera of Kilauea or on branches off this such as the Devastation Trail or the trail to the Thurston Lava Tube.

Hawaii

**Hawaiian Volcanoes National Park

Other features of interest on Hawaii are the Hawaii Tropical Botanical Gardens at Hilo, the tourist resort of Kailua-Kona, Mauna Kea, the Parker Ranch at Waimea, the largest in the United States, and the Puuhonea o Honanau National Historic Park, site of a Hawaiian temple of the late 18th century.

West of the island of Hawaii, separated from it by the Alenuihaha Channel, is Maui. Here too, in the Haleakala National Park, can be seen the results of vulcanism, not in its active form but after the end of activity: the last eruption of Haleakala was in 1790. Large numbers of endemic plants flourish on the volcanic soil of Haleakala's crater, on a scale no longer seen anywhere else in the islands. To the original Polynesian inhabitants the crater was a sacred place where they buried their dead and built their temples.

Maui
**Haleakala National Park

Oahu, the third largest island in the archipelago, is the political, economic and cultural centre of the Hawaiian Islands.

Oahu

The main place of interest on the island is Honolulu, capital of the state of Hawaii, which consists of the three districts of Downtown, Pearl Harbor and Waikiki. In the centre of downtown Honolulu is the modern State Capitol, the architecture of which is designed to reflect the two main elements determining the character of the islands, water and volcanic activity. The Iolani Palace, built by King David Kalakaua in 1879, has the distinction of being the only royal palace in the United States. There are three interesting museums: the Bishop Museum, one of the finest ethnographic museums in the United States; the Hawaii Maritime Museum on Honolulu Harbor; and the Honolulu Academy of Arts (old Hawaiian art). The luxuriant plant world of the Hawaiian Islands can be seen in the Foster Botanic Gardens, to the south of which is Honolulu's Chinatown. In Pearl Harbor is the USS "Arizona" Memorial, erected over the wreck of the battleship "Arizona", sunk by the Japanese on December 7th 1941. The 2 mile/3km long Waikiki Beach is one of the most beautiful town beaches in the world, with Diamonds Head, an extinct volcano which is Honolulu's principal landmark, looming over it.

*Honolulu

Also on Oahu is the Polynesian Cultural Center, with a reconstruction of a Polynesian village and displays of traditional handicrafts and dances.

Houston

U 30

State: Texas
Altitude: 55ft/17m
Population: 1.63 million (Metropolitan Area 3.7 million)

Situation and characteristics

Houston, the fourth largest city in the United States and the greatest metropolis of the South, situated only a few miles inland from the Gulf of Mexico near the border with Louisiana, is a centre for the processing of oil from the Texan oilfields and the offshore drilling rigs; since 1962 it has been the seat of the Mission Control Center of the United States' space programme; and, with the third largest port in the country (the sixth largest in the world), it is a commercial centre of major importance. The port is linked with the Gulf of Mexico by the 50 mile/80km long Houston Ship Canal, which can take ocean-going vessels. The economic importance of Houston, which is also a great banking centre, is reflected in the impressive skyline of its skyscrapers and the plans for further development which are under way.

History

Houston was founded in 1836 by two brothers, John and August Allen, and named after Sam Houston, a hero of the Texan war of liberation and first President of the independent Republic of Texas, of which it was the capital from 1837 to 1839 and from 1842 to 1845, when Austin (see San Antonio, Surroundings) finally took over that function. During the second half of the 19th century Houston was overshadowed by the coastal town of Galveston, but became increasingly important following the construction of a ship channel to the Gulf of Mexico between 1873 and 1914. When Galveston was almost completely destroyed by a hurricane in 1900 Houston succeeded it as the leading port in Texas.

Skyscrapers in downtown Houston

Sights in Houston

The skyscrapers of downtown Houston offer within a relatively small area a cross-section of modern architecture – the 75-storey pentagonal column of the Texas Commerce Bank Tower (by I. M. Pei; viewing hall on 60th floor), the green glass façade of the Allied Bank Plaza (by Edward Basset; 71 storeys), the Pennzoil Place high-rise complex with its prismatic trihedral forms (by Philip Johnson) and the Post-Modern Republic Bank Center (also by Philip Johnson).

Skyscrapers in downtown Houston

The focal point of the city's cultural life is the huge complex of the Houston Civic Center (Capitol Street, between Milam and Bagby Streets), with the Jones Hall for the Performing Arts (home of the Houston Symphony Orchestra), the George R. Brown Convention Center (conventions, exhibitions, concerts), the Nina Vance Alley Theater, the Music Hall, the Sam Houston Coliseum (sporting events, concerts) and the Wortham Center (opera, ballet). On the same site is City Hall.

*Houston Civic Center

The attractive Tranquility Park commemorates the Apollo moon landing programme, with bronze plaques giving information in fifteen different languages.

South of the Sam Houston Coliseum, at 1100 Bagby Street, is the Sam Houston Historical Park, with the Museum of Texas History, an open-air museum with houses in early 19th century style, old shops and a Victorian church.

Sam Houston Historical Park

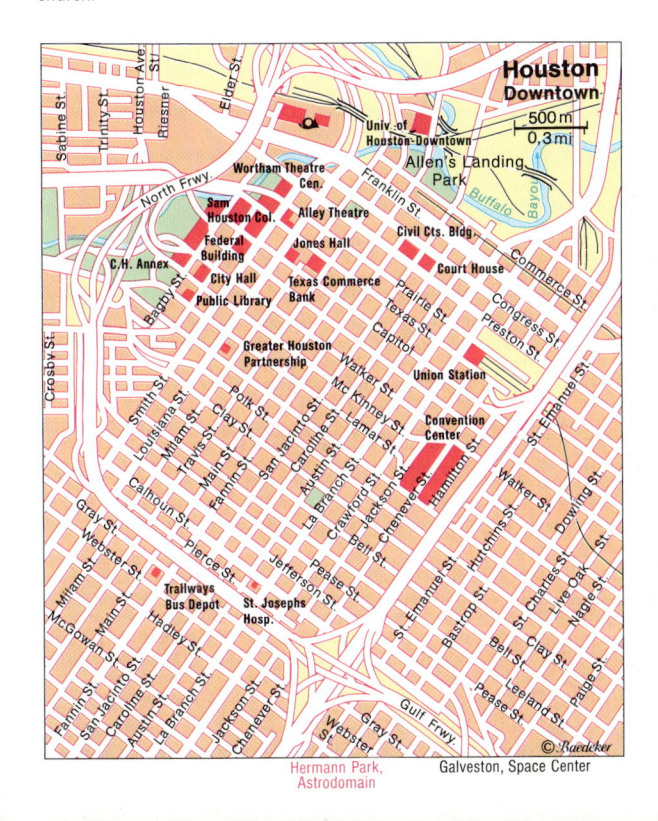

Houston

Art museums in south-west Houston

In the south-western part of the city, between downtown Houston and the Rice University, are three fine art museums: the Contemporary Arts Museum (Montrose Boulevard and Bissonet Street), with periodic special exhibitions of modern art and films; the Museum of Fine Arts (1001 Bissonet Street), largely designed by Mies van der Rohe, with works of art from many countries, including the Kress Collection of High Renaissance art and Indian art of the South-West; and the Menil Museum (1515 Sul Ross Street), housed in a building designed by Renzo Piano, which has an excellent collection of art of all periods and styles.

Rothko Chapel

East of the Menil Museum, at 3900 Yupon Street, is the Rothko Chapel, designed by Philip Johnson, with tapestries by the Russian-American artist Mark Rothko.

Galleria Area

Still farther east is the Galleria Area, dominated by Philip Johnson's 64-storey Transco Tower, with the luxury Galleria shopping centre.

Hermann Park

*Burke Baker Planetarium

To the south of the Museum of Fine Arts, round the Grand Basin, is Hermann Park, in which are the large Houston Museum of Natural Science (open: Mon.–Sat. 9am–6pm, Sun. noon–6pm), with the excellently equipped Burke Baker Planetarium, the Miller Outdoor Theater, the Houston Zoological Gardens and the Kipp Aquarium.

Astrodomain
*Astrodome

To the south of the city is the Astrodomain, an extensive leisure complex. Its central feature is the massive Astrodome (Harris County Domed Stadium), the world's first roofed stadium. This immense hall, fully air-conditioned, is 645ft/196m across and 205ft/63m high and can accommodate between 55,000 and 65,000 spectators according to requirements. Here the Houston Oilers (football) and the Houston Astros (baseball) play their home games. On the south side of the stadium is the lower Astrohall, which is used for exhibitions and rodeos. Still farther south, beyond I 610, is the 460ft/140m high Astroneedle, in Astroworld, a large amusement park, next door to which is Waterworld, an aquatic recreation park.

Port

To the east of the city is the Port of Houston. There are free sightseeing cruises on the "Sam Houston". A good general view can be had from the platform on Pier 9.

Surroundings of Houston

**Lyndon B. Johnson Space Center

Open daily 9am–7pm

25 miles/39km south-east of Houston, on the west side of Clear Lake, is the Lyndon B. Johnson Space Center, with the world-famed Mission Control, the monitoring centre for all NASA manned space flights. In the Visitor Orientation Center is a space exhibition, with film shows, models of space capsules, astronauts' rations, samples of moon rock and a variety of objects from the Mercury, Gemini and Apollo manned space programmes. Visitors can try on astronauts' helmets, steer a spacecraft in the simulator and, in the extensive grounds of the Space Center, wonder at huge space rockets and perhaps meet a real astronaut on his way to the Mission Simulation and Training Facility, where in the course of training he may be hurled around in a centrifuge measuring 100ft/30m across.

San Jacinto Battleground

On April 21st 1836 General Sam Houston inflicted a decisive defeat on the Mexican army at San Jacinto and thus brought the Texan fight for independence to a successful conclusion. The scene of the battle, 20 miles/32km east of Houston, is marked by the San Jacinto Monument, a 570ft/174m high column. From the platform at the top there are magnificent views. The Museum of Texas History on the ground floor of the monument traces the development of Texas from the early Indian cultures by way of the Spanish and Mexican periods to the present time.

Galveston

South-east of Houston, on a narrow island in the Gulf of Mexico which is linked with the mainland by a highway, is Galveston, which in 1836 was briefly capital of the Republic of Texas. During the 19th century Galveston was the largest and wealthiest town in Texas, and its earlier splendour is still recalled by a number of handsome mansions. Examples of such Victorian buildings are Ashton Villa (24th Street and Broadway), Bishop's Palace (1402 Broadway) and the Grand Opera House of 1894 (2020 Post Office). The well restored warehouse district known as the Strand (between Strand and Mechanic Streets) still preserves the original façades, now concealing restaurants and shops. One of Galveston's finest parks is Moody Gardens, whose particular attraction is a large glass pyramid for tropical plants. The 32 mile/51km long beach on Galveston Island has made the city a favourite holiday resort.

Historic buildings

Idaho (State; ID)   B–G 9–14

Area:
  83,557sq.miles/216,412sq.km
Population: 1,039,000
Capital: Boise
Popular name: Gem State

The mountain state of Idaho (a name which probably comes from an Indian word meaning "mountain precious stone") lies in the north-western United States. The northern two-thirds of the state, the most mountainous part, are on the western slope of the northern Rockies, whose highest peaks here rise above 10,000ft/3000m and offer excellent conditions for winter sports. Central Idaho, which includes the plateaux of the Clearwater Mountains and Salmon River Mountains, merges in the south and south-west into the arid, steppe-like Snake River plain, along the edge of which flows the Snake River, in a valley which at some points is deeply indented. The climate is dry in summer. More than 40% of Idaho, particularly in the north and centre, is covered with coniferous forests.

Situation and topography

In 1805 Meriwether Lewis and William Clark travelled through the territory which is now Idaho and opened it up to white settlement. Originally part of the neutral territory of Oregon, it passed in 1846 into the possession of the United States. Large numbers of settlers heading for the north-west coast passed through the area, in which regular settlement began only in 1860. An independent territory from 1863, it was the scene in 1877 and 1879 of fierce fighting between whites and Indians, culminating in the flight of the Nez Perce Indians led by Chief Joseph. On July 3rd 1890 Idaho joined the Union as the 43rd state.

History

The main element in the economy of Idaho, the most thinly populated of the states, is agriculture. In the mountainous parts of the state sheep and cattle are reared and on the irrigated Snake River Plains fodder plants, grain, vegetables, fruit and potatoes (a quarter of the US acreage) are grown. Agriculture and the huge areas of forest provide the raw materials for the foodstuffs and woodworking industries. The mining district of Cœur d'Alene in northern Idaho has the United States' richest reserves of silver, zinc and lead ores. Tourism also makes a major contribution to Idaho's economy, thanks to its beautiful forests and lakes and the winter sports centres to be found all over the state.

Economy

Places of Interest in Idaho

In the centre of the state's capital Boise, originally a French foundation, is the State Capitol. Other features of interest are the Ann Morrison Memorial

Boise

Illinois

Park, the romantic Platt Gardens and above all the Julia Davis Park, in which are the Zoo, the State Historical Museum and the Boise Art Museum.

Cœur d'Alene	The holiday resort and timber-working town of Cœur d'Alene lies amid magnificent forest scenery on the lake of the same name, one of the most beautiful in the United States, with ample facilities for boating and fishing.
*Craters of the Moon	South of Arco in south-eastern Idaho is a lunar landscape created by volcanic eruptions between 15,000 and 2000 years ago. This region of lava flows can be explored on well signposted circular routes.
Lewiston	Lewiston is picturesquely situated at the junction of the Clearwater River with the Snake River, on the border with Washington state. Originally dependent mainly on the timber-working industry, it still has one of the largest woodworking factories in the world, but is now also a popular tourist centre, a good base from which to explore the surrounding area.
*Hell's Canyon	From Lewiston there are boat trips through Hell's Canyon, the deepest on the American continent (6500ft/2000m), carved out by the Snake River for a distance of 95 miles/150km along the border with Washington and Oregon.
Nez Perce National Historical Park	In the Nez Perce National Historical Park are 24 signposted sites illustrating the history and culture of the Nez Perce Indians. The chief place in the park is Spalding, 11 miles/17.5km east of Lewiston.
Pocatello	Pocatello is named after an Indian chief who allowed the railroad to pass through his territory. Features of interest are the Museum of Idaho State University and the Bannock County Historical Museum (culture of the Shoshone Indians, etc.). South of the town in Ross Park, on the banks of the Portneuf River, are Indian hieroglyphic signs.
Sun Valley	Sun Valley in southern Idaho attracts skiing enthusiasts throughout the year with its magnificent facilities for winter sports and its excellent tourist infrastructure.
*Twin Falls	The main sight in the little town of Twin Falls is the Shoshone Falls, over which the Snake River plunges down 200ft/60m – 50ft/15m more than the Niagara Falls (see entry). The falls are best seen in spring and autumn, for during the summer most of the water is diverted for irrigating farmland.

Illinois (State; IL)   G–M 34–38

Area:
  56,400sq.miles/146,076sq.km
Population: 11,543,000
Capital: Springfield
Popular name: Prairie State

Situation and topography	Illinois (from the Indian word *illini*, "men"), one of the northerly states of the Middle West, extends from Lake Michigan in the north to the Mississippi in the west and south-west and the Ohio River in the south. Most of its territory lies in the Central Lowlands, with small upland regions only in the south and north-west; its highest point, in the north-west, is Charles Mound (1240ft/378m). The climate is continental, with extreme temperatures both in summer and in winter, the latter being characterised by sharp inflows of cold air, with heavy snowstorms. In summer cyclones moving north, frequently accompanied by violent storms and heavy rain, can cause great destruction. Most of the land is given up to arable farming and stock-rearing. Only a small part of the state is forest-covered.

Illinois

History

The first whites to reach the territory which is now Illinois in the mid 17th century encountered the Indian tribe from which the state takes its name. In 1680 the Sieur de la Salle built the first French fort on the site of present-day Peoria. In 1763 Illinois passed to Britain. In 1778, during the War of Independence, it was captured by the Americans. On December 3rd 1818 it joined the Union as the 21st state. Indian resistance was broken in the Black Hawk War of 1832.

Economy

Thanks to its highly fertile soil over four-fifths of the state's area is in agricultural use. The main crops are soya beans, maize, grain, potatoes, fruit and vegetables; stock-farming (cattle, pigs) is also important. Illinois also has considerable mineral resources (oil, coal, lead, zinc, fluorspar). Most of its industry is concentrated in the Chicago area (iron and steel, meat-processing, mechanical and electrical engineering, chemicals). Tourism is of relatively little importance except in the skiing areas in the north and on the shores of Lake Michigan.

Places of Interest in Illinois

Arcola

Arcola, in eastern Illinois, has one of the state's largest Amish communities (see Religion, p. 41). Their way of life can be observed in Rocksome Gardens, 5 miles/8km west of the town.

*Cahokia Mounds State Historic Site

The Cahokia Mounds, to the east of St Louis (Missouri), are the remains of an Indian settlement of the 8th century A.D. which comprised more than a hundred buildings. The most prominent feature is the Monks' Mound, on which French Trappist monks established themselves in the early 19th century. Finds from the site are displayed in a small museum.

Chicago

See entry

*Galena

The little town of Galena at the extreme north-western tip of Illinois was originally a French outpost, a base for the exploration of the North-West. In the 19th century lead-mining in the surrounding area made it the wealthiest town in the state. Galena has largely preserved its 19th century aspect, with many handsome antebellum houses bearing witness to its former prosperity. Particularly fine is the Old Market House, once occupied by General (later President) Ulysses S. Grant.

Nauvoo

Nauvoo, situated on the Mississippi, on the border with Iowa, played a prominent part in the history of the Mormons. After their prophet Joseph Smith (see Famous People) was driven out of Missouri they followed him to this area and established a kind of independent state. Conflicts with opponents and within the Mormon church culminated in the lynching and murder of Smith and his brother in the local prison. Brigham Young then led the Mormons to Utah. The Mormon period in Nauvoo is recalled by the Joseph Smith Historic Center and the Brigham Young Home.

Peoria

Peoria, south-west of Chicago on the Illinois River, is the oldest town in the state. Features of interest, in addition to a number of historic old houses, are the Wildlife Prairie Park (native animals of Illinois, houses of the pioneers) and the Wheels o' Time Museum (old automobiles, agricultural machinery, domestic equipment, tools and implements).

Springfield

The capital of Illinois, Springfield, situated roughly in the centre of the state, is a national place of pilgrimage. Here, in Oak Ridge Cemetery, are buried Abraham Lincoln, his wife and three of his four children. Lincoln worked in the town as a lawyer from 1837 to 1861, when he was elected President. His house is now a museum and one of the staging-points on the Lincoln Heritage Trail, which runs through all the places in Illinois associated with Lincoln. Other features of interest are the Illinois State Museum, the Governor's Mansion (the third oldest in the United States) and the Dana Thomas House, designed by Frank Lloyd Wright (see Famous People).

Indiana

Starved Rock State Park — This nature park south-west of Chicago on the Illinois River, noted for its sandstone formations, is named after a group of Illini Indians who were left by their enemies to starve to death on one of the rocks.

Indiana (State; IN)   H–M 38–41

Area:
36,185sq.miles/93,719sq.km
Population: 5,610,000
Capital: Indianapolis
Popular name: Hoosier State

Situation and topography — The Middle Western state of Indiana extends from Lake Michigan in the north to the valley of the Ohio River in the south. The wide gently undulating lowlands and plateaux of the Central Lowlands here reach heights of between 300ft/90m and 1260ft/383m. The landscape, formed during the Ice Age, is dotted in the north-east with numerous small lakes. The climate is temperate continental.

History — The fertile plains of Indiana were settled as early as the 10th century by Indians, who have left traces of their occupation in numerous mounds. The first European to explore this area, in 1679, was a Frenchman, the Sieur de la Salle. The territory passed to Britain in 1763, but twenty years later became part of the United States. At first part of the Northwest Territory, it became a separate territory in 1809, with approximately its present boundaries. After the defeat of the Shawnee Indians at Tippecanoe in 1811 it became the 19th state of the Union on December 11th 1816.

Economy — Indiana's situation in the Corn Belt makes it one of the leading agricultural states of the Union. The main crops are maize, soya beans and grain, providing the basis for intensive pig-farming and a large dairy farming industry. The state's main industries, principally concentrated in the cities on Lake Michigan, are iron and steel, automobile construction, chemicals, oil refineries and foodstuffs. Its mineral resources include oil, limestone and coal (mined by opencast methods in the south-west of the state).

Places of Interest in Indiana

Columbus — In the late 1930s the city fathers of Columbus, situated to the south of Indianapolis (see entry), commissioned the Finnish architect Eliel Saarinen to redevelop part of the city. Saarinen brought in other leading architects, and as a result Columbus is now a museum of modern architecture, with buildings designed by Saarinen, I. M. Pei, J. C. Warnke, Kevin Roche and other distinguished names.

Fort Wayne — Fort Wayne, in north-eastern Indiana, owes its name to General "Mad Anthony" Wayne, who in 1791 defeated the Miami Indians and their chief Little Turtle at the strategically important junction of the St Mary and St Joseph Rivers. This event and the later history of the region are illustrated in the Allen County–Fort Wayne Museum. Other features of interest are the Lincoln Museum and the reconstructed Fort Wayne.

Indiana Dunes State Park — The Indiana Dunes State Park extends for 3 miles/5km along the southern shore of Lake Michigan. Its sandy beaches, backed by beautiful white dunes, offer magnificent bathing.

Indianapolis — See entry

North-west of Indianapolis on the Wabash River is Lafayette, scene of a decisive battle in 1811 between government troops and Shawnee Indians led by the "Prophet", Tecumseh's brother. The event is commemorated on the Tippecanoe Battlefield and in the Tippecanoe County Historical Museum.

Lafayette

Between 1814 and 1824 New Harmony, in south-western Indiana, was the scene of a social experiment. Here a deeply religious German named Georg Rapp and his followers, among whom absolute equality prevailed, settled down to cultivate the land in the expectation that the Last Judgment was near. When this failed to materialise the community returned to Pennsylvania, from which they had come. Their village can be seen on a sign-posted tour.

New Harmony

South Bend, in the extreme north of Indiana, is the seat of the University of Notre Dame, founded in 1842. Features of interest on the campus are the Art Museum and the Church of the Sacred Heart, which has the oldest carillon in North America.

South Bend

Vincennes, in south-western Indiana on the border with Illinois, is the state's oldest town, founded in 1732. The main sights are the George Rogers National Historical Park, which commemorates the revolutionary battles against the British, and Grouseland, the home of William Henry Harrison, 9th President of the United States.

Vincennes

Indianapolis

K 39

State: Indiana
Altitude: 650–915ft (198–279m)
Population: 731,000 (Metropolitan Area 1.2 million)

Indianapolis, a typical Mid Western city and capital of Indiana, lies south-east of Lake Michigan on the White River – almost exactly in the centre of Indiana, on a site selected by ten government commissioners in 1820 for the new capital of the state. Indianapolis is now a university town (Indiana State University/Purdue University and University of Indianapolis) and an important commercial centre. The agricultural products of the fertile surrounding area – cattle and grain – are traded and processed in Indianapolis, and among its main industrial products are medicines (insulin products), automobile parts and electrical apparatus. The city's world fame, however, comes from the "Indianapolis 500", the car race held annually on the Sunday before Memorial Day on the Indianapolis Motor Speedway. This is the world's biggest single-day sporting event, drawing hundreds of thousands of motor sport fans.

Situation and characteristics

Sights in Indianapolis

In Monument Circle, an oasis in the city centre, is the Soldiers' and Sailors' Memorial, erected in 1902 to commemorate the dead of the Civil War. To the north of the Monument whole rows of houses were demolished to make room for the Mausoleum and Memorial Hall. Three blocks to the south have recently disappeared, replaced by the large Circle Center Mall (completed 1994). The National Art Museum of Sport, in the 710ft/216m high Bank One Center Tower (1990), houses a collection of sports-related art.

Monument Circle

Circle Center Mall

In the former City Hall (202 North Alabama Street) is the Indiana State Museum (natural history, art and history of Indiana).

Indiana State Museum

Indianapolis

Indianapolis International Airport

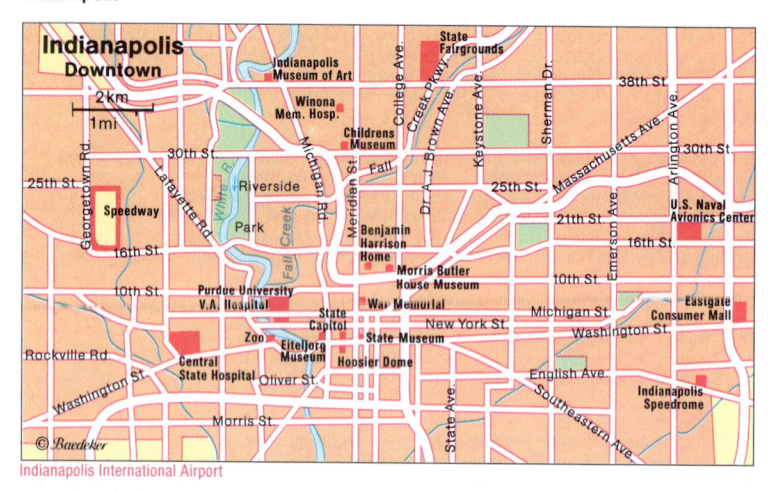

*Eiteljorg Museum of American Indian and Western Art Tue.–Sat. 10am–5pm, Sun. noon–5pm	To the east of Monument Circle, beyond the State Capitol (1888), is the Eiteljorg Museum of American Indian and Western Art, situated at the entrance to the White River State Park (500 Washington Street). Here is displayed the remarkable collection assembled by the Indianapolis businessman Harrison Eiteljorg: painting and sculpture of the West from the early 19th century onwards, including works by the landscapists Albert Bierstadt and Thomas Moran and pictures and sculpture by the leading Western artists Frederick S. Remington and Charles M. Russell; an extensive collection of works of the Taos Society of Artists; and Indian arts and crafts from all over North America.
Canal Walk	For many years the Indiana Central Canal had been an unseemly open sewer, until in the mid eighties its southern section, between the Ohio Street Basin (north-east of the Eiteljorg Museum) and the Walnut Street Basin, was cleaned up and became the central feature of a city centre regeneration scheme – a mile-long promenade along the old waterway.
Hoosier Dome	The construction of the huge Hoosier Dome (100 South Capitol Avenue) in 1984 signalled the beginning of a comprehensive redevelopment of the city centre. This is the home of the local football team, the Indianapolis Colts. The flag-decked Pan American Plaza in the immediate neighbourhood of the Hoosier Dome, the Convention Center and Union Station was laid out to commemorate the Pan American Games of 1987.
Benjamin Harrison Home	Benjamin Harrison, Senator of Indiana (1880), who was re-elected President of the United States in 1888, died in Indianapolis in 1901. His house at 1239 North Delaware Street, with its original Victorian furniture, can be visited.
*Indianapolis Museum of Art Tue.–Sat. 10am–5pm, Sun. noon–5pm	The Indianapolis Museum of Art (1200 West 38th Street) lies to the north of the city centre in a spacious park. The Museum is housed in four pavilions: the Krannert Pavilion, which is devoted to American art from pre-Columbian times to the present day (including Edward Hopper's "Hotel Lobby") and Asian art; the Hulman Pavilion (painting from Baroque to Neo-Impressionism and the Eiteljorg Gallery of African and South Pacific Art); the Clowes Pavilion (medieval and Renaissance art, 18th century British painting, watercolours by Turner); and the Lilly Pavilion (British and American furniture and silver, German porcelain).

Iowa

Full house for the legendary Indy 500

The United States' most celebrated car race, the legendary Indianapolis 500, is run on the Indianapolis Motor Speedway, 7 miles/11km north-west of downtown Indianapolis, which is used only for this one race. The circuit, a 2½ mile/4km oval, was originally designed as an automobile test track, but the first 500 mile race in 1911 was so successful that it became a regular fixture. In the course of time the track, which was originally paved with bricks (still used to mark the finishing line), was adapted to cope with ever-increasing speeds and the accommodation for spectators increased: there is now room for 250,000 in the stands and another 150,000 in the ground. When the track is not in use for practising and training (one month before the race) visitors are taken round it in minibuses. The Speedway Hall of Fame Museum traces the history of the race and displays numerous old racing cars, including 30 winners of the 500.

* **Indianapolis Motor Speedway**

Speedway Hall of Fame Museum

Daily 9am–5pm

Iowa (State; IA)   F–J 29–35

Area:
 56,290sq.miles/145,791sq.km
Population: 2,795,000
Capital: Des Moines
Popular name: Hawkeye State

Iowa (the name of a Sioux tribe) lies in the Middle West, in the Central Lowlands of North America, bounded on the west by the Missouri and on the east by the Mississippi. It is a gently

Situation and topography

Jackson

by the Mississippi. It is a gently undulating region which falls gradually from the north-west (maximum height 1675ft/510m) to the south-east (515ft/157m). Iowa has the best soils (for much of its area loess) in the United States, and is accordingly a region of farmland and prairies. The climate is continental, with very hot summers and winters of extreme cold.

History

The territory that is now Iowa was a favoured Indian hunting ground. Like the neighbouring state of Illinois to the east, it was first discovered by the French, but organised settlement began only in 1788. As part of the French territory of Louisiana it passed to the United States under the Louisiana Purchase of 1803. After the local Indians – now living in a small reservation – had been driven back and replaced by European settlers Iowa was incorporated as an independent territory, and on December 28th 1846 was admitted to the Union as the 29th state.

Economy

Iowa's agriculture is the most productive in the United States. The main crops are maize, soya beans and oats, mainly used for feeding cattle and pigs: Iowa is by a wide margin America's leading pig-farming state, with some 14 million pigs. As a result the state's industries are largely related to agriculture (agricultural machinery, foodstuffs). Also of great importance to the economy is the largest aluminium rolling mill in the United States. Tourism is of secondary importance, though the state has some attractions which draw visitors – the skiing areas in the north and the charming little towns and river scenery on the Mississippi.

Places of Interest in Iowa

Amana Colonies

The settlement of Amana was founded in 1850 by "Inspirationists" of German origin – the first of seven villages in eastern Iowa in which they led a God-fearing life and tilled their communally owned land. A local museum traces the history of the sect, which adopted 20th century ways of life only in 1932.

Des Moines

Iowa's capital, Des Moines, lies approximately in the centre of the state. Features of interest are the State Capitol with its gilded roof (1871), the Victorian-style Governor's house, Terrace Hill (1869), and the Heritage Village, with old agricultural machinery and four "living history farms" in which country life in the 18th and 19th centuries is re-created.

Dubuque

The town of Dubuque, situated on the Mississippi on the border with Illinois, was founded in 1788, the first European settlement in what is now Iowa. Its attractions are its numerous historic old buildings, a beautiful botanical garden and above all paddlewheeler cruises on the Mississippi.

Iowa City

Iowa City, in the east of the state, was its first capital. It is the seat of the University of Iowa, founded in 1847. Its other feature of interest is the birthplace of Herbert Hoover (1874–1964), 31st President of the United States.

Sioux City

Sioux City lies on the border with Nebraska, in the heart of Indian country. Here was buried Sergeant Charles Floyd, the only casualty of Lewis and Clark's expedition from the Mississippi to the Pacific in 1804–05. Woodbury Country Courthouse, a long, low brick structure, is the largest building so far erected by Chicago's "Prairie school" of architecture.

Jackson   F 15

State: Wyoming
Altitude: 6200ft/1890m
Population: 6000

Jacksonville

The little town of Jackson lies on the southern edge of Jackson Hole, a high | Situation and
valley traversed by the Snake River and surrounded by the peaks of Snow | characteristics
King Mountain, the Gros Ventre Range and East Gros Ventre Butte. It is one
of the most visited tourist resorts in the American West and an important
winter sports centre. In spite of heavy commercialisation it is still redolent
of the atmosphere of the Wild West with its saloons, cowboy hats and boots
and country-style jeans. Jackson is an excellent base for excursions into
the Grand Teton and Yellowstone National Parks.

Sights in Jackson

The central feature of the town is the tree-planted Town Square, the four | *Town Square
entrances to which have arched gateways made of hundreds of deer
antlers. Round the square are dozens of saloons, bars, galleries and souvenir stalls. During the main summer season "cowboys" stage a shoot-out
and horse-drawn buggies wait for customers.

The Jackson Hole Museum (105 North Glenwood Street) traces the history | Museums and
of settlement in the valley. The Teton Country Historical Center (105 Mercell | galleries
Avenue) is devoted mainly to the fur trade and the cultural history of the
local Indians. The Wildlife of the American West Art Museum (110 North
Center Street) has the largest collection of pictures and sculpture on the
wild life of the West, including works by Albert Bierstadt, Karl Bodmer,
Charles M. Russell and Ernest Thompson.

The leading galleries are the Wilcox Gallery, the Trailside Galleries and the
Rawson Galleries. In addition to traditional arts and crafts they also display
modern work (bronze miniatures, etc.).

Surroundings of Jackson

From Snow King Mountain (7750ft/2362m; chair-lift), which dominates the | *Snow King
town, there are breathtaking views of the Teton Range. The hill is a popular | Mountain
skiing area in winter.

Above Jackson, to the north-west, is Teton Village, from which a cableway | Rendezvous Peak
runs up to the summit of Rendezvous Peak (10,926ft/3330m). This is also a
good skiing area.

A few miles north of Jackson, in Jackson Hole, is the National Elk Refuge, in | National Elk
which several thousand elk gather at the beginning of winter. From time | Refuge
immemorial animals have wintered here, spending the summer in inaccessible mountain regions within a radius of some 60 miles/100km. In the
winter tourist season horse-drawn sleighs take visitors on tours to observe
the wild life.

For the more adventurous there are rafting trips on the Snake River. Par- | Rafting on the
ticularly spectacular are trips through the Snake River Canyon. | Snake River

See Grand Teton National Park | Tetons

Jacksonville T 44

State: Florida. Altitude: 0–23ft/0–7m
Population: 690,000 (Metropolitan Area 1.2 million)

The city of Jacksonville, situated in the extreme north-west of Florida on | Situation and
the navigable St John's River, only 20 miles/32km from the Atlantic coast, is | characteristics
a major port and industrial centre as well as an important military base. The
largest city in the United States in terms of area, it developed considerably
in the eighties and is now a major business and financial centre.

Jacksonville

History — In pre-Columbian times there was a settlement of the Timucua Indians here. The present town, named after the famous General Jackson, first Governor of Florida, was founded in 1822. It soon developed into an important port, one of the main centres for the export of the produce of the South (cotton, timber, cattle). Around 1884 the Jacksonville area, thanks to its spacious bathing beaches, enjoyed a brief period of prosperity as a holiday resort. During the two world wars Jacksonville was a boom town (shipbuilding, military training areas), though in the thirties and sixties it suffered severe economic setbacks. During the eighties it showed signs of recovery.

Sights in Jacksonville

Central area — In recent years downtown Jacksonville has benefited from a billion-dollar regeneration plan, and now has a series of gleaming new skyscrapers, particularly on the north bank of the St John's River.

*Jacksonville Landing — Jacksonville Landing (1987), on the North Bank, is a modern architectural complex centred on Festival Market Place which has become a popular rendezvous with both young and old.

*Riverwalk — Riverwalk, on the South Bank, is an attractive new area, completed in 1985, on the site of an old shipyard, with hotels, restaurants, shops and a 1¼ mile/2km long boardwalk promenade.

*Museum of Science and History — The Museum of Science and History (1025 Gulf Life Drive/South Main Street; open: daily 10am–5pm) offers an introduction to the world of science and technology. Its main attractions are the "Dinosaurs Alive" show (a dinosaur garden) and the Living World (marine aquarium, songbird aviary, insects, reptiles).

Barnett Bank Tower — The 40-storey Post-Modern Barnett Bank Tower on Bay Street was designed by the German-born architect Helmut Jahn, now based in Chicago.

*Cummer Art Gallery — The remarkable Cummer Art Gallery at 829 Riverside Avenue covers a wide range, from Greek antiquity to the 20th century, including a notable collection of Meissen porcelain.

*Avondale-Riverside Historic District — The old residential district of Avondale and Riverside offers a survey of the architectural styles fashionable in the first three decades of the 20th century. An impressive example is Riverside Baptist Church (by Addison Mizner, 1925). The Avondale Shopping Village is a friendly and attractive neighbourhood, with shops, restaurants and public gardens.

Surroundings of Jacksonville

*Fort Caroline — 10 miles/16km east of the city centre is a reconstruction of the historic old Fort Caroline. In the 16th century French Huguenots attempted to establish a settlement in this area. Here too, in 1565, took place the first clash between France and Spain on the American continent.

Jacksonville Beach — 15 miles/24km east of the city centre is Jacksonville Beach (pop. 20,000), a resort well equipped to cater for the tourist trade. Immediately on the Atlantic is the Seawalk, an attractive seafront promenade. To the south of Mayport Naval Station is Seminole Beach, the most beautiful bathing beach in the area.

**Amelia Island — 32 miles/52km north-east of Jacksonville is Amelia Island (pop. 15,000), an exclusive holiday island of coral limestone which has become a frequent

Joshua Tree National Monument

State: California

The Joshua Tree National Monument lies 143 miles/230km east of Los Angeles (see entry). The northern entrances at Joshua Tree and Twentynine Palms are reached from the west on Interstate 10 or Highway 62 (Twentynine Palms Highway). The southern entrance in Cottonwood Springs (25 miles/40km east of Indio) can also be reached on I 10.	Situation
There no hotels in the area of the Joshua Tree National Monument and only eight primitive campgrounds without either water or fuel. The nearest hotels and motels are in the township of Twentynine Palms (advance reservation essential).	N.B.
This nature reserve (area 870sq.miles/2250sq.km) is partly in the low-lying Colorado Desert to the south-east and partly in the Mojave Desert (see entry) to the north, which is up to 3300ft/1000m higher. In the lower-lying areas the predominant vegetation consists of creosote bushes, together with the cactuses known as "jumping chollas" and aromatic junipers.	Topography
In the higher areas are the Joshua trees which give the National Monument its name. These trees, which belong to the yucca family (*Yucca brevifolia*),	*Joshua trees

Joshua trees

Kansas

were so called by the Mormons who passed this way in the mid 19th century and thought that they resembled the prophet Joshua with his arms raised in prayer.

Kansas (State; KS)   K–M 23–31

Area:
82,277sq.miles/213,097sq.km
Population: 2,495,000
Capital: Topeka
Popular name: Sunflower State

Situation and topography

The state of Kansas (from an Indian term, "people of the south winds") lies in the geographical centre of the United States, in the extensive stepped tableland of the Great Plains, which rises from around 650ft/200m in the east to 3900ft/1200m in the west. In the eastern part of the state the rock formations strike north–south, traversed by valleys up to 330ft/100m deep cut by the Kansas River and its tributaries. Except in the hilly and forest-covered north-east the predominant vegetation pattern before the land was brought into cultivation was short-grass steppeland, familiar to movie-goers as Hollywood's version of the Wild West. The climate is continental, with periods of drought, hot dust storms and tornadoes.

History

The first European to travel over the wide prairies of Kansas was the Spanish conquistador Francisco Coronado in 1541. In 1762 the area, then part of Louisiana, passed to Spain. In 1803 it was acquired by the United States, and in 1817 was declared Indian territory. As a result of the Kansas–Nebraska Act of 1854, which separated the two states, Kansas was drawn into the conflict between North and South over slavery and became known as "bleeding Kansas". On January 29th 1861 it became the 34th state of the Union and threw in its lot with the North.

Economy

Although processing industries (foodstuffs, aircraft construction, helium production, printing) make a larger contribution to the economy than agricultural produce, Kansas is a typically agricultural region: predominantly cattle- and pig-rearing, together with the growing of wheat, millet and maize. The principal minerals worked in Kansas are oil, natural gas, lead and zinc. Tourism is concentrated mainly on the State Parks in the east and the lakes in the centre and south.

A denizen of the prairie

Places of Interest in Kansas

Abilene

The little town of Abilene lies in the north-east of the state. Its wild days as the "cowtown" of Kansas are past, but Abilene Old Town still preserves something of the atmosphere of the Wild West. Apart from this the town is known to fame as the boyhood home of General Dwight D. Eisenhower

Kansas City

(1890–1969), 34th President of the United States, who is commemorated by a museum, the Presidential Library and his tomb in the Eisenhower Center.

In its heyday this famous Wild West town saw a whole posse of sheriffs – Batt Masterson, Bill Tilghman and above all the notorious Wyatt Earp (see Famous People) – and a host of buffalo-hunters, who within a few years slaughtered millions of buffaloes at 100 dollars a time. The town's wild past can be relived in Historic Front Street with its reconstructions of the celebrated Long Branch Saloon, the barber's shop, the general store and many other establishments familiar from Western films. In the Boot Hill Museum, on the hill of that name (the cemetery), are other relics of a bloodstained past.
Dodge City

See entry
Kansas City

North-east of Dodge City is Fort Larned, an important military post on the Santa Fe Trail. Here William T. Sherman, Philip Sheridan, George A. Custer, Kit Carson, Wild Bill Hickock guarded the railroad to the West. Nine of the original buildings are still preserved.
Larned

Topeka (pop. 120,000), lies 60 miles/97km west of Kansas City. Founded in 1859, it is now an industrial city and the state capital. Features of interest are the Capitol and State House. The history of the state can be studied in the headquarters of the Kansas State Historical Society and the Kansas Museum of History. In Gage Park is a beautiful Zoo with a tropical garden and a reproduction of a rain forest.
Topeka

A few miles from Topeka are Cedar Crest, residence of the Governor of Kansas, and the Combat Air Museum, with 75 military aircraft ranging in date from 1917 to 1980.
Cedar Crest

Wichita, now the largest city in Kansas, had humble beginnings in 1865, when Jesse Chisholm began the driving of cattle from here along the famous Chisholm Trail to the Union Pacific railroad station in Abilene. Pioneering days are recalled in the Wichita Historical Museum and the Historic Old Cowtown Museum, a museum village with 40 old buildings.
Wichita

Kansas City   K 31

States: Kansas and Missouri
Altitude: 775ft/236m
Population: 1.6 million (Metropolitan Area)

This double city in the Mid West, straddling the border between Kansas and Missouri, lies at the junction of the Kansas River with the Missouri, extending along the high banks of both rivers (the Bluffs). World-famed for its steaks and its jazz, Kansas City is now the centre of an extensive agricultural region. The great stockyards and packing stations of the 19th century have given place to highly efficient foodstuffs industries and other processing industries (automobile construction, engineering, chemicals, paper, etc.).
Situation and characteristics

Kansas City, Kansas (pop. 186,000) developed in the mid 19th century out of a small town established by white settlers. For a time it was the eastern terminus of the first transcontinental railroad and thus gained importance as a commercial centre. Kansas City, Missouri (pop. 450,000), grew out of a settlement of French fur-traders and a Jesuit mission and during the 19th century rapidly developed into a lively economic and cultural centre. A glance at the ultra-modern skyline of Kansas City, Missouri is enough to show that it remains the more important of the two sister cities.
History

Sights in Kansas City, Kansas

The most interesting feature in Kansas City, Kansas, is the Old Shawnee Town, with an Indian mission school founded in 1839, an old Wells Fargo mail station and other historic buildings.
*Old Shawnee Town

Kennedy Space Center

Bonner Springs	A few miles up the Kansas River is Bonner Springs, with the Wyandotte Historical Museum (regional history) and the Agricultural Hall of Fame (displays on agricultural themes).
Woodlands	In the Woodlands leisure park there are horse and greyhound races throughout the year.

Sights in Kansas City, Missouri

*Crown Center	The Crown Center, an ultra-modern complex of tower blocks of different shapes and sizes built in the 1970s, is the new city centre. It includes many striking buildings by Helmut Jahn and other leading contemporary architects.
Liberty Memorial	From the 215ft/66m high Liberty Memorial there are magnificent views of the city. The Bells of Liberty ring out well known tunes every day.
Museums	For local history there is the Kansas City Museum, for art the rich collections of the Nelson-Atkins Museum of Art and the Kansas City Art Institute. Also of interest is the Toy and Miniature Museum.
*Westport	The old district of Westport has recently been lovingly restored. A magnet for all visitors is the Kelly Tavern, in the city's oldest building.
Country Club Plaza	The Country Club Plaza, which extends along several blocks, with numerous shops, restaurants and theatres, has something of a Spanish air with its fountains and statues.
Swope Park	This 1772-acre (717-hectare) park is the recreation centre for the whole of the Kansas City conurbation, with a variety of leisure facilities, an interesting Zoo and the Starlight Theater.
Worlds of Fun, Oceans of Fun	These two theme parks offer a wide variety of entertainments for families.

Kennedy Space Center

See Cape Canaveral / Kennedy Space Center

Kentucky (State; KY)   K–N 36–43

Area:
40,395sq.miles/104,623sq.km
Population: 3,714,000
Capital: Frankfort
Popular name: Bluegrass State

Situation and topography	The state of Kentucky (from the Indian *ken-tah-keh,* "land of tomorrow") is bounded on the north by the Ohio River. The western end of the state extends into the Mississippi lowlands, while in the south-east is the Cumberland Plateau. From the fertile Bluegrass region in the north-east which gives the state its popular name the land rises to the Cumberland Plateau. Central Kentucky is a region of karstic limestone, with numerous dolines, bizarre rock formations and the magnificent Mammoth Cave. Almost half of the state's area is covered by mixed deciduous forests. The climate is temperate continental.

Kentucky

The first whites to reach the region, from 1670 onwards, were French and British. Permanent settlement began around 1770. During the War of Independence Kentucky suffered severely from raids by Indians allied with the British. On June 1st 1792 it became the 15th state of the Union.

History

The fertile soils of the Bluegrass region yield high-quality tobacco, making Kentucky the largest tobacco producer in the United States after North Carolina. Other important crops are soya beans, maize, grain, vegetables and potatoes. Stock-farming (dairy and beef cattle, pigs, sheep) thrives on the great expanses of pastureland. The state's principal mineral resources are coal, oil and natural gas. The most important branches of industry are engineering, the manufacture of electrical appliances, textiles, foodstuffs (including whiskey) and tobacco. Tourism is of some local importance.

Economy

Places of Interest in Kentucky

3 miles/5km south of Hodgenville is the modest log cabin (now enclosed in a stone Memorial Building) in which Abraham Lincoln was born on February 12th 1809.

Abraham Lincoln Birthplace

ardstown is famous for the old mansion which inspired the composer Stephen Foster (1826–64) to write the popular song "My Old Kentucky Home". Other features of interest are the Old Bardstown Village and Civil War Museum and the Oskar Getz Museum of Whiskey History.

Bardstown

South-eastern Kentucky extends into the Cumberland Mountains. The most important passage through the hills is the Cumberland Gap (1663ft/507m), an 800ft/245m deep cut through the range which was used as a traffic route in Indian times and was discovered by pioneers moving west in the mid 18th century. After the legendary Daniel Boone had driven his Wilderness Trail into Kentucky in 1775 over 200,000 white settlers made their way through the Cumberland Mountains to the West. From Pinnacle Overview (2460ft/750m) there are magnificent views of the hills and the Gap. A popular hike is to the Hensley Settlement, a well preserved old country township.

*Cumberland Gap National Historical Park

30 miles/48km south-west of Louisville is Fort Knox, where most of the United States' gold reserves are stored. There is an interesting Cavalry Museum.

*Fort Knox

Frankfort (pop. 30,000), capital of the state of Kentucky, grew out of a fort established by a pioneer named Frank. It is the chief place in a productive grain- and tobacco-growing region on the Kentucky River. The Museum of the Kentucky Historical Society is housed in the old State Capitol of 1836. Daniel Boone and his wife Rebecca are buried in the town cemetery.

Frankfort

The little country town of Harrodsburg (pop. 8000), south-west of Lexington (see entry), is the oldest settlement of European immigrants west of the Alleghenies, founded around 1774. In Old Fort Harrod State Park is a Living History Museum, with an open-air theatre in which the life story of Daniel Boone is re-enacted.

Harrodsburg

The city of Louisville (pop. 300,000), on the navigable Ohio River, was founded in 1778 and named in honour of King Louis XVI. It is the seat of a university and the headquarters of world-famed brands of tobacco and whiskey (Philip Morris, American Tobacco; Seagram, Schenley and Old Fitzgerald whiskey). The J. B. Speed Art Museum has pictures by Rembrandt, Rubens, Monet and Picasso. Louisville is the scene of the famous Kentucky Derby, which has been held annually since 1875 on the first Sunday in May and draws many thousands of spectators. It is also a port of call for cruises on the Mississippi and Ohio Rivers and the starting-point of trips in the venerable old sternwheeler "Belle of Louisville".

*Louisville

Key West

Natural bridge in the Daniel Boone National Forest (Kentucky)

*Natural Bridge

In the Daniel Boone National Forest south-east of Lexington (see entry) is the Natural Bridge (65ft/20m high, 75ft/23m wide), created by the erosional forces of wind and water. In the surrounding area, now a State Park, are other bizarre rock formations. A few miles north the Red River surges through a wild and romantic gorge.

Other places of interest

Covington (see Cincinnati, Surroundings), Lexington, Mammoth Cave (see entries)

Key West

State: Florida
Altitude: 0–10ft/0–3m
Population: 25,000

**Situation and history

The town of Key West, on an island of coral limestone at the south-west end of the Florida Keys (the natives of which call themselves Conchs), is the most southerly point in the continental United States. In earlier days it was a notorious pirates' lair and later a flourishing port. In 1822 the southern tip of Florida began to be developed as a naval base, and by 1870 Key West was the largest and wealthiest town in Florida. A number of handsome Conch houses still bear witness to the prosperity of the old wreckers and sea-captains. During the 19th century immigrants from Cuba introduced cigar production to Key West.

The carefree Caribbean way of life attracted many artists and writers to the town. Among those who lived and worked here during the thirties and forties were Ernest Hemingway and Tennessee Williams.

Key West

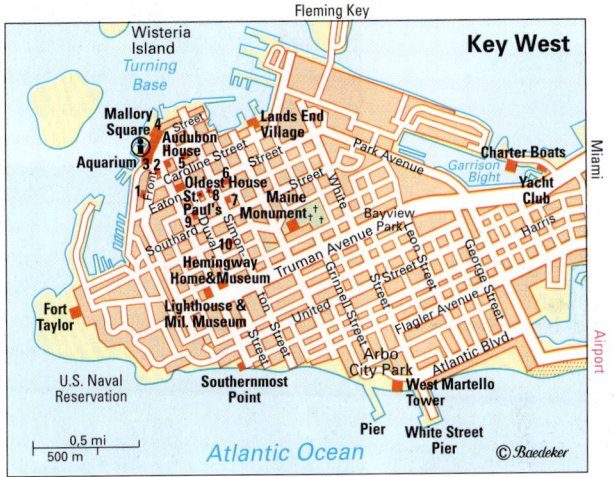

1 The Little White House
2 Mel Fisher Maritime Society Museum
3 Old Post Office/Coast Guard Building
4 Harbor House
5 Sloppy Joe's Bar/Old City Hall
6 Bahama House
7 Marquesa Hotel
8 Old Stone Methodist Church
9 San Carlos Opera House
10 The Piggy Mills House & Garden

Sights in Key West

The Old Town at the south-west end of the island, with its many pastel-coloured 19th century houses, is particularly attractive. Duval Street and its charming side streets are lined with boutiques, art galleries, sidewalk cafés, restaurants and bars.

*Old Town/Duval Street

A particular attraction is the Aquarium (Whitehead Street), with giant turtles, barracudas, Florida lobsters, sharks and other spectacular denizens of the sea.

*Key West Aquarium

Mel Fisher's Treasury Exhibit (200 Green Street/Front Street) displays Spanish gold jewellery, silver coins and other valuable objects recovered in recent years by Mel Gibson from the Spanish galleons "Nuestra Señora de Atocha" and "Santa Margarita", which sank off the Marquesas during a hurricane in 1622. There is also an interesting exhibition on underwater archaeology.

*Mel Fisher's Treasury Exhibit

The famous American bird painter John James Audubon (1785–1851) stayed in Key West in 1832 in a typical Conch house (Whitehead and Greene Streets) which contains some of his original engravings.

Audubon House

Captain Tony's Saloon in Greene Street was known from 1933 to 1937 as Sloppy Joe's Bar and was a favourite haunt of Ernest Hemingway, who often ended the day on the stool which was reserved for him.
The new Sloppy Joe's Bar, just round the corner at 201 Duval Street, is decorated with photographs of Hemingway.

Captain Tony's Saloon

*Sloppy Joe's Bar

Key West's main attraction is the Ernest Hemingway Home and Museum (938 Whitehead Street; open: daily 9am–5pm). This charming house in Spanish colonial style (built 1851) was bought in 1931 by Hemingway, who wrote many of his works here.
The luxuriant tropical garden is occupied by numerous descendants of Hemingway's pet cats.

Ernest Hemingway Home and Museum

271

Key West

The most photographed sight in Key West

Ernest Hemingway's house

Southernmost Point: At the end of Whitehead Street is a large concrete buoy marking the southernmost point in the continental United States. From here it is only 90 miles/145km to Cuba.

Surroundings of Key West

Coral reefs: From the landing-stage at the north end of Duval Street there are trips in glass-bottomed boats to the coral reefs round Key West, still largely undamaged, with their marvellous underwater world.
The south-western outliers of the Florida Keys are the home of a wide variety of birds, including rare terns, cormorants and frigate birds with a wing-span of more that 6ft/2m.

*Marquesas Keys: From Key West there are boat trips westward to the mangrove-fringed Marquesas Keys, the centrepiece of the extensive Key West National Wildlife Refuge.

Dry Tortugas: 70 miles/113km west of Key West are the Dry Tortugas, a group of coral islets and reefs on which Ponce de León discovered great numbers of turtles laying their eggs in 1613.

*Fort Jefferson: In the little island of Garden Key, which can be reached only by visitors sailing their own boat or in a seaplane of the Key West Seaplane Service, is Fort Jefferson, built in 1846 to protect the passage into the Gulf of Mexico. After serving for many years as a military prison it was scheduled in 1935 as a National Monument.

Other keys: See Florida

Lake Tahoe / Squaw Valley K/L 5/6

States: California, Nevada
Altitude: 6235ft/1900m

Among the most beautiful holiday destinations in the American West is Lake Tahoe, which lies on a plateau between the Sierra Nevada and the Carson Range. The plateau has an area of some 200sq.miles/518sq.km, and the lake is just under 22 miles/35km long, up to 12 miles/19km across and up to 1600ft/490m deep. Along its shores, particularly on the Californian side, there are numerous hotels, motels, campgrounds, restaurants and shops, and there are a number of beautiful bathing beaches (e.g. Zephyr Beach) and a variety of other facilities for water sports (including sailing and wind-surfing).

Lake Tahoe
**Topography

On the northern shore of the lake, near Incline Village, is the Ponderosa Ranch, the setting of the popular television series, "Bonanza" (open to visitors from May to October).

Ponderosa Ranch

The chief place in this popular holiday area is South Lake Tahoe (pop. 22,000), through which runs the boundary between California and Nevada. The two sides of the street are very different: on the Californian side there are numbers of small motels and shops, while in Nevada, where gambling is permitted, the street is lined with large and luxurious hotels and casinos (Caesar's, Harrah's, Harvey's, etc.).

South Lake Tahoe

North-west of Lake Tahoe is the beautiful Squaw Valley, venue of the Winter Olympics in 1960. It now boasts the style of "USA Ski Area".

*Squaw Valley

The mountain region round Lake Tahoe is excellently equipped for winter sports. Popular skiing areas, in addition to Squaw Valley, are Mount Rose, Heavenly Valley, Alpine Meadows, the Tahoe Donner Ski Bowl and the Boreal Ski Area.

Other winter sports areas

Lake Tahoe in winter

Las Vegas

Desolation Wilderness Area — South of Lake Tahoe is the imposing Desolation Wilderness Area, with Emerald Bay State Park, a magnificent recreation area dotted with numerous lakes.

Donner Memorial State Park — The Donner Memorial State Park (Donner Lake) commemorates a group heading for the goldfields under the leadership of one Donner, most of whom perished in a violent snowstorm here in October 1846.

Las Vegas   N 10

State: Nevada
Altitude: 2015ft/614m
Population: 258,000 (Metropolitan Area c. 800,000)

Situation and characteristics — Las Vegas, the "world's largest gambling den" and the largest city in the state of Nevada, lies in a pale brown desert landscape surrounded by barren hills. To the east are the Muddy Mountains, with Lake Mead beyond them, to the west the Spring Mountains. It hardly ever rains in Las Vegas, and in summer the temperature can rise above 104°F/40°C.

History — In 1855 a party of Mormons established a settlement in the valley of Las Vegas (Spanish, "fertile plains"), on an old Spanish trade route between Santa Fé and California, but three years later, after unsuccessful lead-mining operations, they moved on. The real history of Las Vegas began in 1905, when the Union Pacific Railroad reached here. A small railroad workers' settlement grew up, equipped with gambling dens, saloons and shops. By 1911 Las Vegas was large enough to be incorporated as a town. Its great boom, however, began twenty years later, when gambling was legalised in Nevada. Another boost was given to its development by the construction of the massive Hoover Dam on the Colorado River, when several thousand men found work in the desert. The power provided by the new hydro-electric station enabled Las Vegas to become a city of light, flashing with gaudy neon signs. The relaxation of marriage and divorce laws brought further visitors to the city. The first hotel in Las Vegas, El Rancho, was built by Los Angeles investors in 1940 – the nucleus of what is now the Strip. Other huge hotels and casinos soon followed, and some rather dubious characters discovered that big money was to be made quickly in Las Vegas. Visitors continue to stream to Las Vegas – over 20 million of them every year.

Sights in Las Vegas

The **Strip — The 2½ mile/4km long central section of Las Vegas Boulevard which runs through the city from north-east to south-west, known as the Strip, is lined with huge entertainment palaces, with revue theatres, night spots, bars, casinos and luxury hotels set in beautiful gardens. The Strip is particularly impressive at night, when the city is illuminated by an endless succession of glittering neon signs. Every evening there are two shows: the dinner show (floor shows and a generous meal) which in most establishments starts around 8pm, and the cocktail show (floor shows and a light supper with cocktails) at 11pm.

Entertainment palaces — The large entertainment palaces are mostly aligned along Las Vegas Boulevard. They are, in alphabetical order: Aladdin (3667 Las Vegas Boulevard South), Bally's Casino Resort (3645 Las Vegas Boulevard South), Caesar's Palace (3570 Las Vegas Boulevard South), Circus Circus (2880 Las Vegas Boulevard), Desert Inn (3145 Las Vegas Boulevard South), Excalibur (3850 Las Vegas Boulevard South), Flamingo Hilton (3555 Las Vegas Boulevard South), Hacienda (3950 Las Vegas Boulevard South), Harrah's (3475 Las Vegas Boulevard South), Imperial Palace (3535 Las Vegas Boulevard South), Las Vegas Hilton (3000 Paradise Road), The Mirage (3400 Las Vegas

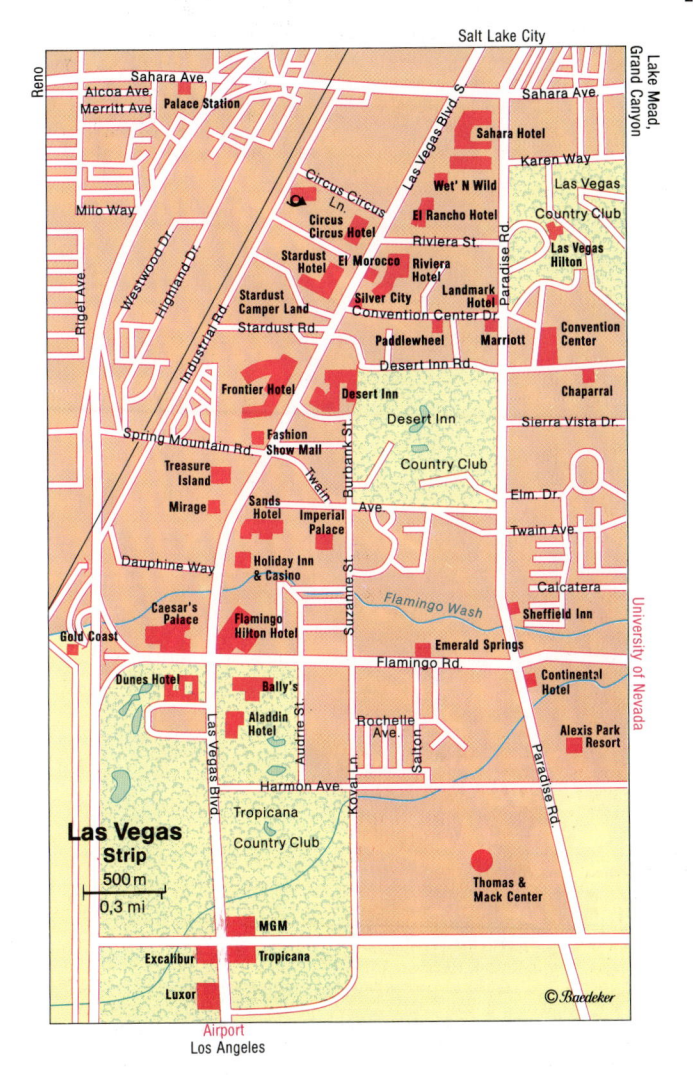

Boulevard South), Riviera (2901 Las Vegas Boulevard South), Sahara (2535 Las Vegas Boulevard South), Stardust (3000 Las Vegas Boulevard South) and Tropicana (3801 Las Vegas Boulevard South).

At 3900 Las Vegas Boulevard is Luxor, a 30-storey pyramid opened in 1993, with 2526 rooms and a covered water park ("Grand Slam Canyon"). Another new arrival in 1993 was the 36-storey Treasure Island (2900 rooms), on a Y-shaped plan, which takes its theme from Robert Louis Stevenson's novel. 1994 saw the opening of the 5005-room MGM Grand Hotel, with an Alice in Wonderland theme.

Latest attractions

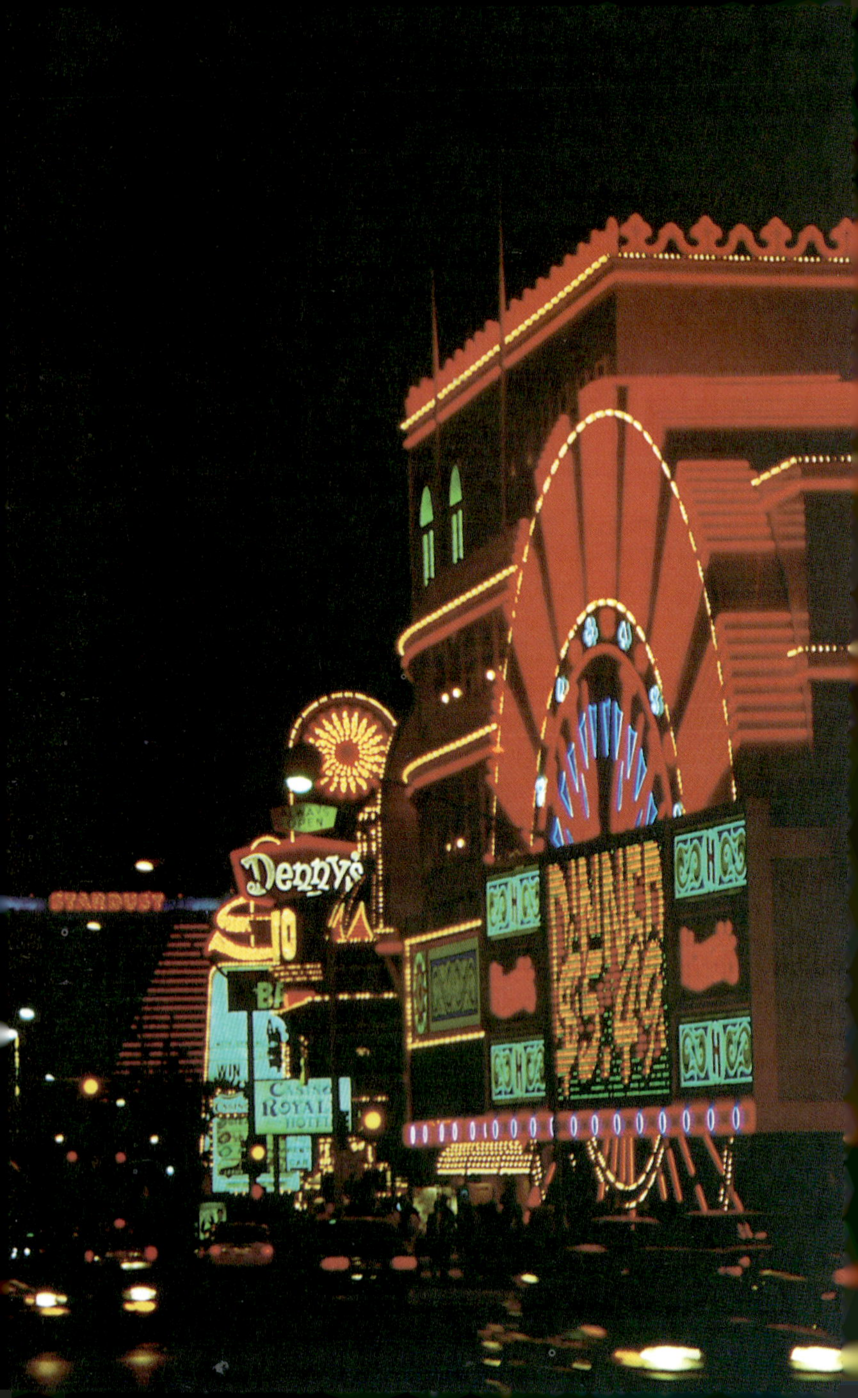
STARDUST
Denny's

The favourite gambling games in the Las Vegas casinos are blackjack, roulette, craps (a dice game, usually fairly noisy) and keno (an American variant of an old Chinese game). Baccarat, poker and bingo are very popular; and there are, of course, the innumerable slot machines ("one-armed bandits"). Betting on races and other sporting events is becoming increasingly popular.   *Gambling*

Other very popular attractions on the Strip are the Guinness World of Records (2780 Las Vegas Boulevard), the Wet 'n' Wild water playground, the exhibition of old-time automobiles in the Imperial Palace (3850 Las Vegas Boulevard) and the Omnimax Theater (a giant-screen movie house) in Caesar's Palace (3570 Las Vegas Boulevard).   *Other attractions on the Strip*

A special feature of Las Vegas is its numerous wedding chapels, in which tens of thousands of couples are married every year.   *Wedding chapels*

To the north of the Strip, near Union Pacific Station, is the Casino Center, with numerous gambling houses (among them the Golden Nugget).   *Casino Center*

The Natural History Museum at 900 Las Vegas Boulevard North offers an interesting survey of the natural history of the desert state of Nevada.   *Natural History Museum*

The exciting National Final Rodeo is held annually in December in the Thomas and Mack Center.   **Final Rodeo*

Surroundings of Las Vegas

40 miles/64km south-east of Las Vegas is the Hoover Dam, built between 1931 and 1936. This gigantic structure (420yd/380m wide, 725ft/221m high; hydro-electric station, with guided tours), which dams the Colorado River to form Lake Mead, is a must for all visitors to the American South-West. Lake Mead itself is popular with water sports enthusiasts; and bathing in the midst of the desert can be enjoyed on Boulder Beach, at the south end of the lake, and Overton Beach at the north end.   ***Hoover Dam**   **Lake Mead*

Farther south the Colorado River flows through the 45 mile/70km long Black Canyon and is then dammed to form the 20 mile/30km long Lake Mohave (hydro-electric station; guided tours).   *Black Canyon/Lake Mohave*

An hour's drive north-west of Las Vegas is Toyabe National Forest.   *Toyabe National Forest*

90 miles/145km south of Las Vegas, at the point where the three states of Nevada, Arizona and California meet, Don Laughlin established a casino on the banks of the Colorado River in 1969. Laughlin has now developed into a boom town with numbers of large casinos and hotels.   *Laughlin*

Lassen Volcanic National Park   J 4

State: California
Area: 165sq.miles/430sq.km
Established: 1916

The National Park is open throughout the year, but its various facilities operate only from June to September. Much of the road through the park is blocked in winter. The winter sports facilities operate from the end of November to the middle of April.   *Season*

Lassen Peak (10,457ft/3187m) in the extreme south of the Cascade Mountains, which takes its name from the Danish pioneer Peter Lassen, is one of   *Situation and *topography*

◀ *The bright lights of Las Vegas*

Lexington / Kentucky Horse Park

the few volcanoes in the United States which have been active in recent times. It is the most southerly of a chain of mighty volcanoes which includes Mount Baker, Mount Rainier, Mount Hood, the former Mount Mazama (Crater Lake), Mount Shasta and Mount St Helens, which erupted in 1980. All these volcanoes belong to the circum-Pacific volcano and earthquake belt known as the "ring of fire".

Lassen Peak is the remnant of Mount Tehama, a volcano which was originally much higher. After 300 years of quiescence Lassen Peak erupted in May 1914 – the start of a period of violent volcanic activity which lasted until 1921. This reached its climax in 1915, when a great cloud of ash mushroomed up to a height of 7 miles/11km and a wave of lava flowed down on the north-east side of the volcano, leaving a trail of destruction.

Sights in Lassen Volcanic National Park

Sulphur Works — A few miles from the south-west entrance to the National Park the road comes to the centre of the former Mount Tehama, at a spot known as the Sulphur Works, a bubbling cauldron of mud pots and sulphurous fumaroles.

Bumpass Hell — Bumpass Hell, 1¼ miles/2km south of Lake Helen, is the largest geothermal field in the National Park. A boardwalk runs past hot springs, simmering mud pots and fumaroles venting sulphurous vapours.

Lassen Peak — From the summit of Lassen Peak (10,457ft/3187m) there are magnificent panoramic views. A hike round the summit on the Lassen Peak Trail (starting from the parking area near Lake Helen) takes 4–5 hours.

Devastated Area — The Devastated Area marks the trail of destruction left by lava flows in 1915, on which vegetation has since begun to revive.

Cinder Cone — In the north-east of the National Park the black Cinder Cone (6907ft/2105m) rises out of the forest. To the south are the Painted Dunes (mounds of volcanic ash) and the Fantastic Lava Beds.

Hot Rock/ Chaos Jumbles — The Hot Rock is a huge boulder weighing several hundred tons which was hurled through the air for many miles by a volcanic eruption. The Chaos Jumbles are a great expanse of volcanic ejecta covering several square miles.

Lexington / Kentucky Horse Park   L 41

State: Kentucky
Altitude: 955ft/291m
Population: 225,000

Situation and characteristics — The city of Lexington, seat of the University of Kentucky and an important economic and cultural centre, lies in the heart of the Bluegrass Country, a fertile rolling plateau on which tobacco is grown. The region is famed for its horse-breeding, and Lexington claims the title of "horse capital of the world". The horse paddocks enclosed by white-painted fences are characteristic features of the landscape.

History — The town was officially founded in 1781, but the place had already been given its name by a group of patriots some years earlier, after the battle of Lexington in Massachusetts. It is now an important centre of the tobacco trade and an industrial town.

Sights in Lexington

**Kentucky Horse Park — The world-famed Kentucky Horse Park (4089 Iron Works Park) lies 10 miles/16km north of Lexington (I 75, exit 120). Here, in typical Bluegrass

Lexington / Kentucky Horse Park

In Kentucky Horse Park

country, everything centres on the horse. There is a Visitor Center which shows films on the park and supplies information on particular activities and events. Open: Mar. 16th–Oct. 31st daily 9am–5pm; rest of year Wed.–Sun. 10am–4pm.

The International Museum of the Horse, with the Calumet Trophy Collection, and the American Saddle Horse Museum give a comprehensive view of the history and importance of the horse, while great race horses are honoured in the Hall of Champions. There is an interesting walk through the park (the Walking Farm Tour) which includes demonstrations of the crafts of blacksmiths, wagoners, harness-makers, etc., and a parade of thoroughbreds (Parade of Breeds Show). Visitors can also enjoy horse trekking and rides in horse-drawn carriages.

The Kentucky Horse Center (3380 Paris Pike; guided tours from April to October) is a training centre for thoroughbreds.

There are race meetings for thoroughbred horses several times annually at the Keeneland Racecourse (4201 Versailles Road) and Red Mile Harness Track (South Broadway and Red Mile Road).

There are several hundred privately owned stud farms of varying size and importance within a radius of some 30 miles/50km of Lexington. Only a few of them are open to visitors.

This handsome house (225 Highbee Mill Road), a fine example of Greek Revival architecture, was built by Daniel Boone's grand-nephew in 1847.

The mansion of Ashland (Richmond and Sycamore Roads) was built in 1806 by Henry Clay, a leading Kentucky politician, and remained in his family until 1948. Now a museum, it illustrates the way of life of a well-to-do 19th century family.

Side notes: Museums and exhibitions; Kentucky Horse Center; Racecourses; Stud farms; Waveland State Historic Site; Ashland

Los Angeles

State: California
Altitude: 0–285ft/0–87m
Population: 3.5 million (Metropolitan Area 14.5 million)

Situation and characteristics	The city of Los Angeles, situated on the Pacific Ocean in southern California, is the centre of the largest conurbation in the United States after New York, which since the First World War has spread crab-wise in all directions and now covers a total area of 460sq.miles/1200sq.km, with a diameter of over 75 miles/120km. The city is bounded on the north-east and east by mountains, and on many days in the year lies under a cloud of smog. Its original nucleus is some 15 miles/25km inland at the foot of the Santa Monica and San Gabriel Mountains.
History and economy	In 1781 a party of Spanish missionaries, among them Junípero Serra, founded the San Gabriel mission on a site 8 miles/13km north-east of the present city centre. The settlement which grew up round it took the name of El Pueblo de Nuestra Señora la Reina de los Angeles de Porciuncula, of which the city's present name is a shortened version. The first inhabitants ("Angelenos") were Spaniards, Mexicans, Indians and blacks. Thereafter the town grew rapidly, and for a time was capital of the Mexican province of Alta California. During the war with Mexico in 1846 the town was occupied by American forces, and under the treaty of Guadalupe Hidalgo passed to the United States. The finding of gold in the Sierra Nevada (1848) gave a boost to its development, and by 1860 it had a population of 5000. With the completion of the first transcontinental railroad, the South Pacific, the first great wave of immigrants began to arrive in 1883, and within a decade the population had risen to over 50,000. Further impetus was given to the town's development by the discovery of oil in the region in 1892 and the construction of artificial harbours at San Pedro and Long Beach between 1899 and 1914. By the early 20th century the population had risen to 250,000. A further economic impulse was given by the development of the film industry, and by 1910 most American films were being made in Los Angeles. The districts of Hollywood and Beverly Hills now came into being, and in 1927 the Academy of Motion Picture Arts and Sciences awarded the first Oscar. The first sound film was produced in 1930. Thereafter Los Angeles developed into the most important industrial and services centre west of the Mississippi. New industries were established – petro-chemicals, automobile manufacture, aircraft and spacecraft construction, engineering, electronics. Numerous major banks and insurance corporations established themselves in the city, and tourism increased steadily in importance, given additional impetus by the siting of the Summer Olympics of 1932 and 1984 in Los Angeles. In recent years, however, the Los Angeles region has been in a state of crisis, mainly as a result of changes in economic structures (e.g. the reduction in the armaments industry) which have affected much of the population either directly or indirectly and have led – most recently in 1992 and 1993 – to violent clashes between different population groups. In January 1994 considerable damage was caused by a severe earthquake.
Population	The Greater Metropolitan Area of Los Angeles now has a population of 14,532,000. The city is a melting-pot of all races, and in recent years the sharp social contrasts between people of different skin colours have led to outbreaks of violence in which chauvinist and racist prejudices ("wealthy" whites, "poor" Latinos and Indians, "stupid" blacks, "crafty" Chinese and Japanese) have played a major part.
Chicanos	Some 5 million people in the Los Angeles region stem from Latin America. Los Angeles is said to be the largest Mexican city outside Mexico, and the name Chicano (an abridged form of Mexicano) is now applied to all Spanish-speaking inhabitants, but more particularly to incomers from the Caribbean and from Central and South America. Although rather pejora-

Los Angeles

Los Angeles Central

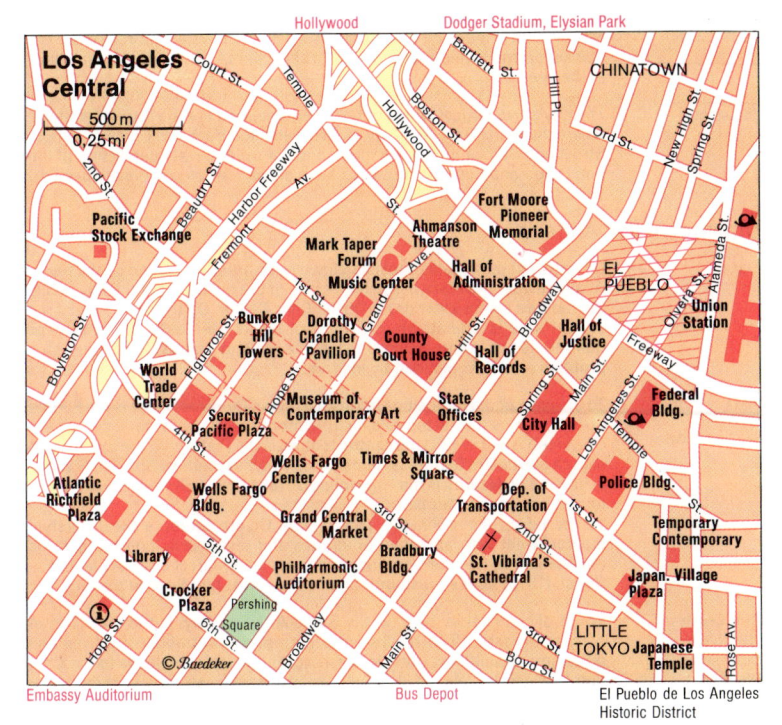

500 m
0.25 mi

(Map labels: Hollywood; Dodger Stadium, Elysian Park; CHINATOWN; Court St.; Temple; Bartlett St.; Hill Pl.; Boston St.; Ord St.; New High St.; Spring St.; Hollywood; 2nd St.; Beaudry Av.; Harbor Freeway; Fremont Av.; Pacific Stock Exchange; Boylston St.; Figueroa St.; 1st St.; Fort Moore Pioneer Memorial; Ahmanson Theatre; Mark Taper Forum; Music Center; Hall of Administration; Broadway; EL PUEBLO; Alameda St.; Union Station; Olvera St.; Bunker Hill Towers; Dorothy Chandler Pavilion; Grand Av.; County Court House; Hall of Records; Hill St.; Hall of Justice; Freeway; World Trade Center; Hope St.; Museum of Contemporary Art; State Offices; Spring St.; City Hall; Main St.; Los Angeles St.; Federal Bldg.; Security Pacific Plaza; 4th St.; Atlantic Richfield Plaza; Wells Fargo Bldg.; Wells Fargo Center; Times & Mirror Square; Dep. of Transportation; 1st St.; Police Bldg.; Grand Central Market; 3rd St.; 2nd St.; Temporary Contemporary; Library; 5th St.; Philharmonic Auditorium; Bradbury Bldg.; St. Vibiana's Cathedral; Japan. Village Plaza; Crocker Plaza; Pershing Square; 6th St.; Broadway; Main St.; 3rd St.; Boyd St.; LITTLE TOKYO; Japanese Temple; Rose Av.; © Baedeker; Embassy Auditorium; Bus Depot; El Pueblo de Los Angeles Historic District)

tive in tone, it is used to distinguish this population group from the Anglo-Americans.

Over 1.2 million black people live in the urbanised region between Pacific Palisades and Laguna Beach. A high proportion of the black population of working age is unemployed, which is a major factor in heightening social tensions in Los Angeles. Many of them feel that they have been "done down" by the whites and the better-off.

Blacks

Asians and immigrants from the Pacific islands are a dramatically increasing population group. Most of them come from Japan, Korea, China, Vietnam, Thailand and the Philippines, and live in their own quarters of the city (Little Tokyo, Chinatown, Koreatown). During the 1970s the Asians moved into districts previously occupied by blacks and Latinos, and some of these areas are notorious for their high crime rate.

Asians and Pacific islanders

Indians play relatively little part in the life of the city. Their numbers are estimated at rather more than 100,000.

American Indians

Until recently the city planners of Los Angeles believed that the only way to deal with the city's traffic problems was to build the world's most elaborate and expensive network of motorways and freeways. Their last achievement in this direction was the 17 mile/27km long eight-lane Century Freeway running across the city from east to west, which cost over 3 billion dollars and involved destroying the homes of 26,000 people. Almost half the built-up area of the city is now taken up by the requirements of traffic (mainly roads and parking lots). Without an automobile a citizen of Los Angeles is lost, for the development of public transport proceeds with little urgency. As a result more than 4 million private automobiles now pour

Smog and the automobile

Los Angeles

their exhaust fumes into the city's air; and a further major contribution to air pollution is made by the aircraft using the four large airports. Hence the blanket of smog which hangs like a portent over Los Angeles on many days in the year.

"Spaghetti junctions"
The city's two largest works of traffic engineering are the four-level Stack, where the Santa Ana, Hollywood, Pasadena and Harbor Freeways, Temple Street and Sunset Boulevard meet, and the seven-level intersection of the San Diego and Century Freeways, with eleven ramps and eleven bridges.

Downtown Los Angeles

Extent
Downtown Los Angeles consists of two main areas separated by the Santa Ana Freeway: the Plaza lies in the centre of the older part of the city, while the modern centre extends round the Civic Center. On the north side of the central area is Chinatown, on the east side Little Tokyo, the Japanese quarter. To the south, beyond extensive parking lots, is South Central, a problem area best avoided by visitors.

Plaza
*El Pueblo de los Angeles Historical Monument
To the west of the imposing Union Passenger Terminal (1939) is the Pueblo de los Angeles (protected as a historic monument), the historic core of the city, established in 1781. Its central feature is the Plaza, with the old mission church of Nuestra Señora la Reina de los Angeles, built by Spanish Franciscans in 1822. Nearby is the Fire House of 1884. In the Sepulveda House is a tourist information bureau.

*Olvera Street
To the north of the Plaza is picturesque Olvera Street, a Mexican-style market street with attractive boutiques and restaurants and many stalls ("puestos") selling craft products. Of particular interest is the Avila Adobe House (1818; now a museum), one of the oldest buildings in the city.

Civic Center

Children's Museum
South of the Pueblo, beyond the Santa Ana Freeway, is the Civic Center with its modern office blocks – the largest concentration of offices and government buildings outside Washington. Main Street leads to the Children's Museum (No. 310), whose motto is "Please touch" rather than "Please do not touch", and the Los Angeles Mall, a huge and well-stocked shopping centre.

*City Hall
The central feature of the Civic Center is the 28-storey City Hall, built in 1928. From the top of City Hall Tower there are – in clear weather – breathtaking panoramic views, extending in the north-east to Mount Wilson with its Observatory, in the east to San Antonio Peak and in the south to the port area of Los Angeles. A short distance away to the south-east is the striking architecture of the Police Building.

Los Angeles Times Building
South-west of City Hall, on Broadway, is the massive Los Angeles Times Building, with its main lobby in the form of a gigantic globe.

*Arthur Will Fountain
Farther north is the Court of Flags, in which the flags of many states flutter in the Californian wind. In the centre, surrounded by tropical vegetation, is the Arthur Will Fountain.

Music Center

*Dorothy Chandler Pavilion
On the west side of the Civic Center is the Music Center, home of the world-famed Los Angeles Philharmonic Orchestra.
The Dorothy Chandler Pavilion, in which concerts and operas are presented, can seat an audience of 3250.

Mark Taper Forum Ahmanson Theatre
The circular Mark Taper Forum (750 seats) and the adjoining Ahmanson Theatre (2100 seats) put on performances of both straight and experimental theatre.

Water and Power Building
To the west the scene is dominated by the massive power station of the Los Angeles Water and Power Department, surrounded by a sheet of water. From here there is a fine view of downtown Los Angeles.

Bunker Hill
To the south-west is Bunker Hill, with its eye-catching complex of high-rise buildings occupied by banks and insurance corporations. Particularly strik-

Los Angeles

ing are the Security Pacific Plaza; the Arco Plaza, with two 52-storey skyscrapers, a large shopping centre and a fountain by the Bauhaus sculptor Herbert Bayer; and the Westin Bonaventure Hotel (1973), with 1500 rooms, a huge atrium and a revolving restaurant with views of the city.

The dominant feature in the landscape is the First Interstate World Center, the tallest building in the American West (1015ft/310m). From here an elaborate staircase resembling the Spanish Steps in Rome leads down to 5th Street.   The Skyway (a complex of pedestrian passageways) links the various buildings and the beautiful roof gardens.

Wells Fargo Court, laid out in gardens, is enclosed by the glass façades of the Wells Fargo Bank and the IBM Building. Beyond Grand Avenue is the California Plaza.

At 250 South Grand Avenue is the important Museum of Contemporary Art (open: Tue.–Sun. 11am–6pm, Thur. to 8pm), housed in a red sandstone building designed by the leading Japanese architect Arata Isozaki. The permanent collection includes spectacular works by Warhol, Lichtenstein, Oldenburg and other contemporary artists.

On Bunker Hill extensive redevelopment is in progress, involving the construction of three new skyscrapers, over 1000 luxury apartments, a hotel and numerous shops and restaurants.

The funicular running up Bunker Hill, popularly known as the Angels' Flight, which was constructed in 1901 and closed down in the sixties, is now being restored at great expense and is due to reopen shortly.

A few minutes' walk east is the Grand Central Market, surrounded by the bustling life of a Chicano quarter. Here a variety of tasty delicatessen and international specialities can be bought.

To the east is the Bradbury Building (1893), with a well preserved Victorian interior.

Farther to the south-west is Pershing Square with its rich tropical vegetation, the busy and attractive central feature of the Financial District, with the elegant Biltmore Hotel. In the surrounding area are a number of striking skyscrapers.

To the west is the Edison Building (1930), with a superb Art Deco interior.

South-east of Pershing Square is the Los Angeles Theater Center, a new cultural focal point.

South-east of the Civic Center and to the east of Broadway is the Japanese quarter, with its shops, tea-houses and restaurants.

Particularly striking is Noguchi Plaza, designed by the Japanese architect Isamo Noguchi. On the square are the American Cultural and Community Center and the Japan American Theatre.

Round the Japanese Village Plaza, to the north, are a number of attractive shops and restaurants. To the north-east is the Japanese American National Museum.

Farther to the north-east is the Temporary Contemporary, the exhibition centre of a new art scene which is still in course of development.

To the north of the Pueblo is New Chinatown, with pagodas, colourful markets and good restaurants, which came into being after the construction of the new Union Station in 1939.

Wilshire Boulevard runs west from downtown Los Angeles, passing MacArthur Park.

Between Highland Avenue and Fairfax Avenue is the famous Miracle Mile, with fashionable shops and striking high-rise buildings.

Just before Fairfax Avenue is Hancock Park, with the Rancho La Brea Tar Pits, famous for the fossils found here – several hundred skeletons of animals who lived between 5000 and 40,000 years ago, including the remains of Ice Age mammoths. There is a very informative site museum.

Los Angeles

*County Museum of Art	At the west end of the park is the County Museum of Art, with a wealth of art treasures, including works by Rembrandt, Holbein, Canaletto, Cézanne, Toulouse-Lautrec, Kandinsky and Chagall.
*Farmers Market	To the north of Hancock Park is the lively Farmers Market (Fairfax Avenue and 3rd Street), overflowing with fruit and delights of all kinds.

**Hollywood

Situation and characteristics	North of Farmers Market is Hollywood, originally a little farming settlement founded around the turn of the century, which was incorporated in Los Angeles in 1910. The first film studio in California – the germ of the world-famed film metropolis – was established here in 1911. Nowadays only a few large film companies (including Universal and Paramount) still operate in Hollywood, along with numerous smaller firms mainly engaged in making television films or audio-visual learning aids.
CBS Studios	Near Farmers Market visitors can see round the studios of the CBS television company (Columbia Broadcasting Systems; Fairfax Avenue and Beverly Boulevard).
Sunset Boulevard *Sunset Strip	A few minutes' drive north, beyond the busy Santa Monica Boulevard, is Sunset Boulevard, which runs west to Beverly Hills. At its western end is the Sunset Strip, the famous entertainments centre with its clubs and restaurants (including the St James Club, the Mondrian and Château Marmont) and the celebrated Hyatt on Sunset.
Hollywood Boulevard	Parallel to Sunset Boulevard on the north is Hollywood Boulevard, the busy main street of this part of Los Angeles.
*Mann's Chinese Theater	This movie house in the style of a Chinese pagoda, with its guardian dragons, is perhaps the most famous cinema in the world, the scene of Oscar presentation ceremonies. In the forecourt are the footprints and handprints of over 150 stars, the first of which were those of Mary Pickford and Douglas Fairbanks in 1929.
*Walk of Fame	At the Chinese Theater begins the most photographed section of Hollywood Boulevard, the Walk of Fame. Set into the black terrazzo paving of the sidewalk are a series of brass plates and pink marble stars bearing the names of famous film stars. There are now 1800 of them, commemorating the greats of the film world and those who consider themselves to be such.
Wax Museum	Farther east is the Hollywood Wax Museum, with figures of famous film actors and politicians.
Schindler House	At 833 North Kings Road is the Schindler House (1921–22), a glass and concrete structure designed by Frank Lloyd Wright.

North-Western Districts

*Beverly Hills	Farther west Sunset Boulevard runs through Beverly Hills, where the stars of film and show business have their luxury – and sometimes quite extraordinary – residences.

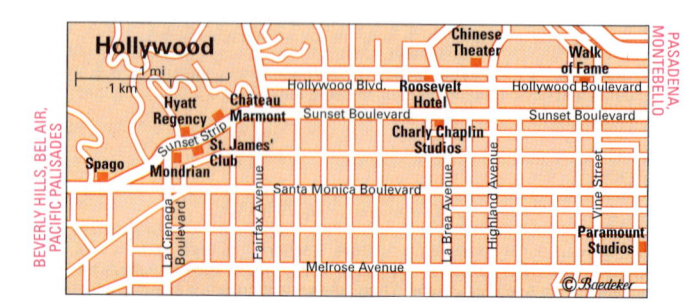

Los Angeles

Walk of Fame at Mann's Chinese Theater   *On Sunset Boulevard*

A must for any visitor to Beverly Hills is Rodeo Drive, a very upstage mile of sinfully expensive shops.	*Rodeo Drive
On the south-western edge of Beverly Hills is Century City, a neighbourhood of modern offices, shops and apartment blocks built on the site of the old 20th Century Fox studios. In Century City Shopping Center is the Dive, built by the famous film director Steven Spielberg ("Jurassic Park", etc.), in which visitors have the feeling of being in a submarine on the bottom of the sea.	Century City
In the Simon Wiesenthal Center in Century City (9760 West Pico Boulevard) is the Museum of the Holocaust, which is devoted to the extermination of the Jews in Hitler's Third Reich.	*Museum of the Holocaust
Sunset Boulevard continues west through the very select residential district of Bel Air. To the south is the scarcely less exclusive district of Westwood.	**Bel Air/ Westwood**
At 10899 Wilshire Boulevard is the very fine Armand Hammer Museum of Art (open: Wed.–Mon. noon–7pm), which is devoted mainly to European art of the last five centuries, including works by Rembrandt, Rubens, Goya and some of the great Impressionists.	*Armand Hammer Museum of Art
Between Bel Air and Westwood is the campus of the University of California (33,000 students), with a beautiful Botanic Garden, the Wight Art Museum and the Franklin Murphy Sculpture Garden (both at 405 Hilgard Avenue), with modern sculpture, including works by Rodin and Henry Moore.	University of California
On Sunset Boulevard beyond the San Diego Freeway is the estate of the film comedian Will Rogers (1879–1935), with stables, corral and riding track.	*Will Rogers State Historic Park
On the Pacific Coast Highway, near Santa Monica Bay with its broad sandy beach, is Pacific Palisades, another residential district for the wealthy.	**Pacific Palisades**

285

Los Angeles

Many villas were destroyed in a great fire, probably started deliberately, in the autumn of 1993. During the Nazi period in Germany a number of German émigrés, including Thomas Mann and Bertolt Brecht, lived here.

Malibu

The beautiful bathing resort of Malibu, celebrated in the songs of the Beach Boys, is also a residential area favoured by stars of show business (among them Bob Dylan).

**J. Paul Getty Museum

The World-famous Getty Art Museum (open: Tue.–Sun. 10am–5pm; closed on public holidays) was personally opened in 1974 by the oil magnate Jean Paul Getty (1892–1976). Situated on a hill above the Pacific, it is a perfect reconstruction of the Villa dei Papiri in Herculaneum, below Vesuvius. The collection includes works of art acquired both by Getty himself and by the 3-billion-dollar Foundation which he established. Among its principal treasures are Greek and Roman sculpture (including the Anadyomenos, probably an original work by Lysippos, 370–300 B.C.), French Rococo furniture and above all an important collection of old master paintings (Rembrandt's "Old Man in Armour", a "Descent from the Cross" of the school of Rogier van der Weyden, etc.). There are also collections of modern decorative art and contemporary photography (including work by Man Ray and Cunningham).

Santa Monica

Wilshire Boulevard ends in Santa Monica (pop. 100,000), a favourite Pacific bathing resort and an important centre of the air and space industries.

Frank Gehry House

At the corner of Washington and 22nd Streets is the Frank Gehry House (1977–78), the rebuilding of an old house with corrugated iron, which caused much controversy at the time. It now ranks as a masterpiece of Deconstructivism.

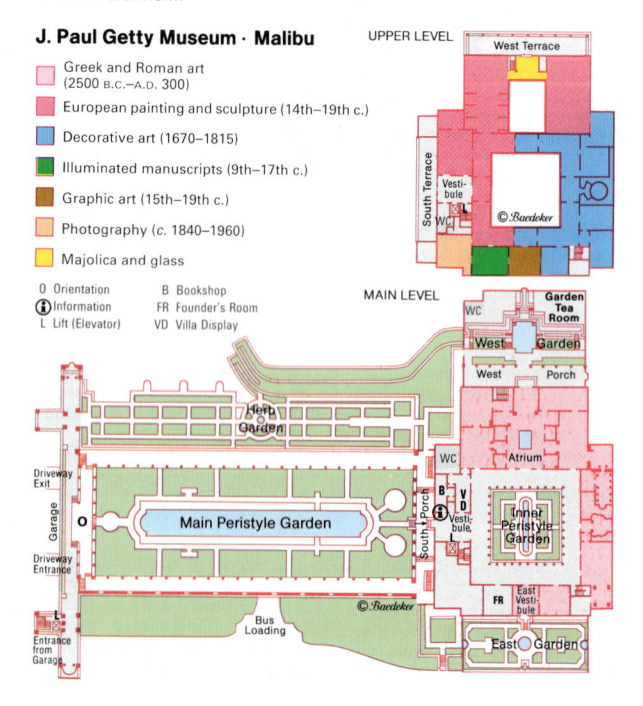

J. Paul Getty Museum · Malibu

- Greek and Roman art (2500 B.C.–A.D. 300)
- European painting and sculpture (14th–19th c.)
- Decorative art (1670–1815)
- Illuminated manuscripts (9th–17th c.)
- Graphic art (15th–19th c.)
- Photography (c. 1840–1960)
- Majolica and glass

O Orientation
ⓘ Information
L Lift (Elevator)
B Bookshop
FR Founder's Room
VD Villa Display

Los Angeles

Beyond Santa Monica is the densely built-up town of Venice, modelled on its Italian prototype, with the resort of Venice Beach, much favoured by roller skating and skateboarding enthusiasts and the fitness-conscious.

Venice

Northern Districts

The main attraction in North Hollywood is Universal Studios (open: daily 8am–5pm), an extensive film city with studios, Wild West sets, waterfalls, artificial lakes and the wardrobes of famous film stars. Visitors are shown the sets for such films as "Back to the Future", "Psycho" and the television series "Columbo" and can experience an attack by the great white shark of "Jaws", Wild West stunt shows and scenes from various thrillers with wild motorboat chases. This is a theme park as much as a studio tour which attracts many thousands of visitors.

North Hollywood
**Universal Studios

Wild West scene in Universal Studios

In the San Fernando Valley (10 miles/16km north-west) are the Busch Gardens, which appeal particularly to families with children. Among the attractions here are the tropical park and a variety of exciting rides.

San Fernando Valley
Busch Gardens

The town of San Fernando (pop. 18,000) grew up round the mission of San Fernando Rey de España, founded by Spanish monks in 1797, which has an interesting museum (Indian art, etc.).

San Fernando

In the suburb of Burbank (pop. 90,000) are the Lockheed Aircraft Company's factory (guided tours) and the headquarters of the National Broadcasting Corporation (NBC; studio tours).

Burbank

On the north side of Los Angeles is Griffith Park, the largest municipal park in the United States (4000 acres/1620 hectares), with a variety of sport and leisure facilities. Among particular attractions are Travel Town (with an open-air transport and fire service museum), the Los Angeles Zoo, the Greek Theatre (open-air), the Ferndell Nature Center (botanical and zoological collections) and the Griffith Observatory, Planetarium and Hall of Science (exhibition on space travel, etc.), from which there is a superb view of Los Angeles.

*Griffith Park

North-east of Los Angeles is Pasadena (pop. 120,000), seat of the California Institute of Technology.
The Norton Simon Museum of Art (411 West Colorado Boulevard) has works by Paul Klee, Lionel Feininger, Wassily Kandinsky, Alexey Jawlensky and many other artists.
Farther north is Angeles National Forest, dominated by Mount Wilson (5709ft/1740m), a peak in the San Gabriel Mountains. Here the Mount Wilson Observatory with its gigantic telescope can be visited.

Pasadena

*Norton Simon Museum of Art

Angeles National Forest/
*Mount Wilson

Los Angeles

*Huntington Library and Art Gallery

A few minutes' drive south-east of Pasadena is the Huntington Library and Art Gallery, a magnificent collection of rare books (including a Gutenberg Bible) and pictures (including Gainsborough's "Blue Boy"). It is set in very beautiful gardens.

San Gabriel

To the south is the suburb of San Gabriel (pop. 35,000), with the fortress-like mission of San Gabriel Arcángel, founded in 1771. Its church is one of the finest in California.

Southern Districts

*Exposition Park

3 miles/5km south-east of the Civic Center are the campus of the University of Southern California and the beautifully laid out Exposition Park, with a large rose garden.

Memorial Coliseum

The central feature of the park is the Memorial Coliseum (1928), which has seating for 100,000 spectators. Some of the events in the 1932 and 1984 Summer Olympics were held here.

*California Museum of Science and Industry

The California Museum of Science and Industry (open: daily 10am–5pm) is devoted to the scientific and technological achievements of the "seventh greatest economic power in the world", as California likes to call itself. Included in the museum are a Hall of Health and a Hall of Economics and Finance.

California Afro-American Museum

Nearby is the California Afro-American Museum, which illustrates the contribution made by blacks to the development of California.

*County Museum of Natural History

The richly stocked County Museum of Natural History (open: Tue.–Sun. 10am–5pm) illuminates the natural history of California with its geological and mineralogical collections (including fossils from the Rancho La Brea Tar Pits).

Watts
*Simon Rodia Towers

In the district of Watts, much troubled in recent years by race riots, are the Simon Rodia Towers (1765 East 107th Street), four towers built by an Italian immigrant of that name from fragments of concrete, glass, pottery and mirrors. Begun in 1921, the task took 33 years. The towers are now protected as a monument of folk art.

San Pedro Bay
Los Angeles Harbor

In San Pedro Bay (15 miles/24km farther south) is Los Angeles Harbor, built around the turn of the century, with the interesting Cabrillo Marine Museum.

Long Beach

A few miles east is the city of Long Beach (pop. 440,000), on the world's largest artificial harbour, which has been steadily enlarged and developed since the beginning of the 20th century.

***"Queen Mary"

The main attraction of Long Beach is the "Queen Mary", which is moored at Pier J (open: daily 10am–4pm). The world's largest passenger liner (over 80,000 tons), it was launched in Britain in 1934 and was until the sixties the flagship of the Cunard line.

*Marineland of the Pacific

10 minutes' drive west of San Pedro Bay is Marineland of the Pacific, one of the largest ocean parks in the world (trained dolphins and whales, etc.).

Buena Park
Movieland Wax Museum

19 miles/30km south-east of downtown Los Angeles is the suburb of Buena Park (pop. 70,000), with the Movieland Wax Museum (famous film and television stars depicted in scenes from their best known films).

*Knott's Berry Farm

To the south, on Beach Boulevard, is Knott's Berry Farm (open: daily 9am to dusk). In the 1920s a farm selling blackberries, it is now a large theme park (gold-diggers' town, Snoopyland). In the more modern part of the park are spectacular roundabouts and roller coasters.

Anaheim

A few miles south of Knott's Berry Farm, on the southern edge of the main Los Angeles conurbation, is Anaheim (pop. 240,000), originally a settlement established by German immigrants in 1857.

**Disneyland

The main attraction in Anaheim is Disneyland, a huge theme park established in 1955.
In this extraordinary world visitors can travel in mail coaches or on an ultra-modern monorail system, in a submarine or a spacecraft. Figures from Walt Disney films are ubiquitous.

Opening times: summer daily 8am–midnight; winter daily 9am–8pm

The entrance leads into a turn-of-the-century Main Street USA, with horse-drawn streetcars and old-time automobiles.

Main Street USA

Beyond this, off to the right, is Tomorrowland, where visitors can experience a rocket launch, ride on a hair-raising roller coaster through the pitch-black universe or dive to the bottom of the sea in a submarine.

Tomorrowland

In Fantasyland you can meet Snow White and visit the Sleeping Beauty's Castle, or fly with Peter Pan and Dumbo.

Fantasyland

Mickey's Toontown is the home of Mickey Mouse, Goofy and Donald and Daisy Duck.

Mickey's Toontown

In Frontierland visitors are taken back to the days of the Wild West and the gold-diggers. A mining railroad runs through deserts, canyons and mountains, and the sternwheeler "Mark Twain" sails on the Rivers of America.

Frontierland
Rivers of America

In Critter Country you will encounter a dancing bear and see Davy Crockett's canoes, and can take an adventurous trip down the rapids.

Critter Country

New Orleans Square re-creates the atmosphere of the city in the Mississippi delta, with 18th century pirates and 19th century street scenes.

New Orleans Square

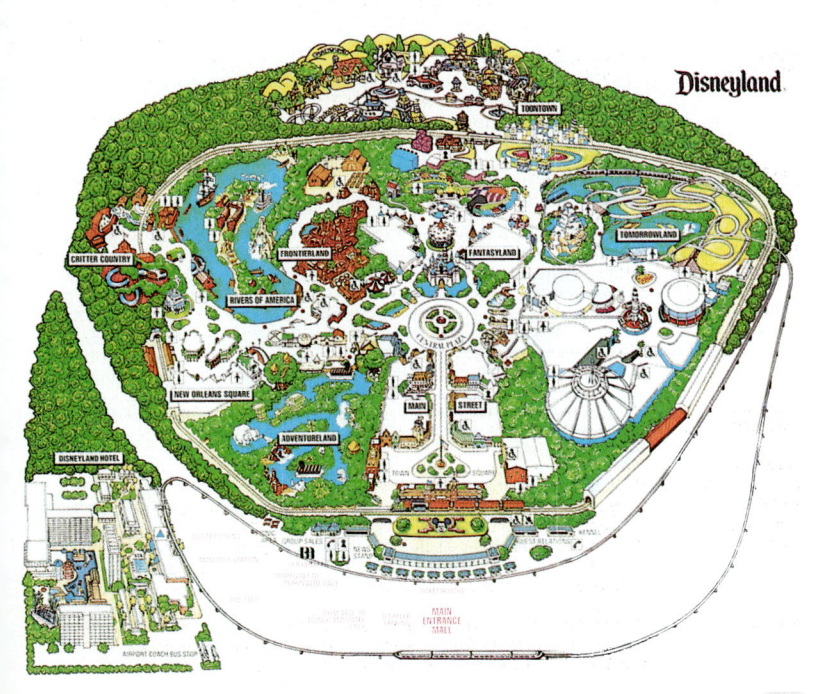

Louisiana

Adventureland — Here visitors sail on an expedition through the jungle, menaced by wild animals, and can visit the Tiki Room with its tropical plants and birds.

Other Places of Interest Round Los Angeles

*Crystal Cathedral — 3 miles/5km south of Disneyland is the Crystal Cathedral (by Philip Johnson, 1980), a futuristic structure of tubular steel clad with mirror glass.

*Santa Catalina Island — 25 miles/40km south of San Pedro Bay, in the Pacific, is Santa Catalina Island. Once a pirates' lair, this rocky islet was developed in 1919 by Wrigley, the chewing-gum king, as a holiday centre, a "second Capri" (diving, swimming, tennis, golf, riding, etc.). At the south-east end of the island is a large colony of seals.

*Channel Islands National Park — Off Santa Monica are the Santa Barbara Islands. The islands of Anacapa, Santa Cruz, Santa Rosa and San Miguel, together with Santa Catalina, form the Channel Islands National Park, which attracts many nature-lovers, water sports enthusiasts and divers.

Louisiana (State; LA) R–V 31–36

Area:
47,752sq.miles/123,677sq.km
Population: 4,252,000
Capital: Baton Rouge
Popular name: Pelican State

Situation and topography — The southern state of Louisiana (named after King Louis XIV of France) occupies the western part of the Gulf Coast plain and the riverine meadowland and delta of the Mississippi (which alone accounts for a third of the state's area). Much of the land, lying at an average height of only 100ft/30m above sea level, has to be protected by levees from flooding; only in the north-west does it rise to around 525ft/160m. The climate is subtropical, with hot and sultry summers, mild winters and occasional devastating hurricanes.

History — The Mississippi delta region, first discovered in 1530 by two Spaniards, Cabeza de Vaca and Panfilo de Narvaez, was occupied in the name of France by the Sieur de la Salle in 1682. After the French failure to prevent the westward extension of the British colonies, in 1762, the territory west of the Mississippi as far north as the Canadian frontier fell to Spain and the territory east of the river to Britain, passing in 1783 to the United States. In 1801 France recovered the Spanish part of the territory and in 1803 sold it to the United States (the "Louisiana Purchase"). On April 30th 1812 Louisiana was admitted to the Union as the 18th state. During the Civil War, in 1862, the Northern states captured much of Louisiana, which supported the Confederates. After the war it remained a state with sharp social and racial tensions.

Economy — The main crops grown on the productive soils of the Mississippi delta and along the Red River are cotton, sugar-cane, soya beans and rice. Cattle-rearing and fishing in the well stocked coastal waters are increasing in importance. The basis of the state's industry is provided by its rich resources of oil, natural gas, sulphur and rock salt, which supply the petrochemical and aluminium smelting plants along the Mississippi between New Orleans and Baton Rouge. New Orleans, Louisiana's largest city and the second most important seaport in the United States, is the tourist centre of the state, whose particular charm lies in its Creole and French heritage.

Places of Interest in Louisiana

The state capital of Baton Rouge, north-west of New Orleans (see entry), owes its name to two Indian tribes who marked the boundaries of their territory with red posts. Its main features of interest are its handsome old mansions, including Mount Hope Plantation (19th c.) and Magnolia Plantation (1791), one of the oldest in the town. Any visit to the town should include a stroll along the river front.

Baton Rouge

St Martinville, south of Baton Rouge, was founded by Acadians from Canada. Two Acadians made famous by Longfellow in his "Evangeline" were Emmeline Labiche (Evangeline) and Louis Arceneaux (Gabriel), who met under an old oak in what is now Port Street. Emmeline is buried in the town cemetery. In the north of the town is the Acadian House Museum (history of the town).

St Martinville

See entry

New Orleans

St Francisville, north-east of Baton Rouge, is a good centre from which to visit the plantation houses of Rosedown (1835), Myrtles Plantation, Catalpa Plantation, Cottage Plantation (1785), Greenwood and Oakley, on which the painter John James Audubon (1785–1851) lived. Here he painted 32 of the finest pictures in his "Birds of America".

St Francisville

Maine (State; ME) B–F 54–58

Area:
   33,215sq.miles/86,027sq.km
Population: 1,235,000
Capital: Augusta
Popular name: Pine Tree State

Maine, the largest and most thinly populated of the New England states, lies in the extreme north-east of the United States, on the frontier with Canada. It consists of three main geographical regions. The much indented Atlantic coast with its innumerable offshore islands runs from south to north-east for a distance of more than 300 miles/500km. To the west of this coastal strip, some 60 miles/100km across, the ground rises gradually into a hilly upland region. Northern Maine is a region of lakes and morainic hills; to the west the White Mountains rise to 5270ft/1606m. More than four-fifths of the state is covered with forests (mainly pine and spruce). In the coastal regions the climate is cool temperate, under strong maritime influence; farther west the maritime influence declines.

Situation and topography

The territory that is now Maine was occupied by Indians of the Algonkian language family when the first Europeans arrived in 1498–99. In the 17th century French settlers established themselves in the area, later followed by British settlers. In 1691 Maine became part of Massachusetts. Thereafter the fur trade, logging, shipbuilding and fishing brought it prosperity. On March 15th 1820 Maine was separated from Massachusetts and became the 23th state of the Union.

History

Thanks to the state's wealth of forests the woodworking and papermaking industries are major elements in its economy. The most important product of the fisheries, now in decline, is lobsters. The predominant agricultural crop is potatoes, followed by other vegetables and poultry feed; dairy farming is also important. Other industries are leather goods, textiles and foodstuffs. Tourism is making a steadily increasing contribution to the economy.

Economy

Maine

Places of Interest in Maine

***Acadia National Park**

The Acadia National Park (area 60sq.miles/156sq.km), one of the most visited nature reserves in the United States (open throughout the year; particularly fine in the fall), lies on the coast of Maine near the Canadian peninsula of Nova Scotia. It is a region of rocky coasts, forests with clear rivers, streams and lakes, and rolling hills, offering ideal conditions for a variety of sports and leisure activities both in summer and in winter.

The core of the National Park is the hilly Mount Desert Island, on the east coast of which is the chief town, Bar Harbor. Particularly attractive are the Otter Cliffs and Otter Point, where a varied Arctic flora can be studied and numbers of birds (cormorants, seagulls, etc.) can be observed. There is a beautiful drive round the National Park on the Park Loop (20 miles/32km).

The park also includes the islands of Isle au Haut, Baker Island, Little Cranberry Island (with the Islesford Historical Museum) and Bald Porcupine as well as the southern tip of the Schoodic Peninsula (magnificent views).

Augusta

Augusta, the state capital, lies some 40 miles/64km inland. Founded by English settlers in 1628, it is now predominantly an industrial town. Features of interest are the massive State House (by Charles Bulfinch, 1832), with the Maine State Museum (natural history, economic and social history of Maine); Blaine House, the Governor's residence; and Old Fort Western (1754), with "living history" presentations.

Bangor

Bangor, formerly a loggers' town, is now a cultural and commercial centre with a number of handsome old houses. Of special interest are the Bangor Historical Museum and the Penobscot Cultural Center Museum on Indian Island.

Baxter State Park

This large nature park lies in the north of the state round Mount Katahdin, Maine's highest peak. At certain times of year a curious astronomical phenomenon can be observed when the first rays of the morning sun on the mainland strike Mount Katahdin.

Brunswick

North-east of the inlets and islands of Casco Bay is Brunswick, a commercial and educational centre. Features of interest are the house in which Harriet Beecher Stowe wrote "Uncle Tom's Cabin", the Museum of Art and the Peary-MacMillan Arctic Museum (Arctic exploration). The two museums are on the campus of the old-established Bowdoin College.

Camden

Thanks to its spectacular situation on the south side of Penobscot Bay, framed by high hills, the little town of Camden is a popular holiday resort, with excellent sport and leisure facilities.

Kennebunkport

The little coastal town of Kennebunkport, 12½ miles/20km south of Portland, was the home of the writers Kenneth Roberts, Booth Tarkington and Rachel Carson. Features of interest are the Seashore Trolley Museum, the local history collection in Town House School and Nott House (1853), with its original furnishings.

Portland

On Casco Bay is Portland (pop. 65,000), the largest town in Maine, best visited in summer (boat trips round the bay). For adults there is the Portland

Museum of Art, for children the Children's Museum of Maine. There are numbers of fine old houses in the town, including particularly the home of the Portland-born poet Longfellow (1807–82), as well as Tate House (1755) and Victoria Mansion (1855), with furniture of the period.

The picturesque little port of Wiscasset is the haunt of artists and writers. Features of interest are the Maine Art Gallery and the Lincoln County Museum. The Musical Wonder House has a collection of old mechanical musical instruments. Wiscasset

Mammoth Cave National Park   M 39

State: Kentucky
Area: 82sq.miles/212sq.km
Established: 1926

The cave is accessible throughout the year. Opening times of the Visitor Center: summer daily 7.30am–7pm, winter 8am–5pm. Season

The constant low temperature (54°F/12°C) and the high humidity of the air (87%) in the interior of the cave call for warm clothing. Stout footwear is essential.

The Mammoth Cave lies in the "Land of 10,00 Sinks" (Caveland Corridor), an area in south-western Kentucky strongly marked by karstic features of all kinds (many dolines and caverns). Situation

With over 300 miles/500km of passages so far surveyed, the Mammoth Cave is one of the world's largest known cave systems. In the course of millions of years rainwater containing small amounts of carbonic acid has dissolved the local limestone and created a labyrinth of chambers and corridors on five levels, with stalactites and stalagmites and deposits of gypsum and saltpetre. Through the lowest level flow the Echo and Styx Rivers, tributaries of the Green River. *Cave system

The part of the cave system round the western entrance was already known to the original Indian inhabitants of the region in the 1st millennium B.C. Around 1812 the recently discovered deposits of saltpetre were used in the manufacture of gunpowder. Later the cave served as a concert hall and for the treatment of lung diseases. History

The National Park administration offers a variety of tours in the cave. The Historic Tour (about 2 hours) takes in the only natural entrance to the cave, the underground Booth's Amphitheater, the 2000-year-old mummified body of an Indian and the old saltpetre quarry. The high points of the tour are the Mammoth Dome (almost 200ft/60m high) and the Ruins of Karnak with their impressive natural columns. The Half-Day Tour (about 4 hours) starts from the Carmichael Entrance and runs past gypsum efflorescences to the Snowball Dining Room, with the extraordinary rock formations (originally snow-white) on its roof, the imposing Frozen Niagara with its beautiful stalactites and stalagmites and the marvellous Crystal Lake with its crystal-clear water. The Echo River Tour (only June–Sept; about 4 hours) follows the Echo and Styx Rivers through a series of chambers and passages. The strenuous Wild Cave Tour is for experienced and properly equipped cave-explorers only. There are also boat trips on the Green River, part of which flows underground. Cave tours

Maryland

Maryland (State; MD) K/L 47–50

Area:
10,460sq.miles/27,092sq.km
Population: 4,860,000
Capital: Annapolis
Popular names: Old Line State,
Free State

Situation and topography

The state of Maryland (named after Queen Henrietta Maria, wife of Charles I) lies on both sides of Chesapeake Bay in the eastern United States, extending inland from the Atlantic to the Allegheny Mountains. The coastal region has numerous inlets and offshore sandbanks. In the west a narrow strip of land reaches into the Appalachians, reaching a height of 3360ft/ 1024m in Backbone Mountain. The eastern part of the state has a humid subtropical climate, the western part a climate of continental type. In the hills hardwood forests predominate; elsewhere the landscape is patterned by meadows and arable land.

History

The area was first explored by Captain John Smith in 1608, and in 1632 a colony was founded by Leonard Calvert, a brother of Lord Baltimore. After the arrival of 200 Catholic refugees from persecution in 1634 the inhabitants of Maryland were guaranteed religious freedom by law in 1649. The Calvert family lost their rights over the colony only in 1776, with the signing of the state's constitution and the Declaration of Independence. Maryland entered the Union as the 7th of the founding states in 1788.

Economy

The agricultural produce of the state – maize, soya beans, tobacco, fruit, potatoes and other vegetables – goes largely to supply the two cities of Baltimore and Washington. Stock-farming and oyster culture also make important contributions to the state's economy. The principal industries are steel production, engineering, foodstuffs and shipbuilding. Maryland also has substantial tourist attractions in its towns and cities, its bathing beaches and its skiing facilities.

Places of Interest in Maryland

Annapolis

The state capital, Annapolis, is the seat of the US Naval Academy, with the Academy Naval Museum. Other features of interest are the Old Senate Chamber in State House, the Governor's Mansion, the William Paca House and Gardens and the Chase-Lloyd House.

Baltimore

See entry

Cambridge

The finest of this old port town's historic houses are on the High Street. Other features of interest are the Brannock Maritime Museum, the Meredith House (1760) and the Neild Museum. The 17th century Old Trinity Church in Church Creek is one of the oldest churches in the United States.

Cumberland

The historic National Road US 40 runs through the Narrows, a wild gorge in the Allegheny Mountains.

Ellicott City

The first terminus of the US railroad system was in Ellicott City. The original station is now in the B and O Railroad Station Museum.

Great Falls of Potomac

The old Chesapeake and Ohio Canal is now a National Historic Park. Its history is documented in Great Falls Tavern and Museum in Potomac.

Ocean City

Ocean City is a busy bathing resort on the Atlantic coast with a magnificent beach of white sand. A rather quieter area is the Assateaque Islands National Seashore to the south of the town.

Massachusetts (State; MA)

Area:
 8257sq.miles/21,386sq.km
Population: 5,996,000
Capital: Boston
Popular names: Bay State,
 Old Colony

Massachusetts (from an Indian term, "big hill in the east"), one of the New England states in the north-eastern United States, is divided into two parts by the Connecticut River, flowing from north to south through the state. To the west of the river the Berkshire Hills (3491ft/1064m) and the Taconic Mountains rise above the rump plateaux of the Appalachians; to the east the central plateau slopes down gradually to the coast. Off the much indented coast, with sandy beaches towards the south end, lie numerous islands and peninsulas. In the east the climate is temperate, in the west more continental in character. Two-thirds of the area of the state is covered by mixed forests, mainly oak, Weymouth pine, spruce and hemlock.

Situation and topography

The Pilgrim Fathers who arrived in the "Mayflower" in 1620 settled in Plymouth, where in 1629 they established a community governed by strict Puritan principles. Their conflicts with the Indian population culminated in 1675–76 in King Philip's War, in which the colonists were victorious. Resistance to British rule and the movement for American independence began in Massachusetts (see Boston), and the first battle in the War of Independence was fought at Lexington in 1775. In 1780 the state adopted the constitution which is still in force. It entered the Union as the 6th state on February 6th 1788.

History

In economic terms Massachusetts is the most important of the New England states. Its highly specialised agriculture achieves high yields in the cultivation of tobacco, vegetables and fruit (particularly cranberries) and in dairy farming and poultry rearing. The state's fisheries, including lobster and shellfish culture, are also important. A major element in the economy, in addition to the commercial and services sectors, is industry, particularly engineering, foodstuffs, metalworking, printing, electrical engineering and electronics. In Harvard Massachusetts has one of the most renowned universities in the United States. The varied beauties of the landscape and the cultural attractions of the cities draw large numbers of visitors every year, making tourism an important factor in the economy.

Economy

Places of Interest in Massachusetts

20 miles/32km north-west of Boston is the Minuteman National Park, scene of the first American resistance to the British in 1775. A number of notable American writers, including Emerson, Hawthorne and Thoreau, lived here; their houses can be visited.

Concord

The inhabitants of this little town on Cape Ann have been since time immemorial fishermen and seamen. This old tradition is commemorated in the bronze statue of the Gloucester Fisherman in the harbour and the museum of the Cape Ann Historical Association. Gloucester is also noted for the artists' colony of Rocks Neck.

Gloucester

Also north-west of Boston is Lexington, where the first battle in the War of Independence took place on April 19th 1775. Features of historic interest in the town are the Minuteman Monument, the Monroe and Buckman

Lexington

Memphis

Taverns, the Hancock-Clarke House and the Museum of Our National Heritage.

Lowell
Lowell lies on the Merrimack River in northern Massachusetts. The heyday of the textile industry is recalled in two open-air museums, the Lowell National Historic Park and the Lowell Heritage State Park. Also in the town is the birthplace of the artist James MacNeill Whistler, which contains some of his pictures.

Rockport
The picturesque little fishing town of Rockport on Cape Ann has been the home of many artists. Features of interest are the Sandy Bay Historical Society and Museum, the Old Castle, the James Babson Museum and the Paper House.

*Salem
Salem, north-east of Boston on Massachusetts Bay, has one of the best historical museums in America, the Essex Institute. It preserves a number of handsome mansions of the 17th–19th centuries with their original interiors, notably the Stephen Philips Memorial Trust House. The House of Seven Gables (1668; guided visits) was the birthplace of the writer Nathaniel Hawthorne (1804–64). A particularly fine example of urban architecture can be seen in Chestnut Street.
The Peabody Museum illustrates Salem's past as a shipbuilding and commercial town (ship models, pictures, nautical equipment, etc.).

Springfield
In Springfield, in the interior of the state on the border with Connecticut, is the oldest American arms factory, where the Springfield M 1903 rifle was manufactured. The Quadrangle is a complex of four museums. The best view of Springfield's handsome old houses is from the Campanile (1905).

Worcester
Worcester lies between Boston and Springfield. Features of interest are the Art Museum (Dutch and Italian paintings) and the Higgins Armory (medieval and Renaissance weapons).

Other places of interest
Boston (see entry), Cambridge (see Boston), Cape Cod (see entry), Plymouth (see Cape Cod)

Memphis

O 35

State: Tennessee
Altitude: 260ft/80m
Population: 610,300 (Metropolitan Area 981,000)

Situation and characteristics
If Nashville (see entry) is the capital of country music, Memphis is the home of Gospel, blues and rhythm and blues. The clubs in Beale Street were for decades the objective of all the singers, mainly black, who hoped for the big chance which would lead to their "discovery". One of them was Elvis Presley, whose grave on his Graceland estate is now the chief tourist attraction of Memphis.
The city, situated at the junction of the Wolf River with the Mississippi, ranks as the greatest market for cotton and hardwoods in the world. These and other products of the surrounding area (alfalfa, soya, rice) are shipped from the second largest inland port in the United States. Industry, with over 1100 firms, also plays an important part in the city's economy.

History
Andrew Jackson, later seventh President of the United States, along with two partners established a settlement here on a site suitable for a harbour, and is therefore regarded as the founder of Memphis. The town was named Memphis because of the similarity of its situation on the high river bank to that of the Egyptian city of Memphis on the Nile. Capital of the Confederation in the early days of the Civil War, the town was taken by Union troops in 1862. In the 1920s, thanks mainly to W. C. Handy ("father of the blues"), Memphis became the great centre of black music. It gained an unhappy place in history when Martin Luther King Jr (see Famous People) was shot here on April 4th 1968.

Memphis

Sun Studios, the launching pad of many pop stars

Sights in Downtown Memphis

One of the most recent additions to the skyline of Memphis is the Great American Pyramid at 1 Auction Avenue, on the banks of the river. The steel and glass façade of this 32-storey structure, modelled on the Pyramid of Cheops, encloses an auditorium with seating for 22,000 spectators as well as multi-media shows on the world of the ancient Egyptians and American music. An elevator runs up the outside to a viewing platform.

*Great American Pyramid

On Mud Island (also known as Festival Island), in the Mississippi, is a ¾ mile/1.2km long model of the course of the river from Cairo, Illinois, to the Gulf of Mexico. The model is part of the Mississippi River Museum, the central feature of this family park (restaurants, boat trips, concerts) on the island.

Mud Island

To the east of Riverside Drive is Beale Street. Little remains of its charm in the days when the blues resounded from the many bars along the street. Almost all the old buildings have been pulled down and replaced by replicas, and the music heard in the present-day establishments is often a mere shadow of the real thing. The great days of the past are recalled only by W. C. Handy's house (No. 325), Handy Park and the statue of Elvis Presley at the corner of Main Street.

Beale Street

A short distance south of Beale Street, at 406 Mulberry Street, is the Lorraine Motel, where Martin Luther King Jr was shot in 1968. The building is now occupied by the National Civil Rights Museum, which traces the history of civil rights movements in the United States. Its centrepiece is the hotel room with the balcony on which Martin Luther King was killed.

*National Civil Rights Museum

West of Beale Street, at 706 Union Avenue, are the legendary Sun Studios, recalling the great days of blues and rock'n'roll. Here began the recording careers of Muddy Waters, B. B. King, Elvis Presley, Jerry Lee Lewis, Roy Orbison and many more.

Sun Studios

Mesa Verde National Park

Outer Districts

Historic houses — On Adams Avenue, which runs east from Mud Island, there are a number of handsome 19th century mansions (restored). The finest are the Magevney House (No. 198) of 1836, the Mallory-Neely House (No. 652) of 1855 and the Woodruff-Fontaine House (No. 680) of 1870, which contains a costume collection.

Overton Park — To the east of downtown Memphis, between Poplar Avenue and East Parkway, are Overton Park and Overton Square, the centre of midtown Memphis's night life. In addition to numerous restaurants and bars there is the Memphis Brooks Museum of Art, the oldest and largest art museum in Tennessee, with a collection which ranges from pictures by way of printed graphic art to textiles. In the north-west corner of the park are Memphis Zoo and Aquarium.

*Pink Palace Museum and Planetarium — South-east of Overton Park, at 3050 Central Avenue, is the Pink Palace Museum (geology, flora and fauna and history of the Middle South). It is housed in a villa which belonged to Clarence Saunders, who in 1916 founded the Piggly Wiggly supermarket chain (still flourishing).

Chucalissa Indian Village — In the south-west of the city is the T. O. Fuller State Park, in which are the excavated and partly restored remains of an Indian village discovered by archaeologists from Memphis State University. The village is believed to have been inhabited from about A.D. 900 to 1500. There is an interesting site museum.

**Graceland

Opening times:
Mar.–Oct.
daily 9am–5pm
(Memorial Day to Labor Day 8am–6pm);
Nov.–Feb.
daily exc. Tue.
9am–5pm

Even though not everyone shares the cult for Elvis Presley (see Famous People), Graceland, the palatial house at 3734 Elvis Presley Boulevard which he acquired in 1957 is a national place of pilgrimage. Here fans of the "King" can walk through his home, lay flowers on his tomb, see his two private jets and his automobiles and stock up in the museum shop with mementoes of their idol, who lived here in his days of glory and in the last unhappy years of alcohol and drugs – though there is no reference to these years on the guided tours of the house.

Mesa Verde National Park M 17

State: Colorado
Area: 80sq.miles/210sq.km
Established: 1906

Season — The National Park, the Museum and Spruce Tree House are open throughout the year; other facilities are closed in winter.

Situation and characteristics — The Mesa Verde ("Green Table") is a tabular hill covered with coniferous forest which reaches a height of 8573ft/2613m, rising abruptly to 2000ft/600m above the semi-desert foreland of the Rockies in the extreme south-west of Colorado. It is of interest not so much for the natural landscape as for the relics of a past Indian culture. Around the beginning of the Christian era the river valleys in this region were occupied by nomadic Indians who later took to a settled life. In the 6th century, for reasons that are not understood, they moved back to the densely forested plateau and its gorges, where they found fertile soils and a sufficiency of water. Here considerable remains of rock habitations (pit houses on the plateau, cliff dwellings on the sides of the canyons), multi-storey houses of adobe or stone built round a central square (pueblos) and cult sites (kivas) of the Anasazi Indians have been preserved. In addition the discovery was made of large quantities of implements and craft objects dating from the heyday of the settlements between the 11th and 13th centuries. Then in the 14th century the inhabitants left their settlements for some unknown reason and moved south-west.

There are an estimated 4000 statutorily protected archaeological sites in the National Park. Admission to the park is restricted and strictly controlled, and some areas can be visited only in the company of a park ranger. *Archaeological sites

From the entrance on the north side of the park a winding road leads to Morfield Village (campground, services). It then continues past Montezuma Valley Overlook and Park Point, the highest point in the park (8572ft/2613m; access road), to the Far View Visitor Center. From there a 13 mile/21km long road runs to Wetherill Mesa (summer only, 8am–4.30pm), with the Step House, which shows remains of two periods of settlement (c. 7th and 13th c.), and the Long House (only under the guidance of a park ranger), the second largest ruin in the park, with a large open space in which dances and ceremonies were performed. The other road leads from the Visitor Center to Chapin Mesa, passing the Far View Ruins (access road), which were occupied between the 10th and 14th centuries, and Cedar Tree Tower (access road), from which it is a short walk to the terraced fields once cultivated by the Indians. In 25 miles/40km the road comes to the Park Headquarters Area, with the Chapin Mesa Museum (archaeological remains, Indian arts and crafts). To the south-east, on the edge of Spruce Canyon, is Spruce Tree House, the best preserved settlement in the park and one of the largest, with 114 rooms and 8 kivas.

Wetherill Mesa

Chaplin Mesa Museum

Spruce Tree House

The Museum is the starting-point of Ruins Road Drive, which takes in the main features of the Mesa Verde in two long loops, with a total length of 12 miles/19km. The high spots in the western part of the park are the Square Tower House, a four-storey structure built against the rock wall of the Navajo Canyon; the Sun Point Pueblo, the remains of a village which was pulled down by its inhabitants in the 13th century to provide material for new dwellings in a cave in nearby Cliff Canyon; and the unfinished Sun Temple, a large cult building on a D-shaped plan. On the eastern loop of the road are the 299-room Cliff Palace, in a large cave on the east side of Cliff Canyon – the largest cave settlement in the park and the first to be discovered in 1888 – and the Balcony House, built into a wide, low recess on the wall of Soda Canyon.

Sun Temple

*Cliff Palace

*Balcony House

A permit must be obtained from the National Park administration (see Practical Information, National Parks) for hiking on the Spruce Canyon Trail (2 miles/3.2km) and the Pictograph Point Trail, in the area of the Chapin Mesa Museum; no permit is required for the Prater Ridge Trail (7¾ miles/12.5km) or the Knife Edge Trail (1½ miles/2.4km), in the Morfield Village area.

Hiking trails

Miami / Miami Beach

Y 45

State: Florida
Altitude: 0–25ft/0–8m
Population: 386,000 (Metropolitan Area 2 million)

The city of Miami lies on the south-east side of the Florida peninsula, separated from the Atlantic Ocean by the Biscayne Bay lagoon and Miami Beach with its huge hotels and apartment blocks. Miami's pleasant winter climate has led to its mushroom growth into a vastly popular holiday resort which draws more than 8 million visitors every year. It has the world's biggest passenger seaport, a port of call for numerous cruise ships, and a

Situation and characteristics

Miami / Miami Beach

large international airport. It has more than 600 large and medium-sized hotels, numerous motels, several thousand restaurants and cafés and some 50 foreign consulates – reflecting the city's importance as a centre for business as well as holiday travellers. Following changes in banking law and the resultant inflow of capital from Latin America and Saudi Arabia Miami has developed into a leading financial centre. There is also considerable industry in the Miami region, notably the aircraft and space and foodstuffs industries. The film industry and bio-medical research institutes have also recently developed.

History

The first European to sail into Biscayne Bay was the Spanish navigator Ponce de León in 1513. In 1567 Spanish Jesuits established the mission station of Tequesta, on the site of Miami, and the settlement which grew up round it became a base for the Spanish silver fleet on its voyage to Europe. After the Spanish withdrawal in 1821 the first American settlers came here to grow cotton and tropical crops. In 1871 William Brickell established a trading post on the estuary of the Miami River (the Indian name Mayami means "Great Water"). Five years later Julia Tuttle, an incomer from the North, acquired a considerable area of land to the north of the river, and on her initiative Henry M. Flagler extended his East Coast Railroad to Miami in 1895–96. The Royal Palm Hotel was then built at the rail terminus. The Spanish–American War of 1898 brought great profits to Miami. The development of the offshore island of Miami Beach now began. During the Second World War Miami was a hospital and recreation centre. After the war began the building boom which is still continuing.

Fidel Castro's revolution on Cuba led many Cubans to leave home and settle in the Miami area, and Cuban refugees played a considerable part in the development of the Miami conurbation. In the early eighties there was a further great wave of refugees from Cuba. This period also saw an influx of refugees from Haiti, who for the most part live the life of underdogs in the Miami area. In August 1992 Hurricane Andrew devastated much of southern Florida. In 1993 Miami acquired an unsavoury reputation for attacks on tourists.

Sights in Miami

Old Town Trolley Tour

Bayside Marketplace is the starting-point of frequent trolley tours of the main sights of Miami and Miami Beach.

Biscayne Boulevard
*Bayfront Park

Miami's main traffic artery is the southern section of palm-lined Biscayne Boulevard, which is flanked by imposing tower blocks.

Bayfront Park, on the east side of Biscayne Boulevard, has recently been completely replanned. An attractive feature is the electronically controlled Pepper Fountain. Also in the park are an amphitheatre which is used for musical performances of all kinds and a tower for laser illuminations, as well as three important monuments: the Torch of Friendship, symbolising Miami's relationships with the countries of Central and South America; the World War II Memorial; and the Challenger Memorial, commemorating the crew of the Challenger spacecraft which exploded in 1986.

*Bayside Marketplace/ Miamarina

Just north of Bayfront Park are Bayside Marketplace and the Miamarina (formerly Pier 5, which features in the television series "Miami Vice"), with good shops and restaurants which attract many visitors. Here too is the "Bounty", a replica of an 18th century three-master on which the film "Mutiny on the Bounty" (with Marlon Brando as Fletcher Christian) was shot in 1962.

Freedom Tower

The most striking building on Biscayne Boulevard is the Freedom Tower (1925), in "wedding-cake" style. One of the oldest skyscrapers in the southeastern United States, it was for many years the headquarters of the "Miami Herald".

Flagler Street

From Biscayne Boulevard the busy Flagler Street runs west to the Guzman Cultural Center (1926; formerly the Olympia Theatre, renovated in 1972 for its present function), Dade County Court House (1926), the ultra-modern

Miami / Miami Beach

Miami Downtown

500 m / 0,3 mi

1. One Biscayne Tower
2. First Federal Building
3. DuPont Building
4. Metro Dade Cultural Center
5. Federal Building
6. Gesù Catholic Church
7. Federal Court House
8. First Methodist Sanctuary
9. First Christian Church
10. Central Baptist Church
11. Freedom Tower
12. Trinity Episcopal Church
13. Flagler Memorial Library
14. Temple Israel
15. First Church of Christ Scientist
16. Museum of Modern Art
17. Miamarina
18. Torch of Friendship
19. Columbus Monument
20. Memorial Library
21. Band Shell
22. World Trade Center
23. Convention Center

— Metro Rail
○ Metro Mover

© Baedeker

Miami / Miami Beach

In Miami Harbor

Federal Building (Government Center) and the attractive Mediterranean-style Metro Dade Cultural Center, with the Center of Fine Arts (periodic special exhibitions), the Main Library and the Historical Museum of Southern Florida (history of southern Florida, early Indian tribes, pirates, pioneers; 3 D film on Miami).

*Centrust Bank Tower

A more recent landmark of downtown Miami is the 52-storey Centrust Bank Tower (1987), which is brilliantly floodlit in many colours at night. It was designed by I. M. Pei, America's best known contemporary architect, in association with Spillis Candela and Partners. The floodlighting scheme, with several hundred 1000-watt lamps and different colours for different occasions (for example green on St Patrick's Day and red on St Valentine's Day) was devised by Douglas Leigh.

Southeast Financial Center

The Centrust Bank is overtopped by the ultra-modern Southeast Financial Center with its 55 storeys.

Little Havana/ *Calle Ocho

From Bayfront Park (Brickell Avenue) 8th Street runs west over the Miami River. Outside the city centre with its skyscrapers it is known as Calle Ocho, and continues into the Tamiami Trail, which runs through the Everglades (see entry). The district on the west side of downtown Miami through which it runs is known as Little Havana because of the many Latinos, particularly Cuban exiles, who live here: hence also the Spanish name Calle Ocho ("Street 8"). Between SW 12th Avenue and SW 27th Avenue is an area of shops, small markets and cheerful cafés and restaurants with a friendly and relaxed atmosphere. The everyday language of Little Havana is Spanish. Planning controls seek to maintain the "Cuban" character of 8th Street.

Orange Bowl

A particular attraction in this area is the Orange Bowl, a football stadium which is also used for the Orange Bowl Musical Festival.

Miami / Miami Beach

The Port of Miami, on two artificial islands (Dodge Island and Lummus Island), is now the world's leading passenger seaport, which can accommodate over a dozen cruise liners at the same time. It handles some 3 million cruise passengers a year, most of them heading for the Bahamas or the Caribbean.

Port of Miami

The MacArthur Causeway, a "road on stilts", crosses Biscayne Bay to Watson Park, with the Japanese Garden (pagoda, tea-house, waterfall), and a Tivoli-style amusement park. Nearby are a helicopter pad (sight seeing flights) and a seaplane landing-stage (excursions to the Bahamas).

Watson Park

Brickell Avenue, a residential street for well-to-do old Miami families, is now lined by modern high-rise office blocks and condominiums. It is famed as the "Wall Street of Miami".

*Brickell Avenue

At the southern tip of Virginia Key is Miami Seaquarium (open: daily 9am–6.30pm; last admissions 5pm), the largest seawater aquarium in southern Florida.

*Seaquarium

The Bear Cut Bridge (toll) leads to the island of Key Biscayne, famed as the venue of major golf and tennis tournaments.

*Key Biscayne

In the 1840s dark-skinned incomers from the Bahamas, known as Conchs, began to settle to the south of Miami. Later the Caribbean atmosphere appealed to artists and intellectuals from New England, who came to spend the winter here. There are now numbers of exclusive shops and restaurants on Grand Avenue, in the Mayfair Shopping Center and on Cocowalk, which was opened in 1991.

*Coconut Grove

To the south of the Rickenbacker Causeway, set in classical-style gardens with fountains, is the beautiful Villa Vizcaya (3251 South Miami Avenue; open: daily 9.30am–4.30pm). The mansion, in Italian Renaissance style, was built in 1912–16 as the winter residence of the wealthy harvester manufacturer James Deering. Its opulently appointed rooms now house a collection of French, Spanish and Italian art, as well as a variety of furniture, tapestries and sculpture and a collection of old Baedekers.

*Villa Vizcaya (Dade County Art Museum)

South of Coconut Grove, on a lagoon, is the select Cable Estate, a district of luxury villas set in beautiful gardens with their own yacht moorings.

*Cable Estate

South-west of the city centre is the suburb – now not quite so select as it originally was – of Coral Gables (pop. 47,000), laid out in Mediterranean style by George Merrick from 1926 onwards to the design of his father, with extensive parks and sports grounds.
Notable features are City Hall, the Miracle Mile, the Colonnade Building, the Venetian Pool (a swimming pool in a quarry of coral limestone) and Coral Way, with Coral Gables House (1907). A striking architectural feature is the former Biltmore Hotel, designed by George Merrick in the 1920s. The Lowe Art Museum of the University of Miami has collections of the arts and crafts of the Pueblo and Navajo Indians, American painting and old masters of the Renaissance and Baroque (the Kress Collection).

*Coral Gables

The main attractions of South Miami are the Parrot Jungle (parrots, flamingoes, etc.), the Metro Zoo and the Moorish-style district of Opa Locka, built in the twenties.

South Miami

In recent years the Miami conurbation has spread ever farther south. Highway US 1 runs south through the suburban districts of South Miami, Kendall, Rockdale, Perrine, Goulds, Princeton and Leisure City to Homestead. This area was ravaged in August 1992 by Hurricane Andrew, which left a trail of devastation across the south of Dade County, destroying large numbers of houses and making tens of thousands of people homeless.

South Dade

Miami / Miami Beach

Miami Beach

Situation and characteristics

From Miami five causeways and bridges cross Biscayne Bay to a narrow strip of land 10 miles/16km long. The small beach settlement which grew up here developed within a few decades into the largest holiday, entertainment and bathing resort in the United States.

History

In 1912 this was merely a small sandy island in Biscayne Bay; then John Collins, founder of the settlement, and Carl Fisher, a millionaire who had already built the Indianapolis motor-racing track, set about developing it. In the twenties, thirties and forties there was a great flowering of Art Deco here. After the Second World War Miami Beach enjoyed a further boom; but regrettably it also attracted many criminals, including drug bosses and arms salesmen.

**Art Deco District

The Art Deco District, now statutorily protected, extends between 5th Street in the south and Indian Creek in the north and between Ocean Drive/Collins Avenue and Lennox Avenue. It contains several hundred buildings, mostly dating from the thirties and restored in recent years. This

Miami / Miami Beach

Bird's eye view of Miami Beach

historic district, decried in the sixties as the "old people's home of the United States", has now taken on an astonishing new lease of life. Many of the old hotels and apartments have been restored to their former splendour, and there are numerous inviting cafés and restaurants advertising their attractions with coloured neon signs.

Ocean Drive is lined with handsome Art Deco buildings, many of which have featured in television advertisements and in films. Particularly notable are the Beacon (732 Ocean Drive; by Henry O. Nelson, 1926), the Colony Hotel (736 Ocean Drive; by Henry Hohauser, 1936), Waldorf Towers (860 Ocean Drive; by Albert Anis, 1937), the Breakwater (940 Ocean Drive; by Anton Skislewicz, 1939), the Cardozo (1300 Ocean Drive; by Henry Hohauser, 1939), with a bar which is busy night and day, and the Cavalier (1320 Ocean Drive; by Roy F. France, 1936).

*Ocean Drive

Below Ocean Drive is a broad beach of firm white sand which is busy throughout the year.

The main traffic artery of Miami Beach is Collins Avenue, known as the Strip, which is also flanked by handsome Art Deco buildings. Among them are Tiffany's (801 Collins Avenue; by L. Murray Dixon, 1939), the Franklin (860 Collins Avenue; by V. H. Nellenbogen, 1934), Fairmont (1000 Collins Avenue; by L. Murray Dixon, 1939), with a famous café terrace, Essex House (1001 Collins Avenue; by Henry Hohauser, 1938), one of Hohauser's most interesting buildings in the style known as Nautical Modernism, the former Hoffman's Cafeteria (1450 Collins Avenue; by Hohauser, 1939), which became the Club Ovo and China Club, Haddon Hall (1500 Collins Avenue; by L. Murray Dixon, 1941), the St Moritz tower block (1565 Collins Avenue; by Roy F. France, 1939), the Surfcomber apartment block (1717 Collins Avenue; by MacKay and Gibbs, 1948) and Greystone (1926 Collins Avenue; by Hohauser, 1939). Also on Collins Avenue are three of the largest

*Collins Avenue

305

Miami / Miami Beach

Art Deco on Ocean Drive

Art Deco hotels, built in the forties, the National, the Delano and the Ritz Plaza. The streamlined structures and architectural detail are designed to recall 20th century means of transport – rockets, submarines, aircraft.

Washington Avenue

Miami Beach's principal business and shopping street is Washington Avenue, which also has a number of notable Art Deco buildings. The George Washington Hotel (534 Washington Avenue; by William P. Brown, 1924) was one of the first seafront hotels in Miami Beach. Other fine examples of Art Deco are the Taft Hotel (1044 Washington Avenue; by Hohauser, 1936), the Kenmore (1050 Washington Avenue; by Antom Skislewicz, 1936), the Main Post Office (1300 Washington Avenue; by Howard L. Cheney, 1939), in Federal Deco style, with a decorative rotunda, and Old City Hall (1130 Washington Avenue; by Martin Luther Hampton, 1927).

*Española Way

Spanish-style Española Way was once favoured by artists, but later degenerated into a red light district. Its former charm has recently been rediscovered. The richly decorated façades were originally designed by Robert Taylor in 1925, and have recently been restored by Polonia Restoration. A particularly striking building is the Cameo Theater (by Robert Collins, 1938) at the end of Española Way.

Euclid Avenue

Notable buildings on Euclid Avenue are the Denis (No. 841; by Arnold Southwell, 1938), the Enjoie (No. 928; by Albert Anis and Henry J. Maloney, 1935–36) and the Siesta (No. 1110; by Edward A. Nolan, 1936).

Meridian Avenue

The Mediterranean-style Palm Gardens complex (No. 760) was built in 1923 to the design of H. H. Mundy.

*21st Street

Notable Art Deco buildings on 21st Street are the former luxury Plymouth Hotel (No. 226; by Anton Skislewicz, 1940) and the neighbouring Adams Hotel (by L. Murray Dixon, 1938). A masterpiece by Henry Hohauser is the

Governor (No. 435; 1939). Nearby is the Tyler Apartment Hotel (No. 430; by L. Murray Dixon, 1937). At No. 300 is the Abbey (by Albert Anis, 1940). At the corner of Washington Avenue and 21st Street is the clubhouse of the municipal golf course (by August Geiger, 1916; restored).

The Bass Museum of Art (Collins Park; open: Tue.–Sat. 10am–5pm, Sun. 1–5pm), built in 1930 to the design of Russell T. Pancoast. Built of coral limestone in a style reminiscent of Maya architecture, it has fine reliefs by Gustav Bohland. The Museum has pictures by both old and modern masters, including works by Dürer, Rubens and some of the Impressionists.

*Bass Museum of Art

Other Sights in Miami Beach

Near Española Way is the Lincoln Road Mall, a shopping street, now pedestrianised, which became known in the fifties as the "Fifth Avenue of the South".

Lincoln Road Mall

The Colony Theatre at 1049 Lincoln Road (by R. A. Benjamin, 1934) is a classic example of Art Deco. Reopened with great pomp in 1976, it is now one of the focal points of the city's cultural life.

*Colony Theatre

The Municipal Park lies almost exactly in the centre of Miami Beach. Its particular features of interest are the modern City Hall (with a piece of sculpture, "Red Sea Road"), the Miami Beach Garden Center and Conservatory (rare tropical plants, flower shows) and the gigantic Convention Center (enlarged 1988).

*Municipal Park

Behind the Convention Center is the Holocaust Memorial, commemorating the 6 million Jews who died a violent death before and during the Second World War.

Holocaust Memorial

Nearby is the Theater of the Performing Arts (3000 seats), which now bears the name of the comedian Jackie F. Gleason. Many Broadway productions are put on here as well as classic plays.

*Theater of the Performing Arts

Adjoining the theatre is the Walk of the Stars, on which many stage stars have left their footprints and signatures.

Walk of the Stars

The dominant building in the northern part of Collins Avenue (No. 4441) is the Fontainebleau Hilton Hotel, built in the sixties, with over 1200 rooms and suites. Among its amenities are a spa pavilion, an artificial grotto complete with waterfall, a tropical lagoon and a swimming pool (which features in the James Bond film "Goldfinger") and an attractive beach bar. On a high wall at the south entrance to the hotel complex is a large mural by Richard Haas depicting what is behind the wall.

*Fontainebleau Hilton ("Big Blue")

Along the beach from 21st Street to 46th Street, a distance of some 2 miles/3km, runs a boardwalk which is frequented from early morning until late at night by promenaders and joggers.

Beachfront Promenade

Indian Creek – frequently the setting for dramatic film chases by land and water – separates northern Miami Beach with its hotels and apartment blocks from the exclusive residential district of Alton Road.

Indian Creek

At the east end of the MacArthur Causeway is an ultra-modern yachting marina with several hundred moorings (boats available for charter, deep-sea angling, diving expeditions, glass-bottomed boats).

International Yacht Harbor

In northern Miami Beach is the Monastery of St Bernard, built in Segovia in 1141, which was transported to this site and re-erected in the 1950s at the expense of the publishing magnate William Randolph Hearst.

Monastery of St Bernard

Miami / Miami Beach

Star Island
Palm Island
Hibiscus Island
— Between the MacArthur and the Venetian Causeway are these three artificial islands, the home of many prominent figures, including Al Capone and Elizabeth Taylor.

Flagler Memorial — On an islet to the north of Star Island is an obelisk commemorating Henry Morrison Flagler, whose Florida East Coast Railroad helped Miami to become a great tourist centre.

Michigan (State; MI) B–H 38–43

Area:
58,525sq.miles/151,585sq.km
Population: 9,368,000
Capital: Lansing
Popular names: Great Lakes State, Wolverine State

Situation and topography — Michigan, a region of many lakes in the Middle West, on the frontier with Canada, is divided into an upper and a lower part by the Straits of Mackinac. Upper Michigan, between Lake Superior in the north and Lake Michigan in the south, consists of an eastern region with a good deal of marshland and a western section which is hillier and more rugged, while Lower Michigan, between Lake Michigan in the west and Lakes Huron and Erie in the east, is a gently undulating tableland. In Upper Michigan, with a moderately continental climate, temperatures in winter, with continuing north-west winds, can fall as low as −47°F/−44°C. Fully half the area of the state is forest-covered, with mixed deciduous forests and, in the north, coniferous forests.

History — From the early 17th century French missionaries and fur-traders began to move into the territory of Michigan, then inhabited by Algonquin Indians, and in 1686 founded the first European settlement at Sault Ste Marie. The French with their Indian allies were defeated by the British in 1763, and twenty years later, under the Peace of Paris in 1783, the area passed to the United States. In 1794, after repeated bloody clashes, the Indian tribes were finally defeated. Michigan was incorporated as an independent territory in 1805, was occupied by British forces in 1812–13 and was admitted to the Union as the 26th state on January 26th 1837.

Economy — Michigan's agriculture produces mainly grain, root crops and soya beans, together with considerable quantities of cattle feed and even wine. The most important element in its economy is industry, lying as it does in the "manufacturing belt" of the United States. Thanks to its convenient situation the dominant automobile industry developed in Detroit, together with various associated supply industries. The state's tourist and holiday trade is increasing in importance, thanks to its facilities for winter sports, hiking and other leisure activities. Lakes Michigan and Superior have some of the most beautiful freshwater beaches in North America.

Places of Interest in Michigan

Ann Arbor — Ann Arbor, to the west of Detroit (see entry), is the seat of the University of Michigan, founded in 1837. Features of interest on the campus are the neo-Gothic Law Quadrangle, several museums (science, art, archaeology) and a botanic garden.

Detroit — See entry

The little town of Frankenmuth, north-west of Detroit, was founded in 1845 by immigrants from Franconia in Germany. Their houses, of traditional Franconian type, strike Americans in particular as quaint.

Frankenmuth

Grand Rapids, in western Lower Michigan, was the boyhood home of Gerald Ford, 38th President of the United States. Among the exhibits in the Museum which bears his name is a model of the President's Oval Office in the White House. The Meyer May House was designed by Frank Lloyd Wright.

Grand Rapids

The Isle Royale (area 430sq.miles/1115sq.km) lies in north-western Lake Superior near the Canadian frontier. Its varied topography, shaped by Ice Age glaciers (with many lakes, streams and fjords), its dense deciduous and coniferous forests and its rich wild life (elks, wolves, foxes, otters, ospreys, herring gulls, falcons, trout, etc.) attract many visitors to this relatively unspoiled tract of country, which can be explored on waymarked hiking trails and boat trips.

*Isle Royale National Park

The state capital, Lansing (to the west of Detroit), has a Capitol modelled on the one in Washington DC, a Historical Museum and a Transport Museum (old-time automobiles and steam engines). East Lansing is the seat of Michigan State University, whose campus is an extremely beautiful park.

Lansing/ East Lansing

The name of this island in the narrow strait between Lakes Huron and Michigan comes from the Algonquin word for "big turtle". It was once of great strategic importance, and a British fort built in the late 18th century above the Straits of Mackinac was the scene of fierce fighting between British and French forces. Fourteen buildings have been restored, and 80% of the island (on which private automobiles are banned) is now a State Park. There are ferry services from St Ignace and Mackinaw City (where there is a restored fur-trading post with "living history" presentations).

*Mackinac Island

The main importance of the American–Canadian double town of Sault Ste Marie (known locally as the Soo) lies in the 1¼ mile/2km long canals on the St Mary River (navigable from mid April to mid December) linking Lakes Huron and Superior – the world's most important waterway, on which 100 million tons of goods are transported annually. The ships pass through two mighty locks (the Soo Locks), one on the Canadian and the other on the American side, which can be seen on boat trips.

*Sault Ste Marie

Milwaukee   F 37

State: Wisconsin. Altitude: 580ft/177m
Population: 610,000 (Metropolitan Area 1.7 million)

The city of Milwaukee lies some 90 miles/145km north of Chicago (see entry) on the west side of Lake Michigan at the inflow of the Milwaukee River, which is joined within the city area by two tributaries, the Menomenee and the Kinickinnic. The town grew out of a trading post established in the 18th century near the Indian village of Melleoki. Much of the population is of German origin, and the city has been called the German Athens of America. Milwaukee is now a commercial and industrial city (Miller, Pabst and Schlitz breweries, Harley Davidson motorcycle factory, engineering, electronics, printing), with an important port accessible all year round on the St Lawrence Seaway. It is also a considerable cultural centre, with several universities and colleges (Marquette University, Wisconsin University, etc.) and a world-famed symphony orchestra.

Situation and characteristics

Sights in Milwaukee

The main sight on the Lakefront is the War Memorial Center (1957; Tue.– Sun. noon–5pm), commemorating the dead of the Second World War and the Korean War; it was designed by the celebrated architect Eero Saarinen.

Lakefront
*War Memorial Centre

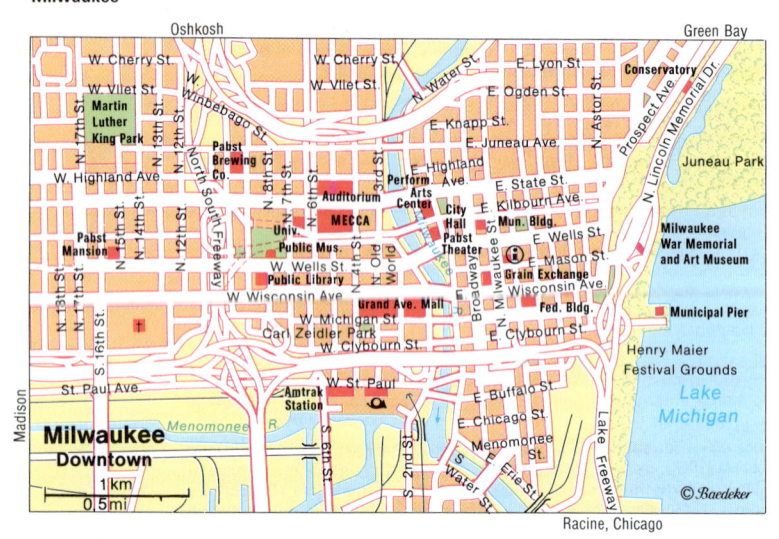

Milwaukee

*Milwaukee Art Museum	In the same complex is the Milwaukee Art Museum (750 North Lincoln Memorial Drive), another striking building, with collections which include pictures by French and German Impressionists and works by contemporary artists.
Municipal Pier/ Henry Maier Festival Grounds	To the south of the War Memorial Center are the Municipal Pier and the Henry Maier Festival Grounds, where the famous SummerFest is held annually in June/July.
Downtown East *First Wisconsin Center	To the west of the Lakefront is the First Wisconsin Center, the city's tallest building, erected in 1974 to the design of the famous architectural firm SOM. From the observatory on the 41st floor there are magnificent panoramic views.
Federal Court	A short distance west is the Federal Court, in a venerable granite building dating from 1892.
Grain Exchange	To the north-west is the Milwaukee Grain Exchange (Milwaukee and Madison Streets).
*City Hall/ *Pabst Theater/ *Performing Arts Center	Farther north-west, on the east bank of the Milwaukee River, is the old heart of the city, with the late 19th century City Hall (by Armand Koch), for many years the great landmark of Milwaukee. Beyond it is another fine late 19th century building, the Pabst Theater, built at the expense of the brewing magnate F. Pabst. To the north of this is the modern Performing Arts Center (by H. Weese, 1969).
Downtown West Père Marquette Park	On the west bank of the Milwaukee River is the Père Marquette Park, commemorating the French Jesuit who was the first European to reach this part of America (1674). Here too is the Milwaukee County Historical Museum.
Old-World 3rd Street	Beyond this, running north–south, is Old-World 3rd Street, on which the city's German immigrants left their stamp (restaurants, shops, etc.).
Civic Center/ MECCA	The heart of Downtown West is the Civic Center, with the Milwaukee Exposition and Convention Center and Arena (MECCA; used for exhibitions, trade fairs, congresses and sporting events), built in 1974. Close by are the Milwaukee Arena and the Milwaukee Auditorium.
*Grand Avenue Mall	The Civic Center and MECCA are linked by skyways (covered walkways high above the traffic) with the imposing Grand Avenue Mall, a multi-storey

Minneapolis / St Paul

consumers' paradise with great numbers of shops, restaurants, fast food stalls and leisure facilities (including the Spirit of Milwaukee Theater). In the immediate neighbourhood are other modern structures – the Federal Building, the Reuss Federal Plaza, the Commerce Building.

Farther west is the Carl Zeidler Park, an oasis of peace bounded on the north by Michigan Avenue.

Carl Zeidler Park

To the west of the Civic Center is the Public Museum (on right), with fascinating natural history displays (dinosaurs, eco-system of tropical rain forest, etc.). Beyond this (on left) is the Public Library, with an interesting exhibition on science and technology, "Discover the World".

*Public Museum

Beyond Interstate 43 is the campus of the private Marquette University (10,000 students), founded in 1864, with two notable sacred buildings, the 15th century St Joan of Arc Chapel, transferred here from its original site in eastern France, and the neo-Gothic Gesù Church, modelled on the original Gesù in Rome.

Westside
Marquette
University

North-east of the university campus is the Pabst Mansion (1893), built for the brewer F. Pabst, with a very elegant interior.

*Pabst Mansion

Farther west is the Tripoli Temple (West Wisconsin Avenue and 30th Street), which resembles a Near Eastern mosque. In fact it has been since the 1920s a freemasons' lodge.

Tripoli Temple

At 9400 West Congress Street is the Greek Orthodox Church of the Annunciation (1961), by Frank Lloyd Wright.

*Greek Orthodox Church

The Miller Brewery on West State Street and the Pabst Brewery on West Juneau Street welcome visitors Mon.–Fri. 10am–3.30pm.

Brewery visits

The world-famed Harley Davidson motorcycle came into being at the corner of Highland Boulevard and 38th Street. Here in 1901 William S. Harley, Arthur and Walter Davidson and a German engineer produced the first Harley Davidson. They went into mass production in 1903, and thereafter the fame of the Harley Davidson spread round the world. The present very modern factory (Harley Davidson Engine Plant, 11700 West Capitol Drive) on Interstate 45 can be visited (guided tours Apr.–Sept. Mon., Wed. and Fri. 9 and 10.30am and 12.30pm).

*Harley Davidson factory

On the western outskirts of the city is Milwaukee County Zoo, which specialises in the breeding of endangered species.

*Milwaukee County Zoo

Minneapolis / St Paul

E 32/33

State: Minnesota
Altitude: 690–980ft/210–299m
Population: Minneapolis 368,400, St Paul 272,000
  (Metropolitan Area 2.46 million

Minneapolis and St Paul, the Twin Cities on the upper course of the Mississippi, together form the largest city in Minnesota, but yet are very different from one another. While the larger city of Minneapolis is the quintessence of the glistening modern American city, the more spaciously laid out St Paul, built on terraces above the Mississippi, has preserved something of the character of an old frontier town (e.g. in Summit Avenue). Features common to both cities, however, are their extensive parks and their economic importance as centres of the electronics, printing and publishing industries. Minneapolis is also the commercial centre of one of the largest farming areas in the United States and has one of the largest grain exchanges in the world.

Situation and characteristics

St Paul, the older of the two cities, originated as a military post established at the junction of the Minnesota River with the Mississippi in 1807 which later became Fort Snelling. From 1823 it became a port of call for river boats. In 1840 fur-traders and trappers established a settlement nearby,

History

Minneapolis / St Paul

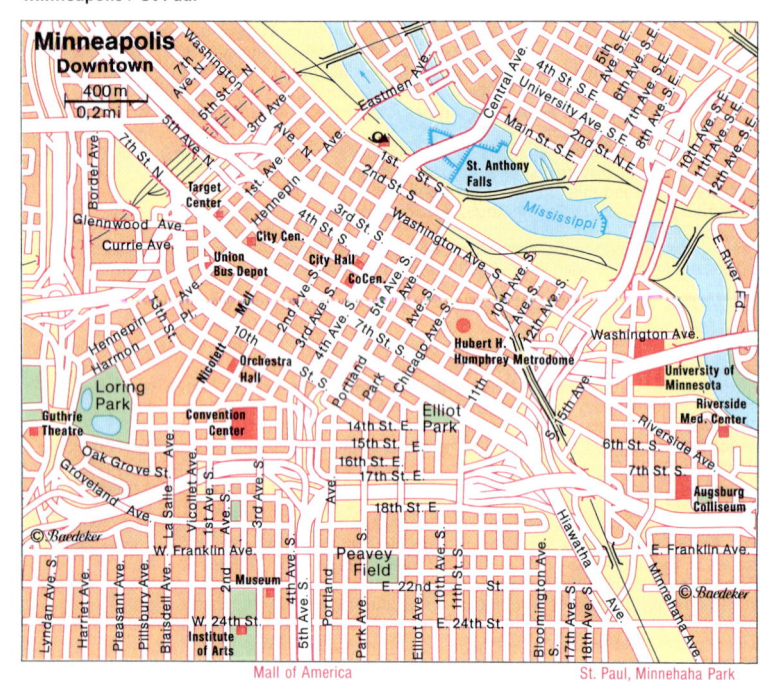

originally called Pig's Eye after the leader of the group, a Frenchman, but renamed St Paul in the following year. When Minnesota was incorporated as a town St Paul was declared state capital.

Minneapolis grew out of two mills built at the St Anthony Falls in 1847. Although this was Indian country, other settlements soon followed, and these displaced the Indians, whose reservation was moved elsewhere. The city's name comes from the Indian word *minne* (water) and the Greek *polis* (city).

Sights in Minneapolis

*Nicollet Mall	The main shopping centre in downtown Minneapolis is Nicollet Mall, a beautifully laid out, traffic-calmed precinct with a great concentration of shops, restaurants, galleries and other attractions like the Minneapolis Planetarium. The central feature of the complex, over which looms the 775ft/236m high tower of the IDS Center, is the Crystal Court, from which a network of glazed skyways lead to other buildings.
City Hall	To the east of Nicollet Mall is City Hall (1891). The statue in the Rotunda, "Father of the Waters", is carved from a single block of Carrara marble.
Grain Exchange	One of the great centres of the world grain trade is the Grain Exchange at 400 South 4th Street S. The busy activity of the Exchange can be watched from the visitors' gallery.
St Anthony Falls	Below the 50ft/15m high St Anthony Falls the Mississippi is navigable all the way down to the Gulf of Mexico.

Minneapolis / St Paul

The Institute of Arts (2300 3rd Avenue S) has a large collection of works from many countries and in many styles, including pictures by European masters (Rubens, Rembrandt).

*Institute of Arts

The Walker Art Center (Vineland Place, south-west of the city centre) is devoted to 20th century art. Opposite it is the Sculpture Garden, the finest work in which is Claes Oldenburg's "Spoonbridge and Cherry".

Walker Art Center

The campus of the University of Minnesota lies on both banks of the Mississippi. On the east bank are the Bell Museum of Natural History and the recently opened Frederick R. Weisman Art Museum, which is worth a visit for its eccentric architecture alone.

University of Minnesota

To the south-east of the city, extending along the banks of the Mississippi at the 55ft/17m high Minnehaha ("Laughing Water") Falls, is Minnehaha Park, with statues of Hiawatha and Minnehaha, the chief characters in Longfellow's "Song of Hiawatha".

Minnehaha Park

To the south of the city, near the airport, is the Mall of America, the world's largest shopping centre, opened in 1992. In addition to 355 shops, restaurants and bars it includes a film centre and Camp Snoopy, the largest roofed theme park in the United States.

**Mall of America

Sights in St Paul

To the south of the State Capitol (1905) is the Minnesota History Center and Museum, which traces the history of the city, using the most modern forms of presentation.

Minnesota History Center and Museum

In the lobby of City Hall (1932; 4th and Washaba Streets) is a 36ft/11m high piece of sculpture by Carl Milles, weighing 60 tons, representing the Indian God of Peace.

City Hall

The Landmark Center (75 West 5th Street) is housed in the finely restored old Federal Courts Building of 1902, which now contains restaurants, gal-

Landmark Center

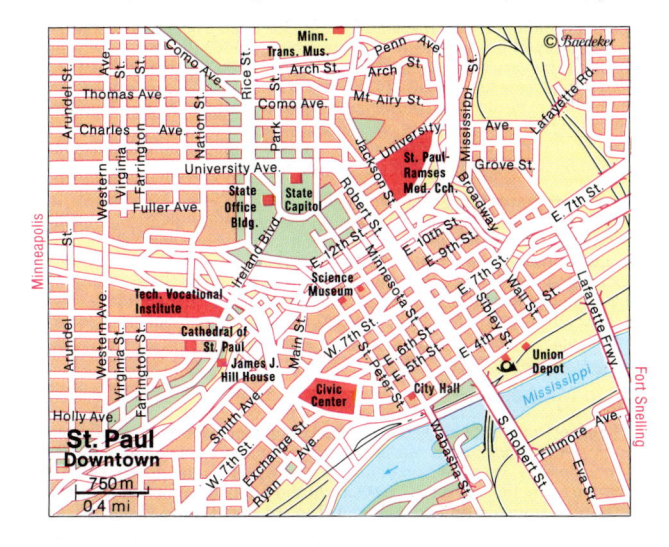

Minnesota

	leries, function rooms and the department of contemporary American art of the Minnesota Museum of Art.
Parks	Among the finest of the more than 90 parks in the city of St Paul are the glass-roofed Town Square Park (7th and Minnesota Streets); Como Park, with the Zoo (Midway and Lexington Parkway); and Indian Mounds Park (in the Dayton's Bluff district), in which are six pre-Columbian mounds.
Fort Snelling	Near the airport is Fort Snelling, which recalls the frontier days of around 1820.

Minnesota (State; MN)   A–F 29–34

Area:
  84,070sq.miles/217,735sq.km
Population: 4,432,000
Capital: St Paul
Popular names: North Star State, Gopher State

Situation and topography	Minnesota (from the Sioux name, "sky-coloured water"), half-way along the northern frontier of the United States, is bounded on the north by Canada, on the north-east by Lake Superior and on the west by the Red River of the North. The Ice Age left behind in this area a gently undulating morainic landscape with more than 11,000 lakes, so that Minnesota is often compared with Finland. The highest point in the state (2228ft/679m) is in the Misquah Hills in the north-west; the south-west of the state is occupied by natural tall-grass prairie. Roughly a third of its total area is occupied by forest (maples and limes in the centre, firs and spruces in the north). The state has a markedly continental climate, with winters which can be extremely severe (an annual average of 60 days of snow cover in the south and 120 days in the north).
History	From the middle of the 17th century French fur-traders began to operate in the territory of present-day Minnesota, which in 1763 passed into British hands. A military post was established in 1820 on the site of Fort Snelling, and this became the nucleus of the city of Minneapolis. Incorporated as an independent territory in 1849, Minnesota joined the Union as the 32nd state on May 11th 1858. Four years later the Sioux rose in arms, in protest against the American failure to observe treaties made with them, but were defeated by the superior strength of government forces.
Economy	Minnesota is an important farming state. Its principal crops are oats, maize, flax, peas, soya beans and sugar-beet, and dairy farming, poultry and cattle rearing also flourish. Mining is mainly for iron: roughly half the US output of iron ore comes from Minnesota, though its reserves are gradually being exhausted. The most important branch of industry is foodstuffs, followed by engineering and tool production, electronics and papermaking. The tourist attractions of Minnesota lie in its vast forests and numerous lakes, which appeal particularly to sportsmen and walkers.

Places of Interest in Minnesota

Duluth	The life of Duluth, at the western tip of Lake Superior, centres on the world's largest inland port, which ocean-going vessels can reach via the St Lawrence Seaway, with the help of a lift bridge which can be raised within a minute from 155ft/47m to 225ft/69m. At the bridge is a museum on the history of shipping on Lake Superior. The old Union Railroad depot now

Mississippi

houses a museum, with old steam locomotives and a street of shops in the style of 1910.

From Duluth North Shore Drive (wide views) runs to Grand Portage, in the extreme north-eastern tip of the state, from which missionaries, fur-traders and trappers used to travel on old Indian trails into the forests of Canada. The old trading post has been partly reconstructed. From Grand Portage there is a ferry to the Isle Royale National Park in Michigan (see entry).
Grand Portage

Ely is a good base for excursions into the unspoiled lake country of the Superior National Forest (canoeing, etc.).
Ely

Hibbing has three claims to fame. It has the world's largest opencast iron ore workings; its local bus company was the germ of the the Greyhound bus system; and it was the birthplace of Bob Dylan.
Hibbing

In Itasca State Park is a little stream which is regarded as the origin of the Mississippi. Round Lake Itasca there is endless scope for recreation, hiking and water sports.
Itasca State Park

The "thousand lakes" were once the heartland of the Dakota Indians. Their history is related in the Mille Lacs Indian Museum.
Mille Lacs Kathio State Park

See entry
Minneapolis-St Paul

The Pipestone National Monument owes its name to the soft reddish stone from which the Indians make their ceremonial pipes. Each tribe has access to this sacred site, where peace must prevail; and even today only Indians are allowed to quarry the stone (an aluminium silicate, known as catlinite after the pioneer and painter of Indian life George Catlin). Examples of Indian pipes can be seen in the Upper Midwest Indian Cultural Center.
Pipestone National Monument

Rochester is the seat of the celebrated Mayo Clinic, famed particularly for its heart operations. There are guided visits on weekdays.
Rochester

Voyageurs National Park, in the far north-west of Minnesota on the Canadian frontier, is a beautiful forest region with more than 30 lakes dotted with over 900 little islands, offering magnificent opportunities for canoeing and fishing. It takes its name from the French *voyageurs* who explored the area in their canoes in the 18th century.
*Voyageurs National Park

Mississippi (State; MS)   P–T 34–37

Area:
47,690sq.miles/123,516sq.km
Population: 2,593,000
Capital: Jackson
Popular name: Magnolia State

The southern state of Mississippi (from the Indian *maesi*, "broad", and *sipu*, "river") is bounded on the west by the riverine meadowland of the Mississippi, which here follows a winding course, and on the south by the Gulf of Mexico. From the terraced Gulf Coast plain to the gently undulating uplands in the interior the land rises only to 820ft/250m. The humid subtropical climate, with occasional extreme temperature fluctuations, fosters a long growing period which produces pine forests in the south-east and mixed deciduous forests (oak, hickory, cypress) in the north-east and west.
Situation and topography

Mississippi

History
The first journey of exploration along the Mississippi was carried out in 1540 by a Spaniard, Hernando de Soto. After the Sieur de la Salle had mapped the river from Illinois to its mouth in 1682 and claimed the area for France the first settlers established themselves near present-day Biloxi in 1699. Thereafter the territory was divided between Spain and Britain, until in 1795 it was taken over by the United States. At first combined with Alabama in a single territory, Mississippi was made an independent territory and on December 10th 1817 was admitted to the Union as the 20th state. Thanks to the use of slave labour in the cotton fields the state prospered. At the beginning of the Civil War Mississippi joined the Confederation, and a number of bloody battles were fought on its soil, in particularly the siege of Vicksburg. In the present century Mississippi stood out against equal rights for all races well into the sixties.

Economy
Cotton is still the characteristic crop of this state, situated as it is in the Cotton Belt. It is no longer a monoculture, however, and other crops such as maize, soya, wheat and rice are grown alongside cotton. The coastal waters are well stocked with fish and yield rich catches. Mississippi's mineral resources include particularly natural gas round Jackson and oil in the south of the state. The principal industries are foodstuffs, textiles, papermaking and furniture manufacture.

Places of Interest in Mississippi

Biloxi
Biloxi, the chief place on the Gulf coast of Mississippi, is the state's oldest town, founded by the French in 1699. Features of interest are the Lighthouse (1849), the harbour (prawn fishing, pleasure craft) and, 5 miles/8km west, Beauvoir Mansion, where Jefferson Davis, President of the Confederation, spent the last twelve years of his life.

Clarksdale
Clarksdale, home of the Delta blues, produced musicians such as John Lee Hooker, Robert Johnson and Howlin' Wolf, mementoes of whom, and of many others, can be seen in the Delta Blues Museum.

Jackson
Jackson (named after Andrew Jackson, 1767–1845, seventh President of the United States), capital of Mississippi, is the economic centre and transport hub of the surrounding area with its oilfields. Here in 1861 the Southern states resolved on secession from the Union. Features of interest are the State Historical Museum in the old Capitol, the Museum of Natural Science and the Mississippi Museum of Art.

Natchez
The little town of Natchez in south-western Mississippi, founded in 1716, was the most important port on the Mississippi in the heyday of the cotton trade, and many handsome mansions and estates, mostly in Greek Revival style, bear witness to the wealth of those days. Among them are the House on Ellicot Hills (1798); Rosalie (1820–23), beautifully situated on high ground above the Mississippi; Stanton Hall (1851–57), with a large ballroom; Magnolia Hall, now housing a museum of fashion and costume; and Longwood, a very large house which was never fully completed.

Natchez Trace Parkway
Still in course of development is the Natchez Trace Parkway, a tourist road following the line of the Natchez Trace, an old route from Natchez to Nashville, Tennessee (see entry), which is first mentioned in 1733. It was at its busiest between 1800 and 1820, when the crews of boats which had sailed down the Mississippi to Natchez returned home on foot or horseback. The Parkway runs past Emerald Mound (12 miles/19km north of Natchez), the second largest pre-Columbian site in the United States, which was occupied between 1250 and 1600 by the Mississippi people, ancestors of the Natchez and Choctaws.

Springfield Plantation
Springfield Plantation House (1786–90), north of Natchez, believed to have been the first in Mississippi, has been preserved almost unchanged. Andrew Jackson was married in the house.

Missouri

Tupelo's most famous son was Elvis Presley (see Famous People), and his birthplace is its great tourist attraction. 23 miles/36km from the little town is Brice's Crossroads, where a Confederate army defeated a larger Union force in 1864.

Tupelo

During the Civil War Vicksburg, part of which lies just above the Mississippi, was a thorn in the flesh of the Union forces, since from there the Confederates controlled shipping on the river. After several unsuccessful attempts to take the town Union troops commanded by General Grant finally captured it in 1863 after a 47-day siege; its fall was one of the bitterest defeats of the Confederates. These events are commemorated in the Vicksburg National Military Park and Cemetery, with the Union gunboat "Cairo" which sank in 1862, and in a museum in the Old Court House. Other features of interest in the town are a number of handsome antebellum houses and the Biedenham Candy Company and Museum of Coca Cola Memorabilia, a restored candy shop where the famous brew was first bottled in 1894.

Vicksburg

Gulf Islands National Seashore (see entry)

Other places of interest

Missouri (State; MO)   J–N 30–36

Area:
  69,695sq.miles/180,515sq.km
Population: 5,158,000
Capital: Jackson City
Popular name: Show Me State

The state of Missouri (from the Indian name "place of the big canoes"), in the central Middle West, is divided by the Missouri River into a northern and a larger southern part. Southern Missouri is occupied by the rolling Ozark Plateau, which is broken up by deep, narrow gorges. The northern part of the state lies in the Central Lowlands, a fertile morainic region covered with loess; the state is bounded on the east by the Mississippi plain, while in the west tall-grass prairie predominates. The climate is warm in summer; there are frequent tornadoes, particularly in the summer months.

Situation and topography

The territory was occupied by Osage Indians when French settlers arrived in the 18th century, founding Ste Genevieve in 1735 and St Louis in 1764. Originally part of the French colony of Louisiana and from 1763 Spanish, the area passed to the United States in 1803 (the Louisiana Purchase). After separating from Arkansas in 1819 Missouri was admitted to the Union on August 10th 1821 as the 24th state. In subsequent decades the state was an area of passage for settlers travelling to the West, and St Louis became the "Gateway to the West". The Civil War threatened to split the state; but although Missouri was a slave-owning state it did not join the Confederates.

History

The main crops grown on the productive loess and clay soils of the plains are maize, rice, cotton and soya beans. Cattle-rearing and, particularly in the Ozark Mountains, sheep-farming play an important part in the economy. Missouri is the largest producer of lead in the United States. In the two industrial centres of Kansas City and St Louis the principal activities are the aircraft and space industries, automobile construction, engineering and metalworking.

Economy

Mojave Desert

Places of Interest in Missouri

Hannibal	Before visiting Hannibal, a small town on the Mississippi, you should read "Tom Sawyer", for it was here that Mark Twain (see Famous People) grew up. Here you will find his boyhood home (now a museum), Becky Thatcher's house, Mark Twain's father's law office and many other places that feature in the novel.
Lake of the Ozarks State Park	This park south-east of Kansas City (see entry) is a popular recreation area. One of the chief places in the park is Osage Beach.
Liberty	Liberty, north of Kansas City, was the scene of the first bank robbery by Jesse James (see Famous People), who was born in nearby Kearney; the bank is now the Jesse James Museum.
St Joseph	St Joseph, in north-western Missouri, has a different claim to fame. It was from here that the first Pony Express rider set out in April 1860 to carry mail to Sacramento (see entry), almost 2000 miles/3200km away in California. The invention of telegraphy put an end to the Pony Express only a year later. Its story is related in the Pony Express Museum and in the Patee House Museum, its old headquarters.
*Table Rock Lake Area	A good base for excursions into this wild and romantic lake district in south-western Missouri, on the border with Arkansas, is the little town of Branson. Features of particular interest are the dam which has formed Table Rock Lake and the Silver Dollar City theme park.
Other places of interest	Kansas City, St Louis (see entries)

Mojave Desert   P 8–12

States: California, Nevada, Arizona
Area: about 15,000sq.miles/39,000sq.km

The huge desert or semi-desert of Mojave extends to the south of the Sierra Nevada from the Coast Range in the west to Nevada and Arizona in the east. The Mojave Desert is a land of extremes: dry salt lakes and luxuriantly green oases, sand dunes and sparse woodland with dwarf trees, abandoned mine workings and closed military areas. This thinly populated arid region, known as the Lonesome Triangle, is one of the hottest places in the United States. It lies at an average height of 2000ft/600m, with hills rising to between 5000ft/1500m and 11,000ft/3300m.

Solar power generation	With over 3000 hours of constant sunshine a year, the Mojave Desert offers almost ideal conditions for alternative means of producing energy. Attention is being concentrated particularly on low-tech methods. In recent years a number of spectacular installations for harnessing solar energy have been established, including a solar tower power station, a "solar dish" and long series of parabolic mirrors in the Dagget area. At Kramer Junction is a modern solar power station which is feeding power into the United States grid.

Sights in the Mojave Desert

Barstow	The little town of Barstow (pop. 22,000), situated at the junction of three highways, is the supply centre for an extensive surrounding area. The California Desert Information Center (831 Barstow Road) has a very informative exhibition on the Mojave Desert and the conditions of life there.

Montana

Near Barstow are the Calico Mountains. Their main attraction is Calico Ghost Town, an abandoned silver-mining settlement which has recently been lovingly restored.

Calico Mountains, Calico Ghost Town

The 20 Mule Team Museum in Boron recalls the days when the borax mined in this region was laboriously transported by mule trains.

Boron

Randsburg, in the Red Mountains, is an old gold-diggers' town which has rather come down in the world but has an interesting Desert Museum.

Randsburg

The streets and houses of Victorville have frequently served as the setting of Western films.

Victorville

In the south-west of the Mojave Desert, where the mule trains with their loads of borax used to halt, is NASA's Ames Dryden Flight Research Facility. Since 1947 the area round Rogers Lake, a dried-out salt lake, has been used by the US Air Force as a test ground; and the almost invariably blue sky in this region is the reason why NASA's space shuttles land on the Edwards Air Force Base when the weather at Cape Canaveral (see entry) is bad. There are guided visits by appointment – tel. (805) 258 3446 or 258 3460 – and when a shuttle landing is imminent.

***Edwards Air Force Base**

Montana (State; MT) A–E 8–21

Area: 139,415sq.miles/
  381,085sq.km
Population: 808,000
Capital: Helena
Popular name: Treasure State

Montana (in Spanish "mountainous") lies in the north-western United States, bounded on the north by Canada. The western third of the state is traversed by the Rocky Mountains, which here reach heights of up to 12,800ft/3900m. The eastern part, in the Great Plains, is a gently undulating plateau rising to a height of 5000ft/1500m, deeply slashed by the upper Missouri and the Yellowstone River. Montana lies in a region of dry continental climate and is particularly arid to the east of the Rockies. The Rocky Mountains are covered by forests which are home to elk, mule deer, grizzlies and brown bears, while in the short grassland of the Great Plains herds of pronghorn antelopes and occasionally bison can still be seen.

Situation and topography

Around the middle of the 18th century the first trappers and fur-traders came into this area, until then inhabited exclusively by Indians, including Gros Ventre and Blackfeet. Lewis and Clark passed through this inhospitable upland world in 1805. Permanent settlements were established only in 1862, after the discovery of gold, and two years later the US territory of Montana was formed. After the discovery of other minerals (silver, copper, etc.) there was a further wave of settlement from 1875 onwards, but the taking of Indian land by the incomers led to bitter fighting with the Sioux and Cheyennes. In the battle of the Little Bighorn the US army commanded by Custer suffered its worst defeat. On November 8th 1889 Montana joined the Union as the 41st state.

History

The economy of Montana is centred on agriculture: cattle and sheep in the Rockies, arable farming on the prairies. The principal crops are lucerne, sugar-beet, maize, beans and vegetables. The main minerals worked in the state are copper, zinc, silver, gold, nickel, platinum, phosphates and oil. The

Economy

Monterey

predominant industries are ore-smelting, foodstuffs and woodworking. The tourist and holiday trade is of great economic importance, for the excellent conditions which Montana can offer for winter sports, fishing, hiking, cycling, bathing in warm springs and canoeing attract large numbers of visitors to this "Big Sky Country".

Places of Interest in Montana

Bozeman	The town of Bozeman, in the south of the state, owes its name to John M. Bozeman, who established a trail from Wyoming to here through Indian country and thus incurred the continuing hostility of the Oglala Indians under their chief Red Cloud (see Famous People). The main attraction of Bozeman is the Museum of Montana State University with its unique dinosaur remains.
Butte	Rather more than a hundred years ago Butte (south-west of Helena) was known as the "richest hill in the world", for the town lay in the centre of an immensely productive silver-, copper- and gold-mining area. The great days of the gold-diggers in Butte are recalled by the Mineral Museum and the World Museum of Mining.
Chinook	At Chinook, near the Canadian frontier, the flight of the Nez Perce Indians, led from Idaho by Chief Joseph, ended in 1877. After a six-day battle with government forces the Indians surrendered – marking the end of Indian resistance in Montana.
Glacier National Park	See Waterton-Glacier National Park
Great Falls	The famous painter of the Wild West, Charles M. Russell, lived and worked in Great Falls, north-east of Helena. His works, displayed in a museum devoted to him, are classics of their kind. The museum also displays his collection of Indian art and everyday objects.
Helena	Montana's capital, Helena, situated in the centre of the western half of the state, was originally known as Last Chance, for a party of disheartened gold-diggers decided to have one final dig here and struck gold – a seam which produced 20 million dollars' worth. In the State Capitol is one of Charles M. Russell's major works, a large mural showing Lewis and Clark meeting the Flathead Indians.
*Little Bighorn Battlefield National Monument	Here, in the Crow Reservation in south-eastern Montana, the US Army suffered its greatest defeat at the hands of the Sioux and Cheyennes. On June 25th 1876 a detachment of the 7th US Cavalry commanded by George Custer attacked a larger Indian force led by Crazy Horse and was annihilated. On the battlefield are a monument commemorating Custer's last stand, erected on the spot where he fell, and a military cemetery.
*National Bison Range	In this reserve, north of Missoula in the Flathead Reservation, bison, antelopes, elks and other animals can be observed from signposted roads.
Virginia City	Virginia City, in south-western Montana, is another old gold-diggers' town, where 300 million dollars' worth of gold was found from 1863 onwards. Twenty historic buildings have been preserved.

Monterey   N 4

State: California
Altitude: sea level
Population: 32,000

Monterey

The town of Monterey lies at the south end of Monterey Bay, 125 miles/ 200km south of San Francisco (see entry). It was founded in 1770, when there was a Spanish military post here. From 1775 to 1822 Monterey was the chief town of the southern part, then in the Spanish sphere of influence, of what is now California, and for a further 24 years it was capital of the Mexican province of Alta California. In 1846 it was occupied by American forces. During the 1930s, when the sardine fishers were bringing in large catches and the fish-canning industry was flourishing, the town enjoyed a considerable economic boom. This period was described by John Steinbeck in his novel "Cannery Row".

The town's main source of income is now the tourist trade in and around Cannery Row.

Situation and history

Sights in Monterey

The Path of History, a route indicated by yellow markings, takes visitors round 35 sites of historical interest.

Path of History

Monterey's main sight is Cannery Row, on which until the 1940s was the greatest concentration of fish canning factories in the world. Some of the canneries have been carefully restored and now house boutiques, souvenir shops, craft shops, galleries and a variety of restaurants and cafés.

*Cannery Row

At 530 Houston Street is Stevenson House, with memorabilia of Robert Louis Stevenson, who stayed here in 1879.

Stevenson House

At 886 Cannery Row is the very interesting Monterey Bay Aquarium (open: daily 10am–6pm), with tanks showing the marine flora and fauna of Monterey Bay and excellent explanatory displays.

**Monterey Bay Aquarium

The Monterey State Historic Park contains a number of well restored historic buildings, including the Custom House Plaza, California's oldest theatre.

*Monterey State Historic Park

A rich man's world: Hearst Castle

Monument Valley

*Fishermen's Wharf — Fishermen's Wharf is now a great tourist attraction, with numerous fish restaurants and souvenir shops. You may be lucky enough to see sea otters or even sealions gambolling in the bay.

Surroundings of Monterey

*17 Mile Drive (toll) — A beautifully engineered road opens up the magnificent scenery of the Monterey peninsula, between Pacific Grove and Carmel. It runs through the Del Monte Forest, passes Pacific Grove (pop. 20,000; Natural History Museum), the Seal Rocks and Cypress Point with its ancient cypresses and finally skirts the world-famous golf course on the equally famous Pebble Beach.

Carmel — A short distance farther on is the beautifully situated former mission station of Carmel, founded by Junípero Serra (whose tomb is in the basilica). Carmel is now an exclusive residential resort.

*Hearst Castle — 100 miles/160km south of Carmel, on the Cuesta Encantada, is Hearst Castle, the sumptuous former residence, begun in 1919, of the newspaper publisher William Randolph Hearst (1863–1951). It is now protected as a historic monument and open to the public.

**Big Sur — From Carmel to 15 miles/24km before San Simeon extends Big Sur, a rugged stretch of the Pacific coast which is of breathtaking beauty. Highway 1 follows a winding course through the hilly coastal scenery, affording magnificent views. There are three inviting State Parks along the route (Andrew Molera S.P., Julia Pfeiffer Burns S.P., Pfeiffer-Big Sur S.P.).

Big Sur (town) — The town of Big Sur lies 33 miles/53km south of Monterey on the river of the same name. In the past it was a sleepy hamlet but since the end of the Second World War it has grown at a tremendous rate, thanks to its beautiful setting and to the prominent figures (including Henry Miller) who have made it their home. Attempts are now being made to restrict its further growth in the interests of the environment.

Monument Valley   M/N 15/16

States: Arizona, Utah
Area: 45sq.miles/115sq.km

Season — Monument Valley is accessible throughout the year, but the best times for a visit are spring and autumn, since the summers are very hot and subject to violent thunderstorms in the afternoon. Not all the facilities are available in winter.

Situation and **topography — Monument Valley, in the north of the Navajo Indian Reservation (see Navajo Country), is one of the most remarkable landscapes in the United States. Since 1960 it has been statutorily protected as the Navajo Tribal Park and is managed by Indians. Out of a great expanse of steppe and desert extraordinary sandstone formations rear up to heights of 1100–2000ft (335–610m) – huge monoliths, pinnacles, sculptured buttes, high mesas, rock arches. The play of colour, ranging from salmon pink to purple, is at its finest in the early morning and at sunset.

Numerous Westerns have been filmed in Monument Valley, including "Stagecoach" (with John Wayne), "Fort Apache" and "The Black Falcon". It was also the setting of the Walt Disney nature film "The Living Desert".

Mount Rainier National Park

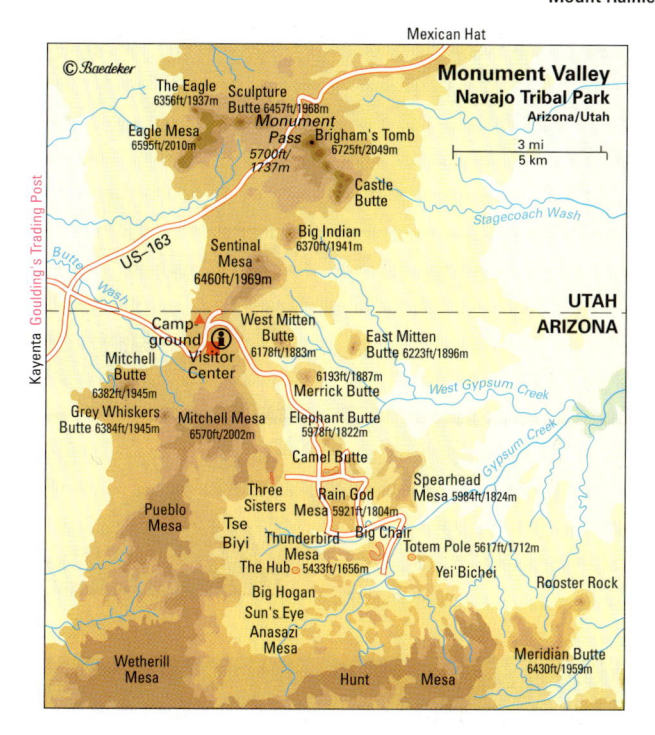

[Map of Monument Valley Navajo Tribal Park, Arizona/Utah, showing features including Mexican Hat, The Eagle 6356ft/1937m, Sculpture Butte 6457ft/1968m, Eagle Mesa 6595ft/2010m, Monument Pass 5700ft/1737m, Brigham's Tomb 6725ft/2049m, Castle Butte, Stagecoach Wash, Sentinal Mesa 6460ft/1969m, Big Indian 6370ft/1941m, US-163, Goulding's Trading Post, Kayenta, Butte Wash, Campground, Visitor Center, Mitchell Butte 6382ft/1945m, West Mitten Butte 6178ft/1883m, East Mitten Butte 6223ft/1896m, Merrick Butte 6193ft/1887m, West Gypsum Creek, Grey Whiskers Butte 6384ft/1945m, Mitchell Mesa 6570ft/2002m, Elephant Butte 5978ft/1822m, Gypsum Creek, Camel Butte, Three Sisters, Rain God Mesa 5921ft/1804m, Spearhead Mesa 5984ft/1824m, Pueblo Mesa, Tse Biyi, Thunderbird Mesa, Big Chair, Totem Pole 5617ft/1712m, The Hub 5433ft/1656m, Yei'Bichei, Rooster Rock, Big Hogan, Sun's Eye, Anasazi Mesa, Wetherill Mesa, Hunt Mesa, Meridian Butte 6430ft/1959m]

The origins of Monument Valley go back some 70 million years to a time when the area was covered by a Mesozoic extension of the Gulf of Mexico. Following a gradual rise in the level of the land the water receded, leaving an extensive plain with numerous faults and clefts which were then subject to erosion. — Origins

Visitors can drive round the park in their own cars on a 16 mile/26km long unsurfaced road, starting from the Visitor Center, but are not allowed to get out. Alternatively there are guided tours starting from Gouldings Trading Post, Kayenta (in all-terrain vehicles on the more rugged roads; also sightseeing flights) and Bluff (geological tours). — Sightseeing

Mount Rainier National Park   C 4

State: Washington
Area: 368sq.miles/953sq.km
Established: 1899

The park is accessible throughout the year, but many roads and tracks are closed in winter. The best time for a visit is summer, when the rich mountain flora is in flower. — Season
The park facilities tend to be overcrowded on summer weekends; it is quieter mid-week. The volcanic massif is often shrouded in cloud for days on end, but on clear days is a landmark visible from many miles away. See Practical Information, National Parks.

323

Mount Rainier National Park

Monument Valley

Mount Rainier rising out of the mist

Mount Rainier (14,410ft/4292m), also known as Mount Tacoma, in the south-west of Washington state, is one of a geologically recent chain of volcanoes in the Cascade Mountains which in the last few years have made news with spectacular eruptions. A strato-volcano, it grew in size from the late Tertiary era onwards, the crater becoming ever larger. Over the last 2000 years it has been highly active. Its last major eruption was in the 19th century, but the clouds of vapour which still rise from the crater are a reminder that the volcano is not yet quiescent. From the fields of névé in the summit region over two dozen glacier tongues reach down on all sides. On Mount Rainier is the largest mass of ice on any mountain in the United States outside Alaska.

Situation and topography

Mount Rainier has a wide variety of flora, ranging from Douglas firs, hemlocks, Sitka spruces and ancient arbor vitae to modest anemones and heath plants. Red deer and roe-deer, marmots and mountain goats are frequently to be seen, and occasionally even bears and cougars.

Flora and fauna

The busiest road in the National Park is the winding mountain road from the Nisqually entrance (2000ft/610m), which runs through beautiful forest country by way of Kautz Creek to Longmire (2765ft/842m; mineral springs; National Park administration) and up to Paradise (5400ft/1645m; winter sports facilities). From here there is a choice of memorable hikes (e.g. to the foot of the Nisqually Glacier).

*The road to Paradise

The eastern part of the National Park can be explored on a road (SR 123) which runs through magnificent scenery from the south-east entrance to the park to the Ohanapecosh Visitor Center (1915ft/585m) and on to Stevens Canyon, a typical glaciated valley with spectacular waterfalls. From there a short side trip (on foot) can be made to the Grove of the Patriarchs with its giant trees hundreds of years old.

Eastern part of the park
*Ohanapecosh

From Stevens Canyon the road climbs northward to the Cayuse Pass (4695ft/1430m), where SR 123 runs into the Mather Memorial Parkway (SR 410), coming from Yakima over the Chinook Pass. From here the Parkway continues north to Tacoma and Seattle.

Mather Memorial Parkway

From the White River entrance (3470ft/1058m), on the Parkway, a road affording wide views runs up to Sunrise (6400ft/1950m), from which in good weather sunrises of breathtaking beauty can be observed.

*Sunrise

The 95 mile/150km long Wonderland Trail runs round Mount Rainier through magnificent scenery with numerous fine viewpoints.

*Wonderland Trail

Napa Valley

L 3

State: California

An hour's drive north of San Francisco (see entry) is the Napa Valley, world-famed for its wine. The valley of the Napa River, the main Californian wine-growing region, is some 30 miles/50km long, with its largest town, Napa (pop. 62,000), at its south end. Other towns are St Helena (pop. 5000) and Calistoga (pop. 4000), at the north end of the valley.

Situation and characteristics

The first wine grapes in this climatically favoured valley were grown by George Yount in 1836. In course of time other wine makers came to the area, mainly from Germany and Italy, and laid out ever increasing areas of vineyards.

History

Sights in the Napa Valley

There are now more than 170 wineries in the Napa Valley, which attract over 3 million visitors a year with their guided visits and wine tastings.

*Wineries

Nashville

	Among the best known are the Beringer Vineyards, the V. Sattui Winery and the Charles Krug Winery in St Helena, the Robert Mondavi Vineyards in Oakville and Hanns Kornell's winery (sparkling wine) at Calistoga.
Wine Train	The Wine Train, an old-time railroad, runs between Napa and Calistoga, offering a comfortable way of seeing the wine-growing area.
St Helena	Features of interest in St Helena are the Napa Valley Wine Museum and the Silverado Museum, which is devoted to Robert Louis Stevenson (author of "The Silverado Squatters" as well as other better known books).
Calistoga	At Calistoga is the "Old Faithful of California", a geyser which shoots a column of hot water into the air at regular intervals. Nearby are a number of mineral springs and remains of a petrified forest.

Surroundings of the Napa Valley

*Sonoma Valley   To the west of the Napa Valley is the Sonoma Valley, which is also famed for its wine. The chief place in the valley is the little town of Sonoma, founded in the 19th century as the last Franciscan mission station in California. Wine-growing was introduced by a variety of wine-makers from Germany, France, Hungary and Italy, and the wines produced here are perhaps the best in the United States. Among the best known producers are the Sebastiani Winery and the Buena Vista Winery, which was established in 1832. North-west of Sonoma, at Glen Ellen, is a ranch which belonged to the writer Jack London (1876–1916; "The Call of the Wild", "The Sea Wolf", etc.), who lived here from 1904 until his death. The ranch is now a museum.

Nashville   N 39

State: Tennessee
Altitude: 440ft/134m
Population: 488,400

Situation and characteristics   Nashville, capital of Tennessee, is situated almost in the centre of the state on the Cumberland River. With its 16 universities and colleges and its reproduction of the Parthenon, it is known as the "Athens of the South". Founded in 1779, Nashville is one of the most important banking and insurance centres in the southern United States, but it is perhaps better known as the capital of country music, which is heard nation-wide in the Grand Ole Opry, a long-running radio programme, as well as in countless bars in the city (many of them no more than tourist traps).

Sights in Nashville

State Capitol	In the centre of the city is the State Capitol (1845–59). Its architect, William Strickland, did not live to see its completion; his tomb is in the building.
Tennessee State Museum	Facing the Capitol on the south is the Tennessee State Museum (history and natural history of Tennessee).
Fort Nashborough	On the banks of the Cumberland River is a reconstruction of Fort Nashborough, the original nucleus of the city, established by pioneers in 1779.
Ryman Auditorium	At 116 5th Avenue N is the Ryman Auditorium, in which the Grand Ole Opry show was performed from 1943 to 1974.
Museum of Tobacco Art and History	The Museum of Tobacco Art and History (800 Harrison Street) is both informative and entertaining. In addition to tracing the history of this ancient American product it displays a large collection of pipes, tobacco tins, advertising material, etc.
Music Row	The area round Music Square, in southwestern downtown Nashville, is the heart of the music industry. Apart from souvenir shops and museums
*Country Music Hall of Fame	devoted to musicians of greater or lesser fame the main sight is the Country Music Hall of Fame, which commemorates the greats of the music business

and displays memorabilia of famous singers. There are also guided tours of the historic RCA Studio B in which many a hit first made its mark. The limousines of the great ones, including Elvis Presley's Cadillac, can be seen in the nearby Car Collectors Hall of Fame (1534 Demonbreun Street).

In the Centennial Park, southwest of the city centre (West End Avenue and 25th Avenue N), is the famous reproduction of the Parthenon, originally built in wood in 1897 to commemorate the centenary of the state of Tennessee and later rebuilt in cement on the same site.

Parthenon

To the south of the park is the Belmont Mansion (1900 Belmont Boulevard), built in the 1850s. One of the finest houses of its kind in the United States, it has thirteen rooms preserving much of their original decoration and furnishings.

*Belmont Mansion

The Belle Meade Plantation (southwest of the city centre at Harding Road), built in 1853, is another handsome old Southern mansion, set in one of the finest plantations in Tennessee.

*Belle Meade Plantation

To the east of Nashville by way of I 40 and Old Hickory Boulevard is Hermitage, the home of Andrew Jackson (1767–1845), seventh President of the United States. In the park surrounding the house (originally built 1819, rebuilt in 1834 after a fire) are the graves of Jackson and his wife.

Hermitage

Northeast of the city (I 40 and Briley Parkway) is the Opryland theme park. The great attractions here are not the usual rides and other amusements but – for country music fans at least – the concerts on Friday and Saturday evenings, when the Grand Ole Opry radio programme, which has been running since 1925, is transmitted from the park's 4400 seat theatre: for tickets dial (615) 889 3060.

Opryland

*Grand Ole Opry

Surroundings of Nashville

15 miles/24km north of Nashville on I 65 is Goodlettsville, with the Museum of Beverage Containers and Advertising, which claims to have the largest collection of drink cans (28,000 items, mainly beer), together with a large collection of advertising material.

Goodlettsville

Navajo Country   N/O 14–16

States: Arizona, New Mexico, Utah
Area: 24,980sq.miles/64,700sq.km

The Navajo Indian Reservation (Navajo Country), established in 1868, is the largest Indian reservation in the United States. Lying for the most part in Arizona, it is bounded on the west by the Colorado River (see Grand Canyon) and on the north by Lake Powell, a long artificial lake formed in a canyon, and the San Juan River; the boundaries on the east and south are ruler straight. Much of the central part of the territory, roughly half of which is barren and infertile, is a desertic tableland slashed by canyons. To the east, striking north–south, are the Chuska Mountains, with Pastora Peak (9413ft/2869m); to the north-east is the Ute Mountain Indian Reservation in Colorado; and to the south-west is the Hopi Indian Reservation, which has an area of some 560sq.miles/1450sq.km. The most interesting parts of Navajo Country, both scenically and culturally, are organised and protected as Tribal Parks or National Monuments. The largest settlements in the reservation are Window Rock (Navajo), the Indian-run administrative centre of the reservation, and Hotevilla (Hopi).

Situation and
**characteristics

Navajo Country

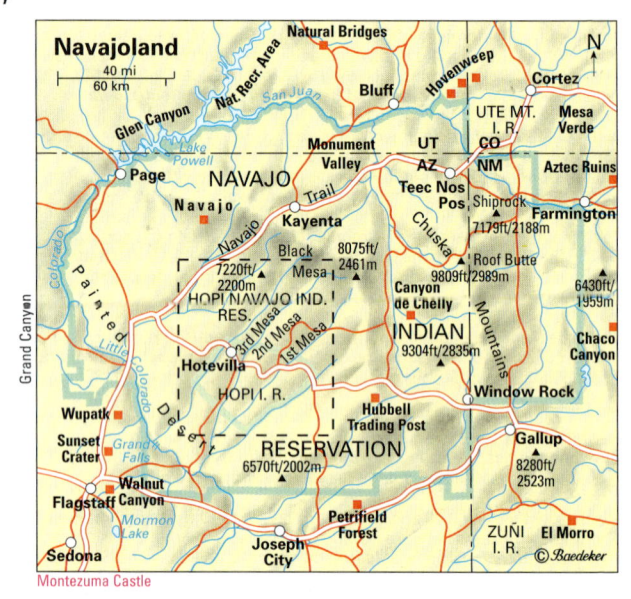

The Navajo

The Navajo or Navaho (pronounced návaho), who call themselves the Diné ("people of the earth"), are the largest of the Indian tribes of the United States, with some 200,000 members. Around the middle of the 16th century the Navajo, then semi-nomadic, ranged over North America from north-western Canada to the south-western United States, where they came in contact with the local Pueblo Indians. From them the Navajo learned weaving and, on a modest scale, farming (maize, pulses). The Spaniards introduced them to the use of tools and firearms and to horses, cattle, sheep and goats, and they then took to stock-rearing (mostly sheep). They put up a fierce resistance to the advance of the whites into their territory, but in 1864, under their chief Manuelito, were compelled to acknowledge defeat after Kit Carson and his forces, avoiding open battle, burned their pastureland, crops and dwellings. The survivors were then forced to undertake a 300 mile/500km trek to Bosque Redondo, by Fort Sumner in New Mexico, on which many died. There the Navajo, now reduced to only 8000, were held prisoner for four years in appalling conditions, after which they were allowed to return to the area of the present reservation on condition that they gave up all resistance to the presence of the whites.

The Navajo now live mainly by cattle-rearing and the sale of craft objects. The mineral resources of the reservation (coal, uranium, etc.) are still mainly worked by whites, the Indians having been bought off with derisory sums. There is little in the way of industry, and the unemployment rate is high. Many of the Navajo, who are reserved but not unfriendly, live in "hogans" – windowless huts of wood, brushwood and clay – and stick to their traditional social structure and beliefs. The reservation is run by a 74 member tribal council based in Window Rock. It has some schools, and in Many Farms is the Navajo Community College, established in 1969.

Art

Navajo art of the early period is represented mainly by pottery vessels and pipe bowls. The Navajo learned their craft skills from the Spaniards and the Pueblo Indians, achieving a great cultural flowering in the 19th century. The weaving techniques of the Pueblo Indians, which were practised by men, were imitated by Navajo women. Their favourite products were the

Navajo Country

patterned blankets which were used for clothing, bed covers, hogan doors or wall decoration. The abstract geometric patterns, rarely repeated, which gave expression in allegorical form to themes from tribal history or the conflict with the whites, consisted originally of plain horizontal stripes (the "chief" pattern), later supplemented by squares, lozenges and zigzag-lines (the "eye-dazzler" pattern). The colours (predominantly shades of brown) were obtained by dyes made from plants. When European yarns and synthetic dyes were introduced in the later 19th century the traditional artistic elements were increasingly abandoned, the weave became looser, the colours brighter, the patterns more standardised, abstract patterns being replaced by representational designs. Textiles imitating the Indian blankets were now manufactured commercially by whites and sold widely throughout the United States. In addition to weaving the Navajo produce attractive silver jewellery inlaid with precious and semi-precious stones (mainly turquoise). Like the Hopi, they practise the ritual art of sand painting.

Apart from rock drawings no written material survives from the early days of the Navajo, but over a thousand Indian legends and hundreds of prescriptions for ceremonies have been handed down orally and in more recent times recorded in writing or on tape. Among traditional rituals is the sacred sun dance, which was prohibited for many years by the United States authorities.

Customs

The Hopi (the Indian term is Moki, the "peaceable people"), numbering only about 7000, belong to the group of sedentary Pueblo Indians (Shoshones) and are totally different from the Navajo, within whose territory their small reservation lies. As village dwelling tillers of the soil and cattle rearers the Hopi inevitably came into conflict with the Navajo, ever looking for new pasturages for their herds. Living in seclusion for more than a thousand years in pueblos on three large tabular hills (the First Mesa, Second and Third Mesas – the village of Orabi on the Third Mesa is probably the oldest continuously occupied settlement in the United States) – the Hopi Indians have a common tribal council, but the individual villages are largely self-governing under a hereditary or elected chief. The Hopi are very reserved in their dealings with outsiders and try to keep "palefaces" away from their traditional religious ceremonies (the fire dance, the eagle dance, the masked dances of the kachina spirits). Before visiting a village the permission of the chief must be obtained, and this is not readily granted; and taking photographs and making sketches are frowned upon.

The Hopi

The Hopi practise various crafts (basketwork, jewellery, pottery), but their speciality is carving figures of kachinas – spirits representing various life forces which form a link between men and their Creator – usually from the roots of poplar trees. The sand painting which is still practised – a ritual in which the medicine man scatters coloured sand in magical symbols, which are wiped away after the ceremony – also has an artistic aspect. In the Hopi Cultural Center on the Second Mesa (on US 264) are an interesting museum and shops selling Indian crafts, as well as a motel.

Art

Museum

It is forbidden to take photographs of people or buildings without permission, and cine cameras, video recorders and tape recorders must not be used at religious ceremonies. On all Indian reserves there is an absolute ban on alcohol which is enforced by the tribal police. The reason for the ban is that the Indians lack a particular enzyme which breaks down alcohol and facilitates its absorption in the body, and in consequence alcohol has a much more powerful effect on them. Visitors must of course themselves observe the ban.

Conduct of visitors

Sights in Navajo Country

The Canyon de Chelly (pronounced de Shay) National Monument, 100 miles/160km north-west of Gallup, New Mexico, is notable for its series

*Canyon de Chelly

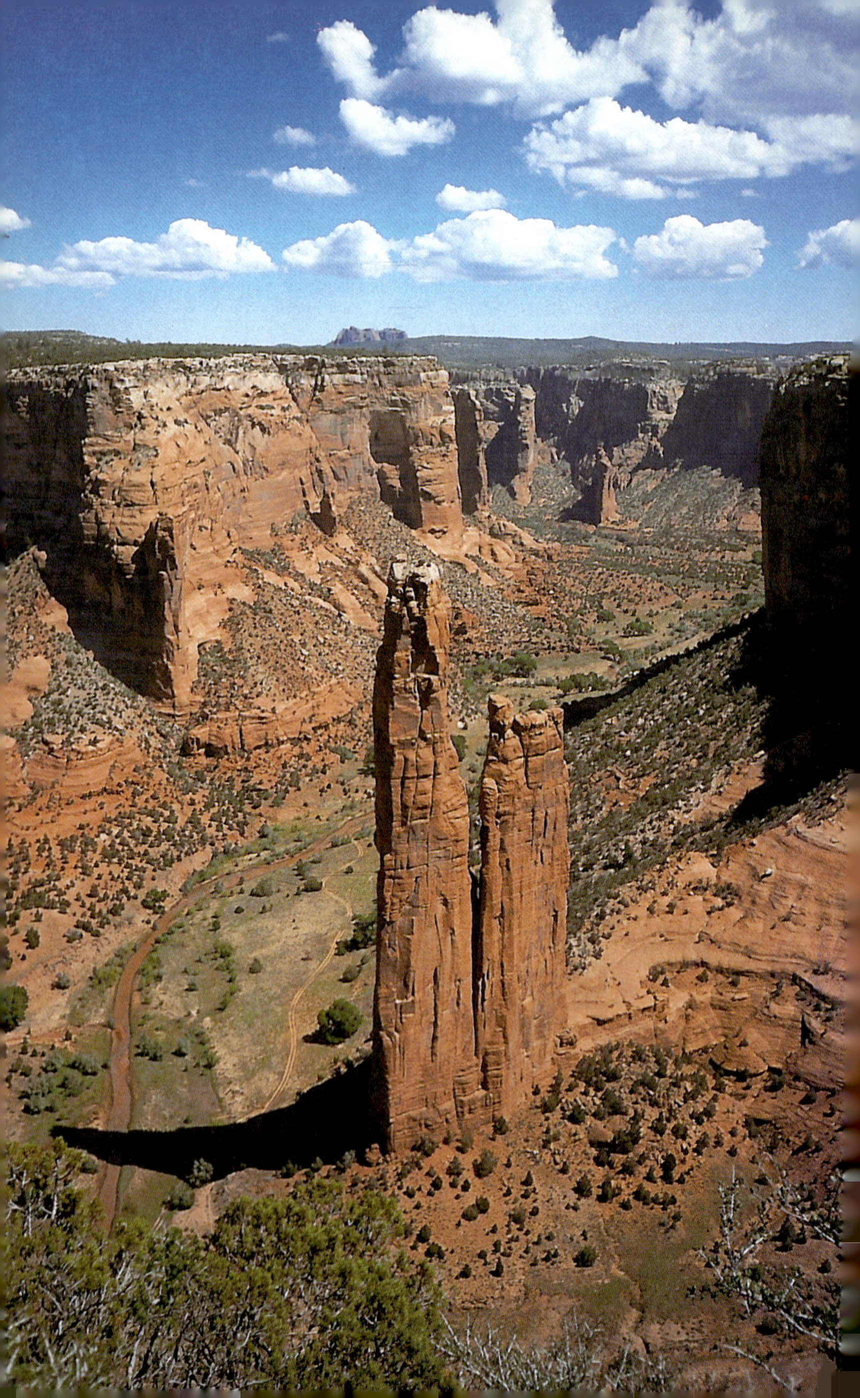

Navajo Country

of steep-sided canyons up to 1000ft/300m deep. In the main canyon are Spider Rock, the most striking rock formation, and the White House (constructed c. 1050, discovered in 1849), the best known of over a hundred cliff dwellings, mostly in inaccessible situations, which were occupied from around A.D. 350 to 1300. Other cliff dwellings are the Antelope House and Mummy Cave (in which mummies were found) in the Canyon del Muerto. In 1864 the Navajo entrenched themselves in the canyons, and the tall cliff known as the Navajo Fortress, the last stronghold against the attacks of Kit Carson's men, in which more than 300 Navajo were besieged and starved out, is a sacred place which may not be entered by whites. There is an informative archaeological museum in the Visitor Center, and there are various guided tours and walks. The only trail open to visitors without a guide is the 2½ mile/4km long White House Trail.

At Ganado, 50 miles/80km west of Gallup, is the Hubbell Trading Post, established by John Lorenzo Hubbell in the late 1870s. The present establishment, which dates from 1885, has an interesting interior and displays an ethnological collection. — Hubbell Trading Post

See entry — Monument Valley

The Painted Desert, round the township of Cameron in the south-west of the reservation, offers a fascinating play of colour. There is a magnificent view of the desert from the Watchtower on the East Rim of the Grand Canyon (see entry). — Painted Desert

The Navajo National Monument (150 miles/240km north-east of Flagstaff, Arizona) consists of three separate 13th century cliff dwellings, some of them accessible only on foot or horseback: Betatakin, constructed around 1200; Keet Seel, the largest and best preserved, built between 1274 and 1286 under a rock overhang; and Inscription House, the smallest of the three. — Navajo National Monument

Rainbow Bridge National Monument (35 miles/56km north-east of Page, Arizona) is a gigantic natural rock arch (span 280ft/85m) on the south side of Lake Powell. — Rainbow Bridge

Round Navajo Country

The well preserved Aztec Ruins, 15 miles/24km north-east of Farmington, New Mexico, are remains of a settlement of some size which was originally occupied between 850 and 1100 and again, briefly, at the beginning of the 13th century. Their name was given to them by early settlers who thought that they resembled the Aztec pyramids of Mexico. — *Aztec Ruins National Monument

Chaco Canyon National Monument, 64 miles/103km north of Thoreau, New Mexico, is reached on unsurfaced roads which are negotiable only in dry weather. There are remains of twelve large and several smaller Indian settlements, the most impressive of which is Pueblo Bonito (c. 800–1300), with 800 rooms and 37 kivas. — Chaco Canyon

See Canyonlands National Park — Glen Canyon

See entry — Grand Canyon National Park

In Hovenweep National Monument, 40 miles/64km west of Cortez, Colorado, are the ruins of Indian pueblos and defensive towers dating from the 12th–14th centuries. — Hovenweep

◀ *Spider Rock in the Canyon de Chelly*

Nebraska

Mesa Verde National Park	See entry
Petrified Forest National Park	See entry
*Sunset Crater National Monument	Sunset Crater, 14 miles/24km north of Flagstaff, Arizona, is the 1000ft/305m high crater of a volcano which erupted in 1065. Round the crater are interesting lava flow formations.
Wupatki	In Wupatki National Monument, 30 miles/48km north of Flagstaff, are extensive remains of 12th and 13th century pueblos. The largest of them, the three-storey Wupatki Pueblo, had more than a hundred rooms with an ingenious heating system.

Nebraska (State; NE) G–J 21–30

Area:
77,225sq.miles/200,018sq.km
Population: 1,593,000
Capital: Lincoln
Popular name: Cornhusker State

Situation and topography

Nebraska (from the Omaha Indian name for the Platte River), in the west central part of the United States, lies on the plateau of the Great Plains. It rises from the Missouri in the east to a height of 5425ft/1654m at the foot of the Rocky Mountains in the west. The south and east of the state have very fertile loess soils, but to the north-west is a great expanse of sand hills and valleys, the characteristic Hills of Nebraska. The climate is continental, with hot summers and cold winters. The original vegetation (grassland in the east, short-grass and wormwood steppe in the west) now survives only in patches, and the huge herds of bison which once roamed here are now represented by small numbers in the National Parks.

History

The territory of Nebraska was originally occupied by Dakota, Omaha, Cheyenne, Pawnee and many other tribes. In 1682 it became part of the French colony of Louisiana, which was acquired by the United States in 1803. For many years it was only sparsely settled; then from the mid 19th century onwards it became an area of transit for pioneers making their way to the West. It was declared a territory of the United States in 1854, and on March 1st 1867 it became the 37th state of the Union.

Economy

Nebraska is one of the leading agricultural states of the US, and large areas of its territory are occupied by stock-farming, mainly cattle (about 6.5 million head). The principal crops on arable farms are maize, wheat, millet, soya beans and sugar-beet. The state also has oil and natural gas. The most important industry is the processing of agricultural produce, in particular meat canning. Other industries include metalworking and electrical engineering. Tourism is of increasing economic importance, since the varied landscapes of Nebraska with their 3000 lakes offer scope for a wide range of leisure and recreational activities (shooting, canoeing, fishing, swimming, riding, skiing).

Places of Interest in Nebraska

Fort Robinson

Fort Robinson, in the extreme north-west of Nebraska, was built in 1874. With its palisades and watchtowers it gives an excellent impression of conditions in the time of the Indian wars. Here in 1877 the Indian chief Crazy Horse, who had come to the fort for peace negotiations, was murdered.

Nevada

Near Grand Island, in the south-east of the state, a recreation area dotted with lakes and ponds extends along the Platte River. Annually in spring and autumn half a million cranes and other migratory birds pause here on their long journey north or south.	*Grand Island Interchange State Wayside
In the east of the state is its capital, Lincoln. Features of interest are the State Capitol, the State University with its museums (including an art museum, with works by Remington and Russell, and the Sheldon Art Gallery, designed by Philip Johnson, with works of the modern American school) and the National Museum of Roller Skating (history of roller skating from 1700 to the present day).	Lincoln
Ogallala, in south-western Nebraska, takes visitors back to the days of cattle-droving, with its saloon, general store, Cowboy Museum (Front Street) and Boot Hill Cemetery.	Ogallala
See entry	Omaha
Within easy reach of Scottsbluff, in the far west of the state, are three places of interest.	**Scottsbluff**
56 miles/90 miles north of the town are the Agate Fossil Beds, where fossils of primeval mammals dating back 20 million years were found.	Agate Fossil Beds National Monument
This 500ft/150m high pinnacle of rock 24 miles/39km south-east on the North Platte River was a landmark on the Oregon Trail, telling the settlers travelling on it that after crossing the Great Plains they had the much more arduous passage of the Rockies ahead of them.	*Chimney Rock
Scotts Bluff, just south of the town, was another landmark for settlers and Pony Express riders on their journey to the West. A circular road takes visitors round the most notable features (including the tracks of wagon wheels) and to the interesting Oregon Trail Museum.	*Scotts Bluff National Monument

---

Nevada (State; NV)   H–O 6–11

Area: 110,560sq.miles/
  286,355sq.km
Population: 1,284,000
Capital: Carson City
Popular name: Silver State

The predominant features of the landscape of Nevada (Spanish "snow-covered") are two great deserts, the Mojave and the Great Basin. The northern two-thirds of the state is occupied by the Great Basin, a region of cold, dry climate which is traversed by numerous ranges of hills striking north–south and rising to over 1000ft/300m. The southern third consists of the hot, dry Mojave Desert (see entry), in which the vegetation is mainly of cacti; only on the eastern slopes of the Sierra Nevada are there forests of conifers.	Situation and topography
The earliest inhabitants of Nevada, who settled in the Moapa Valley around A.D. 100 and belonged to the Pueblo culture, were Anasazi Indians. In 1776 the area was explored by Spaniards, and thereafter became part of the Spanish vice-royalty of New Spain. In 1848 it was ceded by Mexico to the United States. Until 1861 it was joined with Utah in a US territory; then on October 31st 1864 it became the 36th state of the Union. After the Second World War numerous tests of atom bombs were carried out in the Nevada desert.	History
Nevada and the cities of Las Vegas and Reno in particular are famed as centres of legal gambling: not surprisingly, therefore, tourism is the state's	Economy

Nevada

Anasazi rock drawings in the Valley of Fire

principal source of income, to which the holiday areas on Lake Tahoe and Lake Mead also make contributions. Mining (particularly gold, silver, copper and iron) is also an important element in the economy. Nevada's processing industries are mainly iron smelting, the chemical industry and woodworking. Agriculture is almost entirely confined to pastoral farming.

Places of Interest in Nevada

Carson City	The state capital, Carson City, which lies south of Reno, takes its name from the Wild West hero Kit Carson. Features of interest are the State Capitol, with a silver dome, and the Nevada State Museum, which includes a reproduction of a silver-mine.
Ely	Round Ely, in the east of the state, are a number of ghost towns which grew up during the 19th century silver boom and were then abandoned. One of the best known of these is Hamilton, 45 miles/72km west. The White Pine Museum in Ely is informative on the area's silver-mining days.
*Great Basin National Park	The Great Basin National Park, in the desert region on the border with Utah, is centred on Wheeler Peak (13,062ft/3981m). The major attraction is the Lehman Caves, with fantastic rock formations.
Reno	Reno, the "biggest little city in the world", lies in western Nevada. A rather smaller edition of Las Vegas (see entry), it allows visitors to get married or divorced and to lose their money just as expeditiously as in the larger city.
Valley of Fire State Park	37 miles/60km north-east of Las Vegas is the Valley of Fire State Park, with numerous rock drawings scratched on its red sandstone by Indians of the Anasazi culture.
Other places of interest	Lake Tahoe, Las Vegas

New Hampshire (State; NH)   D–G 53–55

Area:
 9280sq.miles/24,030sq.km
Population: 1,105,000
Capital: Concord
Popular name: Granite State

New Hampshire (named after the English county) lies in the north-eastern United States between Maine and Vermont. The northern part of the state is dominated by the granite massif of the White Mountains, part of the Appalachian range, with Mount Washington (6290ft/1917m), the highest peak in the New England states. To the south of the hills is a wooded upland region with innumerable lakes formed during the Ice Age; the largest of them is Lake Winnepesaukee. In the south-east the state reaches the Atlantic coast in a strip only 20 miles/32km wide. Roughly 80% of the state is covered with mixed deciduous and coniferous forests, in the latter of which Weymouth pines predominate. Lying as it does between high ranges of hills and the coast, there are considerable differences in climate in different parts of the state.

Situation and topography

After exploratory voyages in the early 16th century the first Puritan settlers from England landed on the coast in 1623. In 1775 New Hampshire deposed its British Governor and thus became the first colony to break away from the mother country. On June 21st 1788 it became the ninth of the founding states to adopt the US Constitution.

History

New Hampshire's agriculture, now declining, specialises mainly in milk production and poultry rearing. In the south-east of the state is a dense industrial zone in which the most important branches of industry are electrical and mechanical engineering, papermaking and textiles. Tourism is of great economic importance; the hills in the north in particular offer ideal conditions for nature and sporting holidays (excellent skiing).

Economy

Places of Interest in New Hampshire

Concord, on the Merrimack River in southern New Hampshire, has been capital of the state since 1808. Features of interest include State House (1819) and the Historical Society Museum (with an example of the old coaches made in Concord, which had a reputation for indestructibility).

Concord

Laconia's situation near the Winnisquam River and Lake Winnipesaukee makes it a popular holiday resort and a good base from which to explore the beauties of the lakes.

Laconia

The port town of Portsmouth (founded 1630) at the mouth of the Piscataqua River was until 1808 capital of the state. A walk round the recently restored district of Strawbery Banke with its handsome old houses (some of which are open to the public) will introduce visitors to the town's past. In Kittery, Maine, on the opposite side of the river delta, is the Naval Shipyard, the first government shipyard.

*Portsmouth

Nature-lovers, hikers and winter sports enthusiasts will all find what they are looking for in this mountain region. I 93, which traverses the area from north to south, runs through or past the most important places and natural features in the western part of the National Forest.

White Mountains National Forest in New Hampshire

One of the most visited holiday areas in the White Mountains is the Franconia Notch (Gorge) State Park. One of its most striking features is the Old

*Franconia Notch State Park

335

New Jersey

	Man of the Mountains, a 1200ft/365m high crag which suggests the profile of an old man.
*Mount Washington	The easiest way to reach the top of Mount Washington is on the steep cog railway which was opened in 1869. The highest peak in the White Mountains is notorious for its rough and stormy weather: in 1934 the record wind speed of 240 miles/390km an hour was recorded here.
Lake Winnepesaukee	In the centre of the lake district to the south of the White Mountains is Lake Winnepesaukee, which attracts large numbers of visitors, particularly in summer. Weirs Beach, on the west side of the lake, has the widest range of leisure and recreational facilities (two water parks, bathing beaches, steamer trips) but is also the most crowded resort. A quieter place is the old bathing resort of Wolfsboro on the east side of the lake.

New Jersey (State; NJ)   J/K 50/51

Area:
   7835sq.miles/20,295sq.km
Population: 7,760,000
Capital: Trenton
Popular name: Garden State

Situation and topography	New Jersey (named after Jersey in the Channel Islands) is one of the smaller states on the north Atlantic coast. It is bounded on the west by the Delaware River, on the north-east by the Hudson River, on the east by the Atlantic and on the south by Delaware Bay. The north-western part of the state extends into the foothills of the Appalachians and the hilly Piedmont Plateau. Along the edge of the coastal plain are extensive lagoons and spits of land. There are considerable variations in temperature between the dry, cold north and the subtropically humid south. The hardwood forests which originally covered the whole state except the areas of marshland have now largely disappeared, giving place to low coniferous and oak scrub forest and large areas devoted to the growing of bilberries and cranberries.
History	The territory of New Jersey, originally occupied by Lenni-Lenape Indians, was settled in the 17th century by Dutch immigrants. Until 1664 it was part of the colony of Nieuw Holland; thereafter, under pressure from Britain, it became a Quaker colony. In 1701 Britain gained control of New Jersey. During the War of Independence its strategic situation made it the scene of major battles between American and British forces. On December 18th 1787 it signed the US Constitution as the third of the founding states.
Economy	New Jersey's highly developed agriculture is primarily directed towards supplying the large cities with basic foodstuffs (vegetables, fruit, dairy products). It is also one of the leading industrial states of the USA, the most important branches of industry being steel production, engineering and automobile construction. Its long and varied coastline is the main tourist attraction.

Places of Interest in New Jersey

*Atlantic City	Atlantic City, the best known – and by some the most decried – seaside resort on the Atlantic coast of New Jersey, founded in the 1850s, offers visitors its long sandy beaches and an immense range of entertainments and amusements which has earned it the name of the "Las Vegas of the East". It now has a dozen large casinos and innumerable revue theatres which put on shows round the clock. Atlantic City is annually the scene of boxing matches for large purses and the election of Miss America.

New Jersey

Atlantic City: a casino in the Las Vegas of the East

Most of the places of entertainment, restaurants and boutiques are on the Broadwalk, a 5 mile/8km long seafront promenade 60ft/18m wide. The history of the city is traced in the Historic Museum, with particular reference to famous visitors and stars of the night.

This little town in south-western New Jersey has preserved the largest number of historic buildings in the state – over 2000 – dating from the last 300 years.	Bridgeton
The attractions of Cape May, at the southernmost tip of New Jersey, were discovered by the more prosperous citizens of Philadelphia in the 18th century, and in the 19th century it enjoyed a heyday as a fashionable bathing resort. Six Presidents of the United States had houses here. The attraction of the town lies in its handsome holiday homes, rebuilt in Victorian style after a fire in 1878 (National Historical Landmark).	*Cape May
In this National Historical Park in northern New Jersey Washington's forces camped during the winter of 1779/80. Features of interest are the Historical Museum and Fort Nonsense.	Morristown National Historical Park
South of Atlantic City is the popular seaside resort of Ocean City, with a wide range of leisure facilities, including particularly water sports.	Ocean City
See Philadelphia, Surroundings	Princeton
A few miles north of Atlantic City is the lovingly restored museum village of Smithville, which carries visitors back to the early 19th century.	Smithville
In the centre of the state, on the Delaware River, is the state capital, Trenton, which preserves a number of historic buildings and sites. Particular features of interest are the State House, State Museum and State Cultural Center.	Trenton

New Mexico (State; NM) N–S 16–22

Area: 121,595sq.miles/
314,925sq.km
Population: 1,548,000
Capital: Santa Fe
Popular name: Land of
 Enchantment

Situation and topography

The state of New Mexico in the south-western United States is divided between three geographical regions. The western part of the state is occupied by a plateau traversed by ranges of hills and slashed by numerous canyons; in the centre are the southern foothills of the Rocky Mountains (highest point Wheeler Peak, 13,161ft/4011m), through which flows the Rio Grande; and in the east the hills fall dowm to the wide expanses of the Great Plains, with the Llano Estacado. The climate is extremely dry – New Mexico has an annual rainfall of only 14in./350mm, the lowest in the United States – and as a result the country ranges between steppe and desert. Typical trees in the mountain regions are spruce, fir, nut pine and juniper. Yuccas and mesquites grow in the desert regions.

History

In New Mexico – known as Indian Land – impressive cliff dwellings and ruins bear witness to the cultures of the Pueblo, Apache, Navajo and Anasazi Indians. The first European to reach the area round the Rio Grande was Francisco Marcos de Niza, who came here in 1539 in the quest for gold. The territory was colonised in the 17th century by Spaniards, who encountered fierce resistance from the local Indian tribes. In 1821 it was occupied by Mexico; then in 1846, after the outbreak of the Mexican-American War, it was annexed by the United States. In 1850 (combined with Arizona until 1863) it was incorporated as a US territory, and on January 6th 1912 it was admitted to the Union as the 47th state. The first atom bomb was exploded on July 16th 1945 at the Alamogordo test site.

Economy

New Mexico's agriculture is predominantly extensive pastoral farming; arable crops include vegetables, cotton, fruit, wheat and hay. The state has the largest deposits of uranium in the United States, as well as potassium salts, copper, oil and natural gas. Its principal industries are chemicals, foodstuffs, electronics and engineering. The main assets of the tourist trade are natural beauties such as the Carlsbad Caverns and the remains of early Indian cultures.

Places of Interest in New Mexico

Acoma Pueblo

On a 365ft/112mft high mesa south-west of Albuquerque (see entry) are the remains of what is thought to be the oldest continuously inhabited settlement in the United States, securely dated on archaeological evidence to 1150 but quite probably occupied since the beginning of the Christian era. Beside the pueblo Spanish Franciscans established the mission of San Esteban del Rey in 1629.

*Aztec Ruins

In the far north-west of New Mexico, on the border with Colorado, settlers who reached this area around 1800 found a settlement of the Pueblo Indians and thought it was an Aztec town. The settlement, which was occupied between 1100 and 1300, consists of 400 rooms. There is a museum illustrating the old Indian culture.

The Chaco Canyon in north-western New Mexico was a centre of the Anasazi culture between the 10th and 12th centuries. The remains include the extensive settlement of Pueblo Bonito and an elaborate system of paths and flights of steps hewn from the sandstone.

*Chaco Culture National Historical Park

North of the old mining town of Silver City are the Gila cliff dwellings: 42 rooms in six caves in the cliff face constructed by the Mogollon Indians around 1300.

Gila Cliff Dwellings

To the west of Albuquerque (see entry) is the El Morro National Monument, a sandstone cliff over 200ft/60m high topped by a pueblo with pre-Columbian rock drawings. There are also later inscriptions by Spanish conquistadors, including Don Juan de Oñate in 1605.

El Morro National Monument

South-east of Albuquerque is the old Wild West town of Lincoln, scene of the Lincoln County cattle war in 1877–78, in which Billy the Kid (see Famous People) made his debut as a gunman and ended up in jail in the County Courthouse. The Courthouse is now a museum devoted to its most celebrated inmate. There is another museum in the town telling the story of the Buffalo Soldiers, a regiment of black soldiers who fought the Apaches.

Lincoln

Red Rock State Park, north of Gallup in western New Mexico, is the venue, annually in August, of the Intertribal Indian Ceremonial, which is attended by members of 50 different tribes from all over the United States, Canada and Mexico.

Red Rock State Park

South-east of Albuquerque is the Salinas Pueblo National Monument, which contains within its extensive area remains left by the Spanish conquistadors as well as the native Indians: the San Benaventura Mission (begun 1659) and 21 pueblo mounds at Gran Quivira, the ruins of the mission church of San Gregorio de Abó, adjoining a large pueblo to the west of Mountainair and the ruins of the mission of the Purísima Concepción to the north of Mountainair.

*Salinas Pueblo Missions

Albuquerque, Carlsbad Caverns, Santa Fe, White Sands National Monument (see entries)

Other places of interest

New Orleans

U 35

State: Louisiana
Altitude: 0–13ft/0–4m
Population: 533,000 (Metropolitan Area 1.6 million)

New Orleans, the largest city in the state of Louisiana and the second largest inland port (also handling seagoing vessels) in the United States, lies on the Mississippi, 105 miles/170km above its mouth. It is world-famed for its Creole and Cajun life-style, which finds expression not only in its excellent cuisine and programme of festivals but in many aspects of its way of life. And around the turn of the century this was also the birthplace of jazz, which is still actively practised here. This metropolis of the Old South draws hosts of visitors, especially at the time of the Carnival (Mardi Gras), when the climate is particularly agreeable.
The city lies in an area of marshland, formerly malaria-ridden but now drained, between the Mississippi, here up to half a mile (800m) wide, and Lake Pontchartrain, which is drained by a series of bayous (ditches, sluggish waterways). Much of the crescent-shaped city centre lies below the high-tide mark and is protected by a levee 6 miles/10km long and over 13ft/4m high.

Situation and characteristics

Originally dependent mainly on shipping and shipbuilding, the town's economy later centred on the produce of its rich hinterland (particularly cotton, sugar, rice and timber) and on fishing. More recently there has been a major restructuring of the economy as a result of the working of natural

Economy

New Orleans

gas and, even more importantly, offshore oil. The New Orleans region is now one of the leading world centres of the petro-chemical industry. Tourism is an increasingly important source of revenue: with over 7 million visitors annually, New Orleans is now one of the most important tourist centres in the United States.

Population

In the second half of the 19th century the population of New Orleans grew from 120,000 to just under 300,000, and in the 1960s reached its highest point at 628,000. Since then almost 100,000 people have moved out of the city into the Greater Metropolitan Area.

New Orleans is a melting-pot of cultures. In addition to the French-speaking Cajuns (Acadians: descendants of the French settlers who were expelled from Nova Scotia in the 18th century) its population includes Creoles, Italian, Irish and German immigrants and descendants of black slaves. The city's cultural diversity is reflected in its music, its cuisine and of course in its festivals.

Jazz

New Orleans is the home of jazz. The chief protagonists of this new musical style (see Introduction, Music), practised particularly in the entertainment quarter of the city, were "King" Oliver, J. R. Morton and above all Louis Armstrong (see Famous People). The jazz of New Orleans continues to attract fans from all over the world. Black music, i.e. blues and Dixieland, ragtime and swing, Creole jazz and the more recent funky jazz, can be heard in Preservation Hall (726 St Peter Street), the legendary Lulu White's Mahogany Hall (309 Bourbon Street), the Palm Court Jazz Café (1204 Decatur Street) and countless other night spots. Other places that are at present "in" are Tipitina's (501 Napoleon Avenue), Muddy Waters (8301 Oak Street), Mulate's (201 Julia Street) and the Absinthe Bar (400 Bourbon Street).

Mardi Gras

The high spot in the city's programme of festivals is the Carnival (Mardi Gras), which flourished particularly at the turn of the century. During the Carnival, particularly on Rose Monday and Shrove Tuesday, the French Quarter is taken over by the revellers, with a series of lively parades and masked balls.

History

New Orleans was founded in 1718 by the French governor Jean-Baptiste Lemoine de Bienville and named after the Duc d'Orléans, then Regent of France. In 1721 it became capital of Louisiana. Soon afterwards a large party of German immigrants arrived, and by 1732 the population had risen to 5000. In 1762 France was compelled to cede the town to Spain, though for several years the population successfully resisted the takeover. New Orleans was again in French hands from 1800 to 1803, when under the Louisiana Purchase it passed to the United States. In 1815 General Andrew Jackson inflicted a decisive defeat on British forces near the town. During the Civil War New Orleans surrendered to Union forces in 1862.

**Vieux Carré (French Quarter)

Situation and atmosphere

The Vieux Carré or French Quarter of New Orleans, the old town centre, extends along a crescent shaped bend on the Mississippi. French influence is particularly marked in the buildings, some of them between 100 and 260 years old, with their arcades, wrought iron balconies, red-tiled roofs and picturesque fountain decked courtyards. The blacks who settled in the town, together with the old established Creole inhabitants, created jazz around the turn of the century in the entertainment quarter, which was demarcated by municipal ordinance in 1897 and marked out with red lamps, and in nearby Bourbon Street. Nowadays the district contains a profusion of jazz spots and places of entertainment of very varying quality, well-known restaurants, cheerful cafés, souvenir shops, galleries and old hotels, all refurbished and titivated for the tourist trade.

New Orleans

Bourbon Street, in the heart of the French Quarter (see p. 344)

The main square of the old town is tree-planted Jackson Square, with an equestrian statue (1856) of General Andrew Jackson. Very attractively laid out is the area along the banks of the Mississippi, with the Riverboat Docks, the promenade known as the Moon Walk, the Millhouse and the former Jackson Brewery, as well as a variety of boutiques and fast food outlets. | *Jackson Square (Place d'Armes)

On the north side of the square is the St Louis Cathedral (R.C.), built in 1794 on the site of two earlier churches. | St Louis Cathedral

To the north-east is the Presbytère (1817), originally the presbytery, which later housed the Supreme Court of Louisiana and is now occupied by a section of the Louisiana State Museum. | Presbytère

A picturesque and lively little street (many street artists), particularly in spring, is the Ruelle d'Orléans, also known as Pirates' Alley after the freebooters who used to haunt this area. | *Ruelle d'Orleans (Pirates' Alley)

The Cabildo was built in 1795 as the residence of the Spanish governor. The Louisiana Purchase was agreed here in 1803. This building now houses the Louisiana State Museum with its large collections of material on the history of the town and the region. | *Cabildo

To the north-west is the Anthony Garden, in which duels were once fought. Nearby is La Branche House (1835), with beautiful wrought iron balconies. | Anthony Garden/La Branche House

The Pontalba Buildings, the first apartment blocks in America (mid 19th century), extend along two sides of Jackson Square. In the block on the west side is a "Puppetorium" (representations of **historical scenes by mechanical puppets). | Pontalba Buildings

341

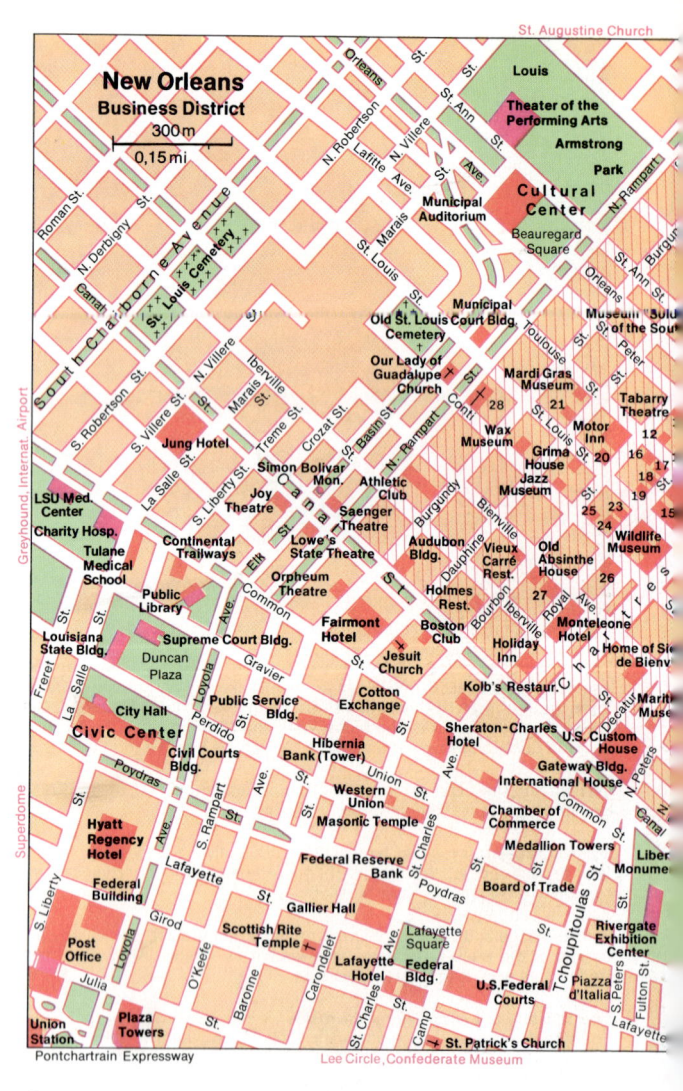

New Orleans

Petit Théâtre	Opposite is the Petit Théâtre (1797). Adjoining is the attractive Petit Salon.
*French Market	At the east corner are the long market halls of the picturesque French Market, with an abundance of culinary delights and a busy flea market. At the near end is the old established Café du Monde.
Old US Mint/ *Mardi Gras and Jazz Museum	At the north-east end of the French Market is the Old US Mint (1835), in which US coins were minted until 1910. It now houses the Mardi Gras and Jazz Museum.

New Orleans

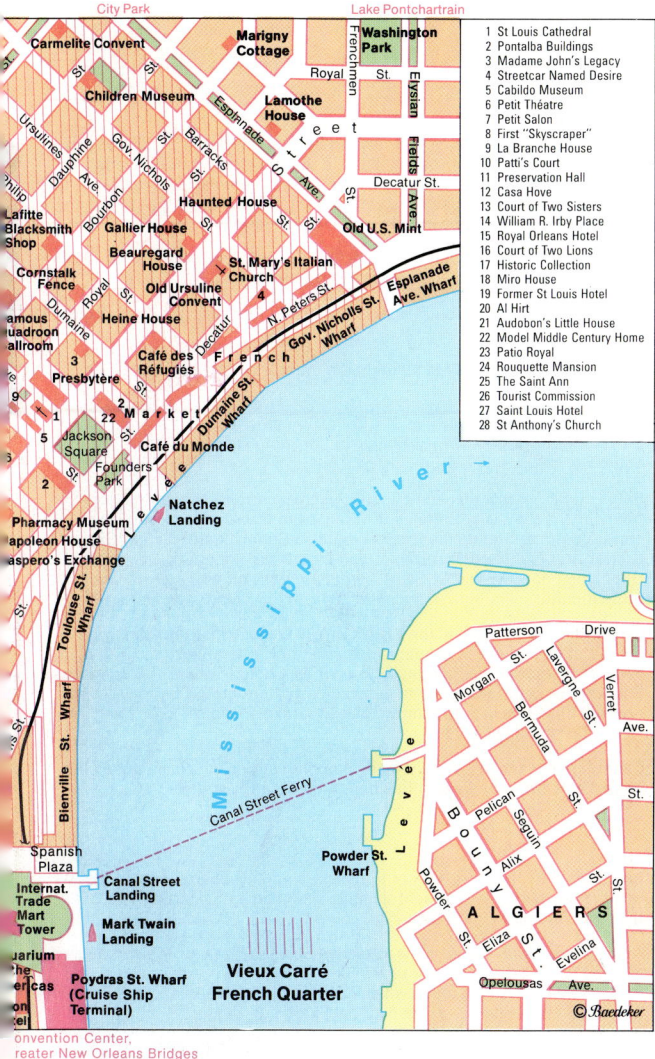

Map legend:
1. St Louis Cathedral
2. Pontalba Buildings
3. Madame John's Legacy
4. Streetcar Named Desire
5. Cabildo Museum
6. Petit Théatre
7. Petit Salon
8. First "Skyscraper"
9. La Branche House
10. Patti's Court
11. Preservation Hall
12. Casa Hove
13. Court of Two Sisters
14. William R. Irby Place
15. Royal Orleans Hotel
16. Court of Two Lions
17. Historic Collection
18. Miro House
19. Former St Louis Hotel
20. Al Hirt
21. Audobon's Little House
22. Model Middle Century Home
23. Patio Royal
24. Rouquette Mansion
25. The Saint Ann
26. Tourist Commission
27. Saint Louis Hotel
28. St Anthony's Church

To the south-west, on Decatur Street, is the original "streetcar named Desire". — Streetcar Named Desire

In Chartres Street is the Ursuline Convent, built about 1735. Adjoining is St Mary's Italian Church (1780). — Ursuline Convent

One of the oldest buildings in the city is the trim house on Dumaine Street known as Madame John's Legacy, built in 1726. It is now a museum. — *Madame John's Legacy

At the south-west end of Decatur Street is the handsome US Custom House (1848), with a sumptuous marble hall. — Custom House

343

New Orleans

*Royal Street	There are a number of fine buildings on Royal Street, including the old Bank of Louisiana, the old established Antoine's Restaurant, the Spanish Governor's House (1784), the Court of Two Sisters (1832), Patti's Court (1860; once occupied by the famous singer Adelina Patti) and Dr Le Monnier's House (1811).
*Bourbon Street	The best known street in New Orleans is Bourbon Street, with famous jazz spots and Old Absinthe House (1807), in which Andrew Jackson and the guerrilla leaders Jean and Pierre Lafitte planned the decisive battle with British forces. The Voodoo Museum illustrates the mingling of Christian elements and pagan African rites in the voodoo cult.
Hermann Grima House	This interesting house with stables (820 St Louis Street) was built in 1831 for a successful businessman named Hermann Grima.
*Brennan's Restaurant	In Conti Street, to the south-east, is Brennan's Restaurant, famed for its cuisine.
Wildlife and Fisheries Building	In the Wildlife and Fisheries Building is a museum illustrating the fauna of Louisiana.
Musée Conti (Wax Museum)	A few minutes' walk north, at 917 Conti Street, is the Musée Conti (Wax Museum), with tableaux by wax figures depicting scenes from the history of the city.
Garden of the Americas	Between Rampart Street and Basin Street, which mark the north-western boundary of the Vieux Carré, is the Garden of the Americas, with monuments commemorating the freedom fighters Benito Juárez García, Simón Bolívar and Francisco Morazán. Close by are the church of Our Lady of Guadalupe and the Old St Louis Cemetery, with numbers of handsome monuments.
Louis Armstrong Park	On the north-west edge of the Vieux Carré is Louis Armstrong Park, with a bronze statue of the legendary musician and entertainer (see Famous People). The area was originally known as Congo Square (Beauregard Square), for negro slaves were allowed to gather here on Sundays. Here now are the Municipal Auditorium, the Theatre of Performing Arts and the Treme Community Center.
Canal Street	Canal Street is the city's lively main shopping street, which separates the Vieux Carré from the Central Business District to the south.

*Riverfront

	In recent years the west bank of the Mississippi has been the subject of a comprehensive redevelopment scheme, designed particularly to appeal to the international tourist trade.
Spanish Plaza	At the end of Canal Street is the attractive Spanish Plaza, on which a lively masked ball takes place on Rose Monday. The square is dominated by the 33-storey World Trade Center, which has a revolving observation platform. Adjoining is the Rivergate International Exhibition Center.
Canal Street Ferry	The Canal Street Ferry crosses the Mississippi, here 700yd/640m wide, to the eastern suburb of Algiers. At 233 Newton Street is Blaine Kern's Mardi Gras World, where the floats for Mardi Gras are prepared.
*Aquarium of the Americas	To the south of the World Trade Center is the Aquarium of the Americas (open: daily 10am–5pm), which attracts great numbers of visitors. Here can be seen more than 7000 different representatives of the freshwater and saltwater fauna of the Mississippi, the Amazon and the Caribbean (Gulf of Mexico). Adjoining is Riverfront Park.
Cruise Ship Terminal	In front of the Aquarium is the New Orleans Cruise Ship Terminal.

New Orleans

An old-time sternwheeler in front of the modern Riverfront

From the Cruise Ship Terminal the Riverwalk runs south, with over 200 boutiques, restaurants and cafés.
Farther south is the modern New Orleans Convention Center.

Riverwalk

Convention Center

Central Business District

To the west of the Riverfront is the Central Business District, with various bank buildings (including the Hibernia Tower), the Cotton Exchange and a number of hotels.

Situation

In the centre of the district is Lafayette Square, with three monuments, including one to Benjamin Franklin. On the west side of the square is the Gallier Hall, formerly City Hall.

*Lafayette Square

Near the Pontchartrain Expressway is the beautifully laid out Lee Circle, with a bronze statue of the Southern General Robert Lee on a tall column. Close by is the Confederate Museum (929 Camp Street), which is devoted to the Civil War.

Lee Circle

To the west of the Central Business District is the 272ft/83m high Louisiana Superdome, one of the largest stadiums in the United States, with seating for 100,000 spectators. To the south are the Union Passenger Terminal and the Head Post Office.

*Louisiana Superdome

To the west of the Pontchartrain Expressway is the 51-storey skyscraper One Shell Plaza, one of the city's tallest buildings.

One Shell Plaza

To the north of the Superdome is the modern Civic Center, with the handsome 11-storey City Hall, a number of court buildings and the Louisiana State Office Building.

Civic Center

Garden District

The Garden District, a prosperous residential area, lies south-west of the Pontchartrain Expressway.

Situation

New York

St Charles Avenue	On St Charles Avenue are a number of handsome mansions with large gardens and parks. Near its north-east end are the headquarters of the United Fruit Company (1920), a business with worldwide interests.
*Audubon Park	In the south-west of the Garden District is Audubon Park, laid out in 1915, with fine stands of oaks, a zoo, hothouses, a golf course and a number of small lakes.
Loyola University/ Tulane University	North of the park are the Tudor-style buildings of the Roman Catholic Loyola University, founded in 1912. Beyond it is the campus of Tulane University, with the 80,000-seat Sugar Bowl stadium.

*City Park

Situation	The beautifully laid out City Park, with numerous lakes and dried-up bayous and several golf courses, lies in the north of the city. Along the east side of the park runs the St John Bayou, a drainage canal which reaches deep into the city area.
*New Orleans Museum of Art	The New Orleans Museum of Art (open: Tue.–Sun. 10am–5pm) has a rich art collection, including Renaissance and Baroque pictures donated by the art collector Samuel H. Kress, ancient Greek vases, pre-Columbian art and modern black African art.
Floral Clock/ Popp Fountain	Particular attractions in the park are the Floral Clock and the illuminated Popp Fountain.

Surroundings of New Orleans

Lake Pontchartrain	To the north of the City Park is Lake Pontchartrain (40 miles/64km long, 25 miles/40km across and only 20ft/6m deep), round the shores of which are numerous speciality restaurants (particularly fish and game). There are also marinas and bathing beaches, and an amusement park which appeals particularly to families with children.
Lake Pontchartrain Causeway	A 25 mile/40km long causeway constructed after the Second World War runs across the lake.
Fat City	Near the south end of the causeway is the new district of Fat City, with attractive restaurants, cafés and shops.
*Chalmette National Historical Park	6 miles/10km east is Chalmette National Historical Park, where General Jackson defeated the British forces in 1815. In the National Cemetery are the graves of 12,000 Union soldiers who fell in the Civil War.
**Boat trips on the Mississippi	There are daily excursions on "Old Man River" in old-time sternwheelers with resounding names. A trip into the fragile amphibious landscape of the Mississippi delta is particularly impressive.
*Plantation Country	Along the banks of the Mississippi between New Orleans and Baton Rouge (see Louisiana) are a string of beautifully restored old plantation houses. The finest are Destrehan Plantation (1787), San Francisco Plantation (1856), Tezcuco Plantation (1855), Houmas Plantation (1840), Oak Alley Plantation and the White Castle (Nottoway Plantation).

New York (State; NY)   F–J 46–52

Area: 48,420sq.miles/128,400sq.km
Population: 18,058,000
Capital: Albany
Popular name: Empire State

New York

Situation and topography

New York State lies in the north-eastern United States on the Canadian frontier, extending northward from New York City to Lake Ontario and north-westward to Lake Erie. The landscape of the state shows great diversity, with high mountain ranges in the north-east, expanses of plain in the centre and a coast fringed with spits of land in the south. It has a cool temperate climate, with inflows of cold air from the north in winter. The plateau and mountain regions are mostly forest covered and rich in game. The plains are predominantly arable land.

History

In 1609 Henry Hudson, then in the Dutch service, sailed up the river which bears his name as far as the site of present-day Albany. In 1623 the Dutch colony of Nieuw Holland was founded here, and settlers were brought in from the Netherlands. In 1664 the colony was ceded to Britain and in 1665 became a Crown colony. The town of New York was occupied by British forces during the whole of the War of Independence. On July 26th 1788 New York became the eleventh of the founding states to adopt the Constitution.

Economy

The produce of the state's highly specialised agriculture (poultry rearing, dairy farming; fruit and vegetables, including potatoes) is mainly devoted to supplying the great city conurbations. It also has the highest industrial output in the United States after the state of California, with roughly half of its total industrial production coming from New York City. The main tourist areas in the state are the Adirondacks and the Great Lakes, with Niagara Falls and New York City as the principal highlights. The world-famed winter sports and Olympic resort of Lake Placid also lies within New York State.

Montauk Lighthouse (New York State)

New York

Places of Interest in New York State

*Adirondacks
The Adirondacks, a range of hills of medium height, forest covered and with numerous lakes, lie in the far north of New York State; geologically they form part of the Canadian Shield. The highest peak is Mount Marcy (5345ft/1629m). The Adirondacks have long been a favourite holiday and recreation area, offering excellent fishing, shooting and walking. The area can be explored by canoe on the 125 mile/200km long waterway from the Old Forge in the west to Saranacs in the north-west of the Adirondack Park.

*Lake Placid
The world-famed winter sports resort of Lake Placid, at the foot of Whiteface Mountain, has twice hosted the Winter Olympics (1932, 1980).

*Albany
The state capital, Albany (pop. 110,000) lies 160 miles/240km north of New York in the valley of the Hudson River. It was given a great boost as an industrial and commercial centre by the opening of the Erie Canal in 1825. There is a fine view of the town and the Hudson River from the Corning Tower of the modern Empire State Plaza. Albany has many fine old 18th and 19th century buildings which have been carefully restored in recent years. The Albany Institute of History and Art has one of the oldest collections in the United States (including pictures of the 19th century Hudson River school).

*Buffalo
At the east end of Lake Erie is Buffalo, the state's second largest city, which since the construction of the St Lawrence Seaway has been one of the leading ports on the Great Lakes. The hub of the city's life is Niagara Square, with a monument to the murdered President William McKinley and the Theodore Roosevelt Inaugural National Historic Site. From the neighbouring 28-storey City Hall there is a fine panoramic view of the western part of the state. The Albright Knox Art Gallery has a fine collection, particularly of European and American art of the 18th–20th centuries. The museum of the Buffalo and Erie County Historical Society traces the history of the Buffalo region and the pioneering period. In the old Allentown district are many finely restored Victorian buildings now housing art galleries, boutiques and small restaurants. A striking early skyscraper is the Guaranty Building in Church Street (by Dankmar Adler and Louis Sullivan, 1896). In the port of Buffalo is the huge Naval and Servicemen Park, with numerous attractions (including Second World War submarines and destroyers).

Cooperstown
To the west of Albany, in central New York State, is Cooperstown, made famous by James Fenimore Cooper, author of the Leatherstocking tales. Its other tourist feature, for devotees of the American national game, is the Baseball Hall of Fame.

Hyde Park
On the east bank of the Hudson River, near Kingston, are Hyde Park, birthplace and residence of President Franklin D. Roosevelt (see Famous People), now a museum, and the palatial Vanderbilt Mansion.

Saratoga Springs
With its handsome 19th century spa facilities (in Saratoga State Park) and other amenities Saratoga Springs, north of Albany on I87, is a very fashionable resort. During the high season (June to August) there are race meetings, and leading dramatic companies from New York and Philadelphia put on shows in the Saratoga Performing Arts Center.

Woodstock
The remote little village of Woodstock in the Catskill Mountains became world-famous at a stroke when it was the scene of the legendary festival of August 1969, "three days of peace and music".

Other places of interest
New York City, Niagara Falls (see entries)

New York City

H/J 51/52

State: New York
Altitude: 0–410ft/0–125m
Population: 7.32 million (Metropolitan Area 18.1 million)

The description of New York in this guide is abridged, since there is a detailed account of the city in the AA/Baedeker guide "New York".

New York City, the largest city in the United States – the "Big Apple", the "world capital of excitement" – lies in the south-east of New York State, at the point where the Hudson River and East River flow into Long Island Bay. New York is the world centre of finance and capital, the seat of the United Nations, a cultural Mecca without equal, a mosaic of nations and a city of stark social contrasts in which extravagant luxury and the bitterest poverty are often only a street apart. Greater New York – officially so designated since 1898 – consists of five boroughs, each of which has a population of over a million: Manhattan, the real economic and cultural centre, together with the Bronx, Brooklyn, Queens and Staten Island. The city is headed by the Mayor (since 1993 a Republican), who controls a great army of municipal officials and police. The city administration faces a host of problems: a volume of traffic which is almost out of control and the resultant pollution of the environment, a desperate financial situation which imposes tight restrictions on public expenditure and has allowed whole quarters of the city such as South Bronx to degenerate into disaster areas, housing shortages and homelessness, and a frighteningly high crime rate (though if the

Situation and characteristics

The Statue of Liberty against the skyline of Lower Manhattan

New York City

statistics are to be believed not by any means the highest in the United States).

Population

The waves of immigrants from all over the world have given New York an unusual diversity of ethnic groups which is reflected in an extraordinary cultural range and also in racial and social tensions. It is not quite accurate to talk of a melting-pot of races, for many population groups in their own special quarter: Afro-Americans in Harlem, Chinese in Chinatown, Italians in Little Italy, Poles and Ukrainians in East Village, Hungarians, Czechs and Germans on East Side, Hispanos in the Barrio, and so on.

Economy

New York City occupies a predominant position in the economy of the United States and is the largest capital market and banking centre in the world. Seven of the ten largest American investment banks have their headquarters on the Hudson River, along with a third of all retail businesses in the United States, almost a fifth of all wholesale firms, three commercial exchanges and innumerable service establishments, including 15,000 restaurants, famous department stores like Macy's and Bloomingdale's and a host of advertising and media people and lawyers. Industry is also strongly represented, a leading position being occupied by the traditional textile industry, followed by foodstuff processing and printing and publishing. New York is also the media capital of the United States, with the headquarters of all the major television and radio companies and publishing houses and an immense range of newspapers and periodicals. The big film companies also have their offices in New York, although the films themselves are mostly produced in California. Tourism is also an important element in the economy: the city attracts 25 million visitors annually, including 5.6 million from overseas.

Culture

New York is also the cultural centre of the United States, with 35 Broadway theatres and perhaps 200 little theatres, two opera houses, including the world-famous Metropolitan Opera, several orchestras of outstanding quality, including the New York Philharmonic (founded 1842), and over a dozen ballet and dance companies. It is also a world art centre, with some of the world's greatest museums, headed by the Metropolitan Museum, and several hundred galleries. Science and education are represented by over 50 universities and colleges, the best known of which is Columbia University. And this is by no means the whole story, for what would New York be without its restaurants, bars, jazz clubs and noisy discothèques and its nightbirds, who would agree with Frank Sinatra's song "I wanna wake up in a city that never sleeps!"?

History

The first European to sail into the bay and see the Manhattan peninsula (though without setting foot on it) was Giovanni da Verrazano, an Italian in the French service, who came here in 1524. The first to land here, in 1609, was Henry Hudson, who was looking for the North-West Passage on behalf of the Dutch East India Company, and he was followed four years later by the first Dutch settlers. The foundation of the town that was to become New York is dated to 1626, when Governor Peter Minnewit or Minuit bought the peninsula from the Manna-Hatta Indians and founded the settlement of Nieuw Amsterdam. Under his successor Peter Stuyvesant, who proved something of a dictator, the town grew, but was increasingly threatened by the British, who captured it in 1664 and consolidated their hold in 1674, when the town was renamed New York.

At the beginning of the War of Independence the Americans were defeated in a battle on Long Island and were compelled to abandon the town, recovering it only in 1783. In 1789 George Washington took the oath as first President of the United States in Federal Hall, and New York briefly became the country's first capital. By 1820 it was the largest city in the United States with a population of 150,000. With the opening of the Erie Canal in 1825 it consolidated its position as the leading port on the eastern seaboard. During the 19th century the city's population was multiplied many times by

New York City

the influx of immigrants from Europe and, after the Civil War, of former slaves from the South. By 1898 the population had risen to 3.5 million, and by 1913 it had passed the 5 million mark. That year also saw the beginning of the skyscraper era with the completion of the Woolworth Building: a development which reached its first peak in 1931 with the Empire State Building, the Chrysler Building and the RCA Building. Two years earlier, however, a different note had been struck on "Black Friday", the stock market crash which marked the beginning of the world economic crisis.

After the Second World War New York became the headquarters of the United Nations. Important postwar dates were 1965, when the city was paralysed by a total power blackout; 1970, when the World Trade Center was completed; 1975, when New York was threatened with bankruptcy; the early eighties, when large numbers of new skyscrapers were built; 1987, when the Stock Exchange suffered a worse crash than in 1929 on "Black Monday"; and 1990, when the city elected its first black Mayor, David Dinkins.

Sights in New York City

A first general view of the city can be had from the observation platform of the World Trade Center or the Empire State Building, which both afford breathtaking panoramic prospects. The city's unique skyline is best appreciated from the sea, either on one of the sightseeing cruises which are offered to visitors or, no less strikingly but much more cheaply (50 cents) by taking the Staten Island Ferry from the southern tip of Manhattan to Staten Island and back again. There are many firms offering coach tours, and there are also sightseeing flights by helicopter. Information about all these various possibilities can be obtained from the New York Convention and Visitors Bureau, 2 Columbus Circle, tel. (212) 397 8222. The best way of getting about New York on your own is by the subway, which has an extensive network covering all the places you will want to see – though it should not be used for visits to the outer districts, cars with few passengers should be avoided and in the late evening you should take a taxi instead.

Sightseeing

Lower Manhattan

Lower Manhattan (Downtown) is the area on the Manhattan peninsula to the south of 14th Street.

Situation

On a rocky island 2½ miles/4km south-west of the southern tip of Manhattan is the world-famed Statue of Liberty holding her torch aloft – for millions of immigrants the first they saw of America and the symbol of their hopes. The 305ft/93m high figure by the Alsatian sculptor Frédéric-Auguste Bartholdi was a gift from France to commemorate the 100th anniversary of the United States. From the observation platforms in the head and in the torch – which are usually crowded – there are marvellous views of the city's skyline and, in the opposite direction, of the Verrazano-Narrows Bridge (one of the world's longest suspension bridges (4567yd/4176m)), which links Staten Island with Brooklyn. In the base of the statue is a small museum recording the creation of the statue and its effect on immigrants.

****Statue of Liberty**

Ferry: daily from 9am from South Ferry

Before entering their new home all immigrants were required to pass through admission procedures on Ellis Island. By the beginning of the First World War some 17 million people had been processed here: their fate was often decided in a few minutes, so that Ellis Island became known as the "island of tears". Since 1990 the immigration buildings have been a museum, in which – more directly than in the Statue of Liberty – visitors can follow the history of immigration. There is also a computerised data base from which they can discover the date of entry of their ancestors or relatives.

Ellis Island

Ferry: daily from 9am from South Ferry

351

New York City

1 One New York Plaza
2 American Express Building
3 Four New York Plaza
4 Watson House
5 St. Elizabeth Ann Seton Shrine
6 Seaman's Church Inst.
7 Old U.S. Custom House
8 Bowling Green
9 Cunard Building
10 Wall Street Journal
11 Fraunces Tavern
12 India House
13 Our Lady of Victory Church
14 Bank of New York
15 Citibank
16 Federal Hall Nat. Mem.
17 Morgan Guaranty Trust
18 New York Stock Exchange
19 Irving Trust Building
20 St. George's Chapel
21 American Stock Exchange
22 Equitable Building
23 Marine Midland Building
24 Chase Manhattan Bank
25 Federal Reserve Bank
26 St. John Method. Church
27 One Liberty Plaza
28 Transportation Building
29 Woolworth Building
30 St. Peter's Church
31 Federal Post Office Bldg.
32 N.Y. Telephone Company
33 Benjamin Franklin Statue Printing House Square
34 Pace College
35 Municipal Building
36 Police Headquaters
37 St. James' Church
38 Chatham Green Houses
39 Chinese Museum
40 True Light Luth. Church
41 Transfiguration Church
42 Buddhist Temple
43 City Prison
44 Criminal Court
45 N.Y. State Office Bldg.
46 N.Y. County Court House
47 U.S. Court House
48 St. Andrew's Church
49 Court Square Building
50 U.S. Customs Court
51 Federal Office Building
52 Family Court
53 New York City Fire Museum

New York City

The southern tip of Manhattan – the Battery, with the South Ferry Plaza – is dominated by the skyscrapers of New York Plaza.

Crouching in their shadow is Fraunces' Tavern, originally the oldest building on Manhattan (1719) but later twice burned down and rebuilt. In this famous tavern (the present version of which is not an exact reproduction of the original) Washington spent his last days as commander-in-chief of the revolutionary forces before retiring to his country house, Mount Vernon (see Washington DC).

North-west of the tavern is the square known as the Bowling Green, with the old Customs House, one of the city's finest Beaux-Arts buildings. It stands at the beginning of Broadway, New York's best known street, which runs north from the southern tip of Manhattan for over 12 miles/20km.

The western half of the southern tip of Manhattan is occupied by Battery Park, with the Castle Clinton National Monument. The castle was completed in 1811, and from 1824 to 1855 housed entertainments and concerts; it was then used as an immigration station, and later, until 1941, was occupied by an Aquarium. It has now been restored to its original state.

To the north is Battery Park City, an ambitious scheme carried out in the eighties to rehabilitate and redevelop the south-western shore of Manhattan, which had come sadly down in the world. The dominant architectural features are now the buildings (designed by Cesar Pelli) of the World Financial Center, with the headquarters of Dow Jones, American Express and Merrill Lynch; particularly notable is the spacious and airy Winter Garden.

To the east of the World Financial Center are the 1380ft/420m high twin towers of the World Trade Center, designed by Minuro Yamasaki and opened in 1973. The two main towers and six other buildings, including the Commodity Futures Exchange, accommodate a total staff of 50,000, who find their way to their offices with the help of 104 elevators. Visitors are taken up to the observation deck in the south tower, from which there are spectacular views. On the 107th floor is the exclusive Windows on the World restaurant.

From the World Trade Center we go east to return to Broadway and, turning south, pass a number of skyscrapers, including the Old AT & T Building and One Liberty Plaza (742ft/226m high), and come to Trinity Church (originally built in 1698; present building 1846). Its churchyard, the oldest in the city, contains the graves of Alexander Hamilton (1755–1804), the first US secretary of the treasury, and Robert Fulton (1765–1815), constructor of the first successful steamship.

Opposite the church, running east, is Wall Street, heart of the American financial world, which takes its name from a wall built by the Dutch as a defence against British attacks. On the corner is the 640ft/195m high tower of the Irving Trust, and beyond this the New York Stock Exchange, housed in a building of 1903 resembling a Roman temple. Activity on the floor of the Exchange (illustration, p. 59) can be watched from the visitors' gallery, and there are also guided tours (open: Mon.–Fri. 9am–4pm). Adjoining the Exchange, at the corner of Broad Street, are the fortress-like headquarters of the J. P. Morgan Bank. At the intersection with Nassau Street is the Federal Hall National Memorial, the city's finest neo-classical building, built in 1842 as the Custom House. It occupies the site of Federal Hall, in which Washington was sworn in as President in 1789 and Congress met for a time. To the north, on Nassau Street, is the 810ft/247m high tower of the Chase Manhattan Bank; the building at 60 Wall Street is only 65ft/20m lower. Wall Street continues east – to the north, at 80 Pine Street, is a 950ft/289m high skyscraper – and finally runs into South Street, on the East River.

On South Street, below the Brooklyn Bridge, is South Street Seaport, once the heart of the Port of New York and now a museum area. Here can be seen

Battery

Fraunces' Tavern

Castle Clinton

*Battery Park City

**World Trade Center

Daily 9.30am–9.30pm

South Broadway/ Trinity Church

*Wall Street

*Stock Exchange

Federal Hall National Memorial

*South Street Seaport

New York City

a number of historic ships, including one of the legendary "flying P Liners", the four-master "Pamir" (1911). There are also harbour cruises in the schooner "Pioneer". Between Water and Front Streets are a number of shops and restaurants. For early risers a visit to the noisy and colourful Fulton Fish Market (April to October, first and third Thursday in the month) can be recommended.

Brooklyn Bridge

From the South Street Seaport there is a good view of the 1150yd/1052m long Brooklyn Bridge, the oldest bridge over the East River (1867–83) and the first to be suspended on steel cables.

City Hall

City Hall, half way down Lower Manhattan, was built in 1803–12 in French Renaissance style. In the Governor's Room are the chair on which Washington sat during his inauguration and the seats used in the first Congress

Woolworth Building

South-west of City Hall, on Broadway, is the neo-Gothic Woolworth Building (by Cass Gilbert, 1913). Until the completion of the Chrysler Building (see below) in 1931 this 790ft/240m high skyscraper was the tallest building in the world.

Civic Center

The area north of City Hall and east of Broadway is occupied by the Civic Center, with the 580ft/177m high Municipal Building, the Federal Building, the Police Headquarters, the United States Courthouse, the New York County Courthouse and the old Tombs Prison.

*Chinatown

To the east of the Civic Center is Chinatown, which with its estimated 100,000 inhabitants is the largest Chinese city outside China. In its narrow lanes, in addition to great numbers of shops selling Chinese wares and numerous Chinese restaurants, visitors will come across Buddhist temples and the Chinese Museum in Mott Street. There are lively celebrations of the Chinese New Year, with colourful parades, between the end of January and mid February.

Little Italy

To the north of Chinatown is Little Italy, a land of pasta and grappa – though it is steadily losing ground to the ever expanding Chinatown.

Lower East Side

Lower East side – the blocks to the east of Chinatown and Little Italy, extending to the East River – is still a slum area occupied by the poorer classes of the population. Here, particularly in Orchard Street, there are many Jewish shops selling good quality fashion goods, shoes and furs at low prices.

SoHo

The name of this district has nothing to do with London's Soho, but merely indicates its situation, South of Houston Street (pronounced House-ton). This old factory and warehouse quarter was "discovered" in the seventies by artists, who brought after them galleries, shops, bars and restaurants. There are many interesting old cast-iron buildings in this area. The brick

Guggenheim SoHo

building at 575 Broadway houses a branch of the Guggenheim Museum of Modern Art, the Guggenheim Museum SoHo, opened in 1992.

*Greenwich Village

Nowadays the "Village", between 14th Street and Broadway, is a handsome (and therefore expensive) residential district. Until the sixties it was the haunt of writers and artists, and something of this reputation still

Washington Square

lingers. Its central feature is the lively Washington Square. Round the square are the buildings of New York City University, and in the centre is a triumphal arch commemorating the centenary of Washington's inauguration as President. Other interesting streets and squares are Bleecker Street (antique shops, restaurants, movie houses, bars, theatres), Commerce Street, Christopher Street (centre of the New York gay scene) and Union Square, once the city's entertainment district.

East Village

To the east, beyond Broadway, is East Village, formerly occupied exclusively by Ukrainians and Poles but discovered in the sixties by the "flower

New York City

children" and now the refuge of all those who can no longer afford a flat in Greenwich Village and have made East Village a fashionable address. Round St Mark's Place are numerous second-hand shops offering an extraordinary variety of wares.

Midtown Manhattan

Midtown Manhattan lies between 14th Street in the south and 57th Street in the north. It is laid out on a regular grid plan, with avenues running north–south, beginning with First Avenue in the east, and streets running east–west, and with Broadway cutting diagonally across it. Its main axis is Fifth Avenue, which begins at Washington Square and runs north for several miles, skirting the east side of Central Park. It divides Manhattan into an eastern and a western half, with streets named accordingly (East 14th Street, West 14th Street, etc.). The Midtown section of Fifth Avenue is the real heart of the city, the scene of the various parades which take place throughout the year. Here, between 34th and 57th Streets, is a great concentration of skyscrapers, on Broadway itself and in the side streets; here too are the city's most exclusive shops, the jewellers Tiffany, Van Cleef and Cartier, the Bergdorf Goodman fashion house, and numbers of luxury hotels.

Situation

**Fifth Avenue
(Map p. 356)

At the corner of Fifth Avenue and 34th Street is the Empire State Building, New York's most celebrated skyscraper, its fame enhanced by its role in the film "King Kong". It is particularly striking when floodlit at night. Built of limestone and granite in 1932, this 1250ft/381m high tower (1475ft/449m including the aerial) was for many years the world's tallest building. From the observation platforms on the 86th and 102nd floors there are incomparable views of New York.

**Empire State Building

Daily 9am–midnight

Two blocks north-east of the Empire State Building, at 29 East 36th Street, is the Pierpont Morgan Library, which houses the collection of rare books and works of art assembled by the banker John Pierpont Morgan (1837–1913). In the East Room are displayed incunabula, manuscripts and autographs; in the West Room are works of art, including the marriage portraits of Martin Luther and Katharina Bora by Lucas Cranach the Elder.

Pierpont Morgan Library

To the west of the Empire State Building, beyond Herald Square, is Macy's, the world's largest department store.

Macy's

Still farther west, between Sixth Avenue (Avenue of the Americas) and Eighth Avenue, is the famous Madison Square Garden Center, its position marked by the 765ft/233m high tower of One Penn Plaza. Underground is the large Pennsylvania Station.

Madison Square Garden Center

From Macy's Broadway runs north-west to Times Square, the heart of the Theater District round Broadway. The former splendour is now somewhat faded, for many theatres have disappeared to give place to porno movie houses and night spots, making this a rather equivocal part of the city, the haunt of drug dealers. Nevertheless Times Square is still one of the great tourist draws, not to be missed if you want to go to the theatre or a first-run movie house. Recently measures have been in train to clean up the area and make Times Square more attractive and safer.

*Times Square

Six blocks east of Times Square along 42nd Street, which runs past New York Public Library (the largest library in the United States after the Library of Congress in Washington DC), is the Chrysler Building. The World Trade Center may be the tallest skyscraper in New York and the Empire State Building the most famous; but in the eyes of New Yorkers the 1045ft/319m high Chrysler Building (1931) is the handsomest, with its fine Art Deco exterior and its fantastic Art Deco entrance lobby.

**Chrysler Building

New York City

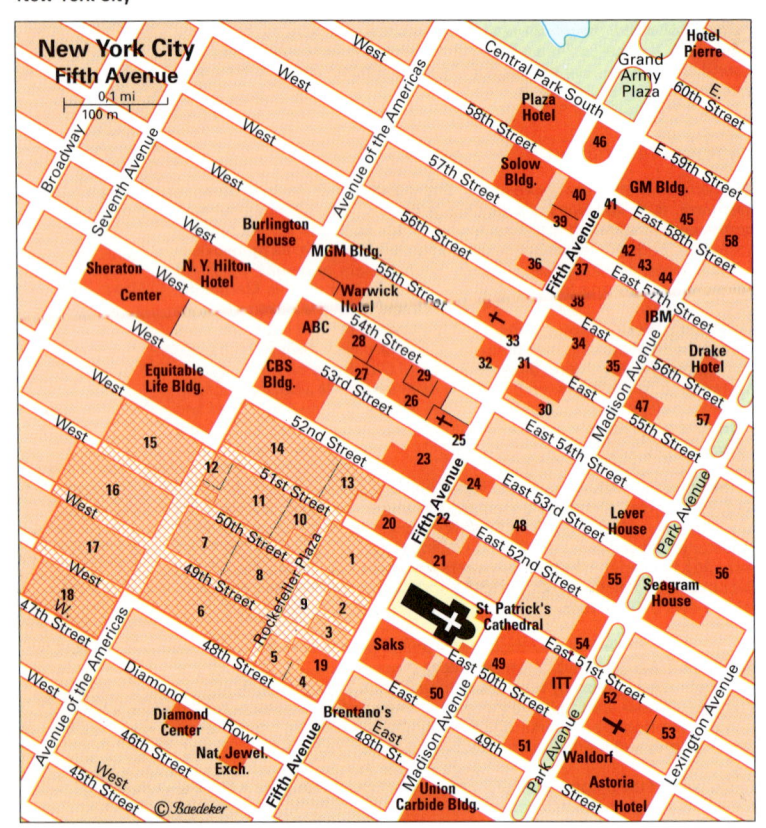

ROCKEFELLER CENTER

1 International Building
2 British Empire Building
3 Maison Française
4 Sinclair Oil Building
5 One Rockefeller Center
6 U.S. Rubber Company
7 General Electric Bldg. West
8 General Electric Bldg. (RCA Bldg)
9 Rockefeller Plaza/Prometheus
10 Associated Press Building
11 Radio City Music Hall
12 Amer. Metal Climax Building
13 15 W. 51st St. Building
14 Sperry Rand Building
15 Time & Life Building
16 Exxon Building
17 McGraw Hill Building
18 Celanese Building
19 Swiss Center
20 640 Fifth Avenue Building
21 Olympic Tower
22 Cartier (Jeweller)
23 Tishman (666 5th Ave.) Building
24 Rolex Building
25 St Thomas Episcopal Church
26 Museum of Modern Art
27 American Craft Museum
28 Hotel Dorset
29 A.A. Rockefeller Garden
30 Elizabeth Arden (Beauty)
31 St Regis Sheraton Hotel
32 Hotel Gotham
33 Fifth Ave. Presbyterian Church
34 Corning Glass Building
35 AT & T Building
36 Doubleday (Bookshop)
37 Tiffany's (Jeweller)
38 Trump Tower
39 Van Cleef (Jeweller)
40 Bergdorf Goodman (Fashion)
41 Bergdorf Goodman (Fashion)
42 Galeries Lafayette
43 Escada (Fashion)
44 Hermès (Fashion)
45 F.A.O. Schwarz (Toys)
46 Pulitzer Memorial Fountain
47 Winslow Hotel
48 Inter-Continental Hotel
49 Palace Hotel
50 Newsweek Building
51 Colgate Palmolive Building
52 St Bartholomew's Church
53 General Electric Building
54 Manuf. Hanover Bank Building
55 Racquet & Tennis Club
56 Citibank Building
57 Mercedes-Benz
58 Standard Brands Building

356

New York City

View over the Avenue of the Americas to the Empire State Building

At the end of 42nd Street, on the East River, is the United Nations Headquarters, occupying a site acquired through the munificence of John D. Rockefeller. It is dominated by the 440ft/134m high Secretariat Building (by Le Corbusier and Niemeyer, 1949–53), with the offices of the Secretary General on the 38th floor. In the Conference Room is a remarkable world clock. Adjoining is the low General Assembly Building, with the chamber in which the General Assembly meets; here too are a souvenir shop and the United Nations post office, whose stamps and special postmarks are much sought after. To sit in on meetings of the General Assembly (at 10.30am and 3.30pm) you must apply in the lobby an hour in advance.

Back along 42nd Street, at the intersection with Park Avenue, is the 807ft/246m high PanAm Building (by Emery Roth, Pietro Belluschi and Walter Gropius, 1963), now occupied by an insurance corporation. At its foot is the huge Grand Central Station.

On three parallel avenues, Park Avenue in the centre, with Lexington Avenue to the east and Madison Avenue to the west, are a series of notable skyscrapers and other buildings. On Park Avenue: Union Carbide Building (No. 270; 705ft/215m high), Chemical Bank (No. 277; 690ft/210m), American Brands (No. 245; 650ft/198m), Seagram Building (No. 375; 525ft/160m; by Mies van der Rohe and Philip Johnson, 1958), Citibank (No. 399; 742ft/226m), Lever House (1952; first glass façade on Park Avenue), the old-established Waldorf Astoria Hotel (No. 301) and the neighbouring St Bartholomew's Church (1919). On Lexington Avenue: Citicorp Tower (No. 575; 915ft/279m; by Hugh Stubbins, 1978, with sloping roof), General Electric Building (No. 570; 640ft/195m) and No. 599 (653ft/199m). On Madison Avenue: IBM Tower (No. 590; 600ft/183m; by E. L. Barnes, 1984), with a marvellous roofed plaza and the IBM Gallery of Science and Art, and the AT & T Building (No. 550; 646ft/197m), the controversial icon of the Post-Modern movement (by Philip Johnson, 1983), with a spectacular roof.

* United Nations Headquarters

Guided visits daily
9.15am–4.45pm

PanAm Building/ Grand Central Station

Park Avenue/ Madison Avenue/ Lexington Avenue

* AT & T Building

New York City

Prometheus in the Rockefeller Center

*St Patrick's Cathedral	In the block bounded by Madison and Fifth Avenues and East 50th and 51st Streets is St Patrick's Cathedral (R.C.), whose 330ft/101m high tower is dwarfed by the surrounding skyscrapers. The cathedral, seat of the Archbishop, was built between 1858 and 1888. In its spacious interior is a figure of Elizabeth Ann Seton (1774–1821), foundress of the Sisters of Charity and the first American saint.
***Rockefeller Center**	Between Fifth and Sixth Avenues and 47th and 52nd Streets is the Rockefeller Center (named after John D. Rockefeller Jr), the world's largest commercial and entertainment complex, decorated with numerous works of art. Its lively centrepiece is the Rockefeller Plaza with its Sunken Plaza (gilded figure of Prometheus), in summer a favourite meeting-place and in winter converted into an ice-rink dominated by a huge and splendidly decorated Christmas tree. Towering above the whole complex is the 850ft/259m high General Electric Building, formerly known as the TCA Building, with the studios of the NBC television company.
General Electric Building	
Radio City Music Hall	Beyond West 50th Street is the Art Deco Radio City Music Hall (1930), with the world's largest auditorium (6200 seats).
Skyscrapers	Other striking skyscrapers in and around the Rockefeller Center are the Exxon Building (1251 Sixth Avenue; 750ft/229m), the McGraw Hill Building (1221 Sixth Avenue; 673ft/205m), the Equitable Center Tower West (787 Seventh Avenue; 750ft/229m), the Olympic Tower (645 Fifth Avenue; 620ft/189m; by Skidmore, Owings and Merrill, 1976) and, rather farther north, the Trump Tower (725 Fifth Avenue; 663ft/202m; by Der Scott), with a terraced exterior and a lavishly decorated atrium.
*Trump Tower	
Museum of TV and Radio	This museum at 25 West 52nd Street offers an impressive survey of the world of film, television and radio in the United States.
***Museum of Modern Art**	North of the Rockefeller Center are the Museum Tower Apartments, a 650ft/198m high apartment block which marks the site of the Museum of

New York City

Museum of Modern Art
('M.O.M.A.')

FOURTH FLOOR

Architecture and Design

A: Architecture
D: Design

THIRD FLOOR

Prints and Illustrated Books

Painting and Sculpture
Prewar A: America before WWII
Postwar E&A: Europe and America after WWII
AE: Abstract Expressionism
EAE: Early Expressionism
C: Contemporary art
M: Matisse ("The Bath")

Drawings

SECOND FLOOR

Photography

Painting and Sculpture

P-I: Post-Impressionism
CUB: Cubism
EXP: Expressionism
SUR: Surrealism
Ky: Kandinsky
M: Monet ("Waterlillies")
MD: Mondrian
MDR: Members' Dining Room

FIRST FLOOR

OR: Office Reception
CR: Check Room
ICG: International Council Galleries
EC: (changing exhibitions) Edward John Noble Education Center
GC: Garden Café
MS: Museum Store

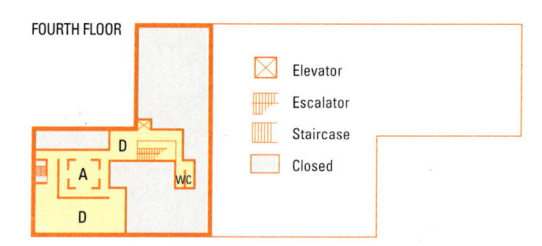

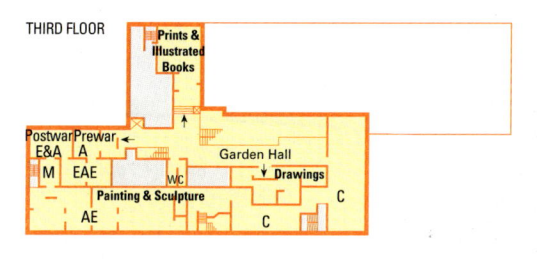

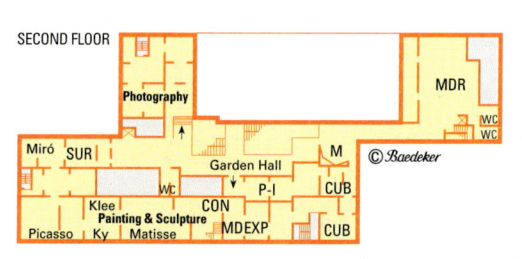

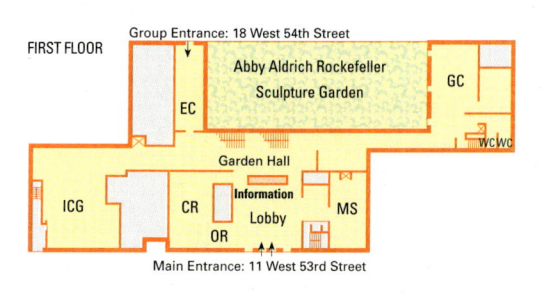

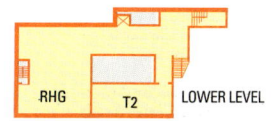

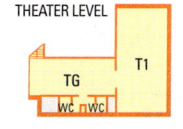

LOWER LEVEL
RHG: René d'Harnoncourt Galleries
T2:   Roy & Niuta Titus Theater 2

THEATER LEVEL
TG: Theater.Gallery
T1:   Roy & Niuta Titus Theater 1

New York
Uptown Manhattan
Central Park

0,3 mi / 500 m
© Baedeker

The Cloisters, Audubon Terrace, Grant's Tomb

MORNINGSIDE HEIGHTS
- Columbia University
- University Hall
- Low Memor. Libr.
- Cathedral of St. John the Divine

HARLEM
- Harlem Meer

WESTSIDE
- Riverside Museum
- Soldiers' & Sailors' Monument
- Jewish Martyrs' Memorial
- Jewish Center
- Hayden Planetarium
- Amer. Museum of Natural History
- N.Y. Historical Society
- Shakespeare Garden
- Strawberry Fields
- The Lake
- The Ramble
- Sheep Meadow
- Heckscher Playground

CENTRAL PARK
- Conservatory Gardens
- Receiving (Croton) Reservoir
- Great Lawn
- Bandshell
- The Mall
- The Pond

YORKVILLE
- Museum of the City of N.Y.
- Mt. Sinai Hospital
- Madison
- Jewish Museum
- Cooper-Hewitt Museum
- Guggenheim Museum
- Metropolitan Museum
- Stuyvesant Mansion
- Whitney Museum
- Frick Collection
- St. James Ch.
- Hunter College
- Temple Emanu-El
- Asia House

- Lincoln Center
- N.Y. Coliseum
- Columbus Circle
- Essex H.
- Zoo
- Arsenal
- Plaza Hotel
- Getty Bldg.
- Carnegie Hall
- Burlington House
- GM Building
- Sheraton Center Hilton
- Mus. of Modern Art
- Rockefeller Center
- St. Thomas Ch.

Hudson River

1. Delacorte Theater
2. Belvedere Castle
3. Cleopatra's Needle
4. Loeb Boat House
5. Bethesda Fountain
6. Wollman Rink
7. Spanish & Portug. Synagogue
8. Holy Trinity Lutheran Church
9. YMCA
10. American Bible Society
11. Hotel Mayflower
12. Gulf & Western Building
13. St. Paul the Apostle Church (R.C.)
14. N.Y. Convention & Visitors Bureau
15. Hotel Ritz Carlton
16. Art Students Legue
17. Hotel Osborne
18. Cami Hall
19. Solow Building
20. N.Y. City Center Theater

Downtown

Modern Art (MOMA). This, the world's finest collection of late 19th and 20th century art, has been housed since 1984 in a light-coloured building by Cesar Pelli at 11 West 53rd Street. Only a brief summary of the artists represented can be given here:

Abby Aldrich Rockefeller Sculpture Garden: modern sculpture by Max Ernst, Alexander Calder, Picasso ("The Goat"), Henry Moore and many others. First floor: Post Impressionists (Degas, Gauguin, Munch, Toulouse-Lautrec, Modigliani), Cubists (Braque, Chagall), Expressionists, Futurists, the Blauer Reiter group (Kokoschka, Schmidt-Rotluff, Nolde, Macke, Heckel), Mondrian, Matisse (the largest collection of his work anywhere), Picasso ("Demoiselles d'Avignon", "Harlequin"), Dada (Max Ernst, Schwitters), Joan Miró, Surrealists. Second floor: mainly American artists (Hopper, O'Keefe, Prendergast), Pop Art (Oldenburg, Lichtenstein, Rauschenberg). Third floor: architecture and design, with original designs by leading architects.

Daily 11am–6pm, Thur. to 9pm; closed Wed.

Adjoining MOMA is the American Craft Museum (40 West 53rd Street), mainly devoted to craft products of the 20th century. North of this, at 157 West 57th Street, is the venerable old Carnegie Hall, the venue of many celebrated concerts.

American Craft Museum/ Carnegie Hall

Uptown Manhattan / Central Park

Uptown Manhattan extends from 57th Street all the way north to the Henry Hudson Bridge, taking in Central Park, the Museum Mile on the east side of the park and the black district of Harlem.

Situation

Central Park, New York's green lung and recreation area, lies between 59th Street in the south and 110th Street in the north and between Fifth and Eighth Avenues in east and west, with a total area of 840 acres/340 hectares. Here you can sunbathe, roller-skate, row on the lake or drive round the park in a horse-drawn carriage. Among features of particular interest in the park are the Zoo at the south-east corner, opened in 1989; the old house known as the Dairy, dating from the park's 19th century origins, with an exhibition on the history of the park; the Mall, a wide avenue lined with statues of writers and composers which leads to the Bethesda Fountain and to the lake with Loeb's Boathouse (boat hire); to the north of this Belvedere Castle, the highest point in the park, and Cleopatra's Needle (counterpart of the one in London), an Egyptian obelisk of about 1500 B.C. from Heliopolis; to the west of the Bethesda Fountain the Strawberry Fields, named after the Beatles' song, which lie opposite the Dakota Building on 72nd Street in front of which John Lennon was murdered in 1980. The northern section of the park is better avoided even during the day.

**Central Park

East of Central Park

On the eastern edge of Central Park, at 1000 Fifth Avenue, is the extensive range of buildings occupied by the Metropolitan Museum of Art. The main building was erected between 1879 and 1898; the middle section was designed by Richard M. Hunt, the side wings by McKim, Meade and White. The Metropolitan Museum of Art, the largest art museum in the world after the British Museum in London and the Hermitage in St Petersburg, was founded in 1870 by a group of New Yorkers, and now contains over 3 million works of art, some 100,000 of which are on permanent display. When visiting the museum you should select on the printed plan the particular sections that interest you most; here only the briefest summary of the museum's contents can be given:

****Metropolitan Museum of Art**

Tue.–Thur. and Sun. 9.30am–5.15pm, Fri. and Sat. to 8.45pm; closed Mon.

Ancient Egyptian art (including the temple from Dendur, taken down during the construction of the Aswan High Dam, presented to the United States and re-erected here, fourteen statues of Queen Hatshepsut

Main floor

New York City

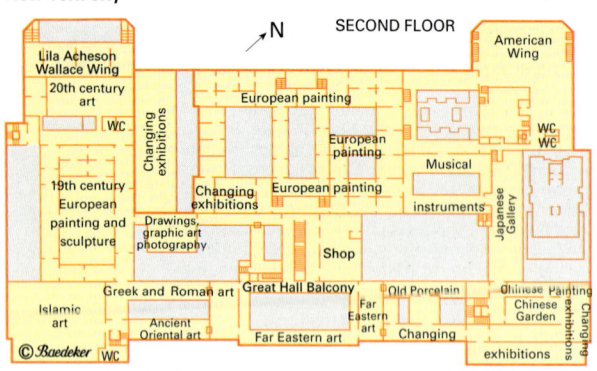

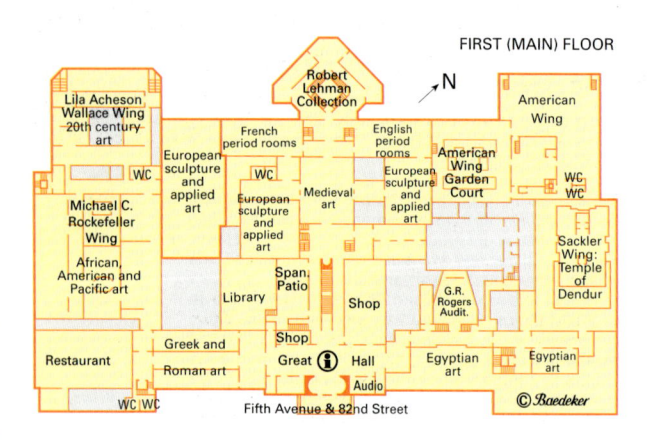

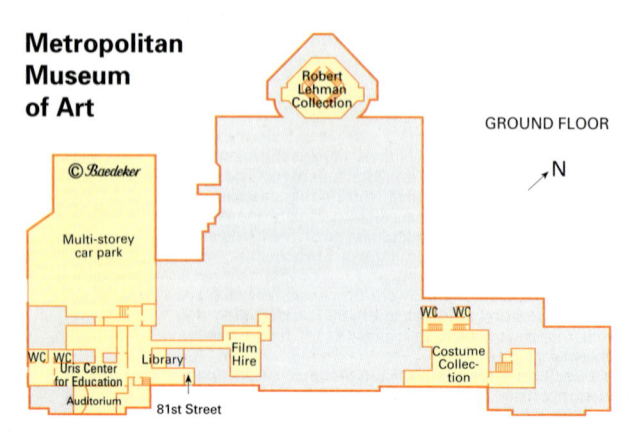

Metropolitan Museum of Art

In Central Park, a green oasis surrounded by skyscrapers

and a princess's gold jewellery dating from about 1900 B.C.); Greek and Roman art (including finds from the palace of Knossos and Roman copies of Hellenistic sculpture); medieval and Byzantine art (sculpture, large tapestry gallery); European sculpture, period rooms (including a marble patio from the Spanish castle of Vélez Blanco, a study from a palace in Gubbio, Sèvres and Meissen porcelain); arms and armour (Viking swords, parade and jousting armour); Robert Lehman Collection (paintings and drawings, with works by Dürer, Memling, Cranach the Elder, El Greco, Goya); American Wing (American art and applied art; continued on second floor); Michael C. Rockefeller Wing (art of the Pacific area); Lila Acheson Wallace Wing (20th century art, including Picasso's portrait of Gertrude Stein, Paul Klee collection, Edward Hopper, sculpture garden; continued on second floor).

Second floor

European painting (Raphael, Titian, Veronese, Frans Hals, Vermeer, van Eyck, van der Weyden, Memling, van der Goes, Cranach the Elder, Holbein the Younger, Dürer, Rembrandt, Rubens, van Dyck, Poussin, Hogarth, Reynolds, Turner, etc.); André Meyer Galleries (19th century European art, including Symbolists, Romantics, Impressionists); Islamic art (woodcarving, ceramics, carpets); ancient Oriental art (Persia, Anatolia, Babylon, etc.); art of the Far East (including Chinese and Japanese lacquerwork, jade and bronzes); drawings and printed graphic art (including Leonardo da Vinci, Michelangelo and Dürer; woodcuts by Goya); musical instruments (including three Stradivariuses).

*Frick Collection

Tue.–Sat. 10am–6pm, Sun. 1–6pm

South of the Metropolitan Museum, at 1 East 70th Street, is the Frick Collection, presented in the very different setting of a sumptuously appointed Empire-style mansion. This very fine private collection assembled by the Pittsburgh steel magnate Henry Clay Frick (1849–1919) concentrates particularly on painting of the 14th–18th centuries (Titian, Bellini, El Greco, Ingres, Vermeer, van Eyck, etc.), Italian Renaissance bronzes and enamelwork.

New York City

*Whitney Museum of American Art

The excellent Whitney Museum of American Art (945 Madison Avenue) is devoted to modern American art, including Pop Art and works left by Edward Hopper. Open: Tue., Wed. and Fri.–Sun. 11am–6pm, Thur. 1–8pm.

**Solomon R. Guggenheim Museum

Daily except Mon. 10am–8pm

The Guggenheim Museum, north of the Metropolitan Museum at 1071 Fifth Avenue, is impressive not only for the fascinating collection assembled by the industrialist Solomon R. Guggenheim (1861–1949) but also for the building in which it is housed (illustration, p. 99). Designed by Frank Lloyd Wright (see Famous People), this is circular in form, each storey larger than the one below. Visitors walk up or down in a spiral as they go round the collection, which includes works by Kandinsky (largest collection in the world), Henri Rousseau, Braque, Picasso, Léger, Cézanne, van Gogh, Chagall and many other artists.

Cooper-Hewitt Museum

A short distance north of the Guggenheim Museum, at 2 East 91st Street, is the Cooper-Hewitt Museum, a branch of the Smithsonian Institution (see Washington DC) devoted to American design.

Jewish Museum

A little farther north again (Fifth Avenue and 92nd Street) is the Jewish Museum, with one of the world's largest collection of Judaica.

Museum of the City of New York

Still farther north (Fifth Avenue and 103rd Street) is the Museum of the City of New York, which is devoted to the history of the city, with old views of New York, rooms furnished in the style of different periods and a wide variety of informative material ranging from baseball to the New York fire service.

West of Central Park

Columbus Circle

At the south-west corner of Central Park Broadway crosses the Columbus Circle, a busy roundabout in the centre of which is a column bearing a

The "Met", one of the world's great opera houses

New York City

statue of Columbus, set up here in 1892. Here is the New York Convention and Visitors Bureau, housed in a Moorish-style building opposite the 680ft/207m high Gulf and Western Building.

North-west of the Columbus Circle is the Lincoln Center for the Performing Arts, the city's cultural heart. The most important buildings in the complex are the Avery Fisher Hall, home of the New York Philharmonic Orchestra; the New York State Theater, home of the New York City Opera and New York City Ballet; and the Metropolitan Opera House, the legendary "Met", one of the world's great opera houses. In the lobby is an Information Center (programmes of performances; guided tours).

*Lincoln Center for the Performing Arts

Metropolitan Opera

On the west side of Central Park (79th Street) is the American Museum of Natural History, New York's largest museum after the Metropolitan Museum of Art. It illustrates the natural history of the United States with a great variety of displays and dioramas, with such outstanding items as the model of a whale in the Hall of Ocean Life and the "Brazilian Princess", the world's largest cut precious stone, a 21,327 carat topaz weighing 9½ pounds (4.3kg). Children will particularly enjoy the Discovery Room, where they can touch and experiment with the exhibits. Attached to the museum is the Hayden Planetarium, which puts on a series of special shows on the general theme of exploring the universe.

**American Museum of Natural History

Daily 10am–5.45pm, Fri. and Sat. till 8.45pm

Between 72nd and 125th Streets the long, narrow Riverside Park extends along the banks of the Hudson River. It contains many monuments, including the tomb of Ulysses S. Grant, Union general and 18th President of the United States, and his wife (at the north end of the park).

Riverside Park

North of Central Park

Immediately north of Central Park is Harlem, home of New York's Afro-American population and still a neglected and dilapidated part of the city. It is better not to explore Harlem on foot, even by day: the best way of seeing its main features of interest – the Abyssinian Baptist Church, All Saints Church, Strivers' Row, the Schomberg Center for Research in Black Culture, etc. – is on a coach tour. In the evening, if you want to visit one of the excellent jazz clubs in the area you should take a taxi.

Harlem

Near the north-west corner of Central Park is the Cathedral Church of St John the Divine, begun in 1891 but still unfinished. If it should ever be completed it will be one of the largest churches in the world.

*St John the Divine

Much farther north (Broadway and 115th Street), on Audubon Terrace, are the Washington Heights Museums, including the Museums of the Hispanic Society and Numismatic Society and the National Museum of the American Indian, a large and very interesting collection of material on the original inhabitants of the whole American continent (open: Tue.–Sat. 10am–5pm, Sun. 1–5pm).

Washington Heights Museums
*Museum of the American Indian

Picturesquely situated above the Hudson River at the northern tip of Manhattan, in Fort Tryon Park, are the Cloisters, which house the Metropolitan Museum's collection of religious art and architecture, including whole cloisters, chapterhouses and chapels, all harmoniously brought together in a modern building to create the atmosphere of a medieval monastery.

The **Cloisters

Daily exc. Mon. 9.30am–5.15pm

Brooklyn / Queens / Bronx / Staten Island

Brooklyn, the largest of New York's boroughs, lies on Long Island, to the east of Manhattan beyond the East River. North of Brooklyn, also on Long Island, is Queens, and north of this again, beyond the East River and

Situation

New York City

separated from Manhattan by the Harlem River, is the Bronx. To the south of Manhattan, bordering on New Jersey, is Staten Island.

Brooklyn — Brooklyn is linked with Manhattan by the Brooklyn–Battery Tunnel, Brooklyn Bridge, Manhattan Bridge and Queensboro Bridge.

*Brooklyn Museum — The principal feature of interest is the Brooklyn Museum (200 Eastern Parkway), which has one of the finest collections anywhere of Egyptian, Near Eastern and Oriental art, together with American and European painting, costumes and applied and decorative art.

Brooklyn Botanic Garden — Beside the Museum is Brooklyn Botanic Garden, with 12,000 different plants, including 900 varieties of roses.

Brooklyn Children's Museum — At 145 Brooklyn Avenue is the Brooklyn Children's Museum, the first children's museum in the world, founded in 1899. It seeks to promote practical experience of technology and nature, allowing children to touch everything and carry out their own experiments.

Greenwood Cemetery — On Gowanus Heights (main entrance 5th Avenue and 25th Street) is Greenwood Cemetery, laid out in 1840. Among those buried here are Samuel Morse (1792–1872), inventor of the telegraph, and Lola Montez (1818–61), the dancer who became the mistress of King Ludwig I of Bavaria.

*Coney Island — At the southern tip of Brooklyn is Coney Island, which before the Second World War was a famous amusement park and bathing beach on the Atlantic but has now rather come down in the world. Nevertheless it is still very attractive and the beach is clean. Here too is the New York Aquarium, with marine fauna from all over the world.

Gateway National Recreation Area — The Gateway National Recreation Area on the coast of Staten Island, to the south of Coney Island across the Verrazano Narrows, offers tired New Yorkers the relaxation of quiet natural surroundings.

Queens
Flushing Meadows — Flushing Meadows Park, where the World's Fairs of 1939–40 and 1964–65 were held, is known to tennis fans all over the world as the place where the US Open Championship is staged – though most of the stars feel that the noise of the traffic and the aircraft using LaGuardia Airport disturbs their concentration. The Shea Stadium is the home ground of the New York Jets football team.

American Museum of the Moving Image — The American Museum of the Moving Image (34–12 36th Street) is devoted to the history of American film.

Bronx

*Bronx Zoo
*Botanical Garden — The Bronx has gained the reputation of a run-down area with a high crime rate; and it is certainly advisable to drive quickly through the broken-down landscape of South Bronx, without getting out, to visit the New York Zoological Park (the Bronx Zoo) in the centre of the Bronx, in which almost all the animals live in open-air enclosures. Immediately north of the Zoo is the New York Botanical Garden (area 290 acres/117 hectares), laid out in 1891 on the model of London's Kew Gardens.

Staten Island
Historic Richmond Town — It is well worth while to take the ferry to Staten Island, not only for the sake of the marvellous view of Manhattan but also to visit Historic Richmond Town, a museum village with 39 houses of the 17th–19th centuries which seeks to re-create the life of the early colonists. Here too is the Mausoleum of the Vanderbilt family.

Surroundings of New York City

*Long Island — This 110 mile/180km long island in the Atlantic is the most popular area of relaxation in the New York region, with beautiful bathing beaches (e.g. on Jones Beach or in Robert Moses State Park). Farther east are the quiet and elegant settlements known as the Hamptons, where there are more fashionable beaches and the rural retreats of the city's intelligentsia, as well as attractive old streets like East Hampton's Main Street, which ends at a fish restaurant. The northern part of the island, round Oyster Bay, is also a favourite getaway for the wealthy.

Niagara Falls F 46/47

New York State – Canadian province of Ontario

The Niagara Falls – among the largest, most impressive and best known falls in the world – lie in the extreme north-west of New York State. Here masses of water from Lake Erie plunge over an almost 200ft/60m drop to flow into Lake Ontario. First described and sketched by a missionary, Louis Hennepin in 1678, they attract over 12 million visitors a year.

Situation and characteristics

The origins of the Niagara Falls go back to the Ice Age, when the river, flowing at a higher level than today over a limestone plateau on the Niagara escarpment, dropped down to the level of Lake Ontario near the present-day town of Lewiston. Then, as a result of retrograde erosion, the falls rapidly moved upstream. Over the last 3000 years they have moved back from the Rainbow Bridge to their present position. The pace of erosion depends on the volume of water going over the falls; but at present rates it can be expected that within a few hundred thousand years the Niagara Falls will be close to the American city of Buffalo.

Formation

The Niagara Falls at present power hydro-electric stations with a total output of 3 million kilowatts. Plans to increase this output are the subject of violent controversy.

Energy potential

Niagara Falls

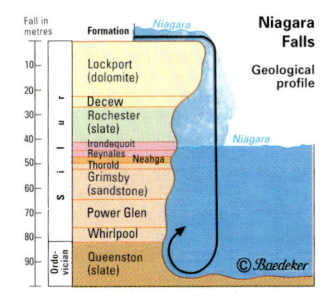

The masses of water from Lake Erie thunder over a horseshoe-shaped rock wall 700yd/640m long at the Horseshoe Falls, which are in Canada, and, a short distance north-east, over the straight American Falls, 360yd/330m long. The frontier between the United States and Canada runs along the middle of the river. Before the falls were harnessed to produce hydro-electricity water poured down at the rate of almost 1,300,000 gallons (6 million litres) per second. A Canadian–American agreement of 1951 on the joint use of the water guarantees a flow of just under half that amount in summer and just under a quarter at night and in winter. In sunny weather the spray at the foot of the falls produces magnificent rainbows.

**Horseshoe Falls
*American Falls

Below the falls the Niagara River flows through a deep gorge varying in width between 90yd/80m and 330yd/300m. To the north-west the gorge narrows and forms a series of rapids (the Whirlpool Rapids).

*Gorge

3 miles/5km below the American Falls the river changes course again, forming the Whirlpool in a great cauldron originally created by tectonic movements and turning north-east over the Lower Rapids towards Lake Ontario.

*Whirlpool

Views of the Falls

The best views of the falls (which are illuminated at night) are to be had from terraces and observation towers on the Canadian side (see below).

Terraces and observation towers

367

Baedeker Special
Daredevils of Niagara

The Niagara Falls have long exerted a fascination on daredevils and publicity-seekers anxious to hit the headlines or appear on television. A small selection:
1825: Three men die in an attempt to go over the falls in boats.
1829: Sam Patch twice jumps a distance of 120ft/37m from a ladder at the Cave of the Winds (near Goat Island) and survives.
1859: M. Blondin, a French rope-dancer, crosses the gorge on a tightrope several times, once carrying his impressario on his back and on another occasion with a stove on which he makes an omelette.
1873: An Italian named Balleni crosses the falls on a tightrope
1876: An Italian woman, Maria Spetterini or Spelterina, becomes the first woman to cross the gorge on a tightrope.
1882: Steve Peer crosses the river on a tightrope several times by day and then falls to his death in attempting to cross by night.
1883: The Channel-swimmer Matthew Webb is drowned in an attempt to swim through the Whirlpool Rapids.
1886: Carlisle D. Graham traverses the Whirlpool Rapids four times in a barrel constructed by himself, Maud Willard is drowned in attempting a similar feat and W. J. Kendall swims through the rapids.
1888: Robert W. Flack is drowned trying to sail down the rapids in a specially constructed boat.
1889: Steve Brodi goes over the Horseshoe Falls in a wooden barrel and survives.
1901: Martha Wagenführer traverses the Whirlpool Rapids in a barrel; a teacher named Annie Edson Taylor goes over the Horseshoe Falls in a wooden barrel weighted with an anvil and suffers only slight injuries; Lincoln Beach flies under the Upper Steel Arch Bridge in a light aircraft.
1910: Claus Larsen negotiates the rapids in a motorboat.
1911: An Englishman, Bobby Leach, goes over the Horseshoe Falls in a barrel but is severely injured.
1920: An English hairdresser named Charles Stephens dies in a plunge over the Horseshoe Falls in a wooden barrel.
1928: Jean Lussier launches himself over the Horseshoe Falls in a large rubber ball and survives.
1930: George L. Stathika survives a plunge over the falls in a steel and timber barrel but dies of suffocation as a result of delay in recovering the barrel.
1951: William "Red" Hill Jr, who along with his father had saved many lives at the falls, dies in a plunge over the falls in a container made from automobile tyres.
1960: A seven-year-old boy named Roger Woodward survives a plunge over the falls after a boating accident.

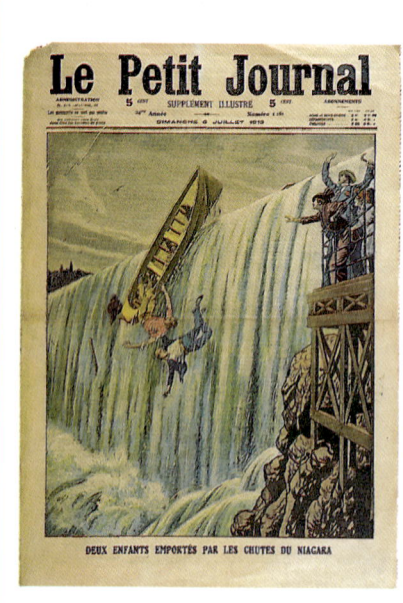

Niagara makes headlines in Europe

Niagara Falls

Rainbow under the Horseshoe Falls

Even more impressive is a rather damp boat trip in the "Maid of the Mist" (waterproof coats and hats provided). The boat sails past the American Falls into the clouds of spray under the Horseshoe Falls.

**"Maid of the Mist"

An elevator runs down to the bottom of the gorge, and a breathtaking trail runs along the side of the gorge above the swirling green water.

*Gorge Trail

A cableway on the Canadian side, the Spanish Aerocar, crosses the surging waters of the Whirlpool.

Whirlpool/Spanish Aerocar

Sightseeing flights in a helicopter are available both on the American side (Goat Island) and on the Canadian side.

Helicopter flights

Niagara Falls, a Double Town

From Prospect Point on the American side there is a fine view of the falls. Here the Observation Tower rises above the bottom of the gorge, offering magnificent panoramic prospects. Elevators run down to the landing-stage from which the "Maid of the Mist" departs. From the foot of the tower wooden gangways run below Prospect Point to the American Falls. On the upper rim of the gorge, across the road, is the New York State Parks Visitor Center (open: mid May to mid September daily 8.30am–8pm; shorter hours at other times of year).

Niagara Falls (USA)

From Prospect Point a path crosses a bridge on to little Green Island, in the middle of the rapids just above the American Falls, and then over another bridge on to Goat Island, between the American and the Horseshoe Falls. From the northern tip of this wooded island a gangway leads on to little Luna Island, beyond the narrow Bridal Veil Falls, which are separated from the American Falls by Luna Island.

Prospect Point

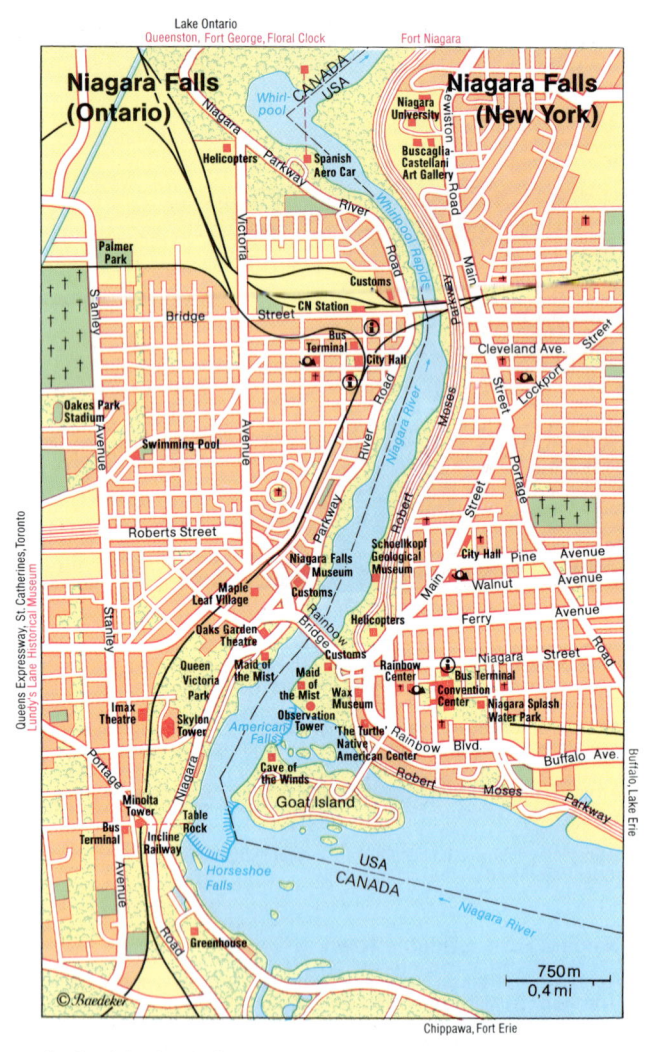

Niagara Falls

Goat Island	On Goat Island, at the foot of the American Falls, is the entrance to the Cave of the Winds (elevators and tunnel), from which boardwalks lead to just under the falls (open: end of May to beginning of September daily 10am–7pm; shorter hours at other times of year). From the end of the tunnel under the American Falls the Horseshoe Falls Lower Gorge Walkway leads to the foot of the Horseshoe Falls.
*Native American Center	On the mainland opposite Goat Island is the Native American Center for the Living Arts (25 Rainbow Boulevard), known as the "Turtle", with displays illustrating the culture of the North American Indians. In summer there are performances of Iroquois dances here.

Niagara Falls

North-east of the Rainbow Bridge is the Schoellkopf Geological Museum, which traces 500 million years of geological history in the Niagara area. From the museum the Upper Gorge Nature Trail leads to Whirlpool Rapids State Park.

*Schoellkopf Geological Museum

Near the museum (Whirlpool Street/Pine Avenue) is the Niagara Falls Aquarium, with a variety of marine animals, including sealions, penguins and otters; natural world of the Great Lakes and North Atlantic.

Aquarium

Maple Leaf Village, on the Canadian side of the Niagara River, is a lively shopping and entertainment centre. From the Maple Leaf Tower there are magnificent panoramic views. Here too is the Niagara Daredevil Museum, devoted to the many daring and often fatal attempts to master the falls and the rapids (see box on p. 368).

Niagara Falls (Canada)
Maple Leaf Village

Upstream, above the gorge, is beautiful Queen Victoria Park, with the Oakes Garden Theatre (an amphitheatre in Greco-Roman style set in attractive gardens, with terraces and promenades; views of the falls), rock gardens and greenhouses.

*Queen Victoria Park

From Table Rock there is an overwhelming view of the Horseshoe Falls. From Table Rock House elevators and three tunnels lead to the foot of the falls (open: mid June to beginning of September daily 9am–10.30pm; at other times of year Mon.–Fri. 9am–4.30pm, Sat. and Sun. 9am–5.30pm). Nearby is the lower station of the Niagara Incline Railway, a funicular running up to the rim of the gorge.

Table Rock

From the observation platform of the Minolta Tower (open: daily 9am–10pm; longer in summer) there are overwhelming views of the Niagara gorge and the falls.

Minolta Tower

On the west side of Queen Victoria Park is the 520ft/158m high Skylon Tower, from which also there are magnificent panoramic views. In the base of the tower is the Niagara International Center (exhibitions, shops).

Skylon Tower

Close by is the Niagara IMAX Theatre (6170 Buchanan Avenue), which presents impressions of Niagara on a screen six storeys high.

Niagara IMAX Theatre

At 4960 Clifton Hill is Ripley's "Believe it or not" Museum. Nearby, at 4915 Clifton Hill, is Louis Tussaud's Waxworks, and at 4943 Clifton Hill is the Guinness World of Records.

Other features of interest

Surroundings of Niagara Falls

On the American side the Robert Moses Parkway runs downstream through Whirlpool State Park and then along the Lower Rapids to Devil's Hole State Park. Ahead is a view of the massive Robert Moses hydroelectric station. Then comes the campus of the old Niagara University, with the Castellani Art Museum (art of the 18th–20th centuries). The road continues to the Robert Moses State Power Plant. Beyond this the parkway turns away from the river and skirts the so-called "Art Park". It then bypasses the town of Lewiston on the east. A few minutes' drive north-east is the Shrine of Our Lady of Fatima (Swan Road), a place of pilgrimage with a church of some architectural interest (1965). Farther north, before the Niagara Escarpment, is a fertile wine and fruit growing area.

American side

To the north of Youngstown, at the point where the Niagara River flows into Lake Ontario, is Old Fort Niagara (State Park). The fort was built in 1726 on the site of an earlier French post established in 1679. There are presentations of historic events in authentic uniforms throughout the year.

Old Fort Niagara

On the Canadian side the Niagara Parkway runs downstream, passing the Whirlpool (see above) and Niagara Glen, to the Sir Adam Beck Generating Plant, the Canadian counterpart of the Robert Moses Plant on the opposite bank.

Canadian side

The beautiful gardens of the Niagara Parks Commission School of Horticulture are well worth a visit. Much photographed are the rose garden (in June) and the floral clock.

*School of Horticulture

North Carolina

Brock's Monument	A few minutes' drive beyond this, on Queenston Heights on the edge of the Niagara Escarpment, is Brock's Monument, commemorating Major-General Isaac Brock, who fell in 1812.
*Fort George	Beyond this are McFarland House (1800; museum) and Fort George, built at the end of the 18th century as a defence against attacks by the rebellious Americans. During the 1812–13 war the fort fell into the hands of the Americans. After 1820 it was abandoned. Recently restored, it is now protected as a National Historic Park. During the main tourist season soldiers put on a show depicting life in the fort in the early 19th century.
Shaw Festival Theater	In the George Bernard Shaw Festival Theater plays by Shaw are performed from the end of April to the middle of October.
*Niagara-on-the-Lake	The little picture postcard town of Niagara-on-the-Lake (pop. 13,000) on Lake Ontario was the first capital of Upper Canada. Its trim little Victorian houses are set in beautiful gardens. Its main street, Queen Street, is lined with shops, restaurants and cafés. In the climatically favoured area round Niagara-on-the-Lake are a number of large vineyards.
Fort Erie	Farther west, opposite Buffalo, at the point where the Niagara River leaves Lake Erie, is the town of Fort Erie (pop. 24,000), founded in 1748 by British loyalists. The two towns are linked by the Peace Bridge. A mile south of the bridge is Fort Erie, established in 1764, which was captured in 1814 by American troops. It is now a kind of open-air military museum.
*Historic Fort Erie	

North Carolina (State; NC) N–P 41–51

Area:
  52,670sq.miles/136,413sq.km
Population: 6,736,000
Capital: Raleigh
Popular names: Tar Heel State,
  Old North State

Situation and topography	North Carolina (named in honour of King Charles I), on the middle Atlantic coast, was one of the thirteen founding states. Some two-fifths of its area is occupied by the swampy coastal plain, off which are the long, narrow Outer Banks; another two-fifths is accounted for by the gently undulating Piedmont Plateau to the west; and beyond this are the Blue Ridge Mountains and Great Smoky Mountains, with Mount Mitchell (6684ft/2037m), the highest peak in the eastern United States. The climate, particularly in the south-east, is subtropical, with hot summers and mild winters; to the west the summers are cooler.
History	In 1585 Sir Walter Raleigh founded the first English settlement on American soil on Roanoke Island, but this was later abandoned. Planned settlement began around 1660, with settlers moving in from Virginia. In 1689 the colony, hitherto known as the Carolinas, was divided into a northern and a southern part. On May 12th 1776 North Carolina became the first British colony in North America to resolve on independence, and on November 21st 1789 it joined the Union as the twelfth state. In 1834 the Cherokees living in the forests of the Appalachians were deported to reservations in Oklahoma on the "Trail of Tears". In April 1861, after the bombardment of Fort Sumter, the state joined the Confederation. On December 17th 1903 the brothers Wilbur and Orville Wright made the first powered flight in history at Kitty Hawk on the Outer Banks.
Economy	North Carolina is the largest producer of tobacco in the United States, and the tobacco industry, centred on Winston-Salem, is a major contributor to the economy, followed by textiles, furniture manufacture, papermaking

North Carolina

and the electrical industry. The principal crops apart from tobacco are maize and soya beans. Tourism is an important source of revenue on the coast.

Places of Interest in North Carolina

Asheville, in the far west of the state, was the birthplace of the writer Thomas Wolfe (1900–38). It is an ideal centre for excursions on the Blue Ridge Parkway and into the Great Smoky Mountains National Park (see entry).

Asheville

Chapel Hill, north-west of Raleigh, is the seat of the University of North Carolina, the oldest state university in the United States. On the university campus is the Morehead Planetarium.

Chapel Hill

Charlotte (pop. 400,000), North Carolina's largest city, lies in the south-west of the state. It is named after Charlotte of Mecklenburg, wife of King George II: hence also the name of Mecklenburg County, in which it is situated. Charlotte/Douglas Airport is one of the most important inland airports in the eastern United States. Features of interest in Charlotte are the Mint Museum of Art (European, African and American art), housed in the former Mint; the Discovery Place, a science museum with the largest planetarium in the United States; and the Charlotte Museum of History, in the Hezekiah Alexander House (1774), the oldest house in Mecklenburg County. For motor sports enthusiasts there is the Charlotte Motor Speedway, for those in quest of entertainment the Carolwinds theme park (10 miles/16km south on I 77), which has no fewer than five roller coasters.

Charlotte

Features of interest in the state capital, Raleigh, are the State Capitol (1840), the Museum of History, the State Museum of Natural Sciences and the North Carolina Museum of Art.

Raleigh

Quayside, Wilmington (North Carolina)

North Dakota

Wilmington	The port of Wilmington has a small and very attractive historic district. Its main tourist attraction is the Second World War battleship "North Carolina", now a museum.
Winston-Salem	In the double town of Winston-Salem is the world's largest cigarette factory (R. J. Reynolds Tobacco Company, 1100 Reynolds Boulevard). The historic district of Salem, founded by the Moravian Brethren in 1766, has been handsomely restored. The Museum of American Art is housed in the mansion of the Reynolds tobacco family.
Other places of interest	Blue Ridge Parkway (see Virginia), Great Smoky Mountains National Park (see entry), Outer Banks (see entry)

North Dakota (State; ND)   A–C 21–29

Area:
70,700sq.miles/183,118sq.km
Population: 635,000
Capital: Bismarck
Popular name: Peace Garden State

Situation and topography	North Dakota (named after the Dakota tribe) lies in the Middle West on the frontier with Canada, in the centre of the North American continent. The landscape of the Great Plains in the west, traversed by the Missouri, changes towards the east from gently undulating ground moraines to steep hills and continues to rise fairly sharply in the Coteau du Missouri. Along the west of the state, on the border with Montana, are the barren Badlands, robbed of their topsoil by erosion. The climate is continental, with extremely cold winters (average January temperatures around 14°F/ −10°C) and short summers. The natural vegetation consists only of grassland and gallery forests along the rivers.
History	The first European, a French fur-trader named La Verendrye, reached the territory of North Dakota, then occupied by Dakota Indians, in 1738. It was part of the French colony of Louisiana until 1803, when it passed to the United States under the Louisiana Purchase. After the division of the territory into a northern and a southern half and the repression of Indian rebellions North Dakota entered the Union as the 39th state on November 2nd 1889.
Economy	On the prairie soils of the wheat belt the growing of grain makes the principal contribution to the economy. Other crops are sunflowers, sugar-beet and flax. The working of minerals is of some importance (brown coal in the west of the state; oil and natural gas). In the industrial sector only the processing industries are of any consequence. The tourist trade centres mainly on the Theodore Roosevelt National Park, Lake Sakakawea and a number of historic sites.

Places of Interest in North Dakota

Bismarck	In the hope of attracting German capital the terminus of the Northern Pacific Railroad was named after the German Chancellor. Having grown into a town, Bismarck became capital of the territory of Dakota in 1883. Features of interest are the Art Deco State Capitol (1933–34) and, to the
Fort Lincoln	south of the twin town of Mandan, Fort Lincoln, from which Custer set out with units of the 7th US Cavalry to encounter defeat at the hands of

Cheyenne and Dakota Indians in the battle of the Little Bighorn; there is a
museum in the fort.

Bottineau, in the far north of the state on the Canadian frontier, is the chief place in an extensive nature reserve and recreation area made up of the J. Clark Salyer National Wildlife Refuge (fishing, observation of wild life), Lake Metigoshe State Park (bathing, boating), the Bottineau Winter Park Ski Area and the International Peace Gardens, a landscaped park symbolising the friendship between Canada and the United States which extends into the Canadian province of Manitoba.

Bottineau

Near Williston in the west of the state, on the border with Montana, is Fort Buford (restored), where Sitting Bull (see Famous People) gave himself up in 1881 after returning to the United States from Canada. A short distance away is the earlier Fort Union (also restored), once an important trading post and fur-trappers' base, where George Catlin and John James Audubon studied and painted the landscape and its inhabitants.

Fort Buford/
Fort Union

North-west of Bismarck the Missouri widens to form Lake Sakakawea, a long lake well stocked with fish which is harnessed to supply power by the Garrison Dam at the south end. The State Park round the lake offers scope for a variety of leisure activities. To the south of the lake, on an old camping ground of the Mandan and Hidatsa Indians, is the Knife River Historic Site, where a number of villages of the Prairie Indians have been rebuilt in an attempt to preserve their culture.

Lake Sakakawea

*Knife River
Indian villages

Half a mile south of Rugby in the north of the state is a monument marking the geographical centre of North America.

Geographical
centre of
North America

The Theodore Roosevelt National Park, in western North Dakota, consists of two separate parts. In these barren Badlands, their soil eroded by wind and weather, visitors may be lucky enough to see a few bison. The park is named after President Roosevelt, who possessed two properties here, the Maltese Cross Cabin near Medora, at the south entrance to the park, and the less easily accessible Elkhorn Ranch.

*Theodore
Roosevelt
National Park

Ohio (State; OH)   H–L 41–45

Area:
  41,330sq.miles/107,044sq.km
Population: 10,939,000
Capital: Columbus
Popular name: Buckeye State

Ohio (named after the river) lies in the northern part of the Central Lowlands between Lake Erie in the north and the Ohio River in the south. In the landscape of ground moraines formed during the ice ages which occupies much of the state's area are innumerable lakes, some of which have degenerated into bogs; the eastern half of the state is part of the Allegheny Plateau. The climate is humid continental. Some 20% of Ohio is covered with mixed forest (maple, oak, ash, hickory, walnut, etc., and conifers).

Situation and
topography

Ohio preserves much evidence of early human settlement in the form of numerous mounds formed by prehistoric men. The first Europeans to reach the territory, then occupied by the Iroquois, were Frenchmen coming

History

Ohio

from Canada. After the French and Indian War the area passed to the British Crown in 1763. At the end of the War of Independence, in 1783, it was incorporated in the United States. After bitter fighting with the Indians the white population rapidly increased from 1787 onwards. On March 1st 1803 Ohio was admitted to the Union as the 17th state.

Economy

Ohio's highly developed agriculture produces maize, wheat, oats, soya beans and vegetables; dairy farming and meat production are also important. The principal minerals are coal, oil and natural gas. Thanks to its convenient situation and proximity to sources of raw materials Ohio developed a large iron and steel industry, which in terms of output takes fourth place in the United States. The most important branches of industry are automobile and aircraft construction, engineering, foodstuffs, porcelain, rubber and electrical engineering. The state's remains of prehistoric Indian culture, interesting cities, skiing areas, lakes, rivers and forests attract large numbers of visitors throughout the year.

Places of Interest in Ohio

Akron

Akron, to the south of Cleveland, is the world's rubber capital, with the headquarters of the three great firms of Goodyear, Bridgestone and Uniroyal. Interested visitors can learn how tyres are made by taking part in a guided tour of the Goodyear factory and looking round the firm's museum.

Columbus

The state capital, Columbus, situated almost exactly in the geographical centre of the state, was founded in 1812 and named after Christopher Columbus. Features of interest are the State Capitol (1861), in the grounds of which is a monument commemorating the murdered President William McKinley (1843–1901), and the Ohio Historical Center, with two "history malls" illustrating the archaeology and history of the state with the most modern methods of presentation. The German Village, south of downtown Columbus, is a refurbished old quarter of the town well equipped with shops and bars.

*Prehistoric Indian mounds

Some of the most interesting of the prehistoric Indian mounds can be seen on a round trip from Columbus, starting on US 23, going south. Among them are the 23 mounds (200 B.C.–A.D. 500) of the Mound City Group National Monument at Chillicothe; the single large mound (250ft/76m long, 30ft/9m high) in the Seip National Monument (17 miles/27km west of Chillicothe); the Serpent Mound State Memorial on SR 73 (total distance 90 miles/144km), a quarter-mile long mound in the form of a snake (800 B.C.–A.D.100), the largest of its kind; and the Fort Ancient State Memorial at Lebanon (total distance 138 miles/220km), a cult site constructed some 1500 years ago by Indians of the Hopewell Culture.

Coshocton

Coshocton, north-east of Columbus on the Ohio-Erie Canal, preserves something of the atmosphere of the 1830s with its restored houses and lock-keeper's house.

Sandusky
Kelleys Island

Sandusky extends for some 6 miles/10km along the shores of Lake Erie, with a wide range of leisure facilities on its beaches. Offshore is Kelleys Island, on which the Kelley family grew wine and reared fish in the early 19th century. On Inscription Rock are old Indian rock drawings. Another vacation centre on the Sandy Lake Erie Beaches is Port Clinton, farther west.

Port Clinton

Toledo

Toledo, at the south-west corner of Lake Erie, has a well stocked art museum ranging from ancient Egyptian art to the modern American school.

Other places of interest

Cincinnati, Cleveland (see entries)

Oklahoma

Oklahoma (State; OK) N–Q 23–31

Area:
  69,920sq.miles/181,090sq.km
Population: 3,175,000
Capital: Oklahoma City
Popular name: Sooner State

The state of Oklahoma (from the Indian term "red people"), in the west central United States, lies mostly in the Inner Plains region. To the west these merge into the flat treeless grassland of the Great Plains, and on the south-west are bounded by the Wichita Mountains and tabular volcanic hills. The eastern part of the state is occupied by the forest-covered (mainly maple and oak) Ouachita and Ozark Mountains, between which runs the valley of the Arkansas River. Climatically Oklahoma lies in a zone of transition between the humid subtropical climate of the south and the dry continental climate of the north. In the 1930s the western part of the state was ravaged by sandstorms.

Situation and topography

Spanish conquistadors passed through the territory of Oklahoma in 1541. In 1682 it was incorporated in the French colony of Louisiana, and in 1803 it was sold to the United States under the Louisiana Purchase. Regarded as worthless land, it was declared Indian territory in 1830. Between 1830 and 1840 the "five civilised tribes" (the Choctaw, Creek, Cherokee, Chickasaw and Seminole Indians) were driven out of their territory in the east and resettled here, and the 50,000 incomers had to share the land with the Comanche, Osage and other Prairie Indians who were already living in the area. From 1889 onwards the American government opened up parts of the territory to white settlement, and thereafter a number of towns with populations of 10,000 or so, like Oklahoma City, sprang up almost overnight. After the adoption of a constitution accepted by both Indians and white settlers in 1907 Oklahoma joined the Union as the 46th state on November 16th in that year.

History

Oklahoma has a very varied farming pattern, ranging from highly developed cattle-rearing to the growing of wheat, cotton and peanuts. The chief minerals are oil and, on a smaller scale, natural gas and brown coal, which are processed in the state's principal industry, petro-chemicals. In the wide range of Oklahoma's tourist attractions the Indian powwows take a leading place.

Economy

Places of Interest in Oklahoma

In Bartlesville, in north-eastern Oklahoma, are the headquarters of a number of oil firms. It can also boast the only high-rise building designed by Frank Lloyd Wright, the 225ft/68m high Price Tower. Another example of modern architecture is Shin'en Kan, a house designed by Bruce Goff. The days of the oil boom are recalled by Nellie Johnstone's Oil Well, the first derrick in the state, still preserved in its original form. The Tom Mix Museum is devoted to the king of movie cowboys.

Bartlesville

The farming town of Lawton in south-western Oklahoma is one of the towns that grew up over night. In Fort Sill the Apache Geronimo spent the last years of his life as a prisoner; he is buried in the adjoining cemetery. The Museum of the Great Plains has a varied collection of material on life in frontier days.

Lawton

Oklahoma City

*Muskogee	In the town of Muskogee in eastern Oklahoma is the very interesting Five Civilised Tribes Museum, which illustrates the cultures of the Cherokee, Chickasaw, Chocktaw, Creek and Seminole Indians.
Oklahoma City	See entry
*Tulsa	The oil capital of Tulsa, the second largest city in Oklahoma, lies in the east of the state. Thanks to the wealth brought by oil, it has a number of excellent museums: the Gilcrease Museum, which is devoted to the move to the West (Indian artifacts, pictures of the Wild West by Remington, Russell and other artists); the Philbrook Museum of Art (art of many periods and styles, including the Italian Renaissance, 19th century English painting and Indian arts and crafts); and the Fenster Museum of Jewish Art.
Indian towns	Many of the Indian nations had their own "capitals", which now have interesting museums devoted to the cultures of the various tribes: Okmulgee for the Creek Indians, Pawhuska for the Osages, Ponca City for the Poncas, Tahlequah for the Cherokees, Wewoka for the Seminoles.

Oklahoma City — O 28

State: Oklahoma
Altitude: 1207ft/368m
Population: 445,000 (Metropolitan Area 1 million)

Situation and characteristics: The capital of the state of Oklahoma lies in the southern Great Plains on the North Canadian River and is now an important industrial centre (aircraft construction, oil processing, etc.). It was founded after the local Indian territory was opened up to white settlement in 1889 and within a short time had a population of 10,000 white settlers. Thereafter it developed rapidly. By 1904 it had its own university, and six years later it became capital of the young state of Oklahoma. It soon developed into an important market centre for cattle, grain and cotton. In 1928 the Midcontinent Field (oil and natural gas) was opened up, and at the peak of the oil boom there were no fewer than 2000 derricks within the city area.

Sights in Oklahoma City

State Capitol	The neo-classical Capitol (without the usual dome) at the intersection of NE 23rd Street and Lincoln Boulevard was completed in 1917 (guided visits daily). Oil was worked in the immediate vicinity of the Capitol until 1986; the pump is now an industrial monument.
State Museum of History	South-east of the Capitol is the State Museum of History, which has a very large collection of Indian artifacts.
Metro Concourse	The Metro Concourse is one of the largest underground pedestrian zones in the United States, with innumerable shops, boutiques, service facilities, restaurants and bars.
*Myriad Gardens	The Myriad Gardens were laid out as part of a scheme for the regeneration and redevelopment of the Central Business District (to the south of the Capitol). They include a botanic garden, an amphitheatre and the very interesting multi-storey Crystal Bridge Tropical Conservatory (tropical plants, etc.).
Art Museum	The Oklahoma City Art Museum (3113 Pershing Boulevard) has collections of European art of the 13th–20th centuries and American art of the 19th and 20th centuries.

Olympic National Park

2 miles/3.2km west of the Myriad Gardens are the Oklahoma National Stockyards, one of the largest stock markets in the world. The noisy auctions held on Mondays, Tuesdays and Wednesdays can be attended by non-dealers.

Oklahoma National Stockyards

The Harn Homestead at 313 NE 16th Street, now protected as an ancient monument, recalls the days of the great takeover of Indian land in 1889.

Harn Homestead

The Oklahoma Heritage Center (fine furniture and furnishings, works of art) occupies a mansion built for the Hefner family in 1917 and recently renovated (201 NW 14th Street).

Oklahoma Heritage Center

A short distance north of the Zoo, at 2100 NE 52nd Street, is the Kirkpatrick Center, with a number of interesting museums, including the Oklahoma Air and Space Museum, the Center of the American Indian, the International Photography Hall of Fame and Museum, the Omniplex Science Museum (a "hands-on" museum; dinosaur two storeys high), a Planetarium and a Japanese Garden.

*Kirkpatrick Center

3 miles/5km north-east of the Capitol, at 1700 NE 63rd Street, is the National Cowboy Hall of Fame and Western Heritage Center, with a large collection of material on the history of the Wild West: pictures and sculpture recalling the days of the pioneers and of Buffalo Bill, the John Wayne Collection (guns and daggers, Indian kachina dolls, etc.). Impressive, too, is the Rodeo Hall of Fame; and the gallery of portraits of Western film heroes appeals to many visitors.

*National Cowboy Hall of Fame and Western Heritage Center

Surroundings of Oklahoma City

57 miles/92km south-west of Oklahoma City is the township of Anadarko, which was the administrative centre for the Indians who were driven out of the eastern states and resettled in the prairies in the 19th century.

Anadarko

A few minutes' drive south-east of Anadarko is its main tourist attraction, Indian Village USA. Here are reconstructions of villages belonging to seven different Indian tribes which give an excellent impression of the daily life of the original inhabitants of North America. In summer there are performances of cult dances.

*Indian City

The Southern Plains Indian Museum, to the east of US 62, has a collection of historic and contemporary Indian art.

Southern Plains Indian Museum

In the National Hall of Fame for Famous American Indians, which also lies to the east of US 62, are bronze busts of famous Indians.

National Hall of Fame for Famous American Indians

Olympic National Park   B 1/2

State: Washington
Area: 1420sq.miles/3678sq.km
Established: 1938. World Heritage Site since 1981

The Olympic National Park lies on the Olympic Peninsula in the north-west of Washington State, which is bounded on the west by the Pacific, on the north by the Strait of Juan de Fuca (the Canadian frontier) and on the east by Puget Sound. On the peninsula is the largest and finest expanse of temperate rain forest in the western hemisphere, declared a National Monument in 1909. The Olympic National Park is one of most visited National Parks in the United States, drawing over 3½ million visitors a year. Within a relatively small area, between sea level and the summit of Mount Olympus (7965ft/2428m), it contains a wide range of different landscapes, the main types of which are covered in the sites described below.

Situation and *topography

379

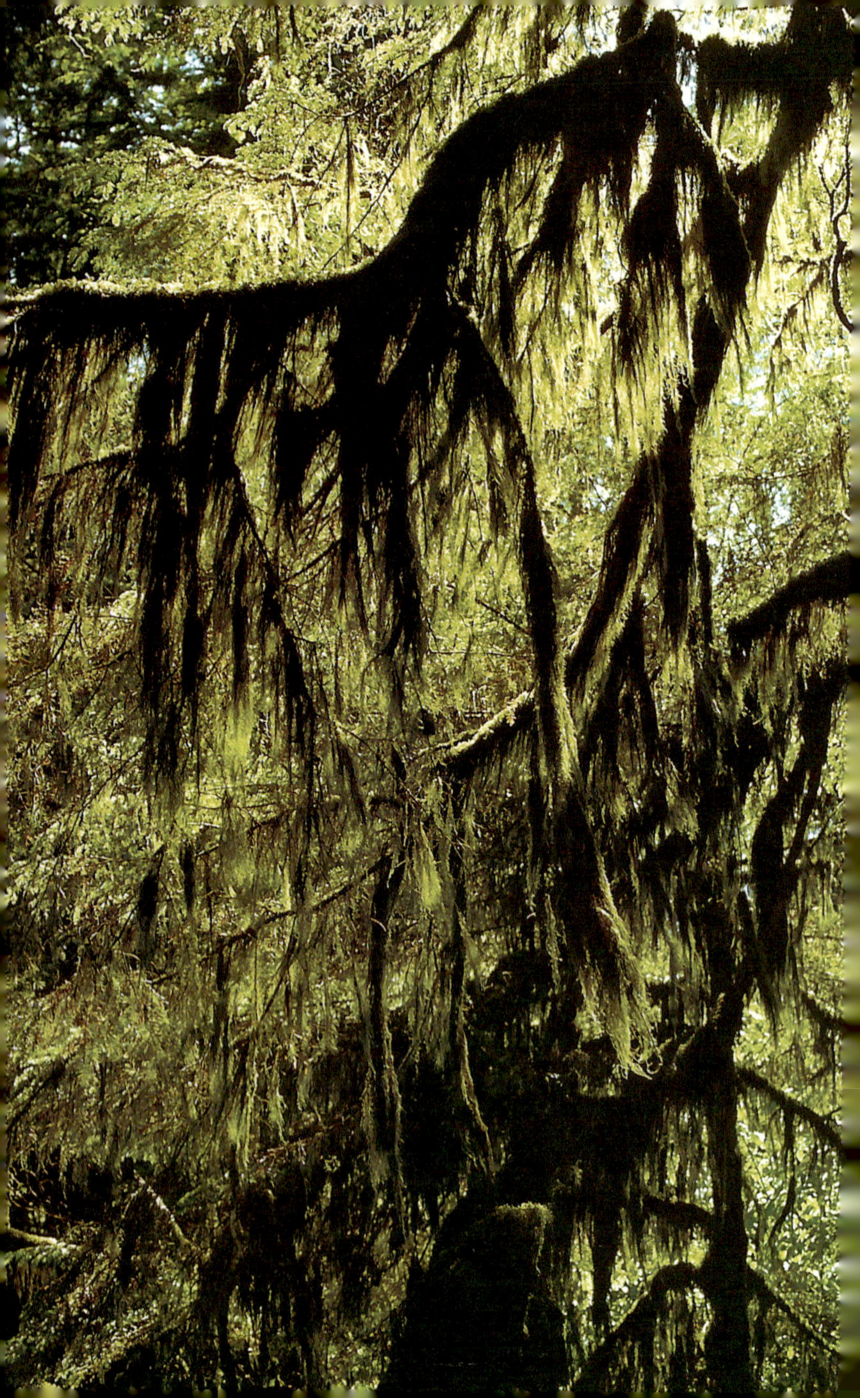

Olympic National Park

The Olympic Mountains, lying in the centre of an area shaped by the encounter of two plates in the process of continental drift, are a geologically young and much folded range. The mountains are deeply fissured, with a complex system of steep-sided valleys. The rocks are mainly marine sediments, with some volcanic intrusions (e.g. cushion lava). There are some 60 glaciers and numerous snowfields. Moraines, travelled granite blocks from Canada, corries, corrie lakes and U-shaped valleys give evidence of strong local glaciation and of the advance of glaciers from the north during the Ice Age, reaching down to Puget Sound. Above the tree-line is a region of alpine meadows with colourful mountain flowers. No roads are permitted in this sensitive vegetation zone. Roe-deer, mountain goats and marmots can be seen here.

The ascent of the highest peaks – Mount Olympus was first climbed in 1854 – is to be recommended only for experienced climbers with proper equipment.

The starting-point for a tour of the National Park is the little town of Port Angeles (pop. 18,000; fishing, woodworking, papermaking, tourism), with the offices of the National Park administration. The park consists of a narrow coastal strip 50 miles/80km long on the Pacific and of the main central area in the Olympic Mountains. Round the central part of the park and the adjoining National Forests to the west, north and east runs the 330 mile/530km long Olympic Peninsula Scenic Drive (US 101 and US 112). From this road ten side roads (partly asphalted) go off into the central area and five others into the coastal strip.

Tour of the National Park

A 20 mile/32km long scenic road runs up to Hurricane Ridge Lodge (alt. 5200ft/1585m; no overnight accommodation), from which there are magnificent views of the glacier-covered mountains of the Olympic range and over the Strait of Juan de Fuca to Vancouver Island in Canada.

Hurricane Ridge

20 miles/32km west of Port Angeles is Lake Crescent, a beautiful mountain lake. A road runs along the south side of the lake to the Marymere Falls, which plunge down from a height of 90ft/27m.

Lake Crescent

Sol Duc Hot Springs are reached on a 12 mile/19km long side road which branches off 2 miles/3km beyond the end of Lake Crescent. Here visitors can bathe in the hot springs.

Sol Duc Hot Springs

The great attraction of the National Park is the magnificent expanse of rain forest – one of the last surviving areas of rain forest in the temperate zone – in the west-facing valleys of the Quinault, Queens and Hoh Rivers. The Hoh Rain Forest, 90 miles/145km from Port Angeles, caters for visitors with its three nature trails, including the very impressive Hall of Mosses Trail. The road up the Hoh valley and then over the Blue Glacier is the most favoured route for the ascent of Mount Olympus.

***Hoh Rain Forest**

The annual cycle of rain coming in from the Pacific and the heavy snowfalls on Mount Olympus in winter, melt-water from which flows down the valleys, have fostered the lush green growth of the forest. While the coastal region lying in the rain shadow of the hills is extremely dry, Mount Olympus has the highest annual precipitations (200in./5000mm) in the United States outside Alaska, which fall mostly during the winter. Rainproof clothing and stout footwear are a must for all visitors.

The four main species of conifer found here – Sitka spruce, hemlock, red cedar and Douglas fir – and the Oregon maple and vine maple grow here to gigantic heights of up to 330ft/100m, with diameters of up to 13ft/4m. The trees and fallen trunks are covered with ferns of unusual size (including liquorice and sword ferns), lichens and moss, on which other trees take root. A fallen trunk which has rotted away will nourish whole colonnades of trees. Particularly striking is Selaginella, a species of moss related to club moss which hangs down from trees (mostly maples) in long garlands and curtains.

Flora and fauna

◀ *Impenetrable rain forest in Olympic National Park*

Omaha

Visitors will rarely see any Roosevelt elk (wapiti) in summer, but the signs of their presence are everywhere: they graze on the rapidly growing vegetation and prevent it from flourishing too luxuriantly. Other animals which may be encountered are black bears, cougars and coyotes, whose tracks can sometimes be seen in the soft soil of the forest. The rivers are well stocked with fish.

Coastal region

The coastal strip is a region of sandy beaches, cliffs rising sheer out of the sea, rock arches, accumulations of driftwood and forests reaching right down to the shore. The northern part of the area is accessible only on side roads branching off US 101; the southern third is traversed by the Scenic Drive between Ruby Beach and Queets. The sea is not particularly inviting for bathers, since the cold current flowing here keeps the water temperature low. When walking on the numerous promontories visitors must keep a watchful eye on the tides. Among the many species of birds to be seen here is the white-headed sea eagle. Seals are common; and sometimes grey whales can be seen swimming past in spring and autumn.

Indian reservations

Within the National Park are four Indian reservations: Makah to the north, with the Makah Cultural Center in Neah Bay; Orette, with a 5 mile/8km hiking trail to Cape Alava, the most westerly point in the continental USA apart from Alaska, and an archaeological museum; Quileute at La Push; and Hoh, on the estuary of the Hoh River.

Omaha H 29

State: Nebraska
Altitude: 1040ft/317m
Population: 336,000 (Metropolitan Area 650,000)

Situation and characteristics

The city of Omaha on the west bank of the Missouri is an important traffic hub and industrial and commercial centre in a prairie region mainly devoted to wheat-growing and stock-rearing. The town was founded in the mid 19th century, when the territory of the local Omaha Indians was opened up to white settlement. From here thousands of immigrants and gold-prospectors set out on the long journey to the West. In the winter of 1846–47 the Mormons paused here on their way to the Salt Lake valley in Utah, and several hundreds of them died in the extreme cold. The town was given an economic boost when the Union Pacific Railroad reached here, and thereafter it developed rapidly into an agricultural and industrial centre which continued to prosper in spite of periodically recurring tornadoes, catastrophic droughts, great floods and devastating plagues of locusts.

Sights in Omaha

Woodman Tower

The modern city centre is dominated by the 445ft/135m high Woodman Tower.

*Joslyn Art Museum

Joslyn Art Museum (2200 Dodge Street) has a fine collection, including work by Indian artists and craftsmen and sketches recording Prince Maximilian zu Wied's journey to the Missouri in 1832–34.

Union Pacific Museum

The Museum of the Union Pacific Railroad (1416 Dodge Street) illustrates the building of the railroad over the Great Plains, and also has mementoes of Abraham Lincoln.

Great Plains Black Museum

The Great Plains Black Museum (2213 Lake Street) illustrates the contribution made by blacks to the opening up of the state of Nebraska.

*Western Heritage Museum

The Union Pacific railroad station (built 1932) is now occupied by the Western Heritage Museum, which surveys the economic and cultural development of the prairies.

Oregon

Round the Old Marketplace, which has been beautifully restored, are a number of attractive restaurants, shops and boutiques.	Old Marketplace
On the north side of the city centre is the campus of Creighton University (founded 1878).	Creighton University
To the north of the city is the Mormon Cemetery, in which the Mormons who died in the winter of 1846–47 are buried. The tragic episode is commemorated by a monument, "Winter Quarters", by A. Fairbank.	Mormon Cemetery
To the west of the city is the Ak-Sar-Ben Field and Coliseum, an arena in which much-frequented cattle auctions and rodeos are held throughout the year.	Ak-Sar-Ben Field and Coliseum
10 miles/16km west of the city centre is Boys Town, an institution for the care of young people founded by Father Edward Joseph Flanagan in 1917.	Boys Town
12 miles/19km south of the city centre is Offutt Air Base, headquarters of the US Strategic Air Command, which has an interesting museum on the history of the American atom bomber fleet.	Strategic Air Command Museum

Surroundings of Omaha

On the opposite (east) bank of the Missouri, in Iowa, is the town of Council Bluffs (pop. 60,000), which in the past was an important Indian meeting-place. The Lewis and Clark expedition reached this area in 1804, and later a fur-trading post was established here. In 1864 the Mormons founded the settlement of Kanesville. A decisive stimulus was given to the town's development by the arrival of the railroad: an event which is commemorated by the Golden Spike Monument.	Council Bluffs

Oregon (State; OR)   D–G 1–9

Area:
 97,073sq.miles/251,419sq.km
Population: 2,922,000
Capital: Salem
Popular name: Beaver State

Oregon (probably from the Indian river name *ouragon*) lies on the Pacific coast, bounded on the south by California and on the north by Washington, from which it is separated by the Columbia River. In the western third of the state the Coast Ranges run parallel to the coast; farther east the state is traversed by the Cascade Mountains, rising to heights of up to 11,237ft/3425m; and between the two ranges is the tectonic depression of the Willamette River. The eastern two-thirds of Oregon are on the steppe-like Columbia Plateau (3900–4900ft/1200–1500m), with the Great Sandy Desert. The Cascade Mountains form a climatic boundary: to the east the climate is dry, with wide fluctuations in temperature, while the land to the west is in the cool temperate zone, with high precipitations on the west side of the hills. As a result the characteristic elements in the vegetation are spruce, Douglas fir and yellow pine, while in the east, on the Columbia Plateau, short grassland and a steppe vegetation of dwarf shrubs predominate.

Situation and topography

The Indian population of Oregon belonged to two different cultures: the coastal tribes like the Nootka and Kwakiutl, who lived by fishing, and

History

Oregon

the hunters and gatherers to the east of the Cascade Mountains, like the Shuswap and Nez Perce. After the first journeys of exploration by James Cook (1778) and George Vancouver (1792) and Lewis and Clark's expedition (1805) the territory, which from 1818 was held by Britain, was first settled by whites in the coastal areas. The main wave of settlement began around 1840, when thousands of settlers streamed into the region, then still relatively unspoiled, most of them travelling on the Oregon Trail. After a frontier dispute between Britain and the United States which was settled by negotiation the US territory of Oregon, taking in broadly the present states of Oregon, Washington and Idaho, was established in 1849. In 1853 the territory was reduced to its present size, and on February 14th 1859 it joined the Union as the 33rd state.

Economy

The forests which cover almost half the area of Oregon provide the basis for the state's most important industry, woodworking, in which 15% of the employed population are engaged. Arable farming (wheat, fodder plants, potatoes and other vegetables, fruit) is possible in much of the state only with the help of irrigation, and accordingly the predominant element in the state's agriculture is meat production. As a result the second most important industry in Oregon is foodstuffs. Other industries include oil refineries, textiles, rubber, synthetic fibres, engineering and electronics. The third element in the economy is tourism; and Oregon offers many attractions to visitors, from the snow-capped mountains with their winter sports facilities to the Pacific coast with its wide range of water sports.

Places of Interest in Oregon

Astoria

The little town of Astoria is beautifully situated on the Pacific coast at the mouth of the Columbia River. From Coxcomb Hill there is a fine view of the river's estuary. The river has a special museum devoted to it, the Columbia River Maritime Museum. 6 miles/10km south-west of the town is Fort Clatsop (restored), where Lewis and Clark's historic expedition ended.

The majestic summit of Mount Hood (Oregon)

Bend lies roughly in the centre of Oregon, in a beautiful setting of lakes and forest. The High Desert Museum has informative displays on the arid regions to the north-west. Among the town's tourist attractions are rafting trips on the Deschutes River and excursions to the volcanic landscapes of Lava Butte (12 miles/19km south) and Newberry National Volcanic Monument (39 miles/63km south). 22 miles/35km south-west of the town is Oregon's largest skiing area, the Mount Bachelor Ski Area (eleven ski-lifts).	*Bend
Eugene, which is separated from its neighbour town of Springfield by the Willamette River, is the seat of the University of Oregon, which has a Museum of Art with an excellent collection of Asian art.	Eugene
From Eugene SR 126 runs west to the coastal town of Florence. 12 miles/19km north on US 101 are the Sea Lion Caves, which are frequented by sealions throughout the year.	**Florence**
To the south of Florence extends the striking landscape of the Oregon Dunes National Recreation Area.	**Oregon Dunes
East of Portland (see entry) along the Columbia River is Hood River, the chief place in the vacation and winter sports area round Mount Hood (11,235ft/3425m), Oregon's highest peak. From the viewpoint half a mile south of the town on SR 35 there are fine views of the mountain and the beautiful valley of the Hood River.	**Hood River**
To the west of Hood River is the Bonneville Dam (salmon ladder) on the Columbia River.	*Bonneville Dam
This attractive old fishing town on the Pacific coast, now a bathing resort, has preserved something of its Victorian atmosphere. In the Undersea Gardens visitors can observe the underwater world of the North Pacific, including a giant octopus named Armstrong.	Newport
This magnificent cave system with its many ramifications lies to the south of the little town of Grants Pass in the south-western corner of Oregon.	*Oregon Caves
The state capital, Salem, lies on the Willamette River to the south of Portland. Features of interest are the State Capitol, a number of museums (Weaving Museum, Museum of Agricultural Machinery) and Oregon's oldest winery, the Honeywood Winery (wine-tasting).	Salem
Crater Lake National Park (see entry), Hell's Canyon (see Idaho), Portland (see entry)	Other places of interest

Orlando   V 44

State: Florida
Altitude: 105ft/32m
Population: 164,000 (Metropolitan Area about 1 million)

The city of Orlando is the chief place in one of the world's most visited tourist regions, which draws some 10 million visitors every year. Among its principal tourist attractions are Walt Disney's second theme park (opened in 1971), the marine park Sea World and Universal Studios Florida, another theme park. Within easy reach, too, is the Kennedy Space Center on Cape Canaveral (see entry). The establishment of these mega amusement parks has encouraged other investors, and there are now around 70,000 hotel and motel beds in the Orlando area, over 2000 restaurants, some fifty golf courses and numerous other attractions great and small.	Situation and characteristics

Sights in the Orlando Area

In recent years there has been much clearing and redevelopment in the city centre. On the site of the old railroad station there has come into being	*Church Street

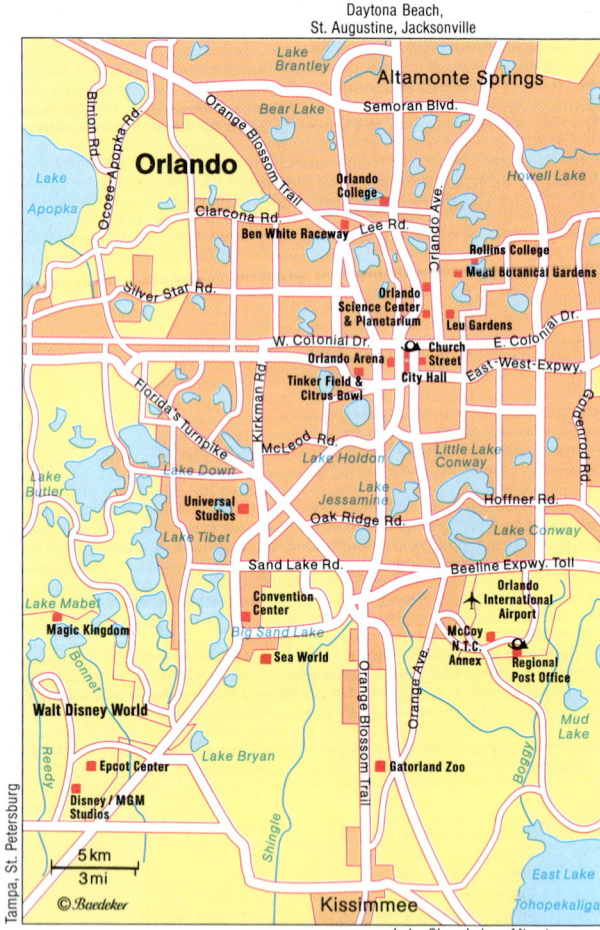

Orlando

	the Church Street Station entertainment and shopping complex (open: daily 11am–2am), with a wide range of shops, restaurants and cafés (including music and entertainment in the style of the twenties and thirties; Rock'n'Roll Palace). A particular attraction is the "Old Duke", a steam engine built in Ohio in 1912 for transcontinental traffic. The old Church Street Exchange has been converted into a shopping centre. A recent addition to the city's shopping facilities is the Church Street Marketplace.
*Orlando Museum of Art	The Orlando Museum of Art (2416 North Mills Avenue) is famed for its excellent collection of pre-Columbian art. The museum also puts on temporary exhibitions of American and African art of the 19th and 20th centuries and travelling exhibitions with loans from international museums.
International Drive	A few miles south-west of the city centre is International Drive, a 3¾ mile/6km long avenue which gives rapid access to the huge theme parks

Orlando

round Orlando. Along the road are numerous hotels and restaurants (some offering "dinner theatre") and a modern office complex, with a congress and trade fair centre.

Wet'n'Wild (6200 International Drive) is a large aquatic play park (open: in spring daily 10am–6pm; in summer daily 9am–9pm; in autumn daily 10am–5pm) which offers a variety of attractions, including swimming pools with waves, breathtaking water slides and white-water trips.

*Wet'n'Wild

The most recent of the major attractions of the Orlando area is Universal Studios Florida at 1000 Universal Studios Plaza (I 4, exit 30B). Here, in "the largest film and television studios outside Hollywood", filming started in October 1988, and the studio complex was opened to the public in 1990. Visitors can either take a tram tour or walk round by themselves, watching filming in progress or sitting in on the recording of television shows. They will see the numerous outdoor sets – streets in New York, 1920s Chicago and San Francisco (Fishermen's Wharf), with actors playing scenes from popular films (e.g. "Blues Brothers", "Ghost Busters"). There are the sets of more than three dozen films, including the house which featured in Hitchcock's "Psycho" and the legendary Hard Rock Café. Particularly nerve-racking is the "Kongfrontation" experience, in which visitors travelling on a reproduction of New York's Elevated Railway are suddenly confronted by King Kong.

**Universal Studios

Daily 9am–11pm; reduced at certain times of year

Sea World is one of the world's largest marine parks, with several aquariums, an artificial coral reef, a pool for sharks and sting-rays, a large enclosure for walruses, sealions, seals, otters and penguins, a flamingo garden and numerous other attractions. The great draws, however, are the Dolphin Stadium, in which highly trained dolphins perform aerobatics, and the Shamu Stadium, in which trained killer whales are put through their paces.

**Sea World

Surroundings of Orlando

19 miles/30km south of Orlando is Kissimmee (pop. 30,000), which in recent decades has grown from a quiet little farming town into a popular holiday resort. Its principal tourist attractions are strung along the Irlo Bronson Memorial Highway – the Elvis Presley Museum (open: daily 9am–10pm), a number of alligator and snake farms, the aquatic playground Water Mania and Xanadu, the "House of the Future".

Kissimmee

**Walt Disney World

25 miles/40km south-west of Orlando is the world-famous Walt Disney World, with three theme parks – the Magic Kingdom, the EPCOT Center and the Disney-MGM Studios – as well as huge hotel complexes and extensive sports facilities. It is most easily reached by way of I 4 and US 192 (Irlo Bronson Highway).

Situation

Walt Disney World was opened on October 1st 1971 and soon developed into the largest entertainment complex in the world. Here in 1963 Walt Disney had found a site on which he could realise his conception of a clean and perfect holiday landscape: a great expanse of open country not too far away from the holiday centres on the coast of Florida, good communications and a climate which made all-year-round operation possible.

Magic Kingdom, daily 9am–6pm; EPCOT Center, daily 9am–8pm; Disney/MGM Studios, daily 9am–7pm. During the main holiday season and on special occasions there are longer opening hours.

Opening times

The centrepiece of the Magic Kingdom is the fantastically towered and turreted Cinderella Castle, around which are seven different sections with 42 shows and rides and innumerable small souvenir shops and restau-

Magic Kingdom

Orlando

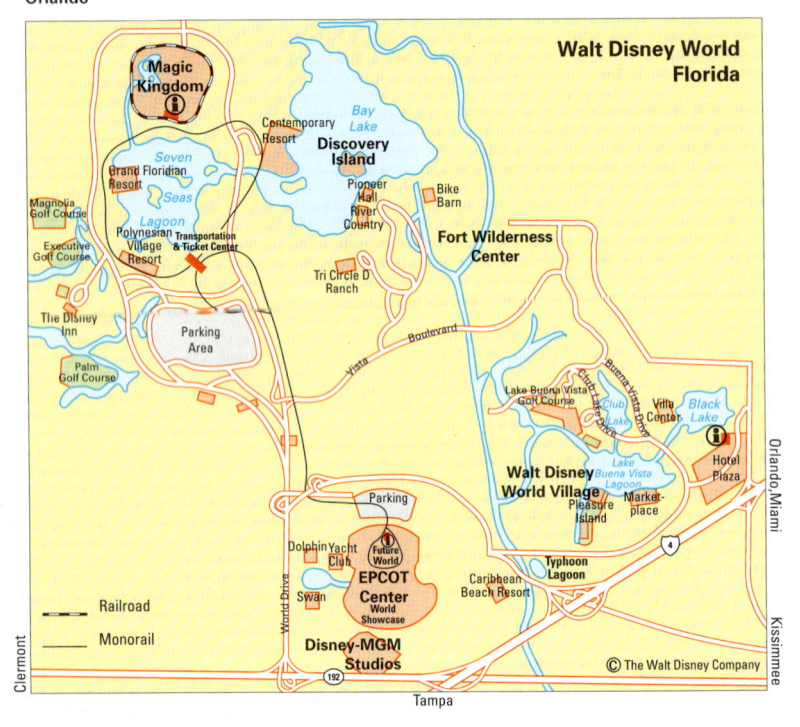

rants. Mickey Mouse and other favourite Disney characters are constantly to be encountered, and every day at 3pm the great Disney Parade with all the familiar figures travels along Main Street into Frontierland, and there is a large live show in front of Cinderella Castle. Particular attractions are Main Street, in turn-of-the-century style, with the Penny Arcade; Adventureland, with the Pirates of the Caribbean and the Jungle Cruise; and Frontierland, with the Big Thunder Mountain Railroad, the Country Bear Jamboree and Tom Sawyer's Island. Liberty Square brings back colonial days. In the Hall of Presidents various US Presidents appear. There is a horrifying Haunted Mansion. In Fantasyland visitors encounter characters from Walt Disney's famous films – Snow White, Peter Pan, Captain Nemo, etc. In Tomorrowland there is a hair-raising roller coaster, Space Mountain.

EPCOT Center

EPCOT – the *Experimental Prototype Community Of Tomorrow* – is the high-tech counterpart of the Magic Kingdom, an area of 260 acres/105 hectares devoted to the past achievements and the future of technology. Here visitors can set out on a journey round the world. Future World, with Spaceship Earth, probes the possibilities of science and technology and looks into the world of the 21st century. World Showcase offers a kind of permanent World's Fair, with pavilions devoted to eleven countries laid out along the 1¼ mile/2km long promenade skirting the World Showcase lagoon.

By horsedrawn tram to Cinderella's Castle ▶

ONE WAY TRANSPORTATION
MAIN STREET
5
TRANSPORTATION CO.
WASTE PLEASE

Outer Banks

Disney-MGM Studios

The newest theme park is the Disney-MGM Studios, opened in 1989: a genuine television and film studio, in which films are in course of production, combined with an amusement park. Visitors may be lucky enough to sit in on the recording of a television show, and the Backstage Studio Tour (1½ hours) which is included in the admission price takes them behind the scenes of current productions. The latest attraction is the adventure movie "Honey, I Shrunk the Kids", a remake of the great Walt Disney success, in which visitors enter an over-size backyard in a Lilliputian world and experience life from the viewpoint of dwarfs. Children will be delighted by this adventure playground, with climbing frames and chutes. In the Backlot Annex there are presentations of exciting film stunts (e.g. the Indiana Jones Epic Stunt Spectacular). Star Tours offers a thrilling space adventure with advanced flight simulation technology, based on the successful George Lucas film "Star Wars",

Other attractions in Disney World

Other attractions in Disney World include Discovery Island with its large colony of scarlet ibises, River Country, Typhoon Lagoon (an exciting bathing pool under palms), Shark Reef (an artificial salt-water reef for snorkellers and divers), Disney Village Marketplace and Pleasure Island, with a popular New Year's Eve party every evening.

Outer Banks   N/O 49/50

States: Virginia, North Carolina

Situation and topography

Off the coasts of Virginia and (for most of the distance) North Carolina lies a chain of long narrow islands extending from Back Bay, Virginia, in the north to Cape Lookout, North Carolina, in the south. These Outer Banks offer, at any rate in the southern two-thirds, an expanse of almost completely unspoiled natural scenery with interesting plants and bird life; the northern

Kitty Hawk: scene of the Wright brothers' first flight

Palm Beach / West Palm Beach

third, however, has been ravaged by the development of the holiday trade and is now a hotchpotch of hotels, motels, holiday homes, restaurants and shopping centres. The Outer Banks can be reached from the north on US 158 or in the south by ferry from Cedar Island or Swan Quarter to Ocracoke (advance reservation necessary during the season).

Sights on the Outer Banks

In the dunes of Kill Devil Hills on Bodie Island (mileposts 7 and 8 on US 158) the brothers Wilbur and Orville Wright made the first powered flight in history on December 17th 1903. Their aircraft, piloted by Orville, rose into the air for 12 seconds, covering the short distance marked by the memorial stones. Close by are the brothers' two shed workshops, and in the Visitor Center is a documentary exhibition. The tall Memorial stands on the hill from which the Wrights launched experimental gliders.

*Wright Brothers National Memorial

On Roanoke Island (reached on US 158) Sir Walter Raleigh founded the first English settlement in 1585, and here on August 18th 1587 Virginia Dare was born – the first child of English parents to be born in North America. Thereafter the settlement mysteriously disappeared; the only trace of it was the enigmatic word "Croatoan" carved on a tree which was found some years later, perhaps referring to an attack by Indians. The Visitor Center tells the story of this "lost colony".

Fort Raleigh National Historic Site

The southern two-thirds of the Outer Banks are now included in the nature reserve formed by the Cape Hatteras National Seashore and Cape Lookout National Seashore. Since these long, thin coastal islands lying between Pamlico Sound to the west and the open Atlantic to the east have been spared the invasion of mass tourism they form an undisturbed habitat for rare plants and for numbers of seabirds and migrants. Beside Bodie Island lighthouse is an observation platform.

*Cape Hatteras National Seashore
*Cape Lookout National Seashore

Palm Beach / West Palm Beach   X 46

State: Florida
Altitude: 0–15ft/0–5m
Population: Palm Beach 10,000, West Palm Beach 68,000

The fashionable bathing resort of Palm Beach lies 75 miles/120km north of Miami (see entry). Here, particularly between Christmas and Easter, the "best people" meet on the wide beach, on the polo ground or on one of the excellent golf courses and tennis courts, and the life of the resort centres on the elegant Worth Avenue (Rodeo Drive) and the many luxury hotels and gourmet restaurants. The old-established and internationally renowned hotels are directly on the beach, and many wealthy families from the worlds of business, politics, culture and fashionable society (the Kennedys, Estée Lauder, Burt Reynolds) have their holiday homes on Ocean Boulevard. Here too is the headquarters of the Professional Golfers' Association (PGA).

Palm Beach

West Palm Beach was originally established to house the large staffs of the hotels and their families. It is now the administrative and business centre of a considerable surrounding area.

West Palm Beach

Palm Beach owes its name to a Spanish ship carrying wine and coconuts which ran aground here in 1878. The few inhabitants of what was then an inhospitable stretch of coast planted the coconuts, and in course of time a grove of palms grew up. The real fathers of Palm Beach were the financier Henry Morrison Flagler and the architect Addison Mizner. From 1874 onwards Flagler spent the winter in Florida and got to know the palm-fringed beach; then in 1894 he extended his Florida East Coast Railroad to

History

Palm Beach / West Palm Beach

Lake Worth and built the legendary Royal Poinciana Hotel in Palm Beach. Thereafter this became a popular resort with the great ones of the world, and a tremendous land and building boom developed. In 1895 Flagler built the less formal Palm Beach Inn (in 1901 renamed the Breakers) directly on the Atlantic, hoping to appeal to a younger public. Among patrons of the hotel were the millionaire industrialist John D. Rockefeller and the newspaper magnate William Randolph Hearst. In 1918 the architect Addison Mizner came to Palm Beach and introduced the Spanish Mediterranean style which was to become characteristic of the resort. His best known buildings are the Boca Raton Hotel and Club and the Everglades Club.

Sights in Palm Beach

*Worth Avenue/ The Esplanade	Worth Avenue is Palm Beach's principal shopping street. In the select shopping centre known as the Esplanade are the establishments of such famous firms as Cartier, Yves Saint-Laurent and Gucci.
*Henry Morrison Flagler Museum	The palatial 73-roomed mansion, Whitehall, built by the railway magnate Henry Morrison Flagler on the shores of Lake Worth in 1901 is now a museum. In the grounds is Flagler's private railway coach.
*The Breakers	The great landmark of Palm Beach, situated directly on the sea, is The Breakers (now protected as a national monument), the famous hotel designed by Leonard Schultze, architect of New York's Waldorf Astoria Hotel.

Sights in West Palm Beach

**Raymond F. Kravis Center for the Performing Arts	The central feature of the old part of West Palm Beach is the Raymond F. Kravis Center for the Performing Arts at 701 Okeechobee Boulevard, opened in 1992, with a large theatre and concert hall (concerts by the Philharmonic Orchestra of Florida and the Palm Beach Symphony Orchestra). This attractive modern building was designed by the German-Canadian architect Eberhard Zeidler.
*Norton Gallery of Art	The Norton Gallery of Art (open: Tue.–Sat. 10am–5pm, Sun. 1–5pm) at 1451 South Olive Avenue (US 1) ranks as one of the best regional art museums in the United States. The collection includes French Impressionists, 20th century American art and Chinese art; there is also a sculpture garden.

Surroundings of Palm Beach and West Palm Beach

Beaches Singer Island	The sewing-machine manufacturer Singer planned a large holiday complex here, but the project never materialised. The beach is one of the finest in the region. Other beautiful bathing beaches are Juni Beach and Boynton Beach.
*Lion Country Safari Park	17 miles/17km west of Palm Beach is the Lion Country Safari Park (Southern Boulevard West/SR 80). Visitors drive their own cars (windows and doors must be kept closed) through the park, in which lions roam freely.
*Morikami Museum and Japanese Gardens	The Morikami Museum (4000 Morikami Park Road) is set in beautiful gardens. There is a flourishing Japanese community here. Japanese tea ceremony, bonsai collection, nature trail. The Hatsume Fair (Japanese arts and crafts) is held at the end of February, the Bon Festival (Summer Festival) in the middle of August.

Palm Springs

10 miles/16km west of Boynton Beach is the Arthur R. Marshall Loxahatchee National Wildlife Refuge, which occupies the north-eastern tip of the Everglades, a region of freshwater wetland biotopes which gives an excellent impression of the sensitive eco-system of the Everglades.

*Arthur R. Marshall Loxahatchee National Wildlife Refuge

The fashionable resort of Boca Raton ("rat's mouth"; pop. 62,000) lies half way between Palm Beach and Fort Lauderdale in a sheltered bay, entrenched behind rocks, on the Atlantic coast. Its 6 miles/10km of coast and agreeably mild climate have made it a popular winter resort. It is famed for the top-class tennis and polo tournaments held here. Steffi Graf and Chris Evert are among the tennis stars who come here, as well as polo-players like the Prince of Wales. The Boca Raton Hotel and Club is a huge complex built by Addison Mizner in 1926. There is an interesting Museum of Art at 801 West Palmetto Park Road.

Boca Raton

Palm Springs   Q 9

State: California
Altitude: 465ft/142m
Population: 40,000

The thermal resort of Palm Springs, the "oasis of the rich", lies in a wide valley between the San Jacinto Mountains in the west and the San Bernardino Mountains in the east, only two hours' drive from Los Angeles (see entry). It was originally a group of seven small settlements which have now developed into one of the most celebrated holiday resorts in California. During the main season (December to March) the temperature here is very agreeable and the hotels are usually fully booked. Formerly this was a resort for the very old and the very wealthy: nowadays it appeals to successful younger people. In recent decades extensive irrigation systems

Situation and characteristics

Palm Springs: an oasis in the desert

Pennsylvania

have been installed and over 50,000 palms have been planted in order to improve the town's amenities. Palm Springs is now the golf metropolis of California, and it is also a Mecca for tennis fans. To the north of the town is a forest of wind-power installations which provide the town with electricity.

History

The hot springs here were discovered by the Spaniards in the 18th century, but Palm Springs became a fashionable resort only in the 1930s, when Hollywood celebrities began to patronise it; since then it has never looked back.

Sights in Palm Springs and Surroundings

Desert Museum

The Desert Museum (101 Museum Drive) has excellently presented displays illustrating the life of the desert. The museum also includes an art gallery, a display of Indian crafts and a sculpture garden.

Moorten's Botanical Garden

At 1701 South Palm Canyon is the beautiful and colourful Moorten's Botanical Garden (open: daily 10am–4pm).

Palm Canyon

6 miles/10km south of Palm Springs, in Indian territory, is Palm Canyon, with some 3000 fan palms.

Living Desert

The Living Desert or Palm Desert (47–900 Potola Avenue) is an expanse of open country in which visitors can study various desert plants and desert animals (in enclosures).

Mount San Jacinto

A trip to the summit of Mount San Jacinto (8516ft/2596m) by cable railway provides an opportunity to observe the different vegetation zones on the way up.

Pennsylvania (State; PA)   G–K 45–50

Area:
  45,308sq.miles/117,348sq.km
Population: 11,962,000
Capital: Harrisburg
Popular name: Keystone State

Situation and topography

The state of Pennsylvania (named after its founder, William Penn) lies in the northeastern United States, reaching from Lake Erie to the Delaware River, on the border with New Jersey. In the east it extends on to the Piedmont Plateau and into the Appalachians and their longitudinal valley; the main part of the state lies on the Allegheny Plateau, which reaches its highest point in Mount Davius (3212ft/979m). In the humid continental climate, with warm summers and cool winters, deciduous forest predominates in fully half the area of the state, with conifers at higher levels.

Pennsylvania is called the Keystone State because some of the key events in the history of the United States took place here, in particular the signing of the Declaration of Independence at Philadelphia in 1776.

History

The first white settlement in the territory of Pennsylvania, then occupied by the Iroquois, was established by Swedes in 1643. Thereafter it became a Dutch colony, and in 1664 passed to Britain. In 1681 Charles II granted the territory to the Quaker William Penn, charging him to speed up the process of settlement. In addition to English Quakers and Scottish and Irish groups the early setttlers were mainly Germans, who left an enduring imprint on

Pennsylvania

Gettysburg: monument to General Meade . . . . . . and the National Soldiers Monument

the state. On December 12th 1787 Pennsylvania became the second state to adopt the Constitution of the United States of America.

Thanks to the deposits of anthracite in the Appalachians Pennsylvania is the leading coal-mining state in the USA. This has led to the development of an important iron and steel industry and a high degree of industrialisation in the state. Agriculture is concentrated mainly on supplying the needs of the industrial areas. The Appalachians and the Pocono Mountains with their excellent winter sports facilities and scope for other outdoor activities are popular tourist and holiday areas.

Economy

Places of Interest in Pennsylvania

This town in the Alleghenies was founded in 1849 by the Pennsylvania Railroad Company, and the town still attracts railway buffs with the Railroader's Memorial Museum and the Horseshoe Curve, where trains turn through a 220 degree curve 795yd/725m long to overcome a height difference of 227ft per mile (43m per kilometre).

Altoona

*Horseshoe Curve

The town of Bethlehem, north of Philadelphia (see entry), was founded by Moravian Brethren from Germany, who have left their mark on the town with the Christmas Festival, when choirs and orchestras join in a celebration which is well known throughout the United States, and in the Gemein Haus of 1741 (now a museum), the Brethren's House of 1748 and the Old Chapel of 1751. In the Moravian Cemetery on Market Street there are graves ranging in date from 1742 to 1910. The Bach Festival held on the campus of Lehigh University is world-famed.

*Bethlehem

The town of Chester, on the Delaware River to the south-west of Philadelphia, is the oldest settlement in Pennsylvania. A memorial stone marks the spot where William Penn landed in the Swedish settlement in 1682. Features of interest are the Courthouse (1724), the oldest in the state, and two

Chester

Pennsylvania Dutch Country

handsome mansions, Morton's Homestead (1655) and the Caleb Pusey Home (1683).

Erie — Erie is Pennsylvania's largest town on the shores of Lake Erie. It was Commodore Perry's headquarters when he defeated an Anglo-Canadian fleet in 1813. His flagship USS "Niagara" has been restored.

**Gettysburg — The decisive battle in the Civil War was fought in southern Pennsylvania, near Gettysburg. It took place over a wide area on July 1st–3rd 1863, when Confederate forces commanded by General Lee which had advanced far into the North were defeated by General Meade's Union army. Altogether 51,000 men on both sides were killed or wounded. Here, four months later, President Abraham Lincoln pronounced his famous Gettysburg Address, in which he set out his ideas on the future of the Union.

National Military Park — The battlefield is now a National Park, traversed by more than 30 miles/48km of roads and tracks, with numerous monuments and memorial stones. Visitors can either find their own way to the main features on the battlefield or take part in a guided tour (2 hours). The course of the battle can be followed in detail on an electric map in the Visitor Center, which also displays a large collection of uniforms and weapons.

On the outskirts of the National Park is a farmhouse which was occupied by President Eisenhower and his wife. In the quiet little town of Gettysburg are a number of museums and memorial sites commemorating the battle. The most notable features are General Lee's headquarters and Wills House, in which Lincoln spent the night.

Harrisburg — Until Chernobyl Harrisburg, the state capital, situated in south-eastern Pennsylvania, had the dubious honour of being the scene of the world's worst nuclear accident, at the Three Mile Island power station on the Susquehanna River. Features of interest in the town are the State Capitol and the informative State Museum.

Hershey — Hershey, to the east of Harrisburg, is known to Americans as the place where the country's favourite chocolate was first made in 1903 by M. S. Hershey – an event and a product which are celebrated in Hershey's Chocolate World.

Scranton — Scranton, in the north-east of the state, was once an anthracite-mining centre; it is now dominated by the electronics industry. Earlier days are recalled by the Pennsylvania Anthracite Heritage Museum and the Scranton Iron Furnaces, four old coal-fired smelting furnaces. The Lackawanna Coal Mine Tour takes visitors 100 yards underground in a disused mine shaft.

York — York, to the south of Harrisburg, was for 90 days capital of the thirteen colonies when Congress was compelled to flee from Philadelphia (see entry). In the Colonial Court House (now a reconstruction) the Articles of Confederation, the founding document of the Union, were adopted in 1777. There are a number of other historic spots in the town. For visitors interested in more modern achievements there is the Harley Davidson motorcycle factory with its museum.

Other places of interest — Pennsylvania Dutch Country, Philadelphia, Pittsburgh (see entries)

Pennsylvania Dutch Country (Lancaster County)   J 49/50

State: Pennsylvania

Situation and characteristics — In south-eastern Pennsylvania, west of Philadelphia, is Pennsylvania Dutch Country, an intensely cultivated and densely populated area with Lancaster

Pennsylvania Dutch Country

Amish Country: an old world idyll

as its chief town. It takes its name from the religious communities of German ("Dutch", from "Deutsch") origin (Amish People, Hutterites, Mennonites: see Baedeker Special, pp. 42–43) who settled here from the 18th century onwards and have preserved their traditional way of life, rejecting all modern aids.

Sights in Pennsylvania Dutch Country

In Bird-in-Hand, 7 miles/11km east of Lancaster, is a well-known Farmers' Market (Wed.–Sat. in summer), at which the Amish People and Mennonites offer their produce for sale.	Bird-in-Hand
The little town of Columbia (pop. 10,700), 10 miles/16km west of Lancaster on the Susquehanna River, has a Watch and Clock Museum with over 8000 exhibits from many centuries.	Columbia
Between Reading and Lancaster (12 miles/19km from the latter town) is Ephrata (pop. 12,100), where German Pietists established a community of monastic type in 1732. Eleven buildings of the Ephrata Cloister (632 West Main Street), erected between 1735 and 1749, have been preserved, and some of them are open to the public, including the Sisters' House, the Meetinghouse and the Householder's Residence.	*Ephrata
South-east of Reading on the Schuylkill River, reached by way of Birdsboro (6 miles/10km) and SR 345, is Hopewell, with a historic ironworks which operated from 1771 to 1883. On the extensive site (Visitor Center) are coal-fired smelting furnaces, a smithy and a variety of other equipment. In summer there are demonstrations of old crafts.	Hopewell Furnace National Historic Site
10 miles/16km east of Lancaster on SR 340 is Intercourse. In People's Place, on Main Street, visitors are introduced to the history and the crafts of the Amish, Mennonites and Hutterites (films, well prepared background	Intercourse

Petrified Forest National Park

	information). Local craft products, cakes and pastries, etc., can be bought in the Country Market and Old Country Store. In Kitchen Kettle Village are 30 shops selling craft goods and local culinary specialities. The Quilt Museum displays beautiful examples of the traditional patchwork quilts.
*Lancaster	Lancaster (pop. 56,000), founded in 1721, is the heart of the Pennsylvania Dutch Country. Features of interest are the Heritage Center Museum in Penn Square; the Central Market, housed in the historic market halls beside the Heritage Center; and the Farmers' Market (Tue., Fri. and Sat.), which has been held without interruption since 1730 – the oldest public farmers' market in the country.
Landis Valley Museum	The Landis Valley Museum (4 miles/6km north of Lancaster on SR 272/ Oregon Pike) is a very large open-air museum illustrating traditional farming life, with many restored farm buildings, some of them transferred here from their original site, together with agricultural implements, shops and other buildings. There are daily demonstrations of old crafts.
Amish farms	The Amish Homestead (2 miles/3km east of Lancaster on SR 462) and the Amish Farm and House (5 miles/8km east on US 30) are two typical Amish farms which are open to visitors (guided tours). 5 miles/8km south of Lancaster is the oldest building in Lancaster County, the Hans Herr House (1719).
Lebanon	The industrial and market town of Lebanon (pop. 25,000; 27 miles/43km north of Lancaster) has two old churches, the Tabor United Church of Christ (10th Street/Walnut Street) and the Salem Lutheran Church (8th Street/ Willow Street), both dating from 1760. A sight of a different kind is the sausage factory of the Weaver's-Baum's Lebanon Bologna Company.
Cornwall Iron Furnace	4 miles/6.4km south of Lebanon on SR 419 (north of I 76) is the Cornwall Iron Furnace, which operated from 1742 to 1883, producing everyday domestic requisites, weapons, etc. A number of old buildings and coal-fired smelting furnaces have been preserved.
Lititz	In Lititz (pop. 8200), 8 miles/13km north of Lancaster, are the Candy Americana Museum and Candy Outlet (48 North Broad Street) and the Sturgis Pretzel House (219 East Main Street), the oldest pretzel bakery in the United States (1784).
Reading	Reading (pop. 78,500; 32 miles/52km north-west of Lancaster), founded in 1748, is the industrial centre of the Pennsylvania Dutch Country, with historic old quarters and fine 18th and 19th century buildings. In the surrounding area are various factory shops and shopping centres selling branded goods at reasonable prices. At 940 Centre Avenue is the Berks County Historical Society Museum (local history, folk art and crafts of the Pennsylvania Dutch).
*Strasburg	Strasburg (pop. 2600), 10 miles/16km south-east of Lancaster, the centre of German immigration in the Pennsylvania Dutch Country, is famed for its railroad museums, in particular the Railroad Museum of Pennsylvania, with a reconstructed station, old locomotives and wagons and an exhibition on railroad history in Pennsylvania. The Strasburg Rail Road Company runs 45-minute trips round Lancaster County in an old steam train. The Toy Train Museum in Paradise Lane displays historic model railways. 2 miles/3km north of the town on SR 896 is the Amish Village, an open-air museum illustrating the houses and way of life of the Amish People.

Petrified Forest National Park   O/P 16

State: Arizona
Area: 147sq.miles/378sq.km
Established: 1906

Petrified Forest National Park

Petrified trees in the Petrified Forest National Park

The National Park is open throughout the year.	Season
The taking of pieces of petrified wood from the Petrified Forest is strictly prohibited. If you plan a long hike in the area you must inform the National Park administration in the Visitor Center and be sure to take a sufficient supply of drinking water.	**N.B.**
The Petrified Forest National Park lies in the arid north-east of Arizona in the Painted Desert (so called because of its brilliantly coloured sandstone in shades of red and blue).	Situation and *topography
In the Mesozoic era this was a plain traversed by numerous watercourses, with a vegetation of horsetails, ferns and coniferous trees in particularly well watered areas. When a tree fell it was covered by river-borne sediments and sealed off from the air, hindering the natural process of decay. In wet periods water containing silicon oxides filtered into the rotten wood, and when it became drier the water evaporated and the silicon oxides crystallised. The concentration gradually became so high that quartz (rock crystal, amethyst, agate, onyx, cornelian, jasper, etc.) was formed, preserving the internal cell structure and the external appearance of the trunk. Then in geologically recent times erosion by wind and weather freed the petrified plant remains from the overlying sandstone and brought to light not only fossilised plant remains (fern leaves, pine cones, etc.) but fossils of shellfish, snails, fish, amphibians and reptiles.	Origins
The 23 mile/42km long Park Road runs through the finest parts of the National Park. After passing through a particularly impressive part of the Painted Desert it comes to the Puerco Indian Ruin, the remains of a settlement occupied by Pueblo Indians 600 years ago. To the south of this is the Newspaper Rock, a huge block of sandstone with Indian rock drawings. In	*Park Road

Philadelphia

the Blue Mesa area it can be seen how the petrified remains of trees have been exposed by erosion. Beyond this the road comes to the Agate Bridge, part of a petrified tree of which both ends are still embedded in the sandstone. Farther south is a viewpoint overlooking the Jasper Forest, a valley filled with the fossil remains of trees. Beyond this again is the Crystal Forest, so named for its wealth of semi-precious stones (rock crystal, amethyst, etc.) and fossil remains of plants. The two Flattops are relics of the layer of sandstone which once covered the whole plain. The road then runs through the Rainbow Forest, with the Long Logs, and comes to the partly restored Indian pueblo known as the Agate House and the Rainbow Forest Museum, behind which are a number of massive petrified tree trunks.

Philadelphia K 50

State: Pennsylvania
Altitude: 0–482ft/0–147m
Population: 1.6 million (Metropolitan Area 4.9 million)

Situation and characteristics

Philadelphia, the "cradle of the nation", lies in the urbanised Atlantic region between Boston and Washington DC (see entries), in the extreme south-east of Pennsylvania, extending along the Delaware River, which is joined here by the Schuylkill River. The city is an important industrial and commercial centre as well as a major port. The most productive branch of

Philadelphia

industry is oil processing; other industries include the electrical industry, chemicals and printing and publishing. Philadelphia's theatres, concert halls, libraries and museums, together with the University of Pennsylvania, Temple University, Drexel University and the famed Philadelphia Orchestra, make it one of the leading cultural centres of the United States.

The first settlers on the site of Philadelphia, in 1640, were Swedes and Finns, later followed by Dutch and British settlers. In 1681 Charles II granted possession of this territory to William Penn (1644–1718), leader of a Quaker colony, who then founded Philadelphia in 1682 as a place of religious freedom. This freedom attracted German Mennonites to settle in the town. In 1683 Penn made a treaty with the Delaware Indians which preserved the town from Indian attacks. In 1701 he granted Philadelphia, which then had a population of 4500, its charter as a town. A fresh impulse was given to the development of the town by Benjamin Franklin, who came to live here in 1723, published a newspaper and was instrumental in founding the University of Pennsylvania. In the liberal climate of Philadelphia the idea of separation from the mother country was first formulated, and on September 5th 1774 the Continental Congress met in Carpenters' Hall. During its second session in Independence Hall the Declaration of Independence was adopted on July 4th 1776. In 1787 the Constitutional Congress met in Philadelphia. Until 1799 it was capital of Pennsylvania, and from 1790 to 1800 was also capital of the United States. In 1848, following the revolutions in Europe, large numbers of Germans settled in the town. The North's rejection of slavery also brought many blacks from the South.

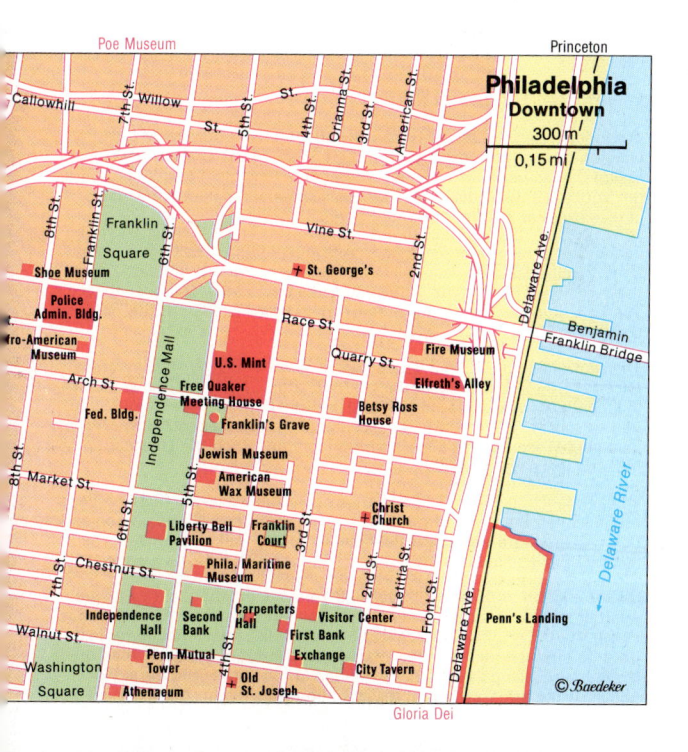

History

Philadelphia

The Liberty Bell, Philadelphia

**Independence National Historical Park

Visitor Center

The Independence National Historical Park contains a number of buildings which have played a great part in the history of the United States. The Visitor Center, beside which is the tower containing the Bicentennial Bell, a gift from the British government on the bicentenary of the United States, is at the corner of 3rd and Chestnut Streets.

*Liberty Bell Pavilion

To the west of the Visitor Center, opposite Independence Hall, is the famous Liberty Bell, cast in England, which was rung for the first time in 1776, on the occasion of the first public reading of the Declaration of Independence. The bell, previously in Independence Hall, was installed in the present pavilion in 1976.

**Independence Hall
Guided visits: summer daily 9am–8pm, winter until 5pm

The central feature of the historic district is the Georgian-style Independence Hall, the "birthplace of the United States". Here the Declaration of Independence was signed in 1776 and the Constitution of the United States was written in 1787. In the restored chamber are a number of historic relics, including Washington's chair and the table on which the Declaration of Independence was signed.

Congress Hall
Old City Hall

Independence Hall is flanked by Congress Hall, in which the first Congress of the United States met from 1790 to 1800 and George Washington and John Adams were elected President, and Old City Hall, which was never in fact the town hall but was the seat of the Supreme Court from 1791 to 1800.

Chestnut Street

On the section of Chestnut Street to the east of Independence Hall are a number of other historic buildings: the Second Bank of the United States (1824–41), now containing a collection of portraits of leading figures in the fight for independence; New Hall, with the Marine Corps Memorial Museum (recalling the role of the Marine Corps in the fight for independence); on the opposite side of the street the Philadelphia Marine Museum

Philadelphia

(history of shipping on the Delaware River and in Delaware Bay); beyond this Pemberton House, a reproduction of the home of the Quaker Joseph Pemberton, now occupied by the Army-Navy Museum; and beyond this again Carpenters' Hall (No. 320), in which the First Continental Congress met in 1774, now a museum of the carpenter's craft.

From Chestnut Street 3rd Street runs south, passing the First Bank of the United States (1797–1811), the country's oldest bank, into Walnut Street. At the corner of 3rd Street is the Merchants' Exchange, originally the seat of the Stock Exchange (founded 1790), the oldest in the United States. At 325 Walnut Street are the headquarters of the Pennsylvania Horticultural Society, the oldest horticultural society in the United States. Farther east, at the corner of 2nd Street, is the City Tavern, in which delegates to the First and Second Continental Congresses used to relax after their labours.

Walnut Street

Concealed between Chestnut and Market Streets is Franklin Court, in which Benjamin Franklin once lived. In one of the reconstructed houses is a museum devoted to the life and work of the great statesman, inventor and journalist.

Franklin Court

South-east of Independence Hall, in Washington Square, once the burial-place of those who died in the fight for independence, is the Tomb of the Unknown Soldier of the Revolution, with an eternal flame.

Washington Square

Other Sights in the Historic District

The area of higher ground to the south of Walnut Street and east of Washington Square, extending almost to Penn's Landing, is called Society Hill after the Free Society of Traders founded by William Penn. Many politicians of the revolutionary period lived in this area, and some of their houses are preserved. At 252 South 4th Street is Old St Mary's Church, with the grave of Commodore John Perry, founder of the US Navy, in the churchyard.

Society Hill

Old St Mary's Church

The Georgian-style Powel House at 244 South 3rd Street was built in 1765 by Samuel Powel, a popular mayor of Philadelphia. South-east of this is the Trouble Tavern (1759). On 2nd Street, between Pine and South Streets, is Headhouse Square, in which a street market has been held since 1745.

Powel House

Headhouse Square

To the north of Independence Hall extends the park-like Independence Mall, laid out in 1948. On its east side, at 55 North 5th Street, is the National Museum of American Jewish History. North of the museum, in Arch Street, is Christ Church Burial Ground, with the graves of Benjamin Franklin and his wife Deborah. Farther north again is the US Mint, established here in 1792, which is now the largest Mint in the world. Opposite the Burial Ground, in the Mall, is the Free Quaker Meeting House, in which the first Free Quaker meeting was held in 1784. South-east of the US Mint, in Arch Street, is the Friends' Meeting House, the city's oldest Quaker meeting house, built on a site acquired by the Quakers in 1693. At the north-west corner of the Mall (7th and Arch Streets) is the Afro-American Historical and Cultural Museum.

Independence Mall

Benjamin Franklin's grave
US Mint

*Afro-American Museum

Half a mile (800m) north of Franklin Square, at 532 North 7th Street, is the Edgar Allan Poe Historic Site, with the house in which Poe lived in 1843–44.

Edgar Allan Poe Museum

To the north, below the Benjamin Franklin Bridge, which crosses the Delaware from Franklin Square, are Old St Augustine's Church (R.C.) and St George's Methodist Church (235 North 4th Street), the oldest Methodist church in the United States, built in 1769.

St George's Methodist Church

403

Philadelphia

Independence Hall, birthplace of the United States of America (see p. 402)

On the Delaware River

Naval Museum — At Pier 11, south of the Benjamin Franklin Bridge, are USS "Olympia", Commodore Dewey's flagship in the battle of Manila Bay during the Spanish–American War (1898) and the Second World War submarine USS "Becuna".

Penn's Landing — At Penn's Landing, where William Penn landed in 1682, there are now a wide range of leisure facilities, including a marina, sports and recreation grounds and old ships.

*New Jersey State Aquarium — From Penn's Landing river buses cross the Delaware to Camden, with the New Jersey State Aquarium, whose principal attractions are an ocean pool (sharks) and a seal pool.

Gloria Dei Church — At the corner of Christian Street and Delaware Avenue (I 95) is the Gloria Dei Church (1700), also known as the Old Swedes, the oldest church in Pennsylvania.

Downtown Philadelphia

*City Hall — From Independence Mall Market Street, lined with shops and department stores, runs west to City Hall (1874–94), at the busy intersection of Market and Broad Streets. The building, in French Renaissance style, was designed by John McArthur; it is crowned by a bronze statue of William Penn.

*Academy of Fine Arts — North of City Hall, at 118 North Broad Street, is the Pennsylvania Academy of Fine Arts, the oldest art school in the United States. It displays a large collection of American art of the last three centuries, including pictures by Peale, West, Sully and Eakins. Open: Tue.–Sat. 10am–5pm, Sun. 11am–5pm.

Philadelphia

North-west of City Hall is the Penn Center, a complex of hotels and high-rise office blocks, including the Central Penn National Bank and the IBM Building. Previously there was a tacit agreement that no buildings in this area should be higher than the statue of William Penn (550ft/168ft), but in recent years a whole series of skyscrapers have been built. Among them are One Liberty Place, at 1650 Market Street, the city's tallest building (945ft/288m), Two Liberty Place (1601 Chestnut Street; 845m/258m) and the Mellon Bank Center (1735 Market Street; 880ft/268m).

*Penn Center

Round Logan Circle

From the Kennedy Plaza, adjoining City Hall, the Benjamin Franklin Parkway runs north-west to Logan Circle with its handsome fountain. On the south side of the square is the Academy of Natural Sciences, the oldest scientific society in the United States. Its extensive collections include dioramas of groups of animals and dinosaur skeletons.

*Logan Circle

The west side of Logan Circle is occupied by the Franklin Institute Science Museum, which is in fact several museums under one roof, and among other things displays many of Franklin's own experiments. It is particularly concerned with the physical bases of technology, and the Science Center offers visitors the opportunity of trying their own experiments, in many fields – computers, information technology, space travel, astronomy, oceanography. Among the exhibits is a large walk-in model of the heart. On the ground floor is an over-life size statue of Benjamin Franklin. The Mandell Futures Center is concerned with the connections between technology and the natural sciences, and forecasts what life will be like in the 21st century. The Tuttleman Omniverse Theatre shows scientific films. There are also exhibitions on electricity and the biological sciences. On the second floor, among much else, is a section on shipbuilding, and on the third is an Observatory. In the basement is a Planetarium.

*Franklin Institute Science Museum

Open: daily 9.30am–5pm

The Rodin Museum (22nd Street and Benjamin Franklin Parkway), opened in 1929, contains the largest collection of Rodin's work outside France, with 124 pieces of sculpture. The collection was assembled in the 1920s by the Philadelphia cinema magnate Jules E. Mastbaum.

*Rodin Museum

Tue.–Sun. 10am–5pm

On the Schuylkill River

At the south end of Fairmount Park is the prominently situated Philadelphia Museum of Art, approached by a broad flight of steps, which has one of the largest art collections in the United States, with some 300,000 exhibits, many of them presented by various foundations. Among the finest sections of the museum are the medieval galleries, which include pictures by Rogier van der Weyden and the van Eyck brothers and complete structures such as a Romanesque cloister and a Gothic chapel. In other rooms are Renaissance and Baroque works and art of the 18th and 19th centuries, including pictures by Van Gogh, Renoir, Toulouse-Lautrec, Manet, Cézanne, Monet and Degas. 20th century European art is represented by Picasso, Chagall, Matisse, Miró, Paul Klee and other artists, American art by the Philadelphia artists Thomas Eakins, Charles Wilson Peale ("The Staircase Group", 1795) and many others. There are also fine collections of Asian art, including a Buddhist and a Chinese temple, porcelain, jade and Oriental carpets.

**Philadelphia Museum of Art

Tue.–Sun. 10am–5pm

Some 550yd/500m north-west of the Museum of Art, along the Schuylkill River and Kelly Drive, is Boathouse Row, with a series of old boathouses belonging to various rowing clubs. Between the Museum and Boathouse Row are the Fairmount Waterworks, with old turbines.

Boathouse Row

1 mile/1.6km south-east of the Zoo is Drexel University, and to the south of this is the campus of the University of Pennsylvania, of which Benjamin

University of Pennsylvania

Phoenix

Franklin was co-founder. On the campus (33rd and Spruce Streets) is the University Museum of Archaeology and Anthropology, with a rich collection of material from Egypt and the Middle East, South and Central America, Greece and Africa.

*Fort Mifflin

Near the junction of the Schuylkill and Delaware Rivers is Fort Mifflin, built by the British in 1772. During the War of Independence it fell into the hands of the American patriots and defended Philadelphia against British attacks.

*Germantown

From City Hall Broad Street runs north into Germantown Avenue, which continues north-east to Germantown (7 miles/11km). Once an independent town occupied by German craftsmen and now a district of Philadelphia with a predominantly black population, it grew up on land which William Penn granted in 1683 to a German Quaker called Daniel Pastorius. The first protests against the import of slaves came from here in 1688. The first German school in North America was established in 1702, and in 1739 the first German newspaper, the "Germantowner Zeitung", was founded by Christoph Sauer.

The Germantown Historical Society in Market Square is a fund of information about Germantown. Other features of interest are the Georgian mansion of Cliveden (6401 Germantown Avenue), built for Judge Benjamin Chew in 1767, Stenton House (1730 18th Street), the Deshler-Morris House of 1773 (5442 Germantown Avenue), Germantown Mennonite Church (6117 Germantown Avenue) and Concord Schoolhouse (6309 Germantown Avenue).

Surroundings of Philadelphia

Princeton

*Princeton University

39 miles/63km north-east of Philadelphia, in the state of New Jersey, is the little town of Princeton, in which the Continental Congress met from June 30th to November 4th 1783. Princeton owes its world fame, however, to its University and its various research institutes, in particular the Institute for Advanced Study, where Albert Einstein worked in his later years. The University, originally founded in 1746 in Elizabeth, New Jersey, as the College of New Jersey, moved to Princeton in 1756. It is one of the elite "Ivy League" universities of the north-eastern United States. A notable modern building is the Woodrow Wilson School of Public and International Affairs (1965), designed by Minoru Yamasaki, an American of Japanese descent; in front of it is the Liberty Fountain. Other striking buildings are Nassau Hall, the Marquand Chapel and the H. S. Firestone Library.

*Valley Forge

On the north-western outskirts of Philadelphia is Valley Forge, where the American army, poorly equipped and inadequately supplied, spent the months from December 1777 to June 1778, in the darkest days of the revolutionary war. Out of a force of between 12,000 and 20,000 men 2000 died of hunger or disease. There are "living history" presentations (daily in summer, at weekends in winter) of the soldiers' ordeal.

Phoenix   Q 13

State: Arizona
Altitude: 1080ft/329m
Population: 985,000 (Metropolitan Area 2.12 million)

Situation and characteristics

Phoenix, capital of the state of Arizona, lies in the valley of the Salt River (which is frequently dry), in a basin known as the Valley of the Sun. The

Phoenix

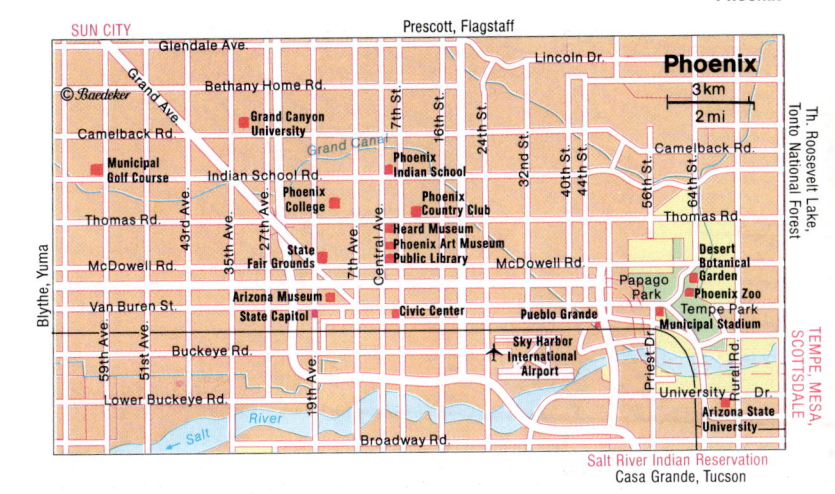

warm, dry climate attracts many sun-lovers, particularly in winter, and also appeals to senior citizens. Irrigation, with water pounded by dams, has made Phoenix and the surrounding area a green oasis in the middle of the desert. Agriculture (cotton, wine grapes, citrus and tropical fruit, vegetables) makes an important contribution to the economy. In recent years many research and development laboratories and firms engaged in the communications technology, aero-space and electronics industries have been established in and around the city. Tourism is showing a sharp increase. The city acquires a special character from the juxtaposition of high-rise modern buildings with architecture showing Indian and Spanish colonial influences, together with a touch of the Wild West. Sport plays a great part in the life of Phoenix, which has numerous golf courses and tennis courts as well as its local football and basketball teams, the Phoenix Cardinals and the Phoenix Suns.

Around 200 B.C. the Phoenix region was occupied by Hohokam Indians, who already knew how to make the desert fertile by irrigation. Amid the remains of settlements and irrigation channels left by the Hohokams, who mysteriously disappeared in the 13th or 14th century, a white settler established himself in 1864 to supply the needs of an army post. In the 1870s a new settlement grew up on the remains of the lost Indian culture and was named after the mythological phoenix which rose from its own ashes. In 1889 Phoenix became capital of Arizona, and after the completion of the Roosevelt Dam in 1911 developed into a regular boom town, which was given an additional boost by the coming of the railroad in 1926. Further stimulus came to the economy after the Second World War and from the "Sun Belt" migration which began in the late sixties. Since the end of the war the population of Phoenix has multiplied more than tenfold.

History

Sights in Phoenix

Set in beautiful gardens is the old State Capitol (Washington Street and 17th Avenue), built in 1900, which was the seat of government until 1974. The imposing state apartments are now a museum on the history of Arizona. Here too can be seen the anchor of USS "Arizona", which was sunk in Pearl Harbor in 1941.

*Arizona State Capitol Museum

Phoenix

Downtown Phoenix

*Heritage Square	In Heritage Square are eight lovingly restored houses dating from the city's early days. Stevens House (between 6th and 7th Streets) contains a collection of dolls and toys. At the corner of 6th and Monroe Streets is Rosson House, an elegant Victorian mansion.
Papago Park/ Zoo/Desert Botanical Garden	In Papago Park are the Phoenix Zoo (455 North Galvin Parkway), which is famed for its Sumatra tigers and orang-utans, and the Desert Botanical Garden (1201 North Galvin Parkway), with examples of vegetation from deserts in different parts of the world and a cactus garden. The flowers are particularly beautiful in spring.
*Heard Museum	The renowned Heard Museum (22 East Monte Vista Road; open: Mon.–Sat. 9.30am–5pm, Wed. to 9pm, Sun. noon–5pm) is devoted to the art and culture of the Indian peoples of the South-West (basketwork, pottery, jewellery, textiles; large collection of kachina dolls).
*Pueblo Grande Museum	In the Pueblo Grande Museum (4619 East Washington Street) are the ruins of a 12th century Hohokam settlement and remains of old irrigation channels.
Arizona Mining and Mineral Museum	The Arizona Mining and Mineral Museum (1502 West Washington Street) is devoted to Arizona's mineral wealth. Its fascinating display of precious stones, many-coloured minerals and various ores bears witness to the state's rich resources of minerals.
*Phoenix Art Museum	The Phoenix Art Museum (1625 North Central Avenue; open: Tue.–Sat. 10am–5pm, Wed. to 9pm, Sun. noon–5pm) has a collection covering the art of the European Renaissance and Baroque, the Far East and the American West.
Hall of Flame/ Museum of Firefighting	The Hall of Flame (6101 East Van Buren Street) illustrates the history of firefighting with exhibits dating back to 1725, including old fire-engines and some very curious types of fire-extinguisher.

Surroundings of Phoenix

The retirement town of Sun City, 11 miles/18km north-west of Phoenix, came into being in the 1960s, and now has a population of 50,000 senior citizens. Offering the attractions of leisure, a pleasant life style, an agreeable climate and beautiful scenery, it is almost entirely residential, with no schools or kindergartens, still less any industry. Another settlement of the same kind, Sun City West, has grown up in the immediate vicinity.

Sun City

Mesa, a Phoenix suburb on a plateau to the south-east, has two museums devoted to the days of the Indians and the pioneers who settled in this area, the Mesa Southwest Museum (53 North MacDonald Street) and the Crismon Farm and Heritage Museum (2345 North Horne Street).

Mesa

The Champlin Fighter Museum (4643 Fighter Aces Drive, Falcon Field) has a collection of fighter planes of the two world wars, the Korean War and the Vietnam War.

Champlin Fighter Museum

To the east of Phoenix is the vacation resort of Scottsdale, with luxury hotels and excellent leisure facilities. Features of interest are the Center for the Arts (art exhibitions) and the McCromick Railroad Park (museum).

Scottsdale

Another popular attraction is Rawhide (23023 Scottsdale Road), a reconstruction of a Western town of around 1880, with a saloon, a steakhouse and wild shoot-ups by professional stuntmen.

*Rawhide

In Taliesin West (108th Street, near Shea Boulevard) was the home and architectural school of the celebrated architect Frank Lloyd Wright (see Famous People).

Taliesin West

Paolo Soleri, who works in the Cosanti Foundation (6433 Doubletree Ranch Road), is another architect whose name is linked with Phoenix. He is at present building the futuristic settlement of Arcosanti, in a beautiful setting north of Phoenix, taking particular account of ecological conditions.

Cosanti Foundation

In the hilly region north-east and east of Phoenix (Tonto National Forest, Mazatzal Mountains, Sierra Ancha Mountains) a series of dams have been built in recent decades, forming artificial lakes to ensure an adequate water supply for the rapidly growing population of the Phoenix Metropolitan Area. The oldest of these lakes is Theodore Roosevelt Lake, to the east of Scottsdale, which was formed by the construction of a dam in 1911. Various water sports (swimming, water-skiing, boating, etc.) are permitted in specially signposted areas.

Artificial lakes

To the south of Theodore Roosevelt Lake, near SR 88, is the Tonto National Monument, a pueblo constructed by Salago Indians in the 14th century.

*Tonto National Monument

Pittsburgh

J 45

State: Pennsylvania
Altitude: 680–1400ft/207–427m
Population: 370,000 (Greater Metropolitan Area 2.1 million)

On the north-western Allegheny Plateau, at the point where the Allegheny and Monongahela Rivers join to form the Ohio, lies the city of Pittsburgh, surrounded by the wooded hills of the western Appalachians. The wealth of the city came from these hills: the coal mined here was the basis of a great steel industry which at one time produced half the total requirements of the United States. This branch of industry is still a major element in the city's economy, but since the crisis of the antiquated American steel industry in the 1970s a process of restructuring has been under way, and Pittsburgh now has a range of other industries as well, in particular service industries, high tech industry and light industry. The city's good communications – it is an important inland port and has a large new airport opened in 1992 – have led major firms like Westinghouse Electric to establish their

Situation and characteristics

Pittsburgh

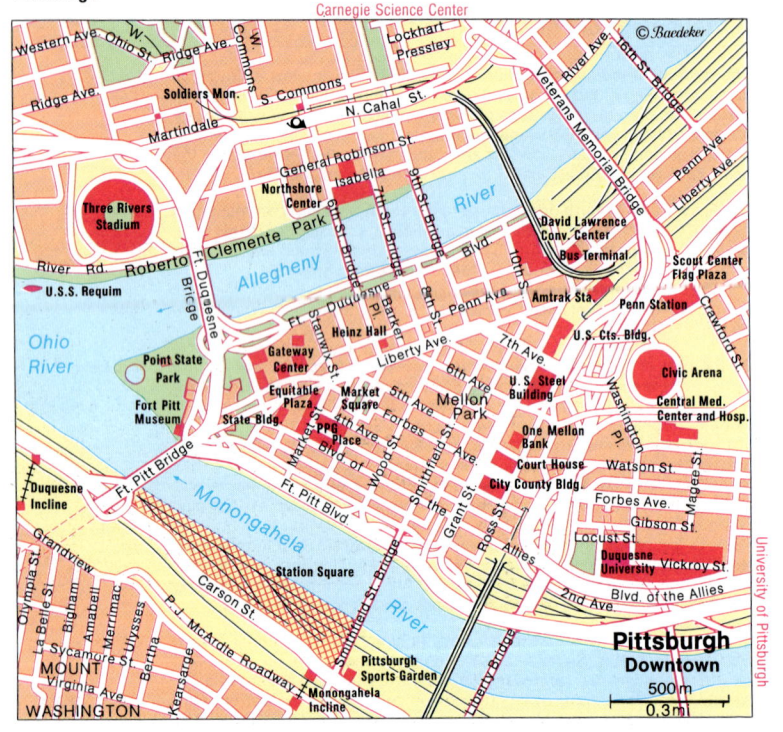

History	headquarters here. Pittsburgh is thus no longer the soot-encrusted coal and steel town of the past, but rather a metropolis with fine parks and gardens flanking the rivers, a modern city centre and established cultural institutions such as the Pittsburgh Symphony Orchestra and the Pittsburgh Opera.
	The first Europeans to reach the "Golden Triangle" between the rivers were Frenchmen, who built Fort Duquesne. The French fort was destroyed by the British in 1758 and replaced by Fort Pitt (named after William Pitt the Elder). The settlement which grew up round the fort was named Pittsburgh; the local coalfields began to be worked and blast furnaces were built. The demand for iron and steel for the Civil War brought prosperity to heavy industry, and thereafter industrialists like Andrew Carnegie and Henry Clay Frick built up their empires. Pittsburgh enjoyed further booms during the two world wars, but thereafter the crisis in the steel industry made a process of readjustment necessary.
	Pittsburgh was one of the birthplaces of the American trade union movement: the American Federation of Labor was founded here in 1881, and the city was frequently the scene of bitter conflicts between workers and employers.

Sights in Pittsburgh

*Golden Triangle Point State Park	The heart of Pittsburgh is the "Golden Triangle" at the junction of the Allegheny and Monongahela Rivers. At the tip of the triangle is Point State

410

Pittsburgh

View of the Golden Triangle

Park, with a large fountain symbolising the birth of the Ohio. This was the site of Fort Pitt, of which there now remains only a blockhouse. The fort's original appearance is shown in dioramas in the Fort Pitt Museum.

With its gardens, its old buildings and its attractive restaurants and shops, picturesque Market Square is a pleasant relief from the rather overpowering skyscrapers which surround it.

Market Square

The 31-storey skyscraper Fifth Avenue Place (Stanwix Street) contains a shopping mall, the Avenue of Shops, lavishly decorated with marble, glass and brass. Between 6th and 7th Streets is the granite-built CNG Tower, a major landmark on the city's skyline. In Grant Street, side by side, are the two tallest buildings in Pittsburgh, One Mellon Bank Center (715ft/218m) and the USX Tower (840ft/256m), the façade of which, constructed of non-stainless steel, is quietly rusting. The Post-Modern complex PPG Place was designed by Philip Johnson. The Alcoa Building (425 5th Avenue) was a pioneering feat of building technology, the aluminium cladding having been applied without any internal scaffolding.

Skyscrapers

The Strip District, on the Allegheny River at the north-east corner of the Golden Triangle, formerly occupied by warehouses and railroad installations, is now the city's wholesale market centre, a scene of lively activity in the early morning and forenoon. There are guided tours of the complex, including the Wholesale Produce Terminal, the largest wholesale vegetable market in western Pennsylvania.

Strip District

In the Mount Washington district on the north bank of the Monongahela River, between Smithfield Street Bridge and Fort Pitt Bridge, is Station Square, once occupied by railway yards but now an elegant shopping centre. Near Smithfield Bridge is the Bessemer Court open-air museum, which is devoted to the city's industrial history and includes among the exhibits a 10-ton Bessemer steel hammer of 1930. Close by, in Station Square, is the Transportation Museum (old cars, bicycles and railroad wagons).

Mount Washington
Station Square

Bessemer Court

Transportation Museum

Portland

Funiculars	From South Side two funiculars run steeply up Mount Washington – the last of the cable railways which used to carry coal from the mines in the hill down to the river for shipment. The Monongahela Incline starts from West Carson Street, opposite Station Square, the Duquesne Incline Railway farther along the street, north-west of Fort Pitt Bridge. From the top of the hill there are fine views of downtown Pittsburgh.
North Side *Carnegie Science Center	In North Side (the north bank of the Allegheny River) is the huge Carnegie Science Center (1 Allegheny Avenue), a museum of science and technology. Among the subjects dealt with are industrial processing methods, the use of energy and socio-cultural aspects of nutrition. The Pacific Coral Reef Aquarium displays a wide range of tropical fishes. In the Rangos Omnimax Theater visitors can make imaginary journeys through the human body; in the Henry Buhl Jr Planetarium and Observatory they can fly into space. Opening times: Mon.–Wed. 10am–5pm, Thur. and Sun. to 9.30pm. Fri. and Sat. to 10.30pm.
Andy Warhol Museum	The Andy Warhol Museum, opened in 1994, is devoted to the life and work of the Pop Art artist, who was born in North Side. Housed in a restored warehouse, it displays paintings, drawings, prints, films and videos by Warhol.
East of the Golden Triangle University of Pittsburgh	To the east of the city centre is the campus of the University of Pittsburgh, dominated by the 535ft/163m high "Cathedral of Learning" (1935) containing lecture rooms, including 22 so-called nationality classrooms for different ethnic groups, including Jews and Armenians. South-east of the building is the Stephen Foster Memorial, commemorating the Pittsburgh-born composer of that name (1826–64), author of the popular song "Oh, Susannah".
*The Carnegie	To the east of the University, at 4400 Forbes Avenue, are the Museum of Natural History, the Museum of Art and the Music Hall, in the complex known simply as "the Carnegie" after its founder Andrew Carnegie. The most interesting is the Museum of Natural History, famed for its large dinosaur collection, the Hillman Hall of Minerals and Gems and its displays of material on the cultures of the North American Indians and the life of the Inuit in the Arctic. Opening times: Tue.–Sat. 10am–9pm, Sun. 1–5pm.
Frick Art Museum	Still farther east is Frick Park, with the Frick Art Museum. This displays the art collection of Helen Clay Frick, with pictures ranging in date from the early Renaissance to the end of the 18th century (open: Tue.–Sat. 10am–5.30pm, Sun. noon–6pm). Farther north is the country house which belonged to the Pittsburgh industrialist Henry Clay Frick.

Portland   D 3

State: Oregon
Altitude: 75ft/23m
Population: 437,000

Situation and characteristics	Portland, the largest city in Oregon, lies in a beautiful setting on the banks of the Willamette River, on the north-western border of the state. An industrial city and port, it has a number of features of interest and attractive open spaces, including in particular the beautiful Washington Park.
History	Portland was founded in 1844 as a little port town on the west bank of the Willamette River. Much of the town was destroyed by a great fire in 1873, but after its rebuilding it developed into a thriving city. When new ports were built on Puget Sound in the early 20th century, however, Portland lost its leading role.

Puerto Rico

Sights in Portland

The Portland Art Museum in Park Avenue has a collection of high quality in a variety of fields, including Indian art and Renaissance pictures in the Kress Collection.

Portland Art Museum

Opposite the Art Museum is the Oregon Historical Museum, with a rich collection of material on the history of the state.

Oregon Historical Museum

At the corner of Madison Street and 5th Avenue is the Portland Building, with a glass and concrete façade with features borrowed from historic buildings which make it one of the forerunners of Post-Modern architecture.

Portland Building

The Old Town of Portland is some blocks north of the present city centre, between 5th and Front Avenues. Only a few buildings survive from the city's earliest days, and in recent years there has been much building of new shops and restaurants. The Saturday Market held at weekends from March to Christmas round the Skidmore Fountain (corner of 1st Avenue and Ankeny Street) attracts large numbers of people. At 9 NW 2nd Avenue is the American Advertising Museum.

Old Town

This large park to the west of the city centre contains a number of features of interest. The best known is the International Rose Test Garden, where new varieties of roses are grown; in the city's mild climate they continue to flower into autumn. An annual event for rose-lovers is the Rose Festival in June. Other attractions are the Zoo, famed for its herd of Asiatic elephants, the Oregon Museum of Science and Industry (supplemented since 1992 by a new museum of science and technology on the banks of the river in the city centre), the Japanese Garden and the Hoyt Arboretum.

*Washington Park

Puerto Rico   Not on map

Political status: Commonwealth of Puerto Rico
Area: 3435sq.miles/8897sq.km
Population: 3.6 million
Capital: San Juan

Puerto Rico, the most easterly and the smallest island in the Greater Antilles, lies 1000 miles/1600km south-east of Miami (see entry) between the Atlantic in the north and the Caribbean in the south. The Commonwealth of Puerto Rico also includes the island of Mona, to the west, and the two eastern offshore islands of Vieques and Culebra. The main island extends for 110 miles/180km from west to east, with a breadth which ranges between 31 miles/50km and 37 miles/60km.

Situation and *topography

Puerto Rico offers a varied landscape pattern. Three main zones can be distinguished – the coastal plains, the uplands north and south of the Cordillera Central and the Cordillera Central itself, which reaches its highest point in the Cerro de Punta (4357ft/1328m). With a climate characteristic of the margins of the tropics, marked by an alternation between wet and dry periods, Puerto Rico has a lush tropical vegetation, at its richest in the rain forest of the Sierra de Luquillo. Round Arecibo, on the north coast, is an area of bizarre karstic landscape. Along the coasts are a series of beautiful beaches offering good bathing, surfing and diving. Temperatures throughout the year are agreeable; between August and October there may be tropical hurricanes.

In spite of much Americanisation Puerto Rico has preserved its typically Caribbean atmosphere. Much of the population lives in the United States, though with the industrialisation of the island since the 1970s many Puerto Ricans have returned home.

Emigration and re-migration

413

Puerto Rico

History
Puerto Rico (Spanish, "rich harbour") was discovered by Columbus in 1493 and settled by Spaniards, under the leadership of Juan Ponce de León, from 1508 onwards. The island was originally inhabited by some 30,000 Arawak Indians, who called their country Boriquén. Originally the main value of Puerto Rico to the Spaniards was its deposits of gold, which were worked by forced Indian labour, but after the gold was exhausted it remained a Spanish base and a safe haven for ships sailing between the South American mainland and Spain. In the 17th and 18th centuries a plantation economy (sugar, tobacco and coffee) developed, with the labour of slaves imported from Africa. In 1897 Luis Muñoz Rivera wrested a kind of dominion status from the Spanish crown; then in the Spanish–American War of 1898 Puerto Rico passed into the hands of the United States. In 1917 the Puerto Ricans were granted American citizenship and a limited degree of internal self-government. In 1948 they elected their first Governor, and since 1952 Puerto Rico has had its own constitution as a Commonwealth in voluntary association with the United States. All Puerto Ricans are United States citizens, but pay no federal taxes and have no vote in United States elections. In a referendum in November 1993 a bare majority of the population voted for the continuance of their commonwealth status and against the incorporation of Puerto Rico in the United States as the 51st state.

Economy
After abandoning its traditional agricultural monoculture in favour of rapid industrial development Puerto Rico now has a prosperous economy. With a per capita income of 6320 US dollars, it is the best-off island in the Greater Antilles. Most of Puerto Rico's industry, however, is owned by American firms, which benefits from the investment incentives and tax advantages available on the island. The second most important branch of the economy is now tourism, which in the last few years has been actively promoted. Only some 4% of the working population is now employed in agriculture.

Places of Interest in Puerto Rico

The description of Puerto Rico in this guide is abridged, since there is a detailed account of the island in the AA/Baedeker guide "Caribbean".

Arecibo
Arecibo (pop. 90,000), the second largest town on the north coast of the island, is a busy industrial town and an important port. To the south and east of Arecibo is the striking scenery of the Karst Country.

Observatory
The town's principal sight is the Observatorio de Arecibo, which has the largest radio-telescope in the world. Another interesting feature is the Río Camuy Cave Park, part of a huge underground river and cave system. In the Reserva Forestal Río Abajo, a tropical nature park, are teak, mahogany and pine trees.

Río Camuy Cave Park

Culebra
The little island of Culebra, with an area of 11sq.miles/28sq.km and a population of 2000, lies 19 miles/30km east of Puerto Rico. Its chief place is Dewy, beautifully situated on the Enseñada Honda. The island offers excellent diving and bathing.

Isla Mona
The island of Mona (area 22sq.miles/58sq.km), to the west of Puerto Rico, is home to numerous colonies of birds and is surrounded by a colourful underwater world.

Mayagüez
The industrial and university town and commercial port of Mayagüez (pop. 100,000) lies on the west coast of Puerto Rico. The hub of the town's life is the Plaza Colón, with a statue of Columbus and sixteen other bronze statues. It has an interesting zoo and an agricultural research centre. To the north of the town is Rincón, near which is the most westerly point on Puerto Rico, Punta Higüero. There are other beaches and good diving and surfing areas at Aguadilla, Punta Boriquén, Isabela, Punta Sardinas and Quebradillas.

Punta Higüero

Puerto Rico

The Ruta Panorámica runs from Mayagüez to Yabucoa in the south-east of the island, passing through the Cordillera Central and nature reserves like the Monte del Estado and the Toro Negro National Forest. The Cordillera reaches its highest point in the Cerro de Punta (4357ft/1328m).

Ruta Panorámica

South-west and south of Mayagüez are San Germán, the oldest town on the island after San Juan, founded in 1511, and the little town of Cabo Rojo. In the south-eastern corner of Puerto Rico is the Cabo Rojo nature reserve. The Bahía Fosforescente is famous for the phosphorescence of the sea at night.

San Germán/ Cabo Rojo

The old colonial town of Ponce (pop. 300,000), the "Pearl of the South", is Puerto Rico's largest town after San Juan. Its central plaza is dominated by the Cathedral of Nuestra Señora de Guadalupe. On the occasion of Columbus Year, the 500th anniversary of Columbus's discovery of America, 600 of the thousand or so historic buildings in the town were renovated. The main sights are the gaudily painted century-old fire station, the Parque de Bombas; the Museo de Arte; a music museum; a new historical museum opened in 1992; and the La Perla theatre. From the Cruz del Vigia, an observation tower, there are fine views of the town.

Ponce

To the east of Ponce is the oldest cemetery in the Antilles, the Tibes Indian Ceremonial Center, with a reconstructed Taino village. North of the town are the Hacienda Buena Vista, a coffee plantation dating from 1833, and the Caguana Indian Ceremonial Park, a cult site of the Taino Indians.

Tibes Indian Ceremonial Center/ Hacienda Buena Vista

Along the coast to the east of Ponce are the bathing resorts of Santa Isabel and Salinas.

San Juan (pop. 450,000, conurbation 1.1 million), on the north coast, is the capital of Puerto Rico and its cultural and economic centre. Roughly a third of the island's population is concentrated here. In the city centre modern high-rise blocks contrast with colonial buildings in Hispano-Mauresque style.

San Juan

A good starting-point for a tour of the old town of San Juan is the Paseo de la Princesa, which was splendidly refurbished for Columbus Year. From the landing-stages used by the cruise ships the historic promenade runs along the town walls to the Fortaleza (the Governor's palace), the Casa Blanca, once the home of the Ponce de León family, and, dominating the scene, the Fuerte de San Felipe del Morro, for centuries regarded as impregnable, now listed by UNESCO as a world cultural monument. The east end of the town was protected by its counterpart, the Fuerte de San Cristóbal. Other features of interest are the Alcaldía (Town Hall), the Cathedral, with the tomb of Juan Ponce de León, and the Iglesia de San José, one of the oldest and finest Gothic churches in the western hemisphere.

*Viejo San Juan

Among the city's most notable museums are the Museum of Puerto Rican Art, the Pablo Casals Museum, the Museo del Mar (Museum of the Sea) and the Casa del Libro (House of the Book).

To the east of the old part of the town is the Puerta de Tierra district, dominated by the Capitol. Other features of interest are the Parque Muñoz Rivera and the Fortín San Gerónimo. The Condado, Miramar, Ocean Park and Isla Verde districts are the tourist centre of the island, with numerous hotels, restaurants, bars and boutiques. The Condado Convention Center is one of the largest in the Caribbean.

In the Río Piedras district, to the south of the tourist districts, is a magnificent botanical garden belonging to the University's agricultural research station, the Estación Experimental Agrícola.

From San Juan an excursion can be made into the Sierra de Luquillo, bordering the northern coastal plain. In this area is the El Yunque Rain Forest, a nature reserve and National Park extending over 28,000 acres/11,340 hectares. It has a very varied tropical flora, and is home to some rare species of parrot.

Sierra de Luquillo El Yunque Rain Forest

The beaches of Luquillo, Sardinera and Humacao are among the finest in Puerto Rico. The Playa de Humacao is a popular diving area.

Beaches

415

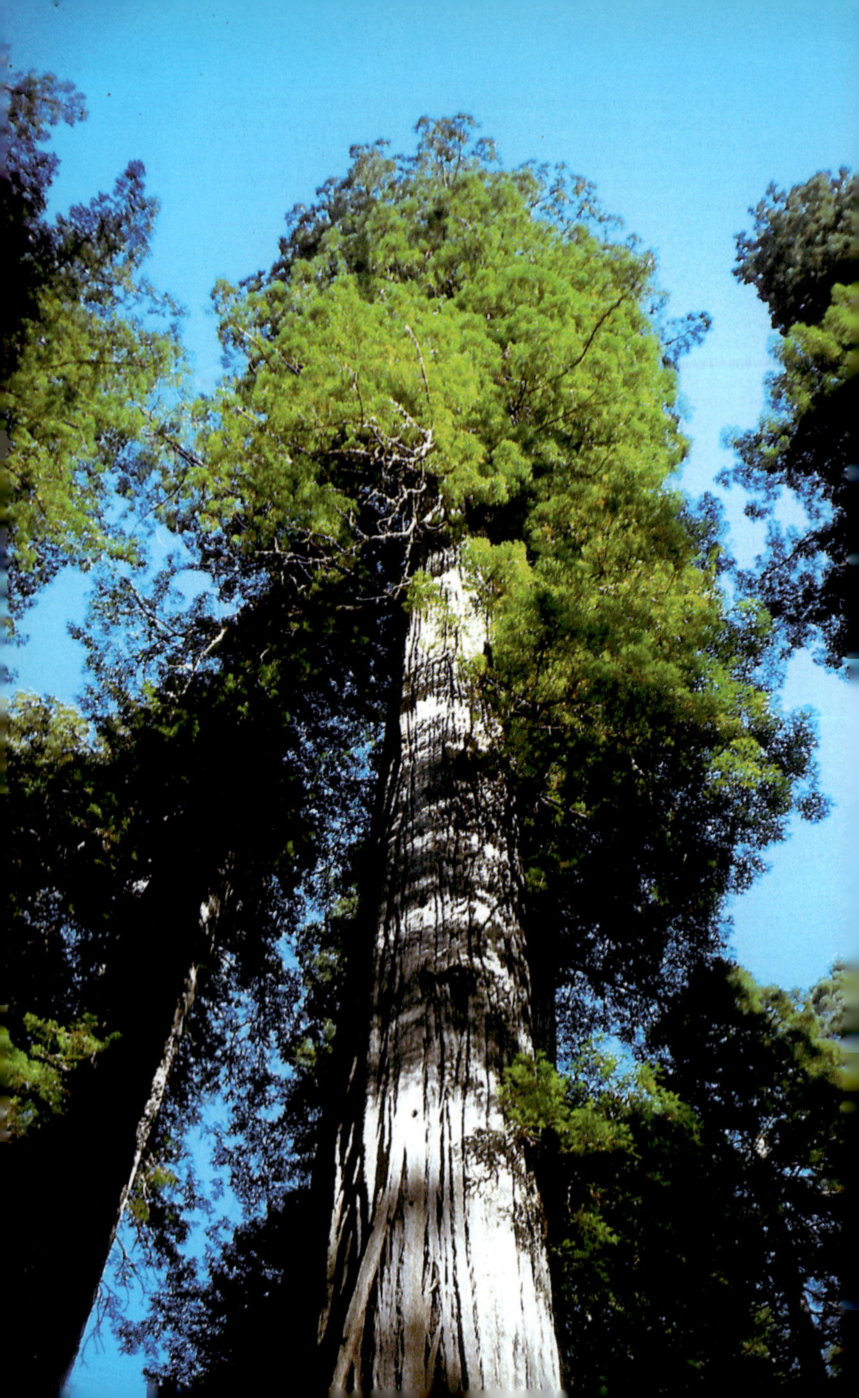

Rhode Island

The former fishing village of Fajardo is now a developing holiday resort. From here there are boats to the offshore islands of Culebra and Vieques.   Fajardo

The island of Vieques (area 52sq.miles/134sq.km) lies 7½ miles/12km east of Puerto Rico, within the Virgin Islands. Most of the island is used as a training area by the US Navy. The chief place is Isabel Segunda.   **Vieques**

Redwood National Park   H 1/2

State: California
Area: 177sq.miles/458sq.km
Established: 1968

The National Park is open throughout the year. The best times for a visit are in spring, when the rhododendrons are in flower, and in autumn for the colouring of the foliage. During the summer the park tends to be crowded with visitors.   Season

The park has some 150 miles/240km of waymarked roads and trails, four campgrounds and some primitive overnight accommodation. There are facilities for swimming, fishing and boating on the Smith River in the Jedediah Smith State Park. Bathing is not recommended on the rugged but beautiful Pacific coast because of its high waves, strong currents and extremely cold water.

The Redwood National Park, which is formed from three smaller nature reserves (Del Norte Coast Redwoods State Park, Jedediah Smith State Park, Prairie Creek Redwoods State Park), lies on the Pacific coast between Orick and Crescent City, 330 miles/530km north of San Francisco (see entry). 50 miles/80km long and up to 7 miles/11km across, it contains some 37,500 acres/15,200 hectares of redwoods.   Situation

The coast redwoods (*Sequoia sempervirens*) grow only in a narrow belt of land along the coast from Oregon, down to the south of San Francisco. They are closely related to the mammoth trees (*Sequoia gigantea*), which grows only on some of the western slopes of the Sierra Nevada. The coast redwoods, which provide much sought after building timber and veneers, are the tallest trees on earth, reaching heights of over 330ft/100m. Trunks with a diameter of 20ft/6m are not uncommon. The average age of these giants is between 500 and 700 years, and some are over 2000 years old. They are almost immune to disease or attack by pests, and their thick bark, up to a foot thick, gives then protection against forest fires, but they have a relatively shallow root system which makes them vulnerable in a storm. Redwoods can be grown from seed, from a cone or from shoots.   **Redwoods

In Tall Trees Grove is the tallest tree on earth. It stands 368ft/112m high, has a circumference of 44ft/13.5m and is 600 years old. Access to it is strictly regulated. A bus (with a very restricted number of seats) runs to the site from the Redwood Information Center.   *Tall Trees Grove

From the Information Center at Orick there is a road to Lady Bird Johnson Grove, a group of immense redwoods named after President Lyndon Johnson's wife.   *Lady Bird Johnson Grove

Rhode Island (State; RI)   H 54

Area: 1214sq.miles/3144sq.km
Population: 1,004,000
Capital: Providence
Popular names: Little Rhody, Ocean State

◀ *Giant redwoods*

Rhode Island

Situation and topography

Rhode Island, the smallest state in the Union, is one of the New England states in the north-east of the USA. The eastern half of the state is occupied by Narragansett Bay, which reaches far inland, and to the west of this are the New England Uplands, the highest point in which is 900ft/274m above sea level. Rhode Island has a maritime climate, with mild winters and wet summers. Over 60% of the state is forest-covered, and its mixed forests of oak, beech, maple, birch, pine, etc., provide a valuable recreation area for the inhabitants of the neighbouring great cities.

History

Refugees from Massachusetts established the first settlements in Rhode Island, where for the first time in a British colony there was a clear line of separation between state and church. Thereafter many refugees from religious persecution found a new home in Rhode Island. In 1675, in the "Great Swamp Fight", the settlers ended the previous predominance of the Narragansett Indians. Rhode Island joined the Union on May 29th 1790, the last of the thirteen founding states to do so.

Economy

The economy of Rhode Island depends mainly on industry. A leading place is taken by the state's traditional textile industry (first cotton spinning mill, 1793), followed by engineering, tool manufacture and jewellery. The rubber and artificial fibre industries are also of some consequence. The state's agriculture (dairy farming, poultry rearing, fruit and vegetables) is geared only to meeting local needs. The fisheries are mainly concerned with mussel culture. Thanks to the state's 375 mile/600km long coast and its great expanses of forest the tourist and holiday trade makes a major contribution to the economy.

Places of Interest in Rhode Island

Bristol

The town of Bristol was founded in 1669, and around 1800 was a considerable port. Shipbuilding brought the town a prosperity to which numerous handsome old houses still bear witness. The Haffenreffer Museum of Anthropology has fine collections of material on the cultures of the Eskimos and the Indians of North and South America. The Coggeshall Farm Museum shows farming life as it was around 1800. The Herreshoff Marine Museum illustrates the history of shipbuilding in Bristol.

**Newport

Newport, in Narragansett Bay, also made its name as a shipbuilding town, and it is still an important yachting port. Its main role, however, has been as an exclusive summer resort patronised by New York society which has preserved much evidence of its past.

**Historic houses

The main tourist attractions of Newport are its sumptuous holiday residences of the 18th and 19th centuries, ranging from English-style country houses to neo-Baroque palaces. The most splendid of them all is The Breakers, a 70-room mansion in the style of an Italian palazzo built for Cornelius Vanderbilt in 1895, still with its original decoration and furnishings. Others worth visiting are the Marble House, The Elms, Rosecliff Hunter House, Belcourt Castle. the Victorian-style Château-sur-Mer and the Samuel Whitehorne House with its exquisite 18th century interior. John F. and Jacqueline Kennedy spent their honeymoon in Hammersmith Farm. From the 3 mile long Cliff Walk, there are superb views of Rhode Island Bay and the houses of Newport.

Two features of unique interest in Newport are the oldest Synagogue in the United States (1763), with a number of treasures, including the oldest Torah in North America, and the Redwood Library and Athenaeum (1750), the earliest library in the United States which is still in use. For tennis fans there are the International Tennis Hall of Fame and the Tennis Museum.

The state capital, Providence, situated at the northern tip of Narragansett Bay, was founded in 1636 and soon developed into a flourishing commercial port. It has a rich stock of restored buildings of the 17th–19th centuries, notably the John Brown House (1786), with a richly appointed interior, and the residence of Governor Stephen Hopkins (1707). Providence also has an unusual number of old churches, including the first Baptist church in America (1775). The imposing domed State House (1901) was designed by the well-known firm of architects McKim, Mead and White. The Rhode Island School of Design has a small but high-quality art collection.

*Providence

Richmond

M 48

State: Virginia
Altitude: 150ft/46m
Population: 203,000 (Metropolitan Area 865,600)

Richmond, capital of Virginia, lies on the James River in the heart of the state. The townscape of Richmond – a banking centre, an industrial town (tobacco, papermaking, printing, chemicals) and the seat of two universities – is dominated by high-rise office blocks, but amid the skyscrapers there are still some reminders (the State Capitol and many old houses) of the town's great past as a centre of the American independence movement and one-time capital of the Confederation.

Situation and characteristics

When, during the revolutionary war, the patriots feared that the capital of Virginia, Williamsburg (see Colonial National Historical Park), might be taken they made Richmond, which had been founded in 1737, the new capital. Here in 1775 Patrick Henry made the famous speech in which he called for separation from Britain with the slogan "Liberty or death!". From 1861 Richmond was capital of the Confederacy until its capture in April 1865. At the end of the war the retreating Southern troops set their storehouses on fire, a fire which spread to the town.

History

Sights in Richmond

In Capitol Square is the imposing State Capitol, built in 1785–88 to the design of Thomas Jefferson, who took as his model the Roman temple known as the Maison Carrée in Nîmes. The Capitol was the scene of major events in American history, including the ratification of Virginia's secession and Robert E. Lee's appointment as commander of the Southern army. The statue of George Washington in the lobby was the work of Jean-Antoine Houdon (1741–1828). In Capitol Square is an equestrian statue of Washington.

*State Capitol

In Clay Street, two blocks north of Capitol Square, is the Valentine Museum (1015 East Clay Street), which is devoted to the social and industrial history of Richmond. The Museum of the Confederacy (1201 East Clay Street) traces the history of the Secession and the subsequent war. The White House of the Confederacy (12th and East Clay Streets) was the seat of Jefferson Davis, President of the Southern states (see Famous People).

Clay Street
Valentine Museum
Museum of the Confederacy
White House of the Confederacy

To the east of the State Capitol, beyond I 95, is the Church Hill Historic Area, with some 70 antebellum houses which give some impression of what Richmond was like before the Civil War.

Church Hill Historic Area

Rocky Mountain National Park

St John's	The district is named after St John's Episcopal Church (1741; 25th and Broad Streets), in which Patrick Henry made his famous speech. The Old Stone House (1737) at 1914 East Main Street, the oldest building in Richmond, now houses the Edgar Allan Poe Museum. Poe lived in the town for several years and worked on a local newspaper.
Edgar Allan Poe Museum	
Virginia Museum of Fine Arts	The principal treasure of the Victoria Museum of Fine Arts is a collection of Fabergé eggs.
Monument Avenue	South of the Museum is Monument Avenue, which is lined with statues of Confederate heroes.
Philip Morris Manufacturing Center	To the south of the city centre (I 95, exit 69) is the Philip Morris Manufacturing Center, where visitors can see round the factory on a guided tour (no charge).

Rocky Mountain National Park J 20

State: Colorado
Area: 414sq.miles/1072sq.km
Established: 1915

Season	The National Park is open throughout the year. The Trail Ridge Road is open from the end of May to October. The park is particularly beautiful in spring (June). Most visitors come in July and August. The country is at its most colourful in early autumn (September). There are excellent winter sports facilities.
Situation and **topography	The Rocky Mountain National Park, 2½ hours' drive north-west of Denver (see entry), includes within its confines the Continental Divide (Watershed), formed by the main ridge of the Rocky Mountains, which on the east side fall abruptly down to the Great Plains in the Front Range. The highest point is Longs Peak (14,256ft/4345m), in the south-east of the National Park. The deep U-shaped valleys were scooped out by glaciers. The icefields and snowfields in the summit zone, the alpine meadows, the quiet lakes and rushing mountain streams and the varied flora and fauna (including wapiti) draw well over 2 million visitors every year.
*Trail Ridge Road	A particularly rewarding trip is a drive along the 50 mile/80km long Trail Ridge Road, which runs through the park from east to west, following an old Indian trail. The starting-point is the Beaver Meadows entrance, above the little resort of Estes Park. From there the road runs by way of Deer Ridge

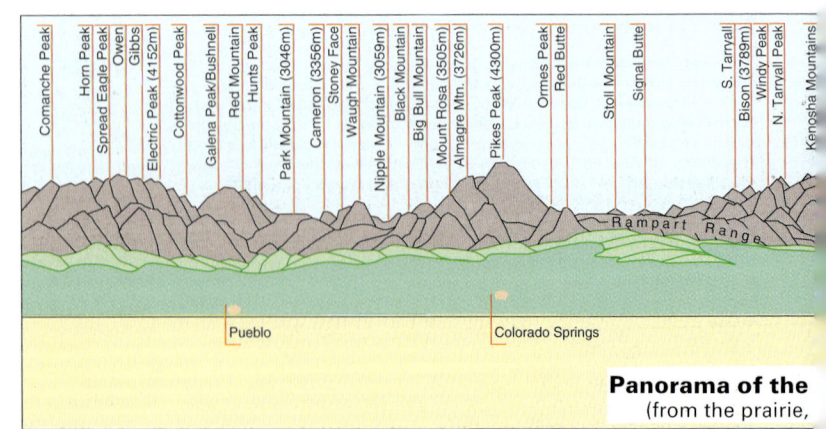

Panorama of the
(from the prairie,

Rocky Mountain National Park

to the Many Parks Curve and on to Forest Canyon Overlook, a viewpoint on a wooded gorge carved out by the Big Thompson River.
From the Rock Cut, some miles farther north-west, there is a magnificent view of the Mummy Range, which strikes in a north-easterly direction, with Ypsilon Mountain (13,514ft/4119m). The High Point (12,182ft/3713m) is, as its name indicates, the highest point on the road. At Fall River Pass is a Visitor Center which can supply full information about the alpine zone of the Rocky Mountains. Here the Old Fall River Road comes in. Beyond the pass the Trail Ridge Road turns south-west to cross the Continental Divide at Milner Pass (10,758ft/3279m) and then runs down, with many bends, into Phantom Valley, through which flows a source stream of the Colorado River. Farther downstream is the Kawuneeche Valley, with the Never Summer Ranch (open-air museum). The road ends at the Grand Lake.

The unsurfaced Old Fall River Road (one-way) runs up from Fall River Entrance Station in a north-westerly direction to the Visitor Center at Fall River Pass (see above), passing Horseshoe Park, the Sheep Lakes and the wild Chasm Falls. | Old Fall River Road

From the Beaver Meadow entrance the Bear Lake Road, a 10 mile/16km long branch road, runs past Moraine Park (Visitor Center) and Glacier Basin to Bear Lake, picturesquely situated among high peaks, from which a variety of magnificent mountain hikes can be undertaken. There is a nature trail round the lake. Above Bear Lake is Dream Lake, sheltering between Flattop Mountain and Hallett Peak. | Bear Lake Road

From SR 7, which runs along the south-eastern edge of the National Park, there is a strenuous mountain hike (a full-day climb) to picturesque Chasm Lake and from there up Longs Peak (14,256ft/4345m), the highest point in the National Park. | Longs Peak/Chasm Lake

On the north-eastern edge of the National Park, in the high valley of the Big Thompson River, is the mountain resort of Estes Park (alt. 7523ft/2293m), named after a pioneer who settled here around 1860. Ten years later a British peer, the Earl of Dunraven, built a hunting lodge in this area, which was famed for its abundance of game and of fish, and soon afterwards the painter Albert Bierstadt came here and was enchanted by the beauty of the scenery. Estes Park is now busy with visitors all year round, offering them a wide range of activities – hiking, riding, fishing, mountain biking, rafting and even golf. There is a cableway up Prospect Mountain (8895ft/2711m). | Estes Park

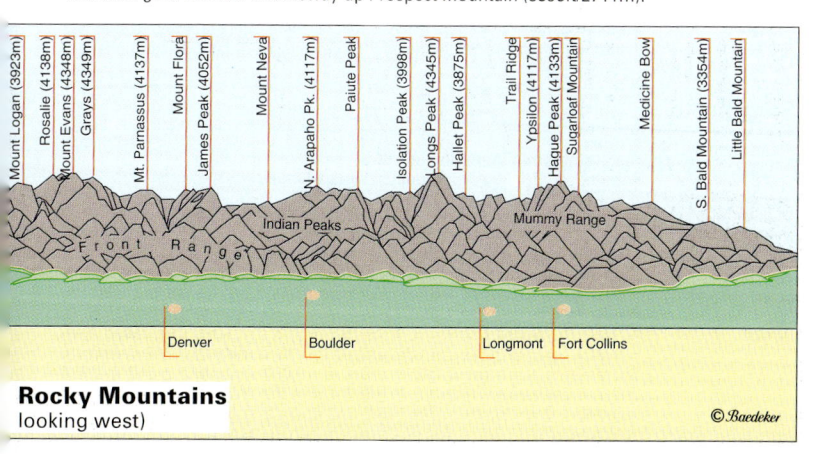

Rocky Mountains
looking west)

© Baedeker

Sacramento

The grandeur of the Rocky Mountains

*Big Thompson River Canyon	The Big Thompson River below Estes Park is a famous trout river which attracts hundreds of anglers. Farther downstream the river turns east towards the Great Plains in a narrow valley shaped by tectonic movement.
Arapaho National Recreation Area	To the south-west, outside the National Park, is the Arapaho National Recreation Area, in the centre of which are the "Great Lakes of Colorado" – Grand Lake, Shadow Mountain Lake, Willow Creek Reservoir, Monarch Lake and Lake Granby, all good fishing lakes.
Arapaho and Roosevelt National Forests	Round Rocky Mountain National Park are great expanses of forest, now a popular recreation area for the people of Denver well equipped to cater for vacationists with scenic highways, cableways, ski-lifts and skiing pistes.

Sacramento L 4

State: California. Altitude: 40ft/12m
Population: 370,000 (Metropolitan Area 1.5 million)

Situation and characteristics	Sacramento, capital of the state of California, lies at the junction of the American River with the Sacramento River. The town, which originally grew up round a fort established here in 1839, is now the commercial centre of a productive agricultural region, an industrial city (aero-space industries, foodstuffs) and an important traffic hub. It is linked with the Pacific by a deep-water canal.
History	In 1839 the Swiss Captain J. A. Sutter built a fort which he called New Helvetia, and the settlement developed rapidly during the 1848 gold rush. Sacramento soon grew into a town of 10,000 inhabitants and in 1854 became capital of California. In 1860 it was the western terminus of the legendary Pony Express. The town was given a further boost by the construction of the Central Pacific transcontinental railroad.

Sights in Sacramento

The most prominent feature of the city centre with its tree-lined streets is the Capitol (1869–74), restored some years ago, which is surrounded by a large park. In neo-classical style, it is crowned by a gilded dome. — *Capitol

The most notable features of the Old Sacramento Historic District are the Central Pacific Passenger Station and the Old Eagle Theatre in Front Street. — Old Sacramento Historic District

The Governor's Mansion (H Street and 16th Street) has been the residence of 13 Governors of California since 1878. — Governor's Mansion

Sutter's Fort Museum (L Street and 27th Street) occupies the site of the first outpost of white settlers in central California. The original adobe building of 1839 has been faithfully reconstructed and now houses mementoes of the pioneering period and the Californian gold rush. — Sutter's Fort

The State Indian Museum (26th Street and K Street) illustrates the way of life of California's original inhabitants. — State Indian Museum

The Crocker Art Museum (216 O Street and 3rd Street) has a collection of 19th century European and American painting and modern Californian art. — *Crocker Art Museum

St Augustine   U 44

State: Florida
Altitude: 0–10ft/0–3m
Population: 13,000

St Augustine, the oldest town in North America founded by Europeans and continuously inhabited since then, lies on the Atlantic coast of north-eastern Florida. Its great tourist attraction is its Spanish heritage, which has been deliberately cultivated in recent years. The atmosphere of old Spain is created by its narrow lanes and colonial-style houses with their characteristic patios, balconies and wrought-iron grilles. — Situation and characteristics

After Ponce de León's discovery of Florida in 1513 the Spaniards sought to populate the new territory. The first settlers, in 1565, were French Huguenots, who built Fort Caroline (see Jacksonville). In the same year the Spanish authorities established their base of San Agustín, on a site which was difficult of access, and this soon developed into the most important military post and mission station in Florida. During the 16th and 17th centuries the young settlement was frequently raided by pirates. When Britain began to promote its interests in the area in the 17th century the Spaniards built the Castillo de San Marcos. In 1763 Florida, and with it St Augustine, passed to Britain. During the War of American Independence the town became a refuge for British loyalists until 1783, when Florida reverted to Spain. In 1821, when the United States acquired Florida, St Augustine was much impoverished. Then at the end of the 19th century, when Henry Flagler built his East Coast Railroad, St Augustine took on a new lease of life as a fashionable bathing resort. — History

Sights in St Augustine

The Old Town of St Augustine has been beautifully refurbished. The Casa Gonzáles-Alvarez (guided visits daily 9am–4.30pm) is believed to be the oldest house in the town. The central Plaza de la Constitución is laid out in typically Spanish colonial style. The Wooden Schoolhouse (now a museum) is over 200 years old. In the fascinating Spanish Quarter Museum (San Agustín Antiguo) a number of old colonial houses form a "living history" museum. — **Old Town

On the north-east side of the Old Town is the Castillo de San Marcos (open: daily 9am–5.30pm), built in the last quarter of the 17th century to protect — *Castillo de San Marcos

St Louis

	the sea route from Cuba to Spain and provide defence against British attacks.
*Lightner Museum	The "Golden Age" collection (Tiffany glass, etc.) of the publisher Otto C. Lightner is housed in a former grand hotel.
Flagler College	The former luxury hotel, the Ponce de León (1888), built by the railway magnate Henry Flagler, is now occupied by an arts college.

Surroundings of St Augustine

*Fort Matanzas National Monument	14 miles/22km south of St Augustine is the little Spanish fort of Matanzas (the name means "slaughter"), in an area which was the scene of bloody clashes in 1565 between the French Huguenot settlers and Spanish troops. The fort also played a key role in the conflicts between Spanish and British forces.
*Marineland of Florida	20 miles/32km south of St Augustine is Marineland of Florida (open: daily 9am–5pm), with spectacular performances by trained dolphins and sea-lions and numbers of sharks, barracudas and giant turtles.

St Louis   L 35

	State: Missouri Altitude: 515ft/157m Population: 397,000 (Metropolitan Area 2.44 million)
Situation and characteristics	St Louis, the largest city in Missouri, lies just below the junction of the Missouri with the Mississippi, which here forms the boundary between the states of Missouri and Illinois. An industrial city (metal-processing, food-stuffs, textiles, furniture, etc.), it is also the seat of the St Louis University (founded 1818), the oldest university west of the Mississippi.
History	In 1764 a French fur-trader named Pierre Laclède established a trading post here, named St Louis after the French King Louis IX (St Louis). In 1803 the town, which then had a population of only 1000, passed to the United States along with the rest of Louisiana under the Louisiana Purchase, and soon developed into an important staging-post for settlers on their way to the West – the "Gateway to the West". The first constitutional assembly of the state of Missouri met in St Louis in 1820. In 1849 most of the town was destroyed in a great fire. During the Civil War St Louis was an important Union base.

Sights in Downtown St Louis

*Jefferson National Expansion Memorial	The tourist centre of St Louis is the Jefferson National Expansion Memorial Park, laid out on a site previously occupied by an old part of the town. It bears the name of President Thomas Jefferson (see Famous People), during whose Presidency the Louisiana Purchase opened up the West to settlement.
**Gateway Arch	In the centre of the park is the Gateway Arch, symbol of the city's role as the "Gateway to the West". This parabolic arch of stainless steel, 625ft/190m high, was erected in 1959–65 to the design of Eero Saarinen, based on an unexecuted project by Adalberto Libera for the entrance to the Esposizione Universale di Roma of 1942. Eight elevators run up to the observation platform on the highest point of the arch. Under the arch are the Visitor Center and the Museum of Westward Expansion.
Old Cathedral	South-west of the Gateway Arch is the Old Cathedral, the Basilica of St Louis of France, built in 1831–34 on the site of an earlier church of 1770,

St Louis

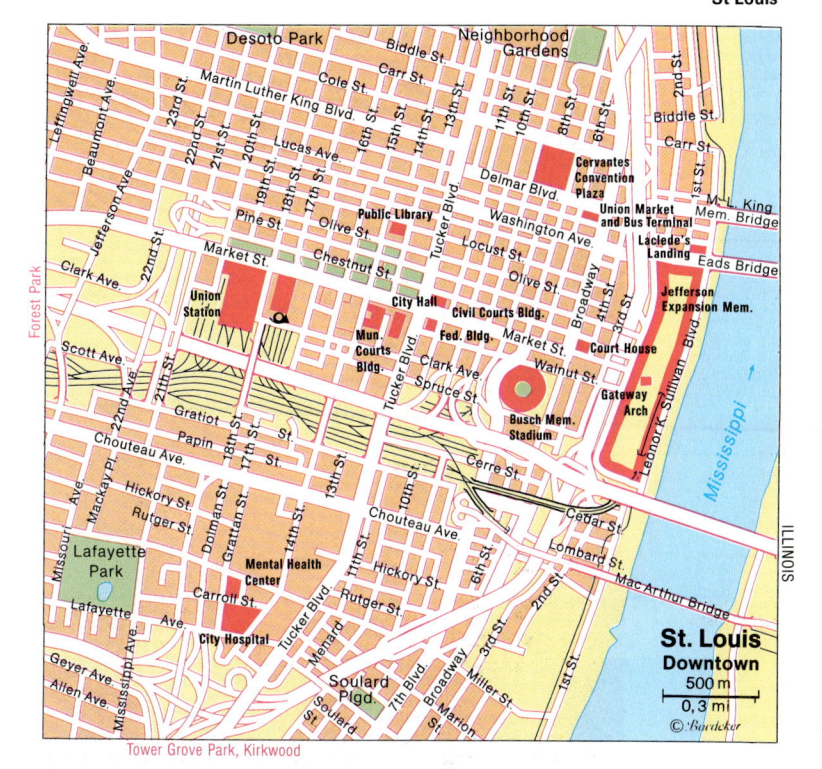

Tower Grove Park, Kirkwood

which survived the 1849 fire unscathed. In the basement is a museum on the history of the city.

On the banks of the Mississippi, to the north of the Gateway Arch, are the Fostaire Heliport, the landing-stage from which sightseeing cruises on the river depart and a variety of entertainment facilities, including the Goldenrod Showboat, built in 1909 (historical melodramas, sightseeing tours, restaurant). Here too is the "Inaugural", a Second World War minesweeper which is now a naval museum.

On the Mississippi

Along the river to the north, between the Martin Luther King Memorial Bridge and the arched steel Eads Bridge (1869–74), is Laclède's Landing, an old port district with a number of old buildings which have been renovated and are now occupied by shops, offices and restaurants.

Laclède's Landing

From the site of the Gateway Arch Market Street runs west to Union Station, a mile away. The city's main street, it is lined by important buildings and, half way along, opens out into St Louis Memorial Plaza.

Market Street

On the right-hand side is a massive domed building, the Old Courthouse (1839–64), now housing the administration of the Jefferson National Expansion Memorial and Museum.

Old Courthouse

On the left-hand side is the gigantic rotunda of the Busch Memorial Stadium (guided visits), which has seating for 50,000 spectators, with the Sports Hall of Fame.

Busch Memorial Stadium

St Louis

Gateway Arch

Eugene Field House

To the south, on Broadway (No. 634), is Eugene Field House (1850; closed Mon.), with a collection of toys and mementoes of Eugene Field, author of children's books.

Back on Market Street, at the corner of 12th Street, on left, is the Federal Building; on the right is the 387ft/118m high Civil Courts Building. Close by are the Bell Telephone Building (400ft/122m) and the equally high Laclède Gas Building.

City Hall

Farther along Market Street, on the left, is City Hall, which was modelled on the Hotel de Ville in Paris. There are some interesting buildings in the streets running north from Market Street. In 14th Street (corner of Chestnut Street) is the Soldiers Memorial Building, commemorating all fallen American soldiers. Farther north are the Public Library and Christ Church Cathedral (Episcopal). To the west of the Public Library is Campbell House, a 19th century town house which is now a museum. At the corner of 14th Street

St Louis

and Market Street is the Kiel Auditorium, which is used for congresses, trade fairs, exhibitions, opera performances and concerts.

550yd/500m farther along Market Street, on the left, is the fortress-like Union Station. In Aloe Plaza, in front of the station, is a fountain by the Swedish sculptor Carl Milles (1875–1955), "Wedding of the Waters", with 14 bronze figures symbolising the union of the Mississippi and the Missouri.

Union Station

Other Sights in St Louis

2 miles/3km west (4431 Lindell Boulevard and Newstead Avenue) is St Louis Cathedral, an imposing neo-Byzantine building (1907) with a gigantic mosaic in the dome (guided visits).

St Louis Cathedral

¾ mile/1km west of St Louis Cathedral is Forest Park, an area of open space 2 miles/3km long by 1 mile/1.5km across. This was the site of the 1904 World's Fair (Louisiana Purchase Exhibition) marking the centenary of the Louisiana Purchase.

Forest Park

On the north side of the park, on Lindell Boulevard, is the Jefferson Memorial (1904), home of the Missouri Historical Society, with rich collections of material on the history of Missouri and St Louis and the Lindbergh Room, commemorating Charles Lindbergh's solo flight over the Atlantic in the "Spirit of St Louis".

Jefferson Memorial

At the south-west corner of the park is the City Art Museum (1904), which has a fine collection of works of art of many different cultures from prehistoric times to the present day, including Meissen porcelain, European and American sculpture and pictures and Chinese bronzes. Also in the park are the Municipal Opera, an open-air theatre with seating for 12,000, the Steinberg Memorial Rink, the Jewel Box, a large hothouse, the distinctively shaped McDonnell Planetarium (1963) and a Zoological Garden with a children's zoo.

*City Art Museum

At the north-west corner of Forest Park is the campus of Washington University, whose medical and science faculties are ranked among the best in the country. On the campus are the Edison Theatre and Steinberg Hall, an art gallery with a collection which includes both old masters and modern art.

Washington University

South-west of the University is the interesting St Louis Museum of Science and Natural History.

2 miles/3km south-east of Forest Park is the large Tower Grove Park. On its north side, along Tower Grove Avenue, is the beautiful Missouri Botanical Garden, also known as the Shaw Garden after the businessman and botanist Henry Shaw (1800–89) who laid it out in 1859. In the south-east part of the gardens are the richly appointed Tower Grove House, Henry Shaw's "garden house" (Henry Shaw Mansion) and his mausoleum.

Tower Grove Park
*Missouri Botanical Garden

In the centre of the gardens is a beautiful rose garden. North of this is the Climatron, a strikingly unusual glasshouse (70ft/21m high, 175ft/53m in diameter) built by R. Buckminster Fuller in 1960, with segments of acrylic glass set in an aluminium framework, which provide a suitable air-conditioned environment for all tropical plants. Other features of the Botanical Garden are an "aqua-tunnel" under a water-lily pool and a herbarium.

In the south of the town (13th and Lynch Streets) is the Anheuser-Busch Brewery, the world's largest (guided visits).

Anheuser-Busch Brewery

St Petersburg

Surroundings of St Louis

National Museum of Transport
South-west of St Louis, near the suburb of Kirkwood, is the interesting National Museum of Transport (3015 Barrett Station Road), which presents a wide-ranging survey of American transport from mule-drawn streetcars to modern air transport (steam, electric and diesel locomotives).

St Petersburg W 43

State: Florida
Altitude: 0–45ft/0–14m
Population: 240,000

Situation and characteristics
The city of St Petersburg, famed for its perpetual sunshine, lies on the Pinellas peninsula on the central Gulf Coast of Florida, between Tampa Bay and Boca Ciega Bay. Off the peninsula is a chain of long, narrow islands. There are wide beaches and numerous marinas along this stretch of coast.

History
The town was founded in 1876 and named after the home town of a Russian businessman who was much involved in the enterprise. In the 1880s the Pinellas Sunshine Coast was already renowned for its healthy climate and attracted a steady increase in population, mainly older people.

The sunshine city
St Petersburg appeared in the Guinness Book of Records when the sun shone on every single day from 1967 to 1969. From 1910 to 1986 the local paper, the "Evening Independent", was given away free on any day on which the sun did not shine, and this cost the publishers only very small losses.

St Petersburg Pier

St Petersburg

Sights in St Petersburg

The Salvador Dalí Museum (Poynter Park, Bayboro Harbor; open: Tue.–Sat. 10am–5pm, Sun./Mon. 1–5pm) has what is probably the largest collection anywhere of Dalí's works.
**Salvador Dalí Museum

Great Explorations (1120 4th Street South) is a hands-on museum which appeals particularly to children.
Great Explorations

St Petersburg Pier is one of the longest of the kind, extending for over a quarter of a mile (400m) into Tampa Bay. At the end of the pier is an inverted pyramid containing shops, restaurants and an observation platform.
**Pier

At the head of the pier is the Historical Museum (history of St Petersburg and surrounding area).
Historical Museum

The Museum of Fine Arts (225 Beach Drive NE), housed in a neo-classical villa, possesses masterpieces of European and American painting of the 17th–20th centuries. Particularly notable is its collection of French Impressionists (Monet, Renoir, Cézanne, etc.). It also has interesting collections of Far Eastern and pre-Columbian art.
*Museum of Fine Arts

North of the city centre are Florida's Sunken Gardens (botanical garden; parrot shows).
*Florida's Sunken Gardens

St Petersburg has a wide beach of white sand extending along the Gulf Coast. Its most notable landmark is the luxury Don Cesar Hotel, built in 1928, which combines Moorish and Mediterranean features in its architecture.
St Petersburg Beach

This 1000-acre (400-hectare) park, named after the Spanish conquistador Hernando de Soto, who landed here in 1539, extends over five islands in Tampa Bay. With its miles of sandy beaches, two piers for anglers, nature trails, cycle tracks, picnic areas and campgrounds it attracts large numbers of visitors throughout the year. At the south-western tip of Mullet Key is the historic Fort de Soto, built during the Spanish-American War of 1898.
*Fort de Soto Park

A must for all visitors is a drive along the Sunshine Skyway (I 275/US 19; toll), a masterpiece of engineering. This multi-lane "highway on stilts", 12 miles/20km long, curves gracefully across the entrance to Tampa Bay. Its central feature is a 4¼ mile/6.8km long high-level bridge, the middle section of which is suspended from two gigantic pylons, allowing the passage of large ocean-going vessels. The old bridge was rammed by a cargo ship in 1980 and partly collapsed; several vehicles were hurled into the sea, and more than 30 people lost their lives. Parts of the old bridge now serve as piers for anglers.
**Sunshine Skyway

Pinellas Suncoast is the name given to a 28 mile/45km long stretch of coast on the Gulf of Mexico. Mile-long beaches of almost snow-white sand and the warm, crystal-clear waters of the Gulf of Mexico with its gentle surf, combined with excellent tourist facilities, create ideal conditions for all kinds of water sports. The season here lasts all year round: even in winter day temperatures are almost invariably above 61°F/16°C. A great variety of water sports can be practised here: sailing, wind-surfing, parasailing, deep-sea angling, diving, water-skiing, etc. The gently sloping beaches are ideal for families. Among favourite bathing resorts and port towns on the coast are Tarpon Springs, originally founded by Greek fishermen; Indian Rocks Beach; the Victorian-style Hamlin's Landing, with wooden quays and pleasant fish restaurants; Madeira Beach; John's Pass Village, a fishing and boating port in turn-of-the-century style; and Treasure Island with its broad sandy beach, once a favourite pirate anchorage. The Suncoast Seabird Sanctuary has a treatment station for injured birds.
*Pinellas Suncoast

Salt Lake City J 14

State: Utah
Altitude: 4328ft/1319m
Population: 160,000

Situation and characteristics

Salt Lake City, the religious centre of the Mormons (Latter Day Saints) and capital of the state of Utah, lies in a high valley of the Jordan River, once an inhospitable tract of country between the rocky summits, rising to over 10,000ft/3000m, of the Wasatch Range in the east, the Great Salt Lake to the north-west and the Great Salt Lake Desert to the west. The rich resources of raw materials in the area led to the development of metal-processing and chemical industries, and the city is now also a prosperous banking and commercial centre. Irrigated farming and tourism also make contributions to its economy.

History

Salt Lake City was founded on July 24th 1847 by Mormons led by Brigham Young who had reached this desert valley after an eighteen-month trek from Illinois. The settlers soon began to irrigate the land and build up a town. Starting from present-day Temple Square, they laid out an ambitious grid plan which still determines the layout of the city. The area, then under Mexican sovereignty, was ceded to the United States under the treaty of Guadalupe Hidalgo in 1848. The Mormons took advantage of this change to establish a state of their own based on their religious ideas. The capital of this state of Deseret ("honey-bee") was Salt Lake City. The young city claimed a similar status for the territory of Utah (named after the Ute Indians), established in 1850, whose first Governor was Brigham Young. The gold rush in the West and the completion of the transcontinental railroad brought increasing numbers of people to the city, which now achieved a modest degree of prosperity. After the Mormons officially renounced polygamy Utah was admitted to the Union as the 45th state.

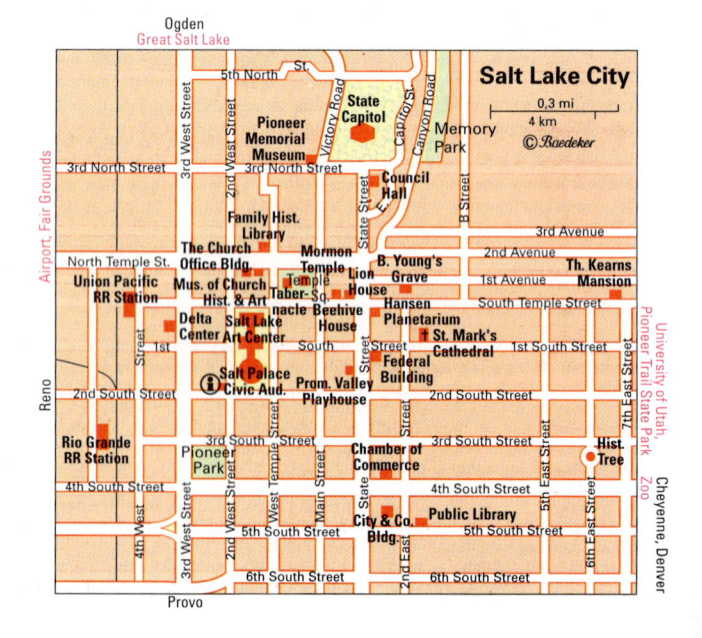

Salt Lake City

Mormon Temple

During the 20th century the city developed at a great pace, tripling its population between 1900 and 1930, and thereafter it grew rapidly into a large modern city.

Sights in Salt Lake City

Temple Square is the holy place of the Mormons. On this large square (10 acres/4 hectares) with its trees and flowerbeds are the Temple, the Tabernacle, the Temple Annex, the Assembly Hall, several monuments and two Information Centers which supply information on the doctrines and the history of the Mormon faith.

*Temple Square

Conducted visits daily 9am–9pm

The Mormon Temple, in the so-called "Mormon style", was built between 1853 and 1893. At each end of this huge granite structure are three towers, the highest of which, at the east end, bears a 13ft/4m high gilded figure of the angel Moroni. The temple may be entered only by Mormons.

Mormon Temple

The Tabernacle is a massive oval building with a dome borne on 44 sandstone piers. The sober interior, with seating for over 6500 people, is noted for its fine acoustics. At the west end is the gallery for the celebrated Tabernacle Choir, and above it is the great organ (choir rehearsals Thur. 8pm, concerts Sun. 9.30am; organ recitals Mon.–Sat. noon, Sun. 2pm).

Tabernacle

The Seagull Monument in Temple Square commemorates the seagulls which saved the Mormons by destroying a plague of locusts which threatened their crops in 1848.

Seagull Monument

The Museum of Church History and Art (45 N. West Temple Street) traces the history of the Mormon church and displays religious art of the 19th and 20th centuries.

Museum of Church History and Art

The high-rise block containing the offices of the Mormon church (50 E. South Temple Street) is the city's tallest building (420ft/128m). From the

LDS Church Office Building

431

Salt Lake City

observation platforms on the 26th floor there are magnificent views of the city, the valley of the Jordan River and the surrounding mountains.

Brigham Young Monument/ Meridian Marker
At the intersection of South Temple Street and Main Street are a bronze statue of Brigham Young and the Meridian Marker, which gives the exact geographical co-ordinates of the city. This was the point at which the original settlement was founded; the numbering of the streets starts from here.

Beehive House
The Beehive House (1854; 67 E. South Temple Street; open: Mon.–Sat. 9.30am–4.30pm, Sun. 10am–1pm), Brigham Young's residence as Governor of Utah and leader of the Mormons and the home of his large family of 19 wives and 56 children. On the turret of the house is a beehive, the symbol of the industriousness of the Mormons, which also appears in the state's coat of arms.

Lion House
The Lion House (63 E. South Temple Street) was built in 1855 to provide additional accommodation for Brigham Young's family. It is now occupied by a restaurant.

Eagle Gate
The Eagle Gate (State Street and E. South Temple Street) was built in 1859 as the entrance to Brigham Young's farm. Originally 22ft/6.70m wide, it was several times enlarged to allow for increasing traffic and is now 75ft/23m wide. The gate is crowned by a massive eagle with a wing-span of over 20ft/6m.

*Hansen Planetarium
One of the main attractions of Salt Lake City is the Hansen Planetarium (15 South State Street; open: Mon.–Thur. 9am–9pm, Fri. and Sat. 9am–midnight, Sun. 1–4pm), with its popular presentations of astronomy (multivision and laser shows, etc.). The Planetarium also has a museum and a specialised library.

*State Capitol
At the north end of State Street, on Capitol Hill, which rises to a height of 295ft/90m above the city, is the Utah State Capitol, a neo-classical domed building 285ft/87m high which houses the House of Representatives, Senate and Supreme Court of Utah. It has a particularly fine interior, with its marble rotunda, the Golden Room (the Governor's reception room) and a small exhibition on the history and economy of Utah.

Brigham Young's Grave
In a small family cemetery on First Avenue, between State Street and A Street, are the graves of Brigham Young (d. 1877) and members of his family.

Pioneer Memorial Museum
The Pioneer Memorial Museum (300 N. Main Street) traces in its 38 rooms the history of the settlement and the cultivation of the originally inhospitable valley to which the Mormons came in 1847, with numerous wagons, agricultural implements and other objects recalling the days of the pioneers.

Governor's Mansion
The Governor's Mansion (603 E. South Temple Street), built by Thomas Kearns, director of mining, in 1901, bears witness to the early prosperity brought by Utah's rich mineral resources. The house, with its period interior, is now the Governor's official residence.

Salt Palace Center
The Salt Palace Center complex at 603 E. South Temple Street takes in Salt Palace (a sports arena), the Salt Lake Art Center (contemporary art; temporary exhibitions) and the Maurice Abravanel Concert Hall (Symphony Hall), home of the famed Utah Symphony Orchestra, which is noted for its fine acoustics.

Family History Library
The Family History Library (35 N. West Temple Street), the largest genealogical library in the world, documents the ancestry of Mormon families, a matter of great importance in their faith.

Council Hall
The Council Hall, to the south of the present Capitol, was originally City Hall and the first State Capitol. It now houses the Utah Travel and State Information Center.

Salt Lake City

University of Utah

2 miles/3km east of the city centre is the University of Utah, which was founded in 1850. On the extensive campus are the Utah Museum of Fine Arts (with pictures by Rubens) and the Museum of Natural History, with a large collection of fossils (including dinosaur skeletons) and interesting departments of geology, palaeontology, biology and anthropology.

Immediately east of the campus, on Wasatch Drive, is the historic Fort Douglas (military museum).

Fort Douglas

When, after the Mormons' 1300 mile/2100km trek, Brigham Young emerged from Emigration Canyon and saw the valley of his visions he exclaimed "This is the place!". The spot is now marked by an imposing monument (2601 E. Sunnyside Avenue). Here too there is a reconstructed 19th century pioneers' village, the Old Desert Village ("living history" presentations).

*Pioneer Trail State Park

The old streetcar depot (600 South Street and 700 East Street), built in 1908, has been transformed into an elegant shopping and entertainment centre, with attractive shops and boutiques, restaurants and various entertainment facilities.

Trolley Square

Liberty Park, a green and pleasant place for recreation, lies between 500–700 East Street and 900–1300 South Street. On the south side of the park is the Tracy Aviary, with over 1000 species of birds.

Liberty Park

The International Peace Gardens (1000 South Street and 900 West Street) have displays of flowers characteristic of different nations, symbolising the peaceful co-existence of different peoples.

International Peace Gardens

Surroundings of Salt Lake City

The Great Salt Lake, half an hour's drive north-west of Salt Lake City, is the largest inland lake west of the Mississippi, 72 miles/116km long, 34 miles/54km wide and up to 50ft/15m deep. It is a remnant of a much larger freshwater lake, Lake Bonneville. Following a fall in the water table this was left with no outlet and shrank as a result of evaporation, leaving the Great Salt Lake Desert. The combination of evaporation with the inflow of surface waters rich in minerals led the salt content of the lake to rise steadily, and at one stage it reached 27% (eight times as high as the world's oceans). In the last few years the water level of the lake has risen as a result of heavy rainfall in the surrounding mountains. At the south end of the lake are bathing beaches and a recreation park (boat hire).

*Great Salt Lake

At Farmington, 15 miles/24km north of Salt Lake City, is this large Wild West theme park, with an impressive reconstruction of a town of pioneering days.

Lagoon Amusement Park

In Ogden, half an hour's drive north of Salt Lake City, are the Browning Firearms Museum and the Union Pacific Railroad Museum.

Ogden

To the east of Ogden are the skiing areas (fine powder snow) of Snow Basin, Nordic Valley and Powder Mountain.

*Skiing areas

55 miles/88km north of Salt Lake City is Brigham City (named after the Mormon leader Brigham Young), with a Mormon tabernacle of 1881 and an informative Pioneer Museum.

Brigham City

On the north side of the Great Salt Lake is the Golden Spike National Historic Site, the point where the Union Pacific and Central Pacific Railroads, starting respectively from Omaha in Nebraska and Sacramento in California, joined up. This first transcontinental railroad was completed on May 10th 1866, when the last spike (the "Golden Spike") was ceremonially driven in. The event is commemorated by an annual re-enactment of the ceremony. The Visitor Center has an exhibition illustrating the importance of the railroad in opening up the West.

*Golden Spike National Historic Site

San Antonio

Logan	25 miles/40km north-east, in a well cultivated high valley, is the little town of Logan, scene of the popular American West Festival held annually in August. Features of interest are the fortress-like Mormon Temple and the 19th century Tabernacle.
Beaver Mountain Ski Area	North-east of Logan are the well-known Beaver Mountain Ski Area and the beautiful Bear Lake.
Big Cottonwood Canyon/ Little Cottonwood Canyon	To the east of Salt Lake City by way of Wasatch Boulevard are Big Cottonwood Canyon and Little Cottonwood Canyon, which attract large numbers of visitors in both summer and winter. Above these two U-shaped valleys are a number of well-known skiing stations (Alta, Snowbird, Solitude Ski Resort, etc.).
Mount Millicent	From Brighton Resort, a vacation centre popular throughout the year, there is a chair-lift up Mount Millicent, from which there are superb panoramic views.
*Alta	Half an hour's drive east of Salt Lake City, at an altitude of 8500ft/2600m, is the winter sports resort of Alta, with first-class skiing areas. There are also good skiing areas round the little town of Park City, farther east.
*Timpanogos Cave National Monument	25 miles/40km south of Salt Lake City, on the northern slopes of Mount Timpanogos (11,750ft/3581m), are three limestone caves linked by underground passages, with marvellous crystal and stalactitic formations.
Provo	47 miles/75km south of Salt Lake City, surrounded by high mountains, is the industrial town of Provo (pop. 90,000), with the Brigham Young University, founded by the Mormons in 1875, which now has 25,000 students (guided visits). There is an interesting Pioneer Museum. To the west of the town, on the shores of Utah Lake, is a State Park. A cable railway leads to the Bridal Veil Falls in Provo Canyon. To the north of Provo is the Sundance Ski Area, which has become increasingly popular in recent years.
**Bingham Canyon Copper Mine	In Bingham Canyon, 25 miles/40km south-west of Salt Lake City near the township of Copperton, is the world's largest opencast copper mine, which is also the largest man-made hole in the earth's surface, almost 2½ miles/4km in diameter and over 2950ft/900m deep. From the Visitor Center (informative displays and video shows on copper-mining) there is a good view into the terraced interior of the mine.

San Antonio U 27

	State: Texas Altitude: 700ft/213m Population: 936,000
Situation and characteristics	San Antonio lies on the San Antonio River and the narrow San Pedro Creek, on the south-eastern edge of the Texan tableland. It is the centre of a prosperous agricultural area (stock-farming), with important industries (engineering, aircraft servicing for the US Air Force, oil). San Antonio, originally a Spanish foundation, reflects more clearly than any other Texan city the influence of different cultures on the history of Texas. The western and southern districts in particular have a distinctly Mexican character. The charming atmosphere of the city attracts many visitors, and its mild climate (an average 54°F/12°C in January, 84°F/29°C in July) makes it a popular winter resort.
History	The Spanish military post of Presidio de Bexar and the Franciscan mission of San Antonio de Valero were established here in 1718, and soon afterwards San Antonio de Bexar became capital of the Spanish province of Texas. After the expulsion of the Spaniards (1821–36) the town was under

San Antonio

Mexican sovereignty, until Texas broke away from Mexico in 1835. The famous battle of the Alamo was fought in the following year. In April 1836 Texas achieved its independence from Mexico, and until the incorporation of Texas in the United States in 1845 San Antonio belonged to the independent republic of Texas.

Sights in San Antonio

On the east side of the city, on Alamo Plaza, is the most famous building in the whole of Texas, the Alamo (from the Spanish word for "cottonwood"), part of the mission station established in 1718. The Alamo church was built by Franciscans in 1744 and made into a fort in 1836. In that year, during the Texan war of independence, a small Texan force entrenched themselves in the Alamo against a Mexican army of 3000 men, and all the 187 defenders (among them Davy Crockett and James Bowie) were killed. Thereafter the Alamo became the "cradle of Texan independence", and "Remember the Alamo!" became the Texan battle-cry. The former mission is now a National Monument, visited annually by 10 million people. The mission buildings (restored) now house the Museum of Texan Independence (open: Mon.–Sat. 9am–5.30pm, Sun. and pub. hols. 10am–5.30pm). In front of the Alamo is a cenotaph (by Pompeo Coppini) commemorating the fallen Texans.

The *Alamo

To the south of the Alamo is the Paseo del Río or River Walk, which follows the windings of the San Antonio River, running below street level. The walk is lined by hotels, restaurants and shops, set amid lush subtropical vegetation; there are a number of departure points for cruises on the river. At the south-eastern bend on the river is the Arneson River Theater, where the audience is separated from the stage by the river.

Paseo del Río/ River Walk

The Alamo, the cradle of Texan independence

San Antonio

La Villita	South of the Arneson Theater is La Villita, a 250-year-old Mexican quarter (restored), with many shops selling folk art, art galleries and restaurants in adobe houses.
HemisFair Park *Tower of the Americas	South-east of the Alamo is HemisFair Park, scene of the World's Fair of 1968. It is dominated by the 750ft/229m high Tower of the Americas, with an observation platform and revolving restaurant. Beyond this are the Institute of Texan Cultures (temporary exhibitions), the Mexican Cultural Institute (contemporary Mexican art) and the Henry B. Gonzalez Convention Center.
Spanish Governor's Palace	To the west of the San Antonio River, reached by way of the Main Plaza and the archiepiscopal San Fernando Cathedral (originally built by settlers from the Canaries in 1738–58), is the Military Plaza/Plaza de Armas, with the low whitewashed palace of the Spanish governor, built in 1749 with materials imported from Spain (open: Mon.–Sat. 9am–5pm, Sun. 10am–5pm).
King William Historic District	To the south of these two plazas is the King William Historic District, built by prosperous German settlers in the 19th century and named after King William of Prussia. The Steves Homestead (1876) is now a museum.
Market Square/ Mercado	Farther west, beyond San Pedro Creek, is the city's Mexican quarter, with the picturesque Market Square/Mercado on West Commerce Street.
Brackenridge Park	North of downtown San Antonio is the spacious Breckenridge Park, with a miniature railway and cableway for children, the Chinese Sunken Gardens and the Japanese Tea Garden. To the east, beyond Funston Place, are the beautiful Botanical Gardens.
Art museums Marion Koogler McNay Art Museum San Antonio Museum of Art	In northern San Antonio are two fine art museums. At 6000 N. New Braunfels Street (to the north of US 81) is the Marion Koogler McNay Art Museum (open: Tue.–Sat. 10am–5pm, Sun. noon–5pm), which specialises in modern art, including contemporary Indian art. The San Antonio Museum of Art at 200 W. Jones Avenue (2 miles/3.2km north-east of the city centre on US 81), housed in a finely restored brewery of 1883, displays North and South American art and Greek and Roman art (open: Mon.–Sat. 10am–6pm, Sun. noon–6pm).

Surroundings of San Antonio

*Mission Trail	South of the city centre, but still within the boundaries of San Antonio, are four other Spanish mission stations founded between 1718 and 1740. They now form part of the San Antonio Missions National Historical Park and can be visited by following the signposted Mission Trail. They are the Mission San Juan Capistrano (1713), the Mission San Concepción (1731–52), the best preserved Franciscan mission in Texas, the Mission San Francisco de la Espada (1731–40) and the "queen of missions", the Mission San José y San Miguel de Aguayo (1720–31), with a beautiful church doorway and carved sacristy window ("Rosa's Window"), Indian huts and corn stores (open: Apr.–Oct. daily 9am–6pm, at other times of year 8am–5pm).
Sea World of Texas	The large marine entertainment showplace, Sea World of Texas, lies 16 miles/26km north-west of San Antonio on Loop 1604 (10500 Sea World Drive). It has over 25 shows, attractions and exhibitions, including the killer whales Shamu and Baby Shamu, Cypress Gardens West Botanical Gardens, a large white-water run and, for children, Capt'n Kid's World. Open: in summer daily 10am–6pm; in winter only at weekends.
*Natural Bridge Caverns	17 miles/27km north-east of San Antonio on I 35 are the Natural Bridge Caverns, the largest stalactitic caves in Texas, with over 10,000 different

stalactitic formations in chambers bearing such romantic names as Sherwood Forest. One of the finest features is the 40ft/12m high King's Throne in the Castle of the White Giants. Open: June–Aug. daily 9am–6pm, at other times of year 9am–4pm.

30 miles/48km north-east of San Antonio on I 35 is New Braunfels, founded by German settlers in 1845. At the beginning of November each year it is the scene of the ten-day Wurstfest (Sausage Festival), which draws over 150,000 visitors. The old settlement of Gruene on the Guadalupe River, with many restored houses, is now part of New Braunfels.

New Braunfels

Austin, capital of Texas, situated 81 miles/130km north-east of San Antonio at the point where the Colorado River leaves the Edwards Plateau, was founded in 1839 and named after Stephen F. Austin (1793–1836), the "father of Texas". It is an educational centre, with the University of Texas, the Lyndon B. Johnson Library and Museum and the Texas Memorial Museum.

Austin

Other features of interest include the red granite State Capitol, modelled on the Capitol in Washington DC, which is the second largest Capitol in the United States; the restored Old Pecan Street (Sixth Street), the town's old main street and still a popular place in the evenings; the museum in the house of the sculptor Elisabeth Ney (1830–1907); and the Governor's Mansion (1010 Colorado Street), a classic Southern mansion dating from 1856.

Sights

San Diego   R 8

State: California
Altitude: 45ft/14m
Population: 1.1 million (Metropolitan Area 2.5 million)

The southern boundary of San Diego, 125 miles/200km south of Los Angeles (see entry) in sunny California, lies along the frontier with Mexico. Thanks to the sheltered situation of its natural harbour with its rocky inlets and miles of sandy beaches the town developed into one of the leading ports on the west coast of the United States. It is the base of the Pacific Fleet and the 11th Squadron of the US Navy. The next most important element in the city's economy after the Navy is the aircraft industry (Convair plant); other major elements are the construction of rockets, oceanographic and bio-medical research, electronics, higher education and tourism. The agreeable climate and scenic beauty of the surrounding area have made San Diego a favourite residential city, whose population has risen by over 25% since 1980.

Situation and characteristics

In 1542 a Spanish expedition led by Juan Rodríguez Cabrillo landed in San Diego Bay and discovered the territory now known as California: this was "the place where California began". Sixty years later Sebastián Vizcaino named the bay after his flagship "San Diego de Alcalá". The foundation of the town, however, dates only from 1769, when the Franciscan friar Junípero Serra built the first of 21 mission stations. (The present mission of San Diego de Alcalá is 6 miles inland from its original site.) In 1822 San Diego came under the control of the new Mexican government, but after the battle of San Pasqual in 1846 it passed into American hands. The admission of California to the Union in 1850 was followed by the establishment of San Diego County. The city's rise to prosperity began, however, after the coming of the Santa Fe Railroad (1885), the development of the port and the moving of the naval base to San Diego in the first half of the 20th century.

History

Sights in Downtown San Diego

In Balboa Park (area 1400 acres/567 hectares), laid out in Spanish/Mexican style for the Panama-California Exhibition of 1915–16, is now the cultural

**Balboa Park

San Diego

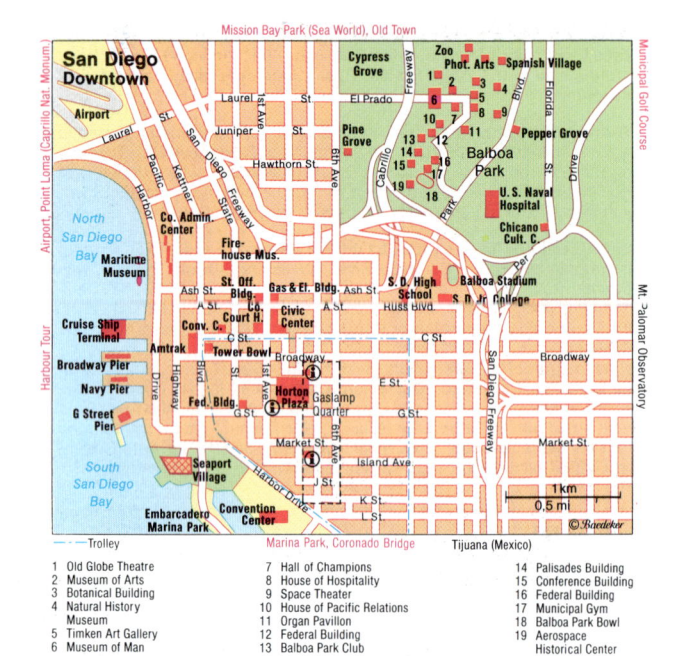

1. Old Globe Theatre
2. Museum of Arts
3. Botanical Building
4. Natural History Museum
5. Timken Art Gallery
6. Museum of Man
7. Hall of Champions
8. House of Hospitality
9. Space Theater
10. House of Pacific Relations
11. Organ Pavillion
12. Federal Building
13. Balboa Park Club
14. Palisades Building
15. Conference Building
16. Federal Building
17. Municipal Gym
18. Balboa Park Bowl
19. Aerospace Historical Center

heart of the city, with a series of museums, theatres, restaurants and various leisure facilities.

*Museums

The Botanical Building, originally designed as a station on the Santa Fe Railroad, contains more than 500 species of tropical and subtropical plants. The House of Pacific Relations has displays on various Latin American countries. The Museum of Man contains material from the Indian pueblos of the south-western United States. The Museum of Photographic Arts in the arcades of the Casa de Balboa presents the work of modern photographers. The San Diego Aerospace Museum contains aviation memorabilia, including a replica of the "Spirit of St Louis" in which Charles Lindbergh (see Famous People) made the first solo transatlantic flight. The collections of the San Diego Museum of Art include works by European masters from the early Renaissance to the 20th century and a large department of American and Asian art; in the adjoining Sculpture Garden are works by Alexander Calder, Barbara Hepworth and Henry Moore. The Natural History Museum, founded more than 100 years ago, is devoted to the flora and fauna of southern California. The Timken Art Gallery has a large collection of Russian icons of the 16th–19th centuries and works by European and American artists. An imposing feature of the park, standing in the open, is the massive Spreckels Organ, with 4000 pipes, which was presented to the city in 1915 by Adolph Spreckels, a millionaire of German origin. In the Spanish Village Arts and Crafts Center visitors can watch various craftsmen at work.

**San Diego Zoo

More than a quarter of Balboa Park is occupied by the famous San Diego Zoo, in which the animals (elephants, bears, giraffes, big cats, reptiles, gorillas, flamingoes, etc.) live in their natural surroundings.

San Diego

Horton Plaza and ... *... La Jolla Cove, San Diego*

In the historic Gaslamp Quarter between Broadway and K Street are 16 blocks of Victorian buildings dating from 1880–1910, with fashionable shops, restaurants and theatres and bars which are favourite haunts of night-birds.

City centre
Gaslamp Quarter

Adjoining the Gaslamp Quarter, between 1st and 4th Avenues, is the modern shopping and entertainment centre of Horton Plaza, named after Alonzo Horton, who in 1867 bought for 265 dollars some 1000 acres/400 hectares of land in what was then a village and now amounts to practically the whole of downtown San Diego.

Horton Plaza

To the north-west, on Harbor Drive, is the San Diego Maritime Museum, with a fine three-master, the "Star of India" (1863), the ferryboat "Berkeley" (1898) and the motor yacht "Medea" (1904).

*San Diego Maritime Museum

To the south-west, also on Harbor Drive, is Seaport Village, which attracts visitors with more than 75 speciality shops and restaurants.

Seaport Village

Sights in Other Districts

The Old Town San Diego State Historic Park, north of downtown San Diego on Presidio Hill, which rises above the San Diego River, takes visitors back to the early days of the city in Mexican and American times with its restored adobe houses and traditional craft workshops. The central feature of the Old Town is the colourful arcading round the Bazaar del Mundo, the lively scene of concerts and folk dancing.

Old Town

From downtown San Diego a bridge high above San Diego Bay leads to the beautiful garden city of Coronado, named after the Coronado Islands which lie off the coast of Baja California (Mexico). The most striking feature is the luxury Hotel del Coronado (1500 Orange Avenue), a four-storey wooden

*Coronado

San Diego

building in Spanish/Mexican style erected in 1888; the installation of the hotel's electricity is said to have been supervised by Thomas Alva Edison (see Famous People). Among illustrious guests have been crowned heads, show business personalities and American Presidents, including Bill Clinton, and the hotel has been the setting of a number of films, including the famous "Some Like It Hot", with Marilyn Monroe, Jack Lemmon and Tony Curtis.

Point Loma
Cabrillo National Monument

At the south end of the Point Loma peninsula, to the west of Coronado, is the Cabrillo National Monument, commemorating the discovery of California by the Portuguese navigator Juan Rodríguez Cabrillo in September 1542. The monument, from which in clear weather there are fine views of the city, draws large numbers of people between mid December and mid February to watch grey whales on their long journey southward from the Bering Sea to the warm bays of Baja California. There are rewarding walks to the old lighthouse on the Bayside Trail and Sylvester Road, with a bizarre mixture of desert and coastal vegetation.

Also on Point Loma are a naval exercise base and the Rosecrans National Cemetery, one of the largest naval cemeteries in the United States.

*Mission Bay

Mission Bay (area 4500 acres/1800 hectares), north-west of downtown San Diego, with its numerous inlets and 25 miles/40km of sandy beaches, is a water sports paradise, with joggers and roller skaters representing the fitness culture of California and elegant yacht clubs and luxury hotels for a more fashionable public.

**Sea World

The highlight of the Mission Bay recreation complex is Sea World of California (1720 South Shore Road), with impressive shows by performing dolphins, sealions, otters and whales.

La Jolla

The idyllic suburb of La Jolla (pronounced La Haw-ya) extends along a 7 mile/11km stretch of coast north of downtown San Diego. Here visitors will find way-out designer boutiques, inviting restaurants and good art galleries in and around Girard Avenue and Prospect Street. The University of California and various research institutes have made this almost village-like suburb a favourite residence of academics, artists and writers. The

*La Jolla Cove

sandy beach of La Jolla Cove is frequented throughout the year by sun-worshippers and also by seals and numbers of seabirds.

University of California

On the campus of the University of California (founded 1912; 16,000 students) are a number of buildings of architectural interest. The Institute of Oceanography (established 1903), which has a fine specialised library, is the oldest and largest oceanographic institute in the United States. Associ-

Scripps Aquarium

ated with it is the Scripps Aquarium, which is devoted to the underwater world of the Californian coast.

Museum of Contemporary Art

The Museum of Contemporary Art is housed in a villa which belonged to Ellen Browning Scripps, a wealthy patroness of the arts who made a major contribution to the development of La Jolla. The villa was originally (from 1941) used as a centre for southern Californian artists and later, after rebuilding, enlarged into a museum of contemporary art.

Surroundings of San Diego

Tijuana

The Mexican frontier town of Tijuana, 16 miles/25km south of San Diego, owed its rise mainly to the Prohibition period in the United States in the 1920s, when thirsty Californians could enjoy the pleasure of drinking alcohol legally only in Mexico. Nowadays it is the duty-free shopping facilities and the night life that stimulate the busy activity round the town's main square, the Parque Municipal Guerrero, the Avenida de la Revolución and the Bulevar Aqua Caliente. In the Centro Cultural is an exhibition on the history and culture of Mexico.

85 miles/136km north-east of San Diego, on the edge of the Colorado Desert, is the Anza-Borrego Desert State Park (area 600,000 acres/240,000 hectares), named after the 18th century Spanish missionary Juan Bautista de Anza. The best time to visit the park is in the spring, when the cacti in the canyons of this fantastic desert region are in flower.

Anza-Borrego
Desert State Park

San Francisco

M 3

State: California
Altitude: 0–910ft/0–277m
Population: 740,000 (Greater Metropolitan Area 6.3 million)

The description of San Francisco in this guide is abridged, since there is a detailed account of the city in the AA/Baedeker guide "San Francisco".

San Francisco, situated at the "Golden Gate" to the Pacific, is only the fourth largest city in California, but it is by a long way the most popular with both Americans and visitors from other countries. It is built on more than forty hills on a 7½ mile/12km wide peninsula between the open sea and San Francisco Bay. The Metropolitan Area of San Francisco takes in the neighbouring Marin, San Mateo, Alameda and Contra Costa Counties. The expanses of water surrounding the city have a moderating effect on the climate, which has the mildness of spring all year round. It is seldom warmer than 77°F/25°C or colder than 50°F/10°C. A cool marine current off the coast contributes to the equable nature of the climate – though it is also responsible for the fog formed in summer when warm mainland air overlies cold sea air. During the colder winter months there may be storms coming in from the Pacific or periods of continuous rain.

Situation and
characteristics

The decisive factor in bringing about San Francisco's rapid population growth was the 1848 gold rush, when immigrants from far and wide headed for the American West. They were followed by Chinese, who provided a cheap labour force. After the Second World War there was an influx of coloured people and Latinos. The present-day population includes 41% whites, 15% blacks and 15% Latinos. The rest of the population consists mainly of Asians, who are relatively more numerous than in any other American city (85,000 Chinese, 30,000 Filipinos, 14,000 Japanese, together with Koreans, Vietnamese, South Sea islanders, Malays, etc.). 42% of the city's inhabitants have a language other than English as their mother tongue. San Francisco has thus become the model of a multicultural society.

Population

The 1950s saw the rise of the beat movement – the term applied to the various dropouts who distanced themselves from the values of American society, gave up the pursuit of dollars and renounced the ideals of consumerism. Many of them gathered in the North Beach district of the city, where they met in bars and bookshops and philosophised. The leading literary representatives of the movement were Allen Ginsberg, William Burroughs and Jack Kerouac. Later the beatniks moved into the Haight-Ashbury district, where in the mid sixties they were reinforced by representatives of the civil rights movements and opponents of the Vietnam War. The hippies now also appeared on the scene, with their long hair, beards, drugs, communes, free love and "Make love, not war" slogan. The 6000 resident hippies were joined at weekends by 20,000 others who came to take part in events such as rock concerts. This milieu, however, also attracted criminals and drug-dealers: violence became increasingly common, and the naïver hippies left, founded country communes, joined the student scene at Berkeley University or simply went home.

Dropouts

A self-confident minority group characteristic of San Francisco is the city's homosexuals, who are well organised and politically very active. No candidate for public office can afford to incur the disfavour of this influential

Homosexuals

San Francisco

group. Since the spread of AIDS, however, the homosexual scene has changed considerably, and the emphasis is now on political demands for more resources to combat the disease and against discrimination against AIDS sufferers. It is estimated that every other homosexual male in San Francisco is HIV positive. A network of organisations are now concerning themselves with all aspects of the disease, from health education and preventive measures to research and the care of AIDS victims.

History

San Francisco Bay was first discovered only in 1769 by a group of Spaniards led by Francisco de Ortega, and in 1776 a Spanish fort (presidio) was built at the Golden Gate as a centre of military administration and the mission of San Francisco de Asís, soon afterwards renamed the Mission Dolores, was established 4 miles/6km inland. Round the mission grew up the village of Yerba Buena, which at first was a place of no particular importance. It was only when the Mexican authorities developed the little harbour into a commercial port that it began to grow. From 1841 onwards the numbers of pioneers moving to the West increased steadily, and soon the population of the area was predominantly American. After the failure of American attempts to buy the territory from Mexico war broke out, and

San Francisco

American settlers fought under the "bear banner" for an independent California (the Bear Banner Rebellion). On July 9th 1846 the American flag was hoisted, and a year later Yerba Buena was renamed San Francisco. The 1848 gold rush brought a dramatic increase in population. At the beginning of 1848 the town's population was 2000: a year later it had risen to 35,000. By the 1860s San Francisco had established its position as the economic centre of the American West. In October 1865 an earthquake caused heavy damage in the town. In 1869 the Central Pacific Railroad reached San Francisco Bay, opening up a rapid transport link with the eastern United States. Economic problems led in July 1877 to serious rioting against the Chinese who had provided a cheap form of labour, mainly employed in railroad construction. On the early morning of April 18th 1906 the town was hit by a severe earthquake with an estimated strength of 8.3 points on the Richter scale. Even more devastating than the earthquake itself were the fires which broke out a few hours later and raged for three days. The bursting of the water mains made it impossible to combat the blazes effectively: much of the town was reduced to ashes, and 674 people were killed. Rebuilding proceeded rapidly, however, with financial aid from all over the United States.

San Francisco

Panorama of downtown San Francisco

A boost was given to the city's economy by the completion of the Golden Gate Bridge and the Oakland Bay Bridge in 1936–37, improving communications with the Bay Area. During the Second World War San Francisco was an important harbour for the US Pacific Fleet. The shipyards worked at high pressure, and within three years the number of jobs had tripled. In the spring of 1945 representatives of 52 states met in the War Memorial Opera House to discuss the final details on the foundation of the United Nations and finally signed the UN Charter.

On October 17th 1989 the city was visited by the worst earthquake (6.9 points on the Richter scale) since the catastrophe of 1906. The Loma Prieta Quake (named after its epicentre) caused most damage in the Marina district, and the partial collapse of the Bay Bridge between San Francisco and Oakland led to the loss of 59 lives.

Downtown San Francisco

Civic Center Plaza — The central feature of the south-western part of downtown San Francisco is the Civic Center Plaza, with City Hall (300ft/91m high dome) and the Civic Auditorium. To the north of City Hall are the State Building, with the Pioneers Museum, and the Federal Office Building. On the east side of the square is the Main Public Library.

Veterans Memorial Building — West of City Hall is the Veterans Memorial Building, in which the Charter of the United Nations was signed in 1945. In the same building are the San Francisco Museum of Modern Art and the Herbst Theater. To the south is the War Memorial Opera House (built 1932).

Symphony Hall — Farther south is the Louise M. Davis Symphony Hall, one of the largest concert halls in the United States, opened in 1980. It is the home of the world-famous San Francisco Symphony Orchestra.

Market Street — From the Civic Center Market Street (San Francisco's "main street") runs south-west. House numbers start from this street, and the streets to the

San Francisco

south-east have a different alignment, heading south-west towards the Twin Peaks and north-east towards Embarcadero Plaza and the Ferry Building on San Francisco Bay.

Beyond the intersection with Powell Street (cable-car turntable) are two striking buildings: the 39-storey Standard Oil Building and the older Standard Oil of California Building, with a handsome plaza and a very interesting exhibition on oil. To the north (Sansome and Pine Streets) is the Pacific Stock Exchange.

Standard Oil Building

The main square of San Francisco's downtown shopping area is palm-shaded Union Square, surrounded by the city's largest department stores and crowded throughout the day by tourists, office workers, street musicians and beggars. In the centre of the square is the Naval Monument, a 100ft/30m high column commemorating George Dewey, commander of the US fleet during the Spanish–American War of 1898, who won the Philippines for the United States. On the east side of the square is Maiden Lane, with a number of buildings designed by Frank Lloyd Wright. Just round the corner are San Francisco's principal theatres.

Union Square/ Downtown shopping area

The very busy Montgomery Street runs through the Financial District, with the 52-storey marble-clad headquarters of the Bank of America (780ft/238m high; built 1969); on the top floor is an observation platform. Diagonally opposite is the 43-storey Wells Fargo Bank, with a History Room containing an excellent exhibition on the Californian gold rush and the hazards of transporting money in the mail-coach era.

Montgomery Street/ Financial District

In the basement of the Bank of California (400 California Street), the oldest bank on the west coast, is the interesting Museum of Money of the American West, with nuggets of gold and silver, 19th century gold coins and banknotes, and historic weapons.

Bank of California

The architectural highlight of the Financial District is the Transamerica Pyramid, built in 1972 to the design of William L. Pereira (see drawing, p. 100). Particularly striking is the (internally illuminated) top section of this steel-framed aluminium-clad structure. There is an observation platform on the 27th floor.

**Transamerica Pyramid

To the north of the Transamerica Pyramid is Jackson Square with its handsome turn-of-the-century buildings (restored) housing a variety of shops.

Jackson Square

Embarcadero

To the south-east of Jackson Square, beyond the Golden Gateway Center and Maritime Plaza, is the Embarcadero Center, with a number of imposing high-rise buildings, including the 42-storey Security Pacific Bank Building, the 31-storey Levi Strauss Building and the unconventional 17-storey Hyatt Regency Hotel with its 187ft/57m high atrium lobby. In Embarcadero Plaza is a striking fountain by Armand Vaillantcourt (1971).

*Embarcadero Center

To the east of Embarcadero Plaza is the Ferry Building, built in 1903 as the headquarters of the ferry company which operated before the construction of the Oakland Bay Bridge. The 235ft/72m high tower is modelled on the tower of Seville Cathedral. The building now houses the Port Authority and an exhibition of minerals and rocks. To the north is the World Trade Center.

Ferry Building

Chinatown

To the west of Montgomery Street, bounded by Kearny Street, Bush Street, Stockton Street and on the north by Broadway, is San Francisco's Chinatown, one of the largest Chinese towns outside Asia, with a population of

Location and **townscape

San Francisco

In Chinatown

100,000, most of them descendants of the immigrants who flocked into California from the mid 19th century onwards. The main street of Chinatown is Grant Avenue, which is entered, when coming from the south, through the picturesque Chinatown Gate, decorated with dragons and other animals. Beyond this is St Mary's Square, with a monument to Sun Yat-sen (1866–1925), founder of the Chinese Republic, who had previously lived in San Francisco. On the north side of the square is Old St Mary's Church (1854).

Particularly attractive is Stockton Street. In central Chinatown is Portsmouth Square, with a monument to the Scottish writer Robert Louis Stevenson (1850–94), who lived for some time in San Francisco. On the north side of the square is the largest Buddhist temple in the United States (1960). From Portsmouth Square a footbridge leads to the Chinese Cultural Center (750 Kearny Street). At the north end of Chinatown is the Chinese Historical Society of America Museum (650 Commercial Street), which traces the history of a hundred years of Chinese immigration.

Chinese New Year

A particularly interesting time to visit Chinatown is during the celebrations of the Chinese New Year.

Nob Hill

Situation

To the west of Chinatown is Nob Hill (338ft/103m), where wealthy families whose money had come from railroad construction and gold-mining – the "nobs" – lived at the turn of the century. On Huntington Park is the famous 29-storey Fairmont Hotel, and opposite this is the 305ft/93m high Mark Hopkins Hotel, with a restaurant offering fine views. On the west side of the park is Grace Cathedral (1928), modelled on Notre-Dame in Paris. Facing it, to the south, is the California Masonic Memorial Temple.

San Francisco

Floral splendour in Lombard Street

San Francisco's cable cars are one of the city's principal attractions. The system was devised by the English engineer Andrew S. Hallidie, who was concerned to relieve horses of the task of hauling street-cars up San Francisco's steep streets. The first section was opened in 1873. Nowadays only three lines still operate – No. 1, the California Street line, No. 2 the Powell Mason line and No. 3 the Powell Hyde line. To avoid long waits at the terminus points the cars can be boarded at any intermediate stop. From the gallery of the Cable Car Barn (Mason and Washington Streets), built in 1887, the operation of the cable winches can be observed. There is a museum, whose exhibits include the first cable car, the cable-gripping and braking mechanisms and samples of cables.

**Cable cars

Russian Hill

North-west of Nob Hill is Russian Hill (295ft/90m), a pleasant residential district with well-kept gardens and outlook terraces.

Situation

Lombard Street, paved with red bricks, winds its way up Russian Hill, overcoming a 40% gradient in ten hairpin bends, flanked by beautifully laid out gardens. The palatial houses lining the street have well maintained façades. Tourists find Lombard Street, which has featured in a number of films (including "The Lady in Red"), highly photogenic.

*Lombard Street

To the north-east, at 800 Chestnut Street, is the San Francisco Art Institute, with an interesting collection of American and European painting and sculpture.

Art Institute

From Russian Hill Union Street runs west into the old district of Cow Hollow, where cows once grazed. There are numerous Victorian-style buildings, now occupied by elegant shops, art galleries and exclusive restaurants.

Cow Hollow

San Francisco

Telegraph Hill

Coit Memorial Tower

*View

On the north side of downtown San Francisco, at the east end of Lombard Street, is Telegraph Hill (295ft/90m), on the slopes of which are artists' studios and handsome old houses. On top of the hill is the Coit Memorial Tower (210ft/64m high), built in 1934 in honour of the firefighting service. From the tower (open: daily 10am–5.30pm) there are magnificent views.

*North Beach

South-west of Telegraph Hill is the North Beach district, which in the sixties became internationally known as the home of the hippies (flower children). The psychedelic movement originated here. Around Washington Square live over 50,000 Americans of Italian descent, whose shops and restaurants give this district its particular stamp. In the south-eastern part of this district, particularly round Broadway and Columbus Avenue, is the pulsating heart of San Francisco's entertainment quarter, with numerous bars, night clubs, jazz spots, cabarets, theatres and restaurants.

North Waterfront

Piers

To the north of Telegraph Hill the Embarcadero, a broad seafront avenue, runs along the northern exit from San Francisco Bay, lined by numerous piers. From Pier 39, with its many shops and places of entertainment, there are fine views of the bay and the city's skyline. Moored at Pier 45 is the three-masted schooner "Balclutha", launched in Glasgow in 1886, with a 144ft/44m mainmast. Pier 43½ is the departure point for ferries and excursion boats.

*Fisherman's Wharf

The Embarcadero ends at Fisherman's Wharf, which has been titivated and developed for the benefit of tourists, with a variety of colourful shops, restaurants, bars and fast food stands. Visitors may even encounter a few fishermen.

*Cannery

On the south-west side of Fisherman's Wharf is the Cannery, an old Del Monte fruit-canning plant which was restored in the sixties and now houses galleries, boutiques, speciality shops, cafés, restaurants and various entertainment facilities. Open-air concerts, poetry readings and other

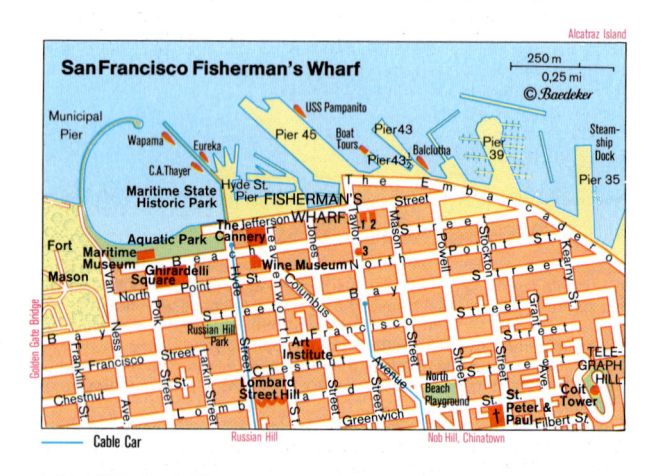

1 Ripley's "Believe it or Not" Museum   2 Wax Museum   3 St. Francis Statue

San Francisco

shows are among the attractions. In nearby Beach Street is the first Wine Museum in the United States.

On the west side of Fisherman's Wharf is the Maritime State Historic Park, with a number of restored vessels of earlier days, including the paddle-steamer "Eureka" of 1890 and the ferry "Alma" of 1891. Nearby is the Maritime Museum, housed in a grandiose former casino, which charts the history of American shipping in the Pacific. *Maritime State Historic Park

To the south of the Maritime Museum is Ghirardelli Square. Here, housed in the restored brick buildings once occupied by Domenico Ghirardelli's chocolate factory, are a variety of shops, restaurants, art galleries and entertainments. *Ghirardelli Square

To the west of Aquatic Park is Fort Mason, from which there is an attractive path leading to the Golden Gate Bridge. Farther west are Marina Park, the Yacht Harbor, Marina Green and the Palace of Fine Arts (1915), now housing the Exploratorium, a museum of science and technology. Other sights

Cathedral Hill

North-west of the Civic Centre is Cathedral Hill (340ft/104m), named after St Mary's Cathedral (R.C.), a very striking modern church with a 200ft/60m high dome, built in 1970 on the site of an earlier church destroyed by fire in 1962. *St Mary's Cathedral

North-west of Cathedral Hill is Japantown (in Japanese Nihomachi), the cultural and economic centre of San Francisco's 14,000 Japanese citizens, with theatres, temples, shrines, restaurants and tea-houses. The Peace Plaza, with beautifully laid out Japanese gardens and a five-tier Peace Pagoda, is entered through the Ronom, a gate designed by Yoshiro Taniguchi. In spring this is the scene of the Cherry Blossom Festival. Japantown

Dolores Street

1¼ miles/2km south-west of the Civic Center is the Mission Dolores (Dolores and 16th Streets). This adobe mission station, built in 1776 and originally dedicated to San Francisco de Asís, was the sixth of the 21 Spanish mission stations on the Californian coast. The adjoining basilica dates from 1918. The cemetery contains the graves of 5000 Indians who died in two mass epidemics in 1804 and 1826. *Mission Dolores

Farther west is Buena Vista Park, from which there are beautiful views. The nearby Josephine D. Randall Junior Museum has a collection of material on the Indian cultures of California. Buena Vista Park

To the south-west are the Twin Peaks (909ft/277m and 902ft/275m). In recent years this has become a favoured residential district. From the hills photographers can take the famous "fog views" of San Francisco. *Twin Peaks

Golden Gate Park

This landscaped park (area 1000 acres/400 hectares), laid out from 1887 onwards to the design of the Scottish landscape gardener John McLaren, is still one of the largest and finest municipal parks in the United States, with over 5000 different species of plants. It contains enclosures with bison and various species of deer, a number of lakes and ponds and a variety of monuments. **Golden Gate Park**

On the east side of the park is the California Academy of Sciences, with the Natural History Museum (open: daily 10am–5pm), the Steinhart Aquarium and the Morrison Planetarium. *California Academy of Sciences

449

San Francisco

M. H. de Young Memorial Museum

North-west of the Academy of Sciences is the M. H. de Young Memorial Museum (open: daily 10am–5pm), with a collection of pictures, sculpture, stained glass, etc., including works by Rembrandt, El Greco, Rubens, Tiepolo and many other masters.

Asian Art Museum

In the west wing of the De Young Museum is the Asian Art Museum, with the Avery Brundage Collection. This contains almost 10,000 works of art from Japan, Korea, China, India, Iran and other Asian cultures. To the south-west is the beautiful Japanese Tea Garden.

Presidio

Situation and characteristics

The Presidio has been so called since Spanish troops set up their first garrison here in 1776. This military area (1460 acres/591 hectares) extending along the northern tip of the San Francisco peninsula to the Pacific is now the headquarters of the US 6th Army. The only building of the Spanish period still surviving in the park, most of which is open to the public (fine views), is the Officers' Club. There is a colours parade daily at 5pm. Within the area of the Presidio are an Army Museum and a large military cemetery. Among those buried in the cemetery is the actress Pauline Tyler, who during the Civil War spied for the Union states.

Golden Gate

**Golden Gate Bridge*

The Golden Gate Bridge, one of the largest and handsomest suspension bridges in the world, spans the Golden Gate, the narrow strait between the San Francisco peninsula and the Marin peninsula. It was built in 1933–37 by the Cincinnati-born engineer Joseph B. Strauss (1870–1938) and was then the world's longest suspension bridge. Technical data: total length 3060yd/2800m, breadth 90ft/27.50m, height of piers 745ft/227m, height

Golden Gate Bridge; in the foreground Fort Point

San Francisco

above water at half tide 220ft/67m. Every week some 2 tons of reddish lead paint are applied to the bridge to protect it from rust. Tolls are payable only when travelling from north to south. It is worth walking across the bridge for the sake of the magnificent views.

At the south end of the bridge are some remains of old fortifications. From Fort Point (Fort Scott) there are superb views.

Fort Point
(Fort Scott)

From the Golden Gate Bridge Lincoln Boulevard (wide views) runs south to Lincoln Park, with the little promontory of Land's End. Near the golf course at the east end of the park is the neo-classical Palace of the Legion of Honor (open: Wed.–Sun. 10am–5pm), which contains a very fine collection of 18th and 19th century European art, including works by Degas, Manet, Monet and Renoir and Rodin's "Thinker". Here too is the Achenbach Foundation's large collection of graphic art.

*Palace of the
Legion of Honor

Below Lincoln Park, to the west, is Cliff House (1858; museum, restaurant), from which there is a fine view of the Seal Rocks.

Cliff House/
Seal Rocks

4 miles/6km beyond Cliff House is the San Francisco Zoo, with animals from many parts of the world, including dwarf hippopotamuses, koala bears and okapis.

*San Francisco
Zoo

Surroundings of San Francisco (Bay Area)

The former prison island of Alcatraz in San Francisco Bay is now a tourist sight. From 1933 to 1963 it was the most notorious jail in the United States, one of its best known inmates being Al Capone. Six years after it was closed the island was occupied by Indians, who remained in possession for several years. There are ferries to the island from Pier 41, near Fisherman's Wharf (in summer daily 9am–5pm, in spring and autumn daily 9am–3pm).

Alcatraz

This 8½ mile/13.5km long two-level bridge, completed in 1936, spans San Francisco Bay from San Francisco to Oakland. It was badly damaged in the 1989 earthquake.

San Francisco–
Oakland Bay
Bridge

At the east end of the bridge is the industrial city of Oakland (pop. 350,000), founded in 1850. The population includes a high proportion of coloured, and the militant Black Panther movement originated here in 1966. In the city centre is Lake Merritt, a small salt-water lake with facilities for recreation. At the south-west end of the lake is the Oakland Museum (natural history, history, art and culture of California).

Oakland

North of the bridge is the town of Berkeley (pop. 110,000), founded in 1841. It is a favoured residential town with major teaching and research institutions. On the east side of the town are important departments of the renowned University of California. Of particular interest are the Robert H. Lowie Museum of Anthropology, the University Art Museum, established on the initiative of the German painter Hans Hofmann, the Pacific Film Archive and the Lawrence Berkeley Laboratory, in which the famous atomic physicist Julius Robert Oppenheimer (1904–67) worked. From the Sather Tower or Campanile there are fine views of San Francisco Bay and the Golden Gate Bridge.

*Berkeley

20 miles/43km east of Berkeley, beyond Walnut Creek, is Mount Diablo (3849ft/1173m), a hill in the Coast Range. From its summit there are wide views, extending in clear weather for almost 200 miles/300km. There are attractive hiking trails in Mount Diablo State Park.

*Mount Diablo

Round the north end of the Golden Gate Bridge is the Golden Gate National Recreation Area. From here there is a fine view of the skyline of San Francisco.

Golden Gate
National
Recreation Area

451

San Jose

*Sausalito	Once a fishing village on Richardson Bay (the northern part of San Francisco Bay), Sausalito is now a popular resort for the citizens of San Francisco. It is a town of picturesque winding lanes, often linked by flights of wooden steps. In the harbour are numerous brightly painted house-boats, some of them of rather eccentric design. The town is now the home of many artists and prosperous citizens who commute to San Francisco. The ferry from San Francisco to Sausalito affords magnificent backward views of the city.

## San Jose					M 4

State: California
Altitude: 95ft/29m
Population: 783,000

Situation and characteristics	The city of San Jose lies between two ranges of hills in the fertile Santa Clara Valley (wine grapes, peaches), now better known as Silicon Valley (see below). It is an important base of the American micro-electronics industry.

History	The town was founded in 1777 under the name of San José de Guadalupe – the oldest incorporated town in the United States – and from 1849 to 1851 was capital of California.

Sights in San Jose

*Rosicrucian Egyptian Museum and Planetarium	In Rosicrucian Park are the headquarters of the Rosicrucian Society, which runs a well stocked Egyptian Museum (Egyptian and Assyrian antiquities) and a Natural History Museum with a Planetarium (open: Tue.–Sun. 9am–4.30pm).

Winchester Mystery House	The Winchester Mystery House (525 S. Winchester Boulevard) was built between 1880 and 1922. Sarah Winchester, owner of the house and heiress to the fortune earned by the Winchester arms factory, continued building operations on the house over many years because a medium had told her that she would not die so long as building was continuing. The result was this extraordinary mansion with 160 rooms, 2000 doors and 10,000 windows.

Surroundings of San Jose

Mount Hamilton/ Lick Observatory	19 miles/30km east of San Jose, on the summit of Mount Hamilton, is the Lick Observatory.

Palo Alto/ Stanford University/ Silicon Valley	17 miles/27km north-west of San Jose is Palo Alto (pop. 60,000; named after a tall redwood tree), with the world-famous Stanford University. The Palo Alto–San Jose–Santa Clara Valley area is now famed world-wide as Silicon Valley. During the 1940s arms factories were established in this area, and later a NASA research centre was sited here. In the sixties and seventies several hundred institutes, laboratories and firms concerned with silicon semi-conductors and computer technology settled in the area, and the close co-operation between the armed forces, industry and the University proved extremely productive.

## Santa Fe					O 19

State: New Mexico
Altitude: 6990ft/2130m
Population: 60,000

Santa Fe

Santa Fe, capital of the state of New Mexico, lies on a tributary of the Rio Grande on the south-western slopes of the very beautiful Sangre de Cristo Mountains. The town gains its particular atmosphere from the mingling of Indian, Spanish/Mexican and Anglo-American cultural influences. Its picturesque streets and lanes, low adobe houses, beautiful churches of the Spanish colonial period and profusion of Indian arts and crafts and contemporary art, combined with its agreeable dry mountain climate, have long attracted visitors. In the forest-covered mountain country round the town, where some mines are still being worked, there are a number of very attractive and interesting Indian pueblos. During the last twenty years, too, excellent winter sports facilities have been developed in the Sangre de Cristo Mountains.

Situation and characteristics

In 1542 the first Spaniards to come here found a populous Indian village. In 1609 they founded a town which became the religious and administrative centre of the province of New Mexico. In 1680 the Spaniards were driven out by the Indians, but returned twelve years later. After Mexico broke away from Spain in 1821 Santa Fe remained capital of New Mexico and built up a lively trade with the Americans. The principal transport route was the Santa Fe Trail, which ran through the valley of the Rio Grande to reach the Missouri at Kansas City. Another important route was the Old Spanish Trail, which led to Los Angeles in California. In 1846, during the Spanish-Mexican War, Santa Fe fell to the United States without any serious fighting and later became capital of the US territory of New Mexico. In 1862 the town fell briefly into the hands of the Confederates. The economy of the town and surrounding area was given a boost by the opening of the Santa Fe Railroad in 1880.

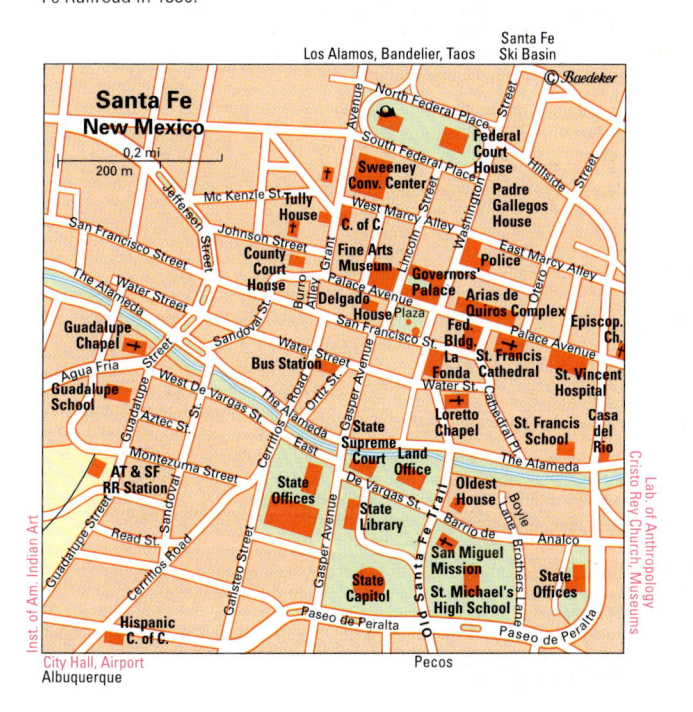

History

Santa Fe

Sights in Santa Fe

Plaza	The busy hub of the town's life is the Plaza, a market square built by the Spaniards where the Santa Fe Trail ended. Here Indian traders offer local arts and crafts for sale. On the north side of the square is the fortress-like Palace of the Governors (1614), which was successively the seat of Spanish, Mexican and American governors and is believed to be the oldest public building in the United States. Here in 1880 Governor Lewis Wallace wrote part of his much-filmed novel "Ben Hur". Exhibitions in the palace trace the history of Santa Fe from prehistoric times to the present day, with particular emphasis on the Indian heritage. In the Hall of the Modern Indian to the north are exhibits illustrating modern Indian culture.
*Palace of the Governors	
Museum of Fine Arts	In an adobe building to the west of the palace is the Museum of Fine Arts (sculpture, pottery, woven fabrics).
Delgado House	Close by, to the south, is Delgado House, built in the adobe style by a businessman of Spanish origin in 1890.
La Fonda Hotel	At the south-east corner of the Plaza is the old-established adobe La Fonda Hotel, which marked the end of the Santa Fe Trail.
Palace Avenue	On Palace Avenue, which runs south-east from the Plaza, are a number of imposing buildings, for example the Prince Plaza (1840), once the centre of the town's social life, and the roomy Sena Plaza, once the property of a major who had fought in the Civil War, which is now occupied by attractive boutiques and galleries.
St Francis Cathedral	The neo-Romanesque Cathedral of St Francis (San Francisco de Asís) was built between 1869 and 1884 on a site occupied by several earlier churches. In a chapel on the north side is La Conquistadora, a figure of the Virgin brought from Spain.
Old Santa Fe Trail Loretto Chapel	From the Plaza the Old Santa Fe Trail runs south. Immediately beyond the La Fonda Hotel is the neo-Gothic Loretto Chapel (1873). The Miraculous Staircase, a spiral staircase leading to the gallery, is said by legend to have been made by St Joseph himself.
*Barrio de Analco	Beyond the Rio de Santa Fe is the Barrio de Analco, an old quarter dating from the early 17th century in which a number of buildings have been lovingly restored. Here too is what is claimed to be the oldest building in the United States, an adobe structure which may have been built around 1200, now housing a restaurant and a number of souvenir shops.
San Miguel	Immediately south is one of the oldest religious buildings in the United States, the chapel of San Miguel (1636), which contains a number of fine statues and a high altar of 1798 with the likeness of St Gertrude (1256–1302; mystic and abbess of a Benedictine convent in Germany).
*State Capitol	South-west of the chapel is the State Capitol (guided visits), a striking circular building (1966) modelled on an Indian kiva (cult building).
De Vargas Street Guadalupe Church	De Vargas Street runs from west to east through the government quarter of the town (State Offices, Supreme Court). At its west end is the Guadalupe Church, which has a beautiful high altar and a number of fine pictures. It is dedicated to Our Lady of Guadalupe, patron saint of Mexico. At its east end De Vargas Street runs into Canyon Road.
*Canyon Road/ Camino del Monte Sol	Along picturesque Canyon Road, an old trade route leading to Pecos, and the equally picturesque Camino del Monte Sol which cuts across it are numerous artists' studios and craftsmen's workshops, some of which can be visited. Farther along Canyon Road is the church of Cristo Rey, the largest adobe church.
Camino Lejo Laboratory of Anthropology/ *Museum of Indian Arts and Culture	On the Camino Lejo are a number of very interesting museums. Housed in an attractive adobe building is the Laboratory of Anthropology, with the Museum of Indian Arts and Culture (open: Mon.–Fri. 10am–5pm), a renowned institution devoted to the traditional folk arts of the American South-West which has impressive displays of Indian arts and crafts (headdresses, textiles, basketwork, jewellery, pottery, weaving).

Santa Fe

A little way south is the Museum of International Folk Art, with folk art and costumes from many different countries.

The Wheelwright Museum (open: daily 10am–5pm) is also concerned with the arts and crafts of the Indians of the American South-West. In addition to a great variety of cult objects, woven fabrics, silverware and sand paintings it also has a collection of old writing and documents inscribed on clay (in particular Indian songs).

Museum of International Folk Art
*Wheelwright Museum

2 miles/3km south-west of the Plaza, on Verillos Road, is the Institute of American Indian Arts (temporary exhibitions on the art of numerous Indian cultures).

*Institute of American Indian Arts

Surroundings of Santa Fe

To the north of Santa Fe is the Hyde Memorial State Park, from which there are magnificent views. Beyond this, in the Sangre de Cristo Mountains, which rise to a height of 11,200ft/3414m, is an excellent skiing area.

Hyde Memorial State Park/ Santa Fe Ski Basin

23 miles/37km south-east of Santa Fe is Pecos, on the southern outskirts of which are the ruins of a Spanish mission station. Nearby is the Pecos National Monument, an Indian pueblo which is believed to have been inhabited from early 14th century until 1838, with a population over 2000.

*Pecos National Monument

10 miles/16km south-west of Santa Fe is the Old Cienaga Village Museum, which re-creates the life of the Spanish colonial period.

Old Cienaga Village Museum

45 miles/72km WNW of Santa Fe, in the volcanic Jemez Mountains, is the wild and romantic Frijoles Canyon, whose principal feature of interest is the Bandelier National Monument. This area, once occupied by Pueblo Indians, was explored by the Swiss-American anthropologist A. F. Bandelier

Frijoles Canyon/ *Bandelier National Monument

Pueblo in the Santa Fe area

Santa Fe

(1840–1914). Between the 13th and 16th centuries the Indians had hewn cave dwellings and cult sites (kivas) out of the easily workable tufa and built multi-storey dwellings, known as talus, against the rock faces. A short distance to the north-west are remains of the pueblo of Tynony, with some 400 rooms and three kivas. In the surrounding area, in country which is difficult of access, are remains of other Indian dwellings and cult sites.

*Painted Cave — In Capulin Canyon is the remarkable Painted Cave, with a whole series of Indian wall paintings of different periods.

Los Alamos — 34 miles/55km north-west of Santa Fe is Los Alamos (alt. 7300ft/2225m; pop. 12,000) – "Atomic City" – an atomic research centre established during the Second World War. Here was constructed the first atomic bomb, which was detonated on July 16th 1945 in what is now the White Sands National Park (see entry). In the Bradbury Science Hall in Los Alamos Scientific Laboratory is an exhibition on the development of nuclear weapons.

**Pueblos

Round Santa Fe are a number of settlements of Pueblo Indians, mostly descendants of the Indians who left the Frijoles Canyon in the 16th century. In these villages old traditions are still maintained, including ritual dances and artistic craft work. They tend to treat strangers with some reserve, and visitors should not photograph or film them except with express permission. Regard should always be had to the particular mentality and sensitivities of the Indians.

The distances and directions of the pueblos listed below are reckoned from Santa Fe.

Southern pueblos — Cochiti Pueblo (30 miles/48km SW) is noted for the manufacture of jewellery and pottery. The inhabitants of Santo Domingo Pueblo (32 miles/51km SW) hold fast to their traditions (particularly ritual dances) but also sell pottery, textiles and silver jewellery. San Felipe Pueblo (34 miles/55km SW) is one of the oldest settlements in a wide surrounding area; it too has skilled craft workers. Sandia Pueblo (50 miles/80km SW) shows the influence of the nearby city of Albuquerque (see entry).

Northern pueblos — San Ildefonso Pueblo (22 miles/35km NW), near Los Alamos, is one of the best known Indian villages, with a lively street market and a very interesting kiva (no admission). In Santa Clara Pueblo (27 miles/43km NW) interesting dances are performed around Christmas. The very picturesque San Juan Pueblo (28 miles/45km NW) is noted for its skilled potters and woodcarvers. The old Picuris (San Lorenzo) Pueblo (55 miles/89km NE) was built in the 13th century.

*Taos

Situation and characteristics — The little town of Taos (pop. 3000), situated in the mountains 70 miles/113km north-east of Santa Fe, was founded in 1615. It has enjoyed a reputation as an artists' colony since the 1880s, but has now unfortunately become a popular tourist centre.

Sights — The central feature of the town is the picturesque Plaza, in which the American flag is always hoisted. In Ledoux Street, to the south-west, are the adobe house of the artist Ernest Blumenschein, who came here in the 19th century, and the Harwood Museum (works by members of the local artists' colony, Indian arts and crafts, the sacred figures called santos). To the east of the Plaza is the house (now a museum) of the legendary pioneer Kit Carson (1809–68). North-east of the Plaza is the art gallery of the Taos Art Association.

2½ miles/4km north-east of Taos is Taos Pueblo, which has been continuously and exclusively occupied by Indians since the 12th century and has preserved its character as a pueblo in the purest form. Round the central plaza, through which flows a stream, are fortress-like houses in the oldest adobe style, but built only of clay and straw, without fired bricks. Particularly notable are the multi-storey community houses, the kivas (cult sites) and the egg-shaped ovens. The Pueblo Indians who live here are still strongly attached to their traditions, and visitors are tolerated only during the day, and then mainly as sources of income.

**Taos Pueblo

To the north of Taos the Rio Grande has gouged out a grandiose gorge 650ft/198m deep, now spanned by a boldly engineered road bridge.

*Rio Grande Gorge Bridge

North-east of Taos, in the Sangre de Cristo Mountains (8900–12,500ft/2700–3800m), is the magically beautiful and excellently equipped winter sports region of the Taos Ski Valley.

*Taos Ski Valley

20 miles/32km north of Taos on a poor road is the D. H. Lawrence Ranch, the last resting-place of the writer D. H. Lawrence (1885–1930), who lived here in 1922–23. Lawrence died in Vence, in southern France, but his wife Frieda von Richthofen brought his ashes back to Taos and had them mixed with sand, cement and water to make an altar which was then set up on a specially built chapel. The ranch is now a conference centre.

D. H. Lawrence Ranch

Savannah

R 44

State: Georgia
Altitude: 45ft/14m
Population: 137,500

Savannah lies on the Atlantic coast at the mouth of the Savannah River, directly on the border with South Carolina. Once the world's most important cotton port, it suffered a period of decline but is now once again a considerable port (mainly container ships and tankers), with oil refineries. Savannah was founded in 1733 by General James E. Oglethorpe in his newly created colony of Georgia – the first town in North America to be laid out on a regular plan. It developed into the leading port for the shipment of cotton and was thus a place of strategic importance in the Civil War. It was badly damaged during the war, but when it was taken by General Sherman's Union troops in December 1864 it was not set on fire but was preserved intact as a Christmas gift to President Lincoln. It has thus one of the largest historic districts in the United States, which with its green streets and shady squares carries visitors back to the great days of the South.

Situation and characteristics

*Townscape

The sailing events of the 1996 Summer Olympics at Atlanta are to be staged at Savannah.

Sights in Savannah

The best way of getting to know Savannah's historic district is to take a stroll along Bull Street and the side streets opening off it. The starting-point is City Hall (1905), opposite which is the US Customs House, built in 1852 on the site of the colony's first public building. To the south of this is Johnson Square, the first square laid out in the new planned town, with Christ Episcopal Church (1838), on the site of the colony's first church of 1733. From Wright Square, the next square on Bull Street, it is a short distance west to the Telfair Mansion (a very handsome Regency house of 1818) and Art Museum (American and European art of the 18th and 19th centuries). Then south, passing the birthplace (1820) of Juliet Gordon Low, who

Bull Street

Telfair Mansion and Art Museum

Savannah

Cotton Exchange and Factors Walk, Savannah

founded the Girl Scouts of the USA, to Oglethorpe Avenue, the southern boundary of the old town. Along this to the east is Abercorn Street, which runs north towards the river, passing the Owens-Thomas House (1816–19) and continuing to Reynolds Square, with the Pink House of 1790.

Factors Walk

*Cotton Exchange

Factors Walk runs from east to west above the river, with iron steps and bridges linking the old cotton warehouses on the river banks with the streets on a higher level. The most important building is the Cotton Exchange (1886), the centre of the cotton trade.

Riverfront

One of the flights of iron steps leads down from Factors Walk to Riverfront, a row of 19th century warehouses now occupied by shops, bars and restaurants. From here there are views, particularly fine in the evening, of the port and the large suspension bridge.

Museums

*Black History Museum

Savannah has a number of interesting museums: the Ships of the Sea Museum (ship models, etc.) at 503 E. River Street; adjoining the Visitor Center at 303 Martin Luther King Jr Boulevard, the Savannah History Museum, housed in a large 19th century engine shed; and the Black History Museum at 514 Huntingdon Street, which organises guided tours of "black Savannah", taking in, for example, the First African Baptist Church (1777), the oldest black church in North America.

Surroundings of Savannah

Forts

15 miles/24km east of Savannah is Fort Pulaski, which was held by the Confederates from 1861 to 1862, when it was taken by Union forces; it has been restored to its condition at that time. 24 miles/40km south of Savannah is Fort McAllister, which was built to defend Savannah; its fall in December 1864 marked the end of Sherman's march to the Atlantic.

Just off the coast to the south of Savannah are a number of islands, including Sea Island, St Simons Island and Jekyll Island, all linked with the mainland by road, which are now popular holiday resorts.

*Golden Isles

Seattle

B 3

State: Washington
Altitude: 0–125ft/0–38m
Population: 503,000 (Greater Metropolitan Area 1.7 million)

Seattle, an important Pacific port and industrial centre and the largest city in Washington State, lies on a narrow strip of land between Puget Sound and Lake Washington, some 140 miles/230km from the open Pacific, with which it is linked by the Strait of Juan de Fuca. The port on Elliot Bay is the principal supply base for Alaska, plays an important part in American trade with Asia and is the most important fishing port in the United States. The city's main branch of industry is the aerospace industry (Boeing Aircraft Co.): more than half of all passenger jet aircraft (in particular jumbo jets) come from Seattle. Other industries include shipbuilding, woodworking, foodstuffs (particularly fish-canning), textiles and above all electronics (Microsoft, etc.).

Situation and characteristics

Seattle lies in a magnificent mountain setting: to the east is the ice pyramid of Mount Rainier (see Mount Rainier National Park), rising out of the Cascade Mountains, to the west the partly snow-capped peaks of the Olympic National Park (see entry). The landscape is variegated by a series of inlets along the coast and a number of lakes.

*Geographical setting

Seattle Downtown

1 White Henry Stuart Building
2 Olympic Hotel
3 First National Bank
4 U.S. Court
5 Federal Reserve Bank
6 Federal Office Building
7 Administration Building
8 Public Safety Building
9 City Hall
10 Smith Tower
11 King County Court House
12 Seattle Art Museum
13 Westlake Center
14 Pacific First Center
15 Convention & Trade Center
Pier 52 Ferry Terminal
Pier 59 Aquarium, Omnidome
Streetcar
Pioneer Square Historic District

459

Seattle

History

The first white settlers in this area were given a friendly welcome in November 1851 by the famous Chief Seattle, and soon after being incorporated as a town Seattle had a population of over 1000. In the early days logging and fishing formed the basis of the town's economy. In 1889 the town was destroyed in a great fire but was quick to recover. In 1893 the transcontinental railroad reached Seattle. In 1896 the first ocean-going vessel from Japan put in at the port, and in that year also the gold rush in Alaska brought a great flood of immigrants to the town. By the turn of the century the population had risen to 80,000.

The opening of the Panama Canal in 1914 and the two world wars gave further boosts to the town's economy, and shipbuilding and aircraft construction developed on a tremendous scale. In 1962 a very successful World's Fair was held in Seattle. More recently the city has played an important part in developing trading relations with the Asian countries, and in the autumn of 1993 President Clinton discussed these matters with statesmen and leading businessmen from states bordering the Pacific.

Sights in Seattle

Pioneer Square
Historic District

The historic core of the city is Pioneer Square, in which stands a 60ft/18m high totem pole. This was the spot where the first white settlers established themselves in 1852. The old Victorian-style brick buildings (including former department stores and hotels) between the 42-storey Smith Tower (observation platform on 35th floor) in the north and King Street Station to the south were restored some years ago and now cater for tourists, with boutiques, souvenir shops and restaurants. The striking Pioneer Building is the starting-point of Bill Speidel's "underground tours", which take visitors round the foundations of buildings destroyed in the 1889 fire.

The skyline of Seattle, with Mount Rainier in the background

Seattle

In the Union Trust Annex Building (117 S. Main Street) is the very interesting Klondike Gold Rush Museum (open: daily 9am–5pm), which brings to life the wild nineties of the 19th century.

To the east of Pioneer Square is the colourful International District, in which the street scene is dominated by immigrants from the Far East (mainly Japanese and Chinese) with their shops and restaurants. At 407 7th Avenue is the Wing Luke Museum, which charts the history of Asian immigration.

To the south of King Street is the Kingdome, a sports arena with seating for over 70,000 spectators. This is the home ground of the Seattle Seahawks football team and is also used for other events such as rock concerts.

*Klondike Gold Rush Museum

*International District

Kingdome

To the north of Pioneer Square is the Central Business District, with City Hall and a number of eye-catching skyscrapers. Among them are the 42-storey Bank of California, the 50-storey First National Bank, the 40-storey circular Washington Plaza Hotel, the two Post-Modern structures Pacific First Center and Westlake Center, and the Rainier Square Shopping Center. At the north-east corner of the Central Business District is the Washington State Convention and Trade Center. On University Street is the Seattle Art Museum, with a collection covering the art of many countries round the world. The Palace of Culture, in Post-Modern style, was designed by Robert Venturi.

Downtown Seattle
Central Business District

*Seattle Art Museum

To the west, on Elliot Bay, is Waterfront Park, from which there are wide views. On "Gold Rush Strip" are a number of old buildings, now occupied by souvenir shops (fine craft products of the Northwest Indians) and attractive restaurants.

From the Alaskan Way Viaduct there is a magnificent view of the waterfront and the port.

On Pier 59 is the Seattle Aquarium (open: daily 10am–5pm, in summer to 7pm), in whose Underwater Dome a variety of Pacific marine creatures (including sea otters, octopuses and dwarf sharks) can be observed.

Close by is the Omnidome, a circular cinema in which visitors can experience on film the 1980 eruption of Mount St Helens. Pier 57 is the departure point of interesting harbour tours.

An old-time streetcar runs along the waterfront between Piers 48 and 70. On the two floors of picturesque Pike Place Market a wide range of wares are offered for sale – fish, fruit, vegetables and all sorts of odds and ends. Here too are a number of cheerful little bars.

Waterfront Park

Alaskan Way Viaduct

*Seattle Aquarium

Omnidome/ Harbour tours

Streetcar
*Pike Place Market

The futuristic Monorail system carries passengers in 1½ minutes from the Westlake Center to the Seattle Center (1¼ miles/2km north-west of the city centre), which was built for the 1962 World's Fair.

The Space Needle, a 605ft/184m high telecommunications tower, has become the great landmark and emblem of Seattle. From the restaurant and the observation platform there are overwhelming panoramic views.

To the south-west are the six buildings of the Pacific Science Center, designed by Minoru Yamasaki (open: daily 10am–6pm), with excellent presentations of various fields of science and mathematics (including astronomy and space travel). The facilities include an IMAX cinema with a giant screen.

To the north-west is the Washington State Coliseum (seating for 18,000 spectators), with a tent roof which requires no internal supports. A cableway runs across the central plaza of the Seattle Center, in which is the International Fountain (illuminated at night).

In Center House are a Children's Museum (many "hands-on" exhibits), the Food Circus and an International Bazaar selling culinary delights and other products from many different countries.

Seattle Center

*Space Needle

*Pacific Science Center

Coliseum
Skyride

Center House

1¼ miles/2km south-east of the Seattle Center, round Denny Way, is a pleasant quarter of the city with attractive restaurants, boutiques and art galleries.

Denny Way

Sequoia and Kings Canyon National Parks

Myrtle Edwards Park/ *Chittenden Locks	North-west of the Seattle Center is the Myrtle Edwards Park. Farther north are the Hiram M. Chittenden Locks, one of the largest and busiest lock complexes in the United States. Nearby are the Fishermen's Terminal (fishing harbour) and Shishole Bay Marina. Beside the locks is a fish ladder which allows salmon and other fish to make their way upstream from the salt water of Puget Sound to the fresh water of Lake Union and Lake Washington.
Lake Union/ Green Lake	To the north-east of the Seattle Center is Lake Union. Farther north is the Green Lake, with an "aqua-theatre". Here too is Woodland Park, with a zoo and a rose garden.
University of Washington	Beyond Portage Bay is the campus of the University of Seattle (36,000 students), which was founded in 1861, with the Thomas Burke Memorial Museum (natural history) and the Henry Art Gallery (mainly modern art). To the south are McCurdy Park, with the Museum of History and Industry, and Washington Park, with the Arboretum and a Japanese tea-garden.

Surroundings of Seattle

Lake Washington	On the northern outskirts of Seattle is Lake Washington (25 miles/40km long), which is popular with sailing enthusiasts. Two long pontoon bridges lead to the quiet suburb of Bellevue.
**Boeing Aircraft Company	Half an hour's drive north of Seattle on US 526, at Everett, is the factory of the Boeing Aircraft Company, with the largest aircraft construction hangar in the world. On a guided tour visitors are shown the latest high-tech aircraft (including the B 747) under construction. Some 20 minutes' drive south of Seattle is an older Boeing works where the Flying Fortresses of the Second World War were built. Nearby is the Red Barn in which W. E. Boeing constructed his first aircraft in 1916.
*Museum of Flight	To the south of the city, at 9404 Marginal Way, is the Museum of Flight (open: daily 9am–5pm), with over three dozen carefully restored old-time aircraft, including one built by the Wright brothers.
*Tillicum Indian Village	From Pier 56 there are boats (¾ hour) to Tillicum Indian Village, which gives visitors an excellent picture of the culture and way of life of the Northwest Indians.
Whidbey Island	To the north of Seattle is Whidbey Island, the largest island in Puget Sound, which was reconnoitred by George Vancouver in 1792 and is now a popular summer resort. On the island are the attractive little townships of Coupeville, Langley and Oak Harbor. To the south of Coupeville is the 19th century Fort Casey.
San Juan Islands	Also popular with vacationists are the San Juan Islands, which preserve a number of buildings dating from the period of British rule. In Friday Harbor is a Whale Museum, and there are boat trips from there to observe whales in the open sea.

Sequoia and Kings Canyon National Parks   M/N 7

	State: California Area: 1350sq.miles/3495sq.km Established: 1890 and 1940
Season	The National Parks are open throughout the year, though the higher levels can be visited only in summer. There are excellent facilities for winter sports.

Sequoia and Kings Canyon National Parks

The 2800-year-old General Sherman Tree in Sequoia National Park

Although established at different times, the Sequoia and Kings Canyon National Parks form a single geographical and administrative unit. They take in a large expanse of grand mountain scenery in the southern part of the Sierra Nevada, extending from the foothills on the edge of the Central Valley of California (San Joaquín Valley) in the west to the main ridge of the Sierra Nevada in the east, with Mount Whitney (14,494ft/4418m), the highest peak in the continental United States (excluding Alaska), the Split Mountain (14,058ft/4285m), Mount Goethe (13,277ft/4047m) and a number of other peaks over 10,000ft/3000m.

Situation and *topography

The two National Parks take in the most impressive part of a 250 mile/400km long belt of vegetation at altitudes between 4000 and 8000ft (1200 and 2400m) in which there are clumps, groves and forests of giant sequoias or mammoth trees (*Sequoiadendron giganteum* or *Sequoia gigantea*). This species and the closely related redwoods of the Pacific

*Giant sequoias

Shenandoah National Park

	coast (*Sequoia sempervirens*) are the only surviving representatives of a genus of sequoias of the swamp cypress family (*Taxodiaceae*) which was once widespread in the northern hemisphere. The giant sequoias can reach a height of between 250 and 300ft (75 and 90m) and a diameter of 40ft/12m and can live for up to 3500 years. Their thick bark (up to 18in./45cm) protects them against fire, and the high tannic acid content of their timber gives them protection against pests and fungal disease. Their only real enemy is man.
Fauna	Visitors who spend some time in the National Parks may be lucky enough to see silver foxes, lynxes and pumas. Commoner are raccoons, skunks, red deer and black bears. A careful watch should be kept for the Pacific rattlesnakes which are by no means rare.
History	The first inhabitants of this mountain region were Potwisha and Kaweah Indians, who lived by hunting, gathering, fishing and farming. The first whites came here only in 1858. Six years later staff of the Geological Survey explored the Sierra Nevada. They were followed by settlers, hunters, lumbermen, gold-prospectors and adventurers, and the Indian inhabitants were almost exterminated, largely as a result of diseases brought by the incomers. By 1890 there were dozens of sawmills in the area, and the sequoias were decimated, for a single giant sequoia provided enough timber for the construction of forty houses. An energetic fighter against the destruction of the sequoia forests was the Scottish-born John Muir, on whose initiative the Sequoia National Park was established.

Sights in Sequoia National Park

*Giant Forest	The Giant Forest in the western part of the Sequoia National Park owes its name to its stands of mammoth trees. The mightiest tree in this area is the General Sherman Tree, which is 275ft/83.8m high and has a circumference of 103ft/31.4m. It is estimated to be 2800 years old, making it one of the largest living organisms on earth. Other impressive groups of mammoth trees are the Senate Group, the Founder's Group and the Cloisters.
Crystal Cove	North-west of the Giant Forest is the very impressive stalactitic cave known as the Crystal Cove.
Moro Rock	A magnificent viewpoint is the 6725ft/2050m high Moro Rock, an isolated granite peak south-east of the Giant Forest.
Crescent Meadow	Crescent Meadow is a very beautiful alpine meadow surrounded by trees. From here there is a road to Tharp's Log, a dwelling contrived by the first white settler in the hollow trunk of a giant sequoia.

Sights in Kings Canyon National Park

*Grant Grove	On the north-west side of Sequoia National Park is Grant Grove, in the northern part of which is the General Grant Tree (266ft/81m high, circumference at the base 108ft/33m), which was discovered in 1862.
*Kings Canyon	Kings Canyon, carved out of the rock by the southern arm of the Kings River, is flanked by steep rock walls and tall granite peaks. From the Cedar Grove tourist centre there are hiking trails to the very beautiful Zumwalt Meadow and the Roaring River and Mist Falls.

Shenandoah National Park

State: Virginia
Area: 305sq.miles/789sq.km
Established: 1936

Shenandoah National Park

The National Park is open throughout the year, though in winter some sections of the Skyline Drive may be closed. The flowers and shrubs are at their finest in spring and summer, but the great glory of the park is its autumn colouring. The most popular time for a visit, therefore, is in October.

Season

**Autumn colouring

The National Park lies roughly in the centre of Virginia, taking in a section of the Blue Ridge Mountains (the most easterly ridge of the Appalachians) some 80 miles/ 128km long but only between 2 and 13 miles (3–21km) wide. The Blue Ridge Mountains, which range in height between 2000 and 4000ft (600 and 1200m), owe their name to the bluish mist which shrouds the tops of the hills, particularly in the early morning. 95% of the park's area is covered by dense mixed forest, the rest by meadowland.

Situation and *topography

Cabin, Big Meadows Lodge

The name of the National Park comes from the Indian name of the Shenandoah River ("daughter of the stars"). None of the original inhabitants, the Monacan and Manahoac Indians, survived the settlement of the area by Europeans, which led, particularly during the 19th century, to the almost complete destruction of the mountain forests by deliberate clearance, mining and stock-farming. Finally in the 1930s, in order to save at least part of the landscape and provide work for the remaining inhabitants, the National Park was established and the Skyline Drive constructed.

History

The most striking feature of the National Park is the density and variety of the forest cover, in which species of oak and pine predominate. In the undergrowth there are ferns and flowers such as the yellow lady's slipper.

Vegetation

The commonest animal is the Virginian white-tailed deer, the ever-popular Bambi. Much rarer – and distinctly less welcome – is an encounter with one of the five or six hundred black bears who live in the National Park.

Fauna

The Skyline Drive, the northern continuation of the Blue Ridge Parkway (see Virginia), runs along the crest of the Blue Ridge Mountains from the north entrance to the National Park at Front Royal (milepost 0.6) to the south entrance at Rockfish (milepost 104.6). Along the road there are numerous stopping points to enjoy the view or see some particular sight. Among them are the Shenandoah Valley Overlook (milepost 17.1), the Swift Run Overlook (milepost 67.2), at an altitude of over 3300ft/1000m, President Hoover's summer residence at the end of the Mill Prong Trail (milepost 52.5) and the old Cave Cemetery below Dark Hollow Falls (milepost 50.7).

*Skyline Drive

Information about hiking trails in the National Park can be obtained at the park entrances or from the park office (see Practical Information, National Parks).

South Carolina (State; SC) O–R 42–47

Area:
19,530sq.miles/80,582sq.km
Population: 3,559,000
Capital: Columbia
Popular name: Palmetto State

Situation and topography

South Carolina (named after King Charles I), one of the thirteen founding states of the Union, lies on the Atlantic coast in the south-eastern United States. The coastal plain has a wet subtropical climate, with summers which can be hot and sultry and mild winters. The climate becomes more temperate towards the north-west as the land rises to the Piedmont Plateau, a well cultivated agricultural region. In the extreme north-west the state takes in part of the Blue Ridge Mountains, a segment of the Appalachians.

History

The first Europeans in this area were Spaniards who landed on the coast in 1526. Systematic settlement, however, began only after Charles II granted possession of the Carolinas to eight "proprietors" in 1663. In 1670 the settlement of Charles Towne was founded near present-day Charleston. The Carolinas were divided into North and South Carolina in 1689. On May 23rd 1788 South Carolina became the eighth state to join the Union, and it was the first of the southern states to secede from it on December 20th 1860. The Civil War began with the bombardment by Union forces of Fort Sumter, at the entrance to Charleston harbour, on April 12th 1861. South Carolina suffered severely during the war, when General Sherman marched through the state and almost completely destroyed Columbia and other towns. It was not readmitted to the Union until 1868, and Union troops were stationed in the state until 1877.

Economy

The principal industry in South Carolina, one of the classic cotton states, is textiles, followed by chemicals and electronics. The second main source of income is the tourist and holiday trade, mainly on the Atlantic coast. The most important agricultural products after cotton are tobacco and soya beans.

Places of Interest in South Carolina

Camden

The little town of Camden, north-east of Columbia, was founded in 1732, and during the revolutionary wars was one of the principal British bases. It is now a horse-racing centre, with an interesting historic district which includes two reconstructed British forts.

Charleston

See entry

Columbia

Columbia (founded 1786), capital of South Carolina, lies roughly in the centre of the state on the Broad and Congaree Rivers. The imposing State House (Main and Gervais Streets) with its dome and its massive granite columns was built between 1855 and 1907. Bronze stars mark hits by Sherman's artillery during the siege of the town. Opposite State House is Trinity Church (1846), one of the largest Episcopal churches in the United States. To the south is the large campus of the University of South Carolina (founded 1801), the central element in which is the brick complex known as the Horseshoe.

A number of antebellum houses have been preserved in the north-east of the town, including the Hampton-Preston Mansion (1818), the Robert Mills Historic House (1823) and the Mann-Simons Cottage (1850). The Woodrow

South Carolina

Myrtle Beach, stretching endlessly into the distance

Wilson Boyhood Home, in which the 28th President of the United States spent his early years, was built after the Civil War.

The South Carolina State Museum, one of the largest museums in the southern states, surveys the history, natural history, science and art of South Carolina.

*South Carolina State Museum

To the east of Columbia, on the Saluda River, is the Riverbanks Zoo, the terrarium, aquarium and bird house of which are particularly remarkable.

*Riverbank Zoo

Georgetown, founded in 1729, is built on the spot where the Spaniards landed in 1526. It has an attractive historic district and offers facilities for deep-sea angling.

Georgetown

Hilton Head Island, off the Atlantic coast in the extreme south-east of the state, is now linked with the mainland by a four-lane highway. It is internationally renowned as a fashionable holiday resort, with clean and well-kept beaches, marvellous golf courses and a wide range of other leisure facilities. The sporting highlights of the season are the golf tournament and the ladies' tennis tournament, both of which attract international stars.

*Hilton Head Island

If Hilton Head Island is the resort for the wealthy, Myrtle Beach is its counterpart for ordinary people. Here they will find endless broad sandy beaches – and, immediately beyond the beaches, equally endless lines of hotels.

Myrtle Beach

Near the little town of Ninety Six on the Piedmont Plateau the first battle of the revolutionary wars in the southern United States was fought in 1775, and, six years later, a British fort was besieged for 28 days. A trail 1 mile/ 1.6km long through the forests takes visitors round the scene of the fighting.

Ninety Six National Historic Site

467

South Dakota (State; SD)   D–F 21–29

Area:
77,115sq.miles/199,730sq.km
Population: 701,000
Capital: Pierre
Popular name: Mount Rushmore State

Situation and topography

South Dakota (from the name of a Sioux tribe, the Dakotas, meaning "allies"), a region of continental climate, lies in the north central United States, in the zone of transition between the Central Lowlands and the Great Plains. It is divided by the Missouri (which is dammed at several points within the state) into two halves. The eastern half is in the Central Lowlands (lowest point 968ft/295m). The western half, mostly consisting of the Missouri Plateau, lies in the Great Plains, a region of grasslands interrupted by tracts of badlands. In the south-west of the state are the Black Hills, which reach a height of 7241ft/2207m in Harney Peak.

History

Some 12,000 years ago the territory of South Dakota was occupied by nomadic bison and mammoth hunters. Later they were succeeded by hunters and gatherers, who buried their dead in long, low mounds. Around A.D. 1200 Mandan and Arikara Indians introduced farming in the Missouri region; then in the 17th and early 18th centuries they were driven farther north by the Sioux. In the 1740s French fur-trappers – the first Europeans in this region – moved into Sioux territory, which then became part of New France (Louisiana) and was acquired by the United States in 1803 under the Louisiana Purchase. Originally the American territory of Dakota also included large areas of the present-day states of Wyoming and Montana. After the reorganisation of the territory the present states of North and South Dakota were formed, and on November 2nd 1889 South Dakota became the 40th state of the Union. The local Indians put up fierce resistance to the takeover of their land by whites, and there were frequent bloody encounters with US troops, causing heavy losses. On December 29th 1890 several hundred Indians were massacred by units of the US Cavalry at Wounded Knee Creek. This inglorious action, which broke Indian resistance, is still not forgotten. In 1973 members of the American Indian Movement occupied the Wounded Knee area, and in 1993 it was the scene of a further protest against the Indian policy of the US government.

Economy

The predominant elements in the state's economy are agriculture and the industries processing agricultural produce. Large areas of the grasslands are now pasturage for livestock (cattle, sheep) and arable land on which grain and fodder crops are grown. Gold and silver mining (Black Hills) also make important contributions to the economy, along with oil and brown coal. An increasingly important source of revenue is tourism. Particular tourist attractions are the Black Hills (Mount Rushmore), a number of spectacular caves and the Badlands National Park (see entry).

Places of Interest in South Dakota

Mitchell

Mitchell (pop. 15,000), in the valley of the James River, is the chief place in a predominantly agricultural area. A sight of international renown is its Moorish-style Corn Palace, which is decorated every year with corn cobs, mosaics made with different colours of corn (maize) and other fruits of the earth and grasses – a tradition which has been maintained since 1892. In mid September there is a large Corn Festival. Other features of interest are

South Dakota

Pine Ridge (South Dakota)

the Friends of the Middle Border Museum (a museum of pioneering days), the Oscar Howe Art Center, the Balloon and Airship Museum and the Enchanted World Doll Museum. To the north of the town is the site of a 10th century Indian village which was excavated some years ago. Nearby is beautiful Lake Mitchell.

Pierre (pop. 13,000), capital of South Dakota, lies in the geographical centre of the state on the Missouri, which is dammed a short distance above the town to form Lake Oahe. Features of interest are Fort Pierre (1832), the State Capitol (1902; recently renovated), the South Dakota Cultural Heritage Center, opened in 1989 (notable for its Indian material), and the Discovery Center and Aquarium (natural history). To the south of the town is the Fort Pierre National Grassland, a stretch of typical prairie vegetation. 60 miles/100km north of Pierre, on the east side of Lake Oahe, is the Whitlock Lakeside Area (recreational activities, particularly angling).

Pierre

Rapid City, the chief town of a wide surrounding area, lies on the eastern edge of the Black Hills (see entry), near Mount Rushmore. It is a good centre from which to explore the Badlands National Park (see entry). The Museum of Geology, in the grounds of the South Dakota School of Mines and Technology, has large geological and mineralogical collections. The Sioux Indian Museum illustrates the history and everyday life of the Sioux Indians. Other popular attractions are the Dinosaur Park (with reproductions of prehistoric animals which once lived in this part of the world) and the Reptile Gardens (giant turtles, etc.). To the east of the town is the Air and Space Museum. The road to Mount Rushmore runs past Bear Country (a park through which visitors can drive in their own cars to see the bears).

Rapid City

In the south-east of the state is its largest town, Sioux Falls (pop. 82,000). Originally founded in 1856, it had soon afterwards to be abandoned because of continual Indian attacks and began to develop only after the

Sioux Falls

469

Tampa

construction of Fort Dakota to provide protection. Features of interest are the Great Plains Zoo and Delbridge Museum of Natural History in Sherman Park and, to the north of this, the battleship USS "South Dakota".

Other places of interest

Badlands National Park, Black Hills (see entries), Mount Rushmore (see Black Hills).

Tampa   W 43

State: Florida. Altitude: 0–55ft/0–17m
Population: 280,000 (Metropolitan Area 2 million)

Situation and history

The city of Tampa, situated on an inlet reaching far into the west coast of Florida, is the economic centre of western Florida. The city centre is an area of high-rise office blocks, but Tampa also has historic old quarters such as Ybor City and Old Hyde Park.

The maps drawn by the Spanish conquistadors show a number of Indian settlements round Tampa Bay. In 1824 the Americans built a fort at the mouth of the Hillsborough River directed against the Seminole Indians. After the Second Seminole War a port and trading centre was established here, and this soon developed into a regional centre. The Civil War brought a period of stagnation, until a boost was given to the town by the construction of the South Florida Railroad.

Towards the end of the 19th century Tampa became a fashionable winter resort. In 1886 the Cuban cigar manufacturer Vincente Martínez Ybor moved his business to Tampa and a new quarter, Ybor City, was built for his Spanish-speaking employees. The mining of phosphates in the surrounding area also gave a stimulus to the city's development.

Sights in Tampa

Downtown Tampa/Franklin Street Mall

The heart of downtown Tampa, at the mouth of the Hillsborough River, is the Franklin Street Mall, a busy pedestrian zone with many shops, attractive restaurants, fountains and trees as well as tall office blocks.

*Tampa Museum of Art

To the west of the city centre, at 601 Doyle Arlton Drive, is Tampa Museum of Art (open: Tue.–Sat. 10am–5pm, Wed. to 9pm, Sun. 1–5pm), which has one of the finest collections of Greek and Roman antiquities in the United States.

Harbor Island

To the south of the city centre, separated from the mainland by the narrow Garrison Channel, is Harbor Island, with the popular Harbor Island Market (boutiques, fast food stands, restaurants). Along the waterfront runs the Waterwalk, a pleasant promenade with fine views.

*University of Tampa

The University of Tampa occupies a building in the style of a Moorish palace which from 1891 to 1929 was a hotel, with furnishings from Europe and the East. In the south wing is the H. B. Plant Museum (turn-of-the-century furniture and objets d'art).

Hyde Park

Hyde Park, between Swann Avenue and Bayshore Boulevard, is Tampa's best preserved old residential district, with many Victorian buildings. In Old Hyde Park Village are fashionable boutiques, galleries and elegant restaurants.

**Ybor City

The townscape pattern of Ybor City, the new district built for the Spanish-speaking workers of Martínez Ybor's cigar factory, is set by old wooden and brick buildings, wrought-iron balconies, arcades and sidewalk cafés. A good starting-point for a tour of the district is the State Museum, housed in a former Cuban bakery (restored). Adjoining is Preservation Park, with six renovated cigar-rolling sheds. On Ybor Square, now a small shopping mall with a variety of shops and restaurants, is the Tampa Rico Cigar Company, where visitors can see cigars being rolled by hand.

**Busch Gardens

Tampa's best known attraction, in the north-east of the city, is the Busch Gardens, a combination of zoo and theme park (Busch Boulevard and 40th

Street/SR 580). The themes of this family leisure park centre mainly on the Dark Continent. In addition it seeks to provide entertainments for every taste – animals, an exotic atmosphere, live shows in several theatres, roller coasters and other adventurous rides. The Zoo has gained a reputation for preserving endangered species, and is particularly proud of its success in breeding such rare species as the black rhinoceros. A recent triumph is the rearing of a large family of koalas, and the Zoo is also co-operating with Peking Zoo in the breeding of pandas. There is an impressive herd of Asiatic elephants.

Dark Continent

The Museum of Science and Industry (4801 E. Fowler Avenue), notable for its unusual architecture, ranks as one of the best museums of technology and natural history in the United States. Particularly interesting is the section devoted to weather and climate, in which visitors can experience, for example, all the power of a hurricane.

Museum of Science and Industry

On the eastern outskirts of the city, beyond I 4, is the Seminole Cultural Center (5221 N. Orient Road), which illustrates the history and culture of the Seminoles. In the Seminole village associated with the Center, with the typical chickees (open living huts), Indian craft skills are demonstrated.

Seminole Cultural Center

Tennessee (State; TN)   N/O 35–44

Area:
 42,145sq.miles/108,152sq.km
Capital: Nashville
Popular name: Volunteer State

The state of Tennessee (after the name of a Cherokee village), in the south-eastern United States, extends from the Mississippi plain in the west to the Appalachians. The southern range of the Appalachians is formed by the Great Smoky Mountains, with Clingmans Dome (6644ft/2025m). To the west of this are the Great Appalachian Valley, through which flows the Tennessee River, the flat Cumberland Plateau and the Nashville Basin, surrounded by ranges of low hills. To the west of the lower Tennessee River (on which are a number of dams) the gently undulating terrain falls down to the Mississippi. As a result of an energetic programme of re-afforestation more than half the state's area is now once again covered with deciduous forest.

Situation and topography

The first Europeans to reach the territory on the Tennessee River, then occupied by Cherokees, were Spaniards, who came here in 1541. They were followed by Frenchmen and then by British settlers, who in 1663 incorporated the area in the British colony of Carolina. Between 1784 and 1789, when Tennessee was separated from Carolina, there existed on the territory of Tennessee an independent but not officially recognised state called Franklin. On June 1st 1796 Tennessee became the 16th state to adopt the Constitution of the Union. In 1861 it left the Union and joined the Confederation. During the Civil War Tennessee was the scene of much fighting, including the battles of Shiloh and Franklin. In 1866 the state was readmitted to the Union. Thirty years earlier most of the Cherokees had been deported to Oklahoma.

History

The state's economic rise began with the establishment in 1933, during the great depression, of the Tennessee Valley Authority, charged to develop the valley of the Tennessee, which harnessed the power of the river to produce electricity. Tennessee's industries include chemicals, engineering,

Economy

471

Tennessee

automobile construction and mining (coal, zinc, phosphates). Its principal agricultural crops are maize, wheat, tobacco and cotton. The main tourist areas are the Great Smoky Mountains, which attract visitors throughout the year, the valley of the Tennessee River with its numerous artificial lakes (water sports), Nashville and Elvis Presley's town of Memphis.

Places of Interest in Tennessee

*Chattanooga

Chattanooga, situated in south-eastern Tennessee on the border with Georgia, was once an outlying settlement of the Cherokee Indians. It is now a city of 150,000 inhabitants in which the first Coca-Cola bottling plant was established and the game of minigolf was invented. The popular song "Chattanooga Choo-Choo" brought it international fame; and visitors can still see the original railroad station of 1909, though it is now converted into a hotel and restaurant arcade. Railway buffs will also find here the largest old-time steam railroad in the South, the Tennessee Valley Railroad. The city has a number of museums, including the Hunter Museum of Art, the Houston Museum of Decorative Arts and the National Knife Museum (knives down the ages). A steep railroad runs up Lookout Mountain, scene of the battle of Chattanooga during the Civil War; on the top, as well as enjoying the view, visitors can study the history of the battle. The Tennessee Aquarium displays the freshwater fishes of the southern United States. 6 miles/10km west of the city, in the Raccoon Mountain recreation area, is one of the largest of the Tennessee Valley Authority's dams.

Knoxville

Knoxville, seat of the University of Tennessee (founded 1794), lies in the east of the state and is a good base from which to explore the Great Smoky Mountains National Park (see entry). It was the first capital of the state, as is evidenced in the Governor William Blount Mansion of 1792. Other features of interest are General James White's Fort (1786) and the Confederate Memorial Hall, which recalls the siege of the city during the Civil War.

Oak Ridge

22 miles/35km west of Knoxville is Oak Ridge, which along with Alamo (see Santa Fe, Surroundings) was involved in the development of the atom bomb. It is still an important centre of nuclear research. The National Laboratory's graphite reactor produced uranium in the form required for the bomb (exhibition). The National Museum of Science and Energy illustrates and explains the development of atomic energy.

*Land between the Lakes

The Land between the Lakes, on the border with Kentucky, was developed by the Tennessee Valley Authority as an extensive recreation area with ample scope for hiking, bathing and various sports. Visitors can also observe a herd of bison and see two museum villages of 1800 and 1850.

Other places of interest

Cumberland Gap National Historic Park (see Kentucky), Great Smoky Mountains National Park, Memphis, Nashville (see entries).

Texas (State; TX)   N–Y 19–32

Area: 267,340sq.miles/
692,405sq.km
Population: 17,348,000
Capital: Austin
Popular name: Lone Star State

Situation and topography

Texas (from an Indian word meaning "friend"), the largest state in the USA after Alaska, consists of three main regions: the Gulf Coast plain, the Great

Plains and the Rocky Mountains. The state extends from the Red River in the north to the Rio Grande in the south and the Gulf of Mexico in the south-east. Characteristic features of the 375 mile/600km long Gulf Coast are the series of coastal lagoons separated from the open sea by long spits of land. To the north-west of the coastal plain are the Great Plains, with hills rising to around 3300ft/1000m, and in the west of the state are the foothills of the Rockies, rising to 8750ft/2667m in the Guadalupe Peak. Here there is a mingling of the landscape pattern of the Great Plains with that of the Cordilleras – deeply indented valleys, canyons, plateaux, volcanic hills and a wide scarpland, all found within a relatively small area.

While in the eastern part of the state a subtropical climate predominates, the climate in the south-west is desertic. Throughout the state there may be periods of intense heat (over 100°F/38°C) in summer and of frost in winter. In the arid regions there are mesquite trees, in the upland areas pines, firs, junipers and oaks; along the rivers, which in their middle and upper courses flow only at certain times of year, there are hickories and cypresses. The characteristic vegetation cover of the Great Plains is grassland, which becomes increasingly scanty towards the west. There are only remnants of the pine and oak forests which once covered the coastal plain.

The coast of Texas was sighted in 1519 by the Spanish navigator Alonso Alvarez de Piñeda, and in 1528 Alvar Núñez Cabeza de Vaca was shipwrecked at what is now Galveston and spent several years exploring the territory. The first permanent Spanish settlements were established only at the end of the 17th century. In 1821 control of the area passed to Mexico. American settlers led by Moses and Stephen F. Austin rebelled against the Mexican government at the end of 1835 and after their victory at San Jacinto in the following year proclaimed the independent republic of Texas. On December 29th 1845 Texas was admitted to the Union as the 28th state. This led to the American–Mexican War, at the end of which the treaty of Guadalupe Hidalgo (1848) laid down the frontier between Mexico and the United States on broadly the present line. During the Civil War Texas fought on the Confederate side. After the war the cattle barons with their huge herds dominated the region and provided the nation's meat supply. The end of the great cattle-rearing era came with the development of cattle-ranching in other states and the discovery of oil in Texas.

History

Texas is one of the USA's leading agricultural states. Almost 30% of its cultivated land is planted with cotton. On the irrigated land of the coastal plain the principal crop is rice, grown in the valley of the Rio Grande. Stock farming (cattle, and also pigs) is still important. In output of minerals (oil, natural gas, graphite, sulphur, magnesium chloride, salt, gypsum, etc.) Texas takes the leading place among American states, and as a result it also has huge oil refineries and a large petro-chemicals industry. The existence of space travel research institutes, mainly in Houston, has led to the development of a strong electronics industry. Other important branches of industry are foodstuffs, engineering and automobile construction. Many big firms, banks, insurance corporations and research institutions have established themselves in Texas.

Economy

The state's grandiose desert landscapes, forest-covered mountains and steppes, and the Gulf Coast plain with its beaches, lakes and rivers offer endless scope for recreation and holidays, earning Texas fourth place among the states in the tourism statistics.

Places of Interest in Texas

Brownsville, the most southerly town in Texas, is connected with the Caribbean by a 17 mile/27km long channel. The American–Mexican War began here on May 8th 1846, as is documented on the Palo Alto Battlefield National Historic Site; and the last battle of the Civil War was fought on the Pallmitto Ranch Battlefield on May 12th and 13th 1865.

Brownsville

Tucson

Within easy reach of Brownsville, beyond the Rio Grande, is the Mexican town of Matamoros.

Corpus Christi The little port of Corpus Christi, on an inlet to the north of Brownsville, has two features of interest: the Texas State Aquarium and the Art Museum of South Texas. From here it is a short distance to the beaches on the Gulf Coast.

*Padre Island National Seashore Padre Island, to the south of Corpus Christi has very beautiful beaches and dunes which are home to 350 different species of birds.

Kingsville South-west of Corpus Christi is Kingsville, where visitors can see the ranch established in 1853 by Richard King, one of the cattle barons.

*El Paso At the western tip of Texas, on the left bank of the Rio Grande, which here forms the frontier with Mexico, is El Paso, the largest American city on the Mexican frontier, with a population of over half a million. On the opposite bank of the river is the Mexican city of Ciudad Juárez. A notable feature of the city is Fort Bliss, occupying the site of a military post established in 1846 and now one of the largest air defence centres in the world, in which soldiers from allied nations are trained. On the site there are three military museums. The El Paso Museum of Art has a fine collection of pre-Columbian and Indian art and the Kress Collection (works of the Italian Renaissance). The Chamizal National Memorial, a beautiful park on the banks of the Rio Grande, commemorates the settlement of the long-standing dispute over the frontier line between the United States and Mexico.

*Mission Trail The Mission Trail, starting from El Paso, leads to a number of former Spanish mission stations in Texas: the Mission Ysleta, the oldest in Texas, established in 1681 as the mission of Nuestra Señora del Carmen; the Mission Socorro, founded in 1682 and moved to its present site after an Indian rising; and San Elizario, with the Spanish garrison church of 1777.

Fredericksburg Fredericksburg, north-west of San Antonio (see entry), was founded in 1846 by German settlers, who left their mark on the town, as can be seen from a number of old houses and the reconstructed Vereins Kirche of 1847.

Langtry Langtry, on the banks of the Rio Grande in western Texas, exemplifies the wildest of the Wild West. Here for 21 years the self-elected Judge Roy Bean, proprietor of a saloon in the town, applied his ideas of law, advertising in the sign above his saloon "ice-cold beer and the law west of Pecos". The saloon is now a museum.

Laredo Laredo, on the Rio Grande at the southern tip of Texas, was briefly capital of the Republic of Rio Grande. Evidence of its former status is provided by the adobe Capitol and a museum in the historic district of the town.

Waco Waco, 2 hours' drive south of Fort Worth, was a centre of the secessionists of Texas. Bailey University, the oldest university in Texas, was founded here in 1845. The Texas Ranger Hall of Fame and Museum charts the history of this legendary police corps. The town hit the headlines in 1993, when police and troops stormed the stronghold of a militant sect.

Other places of interest Austin (see San Antonio), Big Bend National Park, Dallas (see entries), Fort Worth (see Dallas), Galveston (see Houston), Guadalupe Mountains (see Carlsbad Caverns), Houston, San Antonio (see entries).

Tucson R 15

State: Arizona
Altitude: 2420ft/740m
Population: 406,000

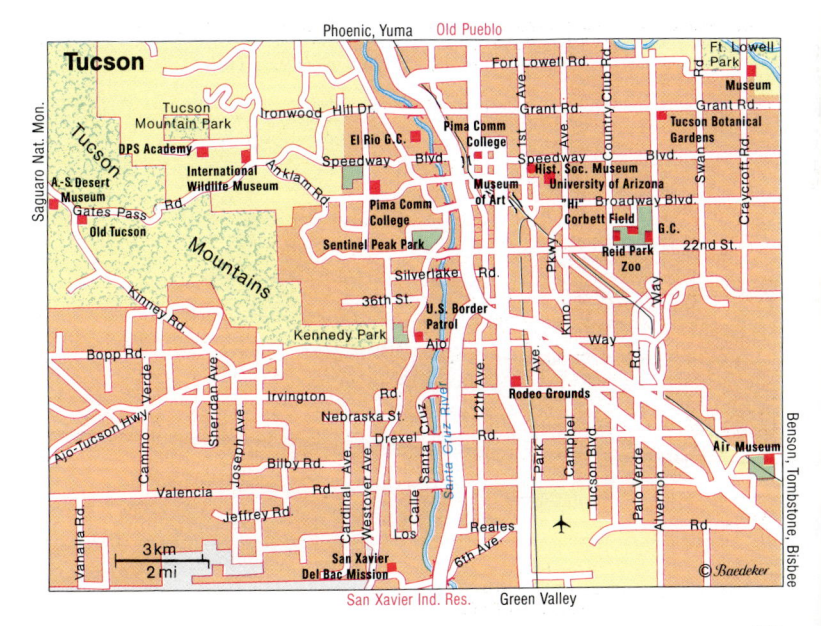

Tucson

Tucson, the "City of Sunshine" and metropolis of the desert-like region of south-eastern Arizona, lies in the wide valley, flanked by high hills, of the Santa River. The main pillars of the local economy in the past were the railway workshops, foodstuffs and textile firms and cattle-rearing. In the surrounding area copper, silver, lead and other minerals are mined. Lucrative irrigated farming (citrus fruits, winter vegetables, cotton) has also developed in the immediate surroundings of the city. In recent years, too, various high-tech industries (anti-aircraft missiles, electronics, etc.) have been established. The warm, dry climate has long attracted tourists, convalescents and people seeking an escape from winter in less favoured areas.

Situation and characteristics

A Jesuit mission station was established here at the end of the 17th century. In the 18th century a permanent settlement was founded which in 1857 became a posting station on the route from San Antonio in Texas to San Diego in California. In the second half of the 19th century Tucson was for a time capital of the territory of Arizona. The construction of the Southern Pacific Railroad increased the importance of the town, in which the University of Arizona was founded in 1891. After the Second World War Tucson developed at an explosive pace, its population rising from 46,000 in 1950 to six times as much in the mid seventies.

History

Sights in Tucson

The El Presidio Historic District with its adobe houses dating from the colonial period has been lovingly renovated. The Museum of Art, housed in six restored buildings, has a rich collection which includes contemporary art and applied art. In the Casa Cordova is the Mexican Heritage Museum.

*El Presidio Historic District

At 151 S. Granada Avenue, in the Community Center complex, is Frémont House, an attractive adobe building of about 1880 which is now a museum run by the Arizona Historical Society.

Frémont House

Tucson

University of Arizona
On the campus of the renowned University of Arizona are the Arizona State Museum, the Mineralogical Museum, the Center for Creative Photography and a fine art collection belonging to the Faculty of Arts. Here too is the Flandreau Planetarium.

*Arizona State Museum
With its large archaeological collection the Arizona State Museum documents 10,000 years of Indian cultural history.

*Mission San Xavier del Bac
This mission station in the south-west of the city was established by Spanish Jesuits in 1770. The mission buildings, in particular the richly furnished church, are fine examples of the Baroque architecture of the colonial period.

Surroundings of Tucson

Mount Lemmon
To the north of the city is Mount Lemmon (9157ft/2791m), which has excellent facilities for winter sports. On its eastern slopes are the Spencer Canyon and the Rose Canyon.

*Biosphere 2
35 miles/56 miles north of Tucson is the giant glass structure known as Biosphere 2, an artificially created, self-maintaining habitat in which four women and four men lived from 1991 to 1993 completely shut off from the outside world, wholly dependent for air, water and food on the productive capacity of this artificial miniature world. Seven "biomes" (tropical rain forest, savanna, desert, lagoon, coral reef, mud-flats, shallow sea, deep sea with poor light) in which over 3500 species of plants and animals were established helped to show that human beings can live a healthy life without destroying their environment.
The project, financed by the billionaire Ed Bass and directed by the scientist John Allen, is planned over a period of a hundred years. Every two years a new team is to inhabit the "biggest test-tube in the world".

Wild West locomotive, Old Tucson

13 miles/20km west of Tucson is Tucson Mountain Park, with a Desert Museum and the reconstructed Western town of Old Tucson. — Tucson Mountain Park

The little Western town of Old Tucson, in the style of the late 19th century, was reconstructed in 1940 as the setting for numerous Western films. Wild shoot-ups are re-enacted here by actors (open: daily 9am–9pm). — *Old Tucson

The Arizona-Sonora Desert Museum is a "living museum" in which desert plants and animals can be seen in their natural habitat. — *Arizona-Sonora Desert Museum

45 miles/73km south-west of Tucson, on Kitt Peak, high in the mountains of the Sonora Desert, is the Kitt Peak Observatory, one of the most important astronomical stations in the world, with 18 telescopes, including a giant solar telescope, and a museum (open: daily 9am–3.45pm; guided visits 1.30pm). — *Kitt Peak National Observatory

20 miles/32km south of Tucson, in Green Valley, is the Titan Missile Museum, where visitors can see Titan II missiles, missile mechanisms, helicopters and a missile silo. — Titan Missile Museum

46 miles/75km south of Tucson is the Tumacacori National Monument, a Franciscan mission station which was abandoned in 1848, with a beautiful church and patio and an interesting museum. — Tumacacori National Monument

US Virgin Islands   Not on map

Political status: US Organised Incorporated Territory
Area: 133sq.miles/344sq.km
Population: 111,000
Capital: Charlotte Amalie, on St Thomas

The US Virgin Islands, lying to the east of Puerto Rico (see entry) in the Lesser Antilles, are the south-western part of the Virgin Islands group, the north-eastern part of which is a British crown colony. In addition to the main islands of St Croix, St Thomas and St John the archipelago contains some 50 smaller islets and reefs.
The pleasant tropical climate, excellent sailing, deep-sea angling and diving, beautiful bathing beaches and duty-free shopping attract thousands of American and European visitors annually. Tourism is the islands' main source of revenue, but contributions are also made to the economy by sugar-cane growing and stock-farming. — Situation and topography

The US Virgin Islands were discovered by Columbus on his second voyage in 1493. Originally colonised by British and Danish settlers, the islands were bought from Denmark by the United States in 1817 for 25 million dollars. The inhabitants are American citizens but have no vote in US elections. — History

Places of Interest in the US Virgin Islands

The description of the US Virgin Islands in this guide is abridged, since there is a detailed account in the AA/Baedeker guide "Caribbean".

The largest of the islands is St Croix, with an area of 83sq.miles/214sq.km. The chief places on the island are Christiansted and Fredriksted. A rewarding excursion from Christiansted is a trip in a glass-bottomed boat to little Buck Island, the only underwater National Park in the United States.
In the Salt River National Park on the north coast of St Croix is the largest mangrove swamp in the US Virgin Islands. — St Croix

Two-thirds of St John, which has an area of only 19sq.miles/50sq.km, is a National Park. The chief place is Cruz Bay, from which there are magnificent — St John

Utah

drives round the island, still relatively unspoiled. Offshore are excellent diving grounds.

St Thomas — On St Thomas (area 31sq.miles/80sq.km) is Charlotte Amalie, the chief place on the US Virgin Islands. The island is a favourite port of call for cruise ships operating in the Caribbean.

Utah (State; UT) H–M 12–16

Area:
84,900sq.miles/219,890sq.km
Population: 1,771,000
Capital: Salt Lake City
Popular name: Beehive State

Situation and topography

The state of Utah (named after the Ute tribe) lies in the western United States in the intermontane upland region, extending into the cold arid desert of the Great Basin, with the Great Salt Lake. Central Utah is occupied by the western foothills of the Rocky Mountains, the Wasatch Range and the Uinta Mountains (Kings Peak, 13,528ft/4123m). The Colorado Plateau to the south thrust upward only in geologically recent times, so that the Colorado River and its tributaries were able to cut their way through the rock, forming deep, narrow gorges and steep-sided canyons in which the sedimentary strata with their variegated colouring are exposed. In the desert regions and on the salt soils only plants adapted to the arid conditions, such as the silver-green sagebrush and the creosote bush, can survive. There is forest cover only in the wetter mountain regions.

History

The first Europeans to travel through the region, then occupied by Ute, Paiute and Shoshone Indians, at the end of the 18th century were Spanish Franciscans, later followed by trappers. Permanent settlement began only in 1847, when the Mormons, led by Brigham Young, reached the Great Salt Lake and founded Salt Lake City. From Salt Lake City they moved out into the surrounding area, cultivating the land and establishing new settlements. The gold rush and the discovery of the region's rich mineral resources led to a sharp increase in population, but it was only on January 4th 1896, after the abolition of polygamy, that the Mormon state was admitted to the Union as its 45th member. Some 70% of all inhabitants of Utah are now Mormons.

Economy

The cultivation of the desert steppeland of the Great Salt Lake Valley was made possible only by irrigation. The principal crops are wheat, sugar-beet and fruit, and there is also much extensive stock-farming. The rich mineral resources of the region include copper (with the world's largest opencast mine in Bingham Canyon), silver, lead and various other metals. The principal industries are ore-smelting, foodstuffs and engineering. The main tourist attractions are the extraordinary landscapes of the various National Parks; the towns, apart from Salt Lake City, are of less tourist importance.

Places of Interest in Utah

*Cedar Breaks National Monument

The same forces of nature that shaped Bryce Canyon were at work also in Cedar Breaks, in south-western Utah, creating a smaller but even more colourful rocky landscape in the form of a gigantic amphitheatre. The best views are to be had from the Rim Drive.

Vermont

In the south-west corner of the state is St George, where Brigham Young spent the winter. Some 17,000 tons of sandstone were used in the Mormon Temple here, and timber had to be brought from 80 miles away. St George owes its popular name of Dixie to the cotton grown in the area.

St George

Arches National Park, Bryce Canyon National Park, Canyonlands National Park, Dinosaur National Monument, Monument Valley, Navajo Country, Salt Lake City, Zion National Park (see entries).

Other places of interest

Vermont (State; VT)   D–G 52–55

Area:
9610sq.miles/24,888sq.km
Population: 567,000
Capital: Montpelier
Popular name: Green Mountain State

The state of Vermont (from French *vert mont*, "green mountain") in the north-eastern United States, between New York State and New Hampshire, extends from the valley of Lake Champlain (125 miles/200km long) in the north-west to the Connecticut River, which forms its eastern boundary. Between them are the Green Mountains which give the state its name – a range in the northern Appalachians, striking from north to south, which reaches its highest point in Mount Mansfield (4393ft/1339m). The cool temperate climate, with heavy snow in the mountains, is continental in character. Almost two-thirds of the state's area is covered with mixed forests.

Situation and topography

In 1609, during a French campaign against the Iroquois, Samuel de Champlain discovered the lake in north-western Vermont which was later named after him. The first American settlers established themselves in the area in 1724. In 1777 Vermont ratified its first constitution – the first constitution of an American state to ban slavery. On March 4th 1791 it joined the Union as the 14th state (the first "non-founding" state).

History

Industrial production in Vermont is concentrated mainly on engineering, the manufacture of electronic parts, foodstuffs, woodworking and papermaking. Agriculture (dairy farming, fruit, potatoes and fodder plants) is practised mainly in the river valleys and the Lake Champlain depression. One of the favourite souvenirs brought back from Vermont by visitors is maple syrup.
Tourism is an important source of income, particularly in the mountain regions.

Economy

Places of Interest in Vermont

The little town of Bennington lies in the extreme south-west of Vermont. The Bennington Battle Monument commemorates a battle during the War of Independence. Other features of interest are a number of handsome 18th century buildings and the Bennington Museum (pictures, etc.).

Bennington

Burlington (pop. 38,000), the largest town in Vermont and the seat of a university, lies in a beautiful setting on the shores of Lake Champlain. The lively town centre offers excellent shopping facilities (for example in the historic Church Street Marketplace). Other features of interest are a branch of the Vermont State Craft Center, the Discovery Museum for children and young people and the memorial museum for the folk hero Ethan Allen.

*Burlington/
Lake Champlain

Virginia

Killington	The village of Killington, to the west of Rutland, has developed in recent years into one of the largest skiing centres in the southern Green Mountains. The main pistes are on the slopes of Killington Peak and Pico Peak.
Manchester	Manchester, in southern Vermont, is a popular holiday resort (walking in summer and skiing in winter).
Middlebury	19 miles/30km south of Burlington is Middlebury, which has preserved an attractive old town centre. Features of interest are two small museums on the history of the town and the Vermont State Craft Center, which has a permanent exhibition of Vermont arts and crafts.
Montpelier	Montpelier is the smallest state capital in the United States, with a population of just under 10,000. Features of interest are the State House, the Vermont Museum (history of the state) and the Kent Museum (local life and life-style).
*Shelburne	Shelburne, 3 miles/5km south of Burlington, is well worth a visit for the sake of the Shelburne Museum alone. This large and unusual open-air museum is a reconstruction of an old village with all its buildings and services, including a railroad station and a paddle-steamer.
St Johnsbury	In St Johnsbury, the largest township in rural north-eastern Vermont, the famous Vermont maple syrup can be bought from the factory. The Fairbanks Museum of Natural Sciences and Planetarium offers visitors an excursion into the Victorian past.
Stowe	The attractive old village of Stowe, beautifully situated at the foot of Vermont's highest hill, Mount Mansfield (4393ft/1339m), is now the state's leading winter sports centre.
Woodstock	The idyllic village of Woodstock, situated on US 4 between Rutland and White River Junction, attracts many visitors with its old-world beauty. On the northern outskirts of the village is Billings Farm and Museum, which re-creates everyday life on the farm around 1900.

Virginia (State; VA)   K–N 42–50

Area:
   40,815sq.miles/105,715sq.km
Population: 6,286,000
Capital: Richmond
Popular name: Old Dominion

Situation and topography	Virginia (named after Elizabeth I, the Virgin Queen), one of the 13 founding states, lies on the middle Atlantic coast of the United States. Here the Atlantic, in the form of Chesapeake Bay, advances deep into the mainland, whose rugged coastline is indented by the broad estuaries of the Potomac, Rappahannock, York and James Rivers. To the west the landscape merges into the gently undulating Piedmont Plateau, which in turn rises gradually into the Blue Ridge Mountains. Beyond this range of hills are the valleys of Virginia, including the beautiful Shenandoah Valley. Virginia has an oceanic climate with warm summers.
History	Virginia, which was the scene of the first permanent British settlement in North America (Jamestown, founded in 1607) and joined the Union as the tenth state on June 25th 1788, played a unique role in the history of the United States. The great leaders of the independence movement – Patrick

Virginia

Henry, George Washington, Thomas Jefferson, George Mason and James Madison – all came from Virginia, and the Declaration of Independence, the Bill of Rights and the Constitution were written here. But Virginia was also a centre of the movement for secession. Jefferson Davis, President of the Confederation, and the Southern general Robert E. Lee also came from Virginia; almost half of all the battles and skirmishes of the Civil War were fought within the state; and finally the surrender of the Confederation was signed here on April 8th 1865.

Virginia's principal industrial products are textiles, automobiles and automobile parts, and electrical and electronic apparatus. Shipbuilding plays a major part in the Norfolk/Portsmouth/Hampton/Newport News conurbation. The most important elements in the state's economy, however, are commerce and the services sector – largely because of the numerous government departments round the federal capital, Washington DC. The main crops grown on the Piedmont Plateau are tobacco, soya beans and peanuts; apples are grown on both sides of the Blue Ridge Mountains, where there is also a productive dairy farming industry. For the tourist Virginia offers a great variety of historic towns and sites.

Economy

Places of Interest in Virginia

In Appomattox Court House, near the little town of that name in western Virginia, on April 9th 1865, the Northern general Ulysses S. Grant and the Confederate leader General Robert E. Lee negotiated the surrender of the Southern army and thus ended the Civil War.

Appomattox Court House National Historic Park

The Blue Ridge Parkway winds its way through the states of Virginia and North Carolina along the Blue Ridge Mountains, the southern outliers of the Appalachians, for a distance of 469 miles/750km. This tourist route

*Blue Ridge Parkway

Peak of Otter, on the Blue Ridge Parkway   *Stalactitic formation in the Luray Caverns*

Washington

(maximum speed 45 mph) begins at Rockfish Gap (milepost 0), on the south side of Shenandoah National Park (see entry), and ends on the edge of the Great Smoky Mountains (see entry), in Cherokee territory. All along the route there are overwhelming views of the dense forests with their variety of wild life and of the valley below; some signs of human settlement can also be seen, such as Mabry Mill (milepost 176; illustration, p. 561). For those with time at their disposal there is magnificent walking on way-marked trails along the way.

Chesapeake Bay Bridge
: The eastern shore of Chesapeake Bay is linked with the Norfolk area by a gigantic feat of engineering, the 17.6 mile/28.2km long Chesapeake Bay Bridge and Tunnel.

Fredericksburg
: Mary Washington, George Washington's mother, lived and died in Fredericksburg, on the Rappahannock River, and James Monroe, fifth President of the United States, also lived here for some time; they are commemorated in Mary Washington House and the James Monroe Museum. Between December 1862 and May 1864 the four fiercest battles of the Civil War were fought in the surrounding area. The battlefields are part of the Fredericksburg and Spotsylvania National Military Park.

George Washington Birthplace
: George Washington was born in 1732 on the estate of Popes Creek, on the banks of the Potomac (east of Fredericksburg on VA 3). The house in which he was born no longer exists, but his life story is vividly presented in an 18th century farmhouse.

Hampton
: On a tongue of land between the York and James Rivers is Hampton, founded in 1610 – the oldest British foundation in the United States which has remained continuously occupied. Features of particular interest are the Virginia Air and Space Center (aircraft, Apollo 12 capsule), St John's Church (1728; liturgical vessels of 1618) and Fort Monroe (where Jefferson Davis, President of the Confederation, was confined after the Civil War), with the Casemate Museum, in which the first naval battle between steam-powered armourclads (the Northern "Monitor" and the Southern "Virginia", formerly the "Merrimac"), fought during the Civil War in Hampton Roads, between Hampton and Norfolk, is fully documented.

*Luray Caverns
: In the Shenandoah Valley (US 211 West) are the Luray Caverns, with magnificent stalactitic formations, including the only stalactite organ in the world.

Norfolk
: Norfolk, which is linked with Hampton by a massive bridge and tunnel structure over the Hampton Roads, is one of the most important ports on the eastern seaboard and the largest naval base in the world (bus tours, Apr.–Oct., starting from Tour and Information Office; harbour cruises). Also of interest is the large Naval Museum. To the east of the town is the very popular Virginia Beach.

Other places of interest
: Alexandria, Arlington (see Washington DC), Charlottesville, Colonial National Historical Park (see entries), Monticello (see Charlottesville), Jamestown (see Colonial National Historical Park), Mount Vernon (see Washington DC), Richmond, Shenandoah National Park (see entries), Williamsburg, Yorktown (see Colonial National Historical Park).

Washington (State; WA)   A–D 1–9

Area: 68,140sq.miles/176,480sq.km
Population: 5,018,000
Capital: Olympia
Popular name: Evergreen State

Washington

Situation and topography

Washington State, in the extreme north-west of the United States, is divided by the Cascade Range into two different climatic zones – a wetter western half, with the Coast Range, and a drier eastern half, with the shallow Puget Sound. Numerous snow- and ice-covered volcanic peaks, including Mount Rainier (14,410ft/4392m), dominate the Cascade Range, which is flanked on the east by the Columbia Basin and on the north-east by the mighty Rockies. The mountains are covered by forests of spruce and Douglas fir, while the vegetation of the Columbia Plateau is of prairie type.

History

The coastal region and the Columbia River were first explored by Spanish and American seamen towards the end of the 18th century. A British captain, John Vancouver, built the fort which bears his name and thus laid the foundations of the profitable fur trade. After the settlement of a dispute between Britain and the United States over the line of the frontier the territory was for a time under joint British–American administration and was finally assigned to the United States in 1848. It was given its present boundaries when Idaho was hived off in 1863, and was admitted to the Union as the 42nd state on November 11th 1889.

Economy

The main branches of the manufacturing sector are the aerospace industries (Boeing, in Seattle), foodstuffs, shipbuilding and aluminium production. The state's agriculture specialises in the growing of wheat, hops, fruit and vegetables and in dairy farming. Thanks to the cool California Current with its abundance of fish the state has a thriving fishing industry. Tourism is concentrated on the Mount Rainier, Olympic and North Cascades National Parks and on the Pacific beaches. The fjord landscape of Puget Sound is particularly attractive.

Places of Interest in Washington State

Coolee City/ Grand Coulee Dam

At the Dry Falls to the south of Coulee City, in the heart of the state, it can be seen how the Columbia River plunged down here for over 300ft/100m over a breadth of 2¾ miles/4.5km before glacial action forced it into a new course. 26 miles/42km north-east the hand of man can be seen at work in the Grand Coulee Dam, which returns part of the river to its old bed.

Lake Chelan

Lake Chelan, which lies between Wenatchee National Forest and Okoanogan National Forest, in the Cascade Mountains, is a happy hunting ground for anglers and water sports enthusiasts alike.

**Mt St Helens National Volcanic Monument

The eruption of Mount St Helens, in the south-west of Washington State, on May 18th 1980 made headlines around the world. A cloud of ash rose 13 miles/21km into the air, almost 150sq.miles/400sq.km of forest were destroyed, houses were overwhelmed by masses of water and mud, and 57 people lost their lives. The mountain itself lost 1300ft/400m in height, and in place of its summit there is now a crater over 2000ft/600m deep. In the area around the volcano, which was declared a National Monument in 1982, visitors are given a unique demonstration of the destructive power of the eruption and can observe the gradual return of animal and plant life. The eruption and its effects are explained in the Information Center in Seaquest State Park.

*North Cascades National Park

The North Cascades National Park in the north of the state, on the Canadian frontier, attracts numbers of anglers, hikers and lovers of unspoiled nature.

Olympia

The main features of interest in Olympia, the state capital, situated on Puget Sound, are the State Capitol and the State Museum. The town also has a number of attractive parks.

483

Washington DC

The Columbia River, separating Washington and Oregon

Spokane	Spokane, in the centre of a farming area, lies in the east of the state, on the border with Idaho. Features of interest are the Museum of Native American Cultures and the Cheney Cowles Museum (local history). There are a number of wineries which offer wine-tastings, and there is skiing on Mount Spokane.
Vancouver	Vancouver, lying directly on the border with Oregon, is the oldest town in the state. The fur-trading post of Fort Vancouver has been partly reconstructed.
Walla Walla	In the south-eastern corner of the state is Walla Walla, an old Indian hunting ground and later a fur-trading fort and a pioneer town. Here Dr Marcus Whitman, the first white settler in the North-West and the only doctor on the Oregon Trail, established himself in 1836. On the site of his house are a memorial and a museum.
Yakima	Yakima, in south central Washington, is named after the Yakima tribe, whose customs and way of life are illustrated in the Yakima Valley Museum and Yakima Nation Indian Cultural Center.
Gingko State Park	North-east of Yakima, near Vantage, are the petrified forests of Gingko State Park.
Other places of interest	Mount Rainier National Park, Olympic National Park, Seattle (see entries).

Washington DC   L 48

District of Columbia
Altitude: 0–410ft/0–125m
Population: 606,900 (Metropolitan Area 3.75 million)

Washington DC

Situation and characteristics

Roughly half way down the Atlantic coast of North America, at the junction of the Anacostia and Potomac Rivers, is Washington DC (District of Columbia), federal capital of the United States, situated on the left bank of the Potomac. The city is the central element in a conurbation with a population of 3.75 million which also includes five counties in Maryland and five in Virginia, in which the hundreds of thousands of federal employees live. Almost 70% of the inhabitants of Washington are Afro-Americans, who live mainly in the south-western, south-eastern and north-eastern quadrants of the city, while the north-western quadrant is mainly occupied by whites. Behind the sumptuous façade of Washington, within a short distance of the Capitol, is another world of poverty and unemployment.

The city was founded and built for one purpose alone, to provide an independent place for the work of government. The site selected, 100 miles/160km above the outflow of the Potomac into Chesapeake Bay, has a climate which does not make work particularly agreeable in summer, when it is so hot and sultry that most of the staff take off their jackets except when they are working in their air-conditioned offices. Accordingly the best times for a visit to Washington are spring and autumn.

Washington DC strikes visitors as an untypical American city, for there are no skyscrapers, which indeed are prohibited by law. The townscape of Washington is one of classical-style buildings, some of them of giant size, laid out along the avenues of enormous width which have earned Washington the name of the "city of magnificent distances". Most of the 20 million people who visit Washington annually are Americans anxious to see the incarnation of American democracy in stone and the sites which are so familiar to them from schooldays and television. Foreign visitors may be surprised to discover how freely accessible – though strictly controlled – even such sensitive areas of government as the Capitol are. They will also find an abundance of museums, some of which are among the most important of their kind in the world.

**Capital of the United States

Washington DC is the seat of Congress (the Senate and the House of Representatives) and of the President of the United States. Over 350,000 people – from drivers to the White House Chief of Staff – are employed by the Administration, and tens of thousands more work in various national and international organisations (the World Bank, the Organisation of American States, the International Monetary Fund) based in Washington, as lobbyists or in various services dependent on government.

Washington has little industry, but there are in the city, in addition to five universities, various research institutes and laboratories concerned with electronics, space travel and armament projects, so that Washington's population has the highest percentage of qualified researchers of any American city. The city's second most important source of revenue – after the work of government – is tourism.

Culture

Culture is represented in Washington by theatres like the National Theatre and orchestras like the National Symphony Orchestra, housed in the extensive John F. Kennedy Center for the Performing Arts. More important, and perhaps of more interest to visitors, are the city's numerous museums, headed by the National Gallery and the Smithsonian Institution. Washington also has the National Archives and the Library of Congress, the largest library in the world. Nor should the culinary world be forgotten: the city's eating-places range from the hamburger stand by way of a variety of foreign cuisines to gourmet French restaurants.

History

After breaking away from Britain in 1776 the young United States had at first no capital and in consequence Congress met in eight different places. In 1789 New York became the capital, but a year later gave place to Philadelphia. Congress then passed the Residence Act, which provided for the establishment of a 10-mile square Federal District responsible only to Congress, and authorised President George Washington to select a site for the new capital. Washington chose an area on the Potomac River near his

Washington DC

country house of Mount Vernon and commissioned Major Pierre-Charles L'Enfant (1754–1825), an officer of French origin who had been dismissed for insubordination, to prepare a plan.

L'Enfant's plan provided for two commanding buildings as "poles" of the layout, the Congress House (Capitol) and the Presidential Palace (White House), to be linked by a wide avenue. By 1800 the Presidential Palace and the Capitol were so far advanced that Congress was able to meet and President John Adams to take up residence in the new buildings in August. Washington suffered a severe setback, however, in 1814, during the British–American war, when British troops took the city and burned down the Capitol and the White House. For many years the new capital was to remain a wish rather than a reality, and Virginia was able to take back the land which it had made over on the right bank of the Potomac.

It was only after the Civil War and the influx of tens of thousands of former slaves that fresh stimulus was given to the development of the capital, mainly due to the energy of Alexander "Boss" Shepherd, and L'Enfant's plans were brought out again. The Washington Memorial, which had been begun in 1848, was completed in 1884, and the much derided city, less than half finished, gradually became the imposing capital of the United States. The appointment in 1901 of the MacMillan Commission on the development of Washington, an Act of 1915 which laid down limits on the height of buildings, the Public Building Act of 1926 (which provided for the construction of magnificent new government buildings), the influx of government officials during the two world wars, the restoration of Pennsylvania

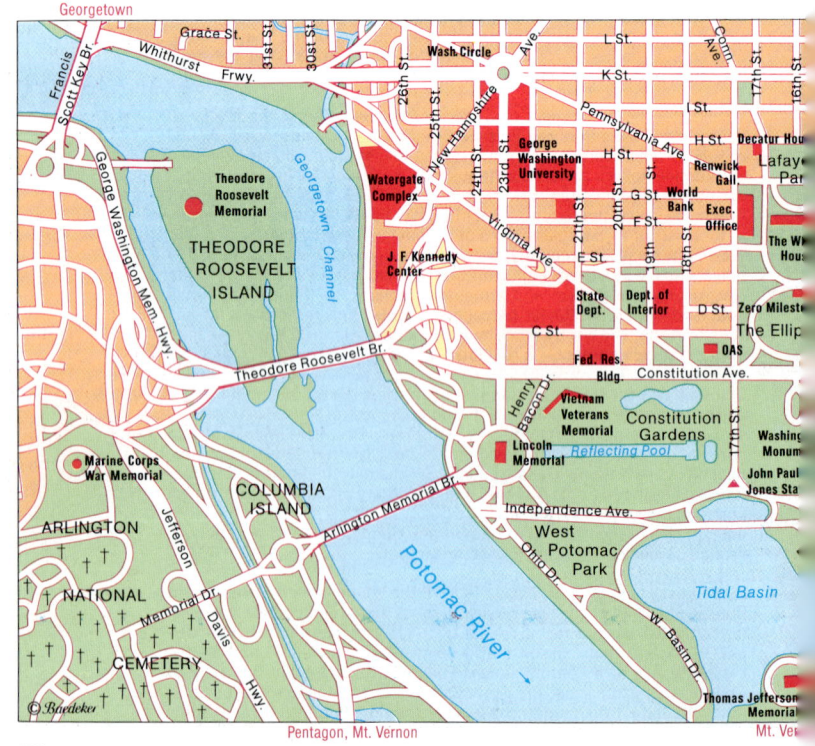

Washington DC

Avenue during the Presidency of John F. Kennedy and the opening of the Metrorail system in 1976 were further milestones in the development of the city. Since 1961 citizens of Washington have been able to take part in the election of the President.

Sights in Washington DC

The townscape of Washington today largely reflects L'Enfant's ideas. The Capitol and the White House are set in a network of streets intersecting at right angles, across which cut thirteen diagonal avenues named after the thirteen founding states. From the Capitol four streets radiate to the points of the compass, dividing the city into four quadrants – Northwest (NW), Northeast (NE), South-west (SW) and Southeast (SE). The north–south streets are numbered, the east–west streets named after the letters of the alphabet. A special position is occupied by the wide Mall running between Capitol Hill and the Lincoln Memorial, which was designed to open up the layout of the capital.

Layout of the city

The principal tourist sights lie almost exclusively in the north-western quadrant, along the Mall and in the immediately surrounding area, and can be seen on foot. The three other quadrants are of little interest and are areas not without danger, certainly not to be visited after dark.

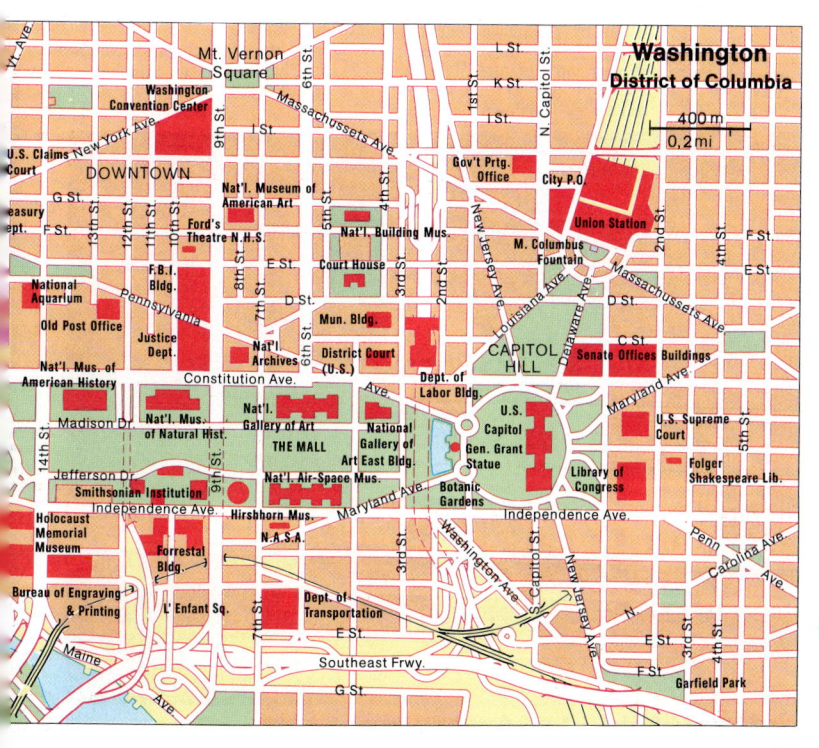

487

Washington DC

Capitol Hill

**Capitol

Daily 9am–4.30pm,
Easter–Labor Day
to 8pm;
guided visits
9am–3.45pm

At the east end of the Mall, commandingly situated on the 100ft/30m high Capitol Hill, is the United States Capitol, seat of the House of Representatives and the Senate. The first building erected by William Thornton between 1793 and 1812, the present Senate Wing, was burned down by the British in 1814. Reconstruction was carried out in several stages: the central block was rebuilt by Latrobe and Bulfinch in 1829, following Thornton's plans; the side wings and the 270ft/82m high dome, modelled on the dome of St Peter's in Rome and crowned by an allegory of Freedom, were built between 1851 and 1865 to the design of Thomas Walter; and finally in 1958–62 the main façade, in front of which each President takes the oath, was enlarged. The Capitol faces east, since it was originally thought that the city would develop in that direction. As a result the Capitol turns its back on the main part of the present city – though it is perhaps some compensation that there is a splendid marble terrace on the rear front which affords a marvellous view of the Mall.

Interior

The interior of the Capitol is as busy as an ant-heap, swarming with Congressmen, lobbyists, security officers and tourists. The entrance on the main floor leads through heavy bronze doors with scenes from the life of Columbus into the Rotunda, under the great cast-iron dome with a ceiling painting of the Apotheosis of Washington (by Constantino Brumidi, 1865). On the walls are huge paintings of scenes from the history of North America. On the south side of the Rotunda is the former Chamber of the House of Representatives, since 1864 the National Hall of Statuary, in which each state has the right to set up statues of two of its leading citizens (some now displayed on the lower floor).

On the north side of the central Rotunda is the small Senate Rotunda, leading into the finely restored Old Senate Chamber in which the Senate met from 1810 to 1859, followed until 1935 by the Supreme Court. Spiral staircases lead down to the lower floor, on which are an interesting exhibi-

The Capitol of the United States in Washington DC

Washington DC

United States Capitol — Principal Floor

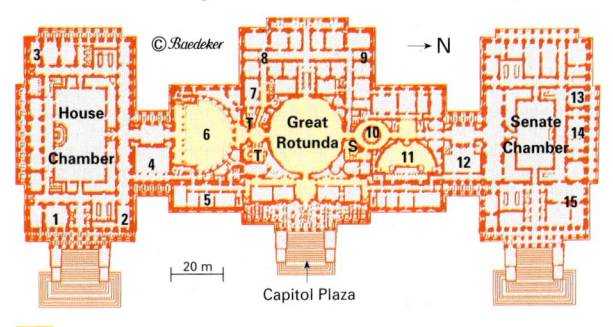

Open to public

1 Speaker's Formal Office
2 Ways and Means Committee
3 Committee on Appropriations
4 House Reception Room
5 Speaker's Office
6 Statuary Hall
7 Foreign Affairs Subcommittee
8 Congressmen's Private Offices
9 Senators' Private Offices
10 Small Senate Rotunda
11 Old Senate Chamber
12 Senate Conference Room
13 President's Room
14 Marble Room
15 Vice President's Office
S Stairs to lower floor

tion on the history of the Capitol and the old Chamber of the Supreme Court.

Beyond the gardens on the main front of the Capitol is the Thomas Jefferson Building, the main building of the Library of Congress, which was modelled on the Paris Opera House. The library is the largest in the world, with some 90 million volumes. Among its principal treasures are one of the three surviving complete Gutenberg Bibles and Thomas Jefferson's manuscript draft of the Declaration of Independence (illustration, p. 65). The guided tours of the Library show visitors these and other rarities, as well as the Great Hall and the large Main Reading Room.

*Library of Congress

Guided tours Mon.–Fri. 10am, 1 and 3pm

On the north side of the Library of Congress is the Supreme Court of the United States (illustration, p. 47). Designed by Cass Gilbert in the form of an ancient temple, this gleaming white building, built between 1929 and 1935, contains the large courtroom in which the nine judges of the Supreme Court hold their sessions.

*Supreme Court

Mon.–Fri. 9am–4.30pm

Ten minutes' walk north along 1st Street is the huge Union Station of 1908, the concourse of which has been converted into an exclusive shopping and restaurant arcade.
In the adjoining City Post Office is the National Postal Museum, opened in 1993.

Union Station

Postal Museum

East Mall – Museums

The eastern half of the Mall, between 15th and 1st Streets, is flanked by a number of museums of outstanding interest. They are open daily from 10am to 5.30pm; admission is free.

Museum Mile

Washington's youngest museum is the National Holocaust Memorial Museum, opened in 1993 and mainly privately financed, which lies just off the south side of the Mall on 14th Street. In this lavishly designed building the history of the extermination of European Jews by Nazi Germany is impressively – and depressingly – documented. On four floors into which

**National Holocaust Memorial Museum

Washington DC

no daylight enters, using the latest methods of presentation, are displayed a great range of original items and other documentation following the development of the Holocaust from the Nazi seizure of power in 1933 and the first measures of discrimination against Jews to planned mass murder and the liberation of the death camps by the Allies. In their tour of the museum visitors enter one of the goods wagons in which so many people were transported to Auschwitz or Treblinka and the high room known as the Stetl whose walls are covered with portraits and family groups of an exterminated Jewish community in Poland. At the end of the route is a light room, intended for meditation and reflection, in which burns an eternal flame.

Bureau of Engraving and Printing

Adjoining the Holocaust Museum is the Bureau of Engraving and Printing, the federal printing office in which banknotes, stamps and state documents are printed (guided tours daily at 2pm, or by appointment in morning until noon).

Smithsonian Institution

Most of the museums along the Mall belong to the Smithsonian Institution, founded in 1846 by the bequest of a British scientist, James Smithson (1765–1829). A total of 14 museums in Washington, together with the Zoo, are run by the Smithsonian, whose headquarters (and an Information Center) are in the Castle, a striking building of 1856 in the style of a Norman castle on the south side of the Mall. Behind the Castle is the restful Enid A. Haupt Garden.

*Freer Gallery

To the right of the main front is the Freer Gallery of Art (reopened in 1993), with a collection of outstanding works of art from Western Asia and the Far East, together with 19th and 20th American art, including an excellent collection of Whistlers.

*Arthur M. Sackler Gallery

On the south side of the Enid A. Haupt Garden is the Arthur M. Sackler Gallery, whose underground rooms supplement the Freer Gallery with another fine collection of Asian art, including a notable collection of jade.

*National Museum of African Art

The National Museum of African Art, also underground, is devoted to the art of Africa south of the Sahara.

Arts and Industries Building

To the left of the Castle is the Arts and Industries Building, which contains reconstructed exhibits and displays (including the steam engine "Jupiter" and various impressively large engines and drive mechanisms) from the Philadelphia World's Fair of 1876 marking the 100th anniversary of the United States.

*Hirshhorn Museum

The adjoining Hirshhorn Museum is notable for the striking architecture (by Gordon Bunshaft) of its circular main building, the "Doughnut of the Mall", as well as for its fine collection of modern European and American art (Picasso, Miró, Archipenko, Mondrian, Hopper, Max Weber, Pop Art, etc.). The Sculpture Garden has a number of works by Rodin.

**National Air and Space Museum

One of the most popular museums of all is the huge National Air and Space Museum. The main entrance hall displays a series of milestones in the history of air and space travel, all originals: the Wright brothers' "Kitty Hawk Flyer", Lindbergh's "Spirit of St Louis", the X 1 (the first supersonic aircraft), the X 15 (the fastest aircraft of all time), the Apollo 11 command module, a piece of genuine moon rock and also terrifying objects like the American Pershing missile and the Soviet SS 20.

The other rooms and galleries are devoted to a variety of themes, including the history of civil aviation (with some very fine original aircraft), the pioneers of flight (Lilienthal's glider, Amelia Earhart's Lockheed Vega, etc.), military aviation (First and Second World Wars, aircraft carrier) and space travel (the Apollo lunar module, astronauts' clothing, a walk-in model of Skylab, etc.). In addition to the large number of original aircraft there are film shows, recordings, diagrams and displays of all kinds.

The newest room has as its motto "What next, Columbus?" and is concerned with future research in space and on earth. The Albert Einstein Planetarium introduces visitors to the wonders of the universe, and the Langley Theater displays films on a huge five-storey-high screen.

Washington DC

The Air Transportation Hall in the National Air and Space Museum

On the site to the east of the Air and Space Museum the Museum of the American Indian is under construction. Its opening is planned for 1996.

Museum of the American Indian

On the north side of the East Mall, opposite the Air and Space Museum, rises the white dome of the National Gallery of Art, one of the world's largest and finest art galleries. (It does not belong to the Smithsonian Institution.)
This sumptuous marble building houses works by masters of the 13th to the 19th century, including Leonardo da Vinci ("Ginevra de' Benci", 1474), Raphael ("Madonna Alba", *c.* 1510), Titian ("Doge Andrea Gritti", 1534–40), van Eyck ("Annunciation", 1435), Dürer ("Portrait of a Priest", *c.* 1516), Grünewald ("Crucifixion", *c.* 1510), Rembrandt (more works than in the Rijksmuseum in Amsterdam), Vermeer ("Woman by Gold Cradle", 1664), El Greco ("Laocoon", 1610), Watteau ("Italian Actors", *c.* 1720), Cézanne ("Pot of Flowers", *c.* 1876) and many more. American painting is represented by Whistler ("The White Girl", 1862), John Singer Sargent ("Repose", 1911) and many others.
The East Building (by I. M. Pei, 1978) is devoted to 20th century art, with works by Matisse, Picasso, Miró, Kandinsky, Max Ernst, Mark Rothko, etc.

**National Gallery of Art

To the east of the National Gallery is the large National Museum of Natural History, which presents all aspects of natural history on its two floors. Among the most notable exhibits are a huge stuffed African elephant, a large model of a blue whale, skeletons of saurians, an insect zoo and – the pride of the mineralogy department – the famous and legendary Hope Diamond.

*National Museum of Natural History

The last museum on the north side of the Mall is the National Museum of American History. The ground floor is devoted to science and technology, including the automobile industry (Model T Ford) and the development of the oil industry. The second floor (European-style first floor) deals with the

*National Museum of American History

Washington DC
National Gallery of Art — West Building · Main Floor

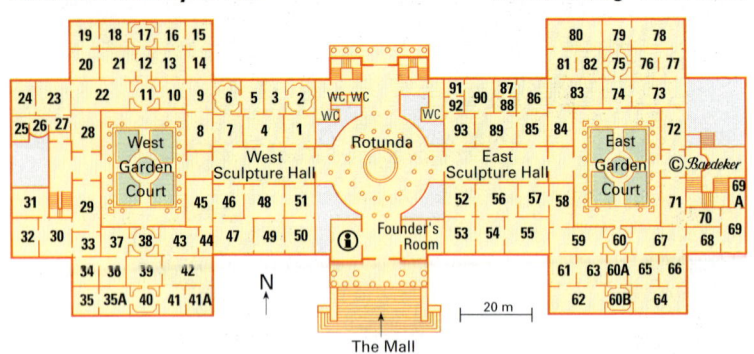

Rooms	Contents
1–10	Florentine and Central Italian Renaissance
11–18	Italian sculpture and furniture of the 13th–16th centuries
19–28	North Italian and Venetian Renaissance
29–33	Italian painting of the 17th and 18th centuries
34–37	Spanish painting of the 16th–20th centuries
38	European sculpture of the 14th and 15th centuries
39–45	Flemish and German painting of the 15th–17th centuries
46–51	Dutch painting of the 17th century
52–56	French painting of the 17th and 18th centuries
57–59	British painting of the 18th and 19th centuries
60, 60A, 60B	American painting of the 18th–20th centuries
61–63	British painting of the 18th and 19th centuries
64–71	American painting of the 18th–20th centuries
72–79	Special exhibitions
80–93	French painting of the 19th century

life and development of the United States, with exhibits which cover a wide range, including the original Star-Spangled Banner of 1814 from Fort Henry, George Washington's false teeth and the dresses of First Ladies. The third floor covers a great variety of subjects, including military history and American elections.

West Mall – Memorials

**Washington Monument

Daily 9am–5pm, April–Labor Day to midnight

The city's dominant landmark, the Washington Monument (illustration, p. 138), stands at the near end of the West Mall, which is laid out in gardens. This 555ft/169m high obelisk of Maryland marble, built to the design of Robert Mills in two phases (1848–55 and 1876–88), is a fitting memorial to George Washington, "father of the nation". A lift (or a flight of 898 steps) takes visitors up to the observation platform at a height of 500ft/152m, from which there are superb views of the capital and the surrounding area.

Jefferson Memorial

To the south of the Washington Monument, beyond the large Tidal Basin, is the Jefferson Memorial, a circular building reminiscent of the Pantheon in Rome which was erected in 1943 on the 200th anniversary of the birth of Thomas Jefferson, one of the authors of the Declaration of Independence. The Memorial and the Tidal Basin are surrounded by Japanese cherry-trees, whose blossoming is celebrated every year with a cherry-blossom festival.

*Lincoln Memorial

To the west of the Washington Monument, at the far end of the Reflecting Pool, in which the obelisk is beautifully mirrored, is the Lincoln Memorial, which stands at the end of the Mall. It was designed by Henry Bacon on the

Washington DC

Abraham Lincoln Memorial

model of the Parthenon in Athens and completed in 1922. The interior is dominated by a 20ft/6m high seated figure (by Chester French) of Lincoln, looking rather sternly past the Washington Monument towards the Capitol. On the walls are extracts from Lincoln's most celebrated speeches.

Leaving the Lincoln Memorial and turning left, we come to the Vietnam Veterans Memorial, at the entrance to which is a realistic piece of bronze sculpture, "Three Servicemen". This simple but impressive memorial, designed by a 21-year-old architectural student, Maya Ying Lin, in 1982 and completed in 1984, commemorates the Americans who died in the Vietnam War. On a 500ft/150m long wall faced with marble slabs are inscribed in chronological order the names of the 58,156 US citizens who were killed or reported missing in Vietnam between 1959 and 1975.

*Vietnam Veterans Memorial

White House Area

On Pennsylvania Avenue, to the north of the Washington Monument, is the White House, the official residence of the President. As with the Capitol, the best-known aspect of the White House, familiar from many television reports, is the rear front: the main façade is on the far side, facing Lafayette Square. The White House, with two main storeys, was originally built by James Hoban in 1792, and after being burned down by British forces in 1814 was rebuilt in 1818. On the guided tours (tickets issued free of charge from 8am at the kiosk on the Ellipse; long queues) visitors do not see a great deal of the interior – a few small rooms in period styles, the East Room, the Ballroom, the State Dining Room and the entrance hall: the rooms where government policy is made, such as the Oval Office, are not open to the public.

*White House

Guided visits Apr.–Oct.

On the east side of the White House grounds is the neo-classical Treasury Building (by Robert Mills, 1838–42).

Treasury Building

South-west of the White House, on 17th Street, are the headquarters of the Daughters of the American Revolution, an association of women belonging to the families of well-known revolutionary heroes founded in 1890, with 33 rooms in 17th, 18th and 19th century styles.

Daughters of the American Revolution

To the north is the Corcoran Gallery of Art, with an excellent collection of American and European art, including works by Frederic Edwin Church and Albert Bierstadt as well as by Rembrandt and Degas.

*Corcoran Gallery of Art

Still farther north is one of the most striking old government buildings in Washington, the Old Executive Building, erected in 1871–88 to house the State Department and the Army and Navy Departments. It is now occupied by White House offices.

Old Executive Building

To the north of the Old Executive Building is the Renwick Gallery, Washington's oldest art gallery. It is now devoted to American (including Indian) art.

Renwick Gallery

Washington DC

The handsome rear front of the White House

Lafayette Square
: At the corners of Lafayette Square, in front of the entrance to the White House, are statues of four heroes of the Revolution who came from Europe to aid the American cause: Friedrich Wilhelm von Steuben (1730–94), Tadeusz Kósciuszko (1746–1817), the Marquis de Lafayette (1757–1843) and the Comte de Rochambeau (1725–1807). In the centre of the square is an equestrian statue of Andrew Jackson, seventh US President (1767–1845).

At the north-east corner of Lafayette Square is Decatur House (1818–19), and on the north side is St John's Church (1816), the "President's church".

Downtown Washington

Federal Triangle
: The triangular area to the north of the Mall which is bounded by Pennsylvania Avenue, Constitution Avenue and 15th Street is known as the Federal Triangle because of the numerous government agencies in this area.

FBI
: The most recent addition is the massive J. Edgar Hoover Building, headquarters of the legendary FBI (Federal Bureau of Investigation) and home of the notorious G-men ("government's men"). There are guided tours on which visitors can see a variety of items from the rich history of crime in the United States.

National Archives
: At the east angle of the Federal Triangle, opposite the National Gallery, are the National Archives, which display the "charters of freedom", the icons of American democracy: the Declaration of Independence, two pages (the preamble and the signatures) of the Constitution and the Bill of Rights.

Pennsylvania Avenue
: The northern boundary of the Federal Triangle, Pennsylvania Avenue, runs diagonally from the Capitol by way of the spacious Freedom Plaza to the White House. The replanning of the avenue began in the time of President Kennedy. Its most striking feature is the Old Post Office, a massive granite structure built in 1889 which after thorough renovation has been converted into a shopping and restaurant arcade.

Washington DC

At 511 10th Street NW is Ford's Theatre (opened in 1863), in which President Lincoln was shot during a performance by John Wilkes Booth on April 14th 1865, five days after the surrender of the Southern states. Performances are still regularly given in the theatre, in which Lincoln's box is preserved as it was on the evening of his murder. The Lincoln Museum commemorates the murder. Lincoln died in Peterson House, opposite the theatre.

*Ford's Theatre/ Peterson House

Daily 9am–5pm

North of Ford's Theatre and east of the large Washington Convention Center, is the National Museum of Women in the Arts (1250 New York Avenue NW), which is devoted exclusively to the work of women artists from the 16th century to the present day, from Indian pottery by way of 19th century portraits to the most modern sculpture.

*National Museum of Women in the Arts

In the north-east of downtown Washington, housed in the old Patent Office Building, is the National Portrait Gallery (8th and F Streets; run by the Smithsonian Institution), with a very fine collection of portraits of great Americans. In the same complex is the National Museum of American Art, with a large collection which includes works by the famous painter of Indian life George Catlin, Frederic Remington, Whistler and John Singer Sargent.

*National Portrait Gallery/ National Museum of American Art

To the east of these two galleries, on the north side of Judiciary Square, is the massive brick Pension Building, built in 1887 to house the department responsible for paying war veterans' pensions. One of the veterans, General Sherman, thought that the worst thing about it was that it couldn't burn down. The building now houses a museum on the history of American architecture.

National Building Museum

Other Sights in Washington DC

Foggy Bottom, the area to the west of the White House extending to the Potomac, was once the site of a German settlement called Hamburg. It is now occupied by government buildings and, round Washington Circle, the campus of George Washington University.

Foggy Bottom

South-west of the White House, on New York Avenue, is the Octagon, a finely appointed house built in 1798–1800 which in spite of its name has only six sides. After the burning of the White House in 1814 President James Madison made this his official residence.

Octagon

Behind the 1960s façade of the State Department (23rd and C/D Streets) are concealed the very elegant and finely furnished 18th century Diplomatic Reception Rooms.

State Department

The focal point of Washington's cultural life, on the banks of the Potomac, is the John F. Kennedy Center for the Performing Arts (1971), with an opera house, a concert hall, three theatres and a movie house.

John F. Kennedy Center

To the north of the John F. Kennedy Center is the Watergate Complex, infamously associated with the late President Nixon. Within the complex are restaurants, a hotel and a marina.

Watergate Complex

North-west of Dupont Circle, at 1600 21st Street, is another fine gallery, the Phillips Collection, which includes both works by unknown artists (B. A. G. Dove, J. Martin, etc.) patronised by Duncan Phillips and paintings by such masters as El Greco, Cézanne, Renoir, Bonnard, Klee and Mondrian.

*Phillips Collection

Georgetown, north-west of Washington, must be visited twice – during the day and at night. By day, visitors will be surprised to discover what an idyllic place much of this old town, founded in 1751 and incorporated in Washington in 1871, still remains. Walking through the streets of the little town, the seat of Georgetown University, they will come across attractive old houses dating from the early days of the United States, like Cox Row and Smith Row in N Street, where the Kennedys once lived, or find a

Georgetown

Washington DC

secluded spot on the quiet Ohio and Chesapeake Canal, on which they can take a trip in a narrow boat. In the evening Georgetown – particularly in M Street and Wisconsin Avenue – offers a profusion of excellent restaurants, bars and music clubs with a lively night life.

*Dumbarton Oaks
Dumbarton Oaks (1703 32nd Street NW) is a sumptuous mansion built in 1800–01 by Senator William Dowsey. Surrounded by marvellous gardens, it now houses a unique collection of Byzantine art, including over 20,000 coins, and a collection of pre-Columbian artifacts. The Music Room has hosted concerts and recitals by leading musicians, among them Igor Stravinsky.

Hillwood Museum
Those interested in Russian art will find an excursion to Hillwood, north of Washington, well worth while. Here can be seen the collection assembled in 1937–30 by Marjorie Post Davies, wife of the US ambassador to the Soviet Union – the largest collection of Russian art outside Russia, including Fabergé eggs which once belonged to the Tsar, icons and furniture.

Surroundings of Washington DC

Arlington
*Arlington National Cemetery

Apr.–Sept. daily 8am–7pm, other times of year to 5pm

Beyond the Potomac in the state of Virginia, reached by way of the Arlington Memorial Bridge, is Arlington, with the National Cemetery of the United States, which can be visited either on foot or by minibus. The Visitor Center has an exhibition on the history of the cemetery, which was established – on land belonging to the Custis and Lee families which was occupied by Union troops during the Civil War – as a burial-place for citizens of the United States, particularly soldiers, who had deserved well of their country. Most visitors will find their way past the endless rows of white headstones to the grave of John F. Kennedy and that of his brother Robert close by. Above the cemetery is Arlington House, now the Robert E. Lee Memorial, from the terrace of which there is a fantastic view of Wash-

Mount Vernon, George Washington's retreat above the Potomac

ington. Here in April 1861 Lee was faced with the choice between taking command of the Confederate army and remaining loyal to the Union. He opted for the South and left Arlington House, which was occupied in May 1861 by Union forces. From the hill on which the house stands it is a short distance to another hill on which is the Tomb of the Unknown Soldier (commemorating the dead of the First and Second World Wars, the Korean and Vietnam Wars and most recently the Gulf War), where the guard is changed every hour.

To the south of the Arlington Cemetery is the famous Pentagon, headquarters of the Department of Defense and the US armed forces (guided tours every half-hour Mon.–Fri. 9.30am–3.30pm).

Pentagon

South of Washington on the George Washington Memorial Parkway is Alexandria, a port town founded by Scottish merchants and laid out on a regular grid plan. It has many fine old buildings, including the Stabler-Leadbeater Apothecary of 1792 (107 S. Fairfax Street), Carlyle House of 1752 (121 N. Fairfax Street) and the house in which Robert E. Lee spent his early years (607 Oronoco Street). The finest church is Christ Church (Cameron and N. Washington Streets), in which the seats occupied by Washington and Lee are marked with silver plaques.

*Alexandria

From Alexandria the George Washington Memorial Parkway continues south through green residential suburbs along the Potomac to Mount Vernon, Washington's beautifully situated country house. The property had belonged to the family since 1674, and when George Washington took it over in 1752 he planned the present house, in which he lived with his family 1759–74, 1783–89 and from 1797 until his death. The Georgian-style house has 19 rooms filled with mementoes of the first President. Among the rooms shown to visitors are Washington's library and study and the room in which he died. Near the house are the kitchen, the secretary's house, stables and workshops. From the terrace there is a marvellous view of the Potomac.

**Mount Vernon

Mar.–Oct.
daily 9am–5pm,
other times of year
to 4pm

In the spacious grounds are the family vault in which George Washington and his wife Martha are buried and the cemetery of his slaves. In the Orangery is a memorial exhibition with many items that belonged to the family.

Waterton-Glacier International Peace Park　　　　　　　　A 11/12

State: Montana
Area: 1788sq.miles/4630sq.km
Established: 1895 (Waterton), 1910 (Glacier). UNESCO World Heritage Site since 1979

The park is open throughout the year, though many roads are closed from November to April. Most visitors come in the summer months, but it is also very pleasant in autumn (until mid October).

Season

Glacier National Park in the United States and Waterton Lakes National Park in Canada have joined since 1932 in the Waterton-Glacier International Peace Park. Although separated by the frontier, the two National Parks form a geographical unit, taking in a relatively unspoiled part of the Rocky Mountains in the area of the Continental Divide (Watershed). This grandiose mountain region, the "crown of the continent", is for the most part an empty wilderness with steep rock faces, more than 50 glaciers and over 200 lakes. Here, in the Lewis and Livingston Ranges, the Rockies have a markedly alpine character. The highest peak is Mount Cleveland (10,448ft/3184m). The landscape of this region was transformed during the ice ages; glaciation reached its peak during the Wisconsin Ice Age, some 12,000 years ago, when only the highest peaks emerged from the ice masses. Characteristic features of the landscape are U-shaped valleys

*Topography

Waterton-Glacier International Peace Park

enclosed between sheer rock walls, lateral hanging valleys from which innumerable waterfalls tumble down into the main valley, narrow, sharp-edged arêtes and ridges, lake-filled corries and lakes formed by terminal moraines.

Flora and fauna

While to the west of the watershed there are dense forests of hemlock and red cedar up to 5900ft/1800m, on the drier east side the tree-line is considerably lower, and the forests of sub-alpine conifers are less dense. In the area of transition to the prairies are stands of aspens. During the short summer when the snow has gone the alpine meadows are a magnificent sea of blossom. The marshland areas (water birches, willows, reeds) are a refuge for beavers, mink, muskrats, ducks, geese and even elk. The narrow prairie zone in the east is the home of coyotes and bison. In the mountain valleys and in the pine and Douglas fir forests on the lower slopes there are red deer, black bears and pumas. The sub-alpine zone, the most important plants in which are spruce. Engelmann fir, larch, white pine, bear-grass and gentian, is the habitat of grizzly bears, and higher up, in the mountain pine zone, there are marmots, Rocky Mountain goats and bighorn sheep. In recent years wolves have been heard howling again in remote mountain valleys.

Bison Paddock

To the north of the park entrance, on Highway 5, is a large enclosure containing a small herd of bison – a relic of the great herds which used to range over the prairies. A road runs through this Bison Paddock.

*Red Rock Canyon Parkway

3 miles/5km beyond the park entrance a road branches off Highway 5 into Red Rock Canyon, following Blakiston Creek, where a large expanse of alluvial soil has been built up between Lower and Middle Waterton Lakes. The road runs through the various bio-climatic zones between the prairie and Mount Blakiston (9646ft/2940m), the highest peak in Waterton Lakes National Park. In 10 miles/16km it comes to Red Rock Canyon with its red ferruginous Pre-Cambrian rocks of the Grinnell formation, patterned by bluish-green algae.

A grand mountain landscape in the Waterton-Glacier International Peace Park

Middle and Upper Waterton Lakes are separated by a narrow strip of land known as the Bosporus, on which stands the majestic Prince of Wales Hotel (1927). From this privileged situation there are views of both lakes and of the surrounding mountain world. Upper Waterton Lake (alt. 4196ft/1279m) is the deepest lake (500ft/152m) in the Canadian Rockies.

Waterton Lakes/ Waterton Townsite

The American and Canadian National Parks are linked by the Chief Mountain International Highway (Hwy 6/SR 17), opened in 1935, which runs partly through the parks and partly through the Blackfoot Indian Reservation, with fine views of the Waterton Valley. The road is open from mid May to mid September.

*Chief Mountain International Highway

Prominently visible is Chief Mountain (9065ft/2763m), an isolated remnant of Pre-Cambrian limestones which has been separated out by erosion and towers high above the gentle hills of the prairies. To the Indians it was a holy mountain, and in earlier days was an important landmark. From the frontier there is a view of Mount Cleveland, the highest peak in Glacier National Park.

9 miles/14km before St Mary, at Babb, a road (closed in winter) goes off to the Many Glacier, a region of great scenic beauty in which Rocky Mountain goats and black bears can be seen. On the shores of Swiftcurrent Lake is the Many Glacier Hotel (built in 1914), from which there are a variety of walks and climbs – to the Grinnell Glacier, the Granite Park area, Iceberg Lake, on whose shimmering green water there are ice floes even in the height of summer, and the Red Rock Falls.
The hotel is the starting-point of the 2½ mile/4km long Swiftcurrent Lake Nature Trail, an informative introduction to beavers, the local geology and the mountain world. From the hotel there are boat trips on the Swiftcurrent and Josephine Lakes.

*Many Glacier

The 50 mile/80km long road (completed in 1932) from St Mary over the Logan Pass (7747ft/2026m) to West Glacier is rated one of the most beautiful mountain roads in North America. Narrow and with many bends, it is usually open only from the second week in June to the middle of September and is closed to vehicles over 7½ft/2.3m wide, including mirrors, and 20ft/6m long. From St Mary the road follows the north side of St Mary Lake (coming in 3 miles/5km, on the south side, to the Triple Divide, the watershed between three drainage systems – to the Pacific, the North Atlantic and the Gulf of Mexico). The view of St Mary Lake and the surrounding peaks from the wide bend beyond Rising Sun is probably the most photographed scene in the park. From the lake the road climbs steeply to the Logan Pass, with the Logan Pass Visitor Center, above which tower the imposing peaks of Reynolds (9128ft/2782m) and Clements Mountain (8773ft/2674m).

*Going-to-the-Sun Road

From the Visitor Center a nature trail (1¼ miles/2km) runs through the Hanging Gardens, which are gay with colour during the short summer season. In this alpine eco-system marmots and Rocky Mountain goats can sometimes be observed. There are rewarding mountain hikes to the Hidden Lake and the Granite Park Chalet. The section of the road between Logan Pass and McDonald Valley is a masterpiece of engineering, winding its way down into the valley in a series of sharp bends and a large loop.

West Virginia J–M 43–47

Area: 24,180sq.miles/62,630sq.km
Population: 1,800,000
Capital: Charleston
Popular name: Mountain State

White Sands National Monument

Situation and topography	West Virginia's popular name, the Mountain State, characterises its topography. Two-thirds of its area is occupied by the Alleghenies in the east of the state, which fall down westward into the Allegheny Plateau, with the Ohio River. Its tourist attractions, therefore, lie in a variety of outdoor activities – hiking, fishing, rafting, winter sports, etc.

West Virginia has relatively cool summers and winters which are frequently cold.

History	The local Indians lived undisturbed by white settlers until 1670. The state of West Virginia came into being when the western counties of Virginia, which did not wish to secede from the Union in 1860, broke away from the rest of the state. It was admitted to the Union on June 20th 1863 as the 35th state.
Economy	West Virginia's industrial base is mining (particularly coal-mining), but this branch of the economy has been badly hit by rationalisation measures and falling demand, and West Virginia is now one of the poorest states in the USA. Other traditional activities are agriculture (fruit, grain), woodworking and glass-blowing. Tourism is now the state's main source of revenue.

Places of Interest in West Virginia

Berkeley Springs	Berkeley Springs, in the extreme north-eastern tip of the state, is the oldest spa in the United States. George Washington established its reputation by his frequent visits to the springs.
Charleston	Charleston, the state capital, lies on the Kanawha River. The Capitol with its golden dome ranks as one of the finest in the United States. In the adjoining Cultural Center are a number of museums.
Harpers Ferry	On October 16th 1859 the fanatical opponent of slavery John Brown (see Famous People) attacked the Union arsenal at Harpers Ferry, in the north-eastern tip of West Virginia, with the idea of establishing a base there and gathering former slaves round him. US troops commanded by Robert E. Lee overwhelmed his small force, and Brown was carried off to Charles Town and hanged in December 1859.
*Monongahela National Forest	The marvellous lonely mountain world of the Alleghenies can be experienced in the Monongahela National Forest (reached by way of US 33). Here both the Potomac and the Ohio rise. There are breathtaking views from the Seneca Rocks.
White Sulphur Springs	White Sulphur Springs, at the south end of the forest, is an elegant spa, whose warm springs were already known to the Indians.
*New Gorge National River	New Gorge River, in the south-west of the state, has cut through the rock to form a gorge up to 1000ft/300m deep. The 52 mile/83km long stretch of the river between Hinton and Fayetteville, with a whole series of rapids, offers good walking and rafting and magnificent views.

White Sands National Monument   R 19

State: New Mexico
Area: 230sq.miles/596sq.km
Established: 1933

White Sands National Monument

White sand and prickly shrubs, White Sands

The White Sands National Monument is half an hour's drive south-west of Alamogordo in the south of New Mexico. It lies in the Tularosa basin, a northern offshoot of the Chihuahua Desert surrounded by hills. Here gleaming white gypsum sand has built up into an extraordinary landscape of dunes up to 60ft/18m high which are constantly being displaced by the wind. Only highly adapted forms of life can stand up to the extreme conditions of this arid and constantly changing habitat. Some plants, for example, have developed roots over 30ft/10m long in order to gain a foothold in the travelling dunes.

Situation and **topography

Access
7am–sunset

Some 250 million years ago this area was occupied by a shallow sea on the bottom of which gypsum was deposited. The present hills were created by the upthrusting and folding of marine sediments. A large section of the earth's crust fell in and the Tularosa basin was formed. In the hills round the basin the deposits of gypsum were dissolved by rain, and water with a high gypsum content gathered in the Tularosa basin, which had no outlet, and formed a lake, now known as Lake Lucero. The lake repeatedly dried out and the gypsum crystallised; and finally small grains of gypsum were blown by wind into the remarkable dunes we see today, which are now under protection as a National Monument.

Origins

It is possible to drive into the fantastic dune landscape on a road which runs into a gypsum track. In 3 miles/5km the Big Dune Nature Trail goes off on the left. The road ends after 8 miles/13km in the heart of the dunes. It is a curious experience to climb one of the dunes in the soft sand, which in spite of the heat is cool.

*Dunes Drive

In walking about in the dunes it is easy to lose your sense of direction, particularly if a sandstorm blows up.

Warning

501

Wisconsin

Surroundings of the White Sands National Monument

White Sands Missile Range
The White Sands National Monument is surrounded on all sides by the White Sands Missile Range, on which captured German missiles were tested during the Second World War. On July 16th 1945 the very first atomic bomb was exploded on the remote Trinity Site. Some 25 miles/40km east of Las Cruces is the military headquarters of the test site, which can be visited (pass required). At the Visitor Center (small museum) a number of missiles are on show.

Alamogordo Space Center
The Space Center, north-east of Alamogordo (open: daily 9am–5pm), has a number of displays (including missiles and space capsules) illustrating the development of space flight.

Wisconsin (State; WI) C–G 33–39

Area:
56,155sq.miles/145,440sq.km
Population: 4,956,000
Capital: Madison
Popular name: Badger State

Situation and topography
Wisconsin (from the Indian term *ouisconsin*, "where the waters meet") lies in the northern Middle West, bounded by Lake Michigan, Lake Superior and the Mississippi. The scarped and lake-strewn region to the north, part of the Canadian Shield, gives place farther south to the sandy Central Lowlands. In this continental climate influenced by the Great Lakes, with its long cold winters and short warm summers, forest is the natural vegetation form, and more than 40% of the state's area is still forest-covered. The steppe country of the Central Lowlands is now for the most part under cultivation.

History
The first European to reach the region round Green Bay on Lake Michigan, then occupied by Algonquin tribes, was a Frenchman, Jean Nicolet, in 1634. The area was under French control until 1763, when it passed to Britain. Although after 1783, following the Revolution, it officially belonged to the United States, it continued to be controlled by Britain until the outbreak of the British–American War in 1812. The mass immigration of farmers and miners began after the Black Hawk War ended the conflict with the Indians. Wisconsin ratified the Constitution on May 29th 1848 as the 30th state, and during the Civil War remained loyal to the Union.

Economy
The predominant form of agriculture is dairy farming: Wisconsin, the "Dairy State", supplies fully 45% of the country's production of cheese. Other agricultural products are maize, potatoes and other vegetables, and tobacco. Logging and mining (zinc, copper, iron) supply important raw materials for industry (mainly engineering, metalworking, papermaking and brewing). There is a particular concentration of industry on the shores of Lake Michigan and in the Milwaukee area. Wisconsin has a flourishing tourist industry, centred mainly on water sports on Lakes Michigan and Superior, winter sports (particularly on Mount Telemark, near Cable) and the summer holiday trade.

Places of Interest in Wisconsin

Apostle Islands
These 22 picturesque little islands in Lake Superior can be reached by ferry from Bayfield. A museum on Madeline Island traces the history of the local Indians and fur-traders.

502

Wyoming

Door County, a peninsula projecting into Lake Michigan to the north of Milwaukee (see entry), is a land of apple and cherry trees, trout streams and romantic strands well supplied with marinas and diving schools. A tasty local speciality is a fish stew of trout, onions and potatoes.

The chief places on the peninsula are Baileys Harbor on Lake Michigan, Ephraim (originally founded by Moravian Brethren from Norway), and Egg Harbor and Ellison Bay on Green Bay. From Ellison Bay there is a ferry to Washington Island (originally settled by Icelanders), with Rock Island State Park.

*Door County

Hayward, in north-western Wisconsin, is the scene of the lumberjacks' world championship, held annually on the last weekend in July.

Hayward

The Land o' Lakes is the region between Boulder Junction, Eagle River and Rhinelander in the north, near the boundary with Michigan, with over 200 lakes set amid forests. It is a very popular holiday region, with good fishing and walking. Bird-watchers may be lucky enough to see one of the few remaining white-tailed eagles.

*Land o' Lakes

The state capital, Madison, lies in southern Wisconsin. More interesting, perhaps, than the Capitol and the State Museum are the many buildings designed by Frank Lloyd Wright (see Famous People), including the headquarters of the First Unitarian Society and several private houses.

Madison

Baraboo (37 miles/60km north-west) will be of interest particularly to circus enthusiasts. This is the home of the world-famous Ringling Brothers' Circus, whose winter quarters open their doors to the public in summer as the Circus World Museum.

Baraboo

A few miles north of Baraboo is Wisconsin Dells, the chief place in the state's most popular holiday region, centred on the gorges carved out by the Wisconsin River. Cruises on the river, good hiking country and a number of amusement parks are among the attractions that draw tens of thousands of visitors every year.

*Wisconsin Dells

The little port of Manitowoc, north of Milwaukee, is a good base for fishing trips on Lake Michigan. The Maritime Museum recalls the time when submarines were built in the yards here.

Manitowoc

See entry

Milwaukee

The town of Oshkosh on Lake Winnebago, north-west of Milwaukee, would be unknown to fame but for the world's largest meet of aviators held here annually in July/August. The total number of aircraft that have attended these meets is now over 10,000. There is an Air Adventure Museum in the town.

*Oshkosh

Wyoming (State; WY)   E–H 14–21

Area:
  90,085sq.miles/253,325sq.km
Population: 503,000
Capital: Cheyenne
Popular names: Equality State,
  Cowboy State

The thinly populated state of Wyoming (from an Indian term meaning "change between mountain and valley") lies in the north-western United States.

Situation and topography

The eastern part of the state, which has a climate of continental type, is occupied by the dry grassland, interspersed with areas of badlands, of the

Wyoming

High Plains, at altitudes of between 3300ft/1000m and 5900ft/1800m. To the north-east the Black Hills (6660ft/2030m) and the spectacular Devil's Tower rise out of the prairies. The heart of the state is the desert-like Wyoming Basin, a depression some 250 miles/400km wide lying at an average altitude of 6500ft/1980m which is surrounded by various ranges of the Rocky Mountains (Bighorn Mountains, Wind River Range, etc.). In the extreme north-west of the state is the Yellowstone Plateau, with numerous post-volcanic features (including spectacular geysers). To the south is the beautiful Teton Range, which is of almost Alpine character. The highest point in the state is the Gannett Peak (13,806ft/4208m) in the Wind River Range, its lowest point on the Belle Fourche River (3101ft/945m) in the extreme north-east.

History

The first Europeans to reach the territory of Wyoming, then occupied by Arapaho and Shoshone Indians, were French prospectors, who came here in the middle of the 18th century. Subsequently a number of French settlements were established. A hundred years later thousands of settlers travelling north-west passed through Wyoming on the Oregon Trail. The Union Pacific Railroad reached the area in 1867, and this led to the establishment of larger settlements and large ranches run by the "cattle barons". Violent clashes between the local Indians and the new white settlers continued into the 1890s. In 1868 Wyoming was officially established as a United States territory. In 1869 the women of Wyoming were given the vote (the first in the United States to receive it). On July 10th 1890 Wyoming became the 44th state of the Union. The first oil well in the state had been drilled in 1884, and by 1908 it experienced its first oil boom. Prospecting for oil increased enormously in 1973, when the Arab oil countries restricted supplies. There was a dramatic collapse in 1982, when world oil prices fell, and the Wyoming oil industry recovered only in the late eighties.

Economy

Wyoming is one of the richest regions in the world in resources of fossil fuel, with an annual output of over 160 million tons of coal, 100 million barrels of oil and huge quantities of natural gas. Some 90% of the soda needed by US chemical and glass industries comes from Wyoming. Stock farming plays an important part in the state's agricultural economy (1.3 million cattle and huge numbers of sheep). More than 5 million visitors are attracted to Wyoming every year by its spectacular National Parks (Yellowstone, Grand Teton) and the lure of the Wild West (e.g. in Buffalo Bill's town of Cody).

Places of Interest in Wyoming

*Bighorn Mountains

In northern Wyoming are the beautiful Bighorn Mountains (13,186ft/4019m). On their eastern slopes are the two little cattle-ranching towns of Buffalo and Sheridan, now tourist centres. For a drive through awe-inspiring mountain scenery, leave Buffalo on US 16, which runs over the Powder River Pass (9666ft/2946m) and then, in Ten Sleep Canyon, through millions of years of the earth's history. The journey ends in Ten Sleep (pop. 440), which still retains something of the atmosphere of the Wild West.

Casper

Casper (pop. 52,000), on the North Platte River, is now the chief town in an area given up to agriculture and the oil industry. It is named after Lieutenant Caspar Collins, who tried to rescue a group of settlers beset by Indians on the Oregon Trail in 1865. Features of interest are the Tate Mineralogical Museum and the reconstructed Fort Caspar on the western outskirts of the town.

Flaming Gorge

Half an hour's drive south of the mining town of Rock Springs is the Flaming Gorge National Recreation Area (water sports, fishing, etc.), which extends into the neighbouring state of Utah. The Green River is dammed here.

Wyoming

Two hours' drive north-east of Cheyenne (see entry), at the junction of the Laramie River with the North Platte River, is Fort Laramie, founded in 1834 as a fur-trading post. In the 1840s, particularly after the discovery of gold in California, the fort was an important staging-point for settlers travelling west on the Oregon Trail. After increasingly violent clashes between the white migrants and the Prairie Indians the fort was taken over by the US Army in 1849 in order to protect the Oregon Trail. From there troops could be sent out against the Indians, and there too treaties were signed with them. In 1868 the Sioux were promised the territory on the Powder River so long as the buffaloes grazed there, but soon afterwards, when gold was discovered in the Black Hills (see entry), the authorities took a different view. In the late 1880s the fort increasingly lost its military importance, and finally was abandoned. Some of the buildings are well preserved or have been restored, including the guard-house, the cavalry barracks, the bakery and some officers' houses. On some summer weekends, particularly around July 4th, there are "living history" presentations.

*Fort Laramie

June–Sept.
8am–7pm,
other times of year
8am–4pm

In south-western Wyoming, west of the township of Kemmerer, is Fossil Butte National Monument, where palaeontologists have been at work since 1856. Here have been found the fossil remains of numerous animals (in particular freshwater fishes).

*Fossil Butte

53 miles/85km south-west of Casper on WY 220, on the north bank of the Sweetwater River, is the granite monolith known as Independence Rock, on which settlers moving west have left records of their passage. Some miles farther south-west is the imposing Devil's Gate.

*Independence Rock

Just under an hour's drive west of Cheyenne is Laramie (pop. 27,000), named after a French trapper who was murdered in this area in 1821. A military post was built here in 1866 to protect workers building the transcontinental railroad, and two years later the first Union Pacific train reached

*Laramie

A quiet day in Laramie

Yellowstone National Park

the town. For a time Laramie was reputedly the "wildest town in the Wild West", frequented by robbers, cattle-rustlers, gamblers, prostitutes and other dubious characters. Violent crime was an everyday matter, and it seemed at times that the life of a steer was worth more than the life of a man. On the other side of the coin, Laramie was the first place in the United States where women were elected to public office. It is also the seat of the University of Wyoming, founded in 1886. The University has a rich Geology Museum (remains of Tyrannosaurus rex), an Anthropology Museum and a new American Heritage and Art Museum (architect Antoine Predock). Other features of interest in the town are the Laramie Plains Museum, the Rocky Mountains Herbarium and the Wyoming Territorial Park, with the Territorial Prison in which Butch Cassidy was once confined.

*Medicine Bow Mountains

In southern Wyoming are the beautiful Medicine Bow Mountains, now also a popular winter sports area. The hills (highest point Medicine Bow Peak, 12,015ft/3662m) were regarded by the Indians as sacred. Here they held powwows and cut arrows from the cedars of the forest.

Thermopolis

Two hours' drive south-east of Cody is the spa of Thermopolis (pop. 5000), founded in 1896, with one of the most abundant hot springs in the western hemisphere (36 gallons/163 litres per second; 135°F/57°C). The healing power of the spring was well known to the Indians.

*Wind River Indian Reservation

In west central Wyoming is the Wind River Indian Reservation, in which a few thousand Shoshone and Arapaho Indians live. The landscape is patterned by Indian villages, great expanses of pastureland – and oil derricks. The chief place in the reservation is Fort Washakie (headquarters of the Bureau of Indian Affairs), near which are the graves of Washakie, a Shoshone chief whose memory is still revered, and Sacajawea. the Indian girl who acted as a guide to the surveyors Lewis and Clark.

Other places of interest

Badlands National Park, Black Hills, Cheyenne, Cody (see entries), Devil's Tower (see Black Hills), Grand Teton National Park, Jackson, Yellowstone National Park (see entries).

Yellowstone National Park   E 14/15

States: Wyoming, Idaho, Montana
Area: 3457sq.miles/8953sq.km
Established: 1872. UNESCO World Heritage Site

Season

The National Park is open throughout the year, but many roads are closed from November to April. Late spring is the time when many animals bring forth their young. Most visitors come in summer, but autumn (until mid October) is also a good time for a visit.

Situation and **topography

Yellowstone, the oldest National Park in the United States, lies on a basalt plateau (average altitude 6600–8200ft/2000–2500m) in the north-western corner of Wyoming, extending a little way into the neighbouring states of Idaho and Montana.

Origins

There were violent volcanic eruptions in the area now occupied by the Yellowstone National Park some 2 million years ago, again 1.2 million years ago and finally 600,000 years ago. After the last eruption and the collapse of the crater a huge caldera was formed. The magma chamber (the "hot spot") which brought about these eruptions still generates a great deal of heat, as is shown by innumerable post-volcanic phenomena, mainly geysers, hot springs, fumaroles and mud volcanoes. The continuing instability of the ground is shown by the frequency of earth tremors in the area.

Yellowstone National Park

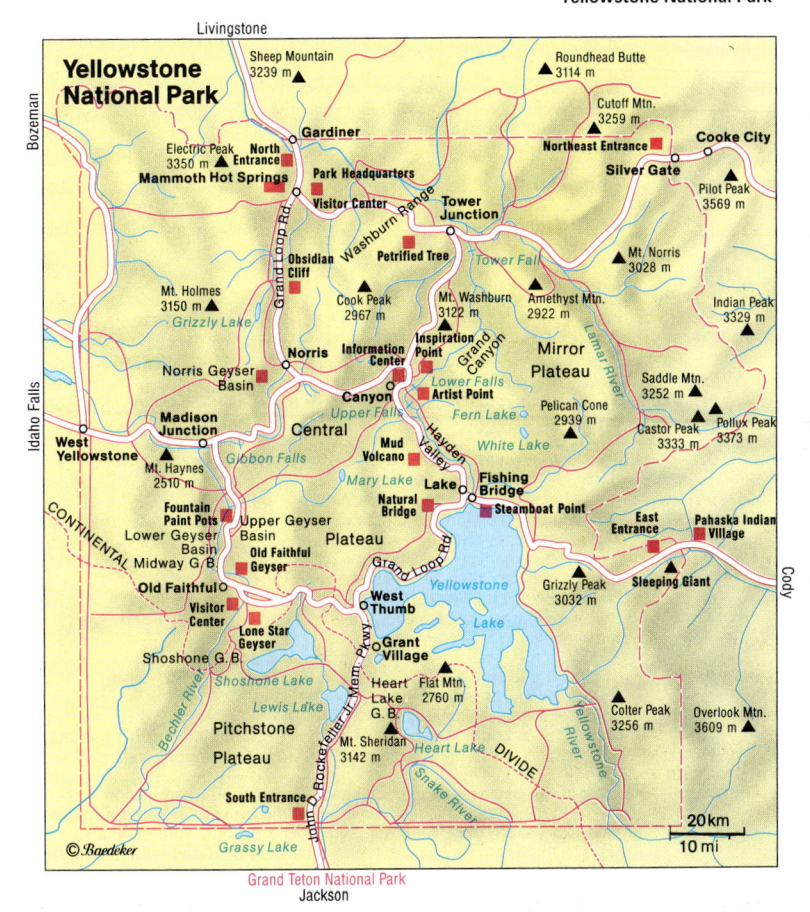

The National Park has a varied range of flora, from desertic vegetation at the north entrance to sub-alpine meadows and forests. The lodgepole pine is a common species, accounting for three-quarters of the forested area. There are from time to time devastating forest fires in the National Park, most recently in the summer of 1988, when large areas of forest in the north-western part of the park were destroyed.

Vegetation/Forest fires

In this relatively intact natural region there is an abundance of wild life. In addition to bison, various species of deer (red deer, wapiti, mule deer), bighorn sheep, beavers and marmots, there are also elk, pronghorn antelopes, black bears, grizzlies and coyotes. In the air swoop ospreys and on water there are pelicans, various species of ducks and geese, and trumpeter swans.

Fauna

*Grand Loop Road

The 142 mile/229km long Grand Loop Road runs round the park in a figure of eight, taking in the most striking of the natural features. The round tour

507

Yellowstone National Park

described below starts and finishes at Mammoth Hot Springs, where the National Park offices are located.

Warning

Before entering the geyser area you should enquire in the Old Faithful Inn or the Visitor Center at the National Park offices about the times of eruption of the various geysers and should check that the paths are safe to use. You must keep exclusively to the marked paths.

**Mammoth Hot Springs

On the east flank of Terrace Mountain (8012ft/2442m) are the Mammoth Hot Springs, which have formed magnificent sinter terraces. They consist of ten sinter basins from 35ft/10m to 200ft/60m high, ranged in "steps" one above the other. There are some 60 hot springs at temperatures of between 64°F/18°C and 165°F/74°C. There is a marvellous play of colour in the evening and early morning.

*Norris Geyser Basin

Farther south is the very impressive Norris Geyser Basin. The hottest place in this area is the Porcelain Basin (with boardwalk). The Echinus Geyser spouts approximately every hour. Here too is the Steamboat Geyser, the largest in the world, which erupts only very irregularly. It can shoot water up to a height of 425ft/130m. In the Norris Museum the operation of geysers is explained.

*Lower Geyser Basin

To the south-west is the Lower Geyser Basin, with the Paint Pot Fountain, in which hot reddish mud simmers. A little way south of this, on the Firehole Lake Drive, is the Great Fountain Geyser, which is a magnificent spectacle every 11 hours or so. On the lush green of Fountain Flat bison and deer can be seen grazing, particularly in the early morning and the evening.

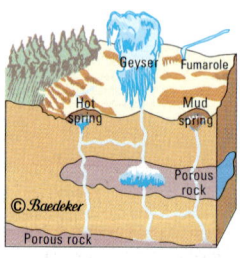

Midway Geyser Basin

The most striking feature in the Midway Geyser Basin (boardwalk) is the mighty crater of the Excelsior Geyser, with a flow of 55 gallons/250 litres of hot water per second. Nearby is the Grand Prismatic Spring (diameter 360ft/110m), one of the finest hot springs in the Yellowstone National Park.

*Upper Geyser Basin

Most of the geysers are in the Upper Geyser Basin, which is only 1 mile/1.5km long. A two-hour trail (boardwalk) through the area takes visitors past Old Faithful, the Giantess Geyser, the Beehive Geyser, the Castle Geyser, the Grand Geyser and fountain basins shimmering in a rainbow of colours.

**Morning Glory Pool

On the north edge of the geyser area is the magically beautiful Morning Glory Pool, named after the flower of that name.

**Old Faithful

One of the star attractions of the Yellowstone is the geyser familiarly known as Old Faithful, famed for the regularity with which it used to shoot columns of water up to a height of 115–165ft/35–50m – though since the last earthquake it has not been so dependable as before. The intervals between eruptions range between half an hour and two hours (at present about three-quarters of an hour); for the approximate times enquire in the Visitor Center or the Old Faithful Inn.

*Old Faithful Inn

The Old Faithful Inn was originally built in log-cabin style in 1904 and has since been several times enlarged. Many famous people have signed the visitors' book.

*Yellowstone Lake

In the southern half of the National Park, at an altitude of 7737ft/2357m, is Yellowstone Lake (area 137sq.miles/355sq.km; depth up to 320ft/98m). Well stocked with fish, it is an angler's paradise. Here too can be seen many species of waterfowl which have become rare elsewhere.

Yellowstone National Park

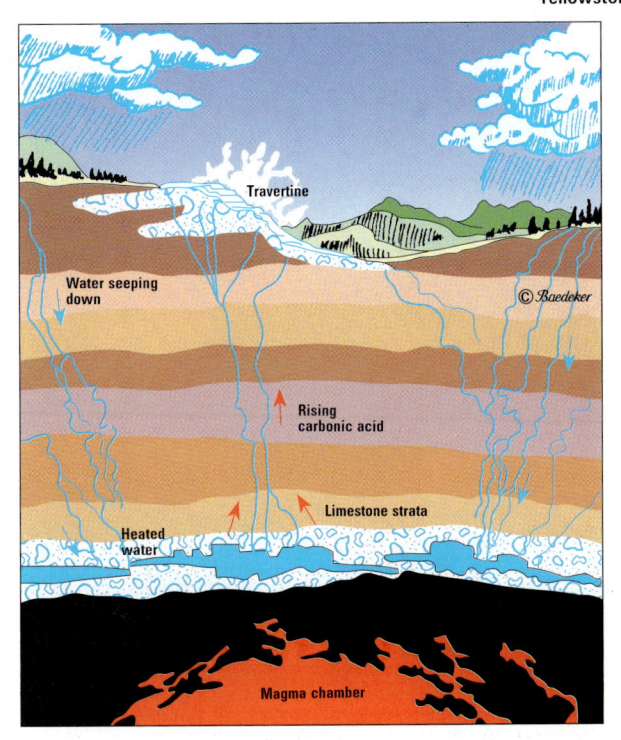

The West Thumb, an offshoot on the west side of Yellowstone Lake, is a water-filled caldera which came into being some 150,000 years ago. On its western edge is the little West Thumb Geyser Basin (boardwalk). In nearby Grant Village is a Visitor Center.

West Thumb/
Grant Village

On the north-west shore of Yellowstone Lake are the little townships of Bridge Bay, Lake Village and Fishing Bridge, with a limited amount of accommodation, campgrounds and various leisure facilities.

Bridge Bay,
Lake Village,
Fishing Bridge

Emerging from the lake, the Yellowstone River flows through a quiet valley, with bison grazing on the meadows; then, to the north of Hayden Valley, it plunges over two spectacular waterfalls into a wild and romantic canyon. There is a fascinating walk along the river which introduces visitors to the geology of the region, passing old lava flows and less well known zones of geo-thermal activity.

*Yellowstone
River

A few miles below Fishing Bridge are the striking mud volcanoes of the Mud Volcano Area and the simmering Sulphur Caldron. Visitors must take care to stay on the boardwalks.

Mud volcanoes/
Sulphur Caldron

In Hayden Valley, a western side valley of almost genial aspect, a variety of wild life can be observed, including bison, deer and sometimes grizzly bears.

Hayden Valley

The easily accessible Upper Falls on the Yellowstone River drop 110ft/33m. A few hundred yards lower down the river plunges 310ft/94m into a gorge with a deafening roar. As a result of chemical reactions in the rhyolite which outcrops here the walls of the gorge shimmer in reddish to yellow tones.

*Upper Falls/
**Lower Falls/
Canyon Village

Yosemite National Park

Morning Glory Pool, Yellowstone National Park

There are very fine views of the falls from Lookout Point and Grandview Point on the north side of the valley, near the holiday settlement of Canyon Village.

Tower-Roosevelt

On the northern edge of the National Park is the little holiday resort of Tower-Roosevelt (alt. 6270ft/1911m), With Roosevelt Lodge. Notable features are the Tower Fall (130ft/40m high) and the Petrified Tree. To the south-east is the Specimen Ridge, with the remains of a number of fossil forests superimposed on one another.

Yosemite National Park   L/M 6

State: California
Area: 1190sq.miles/3082sq.km
Established: 1890

Season

Part of the National Park (the Yosemite Valley) is open throughout the year. The Tioga Road running through the High Sierra is closed in winter. The best time to visit the park is in spring, when the waterfalls, fed by meltwater, are particularly impressive. From June to September the park tends to be overcrowded. There are facilities for winter sports.

Reservation

Since the accommodation available within the National Park and immediately outide it is very limited, it is essential to make reservations well in advance. The Yosemite Lodge is often booked up for years ahead. See Practical Information, National Parks.

Situation and *topography

The Yosemite National Park in eastern California takes in a section of the western Sierra Nevada which has a particularly rich forest cover and

Yosemite National Park

Yosemite Valley

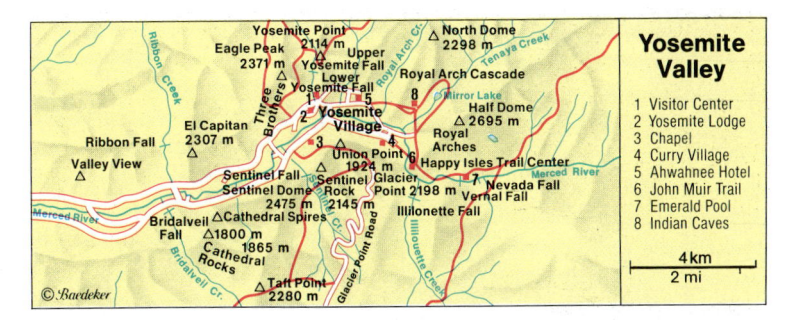

1 Visitor Center
2 Yosemite Lodge
3 Chapel
4 Curry Village
5 Ahwahnee Hotel
6 John Muir Trail
7 Emerald Pool
8 Indian Caves

numerous rivers and lakes. Over 4 million visitors a year throng to the most beautiful parts of the park, with its almost vertical granite walls, imposing waterfalls, alpine meadows, mountain lakes, snowfields and giant sequoias. The flora and fauna of the park are rich and varied. In addition to the giant sequoias there are incense cedars, live oaks, laurels, azaleas, acanthus and rare species of thistle. A variety of animals, including black and brown bears, mule deer, chipmunks and raccoons, are quite frequently to be seen, together with more than 200 species of birds and over two dozen species of reptiles.

More than 4000 years ago men were living in the Yosemite Valley, and many years later they were followed by the Miwok and Ahwahneechee tribes. The first Europeans – fur-trappers – turned up in the area around 1833. Thereafter there were clashes between the local Indians and white gold-prospectors. The first whites to reach the Yosemite Valley, in 1851, were members of a military unit pursuing Indians. Although they did not catch the Indians, they reported to the outside world the extraordinary beauty of this valley, which takes its name from the Indian word for the grizzly bear, a native of this area, *u-zu-ma-ta*. In 1855 a large mounted expedition arrived in the valley, and others followed. In order to ensure that private interests did not spoil the valley Congress passed a law obliging the young state of California to preserve the Yosemite Valley and the Mariposa Grove of giant sequoias. Ten years later a road was built to the valley, and by 1877 there were already organised coach trips to Yosemite. In 1880 the area was taken under federal control, and thereafter was gradually extended to its present size. In 1900 the first automobile made its way into the Yosemite Valley, and in 1907 a railroad line reached the western border of the National Park, remaining in operation until 1945. In 1926 the all-weather motor road to Merced was completed.

History

Sights in the Yosemite National Park

The central feature of the National Park is the Yosemite Valley, through which flows the Merced River: a high valley lying at an altitude of around 4265ft/1300m, 8 miles/13km long and up to 2 miles/3km wide. Huge granite crags rear up another 4600ft/1400m. 3000ft/915m above the valley rises El Capitán (7569ft/2307m), the western buttress of the valley. On the other side of the valley are the Three Brothers, Eagle Peak (8530ft/2600m), Sentinel Rock, the two Cathedral Rocks (first climbed only in the 1940s) and the mighty Half Dome (8842ft/2695m), a monolith closing the east end of the valley in the shape of one half of a dome; whether the missing half ever existed is not known.

**Yosemite Valley

Some 300 million years ago magma was forced upwards into the earth's crust and there were formed the granite massifs of the Sierra Nevada, the upthrust of which began about 150 million years ago and continued into

Origins

Yosemite National Park

A breathtaking view of the Yosemite Falls

the Tertiary era. A predecessor of the present Merced River then carved out a deep canyon on a line marked out by tectonic action. During the ice ages glaciers then gouged out a U-shaped valley, and the rock walls now so characteristic of the valley were shaped. After the last ice age a lake was formed in the valley, and this gradually silted up to form the level valley floor.

Free climbing — El Capitán and the Half Dome are the most celebrated climbing pitches in the Yosemite Valley, and indeed in the whole of California. On these two rocks the technique of free climbing was first tried out and the Alpine scale of difficulty extended beyond grade 6.

***Yosemite Falls** — The renowned Yosemite Falls, half way along the valley, drop down 2425ft/739m in three stages. They usually dry out between June and October, and other falls in the National Park, such as the Bridal Veil Falls, which in full flow are magically beautiful, are reduced in summer to a meagre trickle.

Yosemite Village — At the mouth of the valley is the little settlement of Yosemite Village, from which there is a free shuttle bus up the valley. Here too are the National Park offices, a Visitor Center and the Yosemite Museum, with an exhibition on the culture of the local Indians and a fine picture gallery. In the Indian Village visitors can see something of the life of the Ahwahneechee Indians.

***Giant sequoias** — 2 miles/3km from the south end of the valley is the (fairly easily accessible) Mariposa Grove with its gigantic redwoods. Here there are some 500 of these giant trees, the most striking of which is the Giant Grizzly. In spite of the fact that its crown has been broken off by the weight of snow this huge tree still stands 210ft/64m high and has a diameter of 30ft/9m at the base; and some branches – which start only at a height of 100ft/30m – have a diameter of 6½ft/2m. The tree is estimated to be 2700 years old. Less easily accessible are the redwoods in the remoter but highly interesting biotopes of Merced Grove and Tuolumne Grove.

Zion National Park

Near the Tioga Road (north-west entrance; only negotiable in summer) are a number of beautiful mountain lakes, the finest of which is perhaps the May Lake (alt. 820ft/250m). *Mountain lakes

A climb to Glacier Point (7200ft/2200m) is rewarded by breathtaking views of the peaks in the National Park. *Glacier Point

To the east of El Capitán and the Yosemite Falls is Indian Canyon. The monumental rock wall on the opposite side is known as the Royal Arches because of the recesses in the rock face. Farther east is the Washington Column, a granite pillar over which looms the bare summit of the North Dome (7545ft/2300m). Below this peak the Yosemite Valley divides into the valleys of the Merced River and Tenya Creek, the latter of which flows into the beautifully situated Mirror Lake. **Indian Canyon**

*Mirror Lake

In Merced Canyon are two impressive waterfalls, the Vernon Fall and the Nevada Fall.

Surroundings of the Yosemite National Park

To the east of the National Park, in a beautiful setting, is Mono Lake (alt. 6235ft/1900m; 13 miles/21km long, 8 miles/13km across), an alkaline lake of volcanic origin with no outlet, on whose shores many hundreds of thousands of migrant birds find a resting-place in spring and autumn. On the south side of the lake are a number of bizarrely shaped limestone sinter pinnacles, formed as a result of variations in water level and geo-chemical reactions produced by the meeting of alkaline water and fresh spring water containing lime. *Mono Lake

The eco-system of Mono Lake is in grave danger from the enormous water requirements of the Los Angeles conurbation. Several of its tributaries have already been tapped. In recent years the salt content of the water of the lake has been rising dramatically and the water level has been steadily falling.

Zion National Park   M 12/13

State: Utah
Area: 230sq.miles/596sq.km
Established: 1919

The National Park is open throughout the year, but from December to March there are no bus services to the park and no accommodation for visitors. Between May and October temperatures frequently rise above 99°F/37°C, and there are often short, violent thunderstorms during the afternoon in July and August. The best times for a visit to the National Park, therefore, are spring and autumn. Season

Zion National Park takes in the imposing canyons of the often tumultuous Virgin River, a tributary of the Colorado River, and its tributaries, which in the course of millions of years have carved their way through the horizontally bedded sandstones, limestones and slates of the Markagunt plateau, an offshoot of the Colorado Plateau, creating a magnificent landscape of sheer-walled gorges up to 3000ft/900m deep, mesas (isolated tablelands), rock domes and battlements, in a play of colours ranging from whitish-grey by way of orange and red to deep purple. The predominant colouring of the park is red, in many shades and tones: even the roads are rust-red. A number of Indian cultures (Basketmaker, Anasazi, Paiute) have left their traces in Zion Canyon. When the Mormons came here in 1858 they gave the valley and its most striking features the names they now bear, many of them Biblical. The park area is divided into the south-eastern Zion Canyon section, in which are the main sights, and the north-western Kolob Canyons section, still relatively unprovided with roads and services, which accounts for roughly a third of the total area. Situation and *topography

Zion National Park

Flora and fauna

Ashes, poplars, Douglas firs, spruces, golden aquilegias and maidenhair ferns are only a few of the many species of plants to be found in the National Park. The commonest animals are mule deer, and bighorn sheep are occasionally seen. Small bats flit about in the twilight. Frequent visitors to campgrounds and picnic sites are the comical ground squirrels. Rattlesnakes and cougars, whose main habitat is the Kolob Canyons section, are very rarely seen.

Zion Canyon

From the south entrance of the National Park at Springdale the park road runs past the Watchman (6546ft/1995m; on right) and the West Temple (7809ft/2380m; on left) and up the deeply indented valley of the Virgin River. A short distance from the entrance are the campgrounds (on right) and the Visitor Center (on left).

*Zion Canyon Scenic Drive

The 7½ mile/12km long Zion Canyon Scenic Drive begins after the Zion-Mount Carmel Highway (see below) goes off on the right. On the left are the Sentinel (7156ft/2181m) and the Three Patriarchs (6890ft/2100m), on the right the Mountain of the Sun (6723ft/2049m). Beyond Zion Lodge the road continues up the canyon, passing on the right the Red Arch Mountain (5929ft/1807m) and the Great White Throne (6746ft/2056m) and on the left Angels Landing (5791ft/1765m) and the Organ (5099ft/1554m), to end at the Temple of Sinawava (6014ft/1833m). Open buses take visitors to the main sights on the Zion Canyon Scenic Drive.

*Zion–Mount Carmel Highway

The 11 mile/18km long Zion–Mount Carmel Highway goes off on the right at the junction of Pine Creek with the Virgin River, heading for the east entrance to the National Park. It winds its way up the side of Pine Creek Canyon with many sharp bends and then runs through the 1 mile/1.6km long (unlighted) Zion Tunnel. Shortly before reaching the east entrance it passes on the right the Checkerboard Mesa, eroded into the chessboard pattern which gives it its name.

Hiking trails

At the end of the Watchman Trail (2 miles/3.2km) there are fine views of the lower part of Zion Canyon and into Oak Creek Canyon. The Emerald Pools

In Zion National Park

Zion National Park

Trail (2 miles/3.2km) leads to the Emerald Pools, which are fed by waterfalls. The short Canyon Overlook Trail (1¼ miles/2km) offers a magnificent prospect of Pine Creek Canyon and the Towers of the Virgin on the west rim of Zion Canyon. The Angels Landing Trail (5 miles/8km) is an extremely strenuous route. The steep final section up to Angels Landing calls for a good head for heights; but even without climbing up all the way it is a very rewarding hike.

*Angels Landing Trail

On the Weeping Rock Trail an unusual natural phenomenon can be observed. A nature trail (1¼ miles/2km) leads to the Weeping Rock, a rock overhang overgrown with plants known as the Hanging Gardens. Water seeping down through the rock encounters an impervious stratum and emerges from the rock above the plants; the rock thus "weeps". Other rewarding trails are the Gateway to the Narrows Trail (3 miles/5km), the Sand Bench Trail (3¾ miles/6km), the Hidden Canyon Trail (2½ miles/4km) and the East Rim Trail (8 miles/13km). On the West Rim Trail (27 miles/43km) a tent should be taken for an overnight halt.

From Highway I 15 the Kolob Canyons Road runs past the Visitor Center in the north-west of the park (closed in winter). An unsurfaced mountain road runs from the township of Virgin (to the west of the National Park) by way of the Kolob Terrace Road to Cedar City (65 miles/100km). Although scenically magnificent, this road is negotiable only in dry weather and with an all-terrain vehicle.

Kolob Canyons

In this part of the park is the strenuous Kolob Arch Trail (14 miles/23km), which leads to a free-standing rock arch 310ft/95m high. An overnight halt is necessary on this route.

There are guided pony treks from Zion Lodge. Information on these and other activities in the National Park can be obtained from the park offices (see Practical Information, National Parks).

Pony trekking

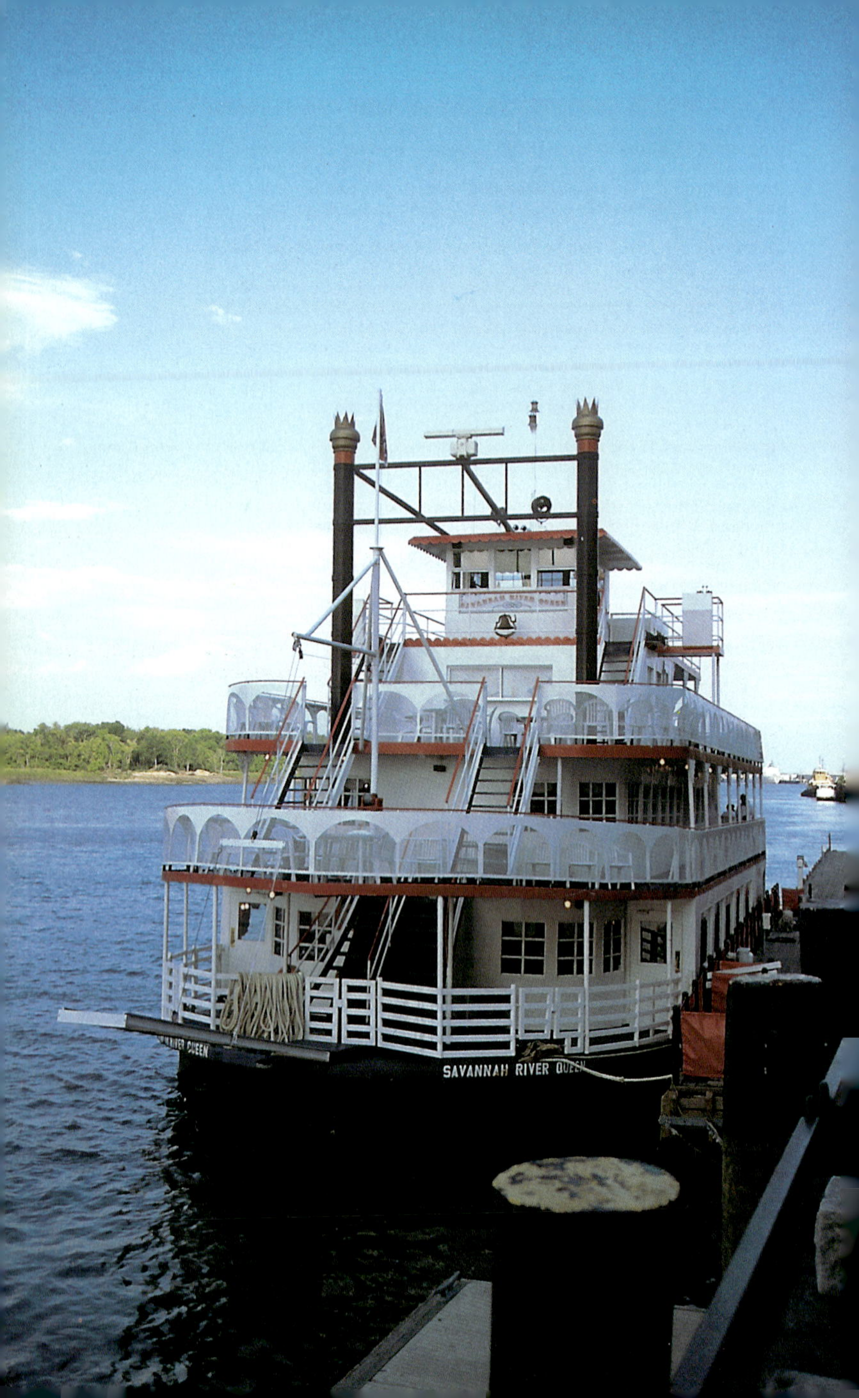
SAVANNAH RIVER QUEEN

Practical Information from A to Z

In view of the immense numbers of hotels and restaurants in the United States no attempt is made in this guide to give detailed listings. Under these headings, and in certain other entries where similar circumstances apply, only the necessary basic information is given. In many cases the telephone "hot lines" (with the prefix 800) are given on which the required information service can be contacted, toll-free, from anywhere in the United States. Also worth consulting are the "yellow page" telephone directories.

General

Accommodation

See Bed and Breakfast, Camping, Hotels and Motels, Young People's Accommodation

Air Travel

Airports

The most important airports for visitors arriving in the United States are New York, Boston, Washington, Chicago, Miami, Atlanta, Los Angeles and San Francisco.

Arrival airports

Service facilities at United States airports are in line with international standards. On arrival from abroad there may be quite long waits at passport control, baggage claim and customs.

Not surprisingly in view of the great distances to be covered, flying is a very popular means of travel in the United States, and by European standards it is relatively cheap. The busiest airports for travel within the United States are New York, Chicago, Miami, Atlanta, Charlotte, Denver, Houston and Los Angeles, followed by Dallas/Fort Worth, Orlando, Cincinnati, Detroit, Minneapolis/St Paul, Kansas City and San Francisco. From these "hub" airports there are services, usually several times daily, to all major US airports.

Domestic flights

There are numerous regional airports and local airstrips linked with the domestic network of services. They are also convenient for private and charter flying.

Regional and local airports

Airlines

The main American airports are served by all the major US airlines and their associates. Airlines which fly international services may be able to offer convenient connections and advantageous fares on domestic flights. US airlines flying non-stop from Britain to the United States: American Airlines (to Boston, Chicago, Dallas/Fort Worth, Los Angeles, Miami, Nashville, New York and Raleigh/Durham), Continental (to Denver, Houston and New York), Delta (to Atlanta, Cincinnati, Detroit and Miami), Northwest (to Boston and Minneapolis), TWA (to St Louis), United (to Los Angeles, New York, San Francisco, Seattle and Washington DC), USAir (to Charlotte).

US airlines

◀ *Another Southern Belle . . .*

Air Travel

On the way to the United States . . .

British airlines	British Airways fly non-stop from London to Atlanta, Baltimore, Boston, Charlotte, Chicago, Dallas/Fort Worth, Houston, Los Angeles, Miami, New York, Orlando, Philadelphia, San Francisco, Seattle and Washington DC, and also from Glasgow and Manchester to New York.
	Virgin Atlantic fly non-stop from London to Boston, Los Angeles, Miami, New York, Orlando and San Francisco.
Fares	Fares on both transatlantic and domestic flights are a confusing jumble of different rates with varying conditions attached. Before booking you should enquire about special fares and reductions. There are usually cheap rates for young people, students and senior citizens. Fares within the United States tend to be higher during the main holiday season, at weekends and around public holidays. Passengers flying the Atlantic on US airlines may be able to get cheap round-trip or excursion rates on domestic flights.
Hot lines	Toll-free lines for airline enquiries from anywhere in the United States:

Air Canada: 1 800 776 3000
American Airlines: 1 800 433 7300
American Eagle: 1 800 433 7300
America West: 1 800 235 9292
British Airways: 1 800 AIRWAYS
Canadian Airlines: 1 800 665 1177
Continental: 1 800 525 0280 (domestic flights),
 1 800 231 0856 (international flights)
Delta: 1 800 241 4141 (international flights)
Northwest: 1 800 225 2525 (domestic flights),
 1 800 447 4747 (international flights)

TWA: 1 800 221 2000 (domestic flights),
1 800 892 4141 (international flights)
United: 1 800 241 6522
USAir: 1 800 428 4322

Transport and airport taxes are payable by passengers on international flights leaving the United States (and Canada). — Taxes

Holders of a pilot's licence and English radiotelephony certificate are allowed to hire an aircraft after passing a test. Further information can be obtained locally. — Private pilots

Alcohol

Statutory restrictions on the consumption of alcohol are a matter for individual states and counties, and thus differ considerably from place to place. In most states alcohol may not be sold to anyone under 21. Wine, beer and other drinks with a low alcohol content are sold in many supermarkets and foodshops; spirits can usually be bought only in special liquor stores. The sale of alcohol on Sundays is restricted or prohibited, depending on the regulations in each state.
The consumption of alcohol is prohibited in public recreation areas (bathing beaches, State Parks, etc.) and on the street. There are heavy penalties for driving under the influence of alcohol: the permitted level of blood alcohol ranges according to state and county between zero and 1 per 1000. It is also prohibited to have in an automobile (even in the boot) an open or empty bottle or can of alcohol.

Amusement Parks

There are innumerable amusement or theme parks all over the United States. The following is merely a selection of the largest.

Disneyland, 1313 Harbor Boulevard, Anaheim, CA 92803, tel. (714) 999 4000 — California
Open: throughout the year; summer daily 8am–1am, winter daily 10am–6pm

Great America, PO Box 1776, 2401 Agnew Road, Santa Clara, CA 95092, tel. (408) 988 1776 and 988 1800
Open: summer daily 10am–midnight, winter daily 10am–6pm

Knott's Berry Farm, 8039 Beach Boulevard, Buena Park, CA 90620, tel. (714) 827 1776
Open: throughout the year daily 10am–midnight

Marine World/Africa USA, Marine World Parkway, Vallejo, CA 94589, tel. (707) 644 4000
Open: throughout the year daily 9.30am–5.30pm

Sea World, 1720 S. Shores Road, Sea World Drive and I 5, San Diego, CA 92109, tel. (619) 222 6363 and 226 3901
Open: throughout the year daily 9am–dusk

Six Flags Magic Mountain, Box 5500, Valencia, CA 91355, tel. (805) 255 4100 and 255 4111
Open: May–Sept. daily 10am–variable times

Boardwalk and Baseball, PO Box 800, Orlando, FL 32802 (I 4 and US 27, Baseball City, FL 33844), tel. (407) 648 5151 — Florida
Open: throughout the year daily 9am–10pm

Amusement Parks

Stars and stripes on the water (Cypress Gardens, Florida)

	Busch Gardens/The Dark Continent, PO Box 9158, 3605 Bougainvillea, Tampa, FL 33674, tel. (813) 988 5171 Open: throughout the year daily 9.30am–6pm
	Sea World of Florida, 7007 Sea World Drive, Orlando, FL 32821–8097, tel. (407) 351 3600 Open: throughout the year; summer daily 8.30am–10pm, winter daily 9am–8pm
	Walt Disney World Resort, PO Box 10000, Lake Buena Vista, FL 32830-1000, tel. (407) 824 4321 Open: throughout the year daily 9am–variable times
Georgia	Six Flags Over Georgia, PO Box 43187, Atlanta, GA 30378 (7561 Six Flags Road, Mapleton), tel. (404) 739 3400 Open: May–Sept. daily 10am–variable times
Illinois	Six Flags Great America, Grand Avenue, Gurnee, IL 60031, tel. (708) 249 1776 Open: May–Sept. daily 10am–variable times
Minnesota	Valleyfair, 1 Valleyfair Drive, Shakopee, MN 55379, tel. (612) 445 7600 Open: May–Sept. daily 10am–variable times
Missouri	Worlds of Fun, 4545 Worlds of Fun Avenue, Kansas City, MO 64161, tel. (816) 454 4545 Open: Apr.–Oct. daily 10am–variable times
New Hampshire	Canobia Lake Park, PO Box 190, North Policy Street, Salem, NH 03079, tel. (603) 893 3506 Open: May–Sept. daily noon–variable times

Angling

Six Flags Great Adventure, PO Box 120, Route 537, Jackson, NJ 08527, tel. (201) 928 2000 Open: Easter–Sept. daily 10am–variable times	New Jersey
The Great Escape, PO Box 511, US 9, Lake George, NY 12845, tel. (518) 792 6568 Open: Memorial Day–Labor Day daily 9.30am–6pm	New York
Carowinds, PO Box 410289, Carowinds Boulevard, Charlotte, NC 28241, tel. (704) 588 2606 Open: Mar.–Oct. daily 10am–8pm	North Carolina
Cedar Point, Sandusky, OH 44871, tel. (419) 626 0830 Open: May–Sept. daily 9am–variable times	Ohio
Kings Island, 6300 Kings Island Drive, Kings Island, OH 45034, tel. (513) 398 5600 Open: Apr.–Sept. daily 9am–10pm	
Sea World of Ohio, 1100 Sea World Drive, Aurora (Cleveland), OH 44202, tel. (216) 562 8101 Open: May–Sept. daily 9am–variable times	
Hersheypark, 100 W Hersheypark Drive, Hershey, PA 17033, tel. 1 800 HERSHEY Open: May–Sept. daily 10.30am–variable times	Pennsylvania
Kennywood, 4800 Kennywood Boulevard, West Mifflin (Pittsburgh), PA 15122, tel. (412) 461 0500 Open: May–Sept. daily 11am–11pm	
Dollywood, 700 Dollywood Lane, Pigeon Forge, TN 37863, tel. (615) 428 9400 Open: May–Oct. daily 9am–variable times	Tennessee
Opryland USA, 2802 Opryland Drive, Nashville, TN 37214, tel. (615) 889 6700 Open: May–Sept. daily 9am–variable times	
Astroworld, 9001 Kirby Drive, Houston, TX 77054, tel. (713) 799 1234 Open: Mar.–Oct. daily 10am–variable times	Texas
Six Flags Over Texas, PO Box 191, 2201 Road to Six Flags, Arlington, TX 76010, tel. (817) 640 8900 Open: Mar.–Nov. daily 10am–variable times	
Lagoon and Pioneer Village, PO Box N, Farmington, UT 84025, tel. (801) 451 0101 Open: May–Sept. daily 11am–variable times	Utah
Busch Gardens "The Old Country", PO Drawer FC, 7901 Pocahontas Trail, Williamsburg, VA 23187, tel. (804) 253 3350 Open: May–Sept. daily 10am–variable times	Virginia
Kings Dominion, I 95 and Route 30, Doswell, VA 23047, tel. (804) 876 5000 Open: June–Sept. daily 9.30am–variable times	

Angling

Local tourist information offices often have very useful brochures listing good fishing waters in the area.	Information

Banks

Fishing permit — In some states anglers must obtain a fishing permit, for which a fee is payable.

Big game fishing — Big game fishing (for swordfish, sailfish, shark, barracuda, tuna, etc.) is a popular sport in the United States. In many ports on the Atlantic, the Gulf Coast and the Pacific boats can be chartered, with crew, fishing tackle and bait. The waters between Florida and the Bahamas are a favourite fishing ground where many record catches have been made.

Freshwater fishing — The prospects for freshwater fishing vary widely from place to place. Enquiry should be made locally about fishing waters and regulations.

Banks

See Currency

Bathing

Beaches — Water sports of all kinds are popular in the United States. Particularly renowned are the crystal-clear water and beaches of fine sand round the Florida peninsula and the Gulf coasts of Alabama (Gulf Islands), Mississippi (Biloxi, etc.), Louisiana and Texas (Texas Gulf Coast, Padre Island National Seashore). There are also beautiful beaches on a number of islands off the coast of Georgia, in South Carolina (Hilton Head Island, Myrtle Beach, etc.) and North Carolina (particularly the Outer Banks and Cape Hatteras), and on the Pacific coast of southern California. For those who do not mind cooler water there are good beaches on the Atlantic coasts of Maryland (Assateague Island), New Jersey (e.g. Atlantic City),

On the beach, Fort Lauderdale

Pennsylvania (Long Beach Island, Beach Island State Park), Massachusetts (particularly Cape Cod, Nantucket Island and Martha's Vineyard) and at various points on the coast of Maine (famed for its lobsters), as well as on the cooler shores of the Pacific (e.g. in the Oregon Dunes National Recreation Area).

Many beaches are equipped with parking areas, showers and lifeguards. Beaches within easy reach of cities, or with large hotel complexes, tend to be crowded, particularly at weekends, but it is often possible to reach more secluded spots by boat.

Both on the Atlantic and Pacific coasts there can be very heavy swells.

In many of the larger tourist centres and in beach hotels boats and equipment for water-skiing can be hired.

Water-skiing

There are good snorkelling areas on the Atlantic coasts of the southeastern United States, on the Gulf Coast and on the Pacific coast of southern California. At many places snorkellers will discover a colourful underwater world with a great variety of marine creatures – denizens of coral reefs, molluscs, crustaceans and fish of many different species. Round some of the islands where there has been water pollution and overfishing certain areas have been closed to snorkellers and divers in order to avoid further damage to marine life.

Snorkelling

It is easy to forget that salt water and a tropical sun can cause severe sunburn: it is a good idea, therefore, to wear a cotton shirt or T-shirt when snorkelling. Caution is required in touching unknown sea creatures (possible danger of a rash): protection can be provided by stout rubber gloves. It is inadvisable to feel into cavities in a coral reef.

Warning

In many places the taking of marine organisms is prohibited, and should not be done even where there is no official prohibition, in order to avoid endangering the delicate biological balance of this habitat.

Wind-surfing is very popular in the United States and is practised wherever bathing is possible. Favourite wind-surfing areas are the waters round Florida, on the coasts of Georgia and South Carolina, along the Gulf of Mexico and at various points on the Pacific coasts of California and in Hawaii. The heavy swell on some coasts offers a challenge to surfboarders, many of whom are to be seen on the Californian coast and in Hawaii.

Wind-surfing and surfboarding

Nude bathing is frowned on in the United States, and offenders caught by the police face a heavy fine. A degree of tolerance prevails on certain stretches of beach in Florida and California.

Nude bathing

See entry

Diving

Bed and Breakfast

Bed and breakfast houses are an increasingly popular form of accommodation in the United States, particularly in tourist areas. Often the rooms offered are in carefully restored old houses, and some of them are of a very high standard of amenity.

Lists of bed and breakfast accommodation can be obtained from state tourist offices (see Information).

Boat Trips

Boating, canoeing and sailing enthusiasts are well catered for in the United States. The Atlantic, Gulf and Pacific coasts and the numerous rivers and lakes in the interior offer endless scope for boating activities of all kinds.

The tourist offices of the various states and the information bureaux of tourist resorts (Chambers of Commerce, Visitor Centers, Welcome Centers: see Information) and National Park offices (see National Parks) supply

Information, boat hire

Business Hours

	information about boating possibilities in their areas and and can provide lists of reliable boat hirers.
House-boats	On some rivers and lakes house-boats can be rented: information from local tourist offices.
Canoe touring	Many inland waters in the United States are suitable for canoe touring. Any expedition of this kind, however, should be carefully prepared, taking account of the need for protection against insects and other dangers of the wilderness. In some of the much ramified waterways, too, it is easy to lose your way. It is advisable, therefore, to inform the canoe-hiring firm (or, in a National or State Park, the park administration) of your proposed route and destination.
Rafting	Rafting (usually in an inflatable or paddle boat) is an increasingly popular sport in the United States. Visitors can choose from a large and increasing range of organised trips in varying degrees of difficulty, from easy paddling trips for the family to exciting white-water trips through spectacular canyons. The organisers of these trips usually supply all the equipment required as well as food, and some trips also include a variety of other activities (riding, climbing, mountain biking, camping, etc.). The best white-water trips are to be had in the mountain country of the West, particularly in Arizona, California, Colorado, Idaho, Montana, Utah and Wyoming, but rafting enthusiasts will also find plenty of scope in West Virginia. Among the most popular rafting rivers are the Colorado (including the Grand Canyon) and some of its tributaries (the Green River, etc.), the upper course of the Snake River (near Jackson) and the Shoshone River (near Cody). Rafting trips are rated very safe, but it should be remembered that the organisers accept no responsibility for possible hazards: each participant in a trip must take out any insurance he considers necessary. Sports shoes, waterproof clothing and waterproof protection against the sun are essential.
Sailing	See entry
Steamboats	See Cruises

Business Hours

Banks	Banks are open Mon.–Fri. 10am–3pm; they stay open until 6pm on either Thursday or Friday.
Chemists	See entry
Post offices	See Postal Services
Shops, shopping malls	Most shops are open Mon.–Fri. 10am–6pm. The larger shopping malls are open Mon.–Sat. 10am–9pm. Some shops are open on Sundays until 6pm. Some are open round the clock.

Bus Travel

Greyhound/ Trailways	The Greyhound/Trailways buses, comfortable and well equipped, run services between all the main cities and tourist centres in the United States.
Greyhound Ameripass	The Ameripass issued by the Greyhound company, valid for 4, 7, 15 or 30 days, offers unlimited travel not only on Greyhound's own services but on

those of numerous other bus lines at very reasonable rates. Passes must be bought before arrival in the United States.

Greyhound/Trailways, PO Box 660362, Dallas, TX 75266–0362, tel. (214) 419 3996, fax (214) 715 7029.

Information

Camping

There are innumerable campgrounds all over the United States. The standard provision is an area to pitch a tent or park a trailer or motorhome, a table, a bench and a place to light a fire. On private campgrounds good sanitary facilities can be taken for granted, and there are frequently additional facilities such as food stores, snack bars, laundry rooms, television rooms, swimming pools and saunas. On many campgrounds small "log cabins" can be hired.
State-run campgrounds (for example in National Parks and State Parks) offer not only very reasonable rates but usually a beautiful setting as well, though the equipment and amenities may sometimes leave something to be desired.

Campgrounds are often crowded, particularly at the main holiday times. Advance booking, therefore, is essential. Some campgrounds belong to a toll-free reservation system: dial 1 800 365 2267 or 1 800 365 CAMP.

Reservations

The largest chain of privately run campgrounds is Kampgrounds of America (KOA). Information and lists of sites:

KOA

Kampgrounds of America, PO Box 30558
Billings, MT 59114, tel. (406) 248 7444.

"Wild" camping (i.e. camping outside recognised campgrounds) is prohibited in the United States. In exceptional cases permission must be obtained from the local authorities.

"Wild" camping prohibited

Canoeing

See Boat Trips

Car Rental

Renting a car is a good way of seeing the United States on your own. Numerous rental firms offer automobiles at attractive rates, weekly hire being particularly good value. But prospective hirers should not allow themselves to be misled by basic rentals which are sometimes temptingly low: it is also necessary to consider the cost of adequate insurance cover (third party – in the USA called liability insurance – or comprehensive, excess allowance), which can be high. In addition account must be taken of state taxes and, where an airport shuttle bus is taken from the airport to the car rental office, airport taxes.
In general it is cheaper to hire a car before leaving home than after arrival.

Tariffs

If the car ordered is not available the person hiring the car is entitled to a vehicle in the next higher category. It is also possible to move up a category with the "upgrade coupons" issued by some travel agencies and airlines. Before taking over the car you should check that it is in good condition and draw attention to any defects.
In some states there are special regulations on car hire. You should check up on these in advance.

Taking over the car

Casinos

Deposit	The car rental firm will ask for a deposit before handing over the car. Usually it is necessary only to present a credit card. Payment in cash is not normal, and if accepted at all is likely to be a substantial amount.
Insurance	Rental firms offer a confusing variety of insurance cover. The main forms are:

CDW: collision damage waiver (for damage to vehicle; desirable)
LDW: loss damage waiver (for loss of vehicle)
PAI: personal accident insurance
PEC: personal effect insurance (baggage insurance)
SLI: supplementary liability insurance (third party insurance additional to the legal minimum requirement)

Driving licence	When hiring a car a national or international driving licence must be produced.
Minimum age	The driver of a hired car must be at least 21.

Rental Firms (a selection)

All the leading rental firms have toll-free "hot lines", whose numbers can be found from the local telephone book. Reservations can be made by ringing these numbers. Almost all firms have desks in international airports and large hotels and offices in cities and tourist centres.

A selection of hot lines:

Alamo	0 800 272 200
Avis	1 800 331 1212
Budget	1 800 527 0700
Dollar	1 800 800 4000
Hertz	1 800 654 3131
National	1 800 CAR RENT
Thrifty	1 800 367 2277
Value	1 800 327 2501
Buying a car for later resale	Visitors who intend to spend some considerable time in the United States may find it worth while to buy a car and resell it at the end of their stay. It may be possible to find a firm which will guarantee to buy the car back.

Casinos

In some states, including Nevada, New Jersey and Colorado, gambling is legal. The great Mecca of gamblers is Las Vegas (see Sights from A to Z). Other gambling towns are Atlantic City (New Jersey), Black Hawk (Colorado) and Laughlin and Reno (Nevada).

Chemists

Drugstores and pharmacies	American drugstores and pharmacies offer a wider range of goods than is usual in British chemists' shops, going well beyond medicines and toilet

articles. Many department stores and supermarkets (e.g. Kroger, Wal Mart, Biggs, Safeway and K-Mart) have their own pharmacies. A wide range of medicines which in Britain are available only on prescription can be freely bought over the counter in the United States.

There is no night service for the supply of medicines outside normal hours. In case of emergency application should be made to the nearest hospital, which is open round the clock and has its own pharmacy.

Emergency services

Drugstores and pharmacies are usually open from 9am to 6pm; some stay open until 9pm or later. Pharmacies in supermarkets are open round the clock.

Opening times

Consulates

See Diplomatic and Consular Offices

Credit Cards

See Currency

Crime

See Safety and Security

Cruises

The two leading cruise ports on the Atlantic coast of the United States are Miami and New York. From New York passenger liners sail north by way of Boston and Cape Cod into Canadian waters. Popular destinations are Halifax, Nova Scotia, and the two French-speaking metropolises of Québec and Montréal on the St Lawrence. There are short cruises from New York to the Bermudas several times weekly.

Ocean cruises
Atlantic

Many visitors to Florida take short cruises to the Bahamas or longer ones to the West Indies or the Gulf of Mexico. Favourite destinations are Nassau and Freeport in the Bahamas, the US Virgin Islands of St Thomas, St Croix and St John, Puerto Rico in the Greater Antilles and the Mexican peninsula of Yucatán with its two offshore islands of Cancún and Cozumel. The "cruise capital of the world" is Miami, which handles well over 3 million passengers a year. Other important cruise ports in Florida are Port Everglades, Palm Beach, Port Canaveral and Tampa.

Florida, Bahamas, Caribbean, Gulf of Mexico

Important cruise ports on the Pacific coast of the United States are Seattle, San Francisco and Los Angeles. Some ships call in at San Diego and the Mexican tourist resort of Acapulco. Many cruise companies operating in the Pacific run cruises to ports in Alaska and the Hawaiian archipelago.

Pacific

A special experience for visitors to the United States is a cruise on the Mississippi in the venerable sternwheel paddle-steamers "Delta Queen" and "Mississippi Queen", which sail upstream from New Orleans to Vicksburg, Memphis, Cairo and St Louis and vice versa. There are also cruises on the Tennessee River and Kentucky Lake to Florence, Decatur and Chattanooga, on the Cumberland River and Lake Barkley to Nashville, and on the Ohio River to Louisville, home of the Kentucky Derby, and on via Madison and Cincinnati to Pittsburgh.

River cruises
Mississippi, Missouri, Tennessee, Ohio

Currency

On a musical cruise to Puerto Rico

Information from any good travel agency or from:
Delta Queen Steamboat Co., 30 Robin Street Wharf
New Orleans, tel. (504) 586 0631.

Currency

The unit of American currency, it hardly needs saying, is the dollar ($), which contains 100 cents. There are bills (banknotes) for 1, 5, 10, 20, 50 and 100 dollars (and for larger amounts in internal bank use) and coins in denominations of 1 cent (a penny), 5 cents (a nickel), 10 cents (a dime) and 25 cents (a quarter); there are also 50 cent and 1 dollar coins, more rarely seen.

The exchange rate of the dollar against most other currencies is subject to fluctuation. The best plan is to change money before leaving home (and to have plenty of small change in coin and low-denomination bills), since the exchange rate is usually better in Europe than in the United States. Foreign currency, however, is not particularly welcome in the United States, and it is better to depend on credit cards, dollar traveller's cheques and a sufficient supply of dollars for the early days of your stay.

Currency regulations
There are no restrictions on either the import or the export of foreign or American currency. If you are taking in more than 10,000 US dollars the amount must be declared in the customs declaration filled in on the aircraft.

Changing money
Money can be changed in the banks at international airports, and there is no difficulty about changing money in tourist centres. It is best to avoid changing money in hotels, which give much poorer rates than the banks.

Traveller's cheques
It is best to come provided with dollar traveller's cheques, which are treated like cash and are normally accepted without question in hotels, restaurants

Customs Regulations

Greenbacks, nickels, dimes and quarters

and shops on presentation of your passport. If traveller's cheques are lost or stolen they will be replaced at once by local branches of the issuing agency on production of the receipt for their purchase.

The commonest method of payment in hotels, restaurants and all kinds of shops is the credit card, and it is essential for putting down the deposit on a rented car. Visitors should therefore be sure to have one or more of the generally recognised cards. The commonest are Mastercard (Eurocard), Visa, American Express, Diners Club and Carte Blanche. Using a credit card with a PIN (personal identity number), it is possible to obtain money from automatic cash-issuing machines; and cash can also be obtained at bank counters on presentation of credit cards and passport.
In spite of the universal use of plastic money it is still, of course, possible to pay for anything with ordinary cash.

Credit cards and cash

In almost every shopping centre and at airports there is at least one bank as well as cash-issuing machines. The banks are usually open from 8.30am to 3 or 3.30pm, on Friday to 6pm. At weekends and on public holidays only the banks at international airports are open.

Banks

Customs Regulations

Visitors arriving in the United States must fill in a customs declaration and an immigration form. The necessary forms will normally be issued on the aircraft.
Personal effects (clothing, toilet articles, jewellery, cameras and cine cameras, films, binoculars, portable typewriters, radios, tape-recorders and television sets, sports equipment, etc.) may be taken into the United States without payment of duty. In addition there are duty-free allowances for

Diplomatic and Consular Offices

adults of 1 quart of alcoholic liquor and 300 cigarettes or 50 cigars or 3 pounds of tobacco. Gifts to the value of 100 dollars per head (including, for adults, up to 1 gallon of alcoholic liquor and 100 cigars) may also be taken in duty-free; any such items should not be gift-wrapped, since they must be available for customs inspection.

There are special regulations on the import of animals, meat and plants. Information about these can be obtained from the US customs authorities.

Diplomatic and Consular Offices

United States Embassies and Consulates

United Kingdom	Embassy: 24–31 Grosvenor Square London W1A 1AE Tel. (0171) 499 9000
	Consulates: 3 Regent Terrace Edinburgh EH7 5BW Tel. (0131) 556 8315
	Queen's House, 14 Queen Street Belfast BT1 6EQ Tel. (0232) 328239
Ireland	Embassy: 42 Elgin Road, Ballsbridge Dublin Tel. (01) 687122
Canada	Embassy: 100 Wellington Street Ottawa, Ontario K1P 5T1 Tel. (613) 238 5335
	Consulates in Calgary, Halifax, Montréal, Québec City, Toronto and Vancouver
Australia	Embassy: Moonah Place Canberra, ACT 2600 Tel. (062) 270 5000
	Consulates in Brisbane, Melbourne, Perth and Sydney
New Zealand	Embassy: 29 Fitzherbert Terrace, Thorndon Wellington Tel. (04) 722068
	Consulate in Auckland

Foreign Embassies and Consulates in the United States

United Kingdom	Embassy: 3100 Massachusetts Avenue NW Washington, DC 20008 Tel. (202) 462 1340

Consulates-General:
Suite 2700, Marquis Tower One
245 Peachtree Center Avenue
Atlanta, GA 30303
Tel. (404) 524 5856

Federal Reserve Plaza, 25th floor
600 Atlantic Avenue
Boston, MA 02210
Tel. (617) 248 9555

33 N. Dearborn Street
Chicago. IL 60602
Tel. (312) 346 1810

1100 Milam Building, Suite 2260
Houston, TX 77002
Tel. (713) 659 6270

11766 Wilshire Boulevard, Suite 400
Los Angeles, CA 90025
Tel. (310) 477 3322

845 Third Avenue
New York, NY 10022
Tel. (212) 745 0200

1 Sansome Street, Suite 850
San Francisco, CA 94104
Tel. (415) 981 3030

Also consulates in Anchorage, Cleveland, Dallas, Kansas City, Miami, New Orleans, Norfolk, Philadelphia, Portland, Puerto Rico, St Louis and Seattle

Ireland

Embassy:
2234 Massachusetts Avenue NW
Washington, DC 20008
Tel. (202) 462 3939

Canada

Embassy:
501 Pennsylvania Avenue NW
Washington, DC 20001
Tel. (202) 682 1740

Consulates in Atlanta, Boston, Buffalo, Chicago, Cleveland, Dallas, Detroit, Honolulu, Los Angeles, Minneapolis, New York, San Francisco and Seattle

Australia

Embassy:
1601 Massachusetts Avenue NW
Washington, DC 20036–2273
Tel. (202) 797 3000

New Zealand

Embassy:
37 Observatory Circle NW
Washington, DC 20008
Tel. (202) 328 4800

Diving

For diving enthusiasts the United States is indeed the "land of unlimited possibilities". The long Atlantic seaboard, extending from the tropical

Dress

shores of the Florida Keys to the cool waters of Maine, the coasts of the Gulf of Mexico, the Pacific coast from California to Canada and great expanses of inland waters offer unrivalled diving opportunities. Much the most inviting diving grounds, however, are to be found in and around Florida, in the Hawaiian archipelago and off the coast of California.

Scuba diving

There are numerous well equipped diving centres where all necessary equipment can be hired. If you bring your own aqualung you may need an adaptor for air cylinders of a different type. When hiring an aqualung you will usually be asked to show evidence of your competence.

Diving Grounds

Florida

The coastal waters of Florida are a diver's paradise. The turquoise-coloured water is of extraordinary clarity, particularly round the more thinly populated islands. Many islands are partly or completely sheltered by coral reefs, home to a colourful underwater world. Off some islands are regular underwater gardens. Round the coasts, too, there are numerous wrecks – including ships of the Spanish silver fleet – which attract treasure-hunters from far and wide.

The best diving grounds are round the Florida Keys. There are well equipped diving stations on Big Pine Key and Cudjoe Key, Islamorada, Key Largo, Key West, Looe Key and Tavernier. Of particular interest are the marine zone of Key Biscayne National Park, Key Largo Coral Reef Preserve, the John Pennekamp Underwater Park and the little islands of coral limestone between Marathon and Key West. There is also good diving off the Gulf Island National Seashore, on the Gulf coast of the Panhandle. There are large diving stations at Destin, Fort Walton Beach, Panama City and Pensacola.

Freshwater spring pools in Florida

A special diving experience is diving in some of the freshwater spring pools in the interior of Florida, in company with manatees and alligators. On some of these (e.g. Live Oak, High Springs) there are diving stations.

California

Although the waters off the Californian coast are relatively cool as well as rough and subject to currents, they offer interesting diving opportunities. Here underwater forests of seaweed swarm with life – sealions, sea-otters, groupers, Garibaldi fish, abalones, colourful purple-shells and a host of other sea creatures. Off Monterey the underwater world is on a giant scale, with bizarre rock formations. Round Point Lobos is an underwater nature reserve, access to which is very strictly regulated. There are other interesting diving grounds off the Californian coast round the Channel Islands, Catalina Island the San Clemente Islands. The wild cliff-fringed coasts of Salt Point State Park to the north of San Francisco will tempt experienced divers.

Hawaii

The Hawaiian islands, particularly the waters round the largest island, Hawaii, have also come into favour with divers in recent years. Among the varied range of marine creatures to be seen here are whales, sharks, mantas, turtles, colourful prawns and squids. An unusual spectacle is provided by the glowing red lava from the volcano Kilauea which is continually flowing down into the sea. The best diving grounds are on the west side of the island of Hawaii between Kailua-Kona and Honaunau. There is relatively safe and easy diving in sheltered Kealakekua Bay.

Dress

Dress in the United States is relatively casual. Between November and March warm clothing is required, since the weather tends to be inhospitable and is sometimes extremely cold.

Formal dress (jacket and tie for men, a dinner dress for women) is expected in top-category hotels and restaurants: guests should enquire about this when booking a table. Visitors should also be equipped with suitable garments for the beach (nude bathing is frowned on), light rainwear and protection against the sun.

Electricity

Electricity in the United States is 110 volts AC, with a frequency of 60 cycles. Electrical appliances (shavers, etc.) must therefore be adjustable to that voltage; and adaptors will be required, since American plugs and sockets are quite different from British or other European ones.

Emergencies

First aid, emergency doctor, police, fire: dial 911.

For help anywhere in the United States, dial 1 800 336 HELP (toll-free).

There are emergency telephones along many highways.

Endangered Species Convention

In the spirit of the Washington Convention on International Trade in Endangered Species of Wild Fauna and Flora, visitors can contribute to the preservation of endangered species by refraining from buying souvenirs made from wild plants or animals or parts of them: e.g. corals, tortoiseshell from wild turtles, living or stuffed lizards or lizard skins, various species of birds and speciments of rare insects. It goes without saying that visitors should not themselves uproot plants or catch any animals.

Events

The tourist offices of the various states (see Information) and the tourist information offices of cities and other local authorities and organisation can usually supply detailed programmes of events month by month.

Major Events (a selection)

January — Breckenridge (CO), Ullr Festival (festival in honour of the Nordic snow god Ullr); Los Angeles (CA), Super Bowl; McCall (ID) and St Paul (MN), Winter Carnival; Miami Beach (FL), Art Deco Weekend; Pasadena (CA), Tournament of Roses Parade; Philadelphia (PA), Mummers' Parade; Tarpon Springs (FL), Greek Epiphany.

February — Apache Junction (AZ), Arizona Renaissance Festival; Daytona (FL), 500 Miles (car race); Miami (FL), Miami Film Festival; Miami Beach (FL), International Boat Show; New Orleans (LA) and Pensacola (FL), Mardi Gras (Carnival); Newport (OR), Seafood and Wine Festival; St Martinsville (LA), La Grande Boucherie des Cajuns (festival of the French-speaking Cajuns); Steamboat Springs (CO), Winter Carnival.

March — Boston (MA), New England Spring Flower Show; Charleston (SC), Festival of Houses and Gardens; Columbus (MS), Spring Pilgrimage; Philadelphia (PA), Flower Show; Sarasota (FL), Medieval Fair; Sebring (FL), Twelve Hours of Sebring (car race); Stone Mountain (GA), Antebellum Jubilee; Westport/Grayland (WA), Whale Fest.

Events

April — Atlanta (GA), Dogwood Festival; Birmingham (AL), Festival of Arts; Juneau (AK), Alaska Folk Festival; Key West (FL), Conch Republic Festival; Knoxville (TN), Dogwood Arts Festival; Mountain View (AR), Arkansas Folk Festival; New Orleans (LA), Jazz and Heritage Festival; Richmond (VA), Historic Garden Week; Sarasota (FL), Sailor Circus; Tucson (AZ), Tucson Festival; Washington DC, National Cherry Blossom Festival; Winchester (VA), Shenandoah Apple Blossom Festival.

May — Baltimore (MD), Preakness Stakes; Biloxi (MI), Shrimp Festival and Blessing of the Fleet; Chicago (IL), International Art Expo; Covington (KY), May Festival in Mainstrasse Village; Fernandina Beach (FL), Isle of Eight Flags Shrimps Festival; Hermann (MO), May Festival; Holland (MI), Tulip Time Festival; Indianapolis (IN), Indianapolis 500 (car race); Louisville (KY), Kentucky Derby; Memphis (TN), International Festival; Moridian (MI), Jimmie Rodgers Memorial Festival; Pensacola (FL), Five Flags Festival; Portland (OR), Rose Festival; Tulsa (OK), International May Festival; Walla Walla (WA), Hot Air Balloon Stampede.

June — Boston (MA), Harbor Festival; Boulder (CO), Shakespeare Festival; Clarinda (IO), Glenn Miller Festival; Detroit (MI), International Freedom Festival; Fort Sisseton (SD), Historical Festival; Frankenmuth (MI), Bavarian Festival; Gettysburg (PA), Civil War Heritage Days; Hannibal (MO), National Tom Sawyer Days; Hardin (MT), Custer's Last Stand Re-enactment; Helena (MT), Montana Traditional Jazz Festival; Honolulu (HI), King Kamehameha Celebration); Jacksonport State Park (AR), Rollin' on the River; Milwaukee (WI), Summer Festival, the Big Gig; Myrtle Beach (SC), Sun and Fun Festival; Norfolk (VA), Harbor Festival; Chicago, A taste of Chicago.

July — Aspen (CO), Music Festival; Bath (ME), Bath Heritage Days; Cedar City (UT), Utah Shakespeare Festival; Cheyenne (WY), Frontier Days; Driggs (ID), Cowboy Festival; Fairbanks (AK), Golden Days; Key West (FL), Hemingway Days; Logan (UT), Festival of the American West; Manti (UT), Mormon Miracle Pageant; Milwaukee (WI), Great Circus Parade; Newport (RI), Newport Music Festival; New Ulm (NM), Heritage Festival; Sturges (WY), Harley Davidson Meeting; Wheeling (WV), Jamboree in the Hills (country music festival).

August — Abingdon (VA), Virginia Highlands Festival; Bethlehem (PA), Music Festival; Charleston (WV), Sternwheel Regatta; Chicago (IL), Jazz Festival; Des Moines (IA), Iowa State Fair; Glenns Ferry (ID), Three Island Crossing; Hugo (OK), Grant's Bluegrass Festival; Middletown (OH), Hot Air Balloon Championship; Rockland (ME), Maine Lobster Festival; Santa Barbara (CA), Old Spanish Days Fiesta; Savannah (GA), Maritime Festival.

September — Albuquerque (NM), New Mexico State Fair; Bismarck (ND), United Tribes International Pow Wow; Cincinnati (OH), Oktoberfest; Dallas (TX), Texas State Fair; Fort Worth (TX), Pioneer Days Celebration and Rodeo; Geneva (OH), Grape Jamboree; Honolulu (HI), Aloha Festival; Knoxville (TN), Tennessee Valley Fair; Lincoln (NH), New Hampshire Highland Games; New Glarus (WI), Wilhelm Tell Festival; Norwalk (CT), Oyster Festival; Ocean City (NJ), Sun Festival; Virginia City (WV), International Camel Race; West Danville (VT), Northeast Kingdom Fall Foliage Festival.

October — Albuquerque (NM), International Balloon Fiesta; Cape May (NJ), Victorian Week; Custer State Park (SD), Buffalo Roundup; Lexington (KY), Equi-Festival; Minot (ND), Norsk Hostfest (Nordic Autumn Festival); Rehoboth Beach (DE), Sea Witch Festival; Vienna (GA), Big Pig Jig; Vincetown (NJ), Chatsworth Cranberry Festival.

November — Kansas City (MS), American Royal Livestock Horse Show and Rodeo; New York (NY), Thanksgiving Day Parade, New York Marathon; Richmond (VA), Thanksgiving Festival; Wheeling (WV), Winter Festival of Lights; Winterthur (DE), Yuletide.

Boston (MA), First Night Celebration (New Year's Night festival); Fort Lauderdale (FL), WinterFest; Hollywood (CA), Christmas Parade on Sunset Boulevard (carriage parade, with many show business personalities); Las Vegas (NV), National Finals Rodeo; Miami (FL), Orange Bowl Festival; Newport (RI), Christmas in Newport; St Augustine (FL), Christmas Regatta; Salt Lake City (UT), Christmas Lights in Temple Square; Walt Disney World (FL), Christmas Parade; Washington DC, Pageant of Peace.

December

Food and Drink

It is sometimes thought that the main specialities of American cuisine are hamburgers and ketchup, hot dogs and chips; but this is very far from the truth. Restaurants serving "American" food are often excellent, and meat and fish dishes are particularly good. There are also tempting regional specialities such as Virginia ham and the Creole and Cajun dishes of the South; and in a good bar even the humble hamburger, freshly made, makes a very appetising meal. And for those who want to look beyond American cuisine there is a wide range of ethnic restaurants.

Meals

Breakfast is best taken in a coffee shop ("America at its best") or in one of the innumerable fast food restaurants. It can be quite a substantial meal, consisting of a glass of pineapple, grapefruit or orange juice, coffee, eggs (boiled, scrambled, fried – "sunny side up" – or an omelette), fried bacon or sausages, sauté potatoes ("hashed browns"), grits, pancakes with maple syrup and toast with butter and various kinds of jam. Many breakfast buffets offer corn flakes and milk, freshly prepared muesli, fresh fruit and different kinds of yoghurt.

Breakfast

On Sundays and holidays brunch – a combination of breakfast and lunch – is a popular meal, usually eaten from around 11 o'clock. This will usually be a buffet offering a wide choice of dishes.

Brunch

Lunch is usually a light meal, which might include salads, something fried, vegetables, etc.

Lunch

The main meal of the day is dinner, which can be a very substantial meal, with fish and meat and a variety of side dishes. Some restaurants put on "dinner shows" to entertain their guests.

Dinner

Food and Drink

Not surprisingly, in view of the great expanses occupied by stock farms and ranches in the United States, meat features prominently on the American menu – T-bone steak, porterhouse steak, sirloin steak and of course the ever-present hamburger. Also very popular are chicken (e.g. fried chicken fingers) and pork (especially prime rib of pork). The main dish is almost always accompanied by a choice of baked potatoes or French fries (chips). Turkey is a meal for a special occasion, particularly Thanksgiving Day.

Meat dishes

The choice of fish dishes includes not only fish and seafood from the Atlantic and Pacific but also a variety of freshwater fish from the country's many lakes and rivers. Particularly tasty are prawns, shrimps, shellfish, oysters, lobsters, grayling, perch and snapper. Stone crabs and conchs are prized as particular delicacies.

Fish

In addition to the all-American steaks, chicken and chef's salad visitors can sample the varied cuisines of all the different races represented in the

Ethnic cuisines

Getting to the United States

United States. The range extends from Italian cuisine by way of Greek and Spanish/Cuban to Mexican, Caribbean and Far Eastern, with the specialities of many different countries. Kosher cooking is also, of course, well represented.

Sweets

Favourite sweets are cheesecake, blueberry cake, and Key lime pie (made with the juice of home-grown limes and cream). Doughnuts are ubiquitous.

Fruit, vegetables

The United States has fresh fruit and vegetables throughout the year. This is true particularly of citrus fruits and easily prepared vegetables (e.g. cucumbers, tomatoes, avocados).

Coffee

American coffee is usually lightly roasted and often served very weak. It is available everywhere and generously supplied; you need only order it once and your cup will be constantly refilled. In areas where there are many Italians or Latinos you can look forward to getting a cup of strong espresso.

Beer

American beers – always served ice-cold – have a relatively low alcohol content (3–3.5% vol), and "light" beers with only 1–1.5% vol are becoming increasingly popular. Bars usually offer a choice of several brands of both bottled and draught beer. Favourite American brands are Budweiser, Busch, Miller, Coors, Michelob and Schlitz. In New England and the Middle West there are numbers of small breweries producing excellent beer. Imported European beer is much dearer than American brands.

Wine

In recent years the United States has developed into one of the world's leading wine-producers. Some four-fifths of the total area of vineyards in the United States is in California, where the growing of vines was introduced by Spanish missionaries in the 18th century. The best known Californian wine-growing areas are Santa Rosa, the Napa Valley, the Sonoma Valley, Mendocino, Livermore, Santa Clara, Monterey, San Benito and the San Joaquín Valley. There is another large wine area in the Finger Lakes region in New York State, an area with a not particularly favoured climate, and smaller areas in the states of Maryland, Virginia, Florida, Ohio, Missouri, Oregon and Washington.

The best known Californian red wines, mostly dry and full-bodied, are Zinfandel, Cabernet, Barbera, Ruby Cabernet, Grenache and Gamay. Predominant among Californian white wines are Chardonnay, French Colombard, Chenin Blanc, Sauvignon Blanc, Pinot Blanc, Semillon, Riesling and Gewürztraminer. Well known red wines from the Finger Lakes area are Concord, Isabella, Baco Noir, Chelois and Delaware; white wines include Duchess, Moore's Diamond, Niagara, Seibel, Vergennes and Elvira. In the United States red wine as well as white wine is often served chilled.

Spirits

Popular spirits – which can be bought only in special liquor stores and can be served in bars only at certain hours – are Scotch whisky and other whiskeys (bourbon, rye, Canadian, Irish), gin, vodka, brandy, rum, vermouth and cordial.

Soft drinks

Fruit juices made from home-grown fruit (oranges, grapefruit, pineapples) are available everywhere. Other popular thirst-quenchers are various colas and other soft drinks, root beer (made from water, sugar, dye and various herbs) and iced tea.

Water

A glass of iced water is served with every meal. This is ordinary tap water with added ice: if you want bottled mineral water, ask for "spring water".

Getting to the United States

By air

Most visitors to the United States go by air. There are numerous scheduled flights from London and other European airports, many of them flying non-stop to major American cities. See Air Travel.

Help for the Disabled

There are also frequent charter flights, chiefly during the main holiday season and to favourite holiday destinations.

Some American airlines (e.g. USAir, American Airlines, Continental, Delta) offer combined air tickets at advantageous rates, covering the transatlantic crossing and onward flights to other US cities or to the Bahamas, the Caribbean or even Hawaii. Information can be obtained from travel agencies.

Special rates

The port of Miami in Florida is the busiest cruise port in the world, the departure point and destination of cruise ships sailing to the Caribbean and Central and South America. Many passenger ships still put in at New York. A combination of sea and air travel is also popular, travelling one way by air and the other by sea. Thus it is possible to sail to New York in the luxury liner "Queen Elizabeth II" and return by Concorde. There are also berths for passengers in some cargo and container ships sailing to ports in the United States. Transatlantic crossings on sailing yachts are also on offer. Again, information can be obtained from travel agencies.

By sea

Golf

The United States is a Mecca for golfers. Golf is a popular American sport; it is not, as in some other countries, a select and expensive one, and there are large numbers of golf courses all over the country: in Florida alone, where golf can be played practically all the year round, there are over a thousand courses. Many American courses, for example the Seminole Golf Club in Palm Beach, are internationally renowned. The stars of the golfing world are frequently to be found playing somewhere in the United States.

Many American golf courses are open to the public, and many golf clubs welcome golfers who are members of foreign clubs. Many hotels and holiday resorts which have their own golf courses or can offer guests the opportunity of playing in a neighbouring golf or country club offer attractive all-in rates.

The tourist offices of the various states (see Information) issue brochures on golfing facilities in their areas.

Information

The newspaper "USA Today" publishes a Golf Atlas of the United States, which can be obtained from:
H. M. Gousha
15 Columbia Circle
New York, NY 10023
Tel. (210) 995 3317.

Golf Atlas

Help for the Disabled

Building regulations vary considerably from state to state. In recent years the authorities have been concerned to ensure that public buildings, airports, railroad stations, hotels, restaurants, etc., have proper facilities for disabled people. Theme parks and other entertainment also try to cater for the disabled, and everywhere there are special parking lots for them.

Facilities for disabled

In Britain the main sources of information and advice on travel by the disabled are the Royal Association for Disability and Rehabilitation (RADAR), 12 City Forum, 250 City Road, London EC1V 8AF, tel. (0171) 250 3222; the Spinal Injuries Association, 76 St James's Lane, London N10 3DF, tel. (0181) 444 2121; and Mobility International, Rue de Manchester, 25 B-1070, Brussels, Belgium, tel. 410 6297, fax. 410 6874.

Information in the UK

"Holiday and Travel Abroad – A Guide for Disabled People", published by RADAR.

Useful publications

Holiday Apartments

"The World Wheelchair Traveller", published by the AA for the Spinal Injuries Association.

"Low Cost Travel Tips for People Using Wheelchairs", published by Mobility International.

The AA also publishes a "Guide for the Disabled Traveller" (free to members).

Information in the USA

Information about travel by disabled persons in the United States can be obtained from:

Information Center for Individuals with Disabilities
Fort Point Place, 27–43 Wormwood Street, 1st floor
Boston, MA 02210
Tel. (617) 727 5540

Other sources of information in the United States are Louise Weiss's "Access to the World: A Travel Guide for the Handicapped" (available from Facts on File, 460 Park Avenue South, New York NY 10016) and the Society for the Advancement of Travel by the Handicapped, 347 Fifth Avenue, 60010 NY 10016, tel. (212) 447 7284.

Holiday Apartments

In the last twenty years or so large numbers of holiday apartments have been built in the holiday regions of the United States. The range extends from luxury villas with their own landing-stage to more modest apartments in tower blocks with a view of the sea. They are usually small furnished apartments with fully equipped kitchens and accommodation for three or four people. Their disadvantage as compared with hotels is that there is a minimum length of stay (usually between 2 and 5 nights). Lists of such apartments can be obtained from local and regional tourist offices (see Information).

Hotels/Motels/Resorts

The range of accommodation for visitors in the United States is enormous, with many hundreds of thousands of rooms in hotels, motels and other forms of accommodation; and more are being built every year. Much of this accommodation is round the coasts, offering the highest standards of comfort and amenity at correspondingly high prices, but there are plenty of hotels and other establishments in more modest price ranges, though they will usually tend to be farther away from bathing beaches and other attractions.

Hotels

Hotels are mostly in the central area of cities and in tourist centres. The larger establishments run courtesy bus services from the nearest airport. In the large hotels there are usually restaurants, coffee shops, snack bars, small shops, beauty parlours, hairdressers and car rental and airline offices.

Resorts

Resorts are luxurious holiday complexes equipped with a wide range of leisure and sports facilities. Often run in the style of country clubs, they have their own bathing beaches, tennis courts, golf courses, horse paddocks, etc., and are usually very expensive.

Motels

Motels are geared to the requirements of motorised tourists. They are usually situated on main roads out of town, have free parking near the

Hotels/Motels/Resorts

rooms and may sometimes have their own swimming pools and sports facilities. The standard of service sometimes leaves something to be desired.

The rate for a double room for one night ranges roughly as follows: Price categories

luxury hotels: over $180
hotels and motels with a high standard of comfort and amenity: $130–200
establishments with a good standard of comfort and amenity: $100–150
good-value hotels and motels: $60–100
modest establishments: $30–80

State taxes may add up to 15% on the cost of a room. There is no additional charge for children occupying the same room as their parents; for an additional adult the charge will range between $5 and $20.
Breakfast is not usually included in the price, and there may also be an additional charge for car parking.
Many hotels, including luxury hotels, offer weekend rates at considerable reductions.

Most hotel rooms have their own bath or shower, air-conditioning, telephone, radio and television. Many hotels, particularly the larger and more luxurious, have one or more restaurants, with prices related to the category of the hotel.

Room keys are normally kept by the guest, not handed in at reception. All hotels have safes (either at reception or in the room) in which objects of value can be deposited.

It is advisable to book hotel and motel rooms in advance, using the "hot lines" (with the 800 code, toll-free) which most hotels have (see below). Lists of hotels can be obtained from local tourist information offices (see Information).   Reservation

Hotel and Motel Chains

Many of the big American hotel chains have offices in Britain through which reservations can be made. Some of them can also provide pre-paid vouchers at advantageous rates. The telephone numbers of these offices are listed in the USA Travelfax obtainable from the United States Travel and Tourism Administration (see Information).

Adam's Mark Hotels: 1 800 231 5858
Best Value Inns/Sundowner/Superior: 1 800 322 8029
Best Western International: 1 800 528 1234
Budgetal Inns: 1 800 428 3438
Canadian Pacific Hotels: 1 800 828 7447
Choice Hotels International: 1 800 221 2222
Clarion Hotels and Resorts: 1 800 4 CHOICE
Comfort Inns: 1 800 4 CHOICE
Courtyards by Marriott: 1 800 321 2211
Days Inn: 1 800 329 7466
Dillon Inns: 1 800 253 7503
Doubletree: 1 800 528 0444
Downtowner/Passport Motor Inns: 1 800 238 6161
Drury Inn: 1 800 325 8300
Econo Lodges: 1 800 4 CHOICE
Embassy Suites: 1 800 EMBASSY
Exel Inns of America: 1 800 356 8013
Fairfield Inn: 1 800 228 2800
Fairmont Hotels: 1 800 527 4727
Four Seasons Hotels and Resorts: 1 800 545 4000

"Hot lines" of hotel chains

Information

Friendship Inns: 1 800 4 CHOICE
Guest Quarters Suite Hotels: 1 800 424 2900
Hampton Inns: 1 800 HAMPTON
Harley Hotels: 1 800 321 2323
Hilton Hotels: 1 800 HILTONS
Holiday Inns: 1 800 HOLIDAY
Homewood Suites: 1 800 CALL HOM(E)
Hospitality International/Master Hosts Red Carpet/Scottish Inns:
  1 800 251 1962
Howard Johnson's Lodges: 1 800 446 4656
Hyatt Hotels: 1 800 223 1234
Inter-Continental Hotels: 1 800 327 0200
Knights Inn: 1 800 722 7220
La Quinta Motor Inns: 1 800 531 5000
Loews Hotels: 1 800 23 LOEWS
Luxbury Hotels: 1 800 CLASS 4 U
Marriott Hotels and Resorts: 1 800 228 9290
Meridien: 1 800 543 4300
Omni Hotels: 1 800 THE OMNI
Preferred Hotels: 1 800 323 7500
Quality Inns: 1 800 4 CHOICE
Radisson Hotel Corporation: 1 800 333 3333
Ramada Inns: 1 800 272 6232
Red Lion Inns: 1 800 548 8010
Red Roof Inns: 1 800 843 7663
Regal Inns: 1 800 851 8888
Regent International Hotels: 1 800 545 4000
Residence Inn by Marriott: 1 800 331 3131
Ritz-Carlton: 1 800 241 3333
Rodeway Inns: 1 800 4 CHOICE
Sheraton Hotels and Motor Inns: 1 800 325 3535
Sleep Inns: 1 800 4 CHOICE
Sonesta Hotels: 1 800 SONESTA
Stouffer Hotels and Inns: 1 800 468 3571
Super 8 Motels: 1 800 848 8888
Suisse Chalet: 1 800 258 1980
Travelodge and Thrift Hotels: 1 800 255 3050
Treadway Inns Corporation: 1 800 873 2392
Trusthouse Forte Hotels: 1 800 225 5843
Vagabond Inns: 1 800 522 1555
West Coast Hotels: 1 800 426 0670
Westin Hotels and Resorts: 1 800 228 3000
Wyndham Hotels and Resorts: 1 800 822 4200

Information

The **US Travel and Tourism Administration** (USTTA) has offices in countries throughout the world. It has a London office (PO Box 1EN, London W1A 1EN) but is best contacted by telephone at (071) 495 4466. It supplies a useful information pack, including a Holiday Planner, a map of the United States, visa information and USA Travelfax.

Destinations with Offices in the United Kingdom

Some states and cities maintain their own offices in the United Kingdom. They can be contacted at the following telephone numbers.

Arizona: (01483) 440460
California: (0171) 405 4746
Delaware: (0171) 379 0344

Information

Daytona: (0171) 935 7756
Florida Division of Tourism: (0171) 727 1661
Florida Gulf Coast: (0181) 651 4742
Florida Keys and Key West: (01564) 794555
Fort Lauderdale: (0171) 630 5995
Hawaii: (0171) 734 0525
Las Vegas/Nevada: (01564) 794999
Massachusetts: (0171) 978 5233
Newport (Rhode Island): (01564) 794999
New York State: (0171) 916 4112
Palm Beach County (Florida): (0181) 681 67762
Pennsylvania: (0171) 379 0344
Rocky Mountains (Wyoming, Montana, S. Dakota, Idaho): (01444) 811991
South Carolina: inquiries to USTTA
Tennessee: (01462) 440784
Tucson (toll-free): (0800) 898307
US Virgin Islands: (0171) 978 5262
Virginia: (0181) 651 4743
Washington DC: (0181) 392 9187

Information Offices in the United States

Alabama Bureau of Tourism and Travel, 401 Adams Avenue, Suite 126, PO Box 4309, Montgomery, AL 36103–4309, tel. (205) 242 4169, fax (205) 242 4554	Alabama
Alaska Division of Tourism, PO Box 110801, Juneau, AK 99811–0801, tel. (907) 465 2010, fax (907) 586 8399	Alaska
Arizona Office of Tourism, 1100 West Washington Street, Phoenix, AZ 85007, tel. (602) 542 8687, fax (602) 542 4068	Arizona
Arkansas Department of Parks and Tourism, One Capitol Mall, Little Rock, AR 72201, tel. (501) 682 7777, fax (501) 682 1364	Arkansas
California Office of Tourism, 801 K Street, Suite 1600, Sacramento, CA 95814, tel. (916) 322 2881, fax (916) 322 3402	California
Colorado Tourism Board, Broadway, Suite 1700, Denver, CO 80202, tel. (303) 592 5510, fax (303) 592 5406	Colorado
Connecticut Department of Economic Development, Tourism Division, Rocky Hill, CT 06067, tel. (203) 258 4355, fax (203) 563 4877	Connecticut
Delaware Tourism Office, 99 Kings Highway, Box 1401, Dover, DE 19903, tel. (302) 739 4271, fax (302) 739 5749	Delaware
Washington DC Convention and Visitors Association, 1212 New York Avenue, Washington, DC 20005, tel. (202) 789 7000, fax (202) 789 7037	District of Columbia/ Washington
Florida Division of Tourism, Department of Commerce, 107 W. Gaines Street, Room 566, Collins Building, Tallahassee, FL 32399–2000, tel. (904) 488 7598 or 9187, fax (904) 487 0132	Florida
Georgia Department of Industry, Trade and Tourism, 285 Peachtree Center Avenue, Marquis Tower Two, 19th floor, Atlanta, GA 30301, tel. (404) 656 3553, fax (404) 651 9063	Georgia
Hawaii State Tourism Office, PO Box 2359, Honolulu, HI 96804, tel. (808) 586 2550, fax (808) 586 2549	Hawaii
Idaho Division of Tourism Development, Department of Commerce, 700 W. State Street, Boise, ID 83720, tel. (208) 334 2470, fax (208) 334 2631	Idaho

Information

Illinois	Illinois Bureau of Tourism, State of Illinois Center, 100 W. Randolph Street, Chicago, IL 60601, tel. (312) 814 4732, fax (312) 314 6581
Indiana	Indiana Tourism Marketing and Film Division, Department of Commerce, One North Capital, Suite 700, Indianapolis, IN 46204–2288, tel. (317) 232 8860, fax (317) 232 4146
Iowa	Iowa Division of Tourism, Department of Economic Development, 200 E. Grand Avenue, Des Moines, IA 50309, tel. (515) 242 4705, fax (515) 242 4749
Kansas	Kansas Travel and Tourism Division, 400 SW 8th Street, 5th floor, Topeka, KS 66603–3712, tel. (913) 296 2009, fax (913) 296 5055
Kentucky	Kentucky Department of Travel, 2200 Capitol Plaza Tower, 500 Mero Street, Frankfort, KY 40602, tel. (502) 564 4930, fax (502) 564 5695
Louisiana	Louisiana Office of Tourism, Department of Culture, Recreation and Tourism, PO Box 94291, Baton Rouge, LA 70804–9291, tel. (504) 342 8100, fax (504) 342 8390
Maine	Maine Office of Tourism, Department of Economic and Community Development, 189 State Street, Station 59, Augusta, ME 04333, tel. (207) 285 5711, fax (207) 287 5701
Maryland	Maryland Office of Tourism Development, Division of Economic and Employment Development, 217 E. Redwood Street, 9th floor, Baltimore, MD 21202, tel. (410) 333 6611, fax (410) 333 6643
Massachusetts	Massachusetts Office of Travel and Tourism, 100 Cambridge Street, 13th floor, Boston, MA 02202, tel. (617) 727 3201, fax (617) 727 6525
Michigan	Michigan Travel Bureau, Department of Commerce, PO Box 30226, Lansing, MI 48909, tel. (517) 373 0670, fax (517) 373 0059
Minnesota	Minnesota Office of Tourism, 121 East 7th Place, St Paul, MN 55101–1810, tel. (612) 296 2755
Mississippi	Mississippi Department of Economic Development and Tourism Division, PO Box 1705, Ocean Springs, MS 395 66–1705, tel. (601) 359 3297, fax (601) 359 2832
Missouri	Missouri Division of Tourism, PO Box 1055, Jefferson City, MO 65102, tel. (314) 751 3051, fax (314) 751 5160
Montana	Montana Promotion Division, Department of Commerce, 1424 9th Avenue, Helena, MT 59620–0411, tel. (406) 444 2654, fax (406) 444 2808
Nebraska	Nebraska Division of Travel and Department of Economic Development, PO Box 94666, 301 Centennial Mall South, Lincoln, NE 68509, tel. (402) 471 3794, fax (402) 471 3778
Nevada	Nevada Division of Travel and Tourism, Capital Complex, Carson City, NV 89710, tel. (702) 687 4322, fax (702) 687 6779
New Hampshire	New Hampshire Office of Travel and Tourism Development, 172 Pembroke Road, PO Box 856, Concord, NH 03302–1856, tel. (603) 271 2343, fax (603) 271 2629
New Jersey	New Jersey Division of Travel and Tourism, Department of Commerce and Economic Development, West State Street, Trenton, NJ 08625–0826, tel. (609) 292 2470, fax (609) 633 7418

Information

New Mexico Department of Tourism, 491 Old Santa Fe Trail, Santa Fe, NM 87503, tel. (505) 827 7400, fax (505) 827 7402	New Mexixo
New York State Division of Tourism, Department of Economic Development, One Commerce Plaza, Albany, NY 12245, tel. (518) 474 4116, fax (518) 486 6446	New York
North Carolina Travel and Tourism Division, Department of Economic and Community Development, 430 N. Salisbury Street, Raleigh, NC 27611, tel. (919) 733 4171, fax (919) 733 8582	North Carolina
North Dakota Tourism Promotion Diivision, Parks and Tourism Department, Liberty Memorial Building, 604 E. Boulevard, Bismarck, ND 58505, tel. (701) 224 2525, fax (701) 223 3081	North Dakota
Ohio Division of Travel and Tourism, Department of Development, PO Box 1001, Columbus, OH 43266–0101, tel. (614) 466 8844, fax (614) 466 6744	Ohio
Oklahoma Tourism and Recreation Department, Travel and Tourism Division, 505 Will Rogers Building, Oklahoma City, OK 73105, tel. (405) 521 3981, fax (405) 521 3992	Oklahoma
Oregon Economic Development Department, Tourism Division, 775 Summer Street NE, Salem, OR 97310, tel. (503) 378 3451, fax (503) 581 5115	Oregon
Pennsylvania Bureau of Travel Marketing, Department of Commerce, 452 Forum Building, Harrisburg, PA 17120, tel. (717) 787 5453, fax (717) 234 4560	Pennsylvania
Rhode Island Tourism Division, Department of Economic Development, 7 Jackson Walkway, Providence, RI 02903, tel. (401) 277 2601, fax (401) 421 7675	Rhode Island
South Carolina Department of Parks, Recreation and Tourism, 1205 Pendleton Street, Suite 104, Edgar A. Brown Building, Columbia, SC 29201, tel. (803) 734 0129, fax (803) 734 0133	South Carolina
South Dakota Department of Tourism, Capitol Lake Plaza, 711 E. Wells Avenue, Pierre, SD 57501–3369, tel. (605) 773 3301, fax (605) 773 3256	South Dakota
Tennessee Department of Tourism, PO Box 23170, Nashville, TN 37202–3170, tel. (615) 741 2158, fax (615) 741 7225	Tennessee
Texas Department of Commerce, Tourism Division, PO Box 12728, Austin, TX 78711, tel. (512) 462 9191, fax (512) 320 9456	Texas
Utah Travel Council, Capitol Hall, 300 N. State Street, Salt Lake City, UT 84114, tel. (801) 538 1030, fax (801) 538 1399	Utah
Vermont Travel Division, Agency of Development and Community Affairs, 134 State Street, Montpelier, VT 05602, tel. (802) 828 3236, fax (802) 828 3233	Vermont
Virginia Tourism Development Group, Department of Economic Development, 1021 E. Cary Street, Richmond, VA 23219, tel. (804) 786 2051, fax (804) 786 1919	Virginia
State of Washington Department of Trade and Economic Development, 101 General Administration Building, Ax–13, Olympia, WA 98504–2500, tel. (206) 586 2088, fax (206) 586 1850	Washington

Information

West Virginia	West Virginia Division of Tourism and Parks, 2101 Washington Street, East Charleston, WV 25305, tel. (304) 558 2200, fax (304) 348 0108
Wisconsin	Wisconsin Division of Tourism, Department of Development, 123 W. Washington Avenue, PO Box 7606, Madison, WI 53707, tel. (608) 266 2161, fax (608) 266 3403
Wyoming	Wyoming Travel Commission, Division of Tourism, Department of Commerce, Frank Norris Jr Travel Center, I 25 and College Drive, Cheyenne, WY 82002–0660, tel. (307) 777 7777, fax (307) 777 6904
American Samoa	American Samoa Government, Office of Tourism, PO Box 1147, Pago Pago, AS 96799, tel. (684) 633 1091/2/3
Guam	Guam Visitors Bureau, 1270 N. Marine Drive, Boon Building, 2nd floor, Suite 201–204, Upper Turnon, Guam 96931, tel. (671) 646 5278 or 5279, fax (671) 646 8861
Puerto Rico	Puerto Rico Tourism Company, PO Box 4435, Old San Juan Station, San Juan, PR 00905, tel. (809) 721 2400, fax (809) 725 4417
US Virgin Islands	US Virgin Islands Division of Tourism, Box 6400, Charlotte Amalie, St Thomas, USVI 00801, tel. (809) 774 8784, fax (809) 774 4390

Language

It may be helpful to list some of the differences between American and British usage.

American	English
aisle	gangway
apartment	flat
bathrobe	dressing gown
bathroom	lavatory
check (in restaurant)	bill
checkroom	cloakroom
closet	cupboard
collect call	reversed charges
cookies, crackers	biscuits
corn	maize
divided highway	dual carriageway
downtown	town centre
drugstore	chemist
elevator	lift
fall	autumn
faucet	tap
flashlight	torch
freeway	motorway
French fries	chips
gas(oline)	petrol
hood (of car)	bonnet
icebox	refrigerator
license plate (of car)	number plate
line	queue
long distance call	trunk call
mail	post
mailman	postman
movie house	cinema
one way ticket	single ticket
pants	trousers

American	English
panty hose	tights
parking lot	car park
potato chips	potato crisps
purse	handbag
restroom	lavatory
round trip ticket	return ticket
sedan (car)	saloon
sidewalk	pavement
store	shop
stove	cooker
streetcar	tram
subway	underground
thread	cotton
traffic circle	roundabout
trunk (of car)	boot
wash cloth	face cloth
wholewheat bread	brown bread
wrench	spanner
zip code	post code

It should also be remembered that the numbering of the floors of a building starts from the ground floor, which in the United States is called the first floor. What in Britain is called the first floor is the second floor in the United States, and so on.

Medical Care

The standard of medical care in the United States is very high, both as regards the numbers and competence of doctors and dentists and in the hospitals. The only problem for visitors is likely to be the high cost: a stay in hospital in particular is extremely expensive. It is essential, therefore, to make sure, before leaving home, that you have adequate insurance cover.

Doctors, dentists, hospitals

Insurance

The supply of medicines is also well organised. Visitors who regularly need a particular medicine should take a copy of the prescription with them so that it can be re-issued by an American doctor if necessary.

Medicines

See also Chemists

Motoring in the United States

Driving Licence

To drive a car in the United States a visitor must have a valid national driving licence. An international driving licence is not essential but may on occasion be helpful; it is accepted only when accompanied by a national driving licence.

Traffic Regulations

There are both federal and state traffic laws. Traffic regulations may thus differ in some respects from state to state. The following general differences from regulations in Europe should be noted.

At uncontrolled intersections the vehicle which gets there first has priority.

Priority

Motoring in the United States

Speed limits

The police are tough on drivers who exceed the speed limit. In traffic-calmed areas in town centres and residential districts the speed limit ranges between 15 miles/24km an hour near schools, hospitals and access roads and 35 miles/56km an hour. On arterial roads and highways with traffic in both directions the limit is normally 45 miles/72km an hour. In areas where game may be crossing the maximum permitted speed at night is 35 miles/56km an hour. On multi-lane highways and motorways (Interstates) the speed limit is 55 miles/88km an hour. Sections of motorway in remote areas with little traffic have a limit of 65 miles/104km an hour.

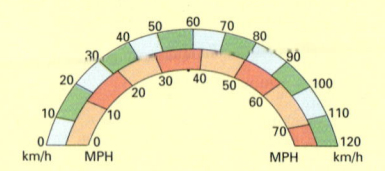

Speed conversion table

1 km = 0.62 mile
1 mile = 1.61 km

© Baedeker

On a road with traffic in both directions all vehicles must stop when a yellow school bus is taking on or discharging passengers. Where a school bus stops on a carriageway which is separated from traffic coming in the other direction by a broad green strip or an impassable barrier this regulation applies only to traffic going in the same direction as the bus. Disregard of the regulation is subject to severe penalties.

Turning right at traffic lights

Traffic lights are situated on the far side of an intersection. It is permissible to turn right against the red provided that you come to a dead stop and give way to any vehicle with priority. At intersections where turning right against the red is not permitted this is indicated by the sign "No Turn on Red".

Dipped headlights

At sunrise and sunset, when visibility is less than 300 yards and on long straight roads with traffic in both directions dipped headlights must be switched on. In some states dipped headlights must be used when the windscreen wipers are in use.

Parking ban

On highways outside built-up areas and on many roads within built-up areas parking is prohibited. If it becomes necessary to stop on a highway you must pull on to the verge or hard shoulder. There are usually roadside signs indicating where and when parking is permitted. Vehicles must not be parked within 15ft/4m of a hydrant.

U turns

On many roads U turns are prohibited. This is indicated by the sign "No Turns".

Overtaking on right

On roads with four or more lanes overtaking on the right is permitted. The same caution must be used in changing to a right-hand lane as in changing to a left-hand one.

Continuous lines

Continuous double yellow or white lines must not be crossed; nor must continuous single lines on the driver's side. Many roads have turn-off lanes, which may be entered only where there is a broken line.

Rush-hour lanes

On multi-lane roads in heavily populated areas one lane may be marked with the sign "HOV 2" or "HOV 3". This means that the lane may be used during the morning and evening rush hours only by cars carrying at least two or three people ("HOV" = "high occupancy vehicle"). Some states use different terms. Improper use of an HOV lane is a punishable offence.

Motoring in the United States

Intercity Highways Subject to Tolls

State	Road	Location	miles	km
Delaware	Kennedy Memorial Highway	Md. State Line to Wilmington	11.2	18.03
Florida	Bee Line Connector	I-4 to Co 436 (Semoran Blvd.)	10	16.1
	Bee Line Expressway	Orlando Airport Plaza to FL-520	22	35.42
	Bee Line East	FL-520 to Cape Canaveral	20	32.2
	Everglades Pwy. (Alligator Alley)	Naples to Andytown	77	123.97
	Florida's Turnpike	I-75 to Miami	260	286
	Florida's Turnpike (Homestead Extention)	Miramar to Florida City	47	75.67
	Sawgrass Expressway	I-75 to I-95	23	37.03
Illinois	Chicago Skyway	I-94, Chicago to Ind. State Line	8	12.88
	East–West Tollway	I-88, Chicago to Rock Falls	97	156.17
	North–South Tollway	I-290. Addison to I-44, Bolingbrook	17.5	28.17
	Northwest Tollway	Des Plaines to South Beloit	76	122.36
	Tri-State Tollway	Ind. State Line to Wis. State Line	83	133.63
Indiana	Indiana Toll Road	Ohio State Line to Ill. State Line	157	252.77
Kansas	Kansas Turnpike	Kansas City to Okla. State Line	233	375.13
Kentucky	Audubon Parkway	Pennyrile Parkway to Owensboro	23	37.03
	Blue Grass Parkway	Elizabethtown to Lexington	72	115.92
	Cumberland Parkway	Bowling Green to Somerset	88.2	142
	Daniel Boone Parkway	London to Hazard	59.4	95.63
	Green River Parkway	Owensboro to Bowling Green	69.7	112.21
	Pennyrile Parkway	Hopkinsville to Henderson	60	96.6
	Purchase Parkway	Fulton to US-62 at Gilbertsville	49	78.89
Maine	Maine Turnpike	York to Augusta	100	161
Maryland	Kennedy Memorial Highway	White Marsh to Del. State Line	42	67.62
Massachusetts	Massachusetts Turnpike	Boston to N.Y. State Line	134	215.74
New Hampshire	F.E. Everett Turnpike	Nashua to Concord	39	62.79
	New Hampshire Turnpike	Portsmouth to Seabrook	16	25.76
	Spaulding Turnpike	Portsmouth to Rochester, N.H.	31	49.91
New Jersey	Atlantic City Expressway	Turnersville to Atlantic City	44	70.84
	Garden State Parkway	Montvale to Cape May	173	278.53
	New Jersey Turnpike	Delaware Memorial Bridge to George Washington Bridge	131	210.91
New York	New York Thruway –			
	Eastbound	Pa. State Line to N.Y.C.	496	798.56
	Westbound	N.Y.C. to Pa. State Line	496	798.56
	Berkshire Section	Selkirk to Mass. Turnpike	24	38.64
	New England Section	N.Y.C. to Conn. State line	15	24.15
	Niagara Section	Buffalo to Niagara Falls	21	33.81
Ohio	J. W. Shocknessy Ohio Turnpike	Pa. State Line to Ind. State Line	241	388.81
Oklahoma	Cimarron Turnpike	I-35 to Tulsa	59.2	95.31
	H.E. Bailey Turnpike	Oklahoma City–Texas State Line	86.4	139.10
	Indian Nation Turnpike	Henryetta to Hugo	105.2	169.37
	Muskogee Turnpike	Tulsa to Webber Falls	53.1	85.49
	Turner Turnpike	Oklahoma City to Tulsa	86	138.46
	Will Rogers Turnpike	Tulsa to Mo. State Line	88.5	142.48
Pennsylvania	Pennsylvania Turnpike	N.J. State Line to Ohio State Line	358	576.38
	Pa. Turnpike (N.E. Sect.)	Norristown to Scranton	110	177.1
Texas	Dallas North Tollway	1-35E, Dallas to FM-544, Dallas	17.2	27.69
	Hardy Toll Road	I-45, Houston to I-610, Houston	21.7	34.93
	Sam Houston Tollway	US-59, Houston to US-290	16	28.98
Virginia	Chesapeake Bay Br. & Tun.	US-13, Norfolk B. to Eastern Shore	17	27.37
	Dulles Toll Road	VA-123 to VA-28	13	20.93
	Powhite Parkway	VA-417 to Old Hundred Rd.	6	9.66
	Richmond–Petersburg Turnpike	Richmond to Petersburg	35	56.35
	Virgin. Bch.–Norfolk Expwy.	US-60, Virgin. Bch. to I-64, Norfolk	12.1	19.48
West Virginia	West Virginia Turnpike	Charleston to Princeton	88	141.68

Motoring in the United States

Distances in miles and kilometres

© Baedeker

Motoring in the United States

Journey times in hours and minutes

549

Motoring in the United States

Crossings	The word "crossing" is frequently abbreviated to "Xing". Thus "Ped Xing" indicates a pedestrian crossing, while "Cattle Xing" is a warning that cattle may be crossing; and in the swamplands of Florida the sign "Gator Xing" invites drivers to keep a lookout for alligators crossing.
Tow-away	Cars parked in a prohibited area or in front of an exit may be towed away, and can be recovered only on payment of a heavy penalty.
Hitch-hiking	Hitch-hiking is permitted in the United States, except on motorways (Interstates) and their access roads.
Traffic signs	See the large map of the United States at the end of this guide.

Highways and Interstate Highways

In a country like the United States which depends on the automobile the road system is necessarily extensive and magnificently engineered. Most roads are toll-free. Important trunk roads and city motorways are multi-lane and without intersections, permitting a smooth flow of traffic.

Interstate highways	The multi-lane interstate highways, without intersections, are the equivalent of the European motorways. They are distinguished from ordinary highways by their blue–white–red signposting. Interstates with even two-digit numbers run east–west; those with odd numbers north–south. Interstates with three-digit numbers are ring roads or bypasses round cities.
Highways	Highways are main roads, usually with several lanes. They are identified by white signs, and may be either federal (e.g. US 17) or state roads (e.g. SR 14 or VA 14). Again odd-numbered roads run broadly north–south and even-numbered roads east–west. The addition of ALT ("alternative") or BUS ("business") to the number indicates that the road is a bypass. Unlike the interstates, highways have intersections. Great care is necessary, therefore, at road junctions and when turning left.
Exits	On roads with separate carriageways exits are normally on the right. Where the road narrows the exit may well be on the left.
Toll roads	On the interstates and highways listed in the table on page 547 tolls are payable. It is advisable to have plenty of small change in order to avoid long waits at the toll-booths. It is then possible to drive straight through the "Exact Fare" gate, throwing the required amount into the baskets provided.

Filling Stations

The United States is covered by a dense network of filling stations (gas stations, service stations). On interstate highways filling stations are sign-posted well in advance. Filling stations now supply almost exclusively lead-free petrol in "regular" and "premium" grades; leaded petrol is rarely available.

At many filling stations, particularly in the evening and at night, payment in advance is required. If payment is made by credit card there is occasionally an additional charge of a few cents per gallon. There are often separate pumps for attendant service and self-service (which is cheaper).

Motoring Organisations

AAA ("Triple A")	American Automobile Association (AAA) 1000 AAA Drive, Heathrow, FL 32746–5063 Tel. 001 407 444 7000.

The AAA is the largest motoring organisation in the United States, with the densest network of branches. Help and information can be obtained by dialling 1 800 AAA HELP.

American Automobile Touring Alliance (AATA) AATA
Bayside Plaza, 188 The Embarcadero
San Francisco, CA 94105
Tel. (415) 777 4000, fax (415) 882 2141.

National Automobile Club (NAC) NAC
150 Vanness
San Francisco, CA 94102–5279
Tel. (415) 565 2012, fax (415) 621 6794

National Automobile Association (NAA) NAA
1730 Northeast Expressway
Atlanta, GA 30329
Tel. (404) 329 0780

Breakdown Assistance

There are emergency telephones along many highways. If assistance of any kind is required the first thing to do is to call 1 800 333 HELP.
The AAA can also help in the event of a breakdown: call 1 800 AAA HELP.
If you have a breakdown in a hired car you should call the rental firm.

Dial 911 for Highway Patrol. Police

Museums

The most important museums are referred to in the Sights from A to Z section of this guide. Before making a visit to a museum it is advisable to check up on opening times either with the museum itself or through the local tourist information office. Many museums are closed on Monday, and some also on Sunday morning or on another weekday. Admission charges can be quite high; at some museums there are reductions for children, students and senior citizens.

National Parks and Reserves

Numerous areas in the United States are under special statutory protection. They fall into three main categories: nature and landscape reserves (National and State Parks, National and State Forests, National Seashores, etc.), areas and sites of historical or archaeological interest (National and State Monuments, Historic Sites, Archaeological Sites) and leisure parks (Recreation Areas). In these areas land use is strictly controlled and there are regulations on the behaviour of visitors. The protected areas are watched over by specially trained park rangers. Certain areas can be visited only with the permission of a park ranger or accompanied by him. The protected areas are mostly well signposted. At many of them admission charges are quite high.

Visitors who are thinking of visiting several National Parks should consider buying a "Golden Eagle" pass. This at present costs $25 and gives free admission to all National Parks for a year. The pass can be obtained at National Park entrances or Visitor Centers. "Golden Eagle" pass

Accommodation in National Parks is available in motels, lodges and cabins. Advance reservation is advisable (see addresses below). Accommodation

National Parks and Reserves

Conduct of visitors — Visitors are not allowed to leave the prescribed roads and trails in National Parks and other protected areas. Camping and lighting fires are permitted only on sites set apart for the purpose. No litter must be left, and wild animals must not be fed. Shooting is prohibited and fishing is allowed only with a special permit. It goes without saying that no plants or animals should be taken.

Sources of Information on National Parks, National Monuments, etc.

The sites listed below are shown in red or green on the large map of the United States at the back of this guide and so can be easily located.

Alabama
- Horseshoe Bend National Military Park, Route 1, Box 103, Daviston, Al 36256, tel. (205) 234 7111
- Russell Cave National Monument, Route 1, Box 175, Bridgeport, AL 35740, tel. (205) 495 2672
- Tuskegee Institute National Historic Site, PO Drawer 10, Tuskegee, AL 36088, tel. (205) 727 6390

Alaska
- Aniakchak National Monument and Preserve, PO Box 7, King Salmon, AK 99613, tel. (907) 246 3305
- Bering Land Bridge National Preserve, PO Box 220, Nome, AK 99762, tel. (907) 443 2522
- Cape Krusenstern National Monument, PO Box 1029, Kotzebue, AK 99752, tel. (907) 442 3890
- Denali National Park and Preserve, PO Box 9, McKinley Park, AK 99755, tel. (907) 683 2294
- Gates of the Arctic National Park and Preserve, PO Box 74680, Fairbanks, AK 99707, tel. (907) 456 0281
- Glacier Bay National Park and Preserve, Gustavus, AK 99826, tel. (907) 697 2230

Grand Canyon country

National Parks and Reserves

Katmai National Park and Preserve, PO Box 7,
  King Salmon, AK 99613, tel. (907) 246 3305
Kenai Fjords National Park, PO Box 1727,
  Seward, AK 99664, tel. (907) 224 3175
Klondike Gold Rush National Historical Park, PO Box 517,
  Skagway, AK 99840, tel. (907) 983 2921
Kobuk Valley National Park, PO Box 1029,
  Kotzebue, AK 99752, tel. (907) 442 3890
Lake Clark National Park and Preserve, 4230 University Drive,
  Suite 311, Anchorage, AK 99508, tel. (907) 271 3751
Noatak National Preserve, PO Box 1029,
  Kotzebue, AK 99752, tel. (907) 442 3890
Sitka National Historical Park, PO Box 738,
  Sitka, AK 99835, tel. (907) 747 6281
Wrangell-St Elias National Park and Preserve, PO Box 29,
  Glennallen, AK 99588, tel. (909) 822 5234
Yukon-Charley Rivers National Preserve, PO Box 167,
  Eagle, AK 99738, tel. (907) 547 2233

Arizona

Canyon de Chelly National Monument, PO Box 588,
  Chinle, AZ 86503, tel. (602) 674 5436
Casa Grande National Monument, 1100 Ruins Drive,
  Coolidge, AZ 85228, tel. (602) 723 3172
Chiricahua National Monument, Dos Cabezas Route, Box 6500,
  Willcox, AZ 85643, tel. (602) 824 3560
Coronado National Memorial, Rural Route 2, Box 126,
  Hereford, AZ 85615, tel. (602) 366 5515 and 458 9333
Fort Bowie National Historic Site, PO Box 158,
  Bowie, AZ 85605, tel. (602) 847 2500
Grand Canyon National Park, PO Box 129,
  Grand Canyon, AZ 86023, tel. (602) 638 7888
Hubbell Trading Post National Historic Site, PO Box 150,
  Ganado, AZ 86505, tel. (602) 755 3475/3477
Montezuma Castle National Monument, PO Box 219,
  Camp Verde, AZ 86322, tel. (602) 567 3322
Navajo National Monument, H.C. 71, Box 3,
  Tonalea, AZ 86044–9704, tel. (602) 672 2366/2367
  (See Sights from A to Z, Navajo Country)
Organ Pipe Cactus National Monument, Route 1, Box 100,
  Ajo, AZ 85321, tel. (602) 387 6849
  (See Sights from A to Z, Arizona)
Petrified Forest National Park,
  AZ 86028, tel. (602) 524 6228
  (See Sights from A to Z)
Pipe Spring National Monument,
  Moccasin, AZ 86022, tel. (602) 643 7105
Saguaro National Monument, 3693 S. Old Spanish Trail,
  Tucson, AZ 85730–5699, tel. (602) 296 8576
  (See Sights from A to Z, Arizona)
Sunset Crater National Monument, 2717 N. Steves Boulevard 3,
  Flagstaff, AZ 86004, tel. (602) 527 7042/7134
Tonto National Monument, PO Box 707,
  Roosevelt, AZ 85545, tel. (602) 467 2241
Tumacacori National Monument, PO Box 67,
  Tumacacori, AZ 85640, tel. (602) 398 2341
Tuzigoot National Monument, PO Box 219,
  Camp Verde, AZ 86322, tel. (602) 634 5564
Walnut Canyon National Monument, Walnut Canyon Road,
  Flagstaff, AZ 86004–9705, tel. (602) 526 3367
Wupatki National Monument, 2717 N. Steves Boulevard, Suite 3,
  Flagstaff, AZ 86004, tel. (602) 527 7134/7040

National Parks and Reserves

Arkansas
: Arkansas Post National Memorial, Route 1, Box 16,
  Gillett, AR 72055, tel. (501) 548 2432
  Buffalo National River, PO Box 1173,
  Harrison, AR 72602, tel. (501) 741 5443
  Fort Smith National Historic Site, PO Box 1406,
  Fort Smith, AR 72902, tel. (501) 783 3961
  Hot Springs National Park, PO Box 1860,
  Hot Springs, AR 71902, tel. (501) 624 3383
  Pea Ridge National Military Park,
  Pea Ridge, AR 72751, tel. (501) 451 8122

California
: Cabrillo National Monument, PO Box 6670,
  San Diego, CA 92106, tel. (619) 557 5450
  Channel Islands National Park, 1901 Spinnaker Drive,
  Ventura, CA 93001, tel. (805) 644 8262
  Death Valley National Monument,
  Death Valley, CA 92328, tel. (619) 786 2331
  (See Sights from A to Z)
  Devil's Postpile National Monument, PO Box 501,
  Mammoth Lakes, CA 93546, tel. summer (619) 934 2289,
  winter (209) 565 3341
  Fort Point National Historic Site, PO Box 29333,
  Presidio of San Francisco, CA 94129, tel. (415) 556 1693/2857
  Golden Gate National Recreation Area, Fort Mason, Building 201,
  San Francisco, CA 94123, tel. (415) 556 0560
  John Muir National Historic Site, 4202 Alhambra Avenue,
  Martinez, CA 94553, tel. 228 8860
  Joshua Tree National Monument, 74485 National Monument Drive,
  Twentynine Palms, CA 92277, tel. (619) 367 7511
  (See Sights from A to Z)
  Kings Canyon National Park,
  Three Rivers, CA 93271, tel. (209) 565 3341
  Lassen Volcanic National Park, PO Box 100,
  Mineral, CA 96063, tel. (916) 595 4444
  (See Sights from A to Z)
  Lava Beds National Monument, PO Box 867,
  Tulelake, CA 96134, tel. (916) 667 2282
  Muir Woods National Monument,
  Mill Valley, CA 94941, tel. (415) 388 2595
  Pinnacles National Monument,
  Paicines, CA 95043, tel. (408) 389 4485
  Point Reyes National Seashore,
  Point Reyes, CA 94956, tel. (415) 663 1092
  Redwood National Park, 1111 Second Street,
  Crescent City, CA 95531, tel. (707) 464 6101
  (See Sights from A to Z)
  Santa Monica Mountains National Recreation Area,
  22900 Ventura Boulevard, Woodland Hills, CA 91364,
  tel. (818) 888 3770
  Sequoia National Park,
  Three Rivers, CA 93271, tel. (209) 565 3341
  (See Sights from A to Z)
  Whiskeytown-Shasta-Trinity National Recreation Area, PO Box 188,
  Whiskeytown, CA 96095, tel. (916) 241 6584
  Yosemite National Park, PO Box 577,
  Yosemite National Park, CA 95389, tel. (209) 372 0200

Colorado
: Bent's Old Fort National Historic Site, 35110 Highway 194 East,
  La Junta, CO 81050–9523, tel. (719) 384 2596
  Black Canyon of the Gunnison National Monument, 2233 East Main,
  Montrose, CO 81401, tel. (303) 249 7036
  Colorado National Monument,
  Fruita, CO 81521, tel. (303) 858 3617

National Parks and Reserves

Indian houses in Mesa Verde National Park

Curecanti National Recreation Area, 102 Elk Creek,
 Gunnison, CO 81230, tel. (303) 641 2337
Dinosaur National Monument (CO, UT), PO Box 210,
 Dinosaur, CO 81610, tel. (303) 374 2216
 (See Sights from A to Z)
Florissant Fossil Beds National Monument, PO Box 185,
 Florissant, CO 80816, tel. (719) 748 3253/3051
Great Sand Dunes National Monument,
 Mosca, CO 81146, tel. (719) 378 2312
Hovenweep National Monument, McElmo Route,
 Cortez, CO 81321, tel. (303) 529 4465
Mesa Verde National Park,
 Mesa Verde National Park, CO 81330, tel. (303) 529 4465
 (See Sights from A to Z)
Rocky Mountain National Park,
 Estes Park, CO 80517, tel. (303) 586 2371
 (See Sights from A to Z)

Constitution Gardens, c/o NCP Central, 900 Ohio Drive SW,   District of
 Washington, DC 20242, tel. (202) 485 9880   Columbia
Ford's Theatre National Historic Site, 511 Tenth Street NW,
 Washington, DC 20004, tel. (202) 426 6924
Frederick Douglass National Historic Site, 1411 W Street SE,
 Washington, DC 20020, tel. (202) 426 5961
Lincoln Memorial, c/o NCP Central, 900 Ohio Drive SW,
 Washington, DC 20242, tel. (202) 485 9880
Lyndon B. Johnson Memorial Grove, Rock Creek Park,
 500 Glover Road NW, Washington, DC 20015,
 tel. (202) 426 6832
Theodore Roosevelt Island: see Virginia, George Washington,
 Memorial Parkway

National Parks and Reserves

Thomas Jefferson Memorial and Tidal Basin, c/o NCP Central,
  900 Ohio Drive SW, Washington, DC 20242, tel. (202) 485 9880
Vietnam Veterans Memorial, c/o NCP Central, 900 Ohio Drive SW,
  Washington, DC 20242, tel. (202) 485 9880
Washington Monument, c/o NCP Central, 900 Ohio Drive SW,
  Washington, DC 20242, tel. (202) 485 9880
White House, c/o NCR, National Park Service, 1100 Ohio Drive SW,
  Washington, DC 20242, tel. (202) 485 9880

Florida

Big Cypress National Preserve, Star Route, Box 110,
  Ochopee, FL 33943, tel. (813) 695 2000 and 262 1066
Biscayne National Park, PO Box 1369,
  Homestead, FL 33090
Canaveral National Seashore, 2532 Garden Street,
  Titusville, FL 32796, tel. (407) 267 1110
Castillo de San Marcos National Monument, 1 Castillo Drive,
  St Augustine, FL 32084, tel. (904) 829 6506
DeSoto National Memorial, PO Box 15390,
  Bradenton, FL 34280, tel. (813) 792 0458
Everglades National Park, PO Box 1279,
  Homestead, FL 33030, tel. (305) 247 6211
  (See Sights from A to Z)
Fort Caroline National Memorial, 12713 Fort Caroline Road,
  Jacksonville, FL 32225, tel. (904) 641 7155
Fort Jefferson National Monument: see Everglades National Park,
Fort Matanzas National Monument: see Castillo de San Marcos
Gulf Islands National Seashore, 1801 Gulf Breeze Parkway,
  Gulf Breeze, FL 32561, tel. (904) 934 2600

Georgia

Andersonville National Historic Site, Route 1, Box 85,
  Andersonvilla, GA 31711, tel. (912) 924 0343
Chattahoochee River National Recreation Area, 1978 Island Ford,
  Parkway, Dunwoody, GA 30350, tel. (404) 394 7912
Chickamauga and Chattanooga National Military Park (GA, TN),
  PO Box 2128, Fort Oglethorpe, GA 30742, tel. (404) 866 9241
Cumberland Island National Seashore, PO Box 806,
  St Marys, GA 31558, tel. (912) 882 4336
Fort Frederica National Monument, Route 9, Box 2860,
  St Simons Island, GA 31522, tel. (912) 638 3639
Fort Pulaski National Monument, PO Box 30757,
  Savannah, GA 31410, tel. (912) 786 5787
Kennesaw Mountain National Battlefield Park, PO Box 1610,
  Marietta, GA 30061, tel. (404) 427 4686
Martin Luther King Jr National Historic Site, 526 Auburn Avenue,
  NE, Atlanta, GA 30312
Ocmulgee National Monument, 1207 Emery Highway,
  Macon, GA 31201, tel. (912) 752 8257

Guam

War in the Pacific National Historical Park, PO Box FA,
  Agana, GU 96910

Hawaii

Haleakala National Park, PO Box 369,
  Makawao, HI 96768, tel. (808) 572 9306
Hawaii Volcanoes National Park,
  Hawaii National Park, HI 96718, tel. (808) 967 7311
Kalaupapa National Historical Park,
  Kalaupapa, HI 96742
Pu'uhonua o Honaunau National Historical Park, PO Box 129,
  Honaunau, Kona, HI 96726, tel. (808) 328 23 26
Puukohola Heiau National Historic Site, PO Box 4963,
  Kawaihae, HI 96743, tel. (808) 882 7218
USS Arizona Memorial, 1 Arizona Memorial Place,
  Honolulu, HI 96818, tel. (808) 422 2771

National Parks and Reserves

Craters of the Moon National Monument, PO Box 29,   Idaho
  Arco, ID 83213, tel. (208) 527 3257
Nez Perce National Historical Park, PO Box 93,
  Spalding, ID 83551, tel. (208) 843 2261

Lincoln Home National Historic Site, 426 S. Seventh Street,   Illinois
  Springfield, IL 62701, tel. (217) 492 4150

George Rogers Clark National Historical Park,   Indiana
  401 S. Second, Street, Vincennes, IN 47591, tel. (812) 882 1776
Indiana Dunes National Lakeshore, 1100 N. Mineral Springs Road,
  Porter, IN 46304, tel. (219) 926 7561
Lincoln Boyhood National Memorial,
  Lincoln City, IN 47552, tel. (812) 937 4541

Effigy Mounds National Monument, Rural Route 1, Box 25A,   Iowa
  Harpers Ferry, IA 52146, tel. (319) 873 3491
Herbert Hoover National Historic Site, PO Box 607,
  West Branch, IA 52358, tel. (319) 643 2541

Fort Larned, National Historic Site, Route 3,   Kansas
  Larned, KS 67550, tel. (316) 285 6911
Fort Scott National Historic Site, Old Fort Boulevard,
  Fort Scott, KS 66701, tel. (316) 223 0310

Abraham Lincoln Birthplace National Historic Site,   Kentucky
  2995 Lincoln Farm Road, Hodgenville, KY 42748,
  tel. (502) 358 3874
Cumberland Gap National Historical Park, PO Box 1848,
  Middlesboro, KY 40965, tel. (606) 248 2817
Mammoth Cave National Park,
  Mammoth Cave, KY 42259, tel. (502) 758 2328
  (See Sights from A to Z)

Jean Lafitte National Historical Park and Preserve,   Louisiana
  423 Canal Street, New Orleans, LA 70130–2341

Acadia National Park, PO Box 177,   Maine
  Bar Harbor, ME 04609, tel. (207) 288 3338
  (See Sights from A to Z, Maine)
St Croix Island International Historic Site:
  see Acadia National Park

Antietam National Battlefield, Box 158,   Maryland
  Sharpsburg, MD 21782, tel. (301) 432 5124
Assateague Island National Seashore, Route 2, Box 294,
  Berlin, MD 21811, tel. (401) 641 1441
Catoctin Mountain Park, 6602 Foxville Road,
  Thurmont, MD 21788, tel. (301) 663 9330
Chesapeake and Ohio Canal National Historical Park, PO Box 4,
  Sharpsburg, MD 21782, tel. (301) 739 4200
Clare Barton National Historic Site: see Virginia, George,
  Washington Memorial Parkway
Fort McHenry National Monument and Historic Shrine, E. Fort,
  Avenue, Baltimore, MD 21230–5393, tel. (301) 962 4299
Fort Washington Park, NCP East, 1900 Anacostia Drive SE,
  Washington, DC 20020, tel. (202) 433 1185 and (301) 763 4600
Greenbelt Park, 6565 Greenbelt Road,
  Greenbelt, MD 20770, tel. (301) 344 3948
Hampton National Historic Site, 535 Hampton Lane,
  Towson, MD 21204, tel. (301) 962 0688

557

National Parks and Reserves

| | Piscataway Park, c/o NCP East, 1900 Anacostia Drive SE, Washington, DC 20020, tel. (301) 763 4600 |

Massachusetts — Adams National Historic Site, PO Box 531, 135 Adams Street, Quincy, MA 02269–0531, tel. (617) 773 1177
Boston National Historical Park, Charlestown Navy Yard, Boston, MA 02129, tel. (617) 242 5644
Cape Cod National Seashore, South Wellfleet, MA 02663, tel. (508) 349 3785
Frederick Law Olmstead National Historic Site, 99 Warren Street, Brookline, MA 02146, tel. (617) 566 1689
John F. Kennedy National Historic Site, 83 Beals Street, Brookline, MA 02146, tel. (617) 566 7937
Longfellow National Historic Site, 105 Brattle Street, Cambridge, MA 02138, tel. (617) 876 4491
Lowell National Historical Park, 169 Merrimack Street, Lowell, MA 01852, tel. (508) 459 1000
Minute Man National Historical Park, PO Box 160, 174 Liberty Street, Concord, MA 01742, tel. (617) 369 6993
Salem Maritime National Historic Site, Custom House, 174 Derby Street, Salem, MA 01970, tel. (508) 745 1470
Saugus Iron Works National Historic Site, 244 Central Street, Saugus, MA 01906, tel. (617) 233 0050
Springfield Armory National Historic Site, 1 Armory Square, Springfield, MA 01105, tel. (413) 734 8551

Michigan — Isle Royale National Park, 87 N. Ripley Street, Houghton, MI 49931, tel. (906) 482 0984 (See Sights from A to Z, Michigan)
Pictured Rocks National Lakeshore, PO Box 40, Munising, MI 49862, tel. (906) 387 3700/2607
Sleeping Bear Dunes National Lakeshore, PO Box 277, 9922 Front Street, Empire, MI 49630, tel. (616) 326 5134

Minnesota — Grand Portage National Monument, PO Box 668, Grand Marais, MN 55604, tel. (218) 387 2788
Pipestone National Monument, PO Box 727, Pipestone, MN 56164, tel. (507) 825 54 64
Voyageurs National Park, HCR 9, Box 600, International Falls, MN 56649, tel. (218) 283 9821 (See Sights from A to Z, Minnesota)

Mississippi — Brices Crossroads National Battlefield Site: see Natchez Trace Parkway
Gulf Islands National Seashore, 3500 Park Road, Ocean Springs, MS 39564, tel. (601) 875 0821
Natchez Trace Parkway, R.R. 1, NT 143, Tupelo, MS 38801, tel. (601) 842 1572
Tupelo National Battlefield: see Natchez Trace Parkway
Vicksburg National Military Park, 3201 Clay Street, Vicksburg, MS 39180, tel. (601) 636 0583

Missouri — George Washington Carver National Monument, PO Box 38, Diamond, MO 64840, tel. (417) 325 4151
Harry S. Truman National Historic Site, 223 N. Main Street, Independence, MO 64050, tel. (816) 254 2720
Jefferson National Expansion Memorial, 11 N. 4th Street, St Louis, MO 63102, tel. (314) 425 4465

National Parks and Reserves

Ozark National Scenic Riverways, PO Box 490,
  Van Buren, MO 63965, tel. (314) 323 4236
Wilson's Creek National Battlefield, Route 2, Box 75,
  Republic, MO 65738, tel. (417) 732 2662

Montana

Big Hole National Battlefield, PO Box 237,
  Wisdom, MT 59761, tel. (406) 689 3155
Bighorn Canyon National Recreation Area, PO Box 458,
  Fort Smith, MT 59035, tel. (406) 666 2412
Custer Battlefield National Monument, PO Box 39,
  Crow Agency, MT 59022, tel. (406) 638 2621
Glacier National Park,
  West Glacier, MT 59936, tel. (406) 888 5441
Grant-Kohrs Ranch National Historic Site, PO Box 790,
  Deer Lodge, MT 59722, tel. (406) 846 2070

Nebraska

Agate Fossil Beds National Monument, PO Box 27,
  Gering, NE 69341, tel. (308) 436 4340
Homestead National Monument of America, Route 3, Box 47,
  Beatrice, NE 68310, tel. (402) 223 3514
Scotts Bluff National Monument, PO Box 27,
  Gering, NE 69341, tel. (308) 436 4340

Nevada

Great Basin National Park,
  Baker, NV 89311, tel. (702) 234 7331
Lake Mead National Recreation Area, 601 Nevada Highway,
  Boulder City, NV 89005–2426, tel. (702) 293 8907

New Hampshire

Saint-Gaudens National Historic Site, R.R. 3, Box 73,
  Cornish, NH 03745–9704, tel. (603) 675 2175

New Jersey

Edison National Historic Site, Main Street and Lakeside Avenue,
  West Orange, NJ 07052, tel. (201) 736 5050
Morristown National Historical Park, Washington Place,
  Morristown, NJ 07960, tel. (201) 539 2085

New Mexico

Aztec Ruins National Monument, PO Box 640,
  Aztec, NM 87410, tel. (505) 334 6174
Bandelier National Monument,
  Los Alamos, NM 87544, tel. (505) 672 3861
Capulin Volcano National Monument,
  Capulin, NM 88414, tel. (505) 278 2201
Carlsbad Caverns National Park, 3225 National Parks Highway,
  Carlsbad, NM 88220, tel. (505) 785 2232
  (See Sights from A to Z)
Chaco Culture National Historical Park, Star Route 4, Box 6500,
  Bloomfield, NM 87413, tel. (505) 988 6727
El Malpais National Monument, PO Box 939,
  Grants, NM 87020, tel. (505) 285 5406
El Morro National Monument,
  Ramah, NM 87321, tel. (505) 783 4226
Fort Union National Monument,
  Watrous, NM 87753, tel. (505) 425 8025
Gila Cliff Dwellings National Monument, Route 11, Box 100,
  Silver City, NM 88061, tel. (505) 536 9461
Pecos National Historical Park, PO Drawer 418,
  Pecos, NM 87552, tel. (505) 757 6414–6032
Salinas National Monument, PO Box 496,
  Mountainair, NM 87036, tel. (505) 847 2585
White Sands National Monument, PO Box 458,
  Alamogordo, NM 88310, tel. (505) 479 6124/6125

New York

Castle Clinton National Monument, Manhattan Sites,
  26 Wall Street, New York, NY 10005, tel. (212) 264 4456

National Parks and Reserves

Eleanor Roosevelt National Historic Site, 519 Albany Post Road,
  Hyde Park, NY 12538, tel. (914) 229 7821
Federal Hall National Memorial, Manhattan Sites, 26 Wall Street,
  New York, NY 10005, tel. (212) 264 4456
Fire Island National Seashore, 120 Laurel Street,
  Patchogue, NY 11772, tel. (516) 289 4810
Fort Stanwix National Monument, 112 E. Park Street,
  Rome, NY 13440, tel. (315) 336 2090
Gateway National Recreation Area, Floyd Bennet Field, Building 69,
  Brooklyn, NY 11234, tel. (718) 338 3575
General Grant National Memorial, 122nd Street and Riverside Drive,
  New York, NY 10027, tel. (212) 264 4456
Hamilton Grange National Memorial, 287 Convent Avenue,
  New York, NY 10031, tel. (212) 264 4456
Home of Franklin D. Roosevelt National Historic Site,
  519 Albany Post Road, Hyde Park, NY 12538,
  tel. (914) 229 7821
Martin Van Buren National Historic Site, PO Box 545, Route 9H,
  Kinderhook, NY 12106, tel. (518) 758 9689
Sagamore Hill National Historic Site, 20 Sagamore Hill Road,
  Oyster Bay, NY 11771–1899, tel. (516) 922 4447
St Paul's Church National Historic Site, 897 S. Columbus Avenue,
  Mount Vernon, NY 10550, tel. (212) 264 4456
Saratoga National Historical Park, R.D. 2, Box 33,
  Stillwater, NY 12170, tel. (518) 664 9821
Statue of Liberty National Monument (NY, NJ),
  Liberty Island, New York, NY 10004, tel. (212) 363 7770
Theodore Roosevelt Birthplace National Historic Site,
  28 E. 20th Street, New York, NY 10003, tel. (212) 264 4456
Theodore Roosevelt Inaugural National Historic Site,
  641 Delaware Avenue, Buffalo, NY 14202, tel. (716) 884 0095
Vanderbilt Mansion National Historic Site, 519 Albany Post Road,
  Hyde Park, NY 12538, tel. (914) 229 7821
Women's Rights National Historical Park, PO Box 70,
  Seneca Falls, NY 13148

North Carolina

Blue Ridge Parkway, 200 BB & T Building, 1 Pack Square,
  Asheville, NC 28801, tel. (704) 259 0779
Cape Hatteras National Seashore, Route 1, Box 675,
  Manteo, NC 27954, tel. (919) 473 2111 and 995 4464
Cape Lookout National Seashore, 3601 Bridges Street, Suite F,
  Morehead City, NC 28557–2913, tel. (919) 240 1409
Carl Sandburg Home National Historic Site, 1928 Little River Road,
  Flat Rock, NC 28731, tel. (704) 693 4178
Fort Raleigh National Historic Site, Cape Hatteras Group,
  Route 1, Box 675, Manteo, NC 27954, tel. (919) 473 5772
Guilford Courthouse National Military Park, PO Box 9806,
  Greensboro, NC 27429, tel. (919) 288 1776
Moores Creek National Battlefield,
  Currie, NC 28435, tel. (919) 283 5591
Wright Brothers National Memorial, Cape Hatteras Group, Route 1,
  Box 675, Manteo, NC 27954, tel. (919) 441 7430

North Dakota

Fort Union Trading Post National Historic Site, Rural Route 3,
  Box 71, Williston, ND 58801, tel. (701) 572 9083
Knife River Indian Villages National Historic Site, R.R. 1,
  Box 168, Stanton, ND 58571, tel. (701) 745 3300
Theodore Roosevelt National Park, PO Box 7,
  Medora, ND 58645, tel. (701) 623 4466

Ohio

Cuyahoga Valley National Recreation Area, 15610 Vaughn Road,
  Brecksville, OH 44141, tel. (216) 650 4636

National Parks and Reserves

Mabry Mill, on the Blue Ridge Parkway

James A. Garfield National Historic Site, Lawnfield,
    8095 Mentor Avenue, Mentor, OH 44060, tel. (216) 255 8722
Mound City Group National Monument, 16062 State Route 104,
    Chillicothe, OH 45601, tel. (614) 774 1125
Perry's Victory and International Peace Memorial, PO Box 549,
    93 Delaware Avenue, Put-in-Bay, OH 43456,
    tel. (419) 285 2184
William Howard Taft National Historic Site, 2038 Auburn Avenue,
    Cincinnati, OH 45219, tel. (513) 684 3262

Chickasaw National Recreation Area, PO Box 201,   Oklahoma
    Sulphur, OK 73086, tel. (405) 622 3161

Crater Lake National Park, PO Box 7,   Oregon
    Crater Lake, OR 97604, tel. (503) 594 2211
    (See Sights from A to Z)
Fort Clatsop National Memorial, Route 3, Box 604–FC,
    Astoria, OR 97103, tel. (503) 861 2471
John Day Fossil Beds National Monument, 420 W. Main Street,
    John Day, OR 97845, tel. (503) 575 0721
Oregon Caves National Monument, 19000 Caves Highway,
    Cave Junction, OR 97523, tel. (503) 592 2100

Allegheny Portage Railroad National Historic Site, PO Box 247,   Pennsylvania
    Cresson, PA 16630, tel. (814) 886 8176
Delaware Water Gap National Recreation Area,
    Bushkill, PA 18324, tel. (717) 588 2435
Edgar Allan Poe National Historic Site: see Independence N.H.P.
Eisenhower National Historic Site,
    Gettysburg, PA 17325, tel. (717) 334 1124
Fort Necessity National Battlefield, National Pike, R.D. 2,
    Box 528, Farmington, PA 15437, tel. (412) 329 5512

National Parks and Reserves

        Friendship Hill National Historic Site: see Fort Necessity, National Battlefield
        Gettysburg National Military Park, PO Box 1080, Gettysburg, PA 17325, tel. (717) 334 1124
        Hopewell Furnace National Historic Site, R.D. 1, Box 345, Elverson, PA 19520, tel. (215) 582 8773
        Independence National Historical Park, 313 Walnut Street, Philadelphia, PA 19106, tel. (215) 627 1776 and 597 8974
        Johnstown Flood National Memorial: see Allegheny Portage Railroad, N.H.S.
        Thaddeus Kósciuszko National Memorial: see Independence N.H.P.
        Upper Delaware Scenic and Recreational River, PO Box C, Narrowsburg, NY 12764
        Valley Forge National Historical Park, Box 953, Valley Forge, PA 19481, tel. (215) 783 1077

Puerto Rico
San Juan National Historic Site, PO Box 712, Old San Juan, PR 00902, tel. (809) 729 6960

Rhode Island
Roger Williams National Memorial, 282 N. Main Street, Providence, RI 02903, tel. (401) 528 5385

South Carolina
Congaree Swamp National Monument, 200 Caroline Sims Road, Hopkins, SC 29061, tel. (803) 776 4396
Cowpens National Battlefield, PO Box 308, Chesnee, SC 29323, tel. (803) 461 2828
Fort Sumter National Monument, 1214 Middle Street, Sullivans Island, SC 29482, tel. (803) 883 3123
Kings Mountain National Military Park, PO Box 40, Kings Mountain, SC 28086, tel. (803) 936 7921
Ninety Six National Historic Site, PO Box 496, Ninety Six, SC 29666, tel. (803) 543 4068

South Dakota
Badlands National Park, PO Box 6, Interior, SD 57750, tel. (605) 433 5361
Jewel Cave National Monument, R.R. 1, Box 60AA, Custer, SD 57730, tel. (605) 673 2288
Mount Rushmore National Memorial, PO Box 268, Keystone, SD 57751, tel. (605) 574 2523
Wind Cave National Park, Hot Springs, SD 57747, tel. (605) 745 4600

Tennessee
Andrew Johnson National Historic Site, PO Box 1088, Greeneville, TN 37744, tel. (615) 638 3551/1326
Big South Fork National River and Recreation Area, Route 3, Box 401, Oneida, TN 37841, tel. (615) 569 9778
Fort Donelson National Battlefield, PO Box 434, Dover, TN 37058-0434, tel. (615) 232 5348/5706
Great Smoky Mountains National Park, Gatlinburg, TN 37738, tel. (615) 436 1200
(See Sights from A to Z)
Obed Wild and Scenic River, PO Box 429, Wartburg, TN 37887, tel. (615) 346 6294
Shiloh National Military Park, PO Box 61, Shiloh, TN 38376, tel. (901) 689 5275
Stones River National Battlefield, 3501 Old Nashville Highway, Murfreesboro, TN 37129, tel. (615) 893 5901

Texas
Alibates Flint Quarries National Monument: see Lake Meredith Recreation Area
Amistad Recreation Area, PO Box 420367, Del Rio, TX 78842-0367, tel. (512) 775 7491

National Parks and Reserves

Big Bend National Park,
   Big Bend, TX 79834, tel. (915) 447 2251
   (See Sights from A to Z)
Big Thicket National Preserve, 3785 Milam,
   Beaumont, TX 77701, tel. (409) 839 2689
Chamizal National Memorial, 800 S. San Marcial,
   El Paso, TX 79905, tel. (915) 532 7273
Fort Davis National Historic Site, PO Box 1456,
   Fort Davis, TX 79734, tel. (915) 426 3224/3225
Guadalupe Mountains National Park, H.C. 60, Box 400,
   Salt Flat, TX 79847–9400, tel. (915) 828 3251
Lake Meredith Recreation Area, PO Box 1438,
   Fritch, TX 79036, tel. (806) 857 3151
Lyndon B. Johnson National Historical Park, PO Box 329,
   Johnson City, TX 78636, tel. (512) 868 7128
Padre Island National Seashore, 9405 S. Padre Island Drive,
   Corpus Christi, TX 78418–5597, tel. (512) 932 2621
San Antonio Missions National Historical Park,
   2202 Roosevelt Avenue, San Antonio, TX 78210–4919,
   tel. (512) 229 5701

Arches National Park, PO Box 907,   Utah
   Moab, UT 84532, tel. (801) 259 8161
   (See Sights from A to Z)
Bryce Canyon National Park,
   Bryce Canyon, UT 84717, tel. (801) 834 5322
   (See Sights from A to Z)
Canyonlands National Park, 125 West 200 South,
   Moab, UT 84532, tel. (801) 259 7164
   (See Sights from A to Z)

Sunrise over Bryce Canyon

National Parks and Reserves

Capitol Reef National Park,
  Torrey, UT 84775, tel. (801) 425 3791
Cedar Breaks National Monument, PO Box 749,
  Cedar City, UT 84720, tel. (801) 586 9451
Glen Canyon National Recreation Area, PO Box 1507,
  Page, AZ 86040, tel. (602) 645 2471
Golden Spike National Historic Site, PO Box 897,
  Brigham City, UT 84302, tel. (801) 471 2209
Natural Bridges National Monument, Box 1,
  Lake Powell, UT 84533, tel. (801) 259 5174
Rainbow Bridge National Monument: see Glen Canyon N.R.A.
Timpanogos Cave National Historic Site, R.R. 3, Box 200,
  American Fork, UT 84003, tel. (801) 756 5238
Zion National Park,
  Springdale, UT 84767–1099, tel. (801) 772 3256
  (See Sights from A to Z)

Virginia

Appomattox Court House National Historical Park, PO Box 218,
  Appomattox, VA 24522, tel. (804) 352 8987
Arlington House, Robert E. Lee Memorial:
  see George Washington Memorial Parkway
Booker T. Washington National Monument, Route 3, Box 310,
  Hardy, VA 24101, tel. (703) 721 2094
Colonial National Historical Park, PO Box 210,
  Yorktown, VA 23690, tel. (804) 898 3400
  (See Sights from A to Z)
Fredericksburg and Spotsylvania National Military Park,
  PO Box 679, Fredericksburg, VA 22404, tel. (703) 373 4461
George Washington Birthplace National Monument, R.R. 1, Box 717,
  Washington's Birthplace, VA 22575, tel. (804) 224 1732
George Washington Memorial Parkway, Turkey Run Park,
  McLean, VA 22101, tel. (703) 285 2598
Great Falls Park, 9200 Old Dominion Drive,
  Great Falls, VA 22066, tel. (703) 285 2966
Maggie L. Walker National Historic Site:
  see Richmond National Battlefield Park
Manassas National Battlefield Park, PO Box 1830,
  Manassas, VA 22110, tel. (703) 361 1865
Petersburg National Battlefield, PO Box 549, Route 36 East,
  Petersburg, VA 23804, tel. (804) 732 3531
Prince William Forest Park, PO Box 209,
  Triangle, VA 22172, tel. (703) 221 7181
Richmond National Battlefield Park, 3215 E. Broad Street,
  Richmond, VA 23223, tel. (804) 226 1981
Shenandoah National Park, Route 4, Box 348,
  Luray, VA 22835, tel. (703) 999 2243
  (See Sights from A to Z)
Wolf Trap Farm Park for the Performing Arts, 1551 Trap Road,
  Vienna, VA 22180, tel. (703) 255 1800

Virgin Islands

Buck Island Reef National Monument, PO Box 160,
  Christiansted, St Croix, VI 00820, tel. (809) 773 1460
Christiansted National Historic Site, PO Box 160,
  Christiansted, St Croix, VI 00820, tel. (809) 773 1460
Virgin Islands National Park, PO Box 7789,
  Charlotte Amalie, St Thomas, VI 00801,
  tel. (809) 776 6201 and 775 6238

Washington

Coulee Dam National Recreation Area, PO Box 37,
  Coulee Dam, WA 99116, tel. (509) 633 9441
Ebey's Landing National Historical Reserve, PO Box 774,
  23 Front Street, Coupeville, WA 98239

Fort Vancouver National Historic Site, 612 E. Reserve Street,
  Vancouver, WA 98661–3897, tel. (206) 696 7655
Klondike Gold Rush National Historical Park, 117 S. Main Street,
  Seattle, WA 98104, tel. (206) 533 7220
Lake Chelan National Recreation Area, PO Box 7,
  Stehekin, WA 98852
Mount Rainier National Park, Tahoma Woods, Star Route,
  Ashford, WA 98304, tel. (206) 569 2211
  (See Sights from A to Z)
North Cascades National Park, 2105 Highway 20,
  Sedro Woolley, WA 98284, tel. (206) 856 5700
Olympic National Park, 600 E. Park Avenue,
  Port Angeles, WA 98362, tel. (206) 452 4501
  (See Sights from A to Z)
Ross Lake National Recreation Area, 2105 Highway 20,
  Sedro Woolley, WA 98284, tel. (206) 857 5700
San Juan Island National Historical Park, PO Box 429,
  Friday Harbor, WA 98250, tel. (206) 378 2240
Whitman Mission National Historic Site, Route 2, Box 247,
  Walla Walla, WA 99362, tel. (509) 527 2761

West Virginia

Appalachian National Scenic Trail, PO Box 807,
  Harpers Ferry, WV 25425, tel. (304) 535 6331
Harpers Ferry National Historical Park, PO Box 65,
  Harpers Ferry, WV 25425, tel. (304) 535 6371
New River Gorge National River, PO Box 246,
  Glen Jean, WV 25846, tel. (304) 465 0508

Wisconsin

Apostle Islands National Lakeshore, Route 1, Box 4,
  Bayfield, WI 54814, tel. (715) 779 3397
St Croix and Lower St Croix National Scenic Riverways, PO Box 708,
  St Croix Falls, WI 54024, tel. (715) 483 3284

Wyoming

Devils Tower National Monument, PO Box 8,
  Devils Tower, WY 82714, tel. (307) 467 5370
Fort Laramie National Historic Site,
  Fort Laramie, WY 82212, tel. (307) 837 2221
Fossil Butte National Monument, PO Box 527,
  Kemmerer, WY 83101, tel. (307) 877 4455
Grand Teton National Park, PO Drawer 170,
  Moose, WY 83012, tel. (307) 733 2880
  (See Sights from A to Z)
John D. Rockefeller Jr Memorial Parkway: see Grand Teton N.P.
Yellowstone National Park, PO Box 168,
  Yellowstone National Park, WY 82190, tel. (307) 344 7381
  (See Sights from A to Z)

Newspapers and Periodicals

News-stands in the United States offer a very wide range of newspapers and periodicals. The weekend editions of newspapers contain detailed calendars of events and full television, radio and cinema programmes.

The leading newspaper that can be called national is "USA Today". Most papers, including such important journals as the "Boston Globe", the "New York Times", the "Washington Post" and the "Miami Herald", have a mainly regional circulation.

Photography

There are no problems about photographing or filming anything you like in the United States. There are good photographic shops all over the country, and in the cities films can be developed and printed within a few hours. Since films tend to be dearer in the United States than in Europe, it is as well to take a good supply with you.

Postal Services

The US Mail is responsible for postal services (including letters, parcels and the remittance of money) in the United States. Telephone and telegraph services are provided by private companies.

Postage rates
The postage on letters within the United States is 29 cents for the first ounce (28 grams) and 23 cents for each additional ounce; postcards cost 14 cents. Airmail letters to Europe cost 50 cents for the first half ounce and 45 cents for each additional half ounce; postcards cost 40 cents. Aerograms with a printed stamp are also 40 cents.

Post offices
Post offices – identified by a US flag – are open Mon.–Fri. 9am to 5 or 6pm, Sat. 8am–noon. Small offices close for lunch. In large cities there are post offices open round the clock.

Poste restante
Poste restante mail should be clearly marked "General Delivery".

Post-boxes
American post-boxes are blue, with "US Mail" in white and a stylised eagle.

Public Holidays

There are relatively few public holidays in the United States, and many shops are open even on holidays other than Thanksgiving Day, Easter Day, Christmas and New Year, though banks, government offices, schools and even some restaurants are closed. On the great Christian festivals (Easter, Whitsun, Christmas) there is no second day's holiday.

Most official holidays are fixed afresh each year and, in order to produce a long weekend, moved to a Monday before or after the actual day.

Public holidays
January 1st: New Year
Third Monday in January: Martin Luther King Jr's Birthday
Third Monday in February: President's Day
Shrove Tuesday: Mardi Gras (Carnival; only regional, mainly in the Panhandle)
Good Friday (only local)
April 26th: Confederate Memorial Day
Last Monday in May: Memorial Day
July 4th: Independence Day
First Monday in September: Labor Day
Second Monday in October: Columbus Day
November 11th: Veterans' Day
Fourth Thursday in November: Thanksgiving Day
December 25th: Christmas Day

Public Transport

With the American dependence on the automobile and the high degree of car ownership, public transport tends to play a subordinate role. Recently, however, constant traffic jams in city centres and the overloading of roads round the great cities have led in some areas to reconsideration of the situation.

In some large cities rapid transit systems (high-speed railways) carry at least part of the heavy city traffic. Among such systems are the old-established subways (underground railways) in New York, Boston and Philadelphia and elevated railways in New York, Chicago and Cleveland. There are modern systems in San Francisco (BART), Washington DC (the Metro), Atlanta (MARTA), Pittsburgh, Chicago, Baltimore and Miami. In recent years the railway system has been developed to provide rapid transit in the Chicago and Miami conurbations. *Rapid transit systems*

Tramway systems (streetcars, trolleys) are now rarely seen. The cable cars of San Francisco are a well-loved feature of the city scene, and elsewhere, as in New Orleans, the old streetcars have taken on a new lease of life as tourist attractions. *Trams*

Most cities have a network – not always a very extensive one – of bus services, reaching out to outlying suburbs. There is usually a flat-rate fare, with no provision for transfer between lines. The fare is paid either in cash to the driver or in the form of tokens put into a box on the bus. *Buses*

See entry *Taxis*

Radio

The programmes of the numerous local and regional radio stations consist mainly of canned music (either serious or light according to the station), frequently interrupted by advertising spots and news headlines. Some stations are directed at particular ethnic groups (Hispanos, Cubans, Haitians, etc.) or religious communities. Others transmit news, sport and music programmes, with or without listener participation, throughout the day.

Some local stations transmit tourist and traffic information on medium wave. The wavelengths on which these programmes can be received are often given on roadside signs. *Tourist information services*

Rafting

See Boat Trips

Rail Travel

Although the economic history of the United States, and with it the growth of tourism, was closely bound up with the development of its railway system, this means of transport is now of only subsidiary importance. In the past express trains with resounding names carried hosts of sun-lovers from the northern states to Florida and winter sports enthusiasts from the great cities of the East to the Rocky Mountains: nowadays there may be no more than a couple of trains a day between the megalopolises on the north-eastern coast and the beaches in the south-east.

Rail Travel

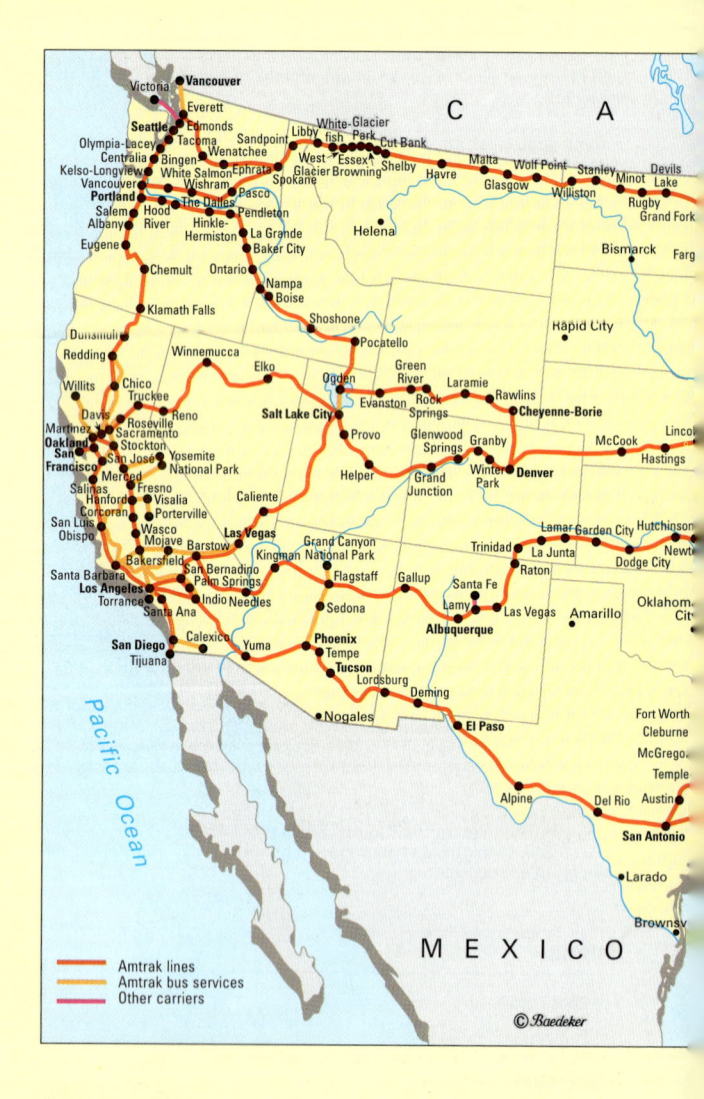

Amtrak

Passenger rail transport and timetabling are the responsibility of the Amtrak organisation. The maintenance of the track and rolling-stock remains in the hands of various railway companies.

Rail passes

Amtrak offers a variety of rail passes, valid for either 15 or 30 days, which can be bought outside the USA at very advantageous rates. A national pass gives unlimited travel over the whole system, and there are also regional passes (Rocky Mountains–Far West, Mississippi–West, East, East or West Coastal).

Rail Travel

Amtrak

Information in the United Kingdom from:
Leisurail, tel. (01733) 033 5599
Destination Marketing, tel. (0171) 978 5212
Explorers Travel, tel. (01753) 681999
Thistle Air, tel. (01563) 71159

Amtrak hot line: 1 800 USA RAIL

Express Trains

Amtrak at present runs the following express trains:

Rail Travel

East	Adirondack: New York–Hudson Valley–Montréal (Canada) Montrealer: Washington DC–Montréal (Canada) Metroliner: New York–Washington DC New England Express: Boston–New York Atlantic City Express: Springfield/Richmond/Harrisburg–Atlantic City Old Dominion: New York–Newport News/Virginia Beach Virginian: New York–Richmond Silver Meteor and Silver Star: New York–Tampa/Miami Carolinian: New York–Charlotte Palmetto: New York–Jacksonville Piedmont: Raleigh–Charlotte Empire and Maple Leaf: New York–Niagara Falls–Toronto (Canada) Lake Shore Limited: Boston/New York–Chicago Capitol Limited: Washington DC–Chicago Broadway Limited and Cardinal: New York–Chicago Pennsylvanian: New York–Pittsburgh Crescent: New York–New Orleans Gulf Breeze: New York–Mobile
Middle West	Chicago Hub: Chicago–Detroit/Toledo/Milwaukee/St Louis/Kansas City/Indianapolis/Quincy/Carbondale/Grand Rapids City of New Orleans: Chicago–New Orleans River Cities: Kansas City/St Louis–New Orleans
West	Texas Eagle: Chicago–Houston/San Antonio–Los Angeles Southwest Chief and Desert Wind: Chicago–Kansas City–Dodge City–Albuquerque–Flagstaff–San Bernardino–Los Angeles California Zephyr: Chicago–Oakland/San Francisco Pioneer: Chicago–Seattle Empire Builder: Chicago–Milwaukee–Minneapolis/St Paul–Minot–Wolf Point–West Glacier–Spokane–Seattle/Portland Coast Starlight: Los Angeles–Seattle
California	Capitols: San Jose–Roseville San Diegans: Santa Barbara–Los Angeles–San Diego San Joaquins: San Francisco/Oakland–Bakersfield
Transcontinental Express	Sunset Limited: Los Angeles–Phoenix–Tucson–San Antonio–Houston–New Orleans–Mobile–Orlando–Miami
Autorail	A train carrying cars runs daily in each direction between Lorton (VA; near Washington DC) and Sanford (FL; near Orlando).

Old-Time Railways

In the United States as in other countries there is a great nostalgia for the old steam trains. All over the country old lines, either standard or narrow gauge, have been brought back into use, mining and lumbering lines have been restored and small railway museums have been established. On some longer stretches of line there are excursions on "dinner trains", sometimes made up of a curious medley of rolling-stock.

The following is a selection of old-time lines, with the point of departure.

Alaska	White Pass and Yukon Route, Skagway
Arizona	Grand Canyon Railway, Williams
Arkansas	Eureka Springs and North Arkansas Railway, Eureka Springs

Restaurants

Napa Valley Railroad; Roaring Camp and Big Trees Narrow Gauge Railroad; Santa Cruz Big Trees and Pacific Railway, Felton	California
Valley Railroad Co., North Cove Express Dinner Train, Essex	Connecticut
Durango and Silverton Narrow Gauge Railroad, Durango; Georgetown Loop Railroad, Georgetown	Colorado
Seminole Gulf Railway, Fort Myers–Bonita Springs	Florida
Lahaina, Kaanapali and Pacific Railroad, Maui Island	Hawaii
The Enter-train-ment Line, Union Bridge	Maryland
Kalamazoo, Lake Shore and Chicago Railway, Paw Paw	Michigan
Osceola and St Croix Valley Railway; Minnesota Zephir Dinner Train, Stillwater	Minnesota
Fremont and Elkhorn Valley Railroad, Fremont	Nebraska
Nevada Northern Railway, East Ely	Nevada
New York and Lake Erie Railroad, Gowanda	New York
Great Smoky Mountains Railway, Dillsboro	North Carolina
Sumpter Valley Railroad, Baker City	Oregon
Strasburg Railroad, Strasburg	Pennsylvania
Black Hills Central Railroad, Hill City	South Dakota
Broadway Dinner Train, Nashville	Tennessee
Texas State Railroad, Rusk–Palestine	Texas
Spirit of Washington Dinner Train, Renton	Washington
Cass Scenic Railroad State Park, Cass	West Virginia

Restaurants

In the tourist regions of the United States there are not only an enormous choice of restaurants but also a surprisingly wide range of ethnic cuisines. In addition to restaurants serving "American" cuisine – which has a great deal more to offer than hamburgers and hot dogs, influenced as it has been by the cuisine of many other countries – there are many Italian and Chinese restaurants, "Tex-Mex" restaurants offering Texan and Mexican specialities, gourmet temples of French cuisine and innumerable German, Swiss, Austrian, Korean, Vietnamese, Thai, Japanese, Brazilian, Argentinian and Arab restaurants. Kosher and vegetarian food is increasingly popular. On the coast there are numerous restaurants specialising in fish and seafood. And visitors will not want to miss the opportunity of sampling the excellent wines produced in the United States.

Restaurants in the United States cover a wide price range, but a good meal need not cost a fortune. Many bars serve tasty snacks such as chilli con carne, chicken fingers, sandwiches and hamburgers. To eat at reasonable cost it is not necessary to patronise restaurant chains such as Taco Bell, Pizza Hut, McDonald's, Burger King and Kentucky Fried Chicken, which are cheap but not always entirely satisfying (though Denny's and Friday's are exceptions). There are better – and not necessarily too expensive – restaurants in areas frequented by tourists, in old town centres which have been regenerated, in holiday resorts and round large hotel complexes.

Riding

Almost all restaurants accept payment by credit card or traveller's cheque as well as in cash.
In the more expensive restaurants, particularly at long weekends and during the main holiday season, it is advisable to book a table in advance. In good restaurants it is usual to wait to be shown to your table by one of the staff. Guests will often be asked "smoking or non-smoking?".

Tipping

See entry

Riding

Trail riding, dude ranches

Riding is a popular form of sport in the United States, and horse-racing is one of the most popular spectator sports. A number of studs in Kentucky, Texas, Arizona, Colorado and other states have international reputations. Trail riding (pony trekking) is also becoming increasingly popular, particularly on "dude ranches" and in some National and State Parks in the West and South-West. At some places Western-style treks lasting several days are on offer.

Information from tourist information offices in the various states (see Information).

Rodeos

At many places, particularly in the cattle-ranching states of the West, there are rodeos during the summer months. In an enclosed arena cowboys show their skill in bull riding (trying to stay as long as possible on the back of a wild steer) and in riding wildly bucking horses (mustangs). There are

Rodeo, Cheyenne

also calf-roping contests (lassooing and tethering young cattle for branding). Other events are likely to include hill billy music, square dancing competitions, chuckwagon races and fairs.
Particularly spectacular are the rodeos held annually in Cheyenne (Wyoming) during the Frontier Days festival in July and every evening in summer at Cody (Wyoming).

Safety and Security

The activities of gangsters like Al Capone and, more recently, "Miami Vice" have made the world familiar with the existence of organised crime in the United States. This is particularly true of the densely populated cities – New York, Washington, Chicago, Los Angeles, Miami – with their sharp social divides, where the financial aristocracy of the United States and the international jet set live side by side with dropouts and castaways and prosperous yuppies cavort in brilliantly neon-lit discos alongside hostels for the old and destitute. Pimps, arms dealers, drug bosses and those who aspire to become so are driven around in luxurious limousines, while round the corner poor blacks, Latinos and Asians compete for the poorest-paid jobs.

Crime

Drug-related crime presents serious problems for the security forces. The country's long coastline and its nearness to the drug-producing countries of Central and South America have made the United States, and the state of Florida in particular, the centre of a large and dangerous drug trade.

Drug-related crime

Visitors should be careful and watchful, particularly in large cities and tourist centres but sometimes also in less populous areas. The danger of criminal attack is greater after dark. In any emergency the police can be called by dialling 911.

Warning

After dark it is advisable to avoid certain areas, particularly parks, bus stations and shady districts in towns. Public transport in the late evening, with few passengers, may also be a possible source of danger. It is worth asking your hotel or a local acquaintance what parts of the town are better avoided. To get back to your hotel at a late hour it is best to take a taxi: it is not advisable to walk about alone after dark.
You should try not to look like a tourist in appearance or behaviour. Keep your camera concealed, and do not think of taking photographs in doubtful areas. It should be remembered that for those concerned poverty has nothing romantic or interesting about it.
You should never carry objects of value or large sums of money, which should be deposited in the hotel safe. Instead of cash it is better to have dollar traveller's cheques and credit cards – though there is something to be said for having a small sum in cash, say 20–50 dollars, which may serve to "buy off" a possible attacker. Showy jewellery should not be worn, and a purse attached to the belt is better than a shoulder or wrist bag.
In your hotel you should lock the door on the inside and not open it to persons unknown to you. On leaving the room take the key with you, and do not leave any objects of value in the room.
In airports and railway stations, at bus stops, in the car parks of car rental firms and in hotels never leave your baggage unattended or give it to anyone who volunteers to take it to a taxi or to your room.
If you feel you are being followed you should call the police from the nearest place of safety.

It is advisable to study your route in advance. If you lose your way and want help the best plan is to stop in a parking place outside a filling station or a shop.

Safety for motorists

Sailing

If you are run into from behind or from the side it is better not to stop at once but to make for the nearest well lighted parking place at a filling station or a shop and call the police from there by dialling 911.
You should not on any account give a lift to hitch-hikers.
You should park your car only in well lighted and easily visible places. It is inadvisable to spend the night in your car.

Sailing

There are numerous marinas where sailing boats can be hired on some stretches of the Atlantic coast (particularly Cape Cod and the Outer Banks), round the Florida peninsula, along the Gulf Coast and on the Pacific coast of California. There are also good sailing waters on the Great Lakes, a number of smaller lakes and the numerous artificial lakes formed by dams on the great rivers. Fuller information can be obtained from the tourist offices of the states concerned (see Information).

Shopping

Shopping streets in the European sense are to be found only in large cities and tourist centres; elsewhere there are only limited shopping facilities in downtown areas. Every town of any consequence, however, has one or more shopping malls, a Marketplace, a Galleria and a flea market. For information apply to the local tourist information office or chamber of commerce.

Sales tax
When shopping in the United States it should be remembered that many goods are subject to a sales tax ranging between 4% and 15% from state to state.

Display of sweet things . . . *. . . in the shopping mall*

Shopping

Shopping malls

Shopping malls, sometimes of enormous size, with parking for cars, are to be found on the outskirts of all large and medium-sized towns. They usually contain branches of a number of department stores (Sears, J. C. Penney, McAlpine, etc.), together with a variety of smaller shops, boutiques, services and restaurants under the same roof. In these shopping malls you can buy practically everything you are likely to want and can compare the price and quality of goods in different shops.

Exclusive boutiques

The most exclusive shops are to be found only in places where the necessary purchasing power is available – in the famous bathing resorts of California and Florida, in some tourist centres in the mountains and in world-famed cities like New York, Boston, Chicago, San Francisco and New Orleans. Elsewhere shops of this quality are much more difficult to find. Even the "yellow pages" telephone book cannot be entirely relied on, since the addresses often change over night or the shops go out of business.

Factory shops

Bargains can often be found in factory outlet shops; but these too are usually to be found only in areas where there is likely to be a sufficient demand from tourists – for example round such tourist magnets as Disneyworld. In some cities there are regular "outlet centers" where several dozen manufacturers offer their products straight from the factory. As a rule these factory shops are run separately from the factories themselves.

Souvenirs

Popular souvenirs are those sold in the large theme parks (e.g. Mickey Mouse T-shirts) and in National Parks and museums. Many visitors like to take home Indian craft products, sold mainly in the reservations but also in some tourist resorts.
Among items which are relatively cheap in the United States are electronic apparatus, cameras and photographic accessories, telephones, answering machines and micro-computers. Other good buys are clothing (especially jeans), underwear, leather goods (particularly shoes) and sports articles (e.g. baseball equipment), since well-known brands cost much less in the United States than in Europe.

Clothing sizes

American clothing sizes sometimes differ from those used in Britain. The following table shows the differences. It is advisable in any case to try things on before buying.

Clothing Sizes								
Men's suits	USA	36	38	40	42	44	46	48
	UK	36	38	40	42	44	46	48
Dress sizes	USA	6	8	10	12	14	16	18
	UK	8	10	12	14	16	18	20
Men's shirts	USA	14	$14\frac{1}{2}$	15	$15\frac{1}{2}$	16	$16\frac{1}{2}$	17
	UK	14	$14\frac{1}{2}$	15	$15\frac{1}{2}$	16	$16\frac{1}{2}$	17
Men's shoes	USA	8	$8\frac{1}{2}$	$9\frac{1}{2}$	$10\frac{1}{2}$	$11\frac{1}{2}$	12	
	UK	7	$7\frac{1}{2}$	$8\frac{1}{2}$	$9\frac{1}{2}$	$10\frac{1}{2}$	11	
Women's shoes	USA	6	$6\frac{1}{2}$	7	$7\frac{1}{2}$	8	$8\frac{1}{2}$	
	UK	$4\frac{1}{2}$	5	$5\frac{1}{2}$	6	$6\frac{1}{2}$	7	

Sometimes items of clothing are labelled with the ill-defined sizes S for small, M for medium, L for large and XL or XXL for extra-large.

Smoking

Smoking is nowadays rather frowned on in the United States. Some airlines have banned it, and it is also prohibited (e.g. in the states of Arizona and Florida) in many public places. Many restaurants have separate sections for smokers and non-smokers.

Souvenirs

See Shopping

Sport

Spectator sports

The most popular – and most telegenic – spectator sports are American football, baseball, basketball and ice hockey. A long way after come tennis and golf. In spite of the fact that the United States hosted the World Cup in 1994 association football is very far from being a mass spectator sport.

American football

The favourite sport, by a long way, is American football. The rules of the game, which originally developed out of rugby, are complicated and difficult for an outsider to understand: what is fascinating is the dynamism of the play and the tactical refinements to which it lends itself. It is played in the National Football League (NFL) in two "conferences", the American Football Conference and the National Football Conference, each of which in turn consists of three divisions (East, Central and West) of four or five teams each. The high point of the season, in January, is the match between the leaders of the two conferences for the Super Bowl, the supreme football trophy. Among the strongest teams in recent years have been the Washington Redskins, the Dallas Cowboys, the New York Giants, the San Francisco 49ers and the Buffalo Bills.

The second football league is the College Football League, in which college teams play in professional conditions but with slightly altered rules. This is the talent nursery of the NFL.

Baseball

Second place in the popularity stakes is taken by baseball, which is even more difficult to follow than American football. There are two leagues, the National League and the American League (each with two divisions), in which Canadian teams are also included. There is no trophy comparable to the Super Bowl. The leading teams are the Pittsburgh Pirates, the Atlanta Braves, the Toronto Blue Jays and the Oakland A's.

Basketball

Thanks to superstars like "Magic" Johnson, Charles Barkley and above all Michael "Air" Jordan (who has declared his intention of retiring), Americans flock to the matches of the National Basketball Association (NBA), which has two "conferences" of two divisions each. It is the ambition of all basketball professionals to play in the NBA with teams such as the Chicago Bulls, the Los Angeles Lakers, the Portland Trail Blazers and the Phoenix Suns.

Ice hockey

Ice hockey also has two "conferences", each with two divisions. The National Hockey League (NHL) is formed by American and Canadian teams, reinforced by Scandinavian, Czech and Russian players. The two teams which reach the final after a series of playoffs play for the Stanley Cup, ice hockey's highest trophy, which is of such importance to the North American professional teams that only second- and third-level players compete in the ice hockey world championships. In recent years the Stanley Cup has been won by the Pittsburgh Penguins, the Edmonton Oilers, the Calgary Flames and the Canadiens of Montréal.

Other popular spectator sports are motor-racing (the Daytona 500, the Indianapolis 500), horse-racing (the Kentucky Derby), tennis, boxing, wrestling, golf, lacrosse and – not to be forgotten – the rodeo (see entry).

Telephoning

Competitive association football is now played in the United States only by college teams and is hardly ever seen on television. Although it is played in schools, the idols of the young are the stars of American football, baseball and basketball, not soccer players. It is doubtful whether the choice of the United States as the venue for the World Cup in June/July 1994 (with matches played in Boston, Chicago, Dallas, New York, Orlando, San Francisco and Washington DC, and the final in Los Angeles) will make much difference. At the end of 1993 only 13% of all Americans knew that the competition for the World Cup was being staged in their country.

World Cup 1994

Angling, bathing, boating, diving, golf, riding, sailing, tennis, walking (see entries)

Active sports

Taxis

In all cities and tourist centres there are sufficient numbers of taxis. They can be hailed in the street.

The basic fare for the first mile is $1–3, plus $1.50 for each additional mile and 20 cents for each minute of waiting time. Since distances in cities and tourist centres are often considerable, the fare can very quickly mount up: thus a trip from Miami International Airport to Miami Beach will cost at least $50. In some areas the fares are fixed by zone.
A tip of 15–20% is expected.

Fares

Telephoning

Public payphones operate with 25 cent, 10 cent and 5 cent coins (quarters, dimes and nickels).

Payphones

United States area codes are three-digit numbers (with no preceding zero).

Area codes

For local calls it is necessary only to dial 1 followed by the subscriber's number.

Local calls

For trunk (long-distance) calls within the USA, dial 1 followed by the area code and the subscriber's number.

Calls within the USA

From private telephones dial 011 followed by the country code and area code, omitting the initial zero, and the subscriber's number. From a public telephone dial 0 or 01 to get the operator, who will tell you what to do.

International calls

To make an international call from the United States, dial 011 followed by the country code: 44 for the United Kingdom, 61 for Australia, 64 for New Zealand.
To telephone to the United States from Britain, dial 010 1, followed by the area code and the subscriber's number.

International dialling codes

A toll-free number for obtaining telephone information will be found in the telephone book.

Telephone information

A direct-dialled three-minute call from the United States to Europe will cost around $5 during the cheap-rate period (evening and night).

Telephone charges

There are reduced rates between 5 and 11pm and considerably reduced rates between 11pm and 8am and at weekends.

Cheap rates

Many payphones can be used only with a Telecard, which can be bought locally.
British visitors can use a BT Chargecard by dialling the operator.

Telecard

Television

AT & T Card — The AT & T company issues its own card, which is comparable to the Telecard but costs less. An AT & T card can be obtained by anyone with a Diners Club or Visa credit card or a bank account in the United States.

Reversed charges (collect calls) — To make a reversed charge call (in the United States "collect call"), call the operator, who will confirm from the recipient of the call that he is willing to accept it and will then put you through.

Telegrams — There are now very few telegraph offices in the United States, and most telegrams (cables) are dictated over the telephone. In hotels they can be handed in at reception or dictated to the telephone switchboard operator. The companies specialising in international cables (e.g. Western Union) are listed in the telephone book.

Television

The United States is the land of television *par excellence*. Scarcely a hotel room in the country is without its television set, and an enormous number of channels operate round the clock, offering a great range of programmes from science fiction to religion – almost invariably interrupted by advertising spots.

Tennis

The United States, and particularly the Sunshine State of Florida, is a Promised Land for tennis enthusiasts. The great stars of the tennis world appear regularly in tournaments at such venues, familiar on television, as Flushing Meadows, Amelia Island, Boca Raton and Key Biscayne; and it is sometimes possible to see qualifying contests elsewhere.
It is possible to play tennis in the United States almost all year round. Many hotels have their own courts.

Time Zones

Travel Documents

Time

The continental United States extend over four time zones: Eastern Time (5 hours behind GMT), Central Time (6 hours behind GMT), Mountain Time (7 hours behind GMT) and Pacific Time (8 hours behind GMT). Alaska and Hawaii have their own time zones, 9 and 10 hours behind GMT. — Time zones

Summer Time (Daylight Saving Time), when clocks are moved one hour forward, is normally in force from the last Sunday in April to the last Sunday in October. — Summer Time

Tipping

In contrast to the general practice in Europe, a service charge is not normally included in hotel and restaurant bills, and tips must be given separately. The staff of hotels and restaurants are often very poorly paid and depend on tips to make up their income.

It is usual to give the boy who takes your luggage to or from your room a tip of $1 dollar per item, and to leave $2 per day for the chambermaid. Staff in reception expect no special tip for normal services. Pool attendants are given $1 per person per day. It is usual to give the hotel porter $1 for fetching a taxi. If a hotel or restaurant offers "valet parking" – that is, if a member of the staff parks your car for you – a tip of $1 should be offered for taking it away and again for bringing it back. — Hotels

The normal tip is 15% of the bill (before the addition of sales tax). The money is usually left on the table. In the better restaurants the head waiter and wine waiter will also expect a tip. — Restaurants

The driver should be given 15% of the amount on the meter, for short journeys rather more. — Taxis

Both men's and women's hairdressers expect a 15–20% tip. — Hairdressers

For bootblacks a tip of between 50 cents and $1 is usual. — Bootblacks

Usherettes are not normally tipped. — Theatres, cinemas

On an organised coach tour the bus driver receives $1.50 per person per day, the tour guide $2.50. — Drivers and tour guides

When paying by credit card you can add the amount of the tip to the total of the bill. — Credit cards

Toilets

It is sometimes difficult to find a toilet, and many public toilets turn out to be closed or are in a filthy condition. The best plan is to use a rest room in a restaurant or shopping centre.

Travel Documents

British citizens visiting the United States for a period of less than 90 days require only a full passport (not a British Visitor's Passport) and a visa waiver form, provided either by a travel agency or by the airline (either at check-in or on the plane). Visitors from Australia and New Zealand must obtain a non-immigrant visitor's visa before leaving home. Canadian citizens require only some form of identity document for a brief visit; for a longer stay a passport should be carried. — Passport

Walking

Immigration form	An immigration form (normally distributed on the aircraft) must be filled in and presented at immigration control.
Financial status	Visitors to the United States must be in possession of a ticket for their return or onward journey and must be able to show that they have enough money to support themselves while in the United States. Visitors travelling on a package tour should have no difficulty.
Inoculations	Evidence of inoculation is only required for visitors coming from an infected country. It is advisable, however, to check up on current regulations at a US consulate.

Walking

National Parks	The numerous National and State Parks and Recreation Areas offer endless scope for walking. There are numerous trails of varying lengths (sometimes on boardwalks over swampy ground) which make exploration of their natural beauties easy and offer magnificent views. The various parks and forests have their own visitor centres and information bureaux, where visitors can get detailed information on the trails. In many parks there are guided walks led by park rangers.
Information	Information about these and other trails – including the 2000 mile/3200 long Appalachian Trail, which runs along the crest of the Appalachians from Maine to Georgia – can be obtained from: American Hiking Society 1015 31st Street NW, Washington, DC 20007

Weights/Measures/Temperatures

Measures of length

1 inch (in.)	= 2.54cm	1cm	= 0.39in.
1 foot (ft)	= 30.48cm	10cm	= 0.33ft
1 yard (yd)	= 91.44cm	1m	= 1.09yd
1 mile	= 1.61km	1km	= 0.62 mile

Measures of area

1 square inch	= 6.45cm^2	1cm^2	= 0.155sq.in.
1 square foot	= 9.288dm^2	1dm^2	= 0.108sq.ft
1 square yard	= 0.386m^2	1m^2	= 1.196sq.yd
1 square mile	= 2.589km^2	1km^2	= 0.386sq.mi
1 acre	= 0.405ha	1ha	= 2.471acres

Measures of volume

1 cubic inch	= 16.386cm^3	1cm^3	= 0.061cu.in.
1 cubic foot	= 28.32dm^3	1dm^3	= 0.035cu.ft
1 cubic yard	= 0.765m^3	1m^3	= 1.308cu.yd

Fluid measures

1 gill	= 0.51181 litre	1 litre	= 8.474 gills
1 pint (pt)	= 0.473 litre	1 litre	= 2.114 pt
1 quart (qt)	= 0.946 litre	1 litre	= 1.057 qt
1 US gallon (gal)	= 3.787 litre	1 litre	= 0.264 gal

Weights

1 ounce (oz)	= 28.35g	100g	= 3.527 oz
1 pound (lb)	= 453.59g	1kg	= 2.205 lb
1 stone	= 6.35kg	10kg	= 1.57 stone

Temperatures

K(elvin)	°C	°F	
373	100	212	*boiling point*
323	50	122	
318	45	113	
313	40	104	
310	37	98.6	*body heat*
308	35	95	
303	30	86	
298	25	77	
293	20	68	
288	15	59	
283	10	50	
278	5	41	
273	0	32	*freezing*
268	− 5	23	*point*
263	−10	14	
258	−15	5	
255.3	−17.7	0	
253	−20	− 4	
248	−25	−13	
243	−30	−22	

$$°C = \frac{5(°F - 32)}{9}$$

$$°F = 1.8 \times °C + 32$$

Winter Sports

When to Go

In a country of such enormous extent it might be supposed that the best time for a visit would be different for each region; but in fact, because of the general north–south orientation of the mountain ranges, which oppose no barrier to the southward movement of cold air masses from the north in winter or to the warm south winds which blow north in summer, this is not entirely true. The coastal ranges prevent the moderating influence of the Pacific from reaching more than a relatively narrow coastal zone, while the influence of the Atlantic, with the warm Gulf Stream and the cold Labrador Current, is felt to a varying extent in different areas.

Much of the United States has a continental climate (see Climate, pp. 18–21), with very cold winters and heavy snow, particularly in the north-east and round the Great Lakes, and hot summers, which in the wet coastal regions in the east and south can be extremely oppressive. The summer heat is more tolerable in the drier west.

For much of the United States the best time for a visit is spring, which quickly gives place to the hot summer. It can also be very pleasant in autumn, which is long and usually dry. From early September to November there is a beautiful Indian summer, when the mountain forests are in the full glory of their autumn colouring. At higher altitudes (above 5000ft/ 1500m or so), for example in the Rockies, on the rim of the Grand Canyon, in the Coastal Range in the west and the Appalachians in the east, and on the cooler coastal strip of California reaching up to the Canadian frontier, under the influence of cold marine currents, warm clothing may be needed even in summer.

For a winter holiday there is Florida, usually warm at this time of year, and at the other climatic extreme the winter sports regions in the mountains (Rockies, Front Range, Sierra Nevada, Cascade Range, Adirondacks, White Mountains).

The best time to visit Alaska is from May to the end of September.

With their equable tropical climates, Hawaii, Puerto Rico and the Virgin Islands offer a pleasant holiday at any time of year.

The main holiday season in the United States is between Memorial Day (end of May) and Labor Day (beginning of September).	Main holiday season

Winter Sports

In recent decades extensive winter sports areas have been developed in the United States – in the mountains of the north-east with their abundance of snow, in the Rocky Mountains, famed for their "champagne snow", in California's Sierra Nevada and even in the desert states of Arizona, Nevada and New Mexico.

In the main skiing areas there are frequently dozens of pistes, well equipped with lifts (cabin cableways, chair-lifts, ski-tows). In some areas there are facilities for heli-skiing. Experienced skiers can then be taken by helicopter to remote and beautiful mountain regions – though from the point of view of the environment this is not a wholly desirable development.	Alpine skiing
Langlauf (Nordic) skiing has become very popular in recent years, and in many areas, particularly in National and State Parks and Recreation Areas, there are prepared langlauf trails.	Langlauf skiing
Also very popular, though not environment-friendly, are trips in snow-mobiles (motor sledges).	Snowmobiles

Winter Sports

Skiing and fun ...   *... in the Rockies*

Winter Sports Regions in the United States

Northern Appalachians	In the Northern Appalachians, which are famed for their abundance of snow, there are a number of fine skiing areas, though because of their nearness to the great cities of the north-east they are frequently overcrowded. As a result the access roads to the most popular areas are often closed quite early in the day.
Adirondacks	The Adirondacks, in the north-east of New York State, are a very popular skiing area. A major skiing centre in this area is Lake Placid, which has twice (in 1932 and again in 1980) hosted the Winter Olympics.
Vermont	The main skiing areas in the state of Vermont are Killington, Mount Snow, Stowe and Sugarbrush.
New Hampshire	In New Hampshire are the White Mountains, with excellent skiing facilities on Mount Washington.
Maine	In the extreme north-east of the United States, in the state of Maine, a number of winter sports areas are still in course of development.
Rocky Mountains	There are superb skiing areas in the Rocky Mountains. Here are some of the oldest, largest and best known winter sports resorts in the United States, well able to stand comparison with Garmisch, Davos and St Moritz.
Front Range: Denver/ Colorado Springs	Round Denver and its neighbouring city of Colorado Springs to the south are numerous excellently equipped skiing areas, all in the Front Range, which rises like an alpine wall to the west of the two cities. Within easy reach of Denver are the pistes above Golden and Boulder, at Idaho Springs (Mount Evans), Arapahoe, Hot Sulphur Springs and in the Rocky Mountain National Park (with the resort of Estes Park). Round Colorado Springs are the beautiful pistes above Manitou Springs and on Pikes Peak.
Vail	Some 2 hours' drive west of Denver is the internationally famed resort of Vail. Within easy reach of Vail are other skiing areas (Beaver Creek, Copper Mountain, etc.).

Young People's Accommodation

The skiing resort in the Rockies, easily reached from Denver, is Aspen, the meeting-place of the international jet set. Round the town are a number of recently developed skiing areas (Aspen Mountain, Aspen Highlands, Snowmass, Buttermilk, etc.). — Aspen

Among other winter sports in Colorado which have come to the fore in recent years are Breckenridge, Keystone, Steamboat Springs, Telluride, Gunnison, Grand Junction, Dolores and Durango. — Other well-known resorts in Colorado

The most popular winter sports resort in Wyoming by a long way is Jackson, from which other skiing areas in the Grand Teton and Yellowstone National Parks are easily reached. — Wyoming

Other skiing areas in course of development are Pinedale (south-east of Jackson), the Bighorn Mountains (above Buffalo and Sheridan) and the Medicine Bow Range (west of Laramie).

There is particularly good powder snow in some skiing areas in the state of Utah. Well-known resorts are Alta, Brighton and Snowbird. Two hours' drive south of Salt Lake City, in the Wasatch Range, is the still relatively undiscovered resort of Sundance. — Utah

In Idaho is the oldest skiing resort in the United States, Sun Valley. There are other good skiing areas at Boise, Grangeville and McCall, and at Montpelier and Soda Springs in the Wasatch Range. — Idaho

The best skiing areas in New Mexico are in the Sangre de Cristo Mountains and the Sacramento Mountains. Particularly popular are the Taos Ski Valley, the Santa Fe Ski Basin and the Sierra Blanca. — New Mexico

In California's Sierra Nevada there are a number of magnificent skiing areas, best reached by way of San Francisco or Reno (Nevada). — **Sierra Nevada**

The best known skiing region in the West is Squaw Valley, where some events in the 1960 Winter Olympics were staged. There are other smaller skiing areas round Lake Tahoe and to the south of South Lake Tahoe. — Squaw Valley, Lake Tahoe

The other large skiing region in California is the Yosemite National Park, where the winter sports season lasts into late spring. — Yosemite National Park

In the Mammoth Lakes/June Mountain area, 300 miles/500km from Los Angeles, there are over 180 pistes, with some three dozen lifts. — Mammoth Lakes/June Mountain

There are good skiing areas, still not overcrowded, in the states of Oregon and Washington. There are excellent facilities in some areas in the Cascade Range (on the Upper Klamath Lake and Crescent Lake, round Timberlin Lodge and on Mount Baker, near the Canadian frontier) and the Olympic National Park. — **Other skiing areas**

Young People's Accommodation

Accommodation specially designed for young people is generally to be found only in areas where there are likely to be numbers of young visitors: that is, mainly in the large cities, in towns with colleges and universities, in the beach resorts of Florida and California favoured by young people and in certain winter sports centres.

Youth Hostels

There are in the United States only some 130 youth hostels run by the American Youth Hostels (AYH) organisation, together with 100 other hostels. It is evidently not possible, therefore, to tour the United States going from hostel to hostel; but there are some areas – in New England and southern Pennsylvania, round the Great Lakes, in the Colorado Rockies, on Puget Sound in the state of Washington and on the Californian Pacific coast – in which it is possible to make shorter tours round a chain of youth hostels.

Young People's Accommodation

Information	American Youth Hostels, 733 15th Street NW, Suite 840, Washington, DC 20005, tel. (202) 783 6161.
Lists of youth hostels	The International Youth Hostel Handbook, available in Britain from the Youth Hostel Association (14 Southampton Street, London WC2, tel. 071–836 1036) contains a comprehensive list of hostels. Fuller information is given by the official AYH Hostelling Handbook, annually updated, which is available at AYH hostels or from the AYH headquarters (above).
Warning	Some youth hostels not run by the AYH organisation fall short of an adequate standard. Genuine youth hostels can be identified by the triangular AYH logo or the internationally recognised "house and tree" symbol.

YMCA and YWCA

In all the larger American cities young people can find accommodation in YMCA and YWCA hostels – though these tend to be fully booked and are sometimes relatively expensive for the accommodation they provide.

Information	YMCA/YWCA Central Office, 291 Broadway, New York, NY 10010.

Student Residences

During university vacations accommodation is often available at reasonable rates in student residences. Information can be obtained from local information offices (see Information) or from the universities and colleges concerned.

Index

Accommodation 517
Air Travel 517
  Airlines 517
  Airports 517
Alabama 139
  Places of Interest 140
Alaska 140
  Features of Interest in Alaska 142
Albuquerque 145
  Sights 145
  Surroundings 146
Alcohol 519
Amusement Parks 519
Angling 521
Arches National Park 146
Architecture 98
Arizona 147
  Places of Interest 148
Arkansas 150
  Places of Interest 151
Art 94
  Painting 94
  Photography 97
  Sculpture 97
Art and Culture 94
Atlanta 152
  Sights 154
  Surroundings 155

Badlands National Park 155
Baltimore 157
  Downtown Baltimore 157
  Inner Harbor 159
Banks 522
Bathing 522
Bed and Breakfast 523
Big Bend National Park 161
Black Hills 161
  Places of Interest in the Black Hills 162
Boat Trips 523
Boston 166
  Back Bay and Brookline 172
  Freedom Trail 167
  Inner Harbor 173
  Surroundings 174
Breakdown Assistance 551
Bryce Canyon National Park 175
Bus Travel 524
Business Hours 524

California 176
  Places of Interest 178

Camping 525
Canoeing 525
Canyonlands National Park 180
  Round Canyonlands National Park 181
Cape Canaveral / Kennedy Space Center 182
  Spaceport USA 183
Cape Cod 184
  Surroundings 185
Car Rental 525
  Rental firms 526
Carlsbad Caverns National Park 185
Casinos 526
Charleston 187
  Historic District 188
  Other Sights in Charleston 189
  Surroundings 190
Charlottesville 191
  Sights 191
  Surroundings 191
Chemists 526
Cheyenne 192
  Sights 193
  Surroundings 194
Chicago 194
  Burnham Park / Chinatown 204
  Grant Park / South Michigan Avenue 202
  Hyde Park / University of Chicago 204
  Lakefront / Old Town / Lincoln Park 205
  Near North Side/Gold Coast 196
  New East Side/Cityfront Center 196
  North Michigan Avenue/ Oak Street 198
  River North 198
  Surroundings 205
  The Loop 199
  West Loop / Near Southwest Side 203
Cincinnati 206
  Sights 207
  Surroundings 207
Cleveland 208
  Sights 208
  Surroundings 209
Climate 20

Cody 209
  Sights 209
  Surroundings 211
Colonial National Historical Park 211
Colorado 212
  Places of Interest 213
Colorado Springs 215
  Sights 215
  Surroundings 215
Connecticut 217
  Places of Interest 217
Consulates 527
Crater Lake National Park 218
Credit Cards 527
Crime 527
Cruises 527
Currency 528
Customs Regulations 529

Dallas 220
  Sights 220
  Surroundings 222
Daredevils of Niagara 368
Death Valley National Monument 222
Delaware 224
  Places of Interest 224
Denver 225
  Sights 225
  Surroundings 229
Detroit 229
  Sights 230
  Surroundings 232
Dinosaur National Monument 233
Diplomatic and Consular Offices 530
Diving 531
  Diving Grounds 532
Dress 532
Driving Licence 545

Economy 50
  Agriculture, Forestry and Fishing 54
  Economic and Social Policy 53
  Energy 56
  Foreign Trade 58
  Industry 57
  Mining 56
  Service Industries 58
  Social Differences 52
  Tourism 59

Index

Education 48
Electricity 533
Emergencies 533
Endangered Species Convention 533
Events 533
　Major Events 533
Everglades National Park 234

Facts and Figures 9
Famous People 81
Fauna 22
Filling Stations 547
Film 118
　Beginnings 118
　Hollywood in Crisis 121
　The Talkies 119
Flora 21
Florida 235
　Places of Interest 236
Food and Drink 535
Foreign Embassies and Consulates in the United States 530

General 9
Georgia 239
　Places of Interest 240
Getting to the United States 536
Golf 537
Government and Society 44
Grand Canyon National Park 241
　Grand Canyon 243
　Sights on the North Rim of the Grand Canyon 245
　Sights on the South Rim of the Grand Canyon 245
　Surroundings 246
Grand Teton National Park 247
Great Smoky Mountains National Park 248
Gulf Islands National Seashore 249

Hawaii / Hawaiian Islands 250
　Places of Interest 251
Help for the Disabled 537
Highways and Interstate Highways 547
History 63
　A New World Order? 80
　Civil War 69
　Colonisation 63
　Crisis and New Hope 77
　Discovery 63
　Foundation, Consolidation and Extension of the Union 66
　From the Cold War to Détente 74
　Prosperity and Neo-Isolationism 72
　Reconstruction and the Rise to World Power 70
　The American Revolution 65
　The United States in the Second World War 73
Holiday Apartments 538
Hotel and Motel Chains 539
Hotels/Motels/Resorts 538
Houston 252
　Sights 253
　Surroundings 254

Idaho 255
　Places of Interest 255
Illinois 256
　Places of Interest 257
Indiana 258
　Places of Interest 258
Indianapolis 259
　Sights 259
Information 540
　Destinations with Offices in the United Kingdom 540
Information Offices in the United States 541
Iowa 261
　Places of Interest 262

Jackson 262
　Sights 263
　Surroundings 263
Jacksonville 263
　Sights 264
　Surroundings 264
Joshua Tree National Monument 265

Kansas 266
　Places of Interest 266
Kansas City 267
　Sights in Kansas City, Kansas 267
　Sights in Kansas City, Missouri 268
Kentucky 268
　Places of Interest 269
Key West 270
　Sights 271
　Surroundings 272

Lake Tahoe / Squaw Valley 273
Language 544

Las Vegas 274
　Sights 274
　Surroundings 277
Lassen Volcanic National Park 277
　Sights 278
Lexington / Kentucky Horse Park 278
　Sights 278
Literature 104
　19th Century 104
　20th Century 106
Living with San Andreas 177
Los Angeles 280
　Disneyland 289
　Downtown Los Angeles 282
　Hollywood 284
　North-Western Districts 284
　Northern Districts 287
　Other Places of Interest Round Los Angeles 290
　Southern Districts 288
Louisiana 290
　Places of Interest 291

Maine 291
　Places of Interest 292
Mammoth Cave National Park 293
Maryland 294
　Places of Interest 294
Massachusetts 295
　Places of Interest 295
Meals 535
Medical Care 545
Memphis 296
　Graceland 298
　Outer Districts 298
　Sights in Downtown Memphis 297
Mesa Verde National Park 298
Miami 299
　Sights 300
Miami Beach 304
　Art Deco District 304
　Other Sights in Miami Beach 307
Michigan 308
　Places of Interest 308
Milwaukee 309
　Sights 309
Minneapolis / St Paul 311
　Sights in Minneapolis 312
　Sights in St Paul 313
Minnesota 314
　Places of Interest 314

586

Index

Mississippi 315
  Places of Interest 316
Missouri 317
  Places of Interest 318
Mojave Desert 318
  Sights 318
Montana 319
  Places of Interest 320
Monterey 320
  Sights 321
  Surroundings 322
Monument Valley 322
Motoring Organisations 550
Motoring in the United States 545
Mount Rainier National Park 323
Museums 551
Music 109
  Dancing in the Street: America's Pop Music 109
  "Hey, Ho! Let's Go!!": But Where To? 116
  "How blue can you get?": Blues 111
  "It don't mean a thing, it ain't got that swing": Jazz 110
  Musicals and Serious Music 117
  "Take me Home Country Roads": Country Music 112
  The Beat Goes On 115
  "The Blues had a Baby and they named it Rock'n'Roll" 113

Napa Valley 325
  Sights 325
  Surroundings 326
Nashville 326
  Sights 326
  Surroundings 327
National Parks and Reserves 551
Navajo Country 327
  Sights 329
  Round Navajo Country 331
Nebraska 332
  Places of Interest 332
Nevada 333
  Places of Interest 334
New Hampshire 335
  Places of Interest 335
New Jersey 336
  Places of Interest 336
New Mexico 338
  Places of Interest 338

New Orleans 339
  Central Business District 345
  City Park 346
  Garden District 345
  Riverfront 344
  Surroundings 346
  Vieux Carré (French Quarter) 340
New York State 346
  Places of Interest in New York State 348
New York City 349
  Brooklyn / Queens / Bronx / Staten Island 365
  East of Central Park 361
  Lower Manhattan 351
  Midtown Manhattan 355
  North of Central Park 365
  Sights in New York City 351
  Surroundings of New York City 366
  Uptown Manhattan / Central Park 361
  West of Central Park 364
Newspapers and Periodicals 565
Niagara Falls 367
  Niagara Falls, a Double Town 369
  Surroundings 371
  Views of the Falls 367
North Carolina 372
  Places of Interest 373
North Dakota 374
  Places of Interest 374

Ohio 375
  Places of Interest 376
Oklahoma 377
  Places of Interest 377
Oklahoma City 378
  Sights 378
  Surroundings 379
Olympic National Park 379
Omaha 382
  Sights 382
  Surroundings 383
Oregon 383
  Places of Interest 384
Orlando 385
  Sights 385
  Surroundings 387
Outer Banks 390
  Sights 391

Palm Beach / West Palm Beach 391
  Sights in Palm Beach 392
  Sights in West Palm Beach 392

Surroundings of Palm Beach and West Palm Beach 392
Palm Springs 393
  Sights in Palm Springs and Surroundings 394
Pennsylvania 394
  Places of Interest 395
Pennsylvania Dutch Country 396
  Sights 397
Petrified Forest National Park 398
Philadelphia 400
  Downtown Philadelphia 404
  Germantown 406
  Independence National Historical Park 402
  On the Delaware River 404
  Other Sights in the Historic District 403
  On the Schuylkill River 405
  Round Logan Circle 405
  Surroundings 406
Phoenix 406
  Sights 407
  Surroundings 409
Photography 565
Pittsburgh 409
  Sights 410
Population; Towns and Other Settlements 25
  Population Groups 26
  Towns and Other Settlements 29
Portland 412
  Sights 413
Postal Services 566
Practical Information from A to Z 517
Protection of Nature and the Environment 23
Public Holidays 566
Public Transport 566
Puerto Rico 413
  Places of Interest 414

Quotations 124

Radio 567
Rafting 567
Rail Travel 567
  Amtrak 568
  Express Trains 569
  Old-Time Railways 570
Redwood National Park 417
Religion 41
Religion and Agriculture 42
Restaurants 571

587

Index

Rhode Island 417
  Places of Interest 418
Richmond 419
  Sights 419
Riding 572
Rocky Mountain National
  Park 420
Rodeos 572

Sacramento 422
  Sights 423
Safety and Security 573
Sailing 574
Salt Lake City 430
  Sights 431
  Surroundings 433
San Antonio 434
  Sights 435
  Surroundings 436
San Diego 437
  Sights in Downtown San
    Diego 437
  Sights in Other
    Districts 439
  Surroundings 440
San Francisco 441
  Cathedral Hill 449
  Chinatown 445
  Dolores Street 449
  Downtown San
    Francisco 444
  Embarcadero 445
  Golden Gate 450
  Golden Gate Park 449
  Nob Hill 446
  North Waterfront 448
  Presidio 450
  Russian Hill 447
  Surroundings of San
    Francisco (Bay
    Area) 451
  Telegraph Hill 448
San Jose 452
  Sights 452
  Surroundings 452
Santa Fe 452
  Pueblos 456
  Sights 454
  Surroundings 455
  Taos 456
Savannah 457
  Sights 457
  Surroundings 458
Seattle 459
  Sights 460
  Surroundings 462
Sequoia and Kings Canyon
  National Parks 462
  Sights in Sequoia National
    Park 464
  Sights in Kings Canyon
    National Park 464

Shenandoah National
  Park 464
Shopping 574
Sights from A to Z 139
Smoking 576
Sources of Information on
  National Parks, National
  Monuments, etc. 552
South Carolina 466
  Places of Interest 466
South Dakota 468
  Places of Interest 468
Souvenirs 576
Sport 576
St Augustine 423
  Surroundings 424
St Louis 424
  Other Sights in St
    Louis 427
  Sights in Downtown St
    Louis 424
  Surroundings 428
St Petersburg 428
  Sights 429
Suggested Routes 128
  By Steamboat on Old Man
    River 134
  Coast to Coast 131
  Dream Roads of the
    USA 128
  East Coast / West
    Coast 131
  Other Scenic Routes 133
  Route 66 128
  Course of Route 66 129
  Special Interest Tours 132
  Through the United States
    by Rail 134

Tampa 470
Taxis 577
Telephoning 577
Television 578
Tennessee 471
  Places of Interest 472
Tennis 578
Texas 472
  Places of Interest 473
The Indians of North
  America 31
Settlement of the
  American Continent 32
The Campaign against the
  Indians 37
The "Discovery" of
  America 33
The Fate of the East Coast
  Indians 34
The Indians of the Prairies
  and Plains 34
US Indian Policy in the
  20th Century 39

Time 579
Tipping 579
Toilets 579
Topography and
  Geology 10
  Minerals 15
  Relief and Geological
    Structure 11
  Rivers and Lakes 16
Traffic Regulations 545
Transport and
  Communications 60
Travel Documents 579
Tucson 474
  Sights 475
  Surroundings 476

USA: Home of the
  Skyscrapers 100
US Virgin Islands 477
  Places of Interest 477
United States Embassies
  and Consulates 530
Utah 478
  Places of Interest 478

Vermont 479
  Places of Interest 479
Virginia 480
  Places of Interest 481

Walking 580
Walt Disney World 387
Washington 482
  Places of Interest in
    Washington State 483
Washington DC 484
  Capitol Hill 488
  Downtown
    Washington 494
  East Mall – Museums 489
  Other Sights in
    Washington DC 495
  Sights in Washington
    DC 487
  Surroundings of
    Washington DC 496
  West Mall –
    Memorials 492
  White House Area 493
Waterton-Glacier
  International Peace
  Park 497
Weights/Measures/
  Temperatures 580
West Virginia 499
  Places of Interest 500
When to Go 581
White Sands National
  Monument 500
  Surroundings 502

Index

Winter Sports 581
  Winter Sports Regions in the United States 582
Wisconsin 502
  Places of Interest 502
Wyoming 503
  Places of Interest 504

Yellowstone National Park 506
  Grand Loop Road 507
Yosemite National Park 510
  Sights 511
  Surroundings 513

Young People's Accommodation 583
  Student Residences 584
  YMCA and YWCA 584
Youth Hostels 583

Zion National Park 513

The Principal Places of Tourist Interest at a Glance (continued from page 6)

*	Page	*	Page
Savannah (GA)	457	Tampa (FL)	470
Seattle (WA)	459	Tucson (AZ)	474
Sequoia and Kings Canyon NP (CA)	462	Voyageurs NP (MN)	315
		Waterton-Glacier NP (MT)	497
Shenandoah NP (VA)	464	Zion NP (UT)	513

The places listed above are merely a selection of the principal sights – places of interest in themselves or for attractions in the surrounding area. There are of course innumerable other sights throughout the United States, to which attention is drawn by either one or two stars.

Source of illustrations:

Archiv für Kunst und Geschichte, Berlin (2); Baedeker-Archiv (5); Bildagentur Schuster, Oberursel (3); Dr Madeleine Cabos, Stuttgart (12); Delta Airlines/Treupel (2); dpa (1); Carin Drechsler-Marx, New York (23); Eichmüller, Reutlingen (2); Rainer Eisenschmid/Gabriele Maier, Stuttgart (23); Florida Department of Tourism (2); Florida State Archives (1); Fotoagentur Helga Lade, Hamburg (1); Frick, Altbach (2); Hamberger, Leutkirch (6); Historia-Photo (1); Sabine Hofmann, Ostfildern (1); IFA, Taufkirchen (3); Christian Jänicke, Munich (2); Helmut Linde, Reutlingen (20); Lindenmuseum, Stuttgart (3); Isolde and Albert Maier, Stuttgart (7); Mangum Management, Munich (2); NCL, Frankfurt am Main (1); Dr Ruth Nestvold, Fellbach (2); Pinellas Suncoast Chamber of Commerce (1); Schapowalow, Hamburg (3); Dr Georg Scherm, Leinfelden-Echterdingen (2); Schröder, Augustdorf (3); Laila Sprattler, Stuttgart (2); Manfred Strobel, Ostfildern (5); Ullstein Verlag, Berlin (16); USTTA, Frankfurt am Main (5); Verlag Der Spiegel, Hamburg (1); Martin Vogel, Frickenhausen (19); Walt Disney Company, Frankfurt am Main (1); Wiechmann Tourism Services, Frankfurt am Main (3); ZEFA, Düsseldorf (2)